Evolution, Early Experience and Human Development

Evolution, Early Experience and Human Development

FROM RESEARCH TO PRACTICE AND POLICY

Edited by
Darcia Narvaez
Jaak Panksepp
Allan N. Schore
and
Tracy R. Gleason

OXFORD
UNIVERSITY PRESS

Oxford University Press

Oxford University Press is a department of the University of Oxford.
It furthers the University's objective of excellence in research, scholarship, and
education by publishing worldwide.

Oxford   New York

Auckland   Cape Town   Dar es Salaam   Hong Kong   Karachi
Kuala   Lumpur   Madrid   Melbourne   Mexico City   Nairobi
New Delhi   Shanghai   Taipei   Toronto

With offices in

Argentina   Austria Brazil   Chile   Czech Republic   France   Greece
Guatemala   Hungary   Italy   Japan   Poland   Portugal   Singapore
South Korea   Switzerland   Thailand   Turkey   Ukraine   Vietnam

Oxford is a registered trademark of Oxford University Press in the UK
and certain other countries.

Published in the United States of America by
Oxford University Press
198 Madison Avenue, New York, NY 10016

Library of Congress Cataloging-in-Publication Data
Evolution, early experience and human development: from research to practice
and policy / edited by Darcia Narvaez ... [et al.].
p. cm.
Includes index.
ISBN 978–0–19–975505–9
1. Developmental psychology.   2. Child development.   3. Neuropsychology.
4.   Human evolution.   I. Narvaez, Darcia.
BF713.E86 2012
155.4'13—dc23
2011051478

1 3 5 7 9 8 6 4 2
Printed in the United States of America
on acid-free paper

Remembering the past to shape the future

{ CONTENTS }

{ PREFACE }

This volume emerged in part from a symposium held in October 2010 at the University of Notre Dame entitled "Human Nature and Early Experience: Addressing the 'Environment of Evolutionary Adaptedness.'" Many of the presenters agreed to write a chapter for this volume. We invited additional chapter and commentary contributions from other leaders in their respective fields. The result is an interdisciplinary glimpse at early life experience through the prism of evolution and John Bowlby's EEA (environment of evolutionary adaptedness). Several authors address experience that matches or mismatches with our evolutionary heritage and its effects on children and parents. Others address early experience and its effects on human nature and the cultures that emerge from both. Some authors question the relevance of early experience to later adaptation. The contributors have a wide range of perspectives.

One note about the organization: The commentaries are organized at appropriate places in the book. If a commentary addresses a particular chapter, it appears right after the chapter. If a commentary is on a set of chapters, it is located after the set. Several more general commentaries appear at the end of the book. We thank all the participants for sharing their insights in the various chapters of this volume, as well as the commentators, many of whom were not present at the symposium, for sharing their perspective on the various chapters and sections of this book.

Readers will notice that there is abundant controversy on various issues, especially those related to the powerful and lasting effects of early experiences on future developmental trajectories. This discussion is healthy for the field, for these debates will be with us for a long time. The material presented here will allow the reader to think about various sides of key issues: How much does early experience matter and for what? Can we integrate findings across subfields of science regarding early life experience? How should ancestral environments inform human developmental science? How malleable is human nature? Are suboptimal outcomes to be expected by evolutionary mechanisms, or do they represent interference by human ideologies and cultural drift from evolutionary behaviors? Do we have enough information now to make recommendations for policy and practice, or must more research be done? We hope the reader will find the volume both informative and stimulating on these and other issues.

Human infants, as those of most species, have abundant resources for resilience. Indeed, to some extent, the capacity to survive despite suboptimal or even harsh conditions forms the nature of organisms, and humans are no exception—we are among the most adaptable of all species. However, as we focus closer and closer on the quality of lived lives, for instance, on the affective sense of comfort and well-being, the more we see that excessive negative early experiences leave a residue of background negativity, pessimism, and ill health that is hard to erase. In contrast, *ceteris paribus*, abundant, happy, prosocial engagements in the early years will tend to solidify the possibility of living a sanguine life where confidence, optimism, and well-being tend to prevail.

{ CONTRIBUTORS }

Veronica M. Afonso, PhD
Department of Psychology
University of Toronto at Mississauga

Lisa H. Amir, MBBS, MMed, PhD
Mother and Child Health Research
La Trobe University
Centre for Women's Health, Gender,
    and Society
University of Melbourne

Helen L. Ball, PhD
Department of Anthropology
Durham University

Jay Belsky, PhD
University of California, Davis
Birkbeck University of London

Adam H. Boyette, PhD candidate
Department of Anthropology
Washington State University

G.A. Bradshaw PhD
The Kerulos Center
Jacksonville, OR

C. Sue Carter, PhD
Brain and Body Center
Department of Psychiatry
University of Illinois, Chicago

Tiffany Field, PhD
Touch Research Institute
University of Miami School of
    Medicine

Joseph L. Flanders, PhD
Department of Psychology
McGill University

Alison S. Fleming, PhD
Department of Psychology
University of Toronto

Lee T. Gettler, PhD
Department of Anthropology
University of Notre Dame

Tracy R. Gleason, PhD
Department of Psychology
Wellesley College

Peter Gray, PhD
Department of Psychology
Boston College

Khalisa N. Herman, PhD
National Institutes of Health

Maria Hernandez-Reif, PhD
Department of Human Development
    and Family Studies
University of Alabama

Barry S. Hewlett, PhD
Department of Anthropology
Washington State University and
    Hawassa University

Jerome Kagan, PhD
Department of Psychology
Harvard University

Melvin Konner, PhD
Department of Anthropology
Emory University

Michael E. Lamb, PhD
Department of Psychology
University of Cambridge

Pranee Liamputtong, PhD
School of Public Health
La Trobe University

David Loye, PhD
The Darwin Project
Pacific Grove, CA

William A. Mason, PhD
Department of Psychology
University of California, Davis

James J. McKenna, PhD
Department of Anthropology
University of Notre Dame

Michael Meaney, PhD
Department of Neurology
McGill University

Viara Mileva-Seitz
Institute of Medical Science
University of Toronto

Darcia Narvaez, PhD
Department of Psychology
University of Notre Dame

Eric E. Nelson, PhD
Section on Development and Affective
  Neuroscience
National Institutes of Mental Health

Jaak Panksepp, PhD
Department of Veterinary
  and Comparative Anatomy,
  Pharmacology, and Physiology
Washington State University

Daniel Paquette, PhD
School of Psychoeducation
University of Montreal

Adam F. A. Pellegrini, PhD candidate
Department of Ecology and
  Evolutionary Biology
Princeton University

Anthony D. Pellegrini, PhD
Department of Educational
  Psychology
University of Minnesota

Bruce D. Perry, MD, PhD
The Child Trauma Academy
  Houston, TX
Department of Psychiatry and
  Behavioral Science
Feinberg School of Medicine
Northwestern University

Stephen W. Porges, PhD
Brain and Body Center
Department of Psychiatry
University of Illinois, Chicago

James W. Prescott, PhD
Institute of Humanistic Science
Lewes, DE

Charlotte K. Russell, PhD
Department of Anthropology
Durham University

Allan N. Schore, PhD
Department of Psychiatry and
  Biobehavioral Sciences
UCLA David Geffen School of
  Medicine

Daniel J. Siegel, MD
UCLA School of Medicine and
  Mindsight Institute
UCLA Center for Culture, Brain, and
  Development
UCLA Mindful Awareness Research
  Center

Howard Steele, PhD
Department of Psychology
New School for Social Research

Zaharah Sulaiman, MBBS
School of Public Health and Human
  Biosciences
La Trobe University

Ross A. Thompson, PhD
Department of Psychology
University of California, Davis

Colwyn Trevarthen, PhD
Department of Psychology
University of Edinburgh

Wenda R. Trevathan, PhD
Department of Anthropology
New Mexico State University

Kerstin Uvnäs-Moberg, MD, PhD
Department of Physiology and
  Pharmacology
Karolinska Institute

{ NOTES FROM THE EDITORS }

Darcia Narvaez thanks the following organizations for their support of the Symposium on "*Human Nature and Early Experience: Addressing the Environment of Evolutionary Adaptedness*" during October 10–12, 2010: local sponsors Memorial Hospital of South Bend, Family and Children's Center of South Bend; University of Notre Dame sponsors: College of Arts and Letters' Institute for Scholarship in the Liberal Arts, Institute for Educational Initiatives, Campus Ministry, Mendoza College of Business, The Graduate School, College of Science. Many of the symposium speakers and guests contributed to this volume. The University of Notre Dame generously supported a sabbatical during which this volume was prepared.

Jaak Panksepp's ongoing work is supported by the Hope for Depression Research Foundation. Our shared goals are to see how positive and negative social emotions promote resilience against and susceptibility to depression, respectively. The invaluable support of the College of Veterinary Medicine at Washington State University along with the Neuropsychoanalysis Society and Fund is also gratefully acknowledged, along with many colleagues here and around the world who recognize the importance of affective neuroscience in promoting a better understanding and implementation of mental health across species and lifespans.

Allan N. Schore's work on the manuscript was supported in part by a grant from the FHL Foundation.

Tracy R. Gleason's work on this manuscript was supported in part by the Brachman-Hoffman Small Grants, a Wellesley College Faculty Award, and the Sophomore Early Research Program. She would like to thank Aryanne DeSilva, Chanelle Lansley, Dana Lee, Michelle Lee, Ayla Nolen, Victoria Nguyen, and Julia Ross for their research assistance.

Human Nature: The Effects of Evolution and Environment

{ 1 }

The Value of Using an Evolutionary Framework for Gauging Children's Well-Being

Darcia Narvaez, Jaak Panksepp, Allan N. Schore, and Tracy R. Gleason

Earlier conceptions of the essential nature of developmental experiences found axiomatic that "early childhood is destiny." This view was deeply embedded in two paradigms—psychoanalysis under the Freudian view, which emphasized parenting influences, and behaviorism, which emphasized early conditioning and reinforcement history (although both psychoanalytic psychotherapists and behaviorists assumed that patterns could be unlearned with some effort). When developmental psychology changed in paradigm to an ecological system perspective that acknowledges multiple levels of influence (Bronfenbrenner, 1979), emphasis shifted to a focus on human resiliency in the face of risk factors (Lester, Masten, & McEwen, 2007). Neuroscience has bolstered the resilient view of development with evidence that the brain remains plastic throughout the life span (e.g., Doidge, 2007; Merzenich et al., 1996). Early childhood is thus viewed within the prism of lifelong interactions among ecosystems and individual neuro-affective propensities, highlighting developmental person-by-context interactions and abundant individual variability in emotional resilience (Suomi, 2006; Worthman, Plotsky, Schechter, & Cummings, 2010).

In the enthusiasm to embrace ideas of life span resiliency, psychology has often soft-pedaled the lasting neurobiological influences of early childhood experience. When researchers have documented the remarkable resiliency of children (e.g., Lester et al., 2007), they often point to better outcomes than might be predicted from certain preclinical studies of early developmental trajectories (Kagan, 1997). In a way, resiliency literature focuses on "good enough" development. As long as children do not end up, for example, as dropouts or inmates, their development is termed a success. Many psychologists and parents seem satisfied with resiliency as a goal for child development. But trends for such outcomes are not always positive. A decade ago, one in four teenagers in the United States was at risk for a poor life outcome (Eccles & Grootman, 2002), and in recent analyses such trends have not improved (Heckman, 2008). The national prevalence of *young* children (under 5 years) with psychosocial problems has been on the increase to between 10% and 21% (Powell, Fixen, & Dunlop, 2003). The rates of *young* children whose behavior displays aggression, delinquency, or hyperactivity are on the increase, at times estimated to be as high as 25% (Raver & Knitze, 2002). The American Academy of Childhood and Adolescent Psychiatry is now describing a "crisis" in children's mental health: 1 in every 5 children has a diagnosable psychiatric disorder, and 1 in every 10 suffers from a mental illness severe enough to impair everyday living (American Academy of Child and Adolescent Psychiatry, 2011). These epidemiological data, as well as recent psychiatric and neurobiological research, seriously challenge the concept of universal resilience, suggesting it may be misleading, simplistic, and incorrect (e.g., Commission on Children at Risk, 2003; Lanius, Vermetten, & Pain, 2010; OECD, 2009; Schore, 2003; Szajnberg, Goldenberg, & Hatari, 2010; UNICEF, 2007).

Another reason to be concerned about the current developmental psychological conception of resilience comes from recent research, which is tempering views that the faults of early childhood can be easily outgrown. Indeed, many cannot be, or if they can, the process requires serious and considerable intervention (Perry, Pollard, Blakely, Baker, & Vigilante, 1995; Schore, 1994, 2001a). The evidence across animal, human psychological, neurobiological, and anthropological research is increasing and converging to demonstrate lifetime vulnerability of brain and body systems among those with poor early care. Even when medicines are available to alleviate symptoms of dysfunction, the underlying suboptimal structures remain (Shonkoff et al., 2012). This problem may be particularly true for emotional and moral functioning (Narvaez, 2008).

A host of public, personal, and social health problems that may have their roots in early experience have been skyrocketing in the United States and increasingly around the world (e.g., psychological problems such as attention deficit/hyperactivity disorder, autism, anxiety, and depression, not to mention psychosomatic conditions such as diabetes, hypertension, obesity, and a variety of autoimmune disorders; see, e.g., Felitti & Anda, 2005; Sanchez, Ladd, & Plotsky, 2001; U.S. Department of Health and Human Services, Substance Abuse and Mental Health Services Administration, 1999; World Health Organization and World Organization of Family Doctors, 2008). Although considerable progress is now being made, science does not have a complete understanding or consistent reliable remedies, nor preventive strategies, for addressing these rising problems.

The emergence and spread of the affective and social neurosciences (Cacioppo & Berntson, 1992; Panksepp, 1998, 2005) make this an auspicious time to reconsider the early life needs of human mammalian systems in light of fostering optimal development (Worthman et al., 2010). This research has provided a greater focus on intrinsic aspects of social functioning—especially primary emotional neuro-affective processes that may need to be enhanced. These disciplines have helped identify the types of brain functions that are typically found in mammalian brains, but they have not scientifically specified how these functions are *normally* (under conditions of optimal development) expressed in humans (but see Schore, 2001b). Nor do we know how they develop and become modified by cultural practices. Without a clear vision of how the emotional foundations of human brains develop and function, psychological science will not be well grounded in scientifically established evolutionary principles (Meaney, this volume; Panksepp, 2010).

The Emotional Foundations of Brain Development, Thought, and Behavior

Affective neuroscience research has specified some of the subcortical anatomies and neurochemistries of basic emotional systems that constitute ancestral memories for a few of the most important feelings that guide human and animal existence (see Panksepp, 1998, for a review). Basic emotion systems constitute genetically ingrained psychobehavioral potentials that help an animal behave adaptively. These potentials are shaped by experience, influencing the functioning of both subcortical and neocortical structures that regulate communication quality (e.g., prosody) and guide adaptive responses to life events (Zinken, Knoll, & Panksepp, 2008). The healthy integration of the lower primary-process emotional-affective powers of the mind and the emergent secondary (learning) and tertiary (thoughtful) cognitive landscapes are left to environmental influences, especially to families and the surrounding cultural milieus (see Worthman et al., 2010).

Developmental science has highlighted sensitive periods in mammalian emotional, social, and cognitive functioning (e.g., Nelson & Panksepp, 1998; Schore, 1994). Only a few of these developmental programs are well mapped in animal models (e.g., vision and other sensory systems, as well as social bonding in several species); fewer still are mapped in the human species (e.g., language), and most cannot be, except for a few psychophysiological correlates of neural activities (e.g., functional magnetic resonance imaging). For ethical reasons, in the domain of emotions, we must resort to animal models to obtain generalizable primary- and secondary-process neurobiological principles relevant to the human condition (LeDoux, 1996; Panksepp, 1998, 2005, 2010). Fortunately, a great deal of evidence now indicates impressive homologies in subcortically concentrated, genetically provided emotional and motivational systems (i.e., key brain areas and chemistries) among all mammals that have been studied; these have substantial cross-species consistencies with abundant predictive robustness in psychiatrically oriented preclinical research (Panksepp & Harro, 2004).[1,2]

The Environment of Evolutionary Adaptedness and Mammalian Needs

Mammals require abundant nurturing care for optimal postnatal development (Weaver, Szyf, & Meaney, 2002). Catarrhine mammals in particular require profound social care (Konner, 2010). John Bowlby (1951; 1980; 1988), psychiatrist-turned-ethologist who created attachment theory, conceptualized the deep human need for profuse sociality as a consequence of our ancestral "environment of evolutionary adaptedness" (EEA; Bowlby, 1951, following Hartman, 1939), the sum of environmental characteristics under which human brains and bodies evolved. We can assume these needs took a specific form when the human genus emerged from ancestral great apes to develop cultural practices that appear to have remained largely stable for 99% of human genus history (e.g., Fry, 2006, 2009). Most of these practices evolved with catarrhine mammals more than 30 million years ago (Konner, 2010). In modern societies, the ancient practices that presumably sustained an implicit understanding of the needs of "the mammalian" brain-mind have been supplanted by "advanced" cultural practices that may be losing touch with our ancestral needs. Thus, we are integrating several literatures—including mammalian animal models and anthropological visions of our evolutionary heritage and evolved, expected care in early life.

Our evolutionary heritage has most often been described in relation to early life experience even though it was experienced over the course of a lifetime. Thus far, scientists have focused primarily on evolved, expected care during infancy and early childhood largely because of confidence that these early phases are more tightly linked to primary-process, primordial biological adaptations rather than to tertiary-process cultural elaborations (but see Levine et al., 1994, for a review emphasizing enculturation in parenting; and see Lumsden & Wilson, 1981, for the influence of culture on fitness-enhancing genetic adaptations). Substantive evidence,

---

[1] Other animals, such as birds, have developed in similar directions (Orosz & Bradshaw, 2007).

[2] Still, the claim of homologies between humans and other animals needs to be made with certain qualifications. Diversity is the hallmark of evolution as different species adapted to different ecological niches (for a review see, West-Eberhard, 2003), so no details of basic emotional and motivational systems are identical across any species (Panksepp, 1998). Moreover, abundant rapidly responding epigenetic effects as well as regulation of protein synthesis by microRNAs distinguish individuals with identical structural genes (e.g., Szyf, McGowan & Meaney, 2008). However, differences in details rarely reflect differences in underlying principles. For instance, oxytocin is now recognized as a brain chemical that helps regulate social bonding in many mammals (Carter, 1998, 2003; Insel, Gingrich, & Young, 2001; Nelson & Panksepp, 1998) with some unique implications and predictions for humans (Panksepp, 2009). At the same time, brain opioids and the ancestral nonapeptide arginine-vasotocin, with a single amino acid difference from oxytocin, carries out homologous functions in birds, such as robust inhibition of separation distress (Panksepp, 1998).

albeit indirect, comes from extant studies of foraging communities around the world, as anthropologists summarize the best current evidence of evolved, expected care for optimal development of infants and young children (e.g., Hewlett & Lamb, 2005). According to the review of findings:

> [Y]oung children in foraging cultures are nursed frequently; held, touched, or kept near others almost constantly; frequently cared for by individuals other than their mothers (fathers and grandmothers, in particular) though seldom by older siblings; experience prompt responses to their fusses and cries; and enjoy multiage play groups in early childhood (Hewlett & Lamb, 2005, p. 15).

These characteristics generally match the early experiences of highly social mammals, especially apes.

In this chapter, we use an evolutionary framework that includes our evolutionary heritage, sometimes referred to as the "environment of evolutionary adaptedness," along dimensions relevant today, to examine early-life-experience effects. We discuss several of these early childrearing characteristics in light of related scientific studies and current practices as known. For most practices, research has not identified exactly when and to what extent compromises of evolved, expected care cause problems. Moreover, these compromises may differ as a function of timing, intensity, length, and context (to name a few variables; also see Davis & Sandman, 2010; Lupien, McEwen, Gunnar, & Heim, 2009). Nevertheless, research reviewed in this volume points to problematic or less than optimal outcomes when these general principles are violated.

NATURAL CHILDBIRTH

Current birthing and childrearing practices no longer come close to the traditional practices of evolved, expected care (see Trevathan, 2011; this volume). Specifically, in the course of childbirth, mammalian parents typically follow the natural rhythms of the mother and child that obviously never involved the many current medical interventions that are common. In contrast, current human societal practices induce physical pain in infants through a variety of perinatal practices, some of which began in an era when infants were presumed to feel no pain. Since World War II, most children in the United States have been born in hospitals (Devitt, 1977), where birth has been medicalized and obstetric practices are the most intrusive in the world, sometimes increasing risks to infants and mothers that lead to high rates of mortality for both groups (Wagner, 2006). Cesarean birth, although sometimes vital for the survival of both mother and baby, now accounts for over 31% of births in the United States (Hamilton, Martin, & Ventura, 2009). Cesarean birth interferes with physiological responsiveness in the mother to the newborn (Swain, Tasgin, Mayes, Feldman, & Leckman, 2008), circumventing the ecstatic wash of hormones that typically accompanies natural vaginal birth (Klaus & Kennel, 1976/1983). Hopefully now mostly in the past, hospitals employed harsh birthing practices (e.g., spanking, separation of mother and child) and imposed such things as bright lights, noxious odors, and painful procedures on neonates, all of which can have detrimental effects on development (see Liu et al., 2007, for a review). Still other current practices also affect later development: Gestational ultrasounds can influence neuronal migration (Ang, Gluncic, Duque, Schafer, & Rakic, 2006), and circumcision obviously causes considerable pain and can impair biological functions (Anders & Chalemian, 1974; Emde, Harmon, Metcal, Koenig, & Wagonfeld, 1971) and social responsivity and attachments (Marshall et al., 1982). And stress, such as that induced by medical birth practices, may foster brain changes that can become permanent if their duration is intense, long, or unmitigated (Lanius et al., 2010). Consequently, common practices around birth in the United States may be disrupting mother-infant entrainment and affecting optimal emotional and social development. What is more, birth experiences can influence mother-child bonding and subsequent breastfeeding success (Klaus & Kennel, 1976/1983; Trevathan, 2011 this volume). Babies who experience skin-to-skin contact immediately after birth are more self-regulated and have a more attuned relationship with their mothers than those who were swaddled or separated; however, the negative influence of swaddling appears to be ameliorated by breastfeeding within the first hours after birth (Bystrova et al., 2009).

BREASTFEEDING: CONTENTS, LENGTH, AND CORRELATES

Mammalian milk is species specific for each of the more than 4,000 mammalian species (American Academy of Pediatrics Section on Breastfeeding, 2005). Human milk is of the thin, rather than thick, variety, which is related to frequent ingestion or at least frequent suckling (on average every 20 minutes for infants as recorded by anthropologists; see Hewlett & Lamb, 2005; Konner & Worthman, 1980). Human mothers, who provided immunity through the placenta, continue to provide immunity after birth, first with colostrum immediately after birth and thereafter with breast milk. Although infants have gastric enzymes for digesting their mother's colostrum and milk, digestive enzymes for other foods do not develop for several months. Breast milk abounds with infection-fighting agents that foster immune and digestive health in the young child. Specific to the environment in which the mother and infant find themselves, mammalian milk produces antibodies for various infective agents (e.g., Slusser & Powers, 1997). Nutritional practices consistent with evolved, expected care would further facilitate survival and enhance thriving.

The American Academy of Pediatrics recommends that human breast milk be the gold standard against which alternative infant food should be weighed in terms of its impact on human growth and development. Human breast milk, besides providing a balanced spectrum of macro- and micronutrients, also contains various enzymes, growth factors, hormones, and other live, health-protective agents including the five basic immunoglobulins, IgG, IgA, IgM, IgD, and IgE (Walker, 1993); breast milk fats and cholesterol co-occur with enzymes, such as lipase, that break down fats (see Goldman, 1993; Goldman, Goldblum, Garza, Nichols, & O'Brien Smith, 1983). Most of these elements are not contained in infant formula. For example, breast milk contains the protein adiponectin that affects how the body processes sugars and fatty substances in the blood; higher levels of adiponectin are related to lower levels of disease and obesity (Martin et al., 2006). Only recently have infant formulas started to supplement tryptophan, the precursor of serotonin, which is linked to the sleep-wake cycle and emotional tone; both are involved in many brain functions including reducing depression (Goldman, 1993; Delgado, 2006). Maternal milk is a rich source of unsaturated fatty acids, bioactive nutrients that are essential to early brain development (Yehuda, Rabinovitz, & Mostofsky, 1999). Not all formulas include DHA (docosahexaenoic acid, an essential omega-3 fatty acid) in presumably optimal proportions, which is important for visual and cognitive development (Hart et al., 2006; Lauritzen, Hansen, Jørgensen, & Michaelsen, 2001; Michaelsen, Lauritzen, Jørgensen, & Mortensen, 2003). Breast milk supports the growth of Lactobacillaceae, found 10 times higher in breastfed infants, which inhibits gram-negative bacteria and parasites (Newburg & Walker, 2007). In comparison to formula, breastfeeding decreases risks in the infant for specific diseases from small to large including infections, diarrhea, meningitis, ear infections, diabetes, and cancer and is protective from disease in general (for a review, see American Academy of Pediatrics Section on Breastfeeding, 2005).

Breastfeeding in the environment of evolutionary adaptedness presumably went on for anywhere from 2 to 5 years or longer (average weaning age of 4 years; for a review, see Hrdy, 2009, also for alloparent provisioning practices). These patterns are still evident in aboriginal populations little influenced by outside cultures. Five to 7 years is about the time needed for the immune system to develop adult-level functioning (Parham, 2004). In the United States, only 11.3% of mothers breastfeed exclusively at 6 months (which is recommended), and only 15.7% are breastfeeding at all at 12 months (Scanlon et al., 2007), although subgroups have different rates (McDowell, Wang, & Kennedy-Stephenson, 2008). See Sulaiman, Amir, and Liamputtong (this volume) for a review of the challenges to breastfeeding in the modern world. A shorter duration of breastfeeding (less than 6 months) may be a predictor of adverse mental health outcomes throughout the developmental trajectory of childhood and early adolescence (Oddy et al., 2010). The World Health Organization recommends a minimum of 2 years of breastfeeding (the American Academy of Pediatrics recommends a minimum of 1 year).

Patterns of mother-infant interaction differ between breastfeeding and bottle-feeding. The amount of mother's gaze, tactile stimulation, and mutual touch are significantly elevated in breastfeeding compared to formula feeding (Lavelli & Poli, 1998). In comparison to formula feeding, breastfeeding is linked to improved mental outcomes such as increased IQ—with longer breastfeeding being better (e.g., Mortensen, Michaelsen, Sanders, & Reinisch, 2002; although see Kramer et al., 2001). The IQs of the 90% of children who have a genetic variant in *FADS2* appear to be benefited especially by breastfeeding (Caspi et al., 2007). For a meta-analysis of the positive effects of breastfeeding on brain development, see Michaelsen and colleagues (2003). Studies suggest a greater degree and severity of illness among formula-fed infants regardless of background (e.g., Garza, 1987; American Academy of Pediatrics Work Group on Breastfeeding, 1997). Note, however, that the positive effects of breastfeeding may well be attenuated in this research. After all, studies comparing formula feeding and breastfeeding often evaluate consequences over short time periods such as 3 or 6 months (for a review see Kramer & Kakuma, 2004). For a more veridical comparison between the experiences of our prehistoric ancestors and modern humans, the comparison group should be children breastfed for at least 2 years if not longer.

PHYSICAL CLOSENESS, AFFECTIONATE TOUCH, AND SOCIAL BONDING

The effects of physical affection on optimal functioning in mammals have garnered attention for some time (e.g., Harlow, 1958). For most mammalian offspring, losing contact with a caregiver is distressing. Even short bouts of separation from the mother cause lifelong changes in stress responsivity for infant rats (Levine, 2005). However, when developmentally appropriate, mild and graded brief separations can help the offspring cope with the stress of longer separations later (Katz et al., 2009), but otherwise can have lasting negative effects. Hofer's (1987, 1994) work with rats has shown that multiple systems are regulated by the presence of the mother and quickly become dysregulated when she is physically absent. Even in species less social than ours, physical separation activates painful emotions (Ladd, Owens, & Nemeroff, 1996; Panksepp, 2003; Sanchez et al., 2001) and influences the dynamics of various emotion-regulating hormones and neuropeptides (Cirulli, Berry, & Alleva, 2002; Cirulli, Francia, Berry, Aloe, Alleva, & Suomi, 2009). Monkeys isolated from adults when young spend their lives with deficits of 5-HIAA, the main metabolite of serotonin, resulting from reduced serotonin production and utilization, which have been linked to impulsive violent and antisocial behavior in mammals (Kalin, 1999; Suomi, 2006). Excessive separation distress during early development sets up the nervous system for depressive disorders later in life, through well-established affective systems of the brain (see Panksepp & Watt, 2011, and Watt & Panksepp, 2009, for overviews).

Physical touch and affection have long-lasting general health effects as well (see Field, this volume). Meaney and colleagues have documented differences in gene expression within the brain-body pituitary-adrenal stress axis, based on the extent of maternal touch soon after birth (Meaney, this volume; Szyf, Weaver, & Meaney, 2007; Weaver et al., 2002). Examining only one of dozens, perhaps even thousands (as observed in unpublished work on primates by Steve Suomi and the aforementioned investigators), of genes affected, Meaney and colleagues found that rats with high-touch (high-licking) mothers in the first

10 days of life had elevated gene expressions for glucocorticoid receptor proteins. Glucocorticoid hormones produced in all mammals in response to stress need to be well regulated to prevent excessive stress, hippocampal dysfunction, and eventual depression (McEwen, 2007). Rats with diminished maternal touch had weaker stress axis regulation, resulting in more anxiety and lifelong heightened responses to stress across a diverse range of brain and behavioral measures (Champagne & Meaney, 2001). Moreover, these effects spiraled across generations. A low-nurturing mother bred low-nurturing daughters, epigenetically further compounding the effects of poor care on brain system development over generations (Weaver et al., 2002). Cross-foster studies show that the effect is environmental and not genetic (Francis, Diorio, Liu, & Meaney, 1999). Meaney, Szyf, and colleagues have now demonstrated the same epigenetic mechanism occurring in the brains of human adults abused as children who subsequently committed suicide (McGowan et al., 2009).

Animal studies on the critical importance of early tactile experience in mammalian development are paralleled by human studies on the essential role of maternal "affective touch" on infant development in the first year of life (Ferber, Feldman, & Makhoul, 2008; Jean, Stack, & Fogel, 2009). The infant and mother utilize "interpersonal touch" as an initial communication system (Gallace & Spence, 2010), especially for the relay and regulation of emotional information (Hertenstein, 2002; Hertenstein & Campos, 2001). Echoing animal research, human studies indicate that a lack of interpersonal touch in mother-infant interactions has an enduring negative effect on psychological, especially emotional, development (e.g., Moszkowski et al., 2009).

In the ancestral context, represented by the EEA, and as is normal for our ape cousins, babies and young children were presumably kept physically in contact with their mothers and others all the time, day and night. McKenna and colleagues (1994) have documented hidden regulators during human mother-child cosleeping, including facilitation of regular feeding/suckling (Ball & Klingaman, 2007; Ball & Russell, this volume; Buswell & Spatz, 2007; McKenna & McDade, 2005; Thoman, 2006). Skin-to-skin contact promotes healthy sleep cycles and adaptive behavioral arousals and exploratory activities (Feldman, Weller, Sirota, & Eidelman, 2002; McKenna, Ball, & Gettler, 2007). Early experiences with physical touch influence brain structures and wiring, facilitating secure attachments, which in turn promote adaptive social and cognitive functioning in adulthood (for a review, see Cushing & Kramer, 2005). Early social loss and insecure attachment are linked to a predisposition for depression and other mental health problems (e.g., Beatson & Taryan, 2003; Watt & Panksepp, 2009). These findings must be considered in light of the fact that only about 13% of US infants regularly sleep in a bed near caregivers (National Institute of Child Health and Human Development, Early Child Care Research Network, 2003).

PROMPT (CARING) RESPONSE

After 9 months of gestational synchrony, human mothers and neonates under natural conditions typically move into an interactional synchrony of sound and movement within the first hours after birth (e.g., Condon & Sander, 1974; Papousek & Papousek, 1992). Some call this right-brain affect regulation (Schore, 1994, 2003) or "limbic regulation" (Lewis, Amini, & Lannon, 2000), in which caregivers act as external regulators of psychological and biological development (Hofer, 1994; Schore, 2001b). This positive emotional entrainment is of clear importance in long-term development after birth (for reviews, see Reddy, 2008; Tronick, 2007). According to the mutual regulation model, the infant is viewed as a subsystem, with the caregiver as the other subsystem, within a "larger dyadic regulatory system" (Tronick, 2007, p. 9) that is in a constant dance of match and mismatch of coordinating intersubjectivity (Reddy, 2008). The infant's experience of repairing communication mismatches with coping strategies (also dependent on mother responsiveness) is believed to lead to a sense of mastery and a positive affective core, whereas opposite outcomes occur for an infant who unsuccessfully uses coping strategies in trying to repair communication mismatches. Consonant with this model, Schore (1994, 2000, this volume) describes the cocreation of an attachment bond of social-emotional communication and interactive regulation between the infant and the sensitive primary caregiver in the first 2 years of life. Optimal human development is thus rooted in social synchrony with others (Reddy, 2008; Schore, 1994; Trevarthen, 2005). Moreover, collective intelligence of human groups is largely based on social sensitivity (Woolley, Chabris, Pentland, Hashmim, & Malone, 2010).

In early life, the right brain is forming its emotional circuitry and structures in collaboration with caregivers (for reviews, see Schore, 1994, 2001b 2003; 2012). Responsive caregivers, in mutual coregulation, shape the infant brain for self-regulation within and across multiple sensory systems (e.g., respiratory, hormonal), influencing multiple levels of functioning (Hofer, 1994) and establishing emotional patterns that promote confidence and mental health. The early developing right brain, which is shaped by the attachment relationship and dominant for the processing of bodily based emotional information, is deeply connected to the autonomic nervous system (Schore, 2005), providing a solid grounding for an emotionally well-integrated personality (McGilchrist, 2009; Nadel & Muir, 2005). Porges's polyvagal theory details how early attachment bonding experiences program the sympathetic and parasympathetic branches of the infant's developing autonomic nervous system, thereby shaping later social and emotional reactivity (Carter & Porges, this volume; Porges, 2007). Indeed, responsive care with coregulated communication patterns is related to good parasympathetic vagal tone, which is critical for well-functioning digestive, cardiac, respiratory, and immune as well as emotional systems (e.g., Donzella, Gunnar, Krueger, & Alwin, 2000; Propper et al., 2008; Stam, Akkermans, & Wiegant, 1997). Nonresponsive parenting leads to poor vagal tone (e.g., Calkins, Smith, Gill, &

Johnson, 1998; Porter, 2003). Other systems are also affected negatively. For example, having a depressed mother (whose nurturing responses are limited) alters the functioning of the hypothalamic-pituitary-adrenal axis (HPA; e.g., Beatson & Taryan, 2003; see Dawson, Ashman, & Carver, 2000, for a review).

Unfortunately, a common cultural misperception, arising partly from the behaviorist tradition, is that letting babies cry themselves to sleep represents adequate, or even appropriate, parenting (Gethin & MacGregor, 2009). When babies are left to cry, with no parental attempt at timely comforting, their brains are flooded with high levels of potentially neurotoxic stress hormones such as cortisol (Blunt Bugental, Martorell, & Barraza, 2003; Gunnar & Donzella, 2002). Brain opioids, which promote feelings of well-being, diminish during human sadness (Zubieta et al., 2003), and psychic pain circuits are aroused (Eisenberger, Lieberman, & Williams, 2003; Panksepp, 2003). Over time, if these experiences are regular and extended, brain stress response systems can be wired permanently for oversensitivity and overreactivity (Anisman, Zaharia, Meaney, & Merali, 1998), leading to predispositions for clinical depression and anxiety (Barbas, Saha, Rempel-Clower, & Ghashghaei, 2003; de Kloet, Sibug, Helmerhorst, & Schmidt, 2005; see Watt & Panksepp, 2009, for a review), poor mental and physical health outcomes, and accelerated aging and mortality (for a review, Preston & de Waal, 2002). Consistent or unrelieved distress during sensitive periods in early life reduces the expression of γ-aminobutyric acid (GABA) genes, leading to anxiety and depression disorders as well as increased use of alcohol for stress relief (Caldji, Francis, Sharma, Plotsky, & Meaney, 2000; Hsu et al., 2003). When emotional dysregulation becomes chronic, it forms the foundation for further psychopathologies (Cole, Michel, & Teti, 1994; Panksepp & Watt, 2011), especially depression. Infant emotional dysregulation is related to subsequent mental illness, including a propensity for violence (Davidson, Putnam, & Larson, 2000). Stress that leads to insecure attachment disrupts emotional functioning, compromises social abilities, and can promote a permanent emotional bias toward anxious self-preservation (Henry & Wang, 1998; also see Schore, 2009, for a review).

Warm, responsive caregiving, as extensively studied (but variably defined; see Richman, Miller, & LeVine, 1992), is shown to have multiple positive effects (Fleming, Mileva-Seitz, & Afonso, this volume). Children raised with abundant care develop systems that respond well to endogenous opioids and oxytocin, leading to better stress regulation (e.g., Fleming, O'Day, & Kraemer, 1999; Heim & Nemeroff, 2001; Liu et al., 1997; Uvnas-Moberg, 1997). Responsive parenting helps children learn to regulate arousal systems both on their own (Haley & Stansbury, 2003) or with others (Schore, 2003) and is linked to heightened moral functioning, including stronger early conscience development (Kochanska, 2002). Well-established vagal tone in adults is correlated with compassion and openheartedness toward others from different backgrounds (summarized by Keltner, 2009). Similarly, children with high vagal tone are more cooperative and giving (for a review, see Eisenberg & Eggum, 2008). And when combined with increased activity in positive affective systems of the brain, high vagal tone promotes human happiness (Sheldon, Kashdan, & Steger, 2011) as opposed to sustained psychological pain (MacDonald & Jensen-Campbell, 2011).

MULTIPLE ALLOMOTHERS

Family life was established on cooperation (Roughgarden & Song, in press). In the ancestral context, with humans living in small, tribal, extended family groups, mothers were probably often assisted by many other adults (e.g., father, grandparents) in caring for infants and children, suggesting that children had in addition to a primary attachment relationship, secondary attachment relationships. Such "cooperative breeding" is corroborated by contemporary observational studies of similar groups (see review by Hrdy, 2009). For example, youngsters require feeding long after weaning, an activity the mother necessarily shares with other adults in documented hunter-gatherer communities until the child is able to help sufficiently to provision the self and others (see Fuentes, in press). Historically, the built-in social safety net for mothers surely increased the chances of the child's survival and decreased the stress burden on the mother. Supportive social contact is known to be a positive influence during birthing and postnatal mother-child communication (Klaus & Kennel, 1976/1983), and in fact some have suggested that, three attentive adults (parents and/or alloparents) appear to be optimal for children to thrive (Sagi et al., 1995; van Ijzendoorn, Sagi, & Lambermon, 1992).

In contrast to our ancestral context, modern life includes several caregiving arrangements that most likely compromise optimal child development. Single parenthood, for instance, can be detrimental to the well-being of the child (Amato, 2007), likely owing to overall decreased social support. Another current practice in the United States is that most children are cared for by nonkin caregivers, who may be less attuned to the needs of individual children than family members might be (Belsky, 2001), and where less than optimal care is often provided due to lack of resources (Peisner-Feinberg, Bernier, Bryant, & Maxwell, 2000). The more time that children spend in any nonmaternal childcare situations across the first 4.5 years of life, the more likely they are to exhibit externalizing problems and conflict with adults at age 4.5 and in kindergarten (National Institute of Child Health and Human Development, Early Child Care Research Network, 2003; although the rare high-quality care may mitigate these effects). In comparison to children at home (a proxy for care that is closer to that provided in the ancestral context), cortisol readings are higher for children in daycare, especially for those under 3 years of age (Vermeer & van Ijzendoorn, 2006), and increase rather than decrease throughout the day (Dettling, Gunnar, & Donzella, 1999). The expulsion rate of prekindergarten children (Gilliam, 2005) and the number of children under age 5 with psychosocial problems (Powell et al., 2003) or on psychotropic medications have increased dramatically in recent years (Zito et al., 2000), and although these trends have not yet been causally connected to deficient childcare, they do suggest that early caregiving is problematic in some way. Poor-quality daycare settings are often not able to cope with children's needs, particularly if they exhibit psychosocial problems or special needs.

PLAY

Mammalian childhoods, especially among primates, are characterized by playful interactions. The natural play of mammals has only recently been ethologically characterized for humans (Scott & Panksepp, 2003) and put under close scientific scrutiny in animal models (Panksepp, Siviy, & Normansell, 1984; Pellis & Pellis, 2009; Siviy & Panksepp, 2011; Spinka, Newberry, & Bekoff, 2001; Vanderschuren, Niesink, & Van Ree, 1997). Fry (in press), Gray (2009; this volume), and Pellegrini (this volume) describe the evolved usefulness of play. Play is now known to promote affectively beneficial gene expression profiles (Burgdorf, Kroes, Beinfeld, Panksepp, & Moskal, 2010), brain development (Gordon, Burke, Akil, Watson, & Panksepp, 2003; Gordon, Kollack-Walker, Akil, & Panksepp, 2002; Panksepp, 2007; van den Berg et al., 1999), and emotion regulation development (Panksepp et al., 2003; van den Berg et al., 1999). Mammals who are deficient in play have difficulty regulating aggressive urges (Potegal & Einon, 1989). Those with little play experience early in life have altered social, sexual, and conflict interactions with peers (van den Berg et al., 1999). Insufficient play may promote behavioral disorders such as attention deficit/hyperactivity disorder (Panksepp, 2007), diminished academic achievement (Barros, Silver, & Stein, 2009), and aggression (Flanders & Herman, this volume). Unfortunately, physical play in kindergarten is disappearing (Miller & Almon, 2009); moreover, educators often have difficulty distinguishing play from aggression and are commonly uncertain about how to manage play urges in young children (Tannock, 2008).

WHAT HAPPENS TO MAMMALS WHO DO NOT RECEIVE WHAT THEY NEED?

Mammalian brains are experience expectant (Greenough & Black, 1992), with age-related regulating sets of experiences and environmental supports promoting brain construction and wiring (e.g., Cushing & Kramer, 2005). Caregiving consistent with evolved, expected care could be conceptualized as a set of experiences anticipated by the human mammalian brain that foster empathy and sociality (Narvaez & Gleason, this volume; Nelson, this volume). Of course, all organisms, including humans, adapt to whatever life-supportive environments they encounter. Mammals, including young humans, adapt to emotionally deficient environments by relying on the more primitive survival modes of their brains, often becoming aggressive, depressive, and/or antisocial (Henry & Wang, 1998; Lewis et al., 2000; Teicher, 2002). Perhaps, then, the increasing incidence of emotionally disorganized children is a form of adaptation that is an "adaptive maladaptation," from a mental health perspective, formed in response to "toxic social environments" (Garbarino,

1995)—environments deficient in the kinds of inclusive social supports our ancestors received. That is, such maladaptations were not part of the evolved adaptive apparatus but reflect a pathological outcome of emotional stressors in human infants reared in socially deficient environments without adequate social supports, resulting in deficient limbic and neocortical development. Schore (1997, 2002), for example, offers interdisciplinary evidence that indicates that relational attachment trauma alters the developmental trajectory of the right brain and thereby imprints a predisposition to later forming psychiatric disorders, including personality disorders.

Under the ancestral conditions (small-band hunter-gatherers; Fry, 2006), individuals would have developed a stronger disposition to cooperate and to exhibit "strong reciprocity" (Gintis, Bowles, Boyd, & Fehr, 2009). Oppositional, aggressive, and/or dangerous individuals would not have earned the trust of the community and likely would have died at younger ages in our ancestral context than cooperative individuals. Poor cooperators may more readily survive today because of the sufficient calories and attention provided through the cultural safety nets of modern societies. Nonetheless, through the neglect of children's various primary social-emotional needs, our society may be starting to normalize abnormality.

ALTERNATIVE VIEWS

Hrdy (1999) has suggested that children reared under adverse conditions (e.g., with stressed parents) may develop personalities (e.g., anxious) that are better prepared for subsisting in a challenging environment. For example, when children are presented with manageable, graded emotional challenges, they can become more resilient (e.g., Katz et al., 2009). However, relational neglect and/or attachment trauma presents the infant not with graded but with highly stressful, undernourishing, and thereby overwhelming experiences. In fact, severe attachment stressors decrease adaptive abilities to respond emotionally, think efficiently, and relate well to others (Lanius et al., 2010). As a result, these children are truly *not* "prepared" for the social environment they face in everyday life. What is more, trauma may not need to be severe to have detrimental effects. Undercare, in terms of our ancestral practices, may also lead to suboptimal functioning (see Narvaez & Gleason, this volume). Surely the range of undercare in ancestral environments was much narrower and limited for our ancestors because children lived within a village of support. They experienced much more physiological stress but many fewer social stresses than childrearing environments today. Social stress has much greater ill effects on child physical and mental well-being than physiological stress (see Konner, 2010, for a review).

Others suggest that humans are demonstrating how adaptive and resilient they are despite the huge spectrum of stressful childhood experiences expressly because they survive in the face of daunting challenges (e.g., Belsky, Steinberg, & Draper, 1991). This perspective, however, ignores the quality of life, and even its length, as important variables in understanding adaptation. Suomi and colleagues (Howell et al., 2007), for example, found that male rhesus monkeys with low central sero-tonin levels early in life, a genetic phenotype that can be modulated environmen-tally, demonstrate high levels of violence and often experience premature death; those that survive to adulthood (10 years later) achieve high rank, but it is not clear how functional they are otherwise (D'Souza & Craig, 2008; Suomi, 2006; Uher & McGuffin, 2008). After all, dominant human males typically do not out-reproduce less dominant males (Lansing et al., 2008).

The wide range of personalities found today (many "pathological") were likely not found in ancestral contexts. Rearing practices that reduced childhood crying were adaptive (Trevathan, 2011); children were probably more "indulged" (Konner, 2005), resulting in apparently conciliatory personalities (Fry, 2006), not the wide range of antisocial personalities that are documented currently. Support for this argument comes from anthropological reports (e.g., Thomas, 1959; Turnbull, 1961) and a review by Prescott (1996), who compared violent and peaceful societ-ies from Textor's (1967) analyses of 400 societies and found that peaceful societies were more physically nurturing (touch, holding, affection) than violent societies. The evolved, expected care we describe appears to lead to not only more coopera-tive personalities but also more peaceful cultures (Fry, 2006; Narvaez & Gleason, this volume).

Perhaps because of a long evolutionary history with relatively egalitarian social structures in ancestral environments (Binmore, 1998) and a deep sense of fairness exhibited among primates (e.g., Brosnan, 2006; Brosnan & de Waal, 2003; de Waal, 2009; now extended to various species), humanity's troubled history during the recent "modern" era of inegalitarianism (the last 10,000 years or so) may be linked to the more powerful members of society exhausting societal resources from a sta-tus race to the top (Diamond, 2005). One reading of modern history is that the human global trajectory is less than optimal (Millennium Ecosystem Assessment, 2005) and seems to be following the same self-destructive pattern as societies that collapsed in the past (Diamond, 2005)—only with worldwide ramifications.

A latent variable that underlies one's reaction to the state of children today is one's subjective view of human nature. If one believes that humans are naturally violent and individualistic, then one is not surprised that so much violence, aggres-sion, and alienation pervade society. However, if one believes that humans are typi-cally nonviolent but prosocial, one is more likely to view aggression and alienation as indicative of an unbalanced state of affairs that can be remedied. Clearly, we take the latter position.

Conclusion

Current US societal practices and accepted childrearing outcomes do not ade-quately consider the original adaptive conditions of our ancestry and the proso-cial emotional dynamics that helped our anthropological and historical ancestors to thrive. Despite the growing evidence for the negative effects of particular early experiences, especially as moderated by emotionally sensitive childrearing practices on the developing brain, scientific research, theory, and policy recommendations do not yet match up with emerging findings. At the same time, we do not wish to romanticize a human ancestral past that cannot be reconstructed precisely, but to provide a plausible thesis, supported by cross-species data, that includes sensitive studies of the emotional-cognitive capacities of our evolutionary ancestors, as gleaned from studies of our closest evolutionary kin, the other great apes (de Waal, 2009). The primordial emotional infrastructure of mammalian brains (Panksepp, 1998, 2005; Panksepp & Biven, Replace 2011 with 2012) clearly coevolved with a particular co-constructing environment such as is described here. In order for science to play an effective role in helping to reverse current negative trends in well-being, we need to foster a widespread understanding of the types of psychobiological needs that humans possess as a result of their evolutionary nature and the type of corresponding care needed to meet those needs. Paying attention to the converging evidence about optimal early care is a place to start. This volume is a contribution to that effort.

Acknowledgments

The first author would like to thank the Spencer Foundation and the University of Notre Dame for their support during the writing of this chapter. The second author thanks the Hope for Depression Research Foundation for support. The fourth author thanks the Brachman-Hoffman Small Grants for support.

References

Amato, P. R. (2007, July). The impact of family formation change on the cognitive, social, and emotional well-being of the next generation. *The Future of Children, 15*(2), 75–96.

American Academy of Child and Adolescent Psychiatry. (2011). *Campaign for America's kids.* Retrieved January 19, 2011, from http://www.campaignforamericaskids.org/

American Academy of Pediatrics Section on Breastfeeding. (2005). Breastfeeding and the use of human milk. *Pediatrics, 115*(2), 496–506.

American Academy of Pediatrics Work Group on Breastfeeding. (1997). Breastfeeding and the use of human milk policy statement. *Pediatrics, 100*(6), 1035–1039.

Anders, T. F., & Chalemian, R. J. (1974). The effects of circumcision on sleep-wake states in human neonates. *Psychosomatic Medicine, 36*(2), 174–179.

Ang, Jr., E. S. B. C, Gluncic, V., Duque, A., Schafer, M. E., & Rakic, P. (2006). Prenatal exposure to ultrasound waves impacts neuronal migration in mice. *PNAS, 103*(34), 12903–12910.

Anisman, H., Zaharia, M. D., Meaney, M. J., & Merali, Z. (1998). Do early-life events permanently alter behavioral and hormonal responses to stressors? *International Journal of Developmental Neuroscience, 16*(3–4), 149–164.

Ball, H. L., & Klingaman, K. P. (2007). Breastfeeding and mother-infant sleep proximity: Implications for infant care. In W. Trevathan, E. O. Smith, & J. J. McKenna (Eds.), *Evolutionary medicine and health: New perspectives* (pp. 226–241). New York, NY: Oxford University Press.

Barbas, H., Saha, S., Rempel-Clower, N., & Ghashghaei, T. (2003). Serial pathways from primate prefrontal cortex to autonomic areas may influence emotional expression. *Neuroscience, 4*(1), 25.

Barros, R. M., Silver, E. J., & Stein, R. E. K. (2009). School recess and group classroom behavior. *Pediatrics, 123*(2), 431–436.

Beatson, J., & Taryan, S. (2003). Predisposition to depression: The role of attachment. *The Australian and New Zealand Journal of Psychiatry, 37*(2), 219–225.

Belsky, J. (2001). Developmental risks (still) associated with early child care. *Journal of Child Psychology and Psychiatry and Allied Disciplines, 42*(7), 845–859.

Belsky, J., Steinberg, L., & Draper, P. (1991). Childhood experience, interpersonal development and reproductive strategy. *Child Development, 62*, 647–670.

Binmore, K. G. (1998). *Game theory and the social contract II. Just playing.* Cambridge, MA: MIT.

Blunt Bugental, D., Martorell, G. A., & Barraza, V. (2003). The hormonal costs of subtle forms of infant maltreatment. *Hormones and Behaviour, 43*(1), 237–244.

Bowlby, J. (1951). *Maternal care and mental health.* New York, NY: Schocken.

Bowlby, J. (1980). *Attachment and loss: Vol 3. Loss: Sadness and depression.* New York, NY: Basic Books.

Bowlby, J. (1988). *A secure base: Parent-child attachment and healthy human development.* New York, NY: Basic Books.

Bronfenbrenner, U. (1979). *The ecology of human development.* Cambridge, MA: Harvard University Press.

Brosnan, S. F. (2006). Nonhuman species' reactions to inequity and their implications for fairness. *Social Justice Research, 19*(2), 153–185.

Brosnan, S. F., & de Waal, F. B. (2003). Monkeys reject unequal pay. *Nature, 425*(6955), 297–299.

Burgdorf, J., Kroes, R. A., Beinfeld, M. C., Panksepp, J., & Moskal, J. R. (2010). Uncovering the molecular basis of positive affect using rough-and-tumble play in rats: A role for insulin-like growth factor I. *Neuroscience, 168*, 769–777.

Buswell, S. D., & Spatz, D. L. (2007). Parent-infant co-sleeping and its relationship to breastfeeding. *Journal of Pediatric Health Care, 21*, 22–28.

Bystrova, K., Ivanova, V., Edhborg, M., Matthiesen, A. S., Ransjö-Arvidson, A. B., Mukhamedrakhimov, R., ... Widström, A. M. (2009). Early contact versus separation: Effects on mother-infant interaction one year later. *Birth, 36*(2), 97–109.

Cacioppo, J. T., & Berntson, G. G. (1992). Social psychological contributions to the decade of the brain: Doctrine of multilevel analysis. *American Psychologist, 47*, 1019–1028.

Caldji, C., Francis, D., Sharma, S., Plotsky, P. M., & Meaney, M. J. (2000). The effects of early rearing environment on the development of GABAA and central benzodiazepine receptor levels and novelty-induced fearfulness in the rat. *Neuropsychopharmacology, 22*, 219–229.

Calkins, S. D., Smith, C. L., Gill, K. L., & Johnson, M. C. (1998). Maternal interactive style across contexts: Relations to emotional, behavioral and physiological regulation during toddlerhood. *Social Development, 7*(3), 350–369.

Carter, C. S. (1998). Neuroendocrine perspectives on social attachment and love. *Psychoneuroendocrinology, 23*(8), 779–818.

Carter, C. S. (2003). Developmental consequences of oxytocin. *Physiology and Behavior, 79*(3), 383–397.

Caspi, A., Williams, B., Kim-Cohen, J., Craig, I. W., Milne, B. J., Poulton, R.,...Moffitt, T. E. (2007). Moderation of breastfeeding effects on the IQ by genetic variation in fatty acid metabolism. *PNAS, 104*(47), 18860–18865.

Champagne, F., & Meaney, M. J. (2001). Like mother, like daughter: Evidence for non-genomic transmission of parental behavior and stress responsivity. *Progress in Brain Research, 133*, 287–302.

Cirulli, F., Berry, A., & Alleva, E. (2002). Early disruption of the mother-infant relationship: Effects on brain plasticity and implications for psychopathology. *Neuroscience and Biobehavioral Reviews, 272*, 73–82.

Cirulli, F., Francia, N., Berry, A., Aloe, L., Alleva, E., & Suomi S. J. (2009). Early life stress as a risk factor for mental health: Role of neurotrophins from rodents to non-human primates. *Neuroscience and Biobehavioral Reviews 33*(4), 573–585., 573–585.

Cole, P. M., Michel, M. K., & Teti, L. O. (1994). The development of emotion regulation and dysregulation: A clinical perspective. *Monographs of the Society for Research in Child Development, 59*(2–3), 73–100.

Commission on Children at Risk. (2003). *Hardwired to connect: The new scientific case for authoritative communities.* New York, NY: Institute for American Values.

Condon, W. S., & Sander, L. W. (1974). Neonate movement is synchronized with adult speech: Interactional participation and language acquisition. *Science, 183*, 99–101.

Cushing, B. S., & Kramer, K. M. (2005). Mechanisms underlying epigenetic effects of early social experience: The role of neuropeptides and steroids. *Neuroscience and Biobehavioral Reviews, 29*(7), 1089–1105.

Davidson, R. J., Putnam, K. M., & Larson, C. L. (2000) Dysfunction in the neural circuitry of emotion regulation—a possible prelude to violence. *Science, 289*(5479), 591–594.

Davis, E. P., & Sandman, C. A. (2010). The timing of prenatal exposure to maternal cortisol and psychosocial stress is associated with human infant cognitive development. *Child Development, 81*(1), 131–148.

Dawson, G., Ashman, S. B., & Carver, L. J. (2000). The role of early experience in shaping behavioral and brain development and its implications for social policy. *Development and Psychopathology, 12*, 695–712.

De Kloet, E. R., Sibug, R. M., Helmerhorst, F. M., & Schmidt, M. (2005). Stress, genes and the mechanism of programming the brain for later life. *Neuroscience and Biobehavioral Reviews, 29*(2), 271–281.

De Waal, F. (2009). Morally evolved: Primate social instincts, human morality and the rise and fall of "veneer theory." In S. Macedo & J. Ober (Eds.), *Primates and philosophers: How morality evolved.* Princeton, NJ: Princeton University Press.

Delgado, P. L. (2006). Monoamine depletion studies: Implications for antidepressant discontinuation syndrome. *Journal of Clinical Psychiatry, 67*(Suppl 4), 22–26.

Dettling, A. C., Gunnar, M. R., & Donzella, B. (1999). Cortisol levels of young children in full-day childcare centers: Relations with age and temperament. *Psychoneuroendocrinology, 24*(5), 519–536.

Devitt, N. (1977). The transition from home to hospital birth in the United States, 1930–1960. *Birth, 4*, 47–58.

Diamond, J. (2005). *Collapse: How societies choose to fail or survive.* New York, NY: Viking.

Doidge, N. (2007). *The brain that changes itself.* New York, NY: Viking.

Donzella, B., Gunnar, M. R., Krueger, W. K., & Alwin, J. (2000). Cortisol and vagal tone responses to competitive challenge in preschoolers: Associations with temperament. *Development Psychobiology, 37*(4), 209–220.

D'Souza, U. M., & Craig, I. W. (2008). Functional genetic polymorphisms in serotonin and dopamine gene systems and their significance in behavioural disorders. *Progress in Brain Research, 172,* 73–98.

Eccles, J., & Grootman, J. A. (2002). *Community programs to promote youth development.* Washington, DC: Committee on Community-Level Programs for Youth. Board on Children, Youth, and Families, Commission on Behavioral and Social Sciences Education, National Research Council and Institute of Medicine.

Eisenberg, N., & Eggum, N. D. (2008). Empathic responding: Sympathy and personal distress. In B. Sullivan, M. Snyder, & J. Sullivan (Eds.), *Cooperation: The political psychology of effective human interaction* (pp. 71–83). Malden, MA: Blackwell Publishing.

Eisenberger, N. I., Lieberman, M. D., & Williams, K. D. (2003). Does rejection hurt? An fMRI study of social exclusion. *Science, 302,* 290–292.

Emde, R. N., Harmon, R. J., Metcal, D., Koenig, K. L., & Wagonfeld, S. (1971). Stress and neonatal sleep. *Psychosomatic Medicine, 33,* 491–497.

Feldman, R., Weller, A., Sirota, L., & Eidelman, A. I. (2002). Skin-to-skin contact (kangaroo care) promotes self-regulation in premature infants: Sleep-wake cyclicity, arousal modulation, and sustained exploration. *Developmental Psychology, 38,* 194–207.

Felitti, V. J., & Anda, R. F. (2005). *The Adverse Childhood Experiences (ACE) study.* Atlanta, GA: Centers for Disease Control and Prevention and Kaiser Permanente.

Ferber, S. G., Feldman, R., & Makhoul, I. R. (2008). The development of maternal touch across the first year of life. *Early Human Development, 84,* 363–370.

Fleming, A. S., O'Day, D. H., & Kraemer, G. W. (1999). Neurobiology of mother infant interactions: Experience and central nervous system plasticity across development and generations. *Neuroscience and Biobehavioral Reviews, 3*(5), 673–685.

Francis, D., Diorio, J., Liu, D., & Meaney, M. J. (1999). Nongenomic transmission across generations of maternal behavior and stress responses in the rat. *Science, 286,* 1155–1158.

Fry, D. P. (2006). *The human potential for peace: An anthropological challenge to assumptions about war and violence.* New York, NY: Oxford University Press.

Fry, D. P. (2009). *Beyond war: The human potential for peace.* New York, NY: Oxford University Press.

Fry, D. (in press). Rough-and-tumble play, and the selection of restraint in human aggression. In D. Narvaez, K. Valentino, A. Fuentes, J. McKenna & P. Gray (Eds.), *Ancestral landscapes in human evolution: Culture, childrearing and social wellbeing.* New York: Oxford University Press

Fuentes, A. (in press). Preliminary steps towards addressing the role of non-adult individuals in human evolution. In D. Narvaez, K. Valentino, A. Fuentes, J. McKenna, & P. Gray (Eds.), *Ancestral landscapes in human evolution: Culture, childrearing and social wellbeing.* New York, NY: Oxford University Press.

Gallace, A., & Spence, C. (2010). The science of interpersonal touch: An overview. *Neuroscience and Biobehavioral Reviews, 34,* 246–259.

Garbarino, J. (1995). *Raising children in a socially toxic environment.* San Francisco, CA: Jossey-Bass.

Garza, C. (1987). Special properties of human milk. *Clinics of Perinatology, 14*, 11–32.

Gethin, A., & Macgregor, B. (2009). *Helping baby sleep: The science and practice of gentle bedtime parenting.* Berkeley, CA: Ten Speed Press.

Gilliam, W. S. (2005). *Prekindergarteners left behind: Expulsion rates in state prekindergarten systems.* New Haven, CT: Yale University Child Study Center.

Gintis, H., Bowles, S., Boyd, R., & Fehr, E. (2009). Moral sentiments and material interests: Origins, evidence, and consequences. In H. Gintis, S. Bowles, R. Boyd, & E. Fehr (Eds.), *Moral sentiments and materials interests: The foundations of cooperation in economic life* (pp. 3–40). Cambridge, MA: MIT Press.

Goldman, A. S. (1993). The immune system of human milk: Antimicrobial anti-inflammatory and immunomodulating properties. *Pediatric Infectious Disease Journal, 12*(8), 664–671.

Goldman, A. S., Goldblum, R. M., Garza, C., Nichols, B. L., & O'Brien Smith, E. (1983). Immunologic components in human milk during weaning. *Acta Paediatrica Scandinavica, 72*(1), 133–134.

Gordon, N. S., Burke, S., Akil, H., Watson, S. J., & Panksepp, J. (2003). Socially-induced brain 'fertilization': play promotes brain derived neurotrophic factor transcription in the amygdala and dorsolateral frontal cortex in juvenile rats. *Neuroscience Letters, 341*(1), 17–20.

Gordon, N. S., Kollack-Walker, S., Akil, H., & Panksepp, J. (2002). Expression of c-fos gene activation during rough and tumble play in juvenile rats. *Brain Research Bulletin, 57*(5), 651–659.

Gray, P. (2009). Play as a foundation for hunter-gatherer social existence. *American Journal of Play, 1*, 476–22.

Greenough, W., & Black, J. (1992). Induction of brain structure by experience: Substrate for cognitive development. In M. R. Gunnar & C. A. Nelson (Eds.), *Minnesota symposia on child psychology 24: Developmental behavioral neuroscience* (pp. 155–200). Hillsdale, NJ: Lawrence Erlbaum.

Gunnar, M. R., & Donzella, B. (2002). Social regulation of the cortisol levels in early human development. *Psychoneuroendocrinology, 27*(1–2), 199–220.

Haley, D. W., & Stansbury, K. (2003). Infant stress and parent responsiveness: Regulation of physiology and behavior during still-face and reunion. *Child Development, 74*, 1523–1535.

Hamilton, B. E., Martin, J. A., & Ventura, S. J. (2009). Births: Preliminary data for 2007. *National Vital Statistics Reports, 57*(12), 2–23.

Harlow, H. (1958). The nature of love. *American Psychologist, 13*, 673–685.

Hart, S., Boylan, L. M. Carroll, S. R., Musick, Y. A., Kuratko, C., Border, B. G., & Lampe, R. L. (2006). Newborn behavior differs with docosahexaenoic acid (DHA) levels in breast milk. *Journal of Pediatric Psychology, 31*, 221–226.

Hartmann, H. (1939). *Ego psychology and the problem of adaptation.* New York, NY: International University Press.

Heckman, J. (2008). *Schools, skills and synapses.* IZA DP No. 3515. Bonn, Germany: Institute for the Study of Labor.

Heim, C., & Nemeroff, C. B. (2001). The role of childhood trauma in the neurobiology of mood and anxiety disorders: Preclinical and clinical studies. *Biological Psychiatry, 49*(12), 1023–1039.

Henry, J. P., & Wang, S. (1998). Effects of early stress on adult affiliative behavior. *Psychoneuroendocrinology, 23*(8), 863–875.

Hertenstein, M. J. (2002). Touch: Its communicative functions in infancy. *Human Development, 45*, 70–94.

Hertenstein, M. J., & Campos, J. J. (2001). Emotion regulation via maternal touch. *Infancy, 2*, 549–566.

Hewlett, B. S., & Lamb, M. E. (2005). *Hunter-gatherer childhoods: Evolutionary, developmental and cultural perspectives*. New Brunswick, NJ: Aldine.

Hofer, M. A. (1987). Early social relationships as regulators of infant physiology and behavior. *Child Development, 58*(3), 633–647.

Hofer, M. A. (1994). Hidden regulators in attachment, separation, and loss. In N. A. Fox (Ed.), *The development of emotion regulation: Behavioral and biological considerations. Monographs of the Society for Research in Child Development, 59* (pp. 192–207). Chicago, IL: University of Chicago Press.

Howell, S., Westergaard, G. C., Hoos, B., Chavanne, T. J., Schoaf, S. E., Cleveland, A.,…Higley, J. D. (2007). Serotonergic influences on life-history outcomes in free-ranging male rhesus macaques. *American Journal of Primatology, 69*, 851–865.

Hrdy, S. (1999). *Mother Nature: Maternal instincts and how they shape the human species*. New York, NY: Ballantine.

Hrdy, S. (2009). *Mothers and others: The evolutionary origins of mutual understanding*. Cambridge, MA: Belknap Press.

Hsu, F. C., Zhang, G. J., Raol, Y. S., Valentino, R. J., Coulter, D. A., & Brooks-Kayal, A. R. (2003). Repeated neonatal handling with maternal separation permanently alters hippocampal GABAA receptors and behavioural stress responses. *PNAS of the United States of America, 155*, 12213–12218.

Insel, T. R., Gingrich, B. S., & Young, L. J. (2001). Oxytocin: Who needs it? *Progress in Brain Research, 133*, 59–66.

Jean, A. D. L., Stack, D. M., & Fogel, A. (2009). A longitudinal investigation of maternal touching across the first 6 months of life: Age and context effects. *Infant Behavior and Development, 32*, 344–349.

Kagan, J. (1997). Conceptualizing psychopathology: The importance of developmental profiles. *Developmental Psychopathology, 9*, 321–334.

Kalin, N. H. (1999). Primate models of understanding human aggression. *Journal of Clinical Psychiatry, 60*(Suppl 15), 29–32.

Katz, M., Liu, C., Schaer, M., Parker, K. J., Ottet, M. C., Epps, A.,…Lyons, D. M. (2009). Prefrontal plasticity and stress inoculation-induced resilience. *Developmental Neuroscience, 31*(4), 293–299.

Keltner, D. (2009). *Born to be good: The science of a meaningful life*. New York, NY: Norton.

Klaus, M. H., & Kennell, J. H. (1976/1983). *Maternal-infant bonding: The impact of early separation or loss on family development*. St. Louis, MO: C. V. Mosby.

Kochanska, G. (2002). Mutually responsive orientation between mothers and their young children: A context for the early development of conscience. *Current Directions in Psychological Science, 11*(6), 191–195. doi:10.1111/1467–8721.00198

Konner, M. (2005). Hunter-gatherer infancy and childhood: The !Kung and others. In B. Hewlett & M. Lamb (Eds.), *Hunter-gatherer childhoods: Evolutionary, developmental and cultural perspectives* (pp. 19–64). New Brunswick, NJ: Transaction.

Konner, M. (2010). *The evolution of childhood*. Cambridge, MA: Belknap Press.

Konner, M., & Worthman, C. (1980). Nursing frequency, gonadal function and birth spacing among !Kung hunger-gatherers. *Science, 207*, 788–791.

Kramer, M. S., Chalmer, S. B., Hodnett, E. D., Sevkovskaya, Z., Dzikovich, I., Shapiro, S.,...Helsing, E. (2001). Promotion of Breastfeeding Intervention Trial (PROBIT): A randomized trial in the Republic of Belarus. *Journal of the American Medical Association, 285*(4), 413–420.

Kramer, M. S., & Kakuma, R. (2004). The optimal duration of exclusive breastfeeding: A systematic review. *Advanced Experimental Medical Biology, 554*, 63–77.

Ladd, C. O., Owens, M. J., & Nemeroff, C. B. (1996). Persistent changes in corticotropin-releasing factor neuronal systems induced by maternal deprivation. *Endocrinology, 137*, 1212–1218.

Lanius, R., Vermetten, E., & Pain, C. (2010). *The impact of early life trauma on health and disease: The hidden epidemic*. New York, NY: Cambridge University Press.

Lansing, J. S., Watkins, J. C., Hallmark, B., Cox, M. P., Karafet, T. M., Sudoyo, H., & Hammer, M. F. (2008). Male dominance rarely skews the frequency distribution of Y chromosome haplotypes in human populations. *PNAS of the United States of America, 105*, 11645–11650.

Lauritzen, L., Hansen, H. S., Jørgensen, M. H., & Michaelsen, K. F. (2001). The essentiality of long chain n-3 fatty acids in relation to development and function of the brain and retina. *Progressive Lipid Research, 40*, 1–94.

Lavelli, M., & Poli, M. (1998). Early mother-infant interaction during breast- and bottle-feeding. *Infant Behavior and Development, 21*, 667–684.

LeDoux, J. E. (1996). *The emotional brain*. New York, NY: Simon and Schuster.

Lester, B. M., Masten, A., & McEwen, B. (Eds.). (2007). *Resilience in children. Annals of the New York Academy of Sciences* (Vol. 1094). New York, NY: Wiley-Blackwell.

Levine, R. A., Dixon, S., LeVine, S. E., Richman, A., Keefer, C., Liederman, P. H., & Brazelton, T. B. (1994). *Child care and culture: Lessons from Africa*. New York, NY: Cambridge University Press.

Levine, S. (2005). Developmental determinants of sensitivity and resistance to stress. *Psychoneuroendocrinology, 30*(10), 939–946.

Lewis, T., Amini, F., & Lannon, R. (2000). *A general theory of love*. New York, NY: Vintage.

Liu, D., Diorio, J., Tannenbaum, B., Caldji, C., Francis, D., Freedman, A.,...Meaney, M. J. (1997). Maternal care, hippocampal glucocorticoid receptors, and hypothalamic-pituitary-adrenal responses to stress. *Science, 277*(5332), 1659–1662.

Liu, W. F., Laudert, S., Perkins, B., MacMillan-York, E., Martin, S., & Graven, S., for the NIC/Q 2005 Physical Environment Exploratory Group. (2007). The development of potentially better practices to support the neurodevelopment of infants in the NICU. *Journal of Perinatology, 27*, S48–S74.

Lumsden, C. J., & Wilson, E. O. (1981). *Genes, mind, and culture: The coevolutionary process*. Cambridge, MA: Harvard University Press.

Lupien, S. J., McEwen, B. S., Gunnar, M. R., & Heim, C. (2009). Effects of stress throughout the lifespan on the brain, behaviour and cognition. *Nature, 10*, 434–445.

MacDonald, G., & Jensen-Campbell, L. A. (Eds.). (2011). *Social pain: Neuropsychological and health implications of loss and exclusion*. Washington, DC: American Psychological Association.

Marshall, R. E., Porter, F. L., Rogers, A. G., Moore, J., Anderson, B., & Boxerman, S. B. (1982). Circumcision II: Effects on mother-infant interaction. *Early Human Development, 7,* 367–374.

Martin, L. J., Woo, J. G., Geraghty, S. R., Altaye, M., Davidson, B. S., Banach, W., ... Morrow, A. L. (2006). Adiponectin is present in human milk and is associated with maternal factors. *American Journal of Clinical Nutrition, 83,* 1106–1111.

McDowell, M. M., Wang, C.-Y., & Kennedy-Stephenson, J. (2008). *Breastfeeding in the United States: Findings from the National Health and Nutrition Examination Survey, 1999–2006.* Data Brief Number 5. Hyattsville, MD: National Center for Health Statistics.

McEwen, B. S. (2007). Physiology and neurobiology of stress and adaptation: Central role of the brain. *Physiological Review, 87,* 873–904.

McGilchrist, I. (2009). *The master and his emissary: The divided brain and the making of the western world.* New Haven, CT: Yale University Press.

McGowan, P. O., Sasaki, A., D'Alessio, A. C., Dymov, S., Labonté, B., Szyf, M., ... Meaney, M. J. (2009). Epigenetic regulation of the glucocorticoid receptor in human brain associates with childhood abuse. *Nature Neuroscience, 12,* 342–348.

McKenna, J., Ball, H., & Gettler, L. (2007). Mother-infant cosleeping, breastfeeding and sudden infant death syndrome: What biological anthropology has discovered about normal infant sleep and pediatric sleep medicine. *Yearbook of Physiological Anthropology, 50,* 133–161.

McKenna, J., & McDade, T. (2005). Why babies should never sleep alone: A review of the co-sleeping controversy in relation to SIDS, bedsharing and breast feeding. *Paediatric Respiratory Reviews, 6*(2), 134–152.

McKenna, J. J., Mosko, S., Richard, C., Drummond, S., Hunt, L., Cetal, M., & Arpaia, J. (1994). Mutual behavioral and physiological influences among solitary and co-sleeping mother-infant pairs: Implications for SIDS. *Early Human Development, 38,* 182–201.

Merzenich, M. M., Wright, B., Jenkins, W., Xerri, C., Byl, N., Miller, S., & Tallal, P. (1996). Cortical plasticity underlying perceptual, motor and cognitive skill development: Implications for neurorehabilitation. *Cold Spring Harbor Symposium on Quantitative Biology, 61,* 1–8.

Michaelsen, K. F., Lauritzen, L., Jørgensen, M. H., & Mortensen, E. L. (2003). Breast-feeding and brain development. *Scandinavian Journal of Nutrition, 47*(3), 147–151.

Millennium Ecosystem Assessment. (2005). *Ecosystems and human well-being: Synthesis.* Washington, DC: Island Press.

Miller, E., & Almon, J. (2009). *Crisis in the kindergarten—why children need to play in school.* College Park, MD: Alliance for Childhood.

Mortensen, E. L., Michaelsen, K. F., Sanders, S. A., & Reinisch, J. M. (2002). The association between duration of breastfeeding and adult intelligence. *Journal of the American Medical Association, 297,* 2365–2371.

Moszkowski, R. J., Stack, D. M., Girouard, N., Field, T. M., Hernandez-Reif, M., & Diego, M. (2009). Touching behaviors of infants of depressed mothers during normal and perturbed interactions. *Infant Behavior and Development, 32,* 183–194.

Nadel, J., & Muir, R. (Eds.). (2005). *Emotional development.* Oxford: Oxford University Press.

Narvaez, D. (2008). Triune ethics: The neurobiological roots of our multiple moralities. *New Ideas in Psychology, 26*, 95–119.

National Institute of Child Health and Human Development, Early Child Care Research Network. (2003). Does amount of time spent in child care predict socioemotional adjustment during the transition to kindergarten? *Child Development, 74*, 976–1005.

Nelson, E. E., & Panksepp, J. (1998). Brain substrates of infant-mother attachment: Contributions of opioids, oxytocin, and norepinephrine. *Neuroscience and Biobehavioral Reviews, 22*, 437–452.

Newburg, D. S., & Walker, W. A. (2007). Protection of the neonate by the innate immune system of developing gut and of human milk. *Pediatric Research, 61*(1), 2–8.

Oddy, W. H., Kendall, G. E., Li, J., Jacoby, P., Robinson, M., de Klerk, N. H., . . . Stanley, F. J. (2010). The long-term effects of breastfeeding on child and adolescent mental health: A pregnancy cohort study followed for 14 years. *Journal of Pediatrics, 156*, 568–574.

Organization for Economic Cooperation and Development. (2009). *Doing better for children.* Paris: OECD Publishing.

Orosz, S. E., & Bradshaw, G. A. (2007). Avian neuroanatomy revisited: From clinical principles to avian cognition. *Veterinary Clinics Exotic Animals Practice, 10*, 775–802.

Panksepp, J. (1998). *Affective neuroscience: The foundations of human and animal emotions.* New York, NY: Oxford University Press.

Panksepp, J. (2003). Neuroscience: Feeling the pain of social loss. *Science, 302*(5643), 237–239.

Panksepp, J. (2005). Affective consciousness: Core emotional feelings in animals and humans. *Consciousness and Cognition, 14*, 19–69.

Panksepp, J. (2007). Can PLAY diminish ADHD and facilitate the construction of the social brain. *Journal of the Canadian Academy of Child and Adolescent Psychiatry, 10*, 57–66.

Panksepp, J. (2009). Primary process affects and brain oxytocin. *Biological Psychiatry, 65*, 725–727.

Panksepp, J. (2010). The basic affective circuits of mammalian brains: Implications for healthy human development and the cultural landscapes of ADHD. In C. M. Worthman, P. M. Plotsky, D. S. Schechter, & C. A. Cummings (Eds.), *Formative experiences: The interaction of caregiving, culture, and developmental psychobiology* (pp. 470–502). New York, NY: Cambridge University Press.

Panksepp, J., & Biven, L. (2012). *The archaeology of mind: Neuroevolutionary origins of human emotions.* New York, NY: Norton.

Panksepp, J., & Harro, J. (2004). The future of neuropeptides in biological psychiatry and emotional psychopharmacology: Goals and strategies. In J. Panksepp (Ed.), *Textbook of biological psychiatry* (pp. 627–660). New York, NY: Wiley.

Panksepp, J., Siviy, S., & Normansell, L. A. (1984). The psychobiology of play: Theoretical and methodological perspectives. *Neuroscience and Biobehavioral Reviews, 8*, 465–492.

Panksepp, J., & Watt, J. (2011). Why does depression hurt? Ancestral primary-process separation-distress (PANIC) and diminished brain reward (SEEKING) processes in the genesis of depressive affect. *Psychiatry, 74*, 5–14.

Papousek, H., & Papousek, M. (1992). Beyond emotional bonding: The role of preverbal communication in mental growth and health. *Infant Mental Health Journal, 13*, 43–53.

Parham, P. (2004). *The immune system.* New York, NY: Garland Publishing.

Peisner-Feinberg, E., Bernier, K., Bryant, D., & Maxwell, K. (2000). *Family child care in North Carolina.* Chapel Hill, NC: Frank Porter Graham Child Development Institute.

Pellis, S. M., & Pellis, V. C. (2009). *The playful brain.* Oxford: Oneworld Publications.

Perry, B. D., Pollard, R., Blakely, T., Baker, W., & Vigilante, D. (1995). Childhood trauma, the neurobiology of adaptation and 'use-dependent' development of the brain: How "states" become "traits." *Infant Mental Health Journal, 16*(4), 271–291.

Porges, S. W. (2007). The polyvagal perspective. *Biological Psychology, 74,* 116–143.

Porter, C. L. (2003). Coregulation in mother-infant dyads: Links to infants' cardiac vagal tone. *Psychological Reports, 92,* 307–319.

Potegal, M., & Einon, D. (1989). Aggressive behaviors in adult rats deprived of playfighting experiences as juveniles. *Developmental Psychobiology, 22,* 159–172.

Powell, D., Fixen, D., & Dunlop, G. (2003). *Pathways to service utilization: A synthesis of evidence relevant to young children with challenging behavior.* Tampa, FL: University of South Florida: Center for Evidence-Based Practice: Young Children with Challenging Behavior.

Prescott, J. W. (1996). The origins of human love and violence. *Pre- and Perinatal Psychology Journal, 10*(3), 143–188.

Preston, S., & de Waal, F. (2002). Empathy: Its ultimate and proximate bases. *Behavioral and Brain Sciences, 25,* 1–72.

Propper, C., Moore, G. A., Mills-Koonce, W. R., Halpern, C. T., Hill-Soderlund, A. L., Calkins, S. D., . . . Cox, M. (2008). Gene–environment contributions to the development of infant vagal reactivity: The interaction of dopamine and maternal sensitivity. *Child Development, 79*(5), 1377–1394.

Raver, C. C., & Knitze, J. (2002). *Ready to enter: What research tells policymakers about strategies to promote social and emotional school readiness among three- and four-year-old children.* New York, NY: National Center for Children in Poverty.

Reddy, V. (2008). *How infants know minds.* Cambridge, MA: Harvard University Press.

Richman, A., Miller, P., & LeVine, R. (1992). Cultural and educational variations in maternal responsiveness. *Developmental Psychology, 28,* 614–621.

Roughgarden, J., & Song, Z. (in press). Incentives in the family I: The family firm, an evolutionary/economic theory for parent-offspring relations. In D. Narvaez, K. Valentino, A. Fuentes, J. McKenna, & P. Gray (Eds.), *Ancestral landscapes in human evolution: Culture, childrearing and social wellbeing.* New York, NY: Oxford University Press.

Sagi, A., van Ijzendoorn, M., Aviezer, O., Donnell, F., Koren-Karie, N., Joels, T., & Harel, Y. (1995). Attachments in a multiple-caregiver and multiple-infant environment: The case of the Israeli kibbutzim. In E. Waters (Ed.), *Caregiving, cultural, and cognitive perspectives on secure-base behavior. Monographs of the Society for Research in Child Development, 60,* (pp. 71–91). Chicago, IL: University of Chicago Press.

Sanchez, M. M., Ladd, C. O., & Plotsky, P. M. (2001). Early adverse experience as a developmental risk factor for later psychopathology. *Development and Psychopathology, 13*(3), 419–449.

Scanlon, K. S., Grummer-Strawn, L., Shealy, K. R., Jefferds, M. E., Chen, J., Singleton, J. A., & Philip, C. M. (2007). Breastfeeding trends and updated national health objectives for exclusive breastfeeding—United States, birth years 2000–2004. *Morbidity and Mortality Weekly Report, 56*(30), 760–763.

Schore, A. N. (1994). *Affect regulation and the origin of the self.* Hillsdale, NJ: Erlbaum.

Schore, A. N. (1997). Early organization of the nonlinear right brain and development of a predisposition to psychiatric disorders. *Development and Psychopathology, 9*, 595–631.

Schore, A. N. (2000). Attachment and the regulation of the right brain. *Attachment and Human Development, 2*, 23–47.

Schore, A. N. (2001a). The effects of early relational trauma on right brain development, affect regulation, and infant mental health. *Infant Mental Health Journal, 22*, 201–269.

Schore, A. N. (2001b). Effects of a secure attachment relationship on right brain development, affect regulation, and infant mental health. *Infant Mental Health Journal, 22*, 7–66.

Schore, A. N. (2002). Dysregulation of the right brain: A fundamental mechanism of traumatic attachment and the psychopathogenesis of posttraumatic stress disorder. *Australian and New Zealand Journal of Psychiatry, 36*, 9–30.

Schore, A. N. (2003). *Affect dysregulation and disorders of the self.* New York, NY: Norton.

Schore, A. N. (2005). Attachment, affect regulation, and the developing right brain: Linking developmental neuroscience to pediatrics. *Pediatrics in Review, 26*, 204–211.

Schore, A. N. (2009). Attachment trauma and the developing right brain: Origins of pathological dissociation. In P. F. Dell & J. A. O'Neil (Eds.), *Dissociation and the dissociative disorders: DMS-V and beyond* (pp. 107–141). New York, NY: Routledge.

Schore, A.N. (2012). *The science of the art of psychotherapy.* New York, NY: Norton.

Scott, E., & Panksepp, J. (2003). Rough-and-tumble play in human children. *Aggressive Behavior, 29*(6), 539–551.

Sheldon, K. M., Kashdan, T. B., & Steger, M. F. (Eds.). (2011). *Designing positive psychology: Taking stock and moving forward.* New York, NY: Oxford University Press.

Shonkoff, J.P., Garner, A.S. The Committee on Psychosocial Childhood, Adoption, and Dependent Care, and Section on Developmental and Behavioral Pediatrics, Dobbins, M.I.,. Earls, M.F., McGuinn, L., ... & Wood, D.L. (2012). The lifelong effects of early childhood adversity and toxic stress. *Pediatrics* 2012;129;e232; originally published online December 26, 2011; DOI: 10.1542/peds.2011–2663

Siviy, S., & Panksepp, J. (2011). In search of neurobiological substrates for social playfulness in mammalian brain. *Neuroscience and Biobehavioral Reviews.* doi:10.1016/j.neubiorev.2011.03.006

Slusser, W., & Powers, N. G. (1997). Breastfeeding update 1: Immunology, nutrition, and advocacy. *Pediatrics in Review, 18*, 111–119.

Spinka, M., Newberry, R. C., & Bekoff, M. (2001). Mammalian play: Training for the unexpected. *Quarterly Review of Biology, 76*, 141–168.

Stam, R., Akkermans, L. M., & Wiegant, V. M. (1997). Trauma and the gut: Interactions between stressful experience and intestinal function. *Gut, 40*, 704–709.

Suomi, S. J. (2006). Risk, resilience, and gene x environment interactions in rhesus monkeys. *Annals of the New York Academy of Sciences, 1094*, 52–62.

Swain, J. E., Tasgin, E., Mayes, L. C., Feldman, R., & Leckman, J. F. (2008). Cesarean delivery affects maternal brain response to own baby cry. *Journal of Child Psychology and Psychiatry, 9*, 1042–1052.

Szajnberg, N., Goldenberg, A., & Hatari, U. (2010). Early trauma, later outcome: Results from longitudinal studies and clinical observations. In R. Lanius, E. Vermetten, & C. Pain (Eds.), *The impact of early life trauma on health and disease: The hidden epidemic* (pp. 33–42). New York, NY: Cambridge University Press.

Szyf, M., Weaver, I., & Meaney, M. (2007). Maternal care, the epigenome and phenotypic differences in behavior. *Reproductive Toxicology, 24*(1), 9–19.

Szyf, M., McGowan, P., & Meaney, M. J. (2008). The social environment and the epigenome. *Environmental and Molecular Mutagenesis, 49,* 46–60.

Tannock, M. T. (2008). Rough and tumble play: An investigation of the perceptions of educators and young children. *Early Childhood Education Journal, 35,* 357–361.

Teicher, M. (2002). Scars that won't heal: The neurobiology of child abuse. *Scientific American, 286*(3), 68–75.

Textor, R. B. (1967). *A cross-cultural summary.* New Haven, CT: HRAF Press.

Thoman, E. B. (2006). Co-sleeping, an ancient practice: Issues of the past and present, and possibilities for the future. *Sleep Medicine Review, 10,* 407–417.

Thomas, E. M. (1959). *The harmless people.* New York, NY: Knopf.

Trevarthen, C. (2005). Action and emotion in development of the human self, its sociability and cultural intelligence: Why infants have feelings like ours. In J. Nadel and D. Muir (Eds.), *Emotional development* (pp. 61–91). Oxford: Oxford University Press.

Trevathan, W. R. (2011). *Human birth: An evolutionary perspective.* New York, NY: Aldine de Gruyter.

Tronick, E. (2007). *The neurobehavioral and social-emotional development of infants and children.* New York, NY: W. W. Norton.

Turnbull, C. M. (1961). *The forest people.* New York, NY: Simon and Schuster.

Uher, R., & McGuffin, P. (2008). The moderation by the serotonin transporter gene of environmental adversity in the aetiology of mental illness: Review and methodological analysis. *Molecular Psychiatry, 13*(2), 131–146.

UNICEF. (2007). *Child poverty in perspective: An overview of child well-being in rich countries, a comprehensive assessment of the lives and well-being of children and adolescents in the economically advanced nations. Report Card 7.* Florence, Italy: United Nations Children's Fund Innocenti Research Centre.

U.S. Department of Health and Human Services, Substance Abuse and Mental Health Services Administration. (1999). *Mental health: A report of the Surgeon General.* Rockville, MD: Center for Mental Health Services, National Institutes of Health, National Institute of Mental Health.

Uvnas-Moberg, K. (1997). Physiological and endocrine effects of social contact. *Annals of the New York Academy of Sciences, 15*(807), 146–163.

Van den Berg, C. L., Hol, T., van Ree, J. M., Spruijt, B. M., Everts, H., & Koolhaas, J. M. (1999). Play is indispensable for an adequate development of coping with social challenges in rats. *Developmental Psychobiology, 34,* 129–138.

Van Ijzendoorn, M., Sagi, A., & Lambermon, M. (1992). The multiple caretaker paradox: Data from Holland and Israel. In R. C. Pianta (Ed.), *Beyond the parents: The role of other adults in children's lives: New directions for child development, 57* (pp. 5–24). San Francisco, CA: Jossey-Bass.

Vanderschuren, L. J., Niesink, R. J., & Van Ree, J. M. (1997). The neurobiology of social play behavior in rats. *Neuroscience and Biobehavioral Reviews, 21,* 309–326.

Vermeer, H. J., & van Ijzendoorn, M. H. (2006). Children's elevated cortisol levels at daycare: A review and meta-analysis. *Early Childhood Research Quarterly, 21*(3), 390–401.

Wagner, M. (2006). *Born in the USA: How a broken maternity system must be fixed to put women and children first.* Berkeley, CA: University of California Press.

Walker, M. (1993). A fresh look at the risks of artificial infant feeding. *Journal of Human Lactation, 9*(2), 97–107.

Watt, D. F., & Panksepp, J. (2009). Depression: An evolutionarily conserved mechanism to terminate separation-distress? A review of aminergic, peptidergic, and neural network perspectives. *Neuropsychoanalysis, 11*, 5–48.

Weaver, I. C., Szyf, M., & Meaney, M. J. (2002). From maternal care to gene expression: DNA methylation and the maternal programming of stress responses. *Endocrine Research, 28*, 699.

West-Eberhard, M. J. (2003). *Developmental plasticity and evolution.* New York, NY: Oxford University Press.

Woolley, A. W., Chabris, C. F., Pentland, A., Hashmim, N., & Malone, T. W. (2010). Evidence for a collective intelligence factor in the performance of human groups. *Science, 330*, 686–688.

World Health Organization and World Organization of Family Doctors. (2008). *Integrating mental health into primary care: A global perspective.* Geneva and London: Author.

Worthman, C. M., Plotsky, P. M., Schechter, D. S., & Cummings, C. A. (Eds.). (2010). *Formative experiences: The interaction of caregiving, culture, and developmental psychobiology.* New York, NY: Cambridge University Press.

Yehuda, S., Rabinovitz, S., & Mostofsky, D. I. (1999). Essential fatty acids are mediators of brain biochemistry and cognitive functions. *Journal of Neuroscience Research, 56*, 565–570.

Zinken, J., Knoll, M., & Panksepp, J. (2008). Universality and diversity in the vocalization of emotions. In K. Izdebski (Ed.), *Emotions in the human voice, Vol. 1. Foundations* (pp. 185–202). San Diego, CA: Plural Publishing.

Zito, J., Safer, D., dos Ries, S., Gardener, J., Boles, M., & Lynch, F. (2000). Trends in prescribing psychotropic medications to preschoolers. *Journal of the American Medical Association, 282*, 1025–1030.

Zubieta, J. K., Ketter, T. A., Bueller, J. A., Xu, Y., Kilbourn, M. R., Young, E. A., & Koeppe, R. A. (2003). Regulation of human affective responses by anterior cingulate and limbic and mu-opioid neurotransmission. *General Psychiatry, 60*(11), 1037–1172.

2

Bowlby's "Environment of Evolutionary Adaptedness"

RECENT STUDIES ON THE INTERPERSONAL NEUROBIOLOGY OF ATTACHMENT AND EMOTIONAL DEVELOPMENT

Allan N. Schore

In a description of the aims of the volume and accompanying symposium, Darcia Narvaez, Jaak Panksepp, and I offer a large body of data from a number of disciplines that disturbingly indicate that "American culture may be deviating increasingly from traditional social practices that emerged in our ancestral 'environment of evolutionary adaptedness'" (Narvaez, Panksepp, & Schore, 2010). This term was devised by John Bowlby, the British psychiatrist-psychoanalyst who created attachment theory. An early pioneer of an interdisciplinary perspective, Bowlby (1969) integrated developmental psychology, psychoanalysis, behavioral biology, and anthropology to offer the organizing principles of his theory in his first of three now classic volumes, *Attachment*. In this seminal statement of the theory, Bowlby proposes, "In the case of biological systems, structure takes a form that is determined by the kind of environment in which the system has been in fact operating during its evolution.... This environment I propose to term the system's 'environment of adaptedness.' Only within its environment of adaptedness can it be expected that a system will work efficiently" (p. 47).

Over the course of this first volume, Bowlby integrates psychoanalytic, ethological, anthropological, and human developmental data to argue that attachment represents not higher cognitive but instinctive behavior. In chapter 4, "Man's Environment of Evolutionary Adaptedness," he asserts,

> [W]hen we come to consider with what *instinctive* behaviour—or, more properly, with what behavioural systems mediating instinctive behaviour—humans may be endowed, a first task to consider is the nature of the environment within they are adapted to operate.... The only relevant criterion by which to consider the natural adaptedness of any particular part of present-day man's behavioural equipment is the degree to which and the way in which it might

contribute to population *survival* in man's primeval environment (Bowlby, 1969, pp. 58–59, my italics).

Turning to ethology, Bowlby offers examples of instinctive survival behavior in subhuman species. He notes that other higher primates also possess "a large repertoire of calls, postures, and gestures that act as a means of communication between members of a group" (p. 63). Importantly, Bowlby postulates that "man's environment of evolutionary adaptedness" (EEA) is a version of a human's "ordinary expectable environment" (p. 64). But this concept is more than just a psychological construct—it also describes events at the biological level. "Not a single feature of a species' *morphology, physiology, and behavior* can be understood or even discussed intelligently except in relation to that species' environment of evolutionary adaptedness" (Bowlby, 1969, p. 64, my italics).

The core of the *Attachment* volume, and, indeed, all of Bowlby's work, elaborates the centrality of the early developing emotional bond between the mother and infant to all later functioning. In chapter 11, "The Child's Tie to Its Mother: Attachment Behaviour," Bowlby proposes, "the child's tie to his mother is a product of a number of behavioural systems that have proximity to mother as a predictable outcome.... The behavioural systems themselves are believed to develop within the infant as a result of his interaction with his environment of evolutionary adaptedness, and especially of his interaction with the principal figure in that environment, namely the mother" (pp. 180–181). Later in the book he observes, "[[B]]ehavioral systems responsible for maternal behavior in a species will work within certain ranges of social and physical environment and not outside them" (p. 470).

Bowlby's speculation that developing structural biological systems are impacted by the environment in which they evolve can now be understood as a principle of interpersonal neurobiology. In modern terms, "biological structure" is currently identified as the *morphology and physiology* of the developing brain that is evolving during the period of attachment, infancy. Indeed, Bowlby gives some clues as to specifically which developing brain systems are influenced by the EEA: those involved in "attachment systems mediating *instinctive* behaviour" that contribute to "population *survival* in man's primeval environment." My work in developmental affective neuroscience indicates that attachment transactions shape the connectivity of specifically the early developing right brain, which is dominant for control of vital functions supporting *survival* and for the processing of emotions (Schore, 1994, 2005). Damasio (1994) argues that emotions are "a powerful manifestation of drives and *instincts.*"

In this chapter, I will argue that the EEA can be identified with the social-emotional relational environment provided by the primary caregiver, which shapes, for better or worse, the experience-dependent maturation of the brain systems involved in attachment. Citing current research in developmental neuroscience, I shall outline recent updates in modern attachment theory (Schore & Schore, 2008), focusing on the early developing right brain and its central role in emotional and social development. Utilizing the perspective of interpersonal neurobiology, I will propose that the EEA facilitates or inhibits the emergence of right lateralized self-regulatory systems. I will also describe later sequelae of significant alterations in the EEA and outline a model of psychobiological evaluations of the EEA that can be used in early diagnosis, intervention, and prevention. Throughout, I will use the actual voices of researchers in various fields in order to show the convergence that is now occurring in an overarching psychoneurobiological model of early human development. This large body of research suggests that the EEA operates within the mother–infant attachment bond at implicit nonverbal levels and molds postnatal right brain development. (For more recent studies on the interpersonal neurobiology of attachment, see Schore 2010a, 2010b, 2010c, 2012).

Interpersonal Neurobiology of Human Brain Development

Neuroscience is now exploring the primacy of developing right brain structure–function relations over the pre- and postnatal stages of life. In classical research, Dobbing and Sands (1973) described the human brain growth spurt, which begins in the last trimester and is at least five-sixths postnatal, and continues to about 18 to 24 months of age. Evidence now clearly indicates that during this rapid period of brain development, the right hemisphere develops before the left. In the middle of the last decade, the pioneer neuroscientist Paul MacLean (1996) asserted, "For the mother the experience during pregnancy of the formless life within, could become after birth a sense of exteriorization and extension of the self that physiologically derives to a large extent from the right hemisphere" (p. 435). In parallel work, Trevarthen (1996) concluded, "The right hemisphere is more advanced than the left in surface features from about the 25th (gestational) week and this advance persists until the left hemisphere shows a postnatal growth spurt starting in the second year" (p. 582). These ideas are supported in later studies by Schleussner et al. (2004), who report "an earlier maturation of certain right than homologous left hemispheric brain areas during fetal brain development" (p. 133). Even more recently, Kasprian et al. (2010) document that at 26 gestational weeks the human fetal right superior temporal sulcus appears earlier and is deeper than the left and conclude, "Our structural data further support the findings of functional neuroimaging studies indicating an earlier maturity of right hemispheric function" (p. 6).

Current interpersonal neurobiological models of perinatal and postnatal development are shifting emphasis from the development of more complex cognitions to the development of the communication and regulation of affect. In a prototypical description Walker-Andrews and Bahrick (2001) observe, "From birth, an infant is plunged into a world of other human beings in which conversation, gestures, and faces are omnipresent during the infant's waking hours.

Moreover, these harbingers of social information are dynamic, multimodal, and reciprocal" (p. 469). Despite the recent overemphasis on cognition, this perspective actually returns to Bowlby's (1969) original description of mother–infant attachment communications that are "accompanied by the strongest of feelings and emotions" and occur within a context of "facial expression, posture, tone of voice, physiological changes, tempo of movement, and incipient action" (p. 120). The bodily based nature of these instinctive attachment communications was stressed by Bowlby's colleague, the pediatrician-psychoanalyst Donald Winnicott, who affirmed, "The main thing is a communication between the baby and the mother in terms of the anatomy and physiology of live bodies" (1986, p. 258).

The psychobiologically attuned mother does more than just receive the infant's affective communications. Subsequently, she regulates these affect-arousal states, thereby minimizing the infant's negative states in comforting transactions but also maximizing his or her positive affective states in interactive play. The primary caregiver is not so much regulating overt behavior as internal states. According to Ovtscharoff and Braun, "The dyadic interaction between the newborn and the mother . . . serves as a regulator of the developing individual's internal homeostasis" (2001, p. 33). Similarly, Pipp and Harmon assert, "It may be that . . . we are biologically connected to those with whom we have close relationships. . . . Homeostatic regulation between members of a dyad is a stable aspect of all intimate relationships throughout the lifespan" (1987, p. 651). The evolutionary mechanism of attachment, the interactive regulation of emotion, thus represents the regulation of biological synchronicity between and within organisms (Bradshaw & Schore, 2007; Schore, 1994).

But even more than this, it is now thought that "the regulatory function of the newborn-mother interaction may be an essential promoter to ensure the normal development and maintenance of synaptic connections during the establishment of functional brain circuits" (Ovtscharoff & Braun, 2001, p. 33). Indeed, affectively laden attachment communications are directly impacting the massive levels of synaptogenesis that characterize the brain growth spurt that spans the last trimester of pregnancy through the second year. A magnetic resonance imaging (MRI) study by Matsuzawa et al. (2001) reveals that the volume of the brain increases rapidly during the first 2 years. These authors document normal adult appearance at 2 years and all major fiber tracts at age 3, and that infants under 2 years show higher right than left hemispheric volumes.

The enormously accelerated growth of the brain during the human brain growth spurt is reflected in the finding that during prenatal and postnatal periods, the rate of synaptogenesis is estimated at 40,000 new synapses every second (Lagercrantz & Ringstedt, 2000). Knickmeyer et al. (2008) report, "Total brain volume increased 101% in the first year, with a 15% increase in the second. . . . The volume of the subcortical area (including brainstem) increased by 130% in the first year and by 14% in the second year" (p. 12178). The subcortical brainstem systems that are actively expressed in the first year generate what Bowlby (1969) termed "attachment systems mediating instinctive behaviour." It is important to emphasize that the structural maturation of these brain systems is not just genetically regulated. Rather, they are characterized as an epigenetic relational process of "experience-dependent maturation." With direct relevance to current interpersonal neurobiological models of attachment, I have suggested that "the self-organization of the developing brain occurs in the context of another self, another brain" (Schore, 1996, p. 60). What do we now know about the intersubjective emotional communications that are transmitted between the mother's and the infant's right brains?

Recent Studies of Right Brain–to–Right Brain Attachment Communications

At about the same time that Bowlby was describing affective attachment communications of facial expression, posture, and tone of voice, Brown and Jaffe's (1975) developmental neuropsychological research indicated, "The right hemisphere can be considered dominant in infancy, for the type of visual and acoustic communication which is relevant for the prelinguistic child" (p. 108). Following Bowlby's lead, in 1994 I suggested that during attachment episodes of *visual-facial, auditory-prosodic,* and *tactile-gestural* affective communications, the psychobiologically attuned caregiver regulates the infant's internal states of arousal.

> The infant's early maturing right hemisphere, which is dominant for the child's processing of visual emotional information, the infant's recognition of the mother's face, and the perception of arousal-inducing maternal facial expressions, is psychobiologically attuned to the output of the mother's right hemisphere, which is involved in the expression and processing of emotional information and in nonverbal communication. (Schore, 1994, p. 63)

A large body of developmental neurobiological research supports the hypothesis that the attachment mechanism is embedded in infant–caregiver right hemisphere–to–right hemisphere affective transactions.

With respect to *visual-facial attachment communications*, it is now established that mutual gaze is critical to early social development (Trevarthen & Aitken, 2001). The development of the capacity to efficiently process information from faces requires visual input to the right (and not left) hemisphere during infancy (Le Grand, Mondloch, Maurer, & Brent, 2003). At 2 months of age, the onset of a critical period during which synaptic connections in the developing occipital cortex are modified by visual experience (Yamada et al., 2000), infants show right hemispheric activation when exposed to a woman's face (Tzourio-Mazoyer et al., 2002). Using an electroencephalographic (EEG) methodology, T. Grossmann, Johnson, Farroni, and Csibra (2007) report that 4-month-old infants presented with images of a female face gazing directly ahead show enhanced gamma electrical activity over right prefrontal areas. Recent near-infrared spectroscopy (NIRS) research (perhaps the most suitable of all neuroscience techniques applicable to human infants) reveals that specifically the 5-month-olds' right hemisphere responds to images of adult female faces (Nakato et al., 2009; Otsuka et al., 2007). By age 6 months infants show a right lateralized left-gaze bias when viewing faces (Guo, Meints, Hall, Hall, & Mills, 2009).

Ongoing studies of prenatal, perinatal, and postnatal *auditory-prosodic attachment communications* also highlight the role of the right brain. In an EEG study of auditory pitch processing in preterm infants born at 30 gestational weeks, Mento, Suppiej, Altoe, and Bisiacchi (2010) conclude, "These findings suggest that the earlier right structural maturation in foetal epochs seems to be paralleled by a right functional development" (p. 1). Using NIRS with 2- to 6-day-old neonates, Telkemeyer et al. (2009) observe "responses to slow acoustic modulations are lateralized to the right hemisphere" (p. 14726). Prosodic processing in 3-month-old infants is known to activate the right temporoparietal region (Homae, Watanabe, Nakano, Asakawa, & Taga, 2006). T. Grossmann, Oberecker, Koch, and Friederici (2010) report that 7-month-old infants respond to emotional voices in a voice-sensitive region of the right superior temporal sulcus, and happy prosody specifically activates the right inferior frontal cortex. These authors conclude, "The pattern of finding suggests that temporal regions specialize in processing voices very early in development and that, already in infancy, emotions differentially modulate voice processing in the right hemisphere" (p. 852). At age 11 months, the voice of a woman's child-directed speech (i.e., with somewhat exaggerated prosody) elicits a right lateralized event-related potential (Thierry, Vihman, & Roberts, 2003).

In terms of *tactile-gestural attachment communications*, Sieratzki and Woll (1996) describe the effects of touch on the developing right hemisphere and assert that the emotional impact of touch is more direct and immediate if an infant is held to the left side of the body. Studies now demonstrate the essential role of maternal "affective touch" on human infant development in the first year of life (Ferber, Feldman, & Makhoul, 2008; Jean, Stack, & Fogel, 2009). This allows the infant and mother to utilize "interpersonal touch" as a communication system (Gallace & Spence, 2010), especially for the communication and regulation of emotional information (Hertenstein, 2002; Hertenstein & Campos, 2001). High levels of tactile stimulation and mutual touch occur in breastfeeding, and Lehtonen, Kononen, Purhonen, Partanen, and Saarikoski (2002) observe an increase in EEG amplitude in right posterior cortical areas in 6-month-old infants during the intense somatosensory tactile contact of breastfeeding.

With respect to gestures, Nagy (2006, p. 227) demonstrates "lateralized system for neonatal imitation" and concludes, "The early advantage of the right hemisphere (Chiron et al., 1997; Schore, 2000; Trevarthen & Aitken, 2001) in the first few months of life may affect the lateralized appearance of the first imitative gestures." Moreover,

Montirosso, Borgatti, and Tronick (2010) document left-sided regulatory gestures when infants are stressed. In summarizing their work on gestures, they state,

> Infants cope with the emotional distress caused by unresponsive mothers through self-regulation behaviors associated with a greater activation of the right hemisphere. In sum, this finding supports the view that during a stressful condition there is a state-dependent activation of the right hemisphere. . . . More generally these findings suggest that the right hemisphere is more involved in the social and biological functions regarding infant caregiver emotional bonding (Schore, 2005, 1999). (p. 108)

Confirming this relational neurobiological model, in very recent functional MRI studies of mother–infant emotional communication, Lenzi et al. (2009) offer data "supporting the theory that the right hemisphere is more involved than the left hemisphere in emotional processing and thus, mothering," and Noriuchi, Kikuchi, and Senoo (2008) report activation of the mother's right orbitofrontal cortex during moments of maternal love triggered by viewing a video of her own infant. Another NIRS study of infant–mother attachment at 12 months concludes, "Our results are in agreement with that of Schore (2000) who addressed the importance of the right hemisphere in the attachment system" (Minagawa-Kawai et al., 2009, p. 289).

Right Brain Dominance Established in the First Year of Human Life

These studies support a central tenet of my work, first articulated in 1994, that attachment impacts the developing right brain. Shortly after, Sieratzki and Woll (1996) definitively stated, "The role of the right hemisphere is crucial in relation to the most precious needs of mothers and infants" (p. 1747), and Chiron et al. (1997) published a study, "The Right Brain Hemisphere Is Dominant in Human Infants." Studies of the unique functions of the right brain subsequently significantly increased, and in 2002 Braun et al. asserted, "The right and left human brain hemispheres differ in macrostructure, ultra-structure, physiology, chemistry, and control of behavior" (p. 97). Indeed, a number of anatomical and imaging studies now show earlier maturation of the right hemisphere in prenatal and postnatal stages of human development (Gupta et al., 2005; Howard & Reggia, 2007; Sun et al., 2005). This research supports the earlier work of Previc (1991), who suggested that the origins of cerebral asymmetry emanate in the intrauterine environment, and that the prenatal positioning of the fetus in the womb allows the inward-facing left ear to receive a greater amount of vestibular stimulation and thus an earlier organization of the right hemispheric vestibular cortex, a brain system involved in emotion processing (Carmona, Holland, & Harrison, 2009).

There is now an emerging consensus that "the emotional experience(s) of the infant . . . are disproportionately stored or processed in the right hemisphere during the formative stages of brain ontogeny" (Semrud-Clikeman & Hynd, 1990, p. 198).

Over the course of the first year, increasingly complex right brain–to–right brain attachment communications imprint first right posterior cerebral areas involved in sensory processing (e.g., right occipital, right fusiform gyrus, right superior temporal sulcus, right temporoparietal regions), and later right anterior cerebral areas. Classical studies reveal regional differences in the time course of cortical synaptogenesis (Huttenlocher, 1990) and that the metabolic activity that underlies regional cerebral function is ontogenetically highest in the posterior sensorimotor cortex and only later rises in the anterior cortex (Chugani & Phelps, 1986). Indeed, although a period of synaptic excess occurs at 4 months in the visual cortex, a similar process does not occur in the prefrontal anterior cortex until the end of the first year of human life (Huttenlocher, 1979).

But maternal–infant emotional transactions allow for more than the experience-dependent maturation of cortical connections within the right cerebral hemisphere. In line with the principle of the sequential caudal-to-rostral structural development of the brain, bodily based attachment transactions also imprint subcortical-cortical connections of the right brain, which is deeply connected into the emotion-processing limbic system. Recall Bowlby's (1969) original description of mother–infant attachment communications that are "accompanied by the strongest of feelings and emotions." Basic research in developmental neuroscience now demonstrates that "the functional maturation of limbic circuits is significantly influenced by early socio-emotional experience" (Helmeke, Ovtscharoff, Poeggel, & Braun, 2001, p. 717). In functional MRI research, Dapretto et al. (2006) contend, "Typically developing children can rely upon a right hemisphere-mirroring neural mechanism—interfacing with the limbic system via the insula—whereby the meaning of imitated (or observed) emotion is directly felt and hence understood" (p. 30). Attachment studies thus strongly support Panksepp's (2008) bold assertion of the primacy of affective neuroscience: "Now cognitive science must re-learn that ancient emotional systems have a power that is quite independent of neocortical cognitive processes" (p. 51).

In addition, prenatal and postnatal interpersonal events also wire the connectivity of structures in the developing central nervous system (CNS) with energy-expending sympathetic and energy-conserving parasympathetic branches of the evolving autonomic nervous system (ANS). There is now consensus that the right brain plays a greater role than the left in autonomic arousal and therefore the somatic aspects of emotional states. Porges (2007) concludes, "Consistent with the views that the right hemisphere appears to play a greater role in affect, especially the adaptive expression of negative affect, the right hemisphere also appears to have a greater role in regulation of cardiac function presumably via shifts in [[parasympathetic]] vagal regulation" (p. 126). According to McGilchrist (2009, p. 437), "The right hemisphere is...more closely in touch with emotion and the body (therefore with the neurologically 'inferior' and more ancient regions of the central nervous system)."

Furthermore, a large body of studies now clearly indicates that maternal care within the attachment relationship shapes the infant's hypothalamic–pituitary–adrenocortical

(HPA) stress-regulating axis (Gunnar, 2000) and that epigenetic programming of maternal behavior alters the development of HPA responses to stress through tissue-specific effects on gene transcription (Weaver et al., 2004). The right hemisphere is known to play a dominant role in regulating the HPA axis and in mediating the human stress response. Indeed, this hemisphere more so than the left is central to the control of vital functions supporting *survival* and enabling the organism to cope with stresses and challenges (Wittling, 1997). Basic research now establishes that optimal stress regulation is dependent on "right hemispheric specialization in regulating stress—and emotion-related processes" (Sullivan & Dufresne, 2006, p. 55).

Environment of Evolutionary Adaptedness and the Emergence of Right Lateralized Self-Regulatory Systems

In a foreword of a reissue of the *Attachment* volume and in a subsequent article in the journal *Attachment & Human Development* (Schore, 2000), I discussed Bowlby's speculation that the environment of evolutionary adaptedness influences the development of a brain system that controls, or regulates, attachment. Bowlby (1969) described "a biological control system" that is centrally involved in instinctive behavior. This control system is structured as a hierarchical mode of organization, and its functions are associated with the organism's "state of arousal" that results from the critical operations of the reticular system and with "the appraisal of organismic states and situations of the midbrain nuclei and limbic system" (p. 110). He even offered a speculation about its anatomical location—the prefrontal lobes (p. 156). This control system, he said, is "open in some degree to influence by the environment in which development occurs" (p. 45). More specifically, it evolves in the infant's interaction with an "environment of adaptedness, and especially of his interaction with the principal figure in that environment, namely his mother" (p. 180). Furthermore, Bowlby speculated that the "upgrading of control during individual development from simple to more sophisticated is no doubt in large part a result of the growth of the central nervous system" (p. 156).

In parallel developmental work, Brazelton and Cramer (1990) speculated,

> The central nervous system, as it develops, drives infants towards mastery of themselves and their world. As they achieve each level of mastery, they seek a kind of homeostasis, until the nervous system presses them on to their next level. Internal equilibrium is always being upset by a new imbalance created as the nervous system matures. Maturation of the nervous system, accompanied by increasing differentiation of skills, drives infants to reorganize their control systems. (p. 98)

Modern developmental neuroscience and interpersonal neurobiology can now identify these attachment control systems (Schore, 2000, 2010c). The neuroanatomy of the emotion-processing limbic system is currently characterized as a system of vertically organized circuits within the brain. Authors are referring to the "rostral limbic system," a hierarchical sequence of interconnected limbic areas in orbito-frontal (ventromedial), anterior cingulate, insular cortex, and amygdala (see Schore, 2003). A large body of evidence shows that the orbitofrontal–insula, medial frontal anterior cingulate, and amygdala systems all interconnect with each other and with brainstem bioaminergic neuromodulatory and neuroendocrine nuclei in the hypo-thalamus, the "head ganglion" of the autonomic nervous system, and therefore each inputs the stress-regulating HPA axis (Schore, 2003). Because they are all com-ponents of the limbic system, each processes and imprints a positive or negative hedonic charge on current exteroceptive information about changes in the external social environment and then integrates it with interoceptive information about con-current alterations in internal bodily states (Schore, 2001a, 2003).

Because each control system directly interconnects with the ANS, and auto-nomic activity is controlled by multiple integrative sites within the CNS that are hierarchically organized, all are involved in the regulation of bodily driven affective states. Although all process exteroceptive and interoceptive information, the later maturing systems in the cortex process this information in a more complex fashion than the earlier subcortical components. The output of the lowest limbic levels is expressed as automatic innate reflexes, while higher processing produces more flexi-ble intuitive responses that allow fine adjustment to environmental circumstances.

In optimal socioemotional environments (EEAs), each limbic level has bidi-rectional connections with the others, and in this manner information can be for-warded both up and down the limbic axis for further appraisal and hierarchical regulation. The earliest and simplest appraisals of exteroceptive and interoceptive affective stimuli are rapid, nonconscious hedonic and aversive affective core pro-cesses in the amygdala; the later and most complex are subjective experiences of pleasure and pain in the orbitofrontal areas. These operations are primarily lateral-ized to the right limbic system, which is preferentially connected downward to the right neurochemical systems associated with arousal, emotion, and motivational states, and upward to the ipsilateral right neocortex.

As applied to the developmental organization of the limbic circuits of the right brain, this conception suggests a three-tiered self-organizing dynamic system. Increased interconnectivity (energy flow) among the three-component circuits would allow for information stored at one level to be transferred to the others. The top level that receives feedback from the lower performs an executive function, and this allows for emergent properties, that is, novel combinations of more complex emotional states. In this hierarchical model, lower subcortical levels of the right brain contain all the major motivational systems (including attachment, fear, play, sexuality, aggression, disgust, etc.) and generate somatic autonomic expressions and arousal intensities of all emotional states. When optimally functioning, higher orbitofrontal-limbic levels of the right cerebral hemisphere generate a conscious emotional state that expresses the affective output of these motivational systems.

In line with the morphogenetic principles of caudal-to-rostral brain development and vertical brain organization, a model of the ontogeny of the limbic system can be offered. Keeping in mind that in humans this development continues postnatally, reversing the sequence of the rostral limbic system (amygdala, anterior cingulate, orbitofrontal) offers specific ideas about how a number of discrete limbic components could come on line and develop connectivity in a defined sequence in the first year. Recall Bowlby's speculation that the limbic system is centrally involved in attachment and that the "upgrading of control during individual development from simple to more sophisticated is no doubt in large part a result of the growth of the central nervous system" (1969, p. 156).

In earlier writings (Schore, 2001a), I proposed that structures in the temporal lobe, the amygdala, especially the central and medial nuclei (Ulfig, Setzer, & Bohl, 2003) and the insula (Afif, Bouvier, Buenerd, Trouillas, & Mertens, 2007), as well as the paraventricular nucleus of the hypothalamus (Myers, Myers, Grober, & Nathanielsz, 1993), are in a critical period of maturation that occurs in the last trimester of pregnancy and continues through the first 2 months of human life. In the second quarter of the first year, a second homeostatic control system emerges in the anterior cingulate (medial frontal) cortex, which hierarchically controls the earlier amygdala-dominated limbic configuration. Ongoing studies in developmental brain research indicate that the orbital prefrontal cortex enters a critical period of growth that spans the last quarter of the first through the middle of the second year, an interval that corresponds with the beginnings of human socialization (Schore, 2003). This ventromedial prefrontal limbic structure is reciprocally interconnected with other limbic areas in the amygdala, insula, and anterior cingulate and represents the hierarchical apex of the right lateralized limbic system. It also forms direct connections with the hypothalamus, the head ganglion of the autonomic nervous system (Barbas, Saha, Rempel-Clower, & Ghashghaei, 2003), as well as bioaminergic neurons in the reticular system that control arousal (Schore, 1994). For the rest of the life span, this system is centrally involved in "the representation of emotional information and the regulator of emotional processes" (Roberts et al., 2004, p. 307) and "acquiring very specific forms of knowledge for regulating interpersonal behavior" (Dolan, 1999, p. 928).

The activity of this frontolimbic system is critical to the modulation of social and emotional behaviors and the homeostatic regulation of body and motivational states, affect-regulating functions that are centrally involved in attachment processes. The dendritic and synaptic maturation of the anterior cingulate and orbitofrontal cortices is specifically influenced by the social environment (Bock, Murmu, Ferdman, Leshem, & Braun, 2008; Schore, 1994, 2003). The orbitofrontal cortex, which is expanded in the right brain, matures at the end of the brain growth spurt in the second year. At this point it acts as the hierarchical apex of the emotion-processing limbic system and as "the highest level of control of behavior, especially in relation to emotion" (Price, Carmichael, & Drevets, 1996, p. 523). A number of writers have noted the importance of this system in early socialization, specifically in the developmental neurobiology of morality (e.g., Narvaez, 2008; Schore, 1994). Indeed, this ventromedial system is a central component of "a 'morality' network in the brain, predominantly in the right hemisphere" (Mendez & Shapira, 2009, p. 165), that is "necessary to oppose personal moral violations...by mediating antic-ipatory, self-focused, emotional reactions that may exert strong influence on moral choice and behavior" (Ciaramelli, Muccioli, Ladavas, & di Pellegrino, 2007, p. 84).

For the rest of the life span, the right and not the left lateralized prefrontal regions are responsible for the regulation of affect and stress (Cerqueira, Almeida, & Sousa, 2008; Czeh et al., 2008; Schore, 1994; Stevenson, Halliday, Marsden, & Mason, 2008; Sullivan & Gratton, 2002; Wang et al., 2005; Wittling, 1997). These data support my earlier proposal: "The co-created environment of evolutionary adaptedness is thus isomorphic to a growth-facilitating environment for the experience-dependent matu-ration of a regulatory system in the orbitofrontal cortex" (Schore, 2000, p. 30).

Legacy of Attachment: Adaptive Right Brain Survival Functions Over the Life Span

In 1994, I proposed that the microarchitecture of the infant's developing orbito-frontal cortex is shaped by the mother's orbitofrontal cortex (Schore, 1994). Ten years later, Nitschke and colleagues (2004) offered a functional MRI study of mothers viewing a photograph of their own infant showing maximal brain activa-tion in the mother's orbitofrontal cortex, especially on the right side. These authors conclude that this cortex plays a critical role in the representation of attachment-related positive affect as described by Bowlby, that it linearly tracks the intensity of positive emotions that underlie maternal attachment, and that individual vari-ations in orbitofrontal activation to infant stimuli reflect an important dimension of maternal attachment. Following this work, an NIRS study of social attachment by Minagawa-Kawai et al. (2009) documents that mothers express increased right orbitofrontal activation when viewing videos of the smiling face of their 12-month-old infants, and that these infants show similar orbitofrontal activation when view-ing their mothers' smile. They conclude, "These results suggest the orbitofrontal cortical role in regulating and encoding the affect in attachment system and also show that infants share similar neuronal functions with mothers, associated with their bonds at 1 year of age" (p. 284).

Over 15 years ago I provided extant developmental data that suggested that subsequent to a child's formation of an attachment to his or her mother in the first year, the child forms another, to the father, in the second year (Schore, 1994). Interestingly, recent magnetoencephalographic research reveals that the medial orbitofrontal cortex of both females and males rapidly and thereby implicitly responds (130 milliseconds) to the image of an infant's face (Kringelbach et al., 2008). These authors conclude that the orbitofrontal cortex expresses a specific and rapid signature for not just maternal but "parental instinct."

The role of the father in child development has been comprehensively summarized by Tamis-LeMonda and Cabrera (2002) and Lamb (2010). Herzog (2001) observes, "The biorhythmicity of man with infant and woman with infant" affords the infant to have "interactive, state-sharing, and state-attuning experiences with two different kinds of caregivers" (p. 55). He further asserts that this paternal function is "entirely contingent on the presence of homeostatic-attuned caregiving by the mother." Though the mother's soothing is essential to the child's attachment security, the father's arousing play is thought to be critical for the child's competent exploration of the physical world (K. Grossmann et al., 2002). Expanding upon these ideas, I have suggested that although the mother is essential to the infant's capacity for fear regulation, in the second year the father is critically involved in male and female toddlers' aggression regulation (Schore, 2003).

Bowlby (1969) proposed that the child's experience with a supportive mother and "a little later father" (p. 378) indicates that the transmission of attachment patterns between mother and infant precedes subsequent transmission between father and child. Building upon this, in *Affect Regulation and the Origin of the Self* I offered the hypothesis that not only the infant's mother but also the father is impacting the growth of the baby's brain:

> I have previously argued that in the first year the mother is the major source of the environmental stimulation that facilitates (or inhibits) the experience-dependent maturation of the child's developing biological (especially neurobiological) structures. In the second year, however, the father now becomes an important source of arousal induction and reduction, and his modulation of stimulation will influence formation of those neural structures that are entering into a critical period of growth. In other words, in the middle of the second year the structural development of the child's brain is shifting from a maternal experience-dependent maturation of one postnatally developing cortical system to a paternal experience-dependent maturation of an even later developing cortical system. (Schore, 1994, p. 233)

In the ensuing decade, the vast majority of developmental neurobiological research has focused on the mechanisms by which specifically one particular adult, a mother, impacts the development of her offspring's developing brain (see Schore, 1994, 2001a, 2003, 2005, 2010b). That said, one laboratory has offered a series of studies clearly demonstrating that paternal care affects synaptic development in the anterior cingulate (Ovtscharoff, Helmeke, & Braun, 2006), orbitofrontal cortex (Helmeke et al., 2009), and somatosensory cortex of the left hemisphere (Pinkernelle, Abraham, Seidel, & Braun, 2009). These authors propose that paternal care significantly affects the development of play behavior. Interestingly, juvenile rough-and-tumble play, a behavior extensively investigated by Panksepp (1998), has been shown to be critically impacted by the father–child relationship (Flanders et al., 2010) and to depend on orbitofrontal activity (Bell, Pellis, & Kolb, 2010; Pellis & Pellis, 2007). Utilizing both EEG and neuroimaging data, Ryan, Kuhl, and Deci (1997) assert

that "the positive emotional exchange resulting from autonomy-supportive parenting involves participation of right hemispheric cortical and subcortical systems that
participate in global, tonic emotional modulation" (p. 719).

The right hemisphere ends its initial growth spurt in the middle/end of the second year, as the left hemisphere begins its own (Thatcher, Walker, & Giudice, 1987).
In later stages the right hemisphere comes back into less intensive growth spurts,
in which its essential functions attain even greater levels of complexity. In ensuing developmental periods, these attachment functions are expressed as implicit
capacities for nonverbal affect communication and interactive stress regulation.
The adaptive capacities unique to the right (and not left) brain are described by
current authors. Brancucci, Lucci, Mazzatenta, and Tommasi (2009) state, "The
neural substrates of the perception of voices, faces, gestures, smells, and pheromones, as evidenced by modern neuroimaging techniques, are characterized by
a general right-hemispheric functional asymmetry" (p. 895). Schutz (2005) notes,
"The right hemisphere operates a distributed network for rapid responding to
danger and other urgent problems. It preferentially processes environmental challenge, stress and pain and manages self-protective responses such as avoidance and
escape" (p. 15). And Uddin, Molnar-Szakacs, Zaidel, and Iacoboni (2006) assert,
"The emerging picture from the current literature seems to suggest a special role of
the right hemisphere in self-related cognition, own body perception, self-awareness
and autobiographical memories" (p. 65).

These adaptive right brain functions are initially imprinted in right brain–to–
right brain affective communications during critical periods of infancy, and such
attachment experiences facilitate the lateralization of the "emotional" right brain
that support its survival functions. According to Rotenberg (2004),

> The main functions of the right hemisphere...the ability to grasp the reality
> as a whole; the emotional attachment to the mother (Schore, 2003); the
> regulation of withdrawal behavior in the appropriate conditions (Davidson &
> Cacioppo, 1992); the integration of affect, behavior and autonomic activity
> (Schore, 2003) are the basic functions of *survival* (Saugstad, 1998) and for this
> reason are the first to appear. (p. 864, my italics)

Later Sequelae of Significant Alterations in the Environment of Evolutionary Adaptedness

Consonant with Bowlby's speculations, these adaptive functions of an efficient lateralized right brain only evolve in an optimal early relational environment of evolutionary adaptedness. However, if the primary caregiver chronically dysregulates
the child's arousal and affective states during early critical periods, this inhibits the
experience-dependent maturation of the right brain. Severe alterations of the EEA
lead to enduring inefficient capacities for coping with interpersonal stressors and

a predisposition to later psychiatric disorders. A large number of studies now demonstrate that alterations of brain development are associated with less than optimal early maternal care, especially with severe "relational trauma" such as abuse and neglect (Schore, 2001c, 2010b). In earlier work I offered interdisciplinary evidence from neuroscience, child psychiatry, and traumatology that suggests that early traumatic environments that generate disorganized/disoriented attachments interfere with the organization of right brain cortical-subcortical limbic circuits and compromise such functions as the capacity to play, attachment, empathy, and the ability to regulate negative affects and pain (Schore, 2002). Severe attachment trauma imprints a permanent physiological reactivity in limbic areas of the right brain, thereby inhibiting its capacity to cope with future stressors. These deficits of affect communication and regulation underlie a predisposition to a number of early forming developmental psychopathologies.

There is now agreement that early stress is associated with alterations in the orbital frontolimbic (ventromedial) cortex and that individuals who experience early adversity such as childhood maltreatment are at a heightened risk for a wide range of psychopathologies (Hanson et al., 2010). Although most of this research focuses on the detrimental effects of deficits of maternal care in the alteration of specifically the right and not left ventromedial cortex (Lyons, Afarian, Schatzberg, Sawyer-Glover, & Moseley, 2002) and the creation of a vulnerability to future psychopathologies (e.g., Korosi & Baram, 2009; Schore, 2003), a small but growing number of studies show that lack of paternal care in infancy is significantly associated with "delayed and partly suppressed development of orbitofrontal circuits" (Helmeke et al., 2009, p. 794).

In my 1994 volume, I proposed that orbitofrontal deficits lie at the core of a number of psychiatric disorders (Schore, 1994), and in 1996, I cited a small but expanding number of studies that reported orbitofrontal involvement and regulation disturbances in a number of developmental psychopathologies (Schore, 1996). Over the last decade, altered morphological and functional development of the orbitofrontal cortex has been documented in a wide variety of early forming neurodevelopmental disorders: schizophrenia (Nakamura et al., 2007); autism (Girgis et al., 2007); affective psychosis (Fahim, Stip, Mancini-Marie, Potvin, & Malaspina, 2007); bipolar disorder (Versace et al., 2008); borderline personality disorder (Chanen et al., 2008); psychopathic personality disorder, aggression, and violence (Craig et al., 2009; Gansler et al., 2009; Kumari et al., 2009); alcohol and drug addiction (Schoenbaum & Shaham, 2008; Volkow et al., 2007); posttraumatic stress disorder (Schore, 2002); dissociative identity disorder (Sar, Unal, & Ozturk, 2007); panic disorder (Roppongi et al., 2010); and depression (Eddington et al., 2009).

Furthermore, prenatal and postnatal stressful experiences also impact the maturation of systems involved in immunocompetence in the developing brain (Garay & McAllister, 2010; Schore, 1994). Individuals with a history of relational trauma are thus at risk for not only later forming psychiatric disorders but also medical

disorders (Felitti & Anda, 2010). The trend of current research on the develop-
mental origins of a vulnerability to later diseases is echoed in the titles of three
representative studies: "Early Childhood Stress Is Associated With Elevated
Antibody Levels to Herpes Simplex Virus Type 1" (Shirtcliff, Coe, & Pollak, 2009);
"Childhood Maltreatment Predicts Adult Inflammation in a Life Course Study"
(Danese, Pariante, Caspi, Taylor, & Poulton, 2007); and "Childhood Maltreatment
as a Risk Factor for Adult Cardiovascular Disease and Depression" (Batten, Aslan,
Maciejewski, & Mazure, 2004).

In a very recent volume, *The Impact of Early Life Trauma on Health and Disease:
The Hidden Epidemic* (Lanius, Vermetten, & Pain, 2010), I present a synopsis of
chapters on "The Impact of Early Life Trauma: Psychobiological Sequelae in
Children." Regarding experimental investigations of attachment trauma, I give an
overview of the state of current research:

> Recent models of early life trauma are altering their focus from deficits in later
> maturing conscious, verbal, explicit and voluntary behavior, to impairments
> of early maturing nonconscious, nonverbal, implicit and automatic adaptive
> social emotional functions. Developmental neuroscience is now moving from
> studies of later maturing left brain conscious verbal cognitive processes into
> the early preverbal development of adaptive emotion processing right brain
> systems in pre- and postnatal periods. (Schore, 2010a, p. 144)

This ongoing trend in the sciences is paralleled by clinical models of early diagnosis,
intervention, and prevention that also focus on right brain development. In the final
sections of this chapter, I utilize recent interdisciplinary data to offer some suggestions on the assessment of extreme deviations in the EEA in stages of early human
development.

Psychoneurobiological Evaluations of the Environment of Evolutionary Adaptedness

A central thesis of this contribution (and indeed all of my work) is that attachment
relationships shape the experience-dependent maturation and lateralization of the
right brain. Early right brain lateralization is thus an interpersonal neurobiological
marker of the EEA. Indeed, the evolving lateralization of right brain structure–
function relationships is an ongoing indicator of the development of "the social
brain" over the human brain growth spurt, which extends from the last trimester
of pregnancy through 18 to 24 months of age. Earlier I cited studies indicating
the emergence of right lateralization in utero. Not only prenatal stress (Alonso,
Navarro, Santana, & Rodriguez, 1997) but also maternal nutritional factors cause
long-lasting changes in the lateralization of the infant brain. In particular, n-3
polyunsaturated fatty acids (PUFAs) such as arachidonic and docosahexanoic
acid (DHA), which are essential to early brain development (Lauritzen, Hansen,

Jorgensen, & Michaelsen, 2001), have been shown to affect brain lateralization. Offspring of mothers fed a diet deficient in PUFA show less DHA and a lower density of cholinergic neurons in the right hemisphere and an impairment of brain maturation in postnatal periods (Vancassel et al., 2005).

According to Schuetze and Reid (2005), although the infant brain has been historically reported to be undifferentiated in terms of cerebral lateralization until 2 years of age, evidence now indicates that lateralized functions are present much earlier in development. Supporting this proposal of the adaptive role of lateralization, Simian-Tov et al. (2008) put forth the following argument:

> Functional hemispheric lateralization is considered crucial for brain efficiency; it enhances neural capacity by allowing separate, parallel, and specialized processing in the hemispheres. Like motor, language, and memory functions, emotional processing has long been considered lateralized. A central role was ascribed to the right hemisphere in perception and processing of either emotions in general or negative emotions in particular. (p. 1782)

Echoing this perspective, Mento et al. (2010) conclude, "The right hemisphere would sustain the functions necessary for the *survival* of the species, such as visuospatial or emotional processes. Consequently the earlier and faster development of the neural substrates underlying these functions is needed to prevent possible impairment during infancy and childhood" (p. 7, my italics). They further note that "early alteration of the normal hemispheric asymmetry in terms of functional development in extremely immature infants has recently been related to several neurocognitive developmental impairments during childhood and adulthood" (p. 8). This model affirms Saugstad's (1998) earlier speculation that neurodevelopmental psychiatric disorders are associated with late and slow cerebral lateralization. After the postnatal period, the right hemisphere subsequently re-enters into (less intense) growth spurts (Thatcher, 1994), but severe alterations of the EEA would alter the later developmental trajectory of the right brain.

The data presented in this chapter strongly suggest that evolving right lateralized visual-facial, auditory-prosodic, and tactile-gestural nonverbal communication functions of "the human social brain" can be assessed over the pre- and postnatal stages of infancy to appraise the ongoing status of emotional and social development. Allman, Watson, Tetreault, and Hakeem (2005) articulate the organizing principle of developmental neuroscience: "The strong and consistent predominance for the right hemisphere emerges postnatally" (p. 367). Giving an overview of their developmental research, T. Grossmann et al. (2010) propose that in postnatal periods, "responses to voices and emotional prosody…might thus serve as one of potentially multiple markers that can help with an early identification of infants at risk for neurodevelopmental disorders" (p. 856). With an eye to diagnostic implications, Montirosso et al. (2010) call for future study of different gestures with simultaneous measurement of brain functions and suggest that "such studies would also be useful with samples of high-risk infants whose behavior and brain organization may be compromised" (p. 109).

Referring to specific lateralized brain regions that are directly impacted by early social-emotional experience, Pinkernelle et al. (2009) observe, *"Environmental factors contribute to the development of hemispheric asymmetry*, as shown here on the cellular and network (dendrites) level. In general, hemispheric lateralization appears to be characteristic for the adequate function of sensory cortices and also for prefrontal and limbic regions" (p. 670, my italics). Earlier I outlined the sequential appearance of critical periods in right lateralized frontal and temporal limbic control systems that regulate stressful levels of arousal and affect. Functional assessments of the experience-dependent maturation of the aforementioned amygdala, insula, cingulate, and orbitofrontal systems would allow for a diagnostic evaluation of the development of more complex self-regulation over the course of infancy. Alterations in the EEA would lead to maturational failures in these right cortical-subcortical regulatory systems in infants who are high risk for right brain social-emotional deficits.

A prime example of a severe alteration in the EEA is children who have spent their entire infancy and toddlerhood in an institutional environment. The early deprivation of institutional rearing disrupts the experience-dependent maturation of right lateralized neural circuitry involved in the recognition of facial emotional expressions (Parker & Nelson, 2005). Studying these infants as young as 7 months, these authors assert,

> The typical trend in brain development is increasing cortical specialization, which often means increasing laterality.... [[F]]ace recognition is typically right lateralized.... The experience of early institutionalization may deprive the proper stimulation to drive this lateralization. Such experience may not offer the developing organism the opportunity to pair social stimuli, such as faces, with special meaning, thereby affecting the specialization of the neural systems involved in recognizing such stimuli. (p. 70)

In adolescence, Romanian orphans with histories of severe early deprivation and neglect show "reduced probability of connection to the frontal pole in the right hemisphere... associated with increased externalizing behavioral problems" (Behen et al., 2009, p. 295). Another study of this population reveals "greater amygdala volumes, especially on the right" (Mehta et al., 2009, p. 943).

Recall that frontal and amygdala regulatory systems are major links between the regulation of emotion, stress reactivity, the HPA axis, and the autonomic nervous system. As previously noted, the development of attachment involves both CNS limbic and ANS autonomic functions. Indeed, research clearly demonstrates that limbic-autonomic circuits are assembled in postnatal periods (Rinaman, Levitt, & Card, 2000). Both the sympathetic and parasympathetic branches of the ANS and their connections up into the cortex and down into the stress-regulating HPA axis continue to mature postnatally. It is now well established that infants with high vagal tone, a measure of parasympathetic activity, present more positive psychophysiological, behavioral, and social capacities (Huffman et al., 1998), and that vagal tone, an index of emotional regulation (Appelhans & Luecken, 2006), is related to parental socialization (Hastings et al., 2008). Chronic low vagal tone (as well as altered resting cortisol levels) over the stages of infancy thus represents a high-risk factor for disturbances of both mind and body. In addition, more attention needs to be paid to pre- and postnatal right lateralized postural and vestibulo-ocular functions, because the right hemisphere is dominant for vestibular disturbances with affective components (Carmona et al., 2009; Dieterich et al., 2003).

Earlier I cited Schutz's (2005) assertion that the right hemisphere preferentially processes environmental challenge, stress, and pain and manages self-protective responses such as avoidance and escape. These functions occur in the first year, and if the primary caregiver is not a haven of safety but a source of fear and distress in critical periods of right brain development, this would represent a severe alteration of the EEA. Indeed, disturbances in right hemispheric maturation are reflected in "very fearful" infants at 7 months who show larger evoked response potentials over the right hemisphere when viewing fearful facial expressions (de Haan, Belsky, Reid, Volein, & Johnson, 2004).

It is important to note that the right hemisphere is also dominant for the regulation of withdrawal behavior (Davidson & Cacioppo, 1992). In 6-month-old infants, withdrawal behavior is associated with elevated cortisol and extreme right frontal EEG activity (Buss et al., 2003). Although states of hyperarousal and fear in infants have been seen as an indicator of disturbance in infant mental health, there is now increased focus on the psychopathogenic nature of hypoarousal and relational withdrawal. Milne, Greenway, Guedeney, and Larroque (2009) describe the long-term negative developmental impact of "social withdrawal" and depression in 6-month-old infants. Citing my right brain model, they conclude, "A withdrawal response in infancy is problematic behavior...not because it leads to later withdrawal per se, but because of the compounding effects on development of not being present in the interpersonal space—the space upon which much of infant development depends" (p. 165).

In the psychiatric literature, Guedeney, Foucault, Bougen, Larroque, and Mentre (2008) report a study of "relational withdrawal" in infants aged 14 to 18 months. This infant reaction reflects inadequate parent–infant interactions and is a feature of most attachment disorders, particularly disorganized attachment. The severe psychopathogenesis of this context is emphasized in their clinical observation: "Sustained withdrawal behavior may be viewed as a chronic diminution of the attachment system, which is gradually generalized into a diminished engagement and lowered reactivity to the environment as a whole" (p. 151). They conclude,

Withdrawn social behavior from as early as 2 months of age, indicated by a lack of either positive (e.g., smiling, eye contact) or negative (e.g., vocal protestations) behavior, is more akin to a state of learned helplessness and should alert the clinician to the possibility that the infant is not displaying age-appropriate emotional/social behavior. Infants may also appear socially withdrawn in several clinical conditions, for example in autism, chronic or severe pain, failure to thrive, or posttraumatic stress disorder. Withdrawal behaviour is also a key symptom of infant depression. (p. 151)

Increased right frontal EEG activity is found in 1-week-old and 3-month-old infants of depressed, withdrawn mothers (Diego, Jones, & Field, 2010). Early relational withdrawal may be a central mechanism in the intergenerational transmission of depression, a clinical syndrome that is now being understood in terms of right hemispheric dysfunction (Hecht, 2010). Relational withdrawal reflects a severe impairment of the attachment mechanism and a marker of a severe decrement in the EEA (for more on withdrawal, disorganized-disoriented attachment, and pathological dissociation in infancy, see Schore, 2009, 2012).

There is now agreement that the essential task of the first year of human life is the creation of a secure attachment bond of emotional communication between the infant and his or her primary caregiver (Schore & Schore, 2008), that learning how to communicate represents the most important developmental process to take place during infancy (Papousek & Papousek, 1997), and that the whole of child development can be basically conceptualized as the enhancement of self-regulation (Fonagy & Target, 2002). All of these emergent functions are dependent upon the structural maturation of the infant's right brain. In line with Bowlby's (1969) conception that the infant's development within the environment of evolutionary adaptedness is impacted by "his interaction with the principal figure in that environment, namely the mother" (p. 181); MacLean's (1996) proposal that "for more than 180 million years, the female has played the central role in mammalian evolution" (p. 422); and Schore's (1996) developmental interpersonal neurobiological tenet, "The self-organization of the developing brain occurs in the context of another self, another brain" (p. 60), assessments of infant mental health and social-emotional development during the human brain growth of the first 2 years must evaluate the *relationship* cocreated by the right brains of both members of an attachment dyad. Ongoing assessments of the developing infant's capacities for nonverbal emotional communication and implicit affect regulation of both positive and negative affective states could be used diagnostically as markers of attachment development, complexity of right brain maturation, infant mental health, and, if indicated, targets of early relational intervention (see Schore, 2012 for a clinical assessment).

Over the ensuing stages of development, right brain functions are essential for the toddler's expanding emotional and social functions. Regulated affective interactions with familiar, predictable caregivers create not only a sense of safety but also a positively charged curiosity that fuels the burgeoning self's exploration of novel socioemotional and physical environments. These advances are critical to the changes in the environment of evolutionary adaptedness that occur in the second year, the stage of human socialization (Schore, 1994). Almost two decades ago Tucker (1992) speculated, "The baby brain must begin participating effectively in the process of social information transmission that offers entry into the culture"

(p. 79). He asserted that social interaction that promotes brain differentiation is the mechanism for teaching "the epigenetic patterns of culture" (p. 122), and that successful social development requires a high degree of skill in negotiating emotional communication, "much of which is nonverbal" (p. 80). Tucker concluded that such emotional information engages "specialized neural networks in humans, within the right hemisphere" (p. 80). I would add that early right brain development not only allows entry into a particular culture but ultimately *shapes the culture itself*.

I propose that Bowlby's concept of environment of evolutionary adaptedness describes the psychological space that a particular culture, at any point of anthropological history, creates to scaffold the emotional bonding between mothers and infants, the evolutionary mechanism of attachment. This relational space operates at implicit levels, and it can either be expansive and facilitating or constrictive and inhibiting. In terms of attachment theory, a decrement in the EEA in a particular culture would be expressed in a decrease in secure and an increase in insecure attachment typologies. This in turn would reflect alterations in right brain maturation and limbic-autonomic functioning and reduced efficiency in implicit stress and affect regulation described earlier.

Thoughts on the Current Decrement in the Environment of Evolutionary Adaptedness in US Culture

In 1994, at the very beginning of my first book, I proposed, "The child's first relationship, the one with the mother, acts as a template, as it permanently molds the individual's capacities to enter into all later emotional relationships" (Schore, 1994, p. 3). In the very last pages I utilized a perspective grounded in interpersonal neurobiology and developmental neuroscience to offer thoughts on a growing trend in American culture that represented a serious departure from an optimal EEA:

> The conclusions of this volume echo and amplify a recent "worrisome" concern expressed by Bretherton (1992) about the experimentally demonstrated increased risk of insecure attachments if day care, as typically provided in present American society, begins in the 1st year and is extensive in duration. In a series of studies Belsky is finding that extensive nonmaternal (and nonparental) care in this 1st year is a risk factor in the increased development of insecure patterns of attachment (Belsky & Rovine, 1988), and that insecure-avoidant infants with such care express more negative affect and engage in less object play in reunion episodes with the mother (Belsky & Braungart, 1991). Other research indicates that even infants in middle- and upper-middle-class families that use in-home baby-sitters for more than 20 hours per week display higher rates of avoidance on reunion with the mother and are more likely to be classified as showing an insecure attachment (Barglow, Vaughn,

& Molitor, 1987). A link between early day care experience and subsequent levels of aggression and noncompliance is also being reported (Haskins, 1985). In an analysis of 13 studies of attachment and child care, Lamb et al. (1992) now concur with Belsky that elevated levels of insecure attachments are consistently found in child care children.... I believe that such disturbing observations must be attended to very seriously.... The matter of caregiving, in not just the first few months but the first 2-years-of-life, is an essential problem for the future of human societies. (Schore, 1994, pp. 540–541)

In the last two decades, these data have been replicated in large-scale studies (NICHD Early Child Care Network, 2006). Recently, Dmitreva, Steinberg, and Belsky (2007) reported, "Evidence indicates clearly that care initiated early in life and experienced for many hours, especially in child-care centers, is associated with somewhat elevated levels of externalizing behavior problems (e.g., aggression and disobedience), and that these effects are not simply a function of low-quality care" (p. 1032). Developmental neuropsychological studies of infants before, during, and after early daycare is now essential, and it should focus not on later maturing language or motor areas, but on brain systems responsible for social-emotional and stress-regulating functions.

Indeed, two out of three American children under 5 years old now receive some form of nonparental childcare, and in most cases, this care begins during the first year of life (Overturf Johnson, 2005). In 2004, 52.9% of mothers with children under the age of 1 year were in the workforce (Bureau of Labor Statistics, n.d.). Highlighting the significant changes over the last 20 years, in the 1960s, 17% of women returned to work by 12 months after delivery, compared with 60% in the early 1990s (52% by 6 months). In the 1990s, of mothers who returned to work within 12 months, more than half did so by 3 months, and 75% by 6 months (Smith, Downs, & O'Connell, 2001). Despite the recommendation of at least 18 weeks of maternity leave by the General Conference of the International Labor Organization (2000), the United States lags seriously behind the other industrialized countries in maternal and paternal leave policies. As a result, most mothers in this country now return to work 6 weeks after delivery

Recall that at 6 weeks the cortical areas of the brain are just beginning to myelinate and to initiate functions such as face processing that are critical to attachment. In this same period, the anterior cingulate (medial frontal) control system that regulates the amygdala and stress-regulating HPA axis enters into a critical period that requires face-to-face social-emotional input. It is at this particular time that many mothers in the United States re-enter the job market and put their infants into daycare, a factor that interferes with the 6-month policy of breastfeeding advocated by the American Academy of Pediatrics, Section on Breastfeeding (2005). Maternal milk is a rich source of unsaturated fatty acids, bioactive nutrients that are essential to early brain development (Yehuda, Rabinovitz, & Mostofsky, 1999). Very recent research indicates that a shorter duration of breastfeeding (less than 6 months) may be a predictor of adverse mental health outcomes throughout the developmental trajectory of childhood and early adolescence (Oddy et al., 2010). Citing my work on brain development, Calnen (2007) asserts, "It is biologically necessary that mothers be with their infants, especially during the first few months postpartum. This is not likely to become a reality until working families are granted a sufficiently long, and paid, maternity leave as a matter of national policy" (p. 39). *Based on the developmental neurobiological data, I would suggest that this country should legislate and implement the strategies now operating in other industrialized nations: maternal leave of 6 months and paternal leave of 2 months.*

To my mind, these data also reflect the fact that for the last two decades American culture has been providing a growth-inhibiting EEA for mother–infant attachment bond formation in the first 2 years of life. Research investigating the short-term effects of maternal employment in the first year after birth demonstrates developmental risks, including insecure attachments (Belsky, 2001) and a negative impact on children's cognitive abilities (Hill, Waldfogel, Brooks-Gunn, & Han, 2005). But a decrement in the EEA is expressed in more than cognitive psychological impairments—rather, it impacts neurobiological development. Recall that the first 2 years of human infancy overlaps the human brain growth spurt, which extends to 18 to 24 months (Dobbing & Sands, 1973). The decrement in the EEA is thus expressed in less than optimal epigenetic influences on the experience-dependent maturation of the early developing emotion-processing right brain. The long-term effect of this altered EEA is a substantial increase in the number of individuals with a neurobiological predisposition for psychiatric disorders.

Evidence for this assertion was offered in 2003 in *Hardwired to Connect*, a report produced by the Commission on Children at Risk, of which I was a member. Citing extensive research that included, among others, the findings that 21% of US children ages 9 to 17 have a diagnosable mental or addictive disorder; that in 2001, 28.3% of adolescents reported episodes of serious depression in the previous year; and that in 2002, at least one of every four adolescents in the United States was found to be at risk of not achieving productive adulthood, the commission of 33 children's doctors, research scientists, and mental health professionals concluded:

> The implications of this research are clear and profound: The declining mental health of many U.S. children is a pressing issue that plays a substantial role in many of today's emerging physical problems. Psychosomatic and psychosocial disorders have pronounced and long-lasting effects on both children's lives and society. (Hardwired to Connect, 2003, p. 71)

In 2005, a National Comorbidity Survey Replication study reported that about half of all Americans will meet the criteria for a *Diagnostic and Statistical Manual of Mental Disorders*, fourth edition (DSM-IV), disorder in their life, with first onset usually in childhood or adolescence (Kessler et al., 2005). In commenting on this study, Insel and Fenton (2005) articulate the widely held principle that "most mental illnesses... begin far earlier in life than was previously believed" (p. 590).

Further confirming the concept of a decrement in the EEA, in 2007, UNICEF published a study of child well-being in 21 rich countries and documented that the United States ranked 21st in health and safety and 20th in the quality of family and peer relationships. The report concludes,

> All families in Organization for Economic Co-operation and Development (OECD) countries today are aware that childhood is being re-shaped by forces whose mainspring is not necessarily the best interests of the child. At the same time, a wide public in the OECD countries is becoming ever more aware that many of the corrosive social problems affecting the quality of life have their genesis in the changing ecology of childhood. Many therefore feel that it is time to attempt to re-gain a degree of understanding, control and direction over what is happening to our children in their most vital, vulnerable years. (UNICEF, 2007, p. 39)

Developmental neuroscience now clearly indicates that the prenatal and postnatal critical periods of early childhood represent the "most vital, vulnerable years." The original embryological concept of critical periods connoted bounded times in development when a rapidly growing tissue in the developing organism is most vulnerable to alterations by external factors. Tucker (1992) described the concept of "psychological embryology" and pointed out that the long period of nurturance and social interaction provided to human children allows "the life experience of other individuals to serve as epigenetic determinants of brain differentiation and intelligence" (p. 122), especially of "specialized neural networks in humans, within the right hemisphere" (p. 80).

In 2001, I offered an article in *The Infant Mental Health Journal* on "The Effects of a Secure Attachment Relationship on Right Brain Development, Affect Regulation, and Infant Mental Health," in which I concluded,

> Adaptive infant mental health can be fundamentally defined as the earliest expression of efficient and resilient strategies for coping with novelty and stress, and maladaptive infant mental health as a deficit in these same coping mechanisms. The former is a resilience factor for coping with psychobiological stressors at later stages of the life cycle, the latter is a risk factor for interruptions of developmental processes and a vulnerability to the coping deficits that define later-forming psychopathologies. (Schore, 2001a, p. 17)

This perspective is consonant with Darwin's principle, "It is not the strongest of the species that survives, nor the most intelligent, but the one most responsive to change."

But this developmental psychoneurobiological model of emotional resilience is not consonant with other current developmental conceptions of cognitive-behavioral resilience. Hrdy (2009) has suggested that children reared under adverse conditions (e.g., with stressed parents) may develop personalities that are better prepared for subsisting in a challenging environment. Indeed, when children are presented with manageable, graded emotional challenges, they can increase resilience (e.g., Katz et al., 2009). However, relational attachment trauma presents the infant with not graded but highly stressful and thereby overwhelming emotional experiences. In fact, severe attachment stressors decrease the adaptive abilities to respond emotionally, think efficiently, or relate well to others. This is due to the fact that significant reductions of "nurturance and social interaction" in human infancy alter the developmental trajectory of the emotional right brain, reducing the capacity of emotional resilience and inducing coping deficits of affect regulation that are associated with a spectrum of developmental psychopathologies. This neurobiological perspective contradicts the idea that having a stressed brain is adaptive.

Most important, the developmental psychological speculation that individuals who experience adverse early environments are better prepared to resiliently face a challenging environment is now being disconfirmed by very recent clinical studies and psychiatric observations (e.g., Baradon, 2010; Lanius et al., 2010). Developmental neuroscience now clearly demonstrates that all children are not "resilient" but "malleable," for better or worse (Leckman & March, 2011). The developmental dogma that most children are able to accommodate variations in the quality of early care without deviation from normal developmental progress and that infants and children show great behavioral and developmental resilience in the face of adverse life experiences also overlooks the documented ongoing dramatic increases in childhood psychopathology, including bipolar disorder (Moreno et al., 2007), attention deficit/hyperactivity disorder (ADHD) (Bloom & Cohen, 2006), and autism (Harpaz-Rotem & Rosenheck, 2004; Landrigan, 2010). Indeed, the American Academy of Child and Adolescent Psychiatry is now describing a "crisis" in children's mental health needs: 1 in every 5 children has a diagnosable psychiatric disorder, and 1 in every 10 suffers from a mental illness severe enough to impair everyday living (Campaign for America's Kids, AACAP). These epidemiological data, as well as current attachment and developmental neurobiological research, seriously challenge the concept of universal resilience as too simplistic if not incorrect (e.g., Hardwired to Connect, Commission on Children at Risk, 2003; Lanius et al., 2010; Schore, 2003; Szajnberg, Goldenberg, & Harai, 2010).

A central tenet of attachment theory and developmental interpersonal neurobiology dictates that the emotional bond between the primary caregiver and her infant will have long-term effects, for better or worse, on the developing right brain, and thereby on both socioemotional and physical health over the entire life span. The clinicians/researchers Fonagy and Target (2005, p. 334) note the paradigm shift in attachment theory: "If the attachment relationship is indeed a major organizer of brain development, as many have accepted and suggested (e.g., Schore, 1997, 2003), then the determinants of attachment relationships are important far beyond the provision of a fundamental sense of safety or security (Bowlby, 1988)." The "brain development" directly impacted by attachment transactions in the first 2 years is the development of the right more so than the later maturing left brain.

The EEA supports or inhibits the experience-dependent maturation of the right brain which is later dominant for processing social interactions (Semrud-Clikeman, Fine, & Zhu, 2011). This chapter suggests that early identification and intervention within the EEA, a period of not only vulnerability but also maximal brain plasticity, will have important practical effects at all later points of the life span. The challenge I made in an issue of *The Infant Mental Health Journal* at the beginning of the last decade applies even more so now:

> [T]he earliest stages of humanhood are critical because they contain within them the representation of our possible futures—they model the potential developmental extension of our individual and collective social identities. . . . When and where shall we place our current resources so as to optimize the future of human societies?. . . How much should we value the very beginnings of human life, in tangible social program dollars? (Schore, 2001b, p. 4)

References

Afif, A., Bouvier, R., Buenerd, A., Trouillas, J., & Mertens, P. (2007). Development of the human fetal insular cortex: Study of the gyration from 13 to 28 gestational weeks. *Brain Structure and Function, 212*, 335–346.

Allman, J. M., Watson, K. K., Tetreault, N. A., & Hakeem, A. Y. (2005). Intuition and autism: A possible role for Von Economo neurons. *Trends in Cognitive Sciences, 9*, 367–373.

Alonso, S. J., Navarro, E., Santana, C., & Rodriguez, M. (1997). Motor lateralization, behavioral despair and dopaminergic brain asymmetry after prenatal stress. *Pharmacology Biochemistry and Behavior, 58*, 443–448.American Academy of Child & Adolescent Psychiatry. (n.d.). *The campaign for America's kids.* Retrieved May 3, 2011, from http://www.campaignforamericaskids.org/

American Academy of Pediatrics, Section on Breastfeeding. (2005). Breastfeeding and the use of human milk. *Pediatrics, 115*, 496–506.

Applehans, B., & Luecken, L. (2006). Heart rate variability as an index of regulated emotional responding. *Review of General Psychology, 10*, 229–240.

Baradon, T. (Ed.). (2010). *Relational trauma in infancy.* London: Routledge.

Barbas, H., Saha, S., Rempel-Clower, N., & Ghashghaei, T. (2003). Serial pathways from primate prefrontal cortex to autonomic areas may influence emotional expression. *BMC Neuroscience, 4*, 25.

Barglow, P., Vaughn, B., & Molitor, N. (1987). Effects of maternal absence due to employment on the quality of infant-attachment in a low-risk sample. *Child Development, 58*, 945–954.

Batten, S. V., Aslan, M., Maciejewski, P. K., & Mazure, C. M. (2004). Childhood maltreatment as a risk factor for adult cardiovascular disease and depression. *Journal of Clinical Psychiatry, 65*, 249–254.

Behen, M. E., Muzik, O., Saporta, A. S. D., Wilson, B. J., Pai, D., Hua, J., & Chugani, H. T. (2009). Abnormal fronto-striatal connectivity in children with histories of early deprivation: A diffusion tensor imaging study. *Brain Imaging and Behavior, 3*, 292–297.

Bell, H. C., Pellis, S. M., & Kolb, B. (2010). Juvenile peer play experience and the development of the orbitofrontal and medial prefrontal cortices. *Behavioural Brain Research, 207*, 7–13.

Belsky, J. (2001). Developmental risks (still) associated with early child care. *Journal of Child Psychology and Psychiatry, 42*, 845–859.

Belsky, J., & Braungart, J. M. (1991). Are insecure-avoidant infants with extensive daycare experience less stressed by and more independent in the strange situation? *Child Development, 62*, 567–571.

Belsky, J., & Rovine, M. J. (1988). Nonmaternal care in the first year of life and the security of infant-parent attachment. *Child Development, 59*, 157–167.

Bloom, B., & Cohen, R. A. (2006). Summary health statistics for U.S. children: National health interview survey. *Vital and Health Statistics, 10*(234), 1–79.

Bock, J., Murmu, R. P., Ferdman, N., Leshem, M., & Braun, K. (2008). Refinement of dendritic and synaptic networks in the rodent anterior cingulate and orbitofrontal cortex: Critical impact of early and late social experience. *Developmental Neurobiology, 68*, 695–698.

Bowlby, J. (1969). *Attachment and loss. Vol. 1: Attachment*. New York, NY: Basic Books.

Bradshaw, G. A., & Schore, A. N. (2007). How elephants are opening doors: Developmental neuroethology, attachment and social context. *Ethology, 113*, 426–436.

Brancucci, A., Lucci, G., Mazzatenta, A., & Tommasi, L. (2009). Asymmetries of the human social brain in the visual, auditory and chemical modalities. *Philosophical Transactions of the Royal Society of London Biological Sciences, 364*, 895–914.

Braun, C. M. J., Boulanger, Y., Labelle, M., Khiat, A., Dumont, M., & Mailloux, C. (2002). Brain metabolic differences as a function of hemisphere, writing hand preference, and gender. *Laterality, 7*, 97–113.

Brazelton, T. B., & Cramer, B. G. (1990). *The earliest relationship*. Reading, MA: Addison-Wesley.

Bretherton, I. (1992). The origins of attachment theory: John Bowlby and Mary Ainsworth. *Developmental Psychology, 28*, 759–775.

Brown, J. W., & Jaffe, J. (1975). Hypothesis on cerebral dominance. *Neuropsychologia, 13*, 107–110.

Bureau of Labor Statistics. (n.d.). *Employment characteristics of families summary*. Retrieved from http://stats.bls.gov/news.release/famee.nr0.htm.

Buss, K. A., Schumacher, J. R. M., Dolski, I., Kalin, N. H., Goldsmith, H. H., & Davidson, R. J. (2003). Right frontal brain activity, cortisol, and withdrawal behavior in 6-month-old infants. *Behavioral Neuroscience, 117*, 11–20.

Calnen, G. (2007). Paid maternity leave and its impact in breastfeeding in the United States: An historic, economic, political, and social perspective. *Breastfeeding Medicine, 2*, 34–44.

Carmona, J. E., Holland, A. K., & Harrison, D. W. (2009). Extending the functional cerebral systems theory of emotion to the vestibular modality: A systematic and integrative approach. *Psychological Bulletin, 135*, 286–302.

Cerqueira, J., Almeida, O. F. X., & Sousa, N. (2008). The stressed prefrontal cortex. Left? Right!! *Brain, Behavior, and Immunity, 22*, 630–638.

Chanen, A. M., Velakoulis, D., Carison, K., Gaunson, K., Wood, S. J., Yuen, H. P.,…Pantelis, C. (2008). Orrbitofrontal, amygdala and hippocampal volumes in teenagers with first-presentation borderline personality disorder. *Psychiatry Research: Neuroimaging, 163*, 116–125.

Chiron, C., Jambaque, I., Nabbout, R., Lounes, R., Syrota, A., & Dulac, O. (1997). The right brain hemisphere is dominant in human infants. *Brain, 120*, 1057–1065.

Chugani, H. T., & Phelps, M. E. (1986). Maturational changes in cerebral function in infants determined by 18FDG positron emission tomography. *Science, 231*, 840–843.

Ciaramelli, E., Muccioli, M., Ladavas, E., & di Pellegrino, G. (2007). Selective deficit in personal moral judgment following damage to ventromedial prefrontal cortex. *SCAN, 2*, 84–92.

Craig, M. C., Catani, M., Deeley, Q., Latham, R., Daly, E., Kanaan, R.,...Murphy, D. G. M. (2009). Altered connections on the road to psychopathy. *Molecular Psychiatry*, advance online publication, June 8, 2009; doi:10.1038/mp.2009.40

Czeh, B., Perez-Cruz, C., Fuchs, E., & Flugge, G. (2008). Chronic stress-induced cellular changes in the medial prefrontal cortex and their potential clinical applications: Does hemisphere location matter? *Behavioural Brain Research*, 190, 1–13.

Damasio, A. R. (1994). *Descartes' error.* New York, NY: Grosset/Putnam.

Danese, A., Pariante, C. M., Caspi, A., Taylor, A., & Poulton, R. (2007). Childhood maltreatment predicts adult inflammation in a life-course study. *PNAS, 104*, 1319–1324.

Dapretto, M., Davies, M. S., Pfeifer, J. H., Scott, A. A., Sigman, M., Bookheimer, S. Y., & Iacoboni, M. (2006). Understanding emotions in others: Mirror neuron dysfunction in children with autism spectrum disorders. *Nature Neuroscience, 9*, 28–31.

Davidson, R. J., & Cacioppo, J. T. (1992). New developments in the scientific study of emotion: An introduction to the special section. *Psychological Science, 3*, 21–22.

De Haan, M., Belsky, J., Reid, V., Volein, A., & Johnson, M. H. (2004). Maternal personality and infants' neural and visual responsivity to facial expressions of emotion. *Journal of Child Psychology and Psychiatry, 45*, 1209–1218.

Diego, M. A., Jones, N. A., & Field, T. (2010). EEG in 1-week, 1-month and 3-month-old infants of depressed and non-depressed mothers. *Biological Psychology, 83*, 7–14.

Dieterich, M., Bense, S., Lutz, S., Drzezga, A., Stephen, T., Bartenstein, P., & Brandt, T. (2003). Dominance for vestibular cortical function in the non-dominant hemisphere. *Cerebral Cortex, 13*, 994–1007.

Dmitreva, J., Steinberg, L., & Belsky, J. (2007). Child-care history classroom composition, and children's functioning in kindergarten. *Psychological Science, 18*, 1032–1039.

Dobbing, J., & Sands, J. (1973). Quantitative growth and development of human brain. *Archives of Diseases of Childhood, 48*, 757–767.

Dolan, R. J. (1999). On the neurology of morals. *Nature Neuroscience, 2*, 927–929.

Eddington, K. M., Dolcos, F., McLean, A. N., Krishnan, K. R., Cabeza, R., & Strauman, T. J. (2009). Neural correlates of idiographic goal priming in depression: Goal-specific dysfunctions in the orbitofrontal cortex. *SCAN, 4*, 238–246.

Fahim, C., Stip, E., Mancini-Marie, A., Potvin, S., & Malaspina, D. (2007). Orbitofrontal dysfunction in a monozygotic twin discordant for postpartum affective psychosis: A functional magnetic resonance imaging study. *Bipolar Disorders, 9*, 541–545.

Felitti, V. J., & Anda, R. F. (2010). The relationship of adverse childhood experiences to adult medical disease, psychiatric disorders and sexual behavior: Implications for healthcare. In R. A. Lanius, E. Vermetten, & C. Pain (Eds.), *The impact of early life trauma on health and disease: The hidden epidemic* (pp. 77–87). Cambridge, UK: Cambridge University Press.

Ferber, S. G., Feldman, R., & Makhoul, I. R. (2008). The development of maternal touch across the first year of life. *Early Human Development, 84*, 363–370.

Flanders, J. L., Simard, M., Paquette, D., Parent, S., Vitaro, F., Pihl, R. O., & Seguin, J. R. (2010). Rough-and-tumble play and the development of physical aggression and emotion regulation: A five-year follow-up study. *Journal of Family Violence, 25*, 357–367.

Fonagy, P., & Target, M. (2002). Early intervention and the development of self-regulation. *Psychoanalytic Inquiry, 22*, 307–335.

Fonagy, P., & Target, M. (2005). Bridging the transmission gap: An end to an important mystery of attachment research? *Attachment and Human Development, 7*, 333–343.

Gallace, A., & Spence, C. (2010). The science of interpersonal touch: An overview. *Neuroscience and Biobehavioral Reviews, 34*, 246–259.

Gansler, D. A., McLaughlin, N. C. R., Iguchi, L., Jerram, M., Moore, D. W., Bhadelia, R., & Fulwiler, C. (2009). A multivariate approach to aggression and the orbital frontal cortex in psychiatric patients. *Psychiatry Research Neuroimaging, 171*, 145–154.

Garay, P. A., & McAllister, A. K. (2010). Novel roles for immune molecules in neural development: Implications for neurodevelopmental disorders. *Frontiers in Synaptic Science, 2*, 1–16.

General Conference of the International Labor Organization. (2000). *C183, maternity protection convention, 2000.* Retrieved May 12, 2011, from http://www.ilo.org/ilolex/cgi-lex/convde.pl?C183

Girgis, R. R., Minshew, N. J., Melhem, N. M., Nutche, J. J., Keshavan, M. S., & Hardan, A. Y. (2007). Volumetric alterations of the orbitofrontal cortex in autism. *Progress in Neuro-Psychopharmacology and Biological Psychiatry, 31*, 41–45.

Grossmann, K., Grossmann, K. E., Fremmer-Bombik, E., Kindler, H., Scheuerer-Englisch, H., & Zimmermann, P. (2002). The uniqueness of the child–father attachment relationship: Father's sensitive and challenging play as a pivotal variable in a 16-year longitudinal study. *Social Development, 11*, 307–331.

Grossmann, T., Johnson, M. H., Farroni, T., & Csibra, G. (2007). Social perception in the infant brain: Gamma oscillatory activity in response to eye gaze. *Social Cognitive and Affective Neuroscience, 2*, 284–291.

Grossmann, T., Oberecker, R., Koch, S. P., & Friederici, A. D. (2010). The developmental origins of voice processing in the human brain. *Neuron, 65*, 852–858.

Guedeney, A., Foucault, C., Bougen, E., Larroque, B., & Mentre, F. (2008). Screening for risk factors of relational withdrawal behaviour in infants aged 14–18 months. *European Psychiatry, 23*, 150–155.

Gunnar, M. R. (2000). Early adversity and the development of stress reactivity and regulation. In C. A. Nelson (Ed.), *Minnesota symposium on child psychology. Vol. 31: The effects of early adversity on neurobehavioral development* (pp. 163–200). Mahweh, NJ: Erlbaum.

Guo, K., Meints, K., Hall C., Hall, S., & Mills, D. (2009). Left gaze bias in humans, rhesus monkeys and domestic dogs. *Animal Cognition, 12*, 409–418.

Gupta, R. K., Hasan, K. M., Trivedi, R., Pradhan, M., Das, V., Parikh, N. A., & Narayana, P. A. (2005). Diffusion tensor imaging of the developing human cerebrum. *Journal of Neuroscience Research, 81*, 172–178.

Hanson, J. L., Chung, M. K., Avants, B. B., Shirtcliff, E. A., Gee, J. C., Davidson, R. J., & Pollak, S. D. (2010). Early stress is associated with alterations in the orbitofrontal cortex: A tensor-based morphometry investigation of brain structure and behavioral risk. *Journal of Neuroscience, 30*, 7466–7472.

Hardwired to Connect. (2003). *The new scientific case for authoritative communities.* New York, NY: Institute for American Values.

Harpaz-Rotem, I., & Rosenheck, R. A. (2004). Changes in outpatient psychiatric diagnosis in privately insured children and adolescents from 1995 to 2000. *Child Psychiatry and Human Development, 34*, 329–340.

Haskins, R. (1985). Public school aggression among children with varying day-care experience. *Child Development, 56*, 689–703.

Hastings, P., Nuselovici, J., Utendale, W., Coutya, J., McShane, K. E., & Sullivan, C. (2008). Applying the polyvagal theory to children's emotion regulation: Social context, socialization, and adjustment. *Biological Psychology, 79*, 299–306.

Hecht, D. (2010). Depression and the hyperactive right hemisphere. *Neuroscience Research, 68*, 77–87.

Helmeke, C., Ovtscharoff, W., Poeggel, G., & Braun, K. (2001). Juvenile emotional experience alters synaptic inputs on pyramidal neurons in the anterior cingulate cortex. *Cerebral Cortex, 11*, 717–727.

Helmeke, C., Seidel, K., Poeggel, G., Bredy, T. W., Abraham, A., & Braun, K. (2009). Paternal deprivation during infancy results in dendrite- and time-specific changes of dendritic development and spine formation in the orbitofrontal cortex of the biparental rodent *Octodon degus. Neuroscience, 163*, 790–798.

Hertenstein, M. J. (2002). Touch: Its communicative functions in infancy. *Human Development, 45*, 70–94.

Hertenstein, M. J., & Campos, J. J. (2001). Emotion regulation via maternal touch. *Infancy, 2*, 549–566.

Herzog, J. M. (2001). *Father hunger: Explorations with adults and children.* Hillsdale, NJ: Analytic Press.

Hill, J. L., Waldfogel, J., Brooks-Gunn, J., & Han, W. J. (2005). Maternal employment and child development: A fresh look using newer methods. *Developmental Psychology, 41*, 833–850.

Homae, F., Watanabe, H., Nakano, T., Asakawa, K., & Taga, G. (2006). The right hemisphere of sleeping infants perceives sentential prosody. *Neuroscience Research, 54*, 276–280.

Howard, M. F., & Reggia, J. A. (2007). A theory of the visual system biology underlying development of spatial frequency lateralization. *Brain and Cognition, 64*, 111–123.

Hrdy, S. (2009). *Mothers and others: The evolutionary origins of mutual understanding.* Cambridge, MA: Belknap Press.

Huffman, L., Bryan, Y., del Carmen, R., Pedersen, F., Doussard-Roosevelt, J., & Porges, S. (1998). Infant temperament and cardiac vagal tone: Assessments at twelve weeks of age. *Child Development, 69*, 624–635.

Huttenlocher, P. R. (1979). Synaptic density in human frontal cortex—developmental changes and effects of aging. *Brain Research, 163*, 195–205.

Huttenlocher, P. R. (1990). Morphometric study of human cerebral cortex development. *Neuropsychologia, 28*, 517–527.

Insel, T. R., & Fenton, W. S. (2005). Psychiatric epidemiology. It's not just about counting anymore. *Archives of General Psychiatry, 62*, 590–592.

Jean, A. D. L., Stack, D. M., & Fogel, A. (2009). A longitudinal investigation of maternal touching across the first 6 months of life: Age and context effects. *Infant Behavior and Development, 32*, 344–349.

Kasprian, G., Langs, G., Brugger, P., Bittner, M., Weber, M., Arantes, M., & Prayer, D. (2010). The prenatal origin of hemispheric asymmetry: An in utero neuroimaging study. *Cerebral Cortex, 21,* 1076–1083.

Katz, M., Liu, C., Schaer, M., Parker, K. J., Ottet, M. C., Epps, A.,…Lyons, D. M. (2009). Prefrontal plasticity and stress inoculation-induced resilience. *Developmental Neuroscience, 31*, 293–299.

Kessler, R. C., Berglund, P., Demler, O., Jin, R., Merikangas, K. R., & Walters, E. E. (2005). Lifetime prevalence and age-of-onset distributions of *DSM-IV* disorders in the national comorbidity survey replication. *Archives of General Psychiatry, 62*, 593–602.

Knickmeyer, R. C., Gouttard, S., Kang, C., Evans, D., Wilber, K., Smith, J. K.,…Gilmore, J. H. (2008). A structural MRI study of human brain development from birth to 2 years. *Journal of Neuroscience, 28*, 12176–12182.

Korosi, A., & Baram, T. Z. (2009). The pathways from mother's love to baby's future. *Frontiers of Behavioral Neuroscience, 3*, 1–8.

Kringelbach, M., Lehtonen, A., Squire, S., Harvey, A. G., Craske, M. G., Holliday, I. E.,…Syein, A. (2008). A specific and rapid neural signature for parental instinct. *PLoS One, 3*, 1–6.

Kumari, V., Bartaki, I., Goswami, S., Flora, S., Das, M., & Taylor, P. (2009). Dysfunctional, but not functional, impulsivity is associated with a history of seriously violent behaviour and reduced orbitofrontal and hippocampal volumes in schizophrenia. *Psychiatry Research: Neuroimaging, 173*, 39–44.

Lagercrantz, H., & Ringstedt, T. (2001). Organization of the neuronal circuits in the central nervous system during development. *Acta Paediatrica, 90*, 707–715.

Lamb, M. E. (2010). *The role of the father in child development.* New York, NY: Wiley.

Lamb, M. E., Sternberg, K. J., & Ketterlinus, R. (1992). Child care in the United States. In M. E. Lamb, K. Sternberg, C. P. Hwang, & A. G. Broberg (Eds.), *Child care in context* (pp. 207–222). Hillsdale, NJ: Lawrence Erlbaum Associates.Landrigan, P. J. (2010). What causes autism? Exploring the environmental contribution. *Current Opinion in Pediatrics, 22*, 219–225.

Lanius, R. A., Vermetten, E., & Pain C. (Eds.). (2010). *The impact of early life trauma on health and disease: The hidden epidemic.* Cambridge: Cambridge University Press.

Lauritzen, L., Hansen, H. S., Jorgensen, M. H., & Michaelsen, K. F. (2001). The essentiality of long chain n-3 fatty acids in relation to development and function of the brain and retina. *Progress in Lipid Research, 40*, 1–94.

Le Grand, R., Mondloch, C., Maurer, D., & Brent, H. P. (2003). Expert face processing requires visual input to the right hemisphere during infancy. *Nature Neuroscience, 6*, 1108–1112.

Leckman, J. F., & March, J. S. (2011). Editorial: Developmental neuroscience comes of age. *Journal of Child Psychology and Psychiatry, 52*, 333–338.

Lehtonen, J., Kononen, M., Purhonen, M., Partanen, J., & Saarikoski, S. (2002). The effects of feeding on the electroencephalogram in 3- and 6-month-old infants. *Psychophysiology, 39*, 73–79.

Lenzi, D., Trentini, C., Pantano, P., Macaluso, E., Iacoboni, M., Lenzi, G. I., & Ammaniti, M. (2009). Neural basis of maternal communication and emotional expression processing during infant preverbal stage. *Cerebral Cortex, 19*, 1124–1133.

Lyons, D. M., Afarian, H., Schatzberg, A. F., Sawyer-Glover, A., & Moseley, M. E. (2002). Experience-dependent asymmetric variation in primate prefrontal morphology. *Behavioural Brain Research, 136*, 51–59.

MacLean, P. D. (1996). Women: A more balanced brain. *Zygon, 31*, 421–439.

Matsuzawa, J., Matsui, M., Konishi, T., Noguchi, K., Gur, R. C., Bilker, W., et al. (2001). Age-related volumetric changes of brain gray and white matter in healthy infants and children. *Cerebral Cortex, 11*, 335–342.

McGilchrist, I. (2009). *The master and his emissary*. New Haven, CT: Yale University Press.

Mehta, M. A., Golembo, N. I., Nosarti, C., Colvert, E., Mota, A., Williams, S. C. R.,...Sonuga-Barke, E. J. S. (2009). Amygdala, hippocampal and corpus callosum size following severe early institutional deprivation: The English and Romanian adoptees study pilot. *Journal of Child Psychology and Psychiatry, 50*, 943–951.

Mendez, M. F., & Shapira, J. S. (2009). Altered emotional morality in frontotemporal dementia. *Cognitive Neuropsychiatry, 14*, 165–179.

Mento, G., Suppiej, A., Altoe, G., & Bisiacchi, P. S. (2010). Functional hemispheric asymmetries in humans: Electrophysiological evidence from preterm infants. *European Journal of Neuroscience*. doi:10.1111/j.1460–9568.2010.07076.x

Milne, L., Greenway, P., Guedeney, A., & Larroque, B. (2009). Long term developmental impact of social withdrawal in infants. *Infant Behavior and Development, 32*, 159–166.

Minagawa-Kawai, Y., Matsuoka, S., Dan, I., Naoi, N., Nakamura, K., & Kojima, S. (2009). Prefrontal activation associated with social attachment: Facial-emotion recognition in mothers and infants. *Cerebral Cortex, 19,* 284–292.

Montirosso, R., Borgatti, R., & Tronick, E. (2010). Lateral asymmetries in infants' regulatory and communicative gestures. In R. A. Lanius, E. Vermetten, & C. Pain (Eds.), *The impact of early life trauma on health and disease: The hidden epidemic* (pp. 103–111). Cambridge, UK: Cambridge University Press.

Moreno, C., Laje, G., Blanco, C., Jiang, H., Schnidt, A. B., & Olfson, M. (2007). National trends in the outpatient diagnosis and treatment of bipolar disorder in youth. *Archives of General Psychiatry, 64*, 1032–1039.

Myers, D. A., Myers, T. R., Grober, M. S., & Nathanielsz, P. W. (1993). Levels of corticotropin-releasing hormone messenger ribonucleic acid (mRNA) in the hypothalamic paraventricular nucleus and proopiomelanocortin mRNA in the anterior pituitary during late gestation in fetal sheep. *Endocrinology, 132*, 2109–2116.

Nagy, E. (2006). From imitation to conversation: The first dialogues with human neonates. *Infant and Child Development, 15*, 223–232.

Nakamura, M., Nestor, P. G., McCarley, R. W., Levitt, J. L., Hsu, L., Kawashima, T.,...Shenton, M. E. (2007). Altered orbitofrontal sulcogyral pattern in schizophrenia. *Brain, 130*, 693–707.

Nakato, E., Otsuka, Y., Kanazawa, S., Yamaguchi, M. K., Watanabe, S., & Kakigi, R. (2009). When do infants differentiate profile face from frontal face? A near-infrared spectroscopic study. *Human Brain Mapping, 30*, 462–472.

Narvaez, D. (2008). Triune ethics: The neurobiological roots of our multiple moralities. *New Ideas in Psychology, 26*, 95–119.

Narvaez, D., Panksepp, J., & Schore, A. (2010). The decline of children and the moral sense. *Psychology Today Blog: Moral Landscapes,* August 15. Retrieved from http://

www.psychologytoday.com/blog/moral-landscapes/201008/the-decline-children-and-the-moral-sense

NICHD Early Child Care Research Network. (2006). Child-care effect sizes for the NICHD Study of Early Child Care and Youth Development. *American Psychologist, 61*, 99–116.

Nitschke, J. B., Nelson E. E., Rusch B. D., Fox A. S., Oakes T. R., & Davidson R. J. (2004). Orbitofrontal cortex tracks positive mood in mothers viewing pictures of their newborn infants. *NeuroImage, 21*, 583–592.

Noriuchi, M., Kikuchi, Y., & Senoo, A. (2008). The functional neuroanatomy of maternal love: Mother's response to infant's attachment behaviors. *Biological Psychiatry, 63*, 415–423.

Oddy, W. H., Kendall, G. E., Li, J., Jacoby, P., Robinson, B., de Klerk, N. H., et al. (2010). The long-term effects of breastfeeding on child and adolescent mental health: A pregnancy cohort study followed for 14 years. *Journal of Pediatrics, 156*, 568–574.

Otsuka, Y., Nakato, E., Kanazawa, S., Yamaguchi, M. K., Watanabe, S., & Kakigi, R. (2007). Neural activation to upright and inverted faces in infants measured by near infrared spectroscopy. *NeuroImage, 34*, 399–406.

Overturf Johnson, J. (2005). *Who's minding the kids? Child care arrangements: Winter 2002* (Current Population Reports No 70–101). Washington, DC: U.S. Census Bureau.

Ovtscharoff, W., & Braun, K. (2001). Maternal separation and social isolation modulate the postnatal development of synaptic composition in the infralimbic cortex of *Octodon degus*. *Neuroscience, 104*, 33–40.

Ovtscharoff, W., Helmeke, C., & Braun, K. (2006). Lack of paternal care affects synaptic development in the anterior cingulate cortex. *Brain Research, 1116*, 58–63.

Panksepp, J. (1998). *Affective neuroscience*. New York, NY: Oxford University Press.

Panksepp, J. (2008). The power of the word may reside in the power of affect. *Integrative Psychological and Behavioral Science, 42*, 47–55.

Papousek, H., & Papousek, M. (1997). Fragile aspects of early social integration. In L. Murray & P. J. Cooper (Eds.), *Postpartum depression and child development* (pp. 35–53). New York, NY: Guilford Press.

Parker, S. W., & Nelson, C. A. (2005). The impact of early institutional rearing on the ability to discriminate facial expressions of emotion: An event-related potential study. *Child Development, 76*, 54–72.

Pellis, S. M., & Pellis, V. C. (2007). Rough-and-tumble play and the development of the social brain. *Current Directions in Psychological Science, 16*, 95–98.

Pinkernelle, J., Abraham, A., Seidel, K., & Braun, K. (2009). Paternal deprivation induces dendritic and synaptic changes and hemispheric asymmetry of pyramidal neurons in somatosensory cortex. *Developmental Neurobiology, 69*, 663–673.

Pipp, S., & Harmon, R. J. (1987). Attachment as regulation: A commentary. *Child Development, 58*, 648–652.

Porges, S. W. (2007). The polyvagal perspective. *Biological Psychology, 74*, 116–143.

Previc, F. H. (1991). A general theory concerning the prenatal origins of cerebral lateralization in humans. *Psychological Review, 98*, 299–334.

Price, J. L., Carmichael, S. T., & Drevets, W. C. (1996). Networks related to the orbital and medial prefrontal cortex: A substrate for emotional behavior? *Progress in Brain Research, 107*, 523–536.

Rinaman, L., Levitt, P., & Card, J. P. (2000). Progressive postnatal assembly of limbic-autonomic circuits revealed by central trans-neuronal transport of pseudo-rabies virus. *Journal of Neuroscience, 20*, 2731–2741.

Roberts, N. A., Beer, J. S., Werner, K. H., Scabini, D., Levens, S. M., Knight, R. T., & Levenson, R. W. (2004). The impact of orbital prefrontal cortex damage on emotional activation to unanticipated and anticipated acoustic startle stimuli. *Cognitive, Affective, and Behavioral Neuroscience, 4*, 307–316.

Roppongi, T., Nakamura, M., Asami, T., Hayano, F., Otsuka, T., Uehara, K.,...Hiraysu, Y. (2010). Posterior orbitofrontal sulcogyral pattern associated with orbitofrontal cortex volume reduction and anxiety trait in panic disorder. *Psychiatry and Clinical Neuroscience, 64*, 318–326.

Rotenberg, V. S. (2004). The ontogeny and asymmetry of the highest brain skills and the pathogenesis of schizophrenia. *Behavioral and Brain Sciences, 27*, 864–865.

Ryan, R. M., Kuhl, J., & Deci, E. L. (1997). Nature and autonomy: An organizational view of social and neurobiological aspects of self-regulation in behavior and development. *Development and Psychopathology, 9*, 701–728.

Sar, V., Unal, S. N., & Ozturk, E. (2007). Frontal and occipital perfusion changes in dissociative identity disorder. *Psychiatry Research: Neuroimaging, 156*, 217–223.

Saugstad, L. F. (1998). Cerebral lateralization and rate of maturation. *International Journal of Psychophysiology, 28*, 37–62.

Schleussner, E., Schneider, U., Arnscheidt, C., Kahler, C., Haueisen, J., & Seewald, H-J. (2004). Prenatal evidence of left-right asymmetries in auditory evoked responses using fetal magnetoencephalography. *Early Human Development, 78*, 133–136.

Schoenbaum, G., & Shaham, Y. (2008). The role of orbitofrontal cortex in drug addiction: A review of preclinical studies. *Biological Psychiatry, 63*, 256–262.

Schore, A. N. (1994). *Affect regulation and the origin of the self.* Mahweh, NJ: Erlbaum.

Schore, A. N. (1996). The experience-dependent maturation of a regulatory system in the orbital prefrontal cortex and the origin of developmental psychopathology. *Development and Psychopathology, 8*, 59–87.

Schore, A. N. (1997). Early organization of the nonlinear right brain and development of a predisposition to psychiatric disorders. *Development and Psychopathology, 9*, 595–631.

Schore, A. N. (2000). Attachment and the regulation of the right brain. *Attachment and Human Development, 2*, 23–47.

Schore, A. N. (2001a). The effects of a secure attachment relationship on right brain development, affect regulation, and infant mental health. *Infant Mental Health Journal, 22*, 7–66.

Schore, A. N. (2001b). Contributions from the decade of the brain to infant mental health: An overview. *Infant Mental Health Journal, 22*, 1–6.

Schore, A. N. (2001c). The effects of relational trauma on right brain development, affect regulation, and infant mental health. *Infant Mental Health Journal, 22*, 201–269.

Schore, A. N. (2002). Dysregulation of the right brain: A fundamental mechanism of traumatic attachment and the psychopathogenesis of posttraumatic stress disorder. *Australian and New Zealand Journal of Psychiatry, 36*, 9–30.

Schore, A. N. (2003). *Affect dysregulation and disorders of the self.* New York, NY: Norton.

Schore, A. N. (2005). Attachment, affect regulation, and the developing right brain: Linking developmental neuroscience to pediatrics. *Pediatrics in Review, 26*, 204–211.

Schore, A. N. (2009). Attachment trauma and the developing right brain: Origins of pathological dissociation. In P. F. Dell & J. A. O'Neil (Eds.), *Dissociation and the dissociative disorders: DSM-V and beyond* (pp. 107–141). New York, NY: Routledge.

Schore, A. N. (2010a). Synopsis. In R. A. Lanius, E. Vermetten, & C. Pain (Eds.), *The impact of early life trauma on health and disease: The hidden epidemic* (pp. 1142–1147). Cambridge, UK: Cambridge University Press.

Schore, A. N. (2010b). Relational trauma and the developing right brain: The neurobiology of broken attachment bonds. In T. Baradon (Ed.), *Relational trauma in infancy* (pp. 19–47). London: Routledge.

Schore, A.N. (2012). *The science of the art of psychotherapy*. New York, NY. Norton.

Schore, A. N. (2010c). A neurobiological perspective of the work of Berry Brazelton. In B. M. Lester & J. D. Sparrow (Eds.), *Nurturing families of young children building on the legacy of T. Berry Brazelton* (pp. 141–153). New York, NY: Wiley Blackwell.

Schore, J. R., & Schore, A. N. (2008). Modern attachment theory: The central role of affect regulation in development and treatment. *Clinical Social Work Journal, 36*, 9–20.

Schuetze, P., & Reid, H. M. (2005). Emotional lateralization in the second year of life: Evidence from oral asymmetries. *Laterality, 10*, 207–217.

Schutz, L. E. (2005). Broad-perspective perceptual disorder of the right hemisphere. *Neuropsychology Review, 15*, 11–27.

Semrud-Clikeman, M., & Hynd, G. W. (1990). Right hemisphere dysfunction in nonverbal learning disabilities: Social, academic, and adaptive functioning in adults and children. *Psychological Bulletin, 107*, 196–209.

Semrud-Clikeman, M., Fine, J.G., Zhu, D.C. (2011). The role of the right hemisphere for processing of social interactions in normal adults using functional magnetic resonance imaging. *Neuropsychobiology, 64*, 47–51.

Shirtcliff, E. A., Coe, C. L., & Pollak, S. D. (2009). Early childhood stress is associated with elevated antibody levels to herpes simplex virus type 1. *PNAS, 106*, 2963–2967.

Siegel, D.J. (1999). *The developing mind: Toward a neurobiology of interpersonal experience*. New York: Guilford Press.

Sieratzki, J. S., & Woll, B. (1996). Why do mothers cradle babies on the left? *The Lancet, 347*, 1746–1748.

Simian-Tov, T., Papo, D., Gadoth, N., Schonberg, T., Mendelsohn, A., Perry, D., & Hendler, T. (2008). Mind your left: Spatial bias in subcortical fear processing. *Journal of Cognitive Neuroscience, 21*, 1782–1789.

Smith, K., Downs, B., & O'Connell, M. (2001, November). *Maternity leave and employment patterns: 1961–1995* (Current Population Reports No. P700-7-9). Washington, DC: U.S. Census Bureau.

Stevenson, C. W., Halliday, D. M., Marsden, C. A., & Mason, R. (2008). Early life programming of hemispheric lateralization and synchronization in the adult medial prefrontal cortex. *Neuroscience, 155*, 852–863.

Sullivan, R. M., & Dufresne, M. M. (2006). Mesocortical dopamine and HPA axis regulation: Role of laterality and early environment. *Brain Research, 1076*, 49–59.

Sullivan, R. M., & Gratton, A. (2002). Prefrontal cortical regulation of hypothalamic-pituitary-adrenal function in the rat and implications for psychopathology: Side matters. *Psychoneuroendocrinology, 27*, 99–114.

Sun, T., Patoine, C., Abu-Khalil, A., Visvader, J., Sum, E., Cherry, T. J.,…Walsh, C. A. (2005). Early asymmetry of gene transcription in embryonic human left and right cerebral cortex. *Science, 308*, 1794–1798.

Szajnberg, N., Goldenberg, A., & Harai, U. (2010). Early trauma, later outcome: results from longitudinal studies and clinical observations. In R. A. Lanius, E. Vermetten, & C. Pain (Eds.), *The impact of early life trauma on health and disease: The hidden epidemic* (pp. 33–42). Cambridge: Cambridge University Press.

Tamis-LeMonda, C. S., & Cabrera, N. (2002). *Handbook of father involvement: Multidisciplinary perspectives.* Mahwah, NJ: Erlbaum.

Telkemeyer, S., Rossi, S., Koch, S. P., Nierhaus, T., Steinbrink, J., Poeppel, D.,…Wartenburger, I. (2009). Sensitivity of newborn auditory cortex to the temporal structure of sounds. *Journal of Neuroscience, 29*, 14726–14733.

Thatcher, R. W. (1994). Cyclical cortical reorganization: Origins of human cognitive development. In G. Dawson & K. W. Fischer (Eds.), *Human behavior and the developing brain* (pp. 232–266). New York, NY: Guilford Press.

Thatcher, R. W., Walker, R. A., & Giudice, S. (1987). Human cerebral hemispheres develop at different rates and ages. *Science, 236*, 1110–1113.

Thierry, G., Vihman, M., & Roberts, M. (2003). Familiar words capture the attention of 11-month-olds in less than 250 ms. *NeuroReport, 14*, 2307–2310.

Trevarthen, C. (1996). Lateral asymmetries in infancy: Implications for the development of the hemispheres. *Neuroscience and Biobehavioral Reviews, 20*, 571–586.

Trevarthen, C., & Aitken, K. J. (2001). Infant intersubjectivity: Research, theory, and clinical application. *Journal of Child Psychology and Psychiatry, 42*, 3–48.

Tucker, D. M. (1992). Developing emotions and cortical networks. In M. R. Gunnar & C. A. Nelson (Eds.), *Minnesota symposium on child psychology. Vol. 24: Developmental behavioral neuroscience* (pp. 75–128). Hillsdale, NJ: Lawrence Erlbaum Associates.

Tzourio-Mazoyer, N., De Schonen, S., Crivello, F., Reutter, B., Aujard, Y., & Mazoyer, B. (2002). Neural correlates of woman face processing by 2-month-old infants. *Neuroimage, 15*, 454–461.

Uddin, L. Q., Molnar-Szakacs, I., Zaidel, E., & Iacoboni, M. (2006). rTMS to the right inferior parietal lobule disrupts self-other discrimination. *SCAN, 1*, 65–71.

Ulfig, N., Setzer, M., & Bohl, J. (2003). Ontogeny of the human amygdala. *Annals of the New York Academy of Sciences, 985*, 22–33.

UNICEF. (2007). *Child poverty in perspective: An overview of child well-being in rich countries, a comprehensive assessment of the lives and well-being of children and adolescents in the economically advanced nations.* Report Card 7. Florence, Italy: United Nations Children's Fund Innocenti Research Centre.

Vancassel, S., Aid, S., Pifferi, F., Morice, E., Nosten-Bertrand, M., Chalon, S., & Lavialle, M. (2005). Cerebral asymmetry and behavioral lateralization in rats chronically lacking n-3 polyunsaturated fatty acids. *Biological Psychiatry, 58*, 805–811.

Versace, A., Almeida, J. R. C., Hassel, S., Walsh, N. D., Novelli, M., Klein, C. R.,…Philips, M. L. (2008). Elevated left and reduced right orbitomedial prefrontal fractional anisotropy in adults with bipolar disorder revealed by tract-based spatial statistics. *Archives of General Psychiatry, 65*, 1041–1052.

Volkow, N. D., Wang, G-J., Telang, F., Fowler, J. S., Logan, J., Jayne, M.,...Wong, C. (2007). Profound decreases in dopamine release in striatum in detoxified alcoholics: Possible orbitofrontal involvement. *Journal of Neuroscience, 27*, 12700–12706.

Walker-Andrews, A. S., & Bahrick, L. E. (2001). Perceiving the real world: Infants' detection of and memory for social information. *Infancy, 2*, 469–481.

Wang, J., Rao, H., Wetmore, G. S., Furlan, P. M., Korczykowski, M., Donges, D. F., & Detre, J. A. (2005). Perfusion functional MRI reveals cerebral blood flow pattern under psychological stress. *Proceedings of the National Academy of Sciences of the United States of America, 102*, 17804–17809.

Weaver, I. C. G., Cervoni, N., Champagne, F. A., D'Alessio, A. C., Sharma, S., Seckl, J. R.,...Meaney, M. J. (2004). Epigenetic programming by maternal behavior. *Nature Neuroscience, 7*, 847–854.

Winnicott, D. W. (1986). *Home is where we start from.* New York, NY: W. W. Norton & Company.

Wittling, W. (1997). The right hemisphere and the human stress response. *Acta Physiologica Scandinavica, Supplement, 640*, 55–59.

Yamada, H., Sadato, N., Konishi, Y., Muramoto, S., Kimura, K., Tanaka, M., et al. (2000). A milestone for normal development of the infantile brain detected by functional MRI. *Neurology, 55*, 218–223.

Yehuda, S., Rabinovitz, S., & Mostofsky, D. I. (1999). Essential fatty acids are mediators of brain biochemistry and cognitive functions. *Journal of Neuroscience Research, 56*, 565–570.

{ Commentary }

Early Experience, Neurobiology, Plasticity, Vulnerability, and Resilience
Michael E. Lamb

In his latest chapter, Allan Schore provides a brief and helpful summary of his many contributions to the field with respect to the neurobiology of attachment and its development. In particular, Schore reviews a growing body of research showing the importance of right hemisphere brain development to social and emotional processes beginning in the first year of life, the period during which human infants form their first emotional relationships or attachments. For many years, Schore has argued, as he does in his latest contribution, that interpersonal experiences during the first year of life have a profound effect on neurobiological development in ways that ensure long-term, perhaps lifelong, effects on both the biological substrates and the behaviors with which they are associated. Allan Schore's lectures, essays, and books on these topics have been greeted with enthusiasm by many profession- als, especially those working in clinical environments, but I worry that some of the claims made or repeated in this chapter are not as well established empirically as Schore believes.

In my commentary, accordingly, I offer alternative explanations based on a dif- ferent reading of the developmental science literature.

My comments on Schore's analysis fall into three broad categories, loosely iden- tifiable as methodological, conceptual, and substantive issues. Let me begin with the "methodological" issues. The last two decades have undeniably brought con- siderable progress in our understanding of neurobiological development and of the associations between neurophysiological and experiential events. Furthermore, it has long been recognized that any behaviors, thoughts, feelings, or actions, includ- ing unconscious, automatic, and autonomic actions, must be associated with neural activity. Similarly, it has been obvious for decades (and evocatively demonstrated by Hebb, 1949) that any future recollection of or learning from such experiences are dependent on neural representations or registrations of the earlier events/experi- ences. In these respects, I am very much in accord with Schore's arguments about the importance of understanding neural correlates of important developmental attain- ments and processes. I also agree that the pace of functional neurodevelopment necessarily sets a limit to the pace of the social, emotional, cognitive, and behavioral developments dependent on those neurological substrates. However, we have to consider these associations in the context of other research and scholarship in developmental psychology and developmental psychobiology and avoid overinterpreting the correlations between neurodevelopmental and behavioral or socioemotional events that are described in Schore's chapter.

Schore does not limit himself to conclusions about the necessary impact of experience on neural pathways and functions. He makes much more profound assertions about the amount and types of experiences that are necessary to shape neural connections in very specific and developmentally salient ways, as well as about the permanence of the neural pathways so created. This vivid narrative effectively draws upon the clinical and scientific literature, but it is important to recognize both that the research in this domain is progressing rapidly and that it has yet to demonstrate the causal connections hypothesized by Schore. In fact, there is very little evidence either that precisely defined particular experiences are "necessary" to ensure "normal" development or that there are narrowly defined critical periods during which long-lasting and developmentally crucial neural pathways and connections are permanently laid down. Indeed, there is considerable evidence to the contrary. Over the last several decades, researchers and scholars have achieved consensus about two broad principles—canalization and plasticity—that are relevant to Schore's assertions. The concept of canalization was captured in Waddington's (1942) proposal three-quarters of a century ago that developmental trajectories were potentiated by rather powerful biologically or maturationally organized tendencies that made development proceed unperturbed despite minor fluctuations in environmental circumstances, thereby ensuring that the vast majority of children developed normally in the absence of grossly deviant circumstances. This concept suggests that children develop "normally" despite minor individual differences in the patterning of early parental behavior, for example. This expectation is also supported by the argument by David Winnicott (a fellow neo-analyst who is cited approvingly by Schore) that children need, not optimal mothering, but "good enough" mothering in order to develop appropriately (Winnicott, 1953). By contrast, Schore argues that variations in the quality of parental care experienced in early infancy are inevitably associated with deficient developmental progression whenever parental care deviates from the optimal.

Although I agree that individual differences in parenting can influence development, the evidence suggests that most children are able to accommodate variations in the quality of care without suffering irreparable damage and resultant deviation from normal developmental progress (Brodzinsky & Palacios, 2005; van IJzendoorn & Juffer, 2006). Furthermore, there is now considerable evidence that infants and children show great behavioral and developmental resilience in the face of contrasting and adverse life experiences, whereas Schore emphasizes the crucial formative importance of finely defined and prespecified experiences during critical periods in order to make normal development possible. It seems likely that individual vulnerabilities and strengths will interact with features of the social and physical environment in determining whether and how infants' development will be affected by their experiences.

In his chapter, Schore focuses on a model of the "environment of evolutionary adaptedness" characterized by exquisitely sensitive parental behavior in almost continuous interactions between mothers and infants in order to make normal or appropriate human socioemotional development possible. Like Bowlby (1969), Schore draws in this regard on Konner's (1972) seminal observations of infant care practices among the !Kung hunter-gatherers of Botswana, observations that drew attention to the amount of time that !Kung infants were held by and the frequency with which they were fed by their mothers. Frequent nursing indeed seems to be a feature of infant care in hunter-gatherer communities (Konner, 2005), but there is considerable variability in the identity of the persons who hold them as well as in the types of social interaction that Western psychologists have come to define as critical (Hewlett & Lamb, 2005)—in particular, the types of face-to-face conversations emphasized by scholars like Schore and Trevarthen (2005) are actually quite rare in many non-Western cultures, where infants seem to develop normally nonetheless. Many researchers have confirmed that sensitive parental responsiveness is a key factor in the development of attachment relationships and in determining the security or quality of those relationships (DeWolff & van Ijzendoorn, 1997; Thompson, 2006), but the ways in which that sensitivity is manifested varies widely from culture to culture. Further, there is substantial evidence that babies become attached even when they enjoy relatively limited amounts of interaction with the attachment figures concerned (e.g., Lamb & Lewis, 2010). Likewise, decades of research by psychologists and anthropologists have shown that human infants develop normally and/or become well adjusted to their native societies and social environments despite a wide range of different early social experiences. Although we often discuss an idealized parenting style that is characterized by an abundance of sensitive and contingent interactions, there is no evidence that children can only develop normally when exposed to very specific types of early experiences. On the contrary, children develop perfectly well despite wide variations with respect to whether, how, and how much they are held; variations with respect to the number of individuals involved in their care; variations in the amounts of face-to-face interaction; and variations in the amount of vocal communication to which they are exposed.

Over the last several decades, researchers have also documented that children's resilience is facilitated by their plasticity. Specifically, even when children are affected by their experiences—as when characteristically insensitive parenting leads to the development of insecure attachments—the effects are not necessarily permanent. Instead, changes in, for example, the quality of social interaction can lead to changes in the quality of the associated attachments, with secure attachments becoming insecure, and insecure attachments becoming secure. Of course, the longer children have experienced a style of interaction with the attachment figure, the more resistant that relationship will be to change, but plasticity remains a defining feature of development, ensuring, for example, that even children who have had appalling early experiences of institutionalization can bounce back dramatically when the children are placed in loving adoptive homes.

In the final section of his chapter, Schore focuses attention on recent increases in the use of out-of-home care in contemporary America. Schore warns that such out-of-home care arrangements involve profound deviations from the childrearing conditions that human infants need to experience in order to develop healthily. By contrast, a diverse array of developmental scientists, including developmental psychologists, anthropologists, and educators, have documented the diversity of childhood experiences in human societies, especially the widespread practice of allocare among not only humans but also many other primate species (Hrdy, 2009), and have cautioned against selective exaggeration and misinterpretation of the available evidence concerning the adverse effects of nonparental care on young children (Lamb & Ahnert, 2006). To be sure, there is evidence that some children who have experienced extensive amounts of early nonparental care manifest dysregulated behavior, both contemporaneously and in the future, and also that the majority of their peers, with similar experiences, are not affected in the same way (NICHD Early Child Care Research Network, 2003, 2005). The interesting questions have to do with understanding the developmental processes and functions determining when and which children are affected in distinctive ways by their experiences of this sort and (stated differently) why some children appear to thrive in circumstances that appear problematic for other children (Lamb, in press). At the very least, existing data argue against assumptions about the narrowness of infants' and children's experiential needs and sensitivity to impact. Such conclusions may accurately describe the developmental trajectory of a small subset of vulnerable children but are not consistent with the literature on normal development across a variety of contexts. Thus, a focus on atypical developmental trajectories may overestimate and misrepresent some of the crucial defining features of our species, notably our extraordinary plasticity and ability to thrive in a diverse array of social environments.

Perhaps the differing conclusions embraced by Schore and me reflect our professional backgrounds: Clinicians tend to focus on atypical development, whereas developmental scientists focus on normative development and resilience. Because the children who are resilient do not find their ways into the clinic, even when their rearing contexts are very challenging, they do not influence the way clinicians think nearly as much as they shape the conclusions reached by developmentalists. By the same token, it is likely that both groups have much to learn from one another.

Acknowledgments

I am grateful to Joe Herbert and Steve Porges for many years of stimulating and edifying discussion as well as for very helpful comments on an earlier draft of this commentary.

References

Bowlby, J. (1969). *Attachment*. New York, NY: Basic Books.

Brodzinsky, D., & Palacios, J. (Eds.). (2005). *Psychological issues in adoption: Research and practice*. London: Praeger.

DeWolff, M. S., & van IJzendoorn, M. H. (1997). Sensitivity and attachment: A meta-analysis on parental antecedents of infant attachment. *Child Development, 68,* 571–591.

Hebb, D. O. (1949). *The organization of behaviour: A neuropsychological theory.* New York, NY: Wiley.

Hewlett, B. S., & Lamb, M. E. (Eds.). (2005). *Hunter-gatherer childhoods*. New Brunswick, NJ: Transaction/Aldine.

Hrdy, S. B. (2009). *Mothers and others: The evolutionary origins of mutual understanding.* Cambridge, MA: Harvard University Press.

Konner, M. J. (1972). Aspects of the developmental ethology of a foraging people. In N. J. Blurton Jones (Ed.), *Ethological studies of child behaviour* (pp. 285–304). Cambridge, UK: Cambridge University Press.

Konner, M. J. (2005). Hunter-gatherer infancy and childhood: The !!Kung and others. In B. S. Hewlett & M. E. Lamb (Eds.), *Hunter-gatherer childhoods* (pp. 19–64). New Brunswick, NJ: Transaction/Aldine.

Lamb, M. E. (in press). Nonparental care and emotional development. In S. Pauen & M. H. Bornstein (Eds.), *Early childhood development and later achievement*. Cambridge, UK: Cambridge University Press.

Lamb, M. E., & Ahnert, L. (2006). Nonparental child care: Context, concepts, correlates, and consequences. In W. Damon, R. M. Lerner, K. A. Renninger, & I. E. Sigel (Eds.), *Handbook of child psychology. Vol. 4: Child psychology in practice* (6th ed., pp. 950–1016). New York, NY: Wiley.

Lamb, M. E., & Lewis, C. (2010). The development and significance of father-child relationships in two-parent families. In M. E. Lamb (Ed.), *The role of the father in child development* (5th ed., pp. 94–153). Hoboken, NJ: Wiley.

NICHD Early Child Care Research Network. (2003). Does amount of time spent in child care predict socioemotional adjustment during the transition to kindergarten? *Child Development, 74,* 976–1005.

NICHD Early Child Care Research Network. (2005). Early child care and children's development in the primary grades: Follow-up results from the NICHD Study of Early Child Care. *American Educational Research Journal, 42,* 537–570.

Thompson, R. A. (2006). Early sociopersonality development. In W. Damon, R. A. Lerner, & N. Eisenberg (Eds.), *Handbook of child development, Vol. 3: Social, emotional, and personality development* (6th ed.). Hoboken, NJ: Wiley.

Trevarthen, C. (2005). "Stepping away from the mirror: Pride and shame in adventures of companionship": Reflections on the nature and emotional needs of infant intersubjectivity. In S. C. Carter, L. Ahnert, K. E. Grossmann, S. B. Hrdy, M. E. Lamb, S. W. Porges, & N. Sachser (Eds.), *Attachment and bonding: A new synthesis* (pp. 55–84). Cambridge, MA: MIT Press.

Van IJzendoorn, M., & Juffer, F. (2006). Adoption as intervention. Meta-analytic evidence for massive catch-up and plasticity in physical, socio-emotional, and cognitive development. *Journal of Child Psychology and Psychiatry, 47*, 1228–1245.

Waddington, C. H. (1942). Canalization of development and the inheritance of acquired characters. *Nature, 150*, 563–565.

Winnicott, D. (1953). Transitional objects and transitional phenomena. *International Journal of Psychoanalysis, 34*, 89–97.

3

How Primary-Process Emotional Systems Guide Child Development

ANCESTRAL REGULATORS OF HUMAN HAPPINESS, THRIVING, AND SUFFERING

Jaak Panksepp

Introduction

The sustained qualities of children's emotional experiences during the first 2 years of life have a decisive influence on the way they feel, and hence on how they behave, for the rest of their lives. It is not known precisely how this happens, but the developmental/epigenetic effects of early social affective experiences probably influence many higher as well as lower brain functions.

Although we are a resilient species, affectively balanced minds are not assured by our genetic heritage. They arise from the primal, inherited emotional forces of infant minds intermingling with the nurturance of caring parenting. These primary-process aspects of human and animal minds are the ancestral tools for living that direct developmental-epigenetic trajectories for both affectively healthy and disturbed child maturation. Thus, parenting styles, as they interact with children's inbuilt and developmentally emergent temperaments, can have lifelong consequences. As summarized in this volume, much has been learned about how this may happen within the human mind. And research on our fellow animals is illuminating diverse developmental pathways that can be carved out in the neural matrices of animal minds (see chapters by Carter & Porges, by Meaney, by Nelson, and by Fleming, Mileva-Seitz, & Afonso, this volume). As a basic foundation for much of what will emerge from our various discussions, my limited introductory goal is to illuminate the primal foundational emotional fabric, self-similar in all mammalian brains, upon which and from which such developmental passages are woven. Without certain genetically endowed kinds of ancestral social-emotional forces, the developmental social enrichment of children's brains, by optimal parenting, might not be possible.

Thus, the role of primary-process emotions in early child development is the focus of this essay, with some reflections on the secondary-process learning/memory mechanisms that parse affective experiences in time and space, as well as object relations. Both are essential for understanding how early experiences mold adult minds, with learning always preceding understanding—namely, the construction of tertiary-process levels of the mind. The primal evolved powers of the mind, shared by all mammals in kind if not detail, emerged long before the Pleistocene. They remain essential for our higher conscious lives (Panksepp, 1998a, 1998b). The primal emotional circuits, initially free of cognitive contents, are essential for the way our children's higher emotional and cognitive minds develop. Our expansive autonoetic (deep, autobiographical memory based) cognitive consciousness arises developmentally from the memorial storehouses provisioned and culturally programmed by life experiences; thoughtfulness arises largely from the initially blank slate of our neocortical random access memory (RAM)–like brain expansions. It is within the self-similar repetitive "columnar" fields of the neocortex that the primal affective and perceptual capacities of children's minds are molded into the idiographic noetic and autonoetic experiences that characterize human cultural life.

These developmental themes apply to all mammals, with some unique aspects in humans. We have a much greater capacity for mental time travel (the *autonoesis* of Tulving, 2005) because we simply have so much more neocortex. Although infants' brains rapidly become enriched cognitively, the ancestral affective forces of the mind are essential for understanding the valued qualities of mental existence. Primal feelings can make life wonderful. They can make life hell. This is the case in all mammalian species (Panksepp, 1998a; Panksepp & Biven, 2012).

If we do not pursue the primal foundations of emotions in neuroscientifically realistic animal models, where the underlying primary processes can be studied, we cannot understand, in scientific detail, how early affective values—various emotional delights and vicissitudes—developmentally impact the minds of our children. What cross-species affective neuroscience can provide are guideposts for considering the impact of the ancestral infrastructure of our primary-process, anoetic emotional minds ("unknowing" affective consciousness) and also the secondary-process basic learning and memory processes (foundational for noetic or "knowing" consciousness, but deeply unconscious in themselves) on the emergence of our sophisticated tertiary-process higher order cognitive mechanisms, with which most developmental psychologists—indeed, all human beings—are rightfully most concerned.

Some Basics of BrainMind[1] Evolution

In the brain, one can see evolutionary progressions more clearly—at morphological, neurochemical, and functional levels—than in any other part of the body. What came first in brain evolution remains situated in the medial regions of the brain. For instance, we can be confident that serotonin neurons of both dorsal and medial raphe nuclei of the mesencephalon (midbrain), which lie right at the midline,

---

[1] Please note that BrainMind and MindBrain will be used synonymously and without hyphenation or apologies throughout this chapter, depending on stylistic preferences. This highlights the need for a fully monistic concept that is both psychological and neuroscientific, without hints of dualistic ambiguities (as in brain-mind).

are among the oldest nerve cells in our highly encephalized brains, and not only influence how the rest of the brain is laid down but also control neuroplasticity throughout life (Sodhi & Sanders-Bush, 2004). More recent developments emerged successively and further laterally. In short, what was genetically crafted most recently in brain evolution depends critically for its eventual functional specializations on what came earlier: Midbrain functions are older than hypothalamic and basal ganglia functions, and all three are critically important for both higher limbic functions and the most recent neocortical endowments. In contrast, the primal emotional circuits—concentrated in the basal ganglia and diencephalon, down to the midbrain and pons—do not rely on the secondary and tertiary processes of the neocortex for their intense feelings. Thus, we should first pay attention to how bottom-up mind emergence matures in our children in order to understand how their upper mind emergence, concentrated in the neocortex, responds to world events that sway the various emotional forces they have inherited. Only through BrainMind maturation and cultural learning do higher regulatory processes consolidate, hopefully progressively promoting the possibility of *phronesis,* the Aristotelian synthesis of emotional-affective and intellectual-cognitive processes, in wisdom.

If we do not pay attention to issues of functional emergence at all levels of BrainMind organization, we can make many mistakes in the way we rear our children. The ancient "natural" ways—from the many environments of evolutionary adaptedness (the so-called EEA, first conceptualized by John Bowlby, 1980)—should be guideposts for our thinking about the emergence of higher brain functions. It is critically important to recognize that bottom-up mind emergence during early brain development, culturally guided by certain positive affects, can provide socially desirable top-down controls at maturity. When negative affect prevails during early development, the consequences can be dire (Heim, Newport, Mletzko, Miller, & Nemeroff et al., 2008). Some mind medicines and psychotherapies may eventually help (Fosha, 2009; Panksepp, 2004a, 2004b), but what was forged in early development often cannot be untangled completely later. As William James (1890, p. 127) put it:

> We are spinning our own fates, good or evil, and never to be undone.... The drunken Rip Van Winkle excuses himself for every fresh dereliction by saying "I won't count this time!!" Well!! he may not count it, and a kind Heaven may not count it; but it is being counted none the less. Down among his nerve cells and fibres the molecules are counting it, registering and storing it up to be used against him when the next temptation comes.

Because it is so important to conceptualize both the brain and mind in evolutionary ways, let me re-emphasize the functional layers of MindBrain emergence we will consider here, in the simplest conceptual terms. As summarized in Table 3.1, the lowest primary-process (anoetic) level lies at the foundation of the mind—composed of neural circuits that govern the fundamental infrastructure of our affective lives—a form of phenomenal experience I call affective consciousness (Panksepp, 2005a, 2005b). This basic subcortical plan of the human BrainMind

TABLE 3.1 Types of Affective Processes

1. **Primary-process, basic primordial *anoetic* affects (subneocortical)**
   a) Homeostatic affects (brain–body interoceptors: hunger, thirst, etc.)
   b) Sensory affects (exteroceptively-sensorially triggered pleasurable and unpleasurable/disgusting feelings)
   c) Emotional affects (emotion action systems; *intentions in action*)
   d) Emotion examples: SEEKING, FEAR, RAGE, LUST, CARE, PANIC, and PLAY
2. **Secondary-process affects (*noetic* learning via basal ganglia)**
   a) Classical conditioning (e.g., FEAR via basolateral and central amygdala)
   b) Instrumental and operant conditioning (SEEKING via nucleus accumbens)
   c) Behavioral and emotional habits (largely unconscious—dorsal striatum)
   d) Behavioral examples: exploration, freezing, attack, sex, maternal, crying, etc.
3. **Tertiary-process affects and neocortical *autonoetic* "awareness" functions**
   a) Cognitive functions: thoughts and planning (associative neocortical)
   b) Affective ruminations and regulations (cingulate, medial, and orbitofrontal)
   c) "Freewill" (executive working-memory functions—*intention to act*)
   d) Higher affective states: desire–wanting, anxiety–worry, hatred, eroticism, loving concern, sadness, grief, fun, and enjoyment

was laid down more than 50 million years ago. At the secondary-process (noetic) level, our affective lives are parsed to fit and adapt to environmental opportunities and exigencies through the deeply unconscious neural mechanisms of learning and memory, which fill our memory banks with the grist for autonoetic consciousness—the tertiary-process forms of both wise and unwise decision making, evoked commonly in the service of our feelings (Vandekerckhove & Panksepp, 2009). The basic plan of our higher brain functions was surely achieved at least 3 to 4 million years ago, probably earlier, as suggested by cranial endocasts of our ancestors, but with the possibility of many changes in association fibers that cannot be measured from fossil remains.

Our massive general-purpose neocortical expansions emerged rapidly in terms of evolutionary time. Much of it happened simply by massive replication of existing circuit functions (e.g., cortical columns), as neocortical expansion was permitted by weakening of the cranial plates. There was insufficient time for much additional intrinsic programming within these rapidly expanding higher brain tissues than was already present in ancestral primates. Thus, much of our neocortex is a generalized and highly plastic learning "machine," as many theoreticians have supposed (Doidge, 2007), rather than a repository of many specialized evolved functions. It is likely that most of our neocortical functions did not arise from genetic modularization, but from developmental programming. At birth, the human neocortex resembles a vast and empty general-purpose RAM space, ready for experience-dependent functional specializations. Dramatic support for this view is available. Consider the simple fact that even visual functions of the occipital cortex are developmentally, rather than evolutionarily, established: If posterior brain regions that typically become "visual cortex" are surgically removed in utero (in mice), the adjacent neocortical regions develop fine visual capacities (Sur & Rubenstein, 2005). In other words, subcortical visual networks have an "urge" to connect with cortical tissues, where they establish functionally specialized territories developmentally. Thus, it is not farfetched to believe that subcortical primary-process emotional systems, which consist of basic motive urges for specific types of bodily actions, also have major roles in helping establish some of the executive and memorial functions of higher regions of the brain, especially frontal, parietal, and temporal association areas. What was genetically dictated was the laying down of looping intracortical connections allowing diverse brain areas to "converse," but the final functionality is more likely due to experience-dependent fertilization and pruning of connections than to any intrinsic "modularity."

The subcortical functions, such as the basic emotions that will be introduced, are more heavily dictated genetically. Why? Because their anatomical and neurochemical similarities across species are striking (Panksepp, 1998a; Panksepp & Biven, 2012). There is also compelling evidence that the qualities of those primal circuits guide learning, and probably also our ways of thinking, as we mature. Indeed, there are reasons to believe that this bottom-up developmental progression emerges through nested hierarchies among levels of control: Lower systems provide the foundational "forces" for higher functions to become developmentally "modularized" (Figure 3.1). There is abundant data for such a new vision of brain organization, and details can be found elsewhere (Northoff, Wiebking, Feinberg, & Panksepp, 2011).

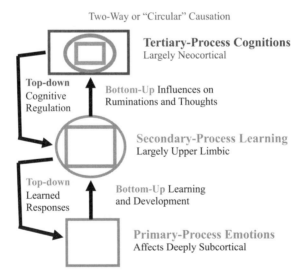

Figure 3.1 *A summary of the hierarchical bottom-up and top-down (circular) causation that operates in every primal emotional system of the brain. The schematic summarizes the hypothesis that in order for higher MindBrain functions to operate, they have to be integrated with the lower BrainMind functions, with primary processes being depicted as squares, secondary learning processes as circles, and tertiary processes, at the top, as rectangles.*

Just as pervasive bottom-up influences during BrainMind maturation guide neo-cortical specializations, top-down controls gradually develop capacities to regulate those ancestral brain powers (see Nelson, this volume). This has vast implications for how our adult minds emerge, with profound implications for how these ancestral powers may be deployed, with wisdom, to promote child development.

The Emotional Primes: Seven Evolutionary Tools for Affective Life

The basic emotional systems have been identified by evocation of distinct emotional actions, similar across mammalian species, by artificial activation of neural systems with localized brain stimulation. Wherever in an animal's brain we can evoke coherent emotional actions by local electrical and chemical brain stimulation, we can also provoke "rewarding" and "punishing" effects as monitored by the learning of various approach, escape, and avoidance behaviors (Panksepp, 1998a, 2005a, 2010b). Stimulation of these same brain networks in humans evokes emotional feelings, with full ownership (Coenen, Schlaepfer, Maedler, & Panksepp, 2011; Panksepp, 1985), providing strong support that basic forms of emotionality were built into the mammalian brain by evolution.

The discovery that diverse affective systems exist in subneocortical regions of the brain has empirically clarified the primary-process neural infrastructure of emotional feelings in all mammals, including humans. These powers of the mind, some especially intense in infancy and childhood, probably guide cognitive development. Indeed, they may be essential for all higher cognitive developments, especially if phenomenal consciousness itself is critically dependent on core affective mechanisms (Holstege & Saper, 2005; Panksepp, 1998b, 2005b, 2007a, 2008a, 2008b, 2010a). Depending on environmental issues and the qualities of rearing, these systems can promote mental health or misery.

After a brief introduction of the affective systems, I will specifically consider each from infant developmental perspectives. Since none of these systems has been *experimentally* well studied in humans, I often have to proceed with generalizations and conjectures from the animal data, which yield abundant hypotheses, none of which are easy to test because they require brain research. However, rather than hinder the flow of narrative with such qualifications, it is worth considering how each may promote and constrain the developmental trajectories of our children. Thorough descriptions of the systems are available in Panksepp (1998a) and Panksepp and Biven (2012).

1.THE SEEKING SYSTEM

This hedonically positive network has traditionally been called "the brain reward system." Animals self-stimulate this system eagerly. Most drug addictions, as well as the garden-variety temptations—from excessive shopping to eager use of the

Internet and compulsive gambling (Knutson, Adams, Fong, & Hommer, 2001; Knutson & Wimmer, 2007)—are among the many manifestations of this system in action, especially when channeled by individual learning. The SEEKING system is of critical importance for springing into action whenever animals deal with key life challenges, giving the young that energized, at times impulsive, "here and thereness" of their behavior. This primal appetitive-motivational system, energized by mesolimbic dopamine circuits, is a general-purpose foundation for all the life-sustaining desires of organisms. In that capacity, it is also of critical importance for many other emotional systems to operate effectively (e.g., from childhood PLAY, to postadolescent LUST, as well as maternal CARE). The cross-species science of the SEEKING system is extensively described elsewhere (Alcaro, Huber, & Panksepp, 2007; Alcaro & Panksepp, 2011; Ikemoto & Panksepp, 1999; Panksepp, 1998a; Panksepp & Moskal, 2008).

SEEKING arousals energize dreaming and provoke infants to engage intensely in exploration—whether searching inquisitively for resources needed to survive or to alleviate boredom and promote entertainment. This system leads all mammals to become excited when they are about to get what they desire (i.e., yielding expectancy arousal to conditioned stimuli). In short, animals use this system to acquire both their daily food and fun. When bodily needs are fulfilled, it promotes enthusiastic exploration of the world, helping to create new knowledge and promote new interests (Silvia & Kashdan, 2009). At its best, the SEEKING urge promotes human creativity and the search for knowledge (Reuter et al., 2005), and perhaps the construction of highly engaging personality structures.

Dopamine-energized SEEKING circuits can coordinate the functions of many medial frontal cortical regions that mediate planning and foresight, as well as psychotic delusions and ruminations. This system exerts more widespread control over cortical functions in humans than in the simpler creatures used for behavioral neuroscience research—that is, not just frontal executive brain regions, but also posterior perceptual functions (Panksepp & Biven, 2012). But still, the SEEKING urge promotes anticipatory eagerness, intentions in action with apparent raw purpose, in both humans and animals. This is the closest we have to a euphoria system in the brain, but it is not the only one to mediate positive affect.

Optimal child development implications. The SEEKING urge can fill the mind with interest while coaxing bodies to move in search of resources that all creatures need and desire—including yearnings evoked by music (Blood & Zatorre, 2001). Healthy use of this system can help fulfill our curiosity, from mundane intellectual interests to sublime pursuits (Kashdan, 2009; Silvia, 2006). Constitutional underactivity of this system can promote helplessness, feelings of stress, and a form of depression characterized by anhedonia (Nestler & Carlezon, 2006; Panksepp & Watt, 2011; Watt & Panksepp, 2009). When the SEEKING urge becomes spontaneously overactive, which can happen as a result of various drugs, thoughts and cravings can become excessive and stereotyped, yielding manic obsessions. Thus, the affectively positive SEEKING urge can be a double-edged sword: While balanced activity promotes diverse and useful world engagements, excessive activity promotes a mania that disrupts balanced living.

Optimal child development is surely promoted by abundant positive life-affirming experiences, providing perhaps a lasting "tonic" for affectively positive personality development. Presumably, the SEEKING urge can be strengthened (sensitized) and channeled to mold positive characterological habits, or negative ones, through early experiences (e.g., adolescents using social media to engage with others vs. using it to conduct acts of cyber-bullying). Clearly, the trajectory of this system for tertiary-process psychological development rests heavily on rearing practices that direct and mediate SEEKING so that young children can develop a storehouse of artistic and scientific-humanistic perspectives and can be coaxed onto paths that optimally instantiate the better side of the human spirit. Much has been written about how such positive psychic energies can be harnessed to promote tolerance, compassion, and acceptance of uncertainty (Kashdan, 2009; Panksepp & Biven, 2012; Silvia, 2006). But for optimal infant development, it should be remembered that the SEEKING system, like all the other emotional primes, is born anoetic ("objectless"—without any initial knowledge). It is within the proper shaping of this system that the conditions for optimal thriving can be created.

2. THE RAGE/ANGER SYSTEM

Working in tandem with, often in opposition to, SEEKING, RAGE is an emotional system that helps organisms defend and procure resources when there is competition; it probably mediates what is typically called "anger" in the vernacular. RAGE is stimulated by frustration arising from any attempts to curtail an animal's freedom of action or aspirations to fulfill one's desires. It has long been known that one can enrage both animals and humans by stimulating specific circuits of the brain—running from the medial amygdala through the hypothalamus to the periaqueductal gray (PAG). The RAGE system invigorates aggressive behaviors when animals are irritated or restrained and also helps animals defend themselves by arousing fear in their opponents. Chronic overactivity of this system is probably a major source of irritable psychiatric disorders, but such conditions are not explicitly recognized in current diagnostic manuals (e.g., *Diagnostic and Statistical Manual of Mental Disorders,* fourth edition [DSM-IV]). In a number of well-documented cases, humans stimulated in these brain regions have exhibited sudden, intense RAGE attacks, with no external provocations (Panksepp, 1985). But this system can also work in tandem with appetitive SEEKING urges, especially in higher regions of the BrainMind (Harmon-Jones, 2007). Key regulatory chemistries in the RAGE system are the neuropeptide substance P and glutamate, which promote arousal of anger, as well as endogenous opioids, which inhibit the system. The cross-species science of the RAGE system is extensively described elsewhere (Guerra, Colonnello, & Panksepp, 2010; Haller & Kruk, 2006, Panksepp & Zellner, 2004; Siegel, 2005).

Optimal child development implications. Raw anger has a mind of its own. When neuroscientists get around to it, they will better understand how arousal of this system can be epigenetically strengthened by repeated use (Adamec & Young, 2000). Thus, children exposed to violence in the media may incorporate what they have seen at deeper affective MindBrain levels than their cognitions (Feshbach & Tangney, 2008). In addition, relevant gene expression patterns may be modified in this emotional system. For example, long ago Ginsburg and Allee (1942) demonstrated that levels of stress early in life influence whether mice would show peaceful or hyperaggressive temperaments as adults. Similarly, when fathers physically play with their children, those fathers who too readily take a submissive role seem to promote future aggression in their children, while dads who show their confident authority in the midst of playful fun do not (Flanders et al., 2010). Of course, more research is needed before we can be confident of a causal tie between such parenting and child outcomes.

Children should be given instruction in anger management, learning how to cognitively understand their anger and dissipate such destructive energies creatively, preferably at the earliest opportunities, especially in the midst of the physical play that they adore. As Aristotle said in advancing his concept of *phronesis*: "Anybody can become angry—that is easy; but to be angry with the right person, and to the right degree, and at the right time, and for the right purpose, and in the right way—that is not within everybody's power and is not easy." It requires an accurate cognitive appraisal of all relevant facts and perspectives, often a rare commodity, providing many opportunities for education. A child should be taught to understand that one of the main roles of anger in his or her life should be to learn to open the gates of "forgiveness," for that is the main path away from the sustained bitterness of anger and hate. Such cultural visions of optimal education may help promote the attainment of a more solid foundation for positive psychology in our children (e.g., Thoresen, Luskin, & Harris, 1998).

3. THE FEAR/ANXIETY SYSTEM

A coherently operating FEAR circuit was designed during brain evolution to help animals reduce pain and the possibility of destruction. When electrically stimulated at low current, this circuit initially promotes freezing, but with higher levels of current animals flee in a coordinated fashion as if they are extremely scared. Humans stimulated in these same brain regions, coursing between the amygdala and PAG along a path that overlaps and interdigitates with the nearby FEAR system, are engulfed by an intense free-floating anxiety that appears to have no environmental cause. Key chemistries that regulate this system are neuropeptide Y and corticotrophin-releasing factor (CRF); specific antianxiety agents such as the benzodiazepines inhibit this system. The cross-species science of the FEAR system is extensively described elsewhere (Panksepp, 1990, 2004a, 2010b).

Modest anxiety in rats can be monitored through their emission of 22-kHz ultrasonic vocalizations, but intense fear (i.e., impending foot shock) terminates these alarm calls. In addition, animals "sigh" (exhibit a double inhalation) when given safety signals in the midst of the signaled punishments commonly used in fear-learning experiments (Soltysik & Jelen, 2005). We currently have no compelling animal models for "worry," but one might anticipate that careful monitoring of more subtle emotional signs than those typically used in animal studies (e.g., rapid shifting of eyes and body orientation during emotionally challenging tasks) might provide further insights that may be more relevant for human development (e.g., Berlyne, 1960) than the rather harsh fear-conditioning procedures so widely used in animal research.

Optimal child development implications. Chronic arousal of this system in early development can promote neuroticism, anxiety disorders, and depression (Heim et al., 2008). Obviously, as with all other negative affect systems, child mental well-being is optimized if the influences of early anxieties are minimized, albeit not totally absent from the banquet of development. This system, like all primary-process emotional systems, can be sensitized (characterized by overreactivity, along with epigenetic changes in gene expression patterns; Szyf, McGowan, & Meaney, 2008). We will focus more extensively on this principle when we come to the CARE system, where selected genetic aspects have been worked out in considerable detail.

Assuming that the vicissitudes of early life have not already molded neurotic tendencies in young minds, as so often happens in war-torn regions of our world, titrated doses of anxiety may even promote emotional growth that is appropriate to local environmental and cultural contexts. The utility of fearfulness probably would need to be approached in as nuanced a manner as our potentials for RAGE. Fear is so intrinsically aversive that perhaps it will suffice for a child to simply better appreciate that everyone has this feeling in various situations. This is the feeling that tells us something is dangerous and that we should reconsider what we are about to do. If a young child feels anxious too often, he or she should gradually be taught methods to minimize or gain control over those feelings. The power of the child's SEEKING system could conceivably be harnessed to help him or her create pleasant psychic "pastures" in which to dwell, perhaps by harnessing mindfulness approaches or even the imaginative power of traditional children's stories.

4.THE LUST/SEXUAL SYSTEM

Sexual urges are controlled by specific neurochemical circuits of the brain, but childhood sexuality remains a debatable topic. The ruling chemistries are overlapping but also quite distinct for males and females. They are aroused by sex hormones, which control the manifestations and maturations of social neuropeptide brain chemistries, especially two neuropeptides whose synthesis is regulated by sex hormones: Vasopressin transmission is promoted by testosterone in males, while oxytocin transmission is promoted by estrogen in females. These sociosexual chemistries help create gender-specific sexual tendencies. Vasopressin promotes assertiveness and aggressiveness (possibly expressed as sexual pushiness in male adolescents?), and perhaps jealous behaviors, in males. Oxytocin promotes sexual readiness postures and warm acceptance attitudes in females. The cross-species science of the LUST system is extensively described elsewhere (Pfaff, 1999).

Distinct male and female sexual circuits are constructed early in life by the capacity of testosterone to differentiate male sexual circuitry from a fundamentally feminine brain; male and female capacities for LUST are activated by maturation of gonadal hormones at puberty. Because brain and bodily sex characteristics are independently organized, it is possible for animals that are externally male to have female-specific sexual urges and, likewise, for some to be female in external appearance but to manifest more malelike sexual urges. Acceptance of these brain-based gender differences that do not always match external sexual characteristics has become a challenge for many modern societies.

Optimal child development implications. There is a vast and growing body of literature on the roles of healthy intimate and/or sexual relationships in adolescence and adulthood for happiness and optimal functioning. Perhaps less has been said about younger children. Overall, children surely never need to be shielded from loving adult relationships where nonsexual affection is abundantly displayed. Obviously, they should never be sexually used or abused but encouraged to develop a healthy age-progressive regard for the life-affirming ways of human sexuality and how such forces operate in most satisfying ways in the midst of solid social bonds. During early childhood, it is probably best to educate by empathic example rather than cognitive instruction, with surely more explicit education in adolescence and young adulthood about the relevance of this basic human emotion.

Perhaps an issue that deserves to be recognized more widely is that if spouses have healthy, mutually supportive affectionate relationships, their children typically recognize this as their implicit positive ground of being (promoting secure bonding). Clearly, the nature of human/mammalian social attachments looms heavily in the discussion of this as well as several other basic emotional processes (especially FEAR and PANIC, which promote insecure attachments, while joint SEEKING and PLAY promote secure attachments). The roles of parental sexuality and dominance in promoting or hindering childhood social attachments are clearly problematic and much underexplored facets of child development.

If adult (not to mention child) relationships are beset by major dominance issues, accompanied by excessive anger and fear, neither partner will find adequate emotional satisfaction from their relationships, and the positive affective development of the children will be impaired (Lanius, Vermetten,& Pain, 2010). In this regard, future research may also need to consider the role of aggression systems in sexuality and bonding patterns across species. For example, among our closest primate relatives, bonobos deploy liberal sexual greetings and interactions, leading to matriarchal solidarity as a staple of their overall social harmony (de Waal, 2009). In contrast, common chimpanzees exhibit more explicit male dominance, with more competitive social structures that often promote higher overall levels of aggression and conflict. No doubt, the model human biological temperament is found somewhere in between.

5. THE CARE/MATERNAL NURTURANCE SYSTEM

Human babies are born extremely immature. As a result, much of what would normally be considered fetal development occurs outside the womb. As Konner (2010) graphically put it, this is the "fourth trimester" and requires parents to take care of infants who will not yet specifically bond with them for months. Still, for human mothers to manage, they need the support of other adults, leading in ancestral environments to extended family groups of aunts and uncles, and so forth, who participate in childcare and protection (Hrdy, 2009). Even so, the child usually selects the mother as the primary focus of his or her affection. The mechanisms by which primal mother–infant and infant–mother bonds are formed can probably be studied in other animals. At least that was our premise, as we generated the first neuroscientific understanding of social comfort and bonding.

Some of the chemistries of female sexuality, for instance, oxytocin, also mediate maternal CARE—nurturance and social bonding—suggesting an intimate relationship between female sexual rewards and maternal devotions. Clearly, brain evolution has provided safeguards to ensure that parents (usually the mother) take care of offspring (but we have all seen the devotions of father penguins, warming and guarding their eggs through the harshest Antarctic winters).

The physiology of maternal urges has been worked out in considerable detail. The massive hormonal changes at the end of pregnancy (declining progesterone and increasing estrogen, prolactin, and oxytocin) set the stage for the activation of maternal urges a few days before the young are born. This symphony of hormonal and neurochemical changes, especially the heightened secretions of oxytocin and prolactin, facilitate maternal moods that ensure strong social bonding with the offspring. Similar neurochemicals, especially oxytocin and endogenous opioids, promote infant bonding to the mother. These changes are foundational for one variant of tertiary-process love. The cross-species science of the CARE system is extensively described elsewhere (Hrdy, 2009; Numan & Insel, 2003; and see the contribution from Alison Fleming's group in this volume).

Optimal child development implications. This system is foundational for key forms of human prosocial attitudes, from the establishment of a secure base for emotional maturation, to the capacity and enthusiasm for sustained playful-friendly interactions, to expertise with and refinement of all the prosocial capacities of our species (Reddy, 2008).

Overall, the major lesson from modern comparative neuroscience perspectives is as follows: Children who experience emotional distress and social loss early in life are less likely to live happy lives than those not beset by such traumas (Heim et al., 2008). If parents learn to distribute their care liberally, they will strengthen children's emotional resilience, multidimensionally, for a lifetime (see the superb work from Steve Suomi's lab [2006] for a discussion of the lifetime benefits of early maternal as opposed to peer rearing). Likewise, Michael Meaney's group at McGill has repeatedly demonstrated how dramatically maternal loving care benefits rat pups for a lifetime, including better regulation of the pituitary–adrenal stress axis and optimization of a diversity of positive, epigenetically promoted BrainMind changes too numerous to summarize here (see Champagne & Meaney, 2001; Szyf et al., 2008).

6. THE PANIC/GRIEF/SEPARATION DISTRESS SYSTEM

All young mammals are dependent on parental care, especially maternal care, for survival. Young mammals have a powerful emotional system to indicate they are in need of care, as reflected in their intense crying when lost or left alone in strange places. These separation calls alert caretakers to seek out, retrieve, and attend to the needs of the offspring. This emotional system that motivates social togetherness engenders separation distress—a psychic pain—that motivates both mother and infant to seek each other (Panksepp, 2005c, 2005d, 2005e, 2006). This is a major system for the construction of social bonds (Nelson & Panksepp, 1998; Panksepp, Siviy, & Normansell, 1985). The separation distress system has now been mapped in several species, including human brain imaging (Panksepp, 2003); it is powerfully inhibited by endogenous opioids, oxytocin, and prolactin—the major social attachment, social bonding chemistries of the mammalian brain. These basic separation distress circuits are also aroused during human sadness, which is accompanied by low brain opioid activity. Sudden arousal of this system in humans may contribute to the psychiatric condition known as "panic attacks" (Panksepp, 1998a). It should be more widely recognized that the affects that characterize "panic attacks" probably emerge from quite different emotional networks than the FEAR system (see Panksepp, 1998a, pp. 274–275). The cross-species science of the PANIC/ GRIEF system is extensively described elsewhere (Swain, Lorberbaum, Korse, & Strathearn, 2007; Watt & Panksepp, 2009), along with developmental implications for the genesis of depression (Panksepp & Watt, 2011).

Optimal child development implications. The role of sadness and grief in negative affect and depression are almost too obvious to discuss. Inadequate social bonds are a main source of insecure attachments, loneliness, and general feelings of negative affect in people's lives. Overarousal of the separation distress system promotes lifelong susceptibility to depression (for a full discussion of the neuroscience evidence, see Watt & Panksepp, 2009). Parents may be able to strengthen social bonds and minimize separation distress in children by freely giving comforting touches, which release opioids (Panksepp, Bean, Bishop, Vilberg, & Sahley, 1980). Though it is common for infants to sleep alone at night, perhaps children's emotional development would benefit from the increased human contact of sleeping with their parents. There is no substantial empirical evidence that cosleeping between mother and infant increases infant mortality by the mother inadvertently smothering the child.

7. THE PLAY/JOYFUL ROUGH-AND-TUMBLE, PHYSICAL SOCIAL-ENGAGEMENT SYSTEM

Young animals have strong urges for physical play. This takes the form of pouncing on each other, chasing, and wrestling. These actions can seem outwardly aggressive, but they are accompanied by positive affect—an intense social joy, reflected best in the happy sounds that our children and young rats make, namely, laughter (children) and high-frequency, approximately 50-kHz ultrasonic chirping sounds that resemble human laughter (rats). Indeed, there are similarities between the sub-neocortical brain circuits that mediate play-induced chirping in rats and the neural controls of human laughter and joy (Panksepp, 2007b). In young rats, these happy sounds are maximal when humans tickle them, leading to rapid social bonding. Similarly, children seem to form fast bonds when laughter is involved.

A key function of the social play system is to promote social exploration and gradually facilitate the natural emergence of confident social dominance. Play helps young animals to acquire subtle social interactions that are not genetically coded into the brain but must be learned—the ability to develop, appreciate, and hold on to friendships. Physical play is a major source of joy in early development, and the resulting friendships can diminish depression that can arise (or at least some data suggest) much more from childhood emotional abuse than either physical or sexual abuse (Powers, Ressler, & Bradley, 2009).

The PLAY urge may be one of the major emotional forces that coaxes children to insistently explore intersubjective spaces (Reddy, 2008), which helps promote the cognitive and epigenetic construction of higher social brain areas. The notion that this is a distinct emotional system of the brain is revealed not only by the fact that young animals and humans tend to spontaneously exhibit various play activities, with many prosocial consequences for early development, but also by the fact that one can diminish play urges by brain lesions, such as in the parafascicular area of the thalamus (Siviy & Panksepp, 1987), that do not affect other basic emotions and motivations. Of course, PLAY, along with all of the other positive social-emotional systems (LUST and CARE, and probably the psychomotor agitation of PANIC), utilizes the energizing power of the general-purpose reward-SEEKING system.

There is far too little clinical research on human play (but see the contribution by Flanders, Herman, & Paquette to this volume), with human rough-and-tumble activities only recently being experimentally documented (Scott & Panksepp, 2003), but a good case can be made that absence of play in early human development can promote adult antisocial behaviors (see Flanders et al. in this volume). Also, father–child play, which should be encouraged, is an ideal time for abundant positive affect and beneficial socialization, especially if well deployed. The cross-species science of the PLAY system is extensively described elsewhere (Panksepp, 2007b; Siviy & Panksepp, 2011).

Optimal child development implications. Playfulness is the major source of human and animal joy (Burgdorf & Panksepp, 2006). All other things being equal, those who do not cultivate ludic tendencies in early development, not to mention all other stages of living, cannot be as happy as those that do. The likelihood that this primal social engagement process—surely fundamental for the emergence of social cooperation and friendships, not to mention empathy and the urge to imitate (learn from) others—is of critical importance for human happiness is obvious, but not all that well used by our society. For instance, recently our educational system regressed to strictly valuing basic educational skills (reading, writing, and arithmetic) without a comparable emphasis on the more playful arts and humanities (the substrates of joyful learning and living). I have developed the idea that some of our major childhood problems, such as attention deficit/hyperactivity disorder (ADHD), are promoted by the impoverished play lives of our children (Panksepp, 1998b). The preclinical data indicate that we may be able to reduce ADHD-type life trajectories by promoting physical play throughout early development (Panksepp, 2007c, 2008c). Perhaps increased early playfulness can promote lifetime resilience against stressors and thereby further promote happy and productive lives. The effects of play in gene expression patterns in the developing cortex are dramatic, with implications for the treatment of depression (Burgdorf, Kroes, Beinfeld, Panksepp, & Moskal, 2010; Burgdorf, Panksepp, & Moskal, 2011).

Conclusion

We all know that human babies are born remarkably immature and hence initially rely heavily on the few psychobehavioral tools that Mother Nature provided for their immediate use—for instance, the emotional instincts such as crying for one's food.

With the evolutionary-developmental perspective advanced here, recognizing levels of organization in BrainMind (Table 3.1 and Figure 3.1), we have a reasonable framework for understanding, neuroscientifically, how healthy affectively tinged, higher cognitive capacities of the human mind arise during brain development. This neuroscientific perspective may inform us on how to best nurture the growth of resilience and optimal mental functioning in our children.

A solid case can presently be made that much of the higher cognitive apparatus is grounded on the unlearned, instinctual affects—the varieties of spontaneous feelings we experience during our daily confrontations with the world. Thus, we can envision the importance of affective consciousness in discussing the evolution of the human mind. Emotions motivate "cognitive" choices, because inbuilt affects encode basic values needed for survival. Hunger tells us to top up our energy reserves. Loving feelings tell us who cares about us. We learn much under the tutelage of our fluctuating affects and more if parents understand these powers of the mind and, with wisdom, guide their children toward lifelong thriving. They are the sources of what learning psychologists envision as the "rewards" and "punishments" that "reinforce" behavior. If we do not sustain an affective focus in human development, especially of the resilience-promoting capacities of primal positive affects, we are bound to make many mistakes that arise from our cognitive beliefs and convictions rather than a solid and sympathetic understanding of our children.

Neither childhood nor adult happiness can be found in the midst of psychic pain, especially those pains that arise from our social nature (MacDonald & Jensen-Campbell, 2010). Children can thrive in the midst of modest sensory pleasures but rarely without the fulfillment of their social urges—to be CARED for, to PLAY, and to be free of social pain. And, too, every child thrives when their pervasive SEEKING urges can be satisfied through any of a variety of outgoing activities that they enjoy (see Sunderland, 2006, for a full description of the developmental implications of all of these emotional systems).

The primal affective foundations of mental life can serve to promote both adult happiness and misery. The epigenetic-developmental progressions by which such inbuilt ancestral values mold the higher regions of the human mind remain largely unknown. However, we can surmise that the core affects are re-represented within the nested hierarchies of higher BrainMind regions. These developments, well cultivated, surely allow positive psychological attitudes to pervade maturing social actions arising from the neocortex, which can positively influence others and help build better communities. Such conceptual extensions I must leave to readers' imaginations and the many other chapters of this volume, especially the previous one by Alan Schore.

Hopefully, the views advanced here may allow us to better understand why the bottom-up developmental processes can have such a profound lifelong impact on the emotional health of individuals (e.g., early trauma, especially sustained separation distress, promoting negative affective temperaments and depression later in life). If emotional development progresses by emotional stressors having a direct impact on the spectrum of primary-process affective strengths and weaknesses (see Meaney's contribution to this volume), and if primal emotional networks advance higher mental developments through nested hierarchies (Figure 3.1), then we can see how early emotional vicissitudes can have lifelong consequences.

In sum, through a better understanding of the lifelong impacts of primary-process affective processes throughout the lifespan, we can begin to scientifically bridge and blend basic neuroscience research traditions that can clarify the nature of evolutionarily engrained mammalian emotional systems with the human tertiary-process complexities that most psychologists focus on. To do that well, we will need to aspire toward integrated scientific views of higher and lower BrainMind functions that do not yet exist in mature forms either in our scientific research, in our academic discussions, or in our educational endeavors. Indeed, much of the evidence will have to come from our understanding of the needs of other mammalian species (Broom, 2001; McMillan, 2005). When we achieve well-integrated levels of scientific understanding, we can better aspire toward the realization of optimal childhood development.

Acknowledgment

Substantial amounts of the empirical work noted in this chapter were supported by research funding from the Hope for Depression Research Foundation. I thank Sheri Six for editorial management of this chapter.

References

Adamec, R. E., & Young, B. (2000). Neuroplasticity in specific limbic system circuits may mediate specific kindling induced changes in animal affect-implications for understanding anxiety associated with epilepsy. *Neuroscience and Biobehavioral Reviews, 24*, 705–723.

Alcaro, A., Huber, R., & Panksepp, J. (2007). Behavioral functions of the mesolimbic dopaminergic system: An affective neuroethological perspective. *Brain Research Reviews, 56*, 283–321.

Alcaro, A., & Panksepp, J. (2011). The SEEKING mind: Primal neuro-affective substrates for appetitive incentive states and their pathological dynamics in addictions and depression. *Neuroscience and Biobehavioral Reviews, 35*, 1805–1820.

Berlyne, D. E. (1960).*Conflict, arousal, and curiosity*. New York, NY: McGraw Hill.

Blood, A., & Zatorre, R. J. (2001). Intensely pleasurable responses to music correlate with activity in brain regions implicated in reward and emotion. *Proceedings of the National Academy of Sciences, 98*, 11818–11823.

Bowlby, J. (1980). *Attachment and loss. Vol. 3: Loss: Sadness and depression*. New York, NY: Basic Books.

Broom, D. M. (Ed.). (2001). *Coping with challenge: Welfare in animals including humans*. Berlin: Dahlem University Press.

Burgdorf, J., Kroes, R. A., Beinfeld, M. C., Panksepp, J., & Moskal, J. R. (2010). Uncovering the molecular basis of positive affect using rough-and-tumble play in rats: A role for insulin-like growth factor I. *Neuroscience, 168*, 769–777.

Burgdorf, J., & Panksepp, J. (2006). The neurobiology of positive emotions. *Neuroscience and Biobehavioral Reviews, 30*, 173–187.

Burgdorf, J., Panksepp, J., & Moskal, J. R. (2011). Frequency-modulated 50 kHz ultrasonic vocalizations a tool for uncovering the molecular substrates of positive affect. *Neuroscience and Biobehavioral Reviews, 35*, 1831–1836.

Champagne, F., & Meaney, M. J. (2001). Like mother, like daughter: Evidence for nongenomic transmission of parental behavior and stress responsivity. *Progress in Brain Research, 133*, 287–302.

Coenen, V. A., Schlaepfer, T. E., Maedler, B., & Panksepp, J. (2011). Cross-species affective functions of the medial forebrain bundle: Implications for the treatment of affective pain and depression in humans. *Neuroscience and Biobehavioral Reviews, 35*, 1971–1981.

De Waal, F. (2009). *Primates and philosophers: How morality evolved.* Princeton, NJ: Princeton University Press.

Doidge, N. (2007). *The brain that changes itself.* New York, NY: Penguin.

Feshbach, S., & Tangney, J. (2008). Television viewing and aggression: Some alternative perspectives. *Perspectives on Psychological Science, 3*(5), 387–389.

Flanders, J. L., Simard, M., Paquette, D., Parent, S., Vitaro, F., Pihl, R. O., & Seguin, J. R. (2010). Rough-and-tumble play and the development of physical aggression and emotion regulation: A five-year follow-up study. *Journal of Family Violence, 25,* 357–367.

Fosha, D. (Ed.). (2009). *The embodied mind: Integration of the body, brain and mind in clinical practice.* New York, NY: Norton.

Ginsburg, B. E., & Allee, W. C. (1942). Some effects of conditioning on social dominance and subordination in inbred strains of mice. *Physiology and Zoology, 15,* 485–506.

Guerra, D. J., Colonnello, V., & Panksepp, J. (2010). The neurobiology of rage and anger & psychiatric implications with a focus on depression. In F. Pahlavan (Ed.), *Multiple facets of anger: Getting mad or restoring justice?* (pp. 81–103). New York, NY: Nova Science Publishers.

Haller, J., & Kruk, M. R. (2006). Normal and abnormal aggression: Human disorders and novel laboratory models. *Neuroscience and Biobehavioral Reviews, 30,* 292–303.

Harmon-Jones, E. (2007). Asymmetrical frontal cortical activity, affective valence, and motivational direction. In E. Harmon-Jones & P. Winkielman (Eds.), *Social neuroscience* (pp. 137–156). New York, NY: Guilford Press.

Heim, C., Newport, D. J., Mletzko, T., Miller, A. H., & Nemeroff, C. B. (2008). The link between childhood trauma and depression: Insights from HPA axis studies in humans. *Psychoneuroendocrinology, 33,* 693–710.

Holstege, G. R., & Saper, C. B. (Eds.). (2005). Special issue entitled "The Anatomy of the Soul." *Journal of Comparative Neurology, 493,* 1–176.

Hrdy, S. (2009). *Mothers and others: The evolutionary origins of mutual understanding.* Cambridge, MA: Harvard University Press.

Ikemoto, S., & Panksepp, J. (1999). The role of nucleus accumbens dopamine in motivated behavior: A unifying interpretation with special reference to reward-seeking. *Brain Research Reviews, 31*(1), 6–41.

James, W. (1890). *The principles of psychology.* New York, NY: Henry Holt & Co.

Kashdan, T. B. (2009). *Curious? Discover the missing ingredient to a fulfilling life.* New York, NY: William Morrow.

Knutson, B., Adams, C. M., Fong, G. W., & Hommer, D. (2001). Anticipation of increasing monetary reward selectively recruits nucleus accumbens. *Journal of Neuroscience, 21,* 1–5.

Knutson, B., & Wimmer, G. E. (2007). Reward: Neural circuitry and social valuation. In E. Harmon-Jones & P. Winkielman (Eds.), *Social neuroscience* (pp. 157–175). New York, NY: Guilford Press.

Konner, M. J. (2010). *The evolution of childhood.* Cambridge, MA: Belknap Press of Harvard University Press.

Lanius, R. A., Vermetten, E., & Pain, C. (2010). *The impact of early life trauma on health and disease: The hidden epidemic.* New York, NY: Cambridge University Press.

MacDonald, G., & Jensen-Campbell, L. A. (Eds.). (2010). *Social pain: Neuropsychological and health implications of loss and exclusion.* Washington, DC: American Psychological Association.

McMillan, F. (Ed.). (2005). *Mental health and well-being in animals.* Oxford: F. Blackwell Publishing.

Nelson, E. E., & Panksepp, J. (1998). Brain substrates of infant-mother attachment: Contributions of opioids, oxytocin, and norepinephrine. *Neuroscience and Biobehavioral Reviews, 22,* 437–452.

Nestler, E. J., & Carlezon, W. A. (2006). The mesolimbic dopamine reward circuit in depression. *Biological Psychiatry, 59,* 1151–1159.

Northoff, G., Wiebking, C., Feinberg, T., & Panksepp, J. (2011). The 'resting-state hypothesis' of major depressive disorder: A translational subcortical-cortical framework for a system disorder *Neuroscience and Biobehavioral Reviews, 35,* 1929–1945.

Numan, M., & Insel, T. R. (2003). *The neurobiology of parental behavior.* New York, NY: Springer-Verlag.

Panksepp, J. (1985). Mood changes: In P. J. Vinken, G. W. Bruyn, & H. L. Klawans (Eds.), *Handbook of clinical neurology* (Rev. Series). *Vol. 1: Clinical neuropsychology* (pp. 271–285). Amsterdam: Elsevier Science Publishers.

Panksepp, J. (1990). The psychoneurology of fear: Evolutionary perspectives and the role of animal models in understanding human anxiety. In G. D. Burrows, M. Roth, & R. J. Noyes (Eds.), *Handbook of anxiety. Vol. 3: The neurobiology of anxiety* (pp. 3–58). Amsterdam: Elsevier/North-Holland Biomedical Press.

Panksepp, J. (1998a). *Affective neuroscience: The foundations of human and animal emotions.* New York, NY: Oxford University Press.

Panksepp, J. (1998b). The periconscious substrates of consciousness: Affective states and the evolutionary origins of the SELF. *Journal of Consciousness Studies, 5,* 566–582.

Panksepp, J. (2003). At the interface between the affective, behavioral and cognitive neurosciences: Decoding the emotional feelings of the brain. *Brain and Cognition, 52,* 4–14.

Panksepp, J. (Ed.). (2004a). *Textbook of biological psychiatry.* New York, NY: Wiley.

Panksepp, J. (2004b). The emerging neuroscience of fear and anxiety disorders. In J. Panksepp (Ed.), *Textbook of biological psychiatry* (pp. 489–520). New York, NY: Wiley.

Panksepp, J. (2005a). On the embodied neural nature of core emotional affects. *Journal of Consciousness Studies, 12,* 161–187.

Panksepp, J. (2005b). Affective consciousness: Core emotional feelings in animals and humans. *Consciousness and Cognition, 14,* 19–69.

Panksepp, J. (2005c). Feelings of social loss: The evolution of pain and the ache of a broken heart. In R. Ellis & N. Newton (Eds.), *Consciousness & emotions* (Vol. 1, pp. 23–55). Amsterdam: John Benjamins.

Panksepp, J. (2005d). Why does separation-distress hurt? A comment on MacDonald and Leary. *Psychological Bulletin, 131,* 224–230.

Panksepp, J. (2005e). Social support and pain: How does the brain feel the ache of a broke heart. *Journal of Cancer Pain and Symptom Palliation, 1,* 59–65.

Panksepp, J. (2006). On the neuro-evolutionary nature of social pain, support, and empathy. In M. Aydede (Ed.), *Pain: New essays on its nature & the methodology of its study* (pp. 367–387). Cambridge, MA: MIT Press.

Panksepp, J. (2007a). Neurologizing the psychology of affects: How appraisal-based constructivism and basic emotion theory can coexist. *Perspectives on Psychological Science, 2,* 281–296.

Panksepp, J. (2007b). Neuroevolutionary sources of laughter and social joy: Modeling primal human laughter in laboratory rats. *Behavioral Brain Research, 182*, 231–244.

Panksepp, J. (2007c). Can PLAY diminish ADHD and facilitate the construction of the social brain. *Journal of the Canadian Academy of Child and Adolescent Psychiatry, 10*, 57–66.

Panksepp, J. (2008a). The power of the word may reside in the power of affect. *Integrative Physiological and Behavioral Science, 42*, 47–55.

Panksepp, J. (2008b). The affective brain and core-consciousness: How does neural activity generate emotional feelings? In M. Lewis, J. M. Haviland, & L. F. Barrett (Eds.), *Handbook of emotions* (pp. 47–67). New York, NY: Guilford.

Panksepp, J. (2008c). Play, ADHD, and the construction of the social brain: Should the first class each day be recess? *American Journal of Play, 1*, 55–79.

Panksepp, J. (2010a). The evolutionary sources of jealousy: Cross-species approaches to fundamental issues. In S. L. Hart & M. Lagerstee (Eds.), *Handbook of jealousy: Theories, principles, and multidisciplinary approaches* (pp. 101–120). New York, NY: Wiley-Blackwell.

Panksepp, J. (2010b). Affective consciousness in animals: Perspectives on dimensional and primary process emotion approaches. *Proceeding of the Royal Society, Biological Sciences, 77*, 2905–2907.

Panksepp, J., Bean, N. J., Bishop, P., Vilberg, T., & Sahley, T. L. (1980). Opioid blockade and social comfort in chicks. *Pharmacology Biochemistry and Behavior, 13*, 673–683.

Panksepp, J., & Biven, L. (2012). *Archaeology of mind*. New York, NY: Norton.

Panksepp, J., & Moskal, J. (2008). Dopamine and SEEKING: Sub-neocortical "reward" systems and appetitive urges. In A. Elliot (Ed.), *Handbook of approach and avoidance motivation* (pp. 67–87). Mahwah, NJ: Lawrence Erlbaum Associates.

Panksepp, J., Siviy, S. M., & Normansell, L. A. (1985). Brain opioids and social emotions. In M. Reite & T. Fields (Eds.), *The psychobiology of attachment and separation* (pp. 3–49). New York, NY: Academic Press.

Panksepp, J., & Watt, D. (2011). Why does depression hurt? Ancestral primary-process separation-distress (PANIC) and diminished brain reward (SEEKING) processes in the genesis of depressive affect. *Psychiatry, 74*, 5–14.

Panksepp, J., & Zellner, M. (2004). Towards a neurobiologically based unified theory of aggression. *Revue Internationale de Psychologie Sociale/International Review of Social Psychology, 17*, 37–61.

Pfaff, D. W. (1999). *Drive: Neurobiological and molecular mechanisms of sexual behavior*. Cambridge, MA: MIT Press.

Powers, A., Ressler, K. J., & Bradley, R. G. (2009). The protective role of friendship on the effects of childhood abuse and depression. *Depression and Anxiety, 26*, 46–53.

Reddy, V. (2008). *How infants know minds*. Cambridge, MA: Harvard University Press.

Reuter, M., Panksepp, J., Schnabel, N., Kellerhoff, N., Kempel, P., & Hennig, J. (2005). Personality and biological markers of creativity. *European Journal of Personality, 19*, 83–95.

Scott, E., & Panksepp, J. (2003). Rough-and-tumble play in human children. *Aggressive Behaviour, 29*, 539–551.

Siegel, A. (2005). *The neurobiology of aggression and rage*. Boca Raton, FL: CRC Press.

Silvia, P. J. (2006). *Exploring the psychology of interest*. New York, NY: Oxford University Press.

Silvia, P. J., & Kashdan, T. B. (2009). Interesting things and curious people: Exploration and engagement as transient states and enduring strengths. *Social Psychology and Personality Compass, 3,* 785–797.

Siviy, S., & Panksepp, J. (2011). In search of neurobiological substrates for social playfulness in mammalian brain. *Neuroscience and Biobehavioral Reviews, 35,* 1821–1830.

Siviy, S. M., & Panksepp, J. (1987). Juvenile play in the rat: Thalamic and brain stem involvement. *Physiology and Behavior, 41*(2), 39–55.

Sodhi, M. S., & Sanders-Bush, E. (2004). Serotonin and brain development. *International Review of Neurobiology, 59,* 111–174.

Soltysik, S., & Jelen, P. (2005). In rats, sighs correlate with relief. *Physiology and Behavior, 85,* 598–602.

Sunderland, M. (2006). *The science of parenting.* London: Doring Kindersley.

Suomi, S. J. (2006). Risk, resilience, and gene x environment interactions in rhesus monkeys. *Annals of the New York Academy of Sciences, 1094,* 52–62.

Sur, M., & Rubenstein, J. L. (2005). Patterning and plasticity of the cerebral cortex. *Science, 310,* 805–810.

Swain, J. E., Lorberbaum, J. P., Korse, S., & Strathearn, L. (2007). Brain basis of early parent-infant interactions: Psychology, physiology, and in vivo function neuroimaging studies. *Journal of Child and Adolescent Psychiatry, 48,* 262–287.

Szyf, M., McGowan, P., & Meaney, M. J. (2008). The social environment and the epigenome. *Environmental and Molecular Mutagenesis, 49,* 46–60.

Thoresen, C. E., Luskin, F. M., & Harris, A. H. (1998). Science and forgiveness interventions: Reflections and recommendations. In E. L. Worthington, Jr. (Ed.), *Dimensions of forgiveness: Psychological research and theological perspectives* (pp. 163–190). Radnor, PA: Templeton Foundation Press.

Tulving, E. (2005). Episodic memory and autonoesis: Uniquely human? In H. S. Terrace & J. Metcalfe (Eds.), *The missing link in cognition: Origins of self-reflective consciousness* (pp. 3–56). New York, NY: Oxford University Press.

Vandekerckhove, M., & Panksepp, J. (2009). The flow of anoetic to noetic and autonoetic consciousness: A vision of unknowing (anoetic) and knowing (noetic) consciousness in the remembrance of things past and imagined futures. *Consciousness and Cognition, 18,* 1018–1028.

Watt, D. F., & Panksepp, J. (2009). Depression: An evolutionarily conserved mechanism to terminate separation-distress? A review of aminergic, peptidergic, and neural network perspectives. *Neuropsychoanalysis, 11,* 7–51.

The Integrative Meaning of Emotion
Daniel J. Siegel

Jaak Panksepp brings a deep passion to his groundbreaking work on the role of subcortical processes in the generation of affective states in humans. His devotion to understanding these deep mechanisms of emotion stems from a view into our membership in a group much larger than our species, *Homo sapiens sapiens*, "the one who knows he knows." This group is larger than our primate cousins, and even broader than our mammalian class-mates. Our experience of "animalian" emotional life is shaped by our membership in the animal kingdom, a membership that our author-guide is so exquisitely attuned to in both his personal and professional vision of what it means to be an emotional being on this planet.

For those who've read the author's *Affective Neuroscience* classic text, you know that there is a richness and depth to the view that "emotion" is an organizing process that shapes all aspects of our lives. All animals have developed from an environment of evolutionary adaptedness (EEA). As mammals, we've acquired a limbic area arising from our deeper and older brainstem origins. As primates, our cortical regions have evolved further still. And as human beings, our prefrontal areas have become more complex, more elaborate, and more able to create representations of aspects of reality far from the physical worlds in which we've arisen. We can think of thinking, imagine the lyrics of love, and write books about evolution and the human mind.

One of our guide's major points is that this later acquisition of a neocortex and its prefrontal chief executive areas should not make us forget the subcortical source of the primordial process of "emotion." At the most basic level, then, this anatomic origin of emotion is an EEA-influenced product of an organism's need to survive and to thrive by organizing its internal operations to best adapt to changing environmental conditions and the internal need for homeostasis. Equilibrium of the organism internally and interactively is the outcome of "emotion" and of "emotion regulation" (Campos, Frankel, & Camras, 2004; Gross, 2007)—the two being essentially inseparable. In children, we see that the development of emotion regulation shapes the fundamental pathways of their lives (Woltering & Lewis, 2009) and has a profound influence on both temperament and parent–child relationships (Alink, Cicchetti, Kim, & Rogosch, 2009; Calkins & Hill, 2007; Lewis, Lamm, Segalowitz,

Stieben, & Zelazo, 2006). The way that parents interact with young children directly shapes the way children acquire the capacity to regulate emotions, as evidenced dramatically in Ed Tronick's Still Face paradigm (Tronick, 2007). Ultimately, these innate and experientially derived influences on emotion regulation are at the heart of how we move toward well-being or pathology (Beauregard, Paquette, & Le`vesque, 2006; Cole & Deater-Deckard, 2009; Fosha, Siegel, & Solomon, 2009). On a larger scale, emotion expression, experience, and regulation are shaped by the interpersonal communication patterns embedded in culture that shape our "display rules" and how we comport ourselves both internally and externally (Raval, Martini, & Raval, 2007; Zahn-Waxler, 2010; Zaalberg, Manstead, & Fischer, 2004).

These issues bring us to one of Panksepp's major points: the role of this thing called "emotion" in human life. Emotion involves seven aspects of our neural circuitry that serve as drive systems that Panksepp calls the "emotional primes" of our evolutionary "tools for affective life." These include the SEEKING; RAGE/anger; FEAR/anxiety; LUST/sexual; CARE/maternal nurturance; PANIC/GRIEF/separation distress; and PLAY/Joyful Rough-and-Tumble, Physical Social-Engagement systems. In essence, these ancient systems organize our internal world and our interactions with others. Influencing both our subjective sense of being alive and the regulation of gene expression and neuroplasticity, these primes are fundamentally how we create ourselves—internally and interactively—across time. In this way, all animals have an emotional life as we link differentiated areas of our bodily and social worlds. And this is a major take-home point: Life is emotional, and emotions give rise to the subjective texture of life. In a deep sense, emotion provides both the text and the context of what it means to be alive in the world.

And so you may be wondering, "Where is the controversy?" Simply put, if emotion is a process (not a noun, but a verb) that arises from throughout the nervous system, then it meets the criteria of an emergent property as Francisco Varela and colleagues beautifully described in their discussions of the "brainweb" of life (Varela, Lachaux, Rodriguez, & Martinerie, 2001). Further, emotion can be seen fundamentally as an emergent process of integration, the linkage of differentiated parts (Siegel, 1999/2011, 2009; Tucker, Derryberry, & Luu, 2000). In this way, we can identify forms of psychopathology that emanate from nonintegrated circuits in the brain (Zhang & Raichle, 2010) that impair the brain's ability to function as organized networks of interrelated parts (Fox et al., 2005). In my own work, I have proposed that the chaos or rigidity that fills the clinician's psychiatric manual of mental disorders, the *Diagnostic and Statistical Manual of Mental Disorders,* fourth edition (DSM-IV), can be viewed as an outcome of impaired integration (Siegel, 2010). These views of emotion are not the usual way health care providers, or average citizens, think of "emotion."

And Panksepp's assertion that emotion is of subcortical origin naturally evokes active discussions of the important role in our human lives of cortical regions in our emotional lives. For example, Wager and colleagues (Wager, Davidson, Hughes, Lindquist, & Ochsner, 2008) summarize their own findings, consistent with others' research, of the importance of the frontal cortical structures in the active, conscious regulation of emotion: "This study shows evidence for a distributed set of lateral frontal, medial frontal, and orbitofrontal regions that together orchestrate reappraisal of the meaning of emotional events" (p. 1048). As the cortex grew, then, we achieved the ability to have intentional shaping of this integrative process we call "emotion." Situated in a neural position to coordinate and balance the lower subcortical firing activity of neural firing, these prefrontal regions serve an important role in emotion regulation. As Allan Schore and Ed Tronick have revealed, a wide array of studies can be explored to demonstrate how parent–child interactions shape development and these regulatory structures that integrate the cortex with the anatomically lower and evolutionarily older regions of the brain (Schore, 2003; Tronick, 2007).

Woltering and Lewis (2009) illuminate this issue in explicating two types of emotion regulation, reactive and deliberate. They focus "on specific neural 'hubs,' such as the anterior cingulate cortex and the orbitofrontal cortex, which serve as epicenters for the coupling of cortical and subcortical processes" and then "propose that an increasing coordination between brain regions during emotional situations subserves more effective and efficient regulation with development" (p. 160). And so Panksepp's framework of subcortically derived emotion systems that arose from our EEA can be integrated (no pun intended) with the evolution of our cortical regions that permit a deliberate form of regulation to shape the more reactive regulation of our subcortical systems. Attachment relationships (Siegel, 1999/2011), psychotherapy (Siegel, 2010), and mindful awareness training (Siegel, 2007) can each be seen as direct mechanisms whereby the focus of attention shapes these integrative regulatory circuits to enable more effective means of emotion regulation and a life well lived.

Integration—the linkage of differentiated parts of a system—is the essential process of emotion and emotion regulation. With this perspective in mind, future research can effectively wrestle with the ways in which neural regions become specialized in their anatomically and functionally unique ways and then how interconnecting circuits can link them so that coordination and balance are achieved. Integration enables regulation to be achieved. Even viewing healthy relationships as honoring differences and then promoting compassionate linkages places integration at the center of how interactive experiences in families, classrooms, and perhaps even our global culture can promote the integration at the heart of health.

References

Alink, L., Cicchetti, D., Kim, J., & Rogosch, F. (2009). Mediating and moderating processes in the relation between maltreatment and psychopathology: Mother-child relationship quality and emotion regulation. *Journal of Abnormal Child Psychology, 37*(6), 831–843.

Beauregard, M., Paquette, V., & Le`vesque, J. (2006). Dysfunction in the neural circuitry of emotional self-regulation in major depressive disorder. *Neuroreport, 17*(8), 843–846.

Calkins, S. D., & Hill, A. (2007). Caregiver influences on emerging emotion regulation: Biological and environmental transactions in early development. In J. J. Gross (Ed.), *Handbook of emotion regulation* (pp. 229–248). New York, NY: Guilford.

Campos, J. J., Frankel, C. B., & Camras, L. (2004). On the nature of emotion regulation. *Child Development, 75*(2), 377–394.

Cole, P. M., & Deater-Deckard, K. (2009). Emotion regulation, risk, and psychopathology. *Journal of Child Psychology and Psychiatry, 50*(1), 1327–1330.

Fosha, D., Siegel, D. J., & Solomon, M. (2009). *The healing power of emotion*. New York, NY: W. W. Norton.

Fox, M. D., Snyder, A. Z., Vincent, J. L., Corbetta, M., Van Essen, D. C., & Raichle, M. D. (2005). The human brain is intrinsically organized into dynamic, anticorrelated functional networks. *Proceedings of the National Academy of Sciences USA, 102,* 9673–9678.

Gross, J. J. (Ed.). (2007). *Handbook of emotion regulation*. New York, NY: Guilford.

Lewis, M., Lamm, C., Segalowitz, S., Stieben, J., & Zelazo, P. (2006). Neurophysiological correlates of emotion regulation in children and adolescents. *Journal of Cognitive Neuroscience, 18*(3), 430–443.

Raval, V. V., Martini, T. S., & Raval, P. H. (2007). 'Would others think it is okay to express my feelings?' Regulation of anger, sadness and physical pain in Gujarati children in India. *Social Development, 16,* 79–105.

Schore, A. N. (2003). *Affect regulation and the repair of the self*. New York, NY: W. W. Norton.

Siegel, D. J. (1999/2011). *The developing mind*. New York, NY: Guilford.

Siegel, D. J. (2007). *The mindful brain*. New York, NY: W. W. Norton.

Siegel, D. J. (2009). Emotion as integration: A possible answer to the question, what is emotion? In D. Fosha, D. J. Siegel, & M. Solomon (Eds.), *The healing power of emotion* (pp. 145–171). New York, NY: W. W. Norton.

Siegel, D. J. (2010). *Mindsight: The new science of personal transformation*. New York, NY: Bantam/Random House.

Tronick, E. (2007). *The neurobehavioral and social-emotional development of infants and children*. New York, NY: W. W. Norton.

Tucker, D. M., Derryberry, D., & Luu, P. (2000). Anatomy and physiology of human emotion: Vertical integration of brainstem, limbic, and cortical systems. In J. Borod (Ed.), *Handbook of the neuropsychology of emotion*. New York, NY: Oxford University Press.

Varela, F., Lachaux, J., Rodriguez, E., & Martinerie, J. (2001). The brainweb: Phase synchronization and large-scale integration. *Nature Reviews Neuroscience, 2,* 229–239.

Wager, T. D., Davidson, M., Hughes, B., Lindquist, M. A., & Ochsner, K. N. (2008). Prefrontal-subcortical pathways mediating successful emotion regulation. *Neuron, 59*(6), 1037–1050.

Woltering, S., & Lewis, M. (2009). Developmental pathways of emotion regulation in childhood: A neuropsychological perspective. *Mind, Brain, and Education, 3*(3), 160–169.

Zaalberg, R., Manstead, A., & Fischer, A. (2004). Relations between emotions, display rules, social motives, and facial behaviour. *Cognition and Emotion, 18*(2), 183–207.

Zahn-Waxler, C. (2010). Socialization of emotion: Who influences whom and how? *New Directions for Child and Adolescent Development, 2010*(128), 101–109.

Zhang, D., & Raichle, M. (2010). Disease and the brain's dark energy. *Nature Reviews Neurology, 6,* 15–28.

4

Epigenetics and the Environmental Regulation of the Genome and Its Function

Michael J. Meaney

The study of personality traits has changed dramatically with the integration of the biological sciences, and especially genetics, into psychology and the neurosciences. Evolutionary approaches established the idea that the brain and its development are subject to evolutionary forces. Behavioral genetics (Ebstein, 2006; Kendler, 2001; Plomin & Rutter, 1998) provided evidence for a relation between genomic variation and neural function. Variation in nucleotide sequence (i.e., polymorphisms) is associated with individual differences in personality and thus with vulnerability and resistance to chronic illness (Ebstein, 2006; Meyer-Lindenberg & Weinberger, 2006; Rutter, 2007). Such variations occur at the level of (1) the single nucleotide (i.e., single nucleotide polymorphisms), (2) the number of nucleotide repeats (i.e., variable number of tandem repeats), or (3) chromosomal reorganization. The current challenge is that of *conceptually* integrating findings from genetics into the social sciences and our understanding of the pathophysiology of mental illness. We argue for the importance of considering the genome not as a static form of background information, but rather as a dynamic and indeed modifiable force, the operation of which is regulated by environmental signals. The integration of epigenetics into the study of neural function provides researchers with a description at the level of biological mechanisms for this process.

The effects of genetic variation depend on context and are best considered as probabilistic. Context regulates cell signaling pathways, including transcription factor expression and activity, and thus cellular function is understood as a constant "dialogue" between the genome and its environment. Transcription factor binding to DNA sites regulates the dynamic changes in transcription. However, such effects are transient and do not explain the enduring effects of environmental programming of gene expression. Epigenetic modifications are an ideal candidate mechanism for the effects of environmental signals, including events such as social interactions, on the structure and function of the genome (Harper, 2005; Meaney & Szyf, 2005). We suggest that epigenetics is one such process and can account, in part, for instances in which environmental events occurring at any time over the life span exert both an immediate and even a sustained effect on genomic function and phenotype.

Epigenetics

Epigenetics refers to chemical modifications to the DNA or to the histone proteins that are physically associated with the DNA (collectively referred to as chromatin). The transcriptional activity of the genome is regulated by signals, transcription factors that bind to specific DNA sites. The importance of epigenetic mechanisms lies in the ability to regulate chromatin structure and thus the ease with which transcription factors access DNA sites. Epigenetic signals can thus determine the capacity for environmentally regulated transcription factors to influence genomic function.

Gene transcription. The transcription of the genome is a highly regulated event that involves the binding of transcription factors to specific binding sites across the DNA and the activation or repression of transcription. The expression and activation of the transcription factors themselves is dynamically regulated by environmental signals. Many of the earliest cellular responses to environmental stimuli involve either the activation of preexisting transcriptional signals through chemical modifications such as phosphorylation, or an increase in gene expression that results in the rapid synthesis of proteins (e.g., immediate early gene products). The binding of transcription factors to DNA sites is the biological machinery for the dynamic gene × environment interactions that alter rates of gene transcription.

Figure 4.1 portrays the organization of the glucocorticoid receptor gene as one example of genomic organization. DNA is organized into units referred to as nucleosomes, about 145 to 150 base pairs wrapped around a core region of histone proteins (Luger, Mader, Richmond, Sargent, & Richmond, 1997; Turner, 2001). There is normally a tight physical relation between the histone protein and its accompanying DNA, resulting in a "closed" nucleosome configuration. This may be considered as the default state. The closed configuration impedes transcription factor binding and is associated with a reduced level of gene expression. An increase in transcription factor binding to DNA and the subsequent activation of gene expression commonly requires chemical modification of the chromatin. The primary targets for such modifications are the amino acids that form the histone tails extending from the nucleosome. These modifications alter chromatin in a manner that either increases or decreases the ability of transcription factors to access regulatory sites on the DNA that control gene transcription.

Chromatin modifications. Chromatin structure is dynamically modified at the amino acids that form the histone protein tails (Figure 4.2) through a series of enzymes that bind to and modify the local chemical properties of specific amino acids (Grunstein, 1997; Hake & Allis, 2006; Jenuwien & Allis, 2001). For example, the enzyme histone acetyltransferase "transfers" an acetyl group onto specific lysines on the histone tails. The addition of the acetyl group loosens the relation

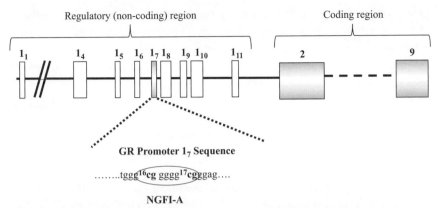

FIGURE 4.1 *A schema describing the organization of the rat glucocorticoid receptor (GR) gene including nine exon regions. Exons 2–9 participate in the coding for the glucocorticoid receptor protein. Exon 1 is composed of multiple regulatory regions, each of which is capable of activating gene transcription (i.e., promoter sequences). The activity of the various exon 1 promoters is tissue specific, with evidence suggesting that certain promoters are more active in areas such as the liver or thymus and others more active in the brain (e.g., exon 1₇; based on McCormick et al., 2000, and see Turner & Muller, 2005, for comparable data in humans). The use of multiple promoters permits regulation in one tissue independently from other regions (i.e., increased glucocorticoid receptor levels in pulmonary tissues prior to birth that are necessary for respiratory competency at parturition, while maintaining reduced glucocorticoid receptor levels in the brain, where glucocorticoid effects might inhibit neurogenesis). The consensus binding site for nerve growth factor–inducible factor A (NGFI-A) lying within the exon 1₇ promoter is highlighted. The reader should note that this organization is not necessarily typical. Regulatory elements (promoters or enhancers) can exist between exons (i.e., within introns) or at sites that are either 5′ or 3′ to the coding region, sometimes at considerable distances.*

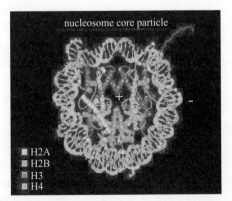

FIGURE 4.2 *Crystallographic image of the nucleosome showing 146 base pairs wrapped around a histone complex that is composed of histone 2A, 2B, 3, and 4 proteins. The tight configuration is maintained, in part, by electrostatic bonds. Modifications, such as acetylation, to the histone regulate transcription factor binding and occur primarily at the histone tails protruding out of the nucleosome (pictured is the blue tail of histone 3).*

between the histones and DNA, opening the chromatin and enhancing the ability of transcription factors to access DNA sites. Thus, histone acetylation at specific lysine sites is commonly associated with active gene transcription (please note that the primary objective of this paper is conceptual, and that our discussion will not refer to all forms of histone modifications).

Enzymes known as histone deacetylases (HDACs) are the functional antagonists of the histone acetyltransferases. Histone deacetylases, of which there are several, remove acetyl groups and prevent further acetylation. Histone deacetylases maintain a closed chromatin structure, decreasing transcription factor and gene expression. Both the acetylation and deacetylation of histones are dynamic and regulated by environmental signals. Indeed, a number of proteins with known transcriptional activity (e.g., transcriptional cofactors) are histone acetyltransferases. These factors enhance the efficacy of transcription factors by opening chromatin and thus increasing the binding of the factor to the regulatory regions of the gene.

Regulation of Glucocorticoid Receptor Expression

Serotonin (5-hydroxytryptamine [5-HT]) regulates glucocorticoid receptor gene transcription in hippocampal neurons (Mitchell, Betito, Rowe, Boksa, & Meaney, 1992; Weaver et al., 2007). This effect is dependent on the binding of nerve growth factor–inducible factor A (NGFI-A), a transcription factor, to a specific binding site on the exon 1_7 glucocorticoid receptor promoter (Figure 4.1). Thus, mutating a single nucleotide in the region of the promoter that normally binds NGFI-A abolishes the ability of NGFI-A to associate with the exon 1_7 promoter and eliminates the effect of NGFI-A on gene transcription (Weaver et al., 2007). However, the ability of NGFI-A to bind to the exon 1_7 promoter is regulated by a transcriptional cofactor, the CREB-binding protein (CREB = cAMP response element binding), that is activated by the same 5-HT/cyclic AMP/PKA (protein kinase) signaling cascade that triggers NGFI-A expression. The CREB-binding protein is a histone acetyltransferase. The association of the CREB-binding protein with the exon 1_7 promoter is accompanied by an increase in the acetylation of a specific lysine on the tail of histone 3 of the exon 1_7 promoter (Weaver et al., 2004; Weaver et al., 2007). Thus, 5-HT activates both NGFI-A and the CREB-binding protein. Interestingly, NGFI-A and the CREB-binding protein physically associate with one another prior to DNA binding.

The effect of 5-HT on glucocorticoid receptor expression reflects the dependence of gene transcription on signals that derive from environmental events (note that the relevant environmental event may be internal or external to the organism; e.g., a change in the availability of glucose, an electrical impulse, or a social interaction). Such effects underlie the dynamic interdependence of gene and environment. However, there are more enduring environmental influences, instances where experience in early life shapes neural development and function in a manner that is sustained into adulthood, providing a basis for environmental influences over the development of individual differences. Recent studies suggest that such environmentally regulated plasticity can exist at the level of the genome and involves the modification of epigenetic marks on DNA.

Environmental Programming of Gene Expression

The objective of our studies is to examine the biological mechanisms whereby a social experience in early life, variations in mother–infant interactions, might influence gene expression and behavior (Meaney, 2001). Such studies focus on variations in maternal behavior within the normal range for the species, in this case the Norway rat, and which occur in the absence of any experimental manipulations (i.e., naturally occurring variations in mother–pup interactions). Variations in maternal care in the rat are quantified with simple observational procedures focusing on the mothers and pups (Champagne, 2008; Champagne, Francis, Mar, & Meaney, 2003). One behavior, pup licking/grooming (LG), emerges as highly variable across mothers. Pup LG is a major source of tactile stimulation for the neonatal rat that regulates endocrine and sympathetic activity in the pup (Hofer, 2005; Levine, 1994; Schanberg, Evoniuk, & Kuhn, 1984) in a manner that enhances somatic growth.

Subsequent findings reveal considerable evidence for the effect of maternal care on the behavioral and endocrine responses to stress in the offspring. The male or female adult offspring of mothers that naturally exhibit increased levels of pup LG (i.e., the offspring of high-LG mothers) show more modest behavioral and endocrine responses to stress compared to animals reared by low-LG mothers (Caldji et al., 1998; Francis, Diorio, Liu, & Meaney, 1999; Liu et al., 1997; Menard, Champagne, & Meaney, 2004; Toki et al., 2007; Weaver et al., 2004). Briefly, the adult offspring of low-LG mothers show increased fearfulness in the presence of novel conditions or in response to well-defined stressors. Thus, actively defensive responses and avoidance are increased in the low-LG offspring. The offspring of high-LG mothers show reduced fearfulness and more modest hypothalamic–pituitary–adrenal (HPA) responses to stress. Cross-fostering studies in which the rearing mother determined the phenotype of the offspring reveal a direct relationship between maternal care and the development of individual differences in stress responses (Caldji, Diorio, & Meaney, 2003; Caldji, Francis, Sharma, Plotsky, & Meaney, 2000; Francis et al., 1999; Weaver et al., 2004).

The effects of maternal care on the development of defensive responses to stress in the rat involve alterations in the function of the corticotrophin-releasing factor (CRF) systems in selected brain regions. Corticotrophin-releasing factor furnishes a critical signal for the activation of behavioral, emotional, autonomic, and endocrine responses to stressors (Bale & Vale, 2004; Koob, Heinrichs, Menzaghi, Pich, & Britton, 1994; Plotsky, Cunningham, & Widmaier, 1989). As adults, the offspring of high-LG mothers show decreased CRF expression in the hypothalamus, as well as reduced plasma ACTH and glucocorticoid responses to acute stress by comparison to the adult offspring of low-LG mothers (Francis et al., 1999; Liu et al., 1997; Weaver et al., 2004; Weaver et al., 2005). Circulating glucocorticoids act at glucocorticoid receptor sites in corticolimbic structures, such as the hippocampus, to regulate HPA activity. Such feedback effects inhibit hypothalamic CRF expression. The high-LG offspring show increased hippocampal glucocorticoid receptor expression, enhanced glucocorticoid negative feedback sensitivity, and decreased hypothalamic CRF levels. Pharmacological manipulations that block the effect of the glucocorticoid receptor serve to eliminate the maternal effect on the HPA response to stress, suggesting that the differences in hippocampal glucocorticoid receptor expression are directly related to those at the level of HPA function.

Pup LG provides tactile stimulation for the neonate. Experimental models that directly apply tactile stimulation, through the stroking of the pup with a brush, provide direct evidence for the importance of tactile stimulation derived from pup LG. Thus, stroking pups over the first week of life increases hippocampal glucocorticoid receptor expression (Jutapakdeegul, Casalotti, Govitrapong, & Kotchabhakdi, 2003) and dampens HPA responses to stress (Burton et al., 2007; Gonzalez, Lovic, Ward, Wainwright, & Fleming, 2001). Likewise, manipulations of lactating mothers that directly increase the frequency of pup LG also increase hippocampal glucocorticoid receptor expression and decrease HPA responses to stress (Francis et al., 1999; Toki et al., 2007). Manipulations, most notably stressors imposed on the mother, that decrease pup LG associate with decreased hippocampal glucocorticoid receptor expression, increased hypothalamic expression of CRF, and enhanced behavioral and HPA responses to stress (Champagne & Meaney, 2006; Fenoglio et al., 2005). Moreover, measures of LG toward individual pups within a litter show that the frequency of licking correlates positively with the level of hippocampal glucocorticoid receptor expression (van Hasselt et al., 2012).

These findings suggest that maternal behavior can "program" stable changes in gene expression that then serve as the basis for individual differences in behavioral and neuroendocrine responses to stress in adulthood. The maternal effects on phenotype are associated with sustained changes in the expression of genes in brain regions that mediate responses to stress and form the basis for stable individual differences in stress reactivity. The question is, *How* might maternal care stably affect gene expression?

Epigenetic Regulation of Glucocorticoid Receptor Expression

The initiation of gene transcription involves modifications to the histone proteins, alterations of chromatin conformation that facilitate transcription factor binding, and activation of gene transcription. A second level of regulation occurs not on the histone proteins, but directly on the DNA. Indeed, the classic epigenetic alteration is that of DNA methylation, which involves the addition of a methyl group (CH_3)

onto cytosines in the DNA (Bird, 1986; Holliday, 1989; Razin & Cedar, 1993; Razin & Riggs, 1980). DNA methylation associates with the silencing of gene transcription in one of two ways (Bird, 2002). First, densely methylated DNA precludes transcription factor binding to DNA sites. The second manner is subtler, and probably far more prevalent in regions with more dynamic variations in gene transcription, such as the brain. Here selected cytosines are methylated, and the presence of the methyl group attracts a class of proteins known as methylated DNA-binding proteins (Klose & Bird, 2006). Methyl CpG–binding protein 2 (MeCP2) and MBD2 (methyl-CpG-binding domain protein 2) are the best studied examples of these proteins. These proteins attract a cluster of proteins that form a repressor complex, which includes active mediators of gene silencing, including HDACs. Histone deacetylases prevent histone acetylation and favor a closed chromatin state that constrains transcription factor binding and gene expression. Compounds that inhibit HDACs can thus increase transcription from methylated DNA.

Despite the reverence afforded DNA, a nucleotide sequence is subject to physical modifications like any other molecule. Collectively, the modifications to the DNA and its chromatin environment can be considered as an additional layer of information that is contained within the genome. This information is thus *epigenetic* in nature (the name derives from the Greek *epi,* meaning "upon," and *genetics*). The acetylation of histones and the methylation of DNA are examples of epigenetic modifications. Epigenetic modifications do not alter the sequence composition of the genome. Instead, these epigenetic marks on the DNA and the histone proteins of the chromatin regulate the structure and operation of the genome. Thus, *epigenetics* is defined as a functional modification to the DNA that does not involve an alteration of sequence (Waddington, 1957; also see Bird, 2007; Hake & Allis, 2006).

The methylation of DNA in mammals is an active biochemical modification that selectively targets cytosines and is achieved through the actions of enzymes, DNA methyltransferases that transfer the methyl groups from methyl donors. There are two critical features to DNA methylation: First, it is a potentially stable chemical modification, and second, when found within regulatory regions of the DNA that include promoters and enhancers, it is associated with the silencing of gene transcription (Bestor, 1998; Bird, 2002; Bird & Wolffe, 1999; Razin, 1998; note, methylation of DNA in other regions of the genome can have very different effects; e.g., Weber et al., 2007). Until recently it was held in some quarters that DNA methylation patterns were overlaid upon the genome only during early periods in embryonic development. This is truly a period of dynamic changes in the methylation of the DNA. Indeed, DNA methylation is a fundamental feature of cell differentiation, a process whereby selected regions of the genome are inactivated in order to define the function of the cell. Thus, DNA methylation was considered both unique to early periods in development and irreversible. Experimental models commonly used to study DNA methylation, including X-chromosome inactivation and parent-of-origin and gene imprinting, reinforced this view (Charalambous, da Rocha, & Ferguson-Smith, 2007; da Rocha & Ferguson-Smith, 2004; Mohandas, Sparkes, & Shapiro, 1981; Riggs & Pfieffer, 1992; but also see Hellman & Chess, 2007, for a more current update on X-chromosome inactivation). Here, too, however, the dogma is falling. Some parental imprinting patterns appear to change over the course of development (Gregg et al., 2010), suggesting a dynamic alteration in underlying epigenetic states. Collectively, these models had left biologists with the impression that under normal conditions DNA methylation occurs early in embryonic life and is irreversible (although see Reik & Walter, 2001). Moreover, the extensive loss of cytosine methylation at certain regions of the genome can associate with pathology; alteration of DNA methylation at tumor suppressors is associated with cancer (Eden, Gaudet, Waghmare, & Jaenisch, 2003; Feinberg, 2007; Laird, 2005).

The issue for the behavioral sciences concerns less the process by which cells specialize as neurons and more the issues related to why neurons in one individual function differently from those of another, or how neurons might dynamically influence later functional properties in relation to experience (i.e., activity-dependent neuronal plasticity). There is now considerable evidence in neuroscience and other fields, including immunology and endocrinology/metabolism, that the state of DNA methylation at specific genomic sites is indeed dynamic even in adult animals (Bird, 2007; Jirtle & Skinner, 2007; Meaney & Szyf, 2005; Sweatt, 2009). Moreover, alterations in DNA methylation are emerging as a candidate mechanism for the effects of early experience in individual differences in neural function as well as in learning and memory. Thus, while the assumptions concerning DNA methylation appear valid for the examples cited earlier, recent studies reveal that DNA methylation patterns are actively modified in mature (i.e., fully differentiated) cells, including, and perhaps especially, neurons, and that such modifications can occur in animals in response to cellular signals driven by environmental events (Jirtle & Skinner, 2007; Meaney & Szyf, 2005; Sweatt, 2009). For example, variations in the diet of mice during gestation or later in development, such as the early postweaning period, can stably alter the methylation status of the DNA (Cooney, Dave, & Wolff, 2002; Waterland & Jirtle, 2003; Waterland, Lin, Smith, & Jirtle, 2006; Whitelaw & Whitelaw, 2006). Likewise, both mature lymphocytes (Bruniquel & Schwartz, 2003; Murayama et al., 2006) and neurons (e.g., Champagne, 2008; Lubin, Roth, & Sweatt, 2008; Martinowich et al., 2003; Sweatt, 2009) show changes in the DNA methylation patterns in response to environmental stimuli. Such epigenetic modifications are thus a candidate mechanism for the environmental "programming" of gene expression.

Epigenetics and the Social Environment

The critical feature of the maternal effects described earlier is that of persistence. The differences in the frequency of pup LG between high- and low-LG mothers are limited to the first week of postnatal life, while the effects on gene expression and neural function are apparent in adulthood. The focus of the epigenetic studies is the NGFI-A consensus sequence in the exon 1_7 promoter (Figure 4.1) that activates glucocorticoid receptor expression in hippocampal neurons. The tactile stimulation associated with pup LG increases 5-HT activity in the hippocampus. In vitro studies with cultured hippocampal neurons show that 5-HT acts on 5-HT_7 receptors to initiate a series of intracellular signals that culminate with an increase in the expression of NGFI-A as well as in the CREB-binding protein. Comparable effects occur in vivo. Manipulations that increase pup LG by lactating rats result in an increased level of cyclic AMP as well as NGFI-A (Meaney et al., 2000). Pups reared by high-LG mothers show increased NGFI-A expression in hippocampal neurons as well as an increased binding of NGFI-A to the exon 1_7 promoter sequence (Weaver et al., 2007). Moreover, the binding of NGFI-A to the exon 1_7 promoter sequence is actively regulated by mother–pup interactions, such that there is increased NGFI-A bound to the exon 1_7 promoter immediately following a nursing bout, but not at a period that follows 25 minutes without mother–pup contact (Hellstrom et al., in preparation).

Nerve growth factor–inducible factor A and the CREB-binding protein form a complex that binds directly to the exon 1_7 promoter sequence and actively participates in the processes that redesign the methylation pattern at this region of the genome (Weaver et al., 2004; Weaver et al., 2007). The adult offspring reared by high-LG mothers show very modest levels of methylation at the 5′ CpG site of the NGFI-A consensus sequence. This effect on methylation is very precise. Lying only a few nucleotides removed from this site is the 3′ CpG site; the methylation status of this site is unaffected by maternal care.

A novel feature of the effect of maternal care on DNA methylation emerged in the results of a developmental study examining the methylation status of the 5′ and 3′ CpG sites from late in fetal life to adulthood (Weaver et al., 2004). Neither the 5′ nor the 3′ CpG site within the NGFI-A-binding region is methylated in hippocampal neurons from fetal rats, whereas both sites are heavily methylated on the day following birth, with no difference as a function of maternal care. These findings reflect de novo methylation, whereby a methyl group is applied to previously unmethylated sites. However, between the day following birth and the end of the first week of life, the 5′ CpG site is "demethylated" in pups reared by high-LG, but not low-LG, mothers. This difference then persists into adulthood. The period for the demethylation occurs within that time when high- and low-LG mothers differ in the frequency of pup LG; the difference in pup LG between high- and low-LG mothers is not apparent in the second week of postnatal life (Caldji et al., 1998; Champagne, 2008; Champagne et al., 2003).

The demethylation of the 5′ CpG site occurs as a function of the same 5-HT-activated signals that regulate glucocorticoid receptor gene expression in cultured hippocampal neurons (Weaver et al., 2007). In hippocampal neurons in culture and treated with 5-HT, which mimics the extracellular signal associated with maternal

LG, the 5′ CpG site is demethylated, with no effect at the 3′ CpG site. The binding of NGFI-A to the exon 1₇ site is critical. Hippocampal neurons that are rendered incapable of increasing NGFI-A expression through antisense or small interfering RNA (siRNA) treatment show neither the demethylation of the 5′ CpG site nor the increase in glucocorticoid receptor expression (Weaver et al., 2007). Likewise, a mutation of the NGFI-A site (exchanging a C for an A at the 3′ CpG site) that completely abolishes the binding of NGFI-A to the exon 1₇ promoter prevents the demethylation of the 5′ CpG site. Finally, the infection of hippocampal neurons with a virus containing a nucleotide construct engineered to express high levels of NGFI-A produces demethylation of the 5′ CpG site of the exon 1₇ promoter sequence and increased glucocorticoid receptor expression.

These findings suggest that maternal licking of pups increases NGFI-A levels in the hippocampal neurons of the offspring, altering DNA methylation. But if DNA methylation blocks transcription factor binding and the 5′ CpG site of the exon 1₇ promoter is heavily methylated in neonates, then how might maternally activated NGFI-A bind to and remodel the exon 1₇ region? And why is the effect apparent at the 5′, but not the 3′, CpG site? The answer to these questions appears to involve other transcriptional signals affected by maternal care. Levels of the transcription factor specific protein-1 (SP-1) and the CREB-binding protein are also increased in the hippocampus of pups reared by High LG mothers (Hellstrom et al., in preparation; Weaver et al., 2007). The exon 1₇ promoter contains a DNA sequence that binds SP-1, and this region overlaps with that for NGFI-A. Specific protein-1 can actively target both methylation and demethylation of CpG sites (Brandeis et al., 1994). The 5′ CpG site is the region of overlap in the binding sites. The CREB-binding protein, on the other hand, acts as a histone acetyltransferase, an enzyme capable of acetylating histone tails, including the exon 1₇ region, opening chromatin and permitting the binding of transcription factors such as NGFI-A and SP-1. Increasing histone acetylation leads to transcription factor binding at previously methylated sites and the subsequent demethylation of these regions (Szyf, Weaver, Champagne, Diorio, & Meaney, 2005). Thus, we suggest that the binding of this complex of proteins, NGFI-A, the CREB-binding protein, and SP-1, is critical in activating the process of demethylation. The results to date are certainly consistent with this model, but we should note that we have yet to firmly establish the identity of the enzyme that is responsible for the demethylation of the 5′ CpG site.

These findings suggest that maternally induced increases in hippocampal NGFI-A levels trigger a process that remodels DNA methylation at the regions of the DNA that regulate glucocorticoid receptor expression. The NGFI-A transcription factor binds to multiple sites across the genome. If NGFI-A-related complexes affect DNA methylation, then one might assume that other NGFI-A-sensitive regions should show a maternal effect on DNA methylation and gene expression comparable to that observed with the glucocorticoid receptor. Zhang and colleagues (Zhang et al., 2010) showed that the hippocampal expression of the *GAD1* gene that encodes for glutamic acid decarboxylase, an enzyme critical for the production of the neurotransmitter γ-aminobutyric acid (GABA), is increased in the adult offspring of high-LG mothers. This effect is associated with altered DNA methylation of an NGFI-A response element in a manner comparable to that for the glucocorticoid receptor gene. Moreover, as with the effect on the glucocorticoid receptor, an in vitro increase in NGFI-A expression mimics the effects of increased pup LG. The function of GABAergic neurons in the limbic system is also regulated by maternal care (Caldji et al., 2003; Caldji et al., 2000; Caldji et al., 1998). These findings are therefore likely relevant for the decreased fearfulness observed in the adult offspring of high-LG mothers.

Taken together, these findings suggest a model whereby a social event may stably alter the function of the genome. This conclusion is supported by the findings from studies of Murgatroyd et al. (2009), who examined the effects of prolonged periods of maternal separation on the development of HPA responses to stress in the mouse. Maternal separation in rodents increases the magnitude of HPA responses to acute stress (e.g., Plotsky et al., 2005). Increased HPA activity associated with maternal separation is accompanied by a persistent increase in arginine vasopressin (AVP) expression in neurons of the hypothalamic paraventricular nucleus and is reversed by an AVP receptor antagonist. Arginine vasopressin acts in synergy with CRF to increase pituitary ACTH synthesis and HPA activity. The altered *avp* expression associates with sustained DNA hypomethylation of a regulatory region containing CpG residues that serve as DNA-binding sites for MeCP2. MeCP2 binding regulates *avp* expression. As in the case with glucocorticoid receptor regulation, *avp* expression correlates with the methylation status of a single CpG site. A rather unique analysis showed that the difference in the methylation of this CpG site remained stable from 3 to 12 months of age, reflecting the potential stability of early environmental effects.

The Functional Importance of the Social Imprint

A critical issue is that of relating the epigenetic modifications at specific DNA regions to genomic function. In vitro studies reveal that the methylation of the 5′ CpG site reduces the ability of NGFI-A to bind to the exon 1_7 promoter and activate glucocorticoid receptor transcription (Weaver et al., 2007). These findings are consistent with the model described earlier, whereby DNA methylation impedes transcription factor binding and thus the activation of gene expression. The next question concerns the in vivo situation and function at a level beyond that of gene expression. In contrast to the situation with neonates, there is no difference in NGFI-A expression as a function of maternal care among adult animals: Hippocampal levels of NGFI-A are comparable in the adult offspring of high- and low-LG mothers. However, the altered methylation of the exon 1_7 promoter would suggest differences in the ability of NGFI-A to *access* its binding site on the exon 1_7

promoter. Chromatin-immunoprecipitation assays, which permit measurement of the interaction between a specific protein and a defined region of the DNA, reveal increased NGFI-A association with the exon 1_7 promoter in hippocampi from adult offspring of high-LG compared to low-LG mothers (Weaver et al., 2004; Weaver et al., 2005). This difference occurs despite the comparable levels of NGFI-A and suggests that under normal conditions, there is more NGFI-A associated with the exon 1_7 promoter in hippocampal neurons of adult animals reared by high-LG compared with low-LG mothers.

There is also evidence that directly links the maternal effect on the epigenetic state of the exon 1_7 promoter to the changes in glucocorticoid receptor expression and HPA responses to stress. Recall that the methylation of specific CpG sites can diminish transcription factor binding through the recruitment of repressor complexes that include HDACs. The HDACs deacetylate histone tails, thus favoring a closed chromatin configuration. Indeed, the exon 1_7 promoter is more prominently acetylated in hippocampi from adult offspring of high-LG compared with low-LG mothers (Weaver et al., 2004; Weaver et al., 2005). This finding is consistent with the increased transcription of the glucocorticoid receptor gene in animals reared by high- versus low-LG mothers. One study (Weaver et al., 2004) examined the effects of directly blocking the actions of the HDACs in the adult offspring of high- and low-LG mothers by directly infusing an HDAC inhibitor into the hippocampus daily for 4 consecutive days. First, as expected, HDAC blockade eliminates the differences in the acetylation of the histone tails (open chromatin) of the exon 1_7 promoter in hippocampal samples from high- and low-LG mothers. Second, the increased histone acetylation of the exon 1_7 promoter in the offspring of low-LG mothers is associated with an increase in the binding of NGFI-A to the exon 1_7 promoter in the offspring of low-LG mothers, eliminating the maternal effect on NGFI-A binding to the exon 1_7 promoter. Comparable levels of NGFI-A binding to the exon 1_7 promoter then eliminate the maternal effect on hippocampal glucocorticoid receptor expression, such that glucocorticoid receptor levels in the adult offspring of low-LG mothers treated with the HDAC inhibitor are comparable to those in animals reared by high-LG mothers. And most important, the infusion of the HDAC inhibitor reverses the differences in the HPA response to stress.

Histone deacetylase inhibition increases NGFI-A binding to the exon 1_7 promoter in the offspring of low-LG mothers. The studies with neonates reveal that increased NGFI-A binding results in the demethylation of the 5′ CpG site. In vitro, the introduction of a viral tool that leads to the increased expression of NGFI-A is sufficient to demethylate the exon 1_7 promoter. We (Weaver et al., 2007) argue that the binding of NGFI-A is critical for the demethylation of the 5′ CpG site. The same effect is apparent in vivo and even with the adult animals used in the studies described previously. Histone deacetylase infusion into the hippocampus increases NGFI-A binding to the exon 1_7 promoter in the adult offspring of low-LG mothers and decreases the level of methylation of the 5′ CpG site on the exon 1_7 promoter. Thus, the reverse pattern of results is apparent in response to the infusion of methionine into the hippocampus. The methionine infusion produced greater methylation of the 5′ CpG site in the offspring of high-LG mothers, decreased NGFI-A binding and glucocorticoid receptor expression, and increased HPA responses to stress (Weaver et al., 2005).

While these studies employ rather crude manipulations, the results suggest that fully mature neurons in an adult animal express the necessary enzymatic machinery to demethylate or remethylate DNA. The importance of this "plasticity" at the level of DNA methylation is revealed in subsequent studies of cognition (see later), which suggest that dynamic modification of DNA methylation in critical neuronal populations in adult animals is involved in specific forms of learning and memory.

Activity-Dependent Regulation of the Epigenome

An increase in the expression of NGFI-A is associated with synaptic plasticity and with learning and memory (Dragunow, 1996; Jones et al., 2001; Knapska & Kaczmarek, 2004; O'Donovan, Tourtellotte, Millbrandt, & Baraban, 1999). Thus, it is not surprising that the offspring of high-LG mothers show increased synaptic density both in early life (Liu et al., 2000) and in adulthood (Bagot et al., 2009; Bredy, Humpartzoomian, Cain, & Meaney, 2003; Liu et al., 2000). Such events occur as a function of a series of activity-dependent changes in neuronal activity triggered by the action of glutamate at the NMDA receptor site (Ali & Salter, 2001; Bear & Malenka, 1994; Malenka & Nicoll, 1993; Morris & Frey, 1997). Thus, it is possible that environmentally driven changes in neuronal transcriptional signals could potentially remodel the methylation state of specific regions of the DNA. These effects could, in turn, prove essential for sustained alterations in synaptic function.

Learning and long-term memory commonly require changes in gene expression and protein synthesis (Alberini, Ghirardi, Huang, Nguyen, & Kandel, 1995; Kandel, 2001; Lynch, 2004). Gene transcription is associated with chromatin remodeling engineered by enzymes that modify the histone proteins within chromatin complexes. A number of the intracellular signals that are crucial for learning and memory are in fact enzymes that modify histone proteins. One example is that of the CREB-binding protein, which functions as a histone acetyltransferase and is strongly implicated in cognitive function (e.g., Alarcon et al., 2004). Thus, contextual fear conditioning, which is a hippocampus-dependent learning paradigm whereby an animal associates a novel context with an aversive stimulus, is accompanied by increased acetylation of histone H3 (Levenson et al., 2004). Likewise, there is evidence for the importance of epigenetic modifications of histones in the amygdala during fear conditioning (Yeh, Lin, & Gean, 2004). Interestingly, extinction of the conditioned fear response is associated with increased histone acetylation in the prefrontal cortex, which mediates the inhibition of conditioned fear responses (Bredy et al., 2007). The CREB-binding protein is probably involved in the relevant histone modifications. Mice that are heterozygous for a dysfunctional form of the CREB-binding protein show significant impairments in multiple forms of hippocampal-dependent, long-term memory (Bourtchouladze et al., 2003; Korzus, Rosenfeld, & Mayford, 2004; Wood, Attner, Oliveira, Brindle, & Abel, 2006; also see Guan et al., 2002, and Vecsey et al., 2007). Importantly, the cognitive impairments are reversed with HDAC administration, suggesting that CREB-binding protein–induced histone acetylation mediates effects on learning and memory.

There is also evidence for the importance of dynamic changes in DNA methylation at specific sites during learning and memory. Fear conditioning results in the rapid methylation and transcriptional silencing of the gene for protein phosphatase 1 (PP1), which suppresses learning. The same training results in the demethylation and transcriptional activation of the synaptic plasticity gene reelin. These findings imply that both DNA methylation and demethylation might be involved in long-term memory consolidation.

Brain-derived neurotrophic factor (BDNF) is implicated in adult neural plasticity, including learning and memory (West et al., 2001). The genomic structure of the Bdnf gene contains multiple promoters that generate messenger RNAs (mRNAs) containing different noncoding exons spliced upstream of a common coding exon (Timmusk et al., 1993), somewhat like that described earlier for the glucocorticoid receptor. In the case of BDNF, the exon IV promoter in rats is activated upon membrane depolarization in cultured cortical and hippocampal neurons by means of KCl, which leads to calcium influx, activating signaling cascades and inducing the expression of an array of genes that are involved in neural plasticity (West et al., 2001).

The activity-dependent Bdnf gene is also regulated through epigenetic modifications that involve dynamic changes in DNA methylation and the association of methylated DNA-binding proteins to the relevant sites on the bdnf promoter. Thus, increased DNA methylation of the exon IV promoter at sites that bind to transcriptional activators is associated with the presence of the methylated DNA-binding protein, MeCP2, and a decreased level of bdnf expression. This transcriptionally quiescent state prior to depolarization is also associated with the presence of histone deacetylases (i.e., HDAC1) and mSIN3A, which form a common repressor complex. Membrane depolarization of the neuron leads to a decrease in CpG methylation and a dissociation of the MeCP2-related repressor complex from the exon IV promoter. As described earlier for the glucocorticoid receptor, the decrease in CpG methylation is then associated with an increase in histone acetylation and the binding of the transcription factor CREB. CREB is known to activate bdnf expression. These data suggest that DNA methylation at a particular site can suppress activity-dependent transcription of Bdnf. These findings also indicate that DNA methylation patterns in postmitotic neurons can undergo dynamic changes in response to neuronal activation, and a lower level of DNA methylation correlates with a higher level of Bdnf gene transcription in neurons.

Interestingly, MeCP2 levels increase as neurons mature (Zoghbi, 2003). Increased MeCP2 protein in mature neurons is consistent with a possible role for MeCP2 in synaptic remodeling associated with learning and memory (Zhou et al., 2006). Further supporting a role for MeCP2 in mature synaptic function and plasticity, Mecp2-null mice exhibit abnormalities in basal synaptic transmission (Moretti et al., 2006), presynaptic function (Moretti et al., 2006), excitatory synaptic plasticity (Moretti et al., 2006), and hippocampal and amygdalar learning (Moretti et al., 2006). Zhou et al. (2006) found that neuronal activity (membrane depolarization) is associated with a phosphorylation of MeCP2 at serine 421 that led to its dissociation from the *bdnf* exon IV promoter and an increase in *bdnf* expression (also see Chen et al., 2003). Importantly, activity-dependent increases in BDNF levels are blocked in cells bearing a mutant version of MeCP2 that is unable to undergo phosphorylation. Glutamate is a primary neural signal for synaptic plasticity, and both glutamate and the direct activation of its NMDA receptor produced MeCP2 phosphorylation in neurons. Glutamate activates NMDA receptors, resulting in a neuronal calcium influx and the activation of calcium-modulated kinase II (CaMKII), which regulates synaptic plasticity (Lisman, Schulman, & Cline, 2002). Zhou et al. (2006) found that CaMKII actively phosphorylates MeCP2.

The protein phosphorylation occurring at MeCP2 in response to neuronal activation is a transient event. The results described earlier (Martinowhich et al., 2003) suggest that neuronal activation can lead to changes in DNA methylation, which is a potentially more stable, epigenetic alteration that could conceivably result in a long-term change in *bdnf* expression. Thus far, this chapter has considered the relation between DNA methylation, histone acetylation/deacetylation, transcription factor binding, and gene expression. However, there is evidence that the chromatin alterations can alter DNA methylation. Thus, HDAC inhibitors result in an increase in histone acetylation, enhanced transcription factor binding, and decreased DNA methylation. Such effects were described earlier in relation to DNA methylation and glucocorticoid receptor expression (Weaver et al., 2004; Weaver et al., 2005). Thus, it is possible that neuronal activation leads to (1) the transient phosphorylation of MeCP2 and its dissociation from the exon IV *bdnf* promoter or (2) an increase in histone acetylation and CREB binding producing increased *bdnf* expression, and that (3) the histone acetylation and CREB binding are also associated with DNA demethylation, as described previously in the case of the glucocorticoid receptor for histone acetylation and NGFI-A binding. Such events could underlie a common process of activity-dependent modification of DNA methylation (Weaver, Meaney, & Szyf, 2006).

Studies by Sweatt and colleagues suggest that the changes in DNA methylation at the exon IV *bdnf* promoter are involved in specific forms of learning and memory (Sweatt, 2009). *Bdnf* gene expression increases in the hippocampus with contextual and spatial learning and appears essential for the synaptic remodeling that accompanies such forms of learning and memory (Hall, Thomas, & Everitt, 2000;

Linnarsson, Björklund, & Ernfors, 1997). Activation of the NMDA receptor is critical for both contextual (Maren & Quirk, 2000) and spatial (Morris et al., 2003)
learning, as well as for the increase in *bdnf* expression that accompanies such events.
Lubin et al. (2008) found that contextual fear conditioning was associated with
a demethylation of the exon IV *bdnf* promoter and an increase in *bdnf* expression:
Both effects were blocked with a glutamate receptor antagonist. Taken together,
these findings suggest that the activity-dependent changes in neuronal activity that
associate with learning and memory induce a dynamic alteration in DNA methylation that, in turn, subserves the sustained changes in gene expression critical for
long-term memory. While this remains a working hypothesis, the findings discussed
earlier further emphasize the degree to which neuronal activation can structurally
remodel the genome and alter its operation.

There is also evidence that environmental influences prevailing during early
development may determine the capacity for such activity-driven, epigenetic modifications. Disruptions to mother–infant interactions during early development
are associated with alterations in hippocampal *bdnf* expression (Lippman, Bress,
Nemeroff, Plotsky, & Monteggia, 2007; Roceri, Hendriks, Racagni, Ellenbroek, &
Riva, 2002; Roceri et al., 2004; but also see Greisen, Altar, Bolwig, Whitehead, &
Wortwein, 2005) and increased DNA methylation at the exon IV *bdnf* promoter
(Roth, Lubin, Funk, & Sweatt, 2009). In mice, rearing in a communal nest, with
three mothers and their litters, increases maternal care toward the offspring, which
in turn associates with increased BDNF expression (Branchi, D'Andrea, Fiore,
et al., 2006). And in the rat, the offspring of high-LG mothers show decreased
MeCP2 association with the exon IV *bdnf* promoter (Weaver et al., 2007) and
increased *bdnf* expression (Liu et al., 2000; Shahrohk & Meaney, unpublished).
Such maternal effects might bias in favor of reduced capacity for epigenetic remodeling at this critical site and restrain synaptic plasticity associated with learning and
memory.

Epigenetics and Mental Health

Recent studies from Nestler and colleagues reveal considerable epigenetic modification at specific genomic sites associated with chronic stress or repeated exposure
to psychostimulant drugs, both of which produce sustained influences on behavior (Nestler, 2009; Renthal & Nestler, 2009). While such effects have yet to be
reported for DNA methylation, modifications of histone proteins are associated
with exposure to drugs of abuse and stressors in rodent models (Renthal & Nestler,
2008, 2009). These findings suggest that epigenetic states, including DNA methylation, are altered by a wide range of biologically relevant events (Meaney & Szyf,
2005; Renthal & Nestler, 2008; Szyf et al., 2005). Such epigenetic modifications
might therefore underlie a wide range of stable changes in neural function following
exposure to highly salient events (e.g., chronic stress, drugs of abuse, reproductive

phases such as parenting, etc.) and are thus logical mechanisms for environmentally induced alterations in mental health (Akbarian & Huang, 2009; Jiang et al., 2008; Tsankova, Renthal, Kumar, & Nestler, 2007).

There is emerging evidence that links the alterations in gene expression associated with DNA methylation to psychiatric illness. Cortical dysfunction in schizophrenia is associated with changes in GABAergic circuitry (Benes & Beretta, 2001). This effect is associated with a decrease in the expression of the *GAD1* gene that encodes for a specific form of glutamic acid decarboxylase (GAD_{67}), one of two key enzymes for GABA synthesis in cortical interneurons. There is compelling evidence for the decreased expression of GAD_{67} in cortical tissues from schizophrenic patients (Akbarian & Huang, 2006; Costa et al., 2004). The dysregulated GAD_{67} expression in the chandelier GABA neurons is thought to result in disruption of synchronized cortical activity and impairment of executive functions in schizophrenia subjects (Lewis, Hashimoto, & Volk, 2005). Likewise, allelic variation in *GAD1* is associated with schizophrenia (Straub, Lipska, Egan, Goldberg, & Kleinman, 2007).

In addition to GAD_{67}, there is also a decrease in cortical expression of reelin in schizophrenic brains (Eastwood & Harrison, 2003); reelin is closely associated with synaptic plasticity. The same GABAergic neurons in the schizophrenic brain that express reelin and GAD_{67} exhibit an increase in DNA methyltransferase 1 (DNMT1; Veldic et al., 2004). DNA methyltransferase 1 is a member of a family of enzymes that transfers a methyl group from the methyl donor *S*-adenosylmethionine (SAM) onto cytosines, thus producing DNA methylation. The promoter for the *reelin* gene shows increased methylation in the brains of patients with schizophrenia compared with control subjects (Abdolmaleky et al., 2005; Grayson et al., 2005). Kundakovic, Chen, Costa, and Grayson (2007) showed that the inhibition of DNMT1 in neuronal cell lines resulted in the increased expression of both reelin and GAD_{67}. The increase in gene expression was associated with a decreased association of MeCP2, further suggesting that these differences are associated with alteration in DNA methylation. Recall that maternal care directly alters DNA methylation of the GAD_{67} promoter in the rat. This effect is associated with a decrease in DNMT1 expression and a reduced MeCP2 association with the *GAD1* promoter.

An important question is that of the developmental origins of such differences in DNA methylation. A set of recent studies (McGowan et al., 2009) suggests that epigenetic modifications might occur in humans in response to variations in parent–offspring interactions. DNA was extracted from hippocampal samples obtained from victims of suicide or from individuals who had died suddenly from other causes (auto accidents, heart attacks, etc.). The samples were obtained from the Québec Suicide Brain Bank, which conducts forensic phenotyping that includes a validated assessment of psychiatric status and developmental history (e.g., McGirr, Renaud, Seguin, Alda, & Turecki, 2008). The studies examined the methylation status of the exon 1_F promoter of the glucocorticoid receptor, which corresponds to the exon 1_7 promoter in the rat (Turner & Muller, 2005). The results showed increased DNA methylation of the exon 1_F promoter in hippocampal samples from suicide victims compared with controls, but only if suicide was accompanied with a developmental history of child maltreatment. Child maltreatment, independent of psychiatric state, predicted the DNA methylation status of the exon 1_F promoter. As in the previous rodent studies, the methylation state of the exon 1_F promoter also determined the ability of NGFI-A to bind to the promoter and activate gene transcription. While such studies are obviously correlational, and limited by postmortem approaches, the results are nevertheless consistent with the hypothesis that variations in parental care can modify the epigenetic state of selected sites of the human genome. Moreover, the findings are also consistent with studies that link childhood abuse to individual differences in stress responses (Heim et al., 2000). Childhood abuse associates with an increase in pituitary ACTH responses to stress among individuals with or without concurrent major depression. These findings are particularly relevant because pituitary ACTH directly reflects central activation of the HPA stress response and hippocampal glucocorticoid receptor activation dampens HPA activity. The findings in humans are consistent with the rodent studies cited earlier investigating epigenetic regulation of the glucocorticoid receptor gene and with the hypothesis that early life events can alter the epigenetic state of relevant genomic regions, the expression of which may contribute to individual differences in the risk for psychopathology (Holsboer, 2000; Neigh & Nemeroff, 2006; Schatzberg, Rothschild, Langlais, Bird, & Cole, 1985).

There are certain limitations that need to be considered as we integrate epigenetics into the study of psychopathology. The study of epigenetic mechanisms in humans is complicated by the fact that epigenetic marks are often tissue specific. For example, the brain contains some neurons that synthesize and release dopamine as a neurotransmitter and others that rely on acetylcholine. We might assume that among dopaminergic neurons, the genes associated with the capacity for acetylcholine production are silenced, likely through some level of epigenetic regulation. Such processes are inherent in the specialization of brain cells, as with all other differentiated cells in the body. This process of specialization involves epigenetic regulation and implies that the epigenetic marks vary from cell type to cell type. Indeed, there is considerable variation in epigenetic marks from one brain region to another, perhaps even more so than variation within the same brain region across individuals (Ladd-Acosta et al., 2007). Brain samples are for the most part beyond direct examination in the living individual at the level of molecular analysis. This often leaves us with measures of DNA extracted from blood or saliva, and with the question of whether the epigenetic marks within such samples actually reflect those within the relevant neuronal population. Thus, for the time being, advances in the study of "neuroepigenetics" will rely heavily on relevant models with nonhuman species as well as complementary studies of samples from postmortem human brains.

Conclusions

Genomic variation associates with individual differences in personality and predicts vulnerability and resistance to a wide range of chronic illnesses. The challenge is to conceptually integrate the findings from genetics into the biological sciences. The operation of the genome is an actively regulated process that involves environmentally sensitive, cellular signals. Genetic variations influence cellular activity and, depending on current and past environmental conditions, will bias toward particular functional outcomes. The molecular events that mediate gene transcription reveal the *interdependence* of gene and environment (Sokolowski, 2001).

There is considerable enthusiasm for the environmental epigenetic hypothesis. The studies reviewed here provide some initial support and suggest that (1) epigenetic remodeling occurs in response to the environmental activation of the classic "activity dependent" cellular signaling pathways that associate with synaptic plasticity; (2) epigenetic marks, particularly DNA methylation, are actively remodeled over early development in response to environmental events that regulate neural development and function; and (3) epigenetic marks at histone proteins and the DNA are subject to remodeling in response to environmental influences even at later stages in development.

These findings suggest that epigenetic remodeling might serve as an ideal mechanism for phenotypic plasticity—the process whereby the environment interacts with the genome to produce individual differences in the expression of specific traits. One could easily imagine that such processes mediate observed discordances between monozygotic twins (Petronis, 2006; Weksberg et al., 2002). Thus, differences at the level of experience might lead to discordance in the nature of the epigenetic marks at specific sites in the genome, leading to differences in phenotype, despite a common genotype. Indeed, there is evidence for an increasing degree of discordance in epigenetic marks over time among monozygotic twins (e.g., Fraga et al., 2005). An accumulation of environmentally driven epigenetic marks that regulate genomic function might underlie divergence of phenotype. The same processes are likely to account for instances of statistical gene × environment interactions, whereby the genotype–phenotype relation is apparent in one environmental context but not in another (Sokolowski & Wahlsten, 2001). An environmentally regulated epigenetic mark might alter the functional consequences of a genomic variation in sequence (Petronis, 2006).

The study of epigenetics has experienced considerable "penetrance" in the fields of physiology, neuroscience, psychology, and even epidemiology. It is important to note that these are the early days. Outside of the fields of cell differentiation, gene imprinting, and cancer, epigenetics studies rely on a rather narrow range of experimental models. The use of genome-wide approaches (e.g., ChIP-ChIP, ChIP-seq, etc.) is revealing findings that challenge entrenched assumptions concerning even rather basic issues, such as the relation between CpG methylation and gene transcription. While DNA methylation continues to be linked to transcriptional silencing, such relations are not universal, and the strength of the relationship may be determined by the underlying genomic sequence. For example, among promoters with a lower percentage of CpG dinucleotides, there appears to be a weaker relationship between the overall level of methylation and that of gene transcription. Likewise, the presence of histone modifications (H3K4me) that associate with transcriptionally active genes appears to be determined not only by DNA methylation but also by the underlying genomic sequence. Such findings should dissuade us from assuming that genomic sequence is merely a passive player in the definition of epigenetic states (Meaney & Ferguson-Smith, 2010). The underlying genomic sequence may influence both the nature of potential epigenetic states and their importance for gene transcription.

Another source of constraint lies in studies suggesting that orthodox mediators of DNA methylation–induced gene silencing may also act to enhance transcriptional activity. Chahrour et al. (2008) examined hypothalamic gene expression patterns of mice that lacked or overexpressed MeCP2. Altered MeCP2 expression associates with widespread changes in transcriptional activity, but in many cases the evidence suggested transcriptional activation, not repression, through MeCP2. Transcriptional activation through MeCP2 appears to associate with CREB binding, and thus the activity of methylated DNA-binding proteins may be contextually regulated. This point may be critical in the hunt for enzymes that directly alter cytosine methylation. Thus, one such protein, MBD2, associates with both DNA methylation and DNA demethylation. We are some ways off from a complete understanding of the pathways linking environmental events to epigenetic states and functional outcomes. In the example of the glucocorticoid receptor described at length here, the critical enzyme necessary for the apparent demethylation has yet to be identified.

The final consideration may well prove to be the most interesting. The attentive reader will have noted that the environmental epigenetics hypothesis contains a serious paradox: If epigenetic states are readily modifiable, then how do such marks support the enduring effects of environmental events? This question raises the possibility that specific epigenetic modifications, once established, might be actively maintained. There is some evidence for such a process. The methylation of the GAD1 promoter in cortical neurons appears dependent on the expression, and presumably the activity, of DNMT1 (Kundakovic et al., 2007; Zhang et al., 2010).

These caveats notwithstanding, we suggest that active modification of the methylation state of specific regions of the genome is a candidate mechanism for environmental effects on the phenotype of the offspring. The capacity for tissue-specific, environmentally driven remodeling of DNA methylation marks provides an ideal process by which environmental signals might act across multiple stages in development to produce coordinated changes in gene expression that then directly mediate variation in phenotype.

Acknowledgments

Research support for M. J. M. is provided by the National Institutes of Health, the Canadian Institutes for Health Research, the Natural Sciences and Engineering Research Council of Canada, and the Human Frontiers Science Program.

References

Abdolmaleky, H. M., Cheng, K., Russo, A., Smith, C. L., Faraone, S. V., Wilcox, M., . . . Ponte, J. F. (2005). Hypermethylation of the reelin (RELN) promoter in the brain of schizophrenic patients: A preliminary report. *American Journal of Medicine and Genetics B: Neuropsychiatric Genetics, 134,* 60–66.

Akbarian, S., & Huang, H. S. (2006). Molecular and cellular mechanisms of altered GAD1/GAD67 expression in schizophrenia and related disorders. *Brain Research: Brain Research Reviews, 52,* 293–304.

Akbarian, S., & Huang, H. S. (2009). Epigenetic regulation in human brain-focus on histone lysine methylation. *Biological Psychiatry, 65,* 198–203.

Alarcon, J. M., Malleret, G., Touzani, K., Vronskaya, S., Ishii, S., Kandel, E. R., & Barco, A. (2004). Chromatin acetylation, memory, and LTP are impaired in CBP++/- mice: A model for the cognitive deficit in Rubinstein-Taybi syndrome and its amelioration. *Neuron, 42*(6), 947–959.

Alberini, C. M., Ghirardi, M., Huang, Y. Y., Nguyen, P. V., & Kandel, E. R. (1995). A molecular switch for the consolidation of long-term memory: cAMP-inducible gene expression. *Annals of the New York Academy of Sciences, 758,* 261–286.

Ali, D. W., & Salter, M. W. (2001). NMDA receptor regulation by Src kinase signalling in excitatory synaptic transmission and plasticity. *Current Opinion in Neurobiology, 11*(3), 336–342.

Bagot, R. C., van Hasselt, F. N., Champagne, D. L., Meaney, M. J., Krugers, H. J., & Joëls, M. (2009). Maternal care determines rapid effects of stress mediators on synaptic plasticity in adult rat hippocampal dentate gyrus. *Neurobiology of Learning and Memory, 92*(3), 292–300.

Bale, T. L., & Vale, W. W. (2004). CRF and CRF receptors: Role in stress responsivity and other behaviors. *Annual Review of Pharmacology and Toxicology, 44,* 525–557.

Bear, M. F., & Malenka, R. C. (1994). Synaptic plasticity: LTP and LTD. *Current Opinion in Neurobiology, 4*(3), 389–399.

Benes, F. M., & Berretta, S. (2001). GABAergic interneurons: Implications for understanding schizophrenia and bipolar disorder. *Neuropsychopharmacology, 25,* 1–27.

Bestor, T. H. (1998). Gene silencing. Methylation meets acetylation. *Nature, 393,* 311–312.

Bird, A. (2007). Perceptions of epigenetics. *Nature, 447,* 396–398.

Bird, A. P. (1986). CpG-rich islands and the function of DNA methylation. *Nature, 321,* 209–213.

Bird, A. P. (2002). DNA methylation patterns and epigenetic memory. *Genes Development, 16,* 6–21.

Bird, A. P., & Wolffe, A. P. (1999). Methylation-induced repression—Belts, braces, and chromatin. *Cell, 99,* 451–454.

Bourtchouladze, R., Lidge, R., Catapano, R., Stanley, J., Gossweiler, S., Romashko, D., ... Tully, T. (2003). A mouse model of Rubinstein–Taybi syndrome: Defective long-term memory isameliorated by inhibitors of phosphodiesterase 4. *Proceedings of the National Academy of Sciences USA, 100,* 10518–10522.

Branchi, I., D'Andrea, I., Sietzema, J., Fiore, M., Di Fausto, V., Aloe, L., & Alleva, E. (2006). Early social enrichment augments adult hippocampal BDNF levels and survival of BrdU-positive cells while increasing anxiety- and "depression"-like behavior. *Journal of Neuroscience Research, 83,* 965–973.

Brandeis, M., Frank, D., Keshet, I., Siegfried, Z., Mendelsohn, M., Nemes, A., ... Cedar, H. (1994). Sp1 elements protect a CpG island from de novo methylation. *Nature, 371,* 435–438.

Bredy, T. W., Humpartzoomian, R. A., Cain, D. P., & Meaney, M. J. (2003). The influence of maternal care and environmental enrichment on hippocampal development and function in the rat. *Neuroscience, 118,* 571–576.

Bredy, T. W., Wu, H., Crego, C., Zellhoefer, J., Sun, Y. E., & Barad, M. (2007). Histone modifications around individual BDNF gene promoters in prefrontal cortex are associated with extinction of conditioned fear. *Learning and Memory, 14,* 268–276.

Bruniquel, D., & Schwartz, R. H. (2003). Selective, stable demethylation of the interleukin-2 gene enhances transcription by an active process. *Nature Immunology, 4,* 235–240.

Burton, C. L., Chatterjee, D., Chatterjee-Chakraborty, M., Lovic, V., Grella, S. L., Steiner, M., & Fleming, A. S. (2007). Prenatal restraint stress and motherless rearing disrupts expression of plasticity markers and stress-induced corticosterone release in adult female Sprague-Dawley rats. *Brain Research, 1158,* 28–38.

Caldji, C., Diorio, J., & Meaney, M. J. (2003). Variations in maternal care alter GABAA receptor subunit expression in brain regions associated with fear. *Neuropsychopharmacology, 28,* 150–159.

Caldji, C., Francis, D. D., Sharma, S., Plotsky, P. M., & Meaney, M. J. (2000). The effects of early rearing environment on the development of GABAA and central benzodiazepine receptor levels and novelty-induced fearfulness in the rat. *Neuropsychopharmacology, 22,* 219–229.

Caldji, C., Tannenbaum, B., Sharma, S., Francis, D. D., Plotsky, P. M., & Meaney, M. J. (1998). Maternal care during infancy regulates the development of neural systems mediating the expression of behavioral fearfulness in adulthood in the rat. *Proceedings of the National Academy of Sciences USA, 95,* 5335–5340.

Chahrour, M., Jung, S. Y., Shaw, C., Zhou, X., Wong, S. T., Qin, J., & Zoghbi, H. Y. (2008). MeCP2, a key contributor to neurological disease, activates and represses transcription. *Science 320,* 1224–1229.

Champagne, F. A. (2008). Epigenetic mechanisms and the transgenerational effects of maternal care. *Frontiers in Neuroendocrinology, 29,* 386–397.

Champagne, F. A., Francis, D. D., Mar, A., & Meaney, M. J. (2003). Naturally-occurring variations in maternal care in the rat as a mediating influence for the effects of environment on the development of individual differences in stress reactivity. *Physiology and Behavior, 79*, 359–371.

Champagne, F. A., & Meaney, M. J. (2006). Stress during gestation alters postpartum maternal care and the development of the offspring in a rodent model. *Biological Psychiatry, 59*, 1227–1235.

Charalambous, M., da Rocha, S. T., & Ferguson-Smith, A. C. (2007). Genomic imprinting, growth control and the allocation of nutritional resources: Consequences for postnatal life. *Current Opinion in Endocrinology, Diabetes and Obesity, 14*, 3–12.

Chen, E., Matthews, K. A., & Boyce, W. T. (2002). Socioeconomic differences in children's health: How and why do these relationships change with age? *Psychological Bulletin, 128*, 295–329.

Chen, W. G., Chang, Q., Lin, Y., Meissner, A., West, A. E., Griffith, E. C., … Greenberg, M. E. (2003). Derepression of BDNF transcription involves calcium-dependent phosphorylation of MeCP2. *Science, 302*, 793–795.

Cooney, C. A., Dave, A. A., & Wolff, G. L. (2002). Maternal methyl supplements in mice affect epigenetic variation and DNA methylation of offspring. *Journal of Nutrition, 132*, 2393–2400.

Costa, E., Davis, J. M., Dong, E., Grayson, D. R., Guidotti, A., Tremolizzo, L., & Veldic, M. (2004). A GABAergic cortical deficit dominates schizophrenia pathophysiology. *Critical Reviews in Neurobiology, 16*, 1–23.

Da Rocha, S. T., & Ferguson-Smith, A. C. (2004). Genomic imprinting. *Current Biology, 14*, R646–R499.

Dragunow, M. (1996). A role for immediate-early transcription factors in learning and memory. *Behavior Genetics, 26*(3), 293–299.

Eastwood, S. L., & Harrison, P. J. (2003). Interstitial white matter neurons express less reelin and are abnormally distributed in schizophrenia: Towards an integration of molecular and morphologic aspects of the neurodevelopmental hypothesis. *Molecular Psychiatry, 769*, 821–831.

Ebstein, R. P. (2006). The molecular genetic architecture of human personality: Beyond self-report questionnaires. *Molecular Psychiatry, 11*, 427–445.

Eden, A., Gaudet, F., Waghmare, A., & Jaenisch, R. (2003). Chromosomal instability and tumors promoted by DNA hypomethylation. *Science, 300*, 455.

Feinberg, A. P. (2007). Phenotypic plasticity and the epigenetics of human disease. *Nature, 447*, 433–440.

Fenoglio, K. A., Brunson, K. L., Avishai-Eliner, S., Stone, B. A., Kapadia, B. J., & Baram, T. Z. (2005). Enduring, handling-evoked enhancement of hippocampal memory function and glucocorticoid receptor expression involves activation of the corticotropin-releasing factor type 1 receptor. *Endocrinology, 146*, 4090–4096.

Fraga, M. F., Ballestar, E., Villar-Garea, A., Boix-Chornet, M., Espada, J., Schotta, G., … Petrie, K. (2005). Epigenetic drift in aging identical twins. *Proceedings of the National Academy of Sciences, 102*(30), 10413–10414.

Francis, D. D., Diorio, J., Liu, D., & Meaney, M. J. (1999). Nongenomic transmission across generations in maternal behavior and stress responses in the rat. *Science, 286*, 1155–1158.

Gonzalez, A., Lovic, V., Ward, G. R., Wainwright, P. E., & Fleming, A. S. (2001). Intergenerational effects of complete maternal deprivation and replacement stimulation on maternal behavior and emotionality in female rats. *Developmental Psychobiology, 38*, 11–32.

Grayson, D. R., Jia, X., Chen, Y., Sharma, R. P., Mitchell, C. P., Guidotti, A., & Costa, E. (2005). Reelin promoter hypermethylation in schizophrenia. *Proceedings of the National Academy of Sciences USA, 102*, 9341–9346.

Gregg, C., Zhang, J., Weissbourd, B., Luo, S., Schroth, G. P., Haig, D., & Dulac, C. (2010). High-resolution analysis of parent-of-origin allelic expression in the mouse brain. *Science, 329*(5992), 643–648.

Greisen, M. H., Altar, C. A., Bolwig, T. G., Whitehead, R., & Wortwein, G., (2005). Increased adult hippocampal brain-derived neurotrophic factor and normal levels of neurogenesis in maternal separation rats. *Journal of Neuroscience Research, 79*, 772–778.

Grunstein, M. (1997). Histone acetylation in chromatin structure and transcription. *Nature, 389*, 349–352.

Guan, Z., Giustetto, M., Lomvardas, S., Kim, J. H., Miniaci, M. C., Schwartz, J. H., …Kandel, E. R. (2002). Integration of long-term-memory-related synaptic plasticity involves bidirectional regulation of gene expression and chromatin structure. *Cell, 111*, 483–493.

Hake, S. B., & Allis, C. D. (2006). Histone H3 variants and their potential role in index-ing mammalian genomes: The "H3 barcode hypothesis." *Proceedings of the National Academy of Sciences USA, 103*, 6428–6435.

Hall, J., Thomas, K. L., & Everitt, B. J. (2000). Rapid and selective induction of BDNF expression in the hippocampus during contextual learning. *Nature Neuroscience, 3*, 533–535.

Harper, L. V. (2005). Epigenetic inheritance and the intergenerational transfer of experi-ence. *Psychological Bulletin, 131*, 340–360.

Heim, C., Newport, D. J., Heit, S., Graham, Y. P., Wilcox, M., Bonsall, R.,…Nemeroff, C. B. (2000). Pituitary-adrenal and autonomic responses to stress in women after sexual and physical abuse in childhood. *Journal of the American Medical Association, 284*, 592–597.

Hellman, A., & Chess, A. (2007). Gene body-specific methylation on the active X chromo-some. *Science, 315*, 1141–1143.

Hofer, M. A. (2005). The psychobiology of early attachment. *Clinical Neuroscience Research, 4*, 291–300.

Holliday, R. (1989). DNA methylation and epigenetic mechanisms. *Cell Biophysics, 15*, 15–20.

Holsboer, F. (2000). The corticosteroid receptor hypothesis of depression. *Neuropsycho-pharmacology, 23*, 477–501.

Jenuwien, T., & Allis, C. D. (2001). Translating the histone code. *Science, 293*, 1074–1080.

Jiang, Y., Langley, B., Lubin, F. D., Renthal, W., Wood, M. A., Yasui, D. H.,…Beckel-Mitchener, A. C. (2008). Epigenetics in the nervous system. *Journal of Neuroscience, 28*, 11753–11759.

Jirtle, R. L., & Skinner, M. K. (2007). Environmental epigenomics and disease susceptibil-ity. *Nature Reviews Genetics, 8*, 253–262.

Jones, M. W., Errington, M. L., French, P. J., Fine, A., Bliss, T. V., Garel, S.,…Davis, S. (2001). A requirement for the immediate early gene Zif268 in the expression of late LTP and long-term memories. *Nature Neuroscience, 4*, 289–296.

Jutapakdeegul, N., Casalotti, S. O., Govitrapong, P., & Kotchabhakdi, N. (2003). Postnatal touch stimulation acutely alters corticosterone levels and glucocorticoid receptor gene expression in the neonatal rat. *Developmental Neuroscience, 25*, 26–33.

Kandel, E. R. (2001). The molecular biology of memory storage: A dialogue between genes and synapses. *Science, 294*(5544), 1030–1038.

Kendler, K. S. (2001). Twin studies of psychiatric illness: An update. *Archives of General Psychiatry, 58*(11), 1005–1014.

Klose, R. J., & Bird, A. P. (2006). Genomic DNA methylation: The mark and its mediators. *Trends in Biochemical Sciences, 31*, 89–97.

Knapska, E., & Kaczmarek, L. (2004). A gene for neuronal plasticity in the mammalian brain: Zif268/Egr-1/NGFI-A/Krox-24/TIS8/ZENK? *Progress in Neurobiology, 74*(4), 183–211.

Koob, G. F., Heinrichs, S. C., Menzaghi, F., Pich, E. M., & Britton, K. T. (1994). Corticotropin-releasing factor, stress and behavior. *Seminars in Neuroscience, 6*, 221–229.

Korzus, E., Rosenfeld, M. G., & Mayford, M. (2004). CBP histone acetyltransferase activity is a critical component of memory consolidation. *Neuron, 42*, 961–972.

Kundakovic, M., Chen, Y., Costa, E., & Grayson, D. R. (2007). DNA methyltransferase inhibitors coordinately induce expression of the human reelin and glutamic acid decarboxylase 67 genes. *Molecular Pharmacology, 71*(3), 644–653.

Ladd-Acosta, C., Pevsner, J., Sabunciyan, S., Yolken, R. H., Webster, M. J., Dinkins, T., ... Feinberg, A. P. (2007). DNA methylation signatures within the human brain. *American Journal of Human Genetics, 81*, 1304–1315.

Laird, P. W. (2005). Cancer epigenetics. *Human Molecular Genetics, 14*(Spec. No. 1), R65–R76.

Levenson, J. M., O'Riordan, K. J., Brown, K. D., Trinh, M. A., Molfese, D. L., & Sweatt, J. D. (2004). Regulation of histone acetylation during memory formation in the hippocampus. *Journal of Biological Chemistry, 279*, 40545–40559.

Levine, S. (1994). The ontogeny of the hypothalamic-pituitary-adrenal axis. The influence of maternal factors. *Annals of the New York Academy of Sciences, 746*, 275–288.

Lewis, D. A., Hashimoto, T., & Volk, D. W. (2005). Cortical inhibitory neurons and schizophrenia. *Nature Reviews Neurosciences, 6*, 312–324.

Linnarsson, S., Björklund, A., & Ernfors, P. (1997). Learning deficit in BDNF mutant mice. *European Journal of Neuroscience, 9*, 2581–2587.

Lippmann, M., Bress, A., Nemeroff, C. B., Plotsky, P. M., & Monteggia, L. M. (2007). Long-term behavioural and molecular alterations associated with maternal separation in rats. *European Journal of Neuroscience, 25*, 3091–3098.

Lisman, J., Schulman, H., & Cline, H. (2002). The molecular basis of CaMKII function in synaptic and behavioral memory. *Nature Reviews Neuroscience, 3*, 175–190.

Liu, D., Diorio, J., Day, J. C., Francis, D. D., Mar, A., & Meaney, M. J. (2000). Maternal care, hippocampal synaptogenesis and cognitive development in the rat. *Nature Neuroscience, 3*, 799–806.

Liu, D., Diorio, J., Tannenbaum, B., Caldji, C., Francis, D. D., Freedman, A., ... Meaney, M. J. (1997). Maternal care, hippocampal glucocorticoid receptors and HPA responses to stress. *Science, 277*, 1659–1662.

Lubin, F. D., Roth, T. L., & Sweatt, J. D. (2008). Epigenetic regulation of *bdnf* gene transcription in the consolidation of fear memory. *Journal of Neuroscience, 28*, 10576–10586.

Luger, K., Mader, A. W., Richmond, R. K., Sargent, D. F., & Richmond, T. J. (1997). Crystal structure of the nucleosome coreparticle at 2.8 A resolution. *Nature, 389*, 251–260.

Lynch, M. A. (2004). Long-term potentiation and memory. *Physiological Reviews, 84*, 87–136.

Malenka, R. C., & Nicoll, R. A. (1993). NMDA-receptor-dependent synaptic plasticity: Multiple forms and mechanisms. *Trends in Neurosciences, 16*(12), 521–527.

Maren, S., & Quirk, G. J. (2000). Neuronal signalling of fear memory. *Nature Reviews Neuroscience, 5*, 844–852.

Martinowich, K., Hattori, D., Wu, H., Fouse, S., He, F., Hu, Y., . . . Sun, Y. E. (2003). DNA methylation-related chromatin remodeling in activity-dependent BDNF gene regulation. *Science, 302*, 890–893.

McCormick, J.A., Lyons, V., Jacobson, M.D., Noble, J., Diorio, J., Nyirenda, M., Weaver, S., Ester, W., Yau, J.L., Meaney, M.J., et al. (2000). 5′-Heterogeneity of glucocorticoid receptor messenger RNA is tissue specific: Differential regulation of variant transcripts by early-life events. *Molecular Endocrinology, 14*, 506–517.

McGirr, A., Renaud, J., Seguin, M., Alda, M., & Turecki, G. (2008). Course of major depressive disorder and suicide outcome: A psychological autopsy study. *Journal of Clinical Psychiatry, 69*, 966–970.

McGowan, P. O., Sasaki, A., D'Alessio, A. C., Dymov, S., Labonté, B., Szyf, M., . . . Meaney, M. J. (2009). Epigenetic regulation of the glucocorticoid receptor in human brain associates with childhood abuse. *Nature Neuroscience 12*, 342–348. doi:10.1038/nn.2270

Meaney, M. J. (2001). The development of individual differences in behavioral and endocrine responses to stress. *Annual Review of Neuroscience, 24*, 1161–1192.

Meaney, M. J., Diorio, J., Donaldson, L., Yau, J., Chapman, K., & Seckl, J. R. (2000). Handling alters the expression of messenger RNAs for AP-2, NGFI-A and NGFI-B in the hippocampus of neonatal rats. *Journal of Neuroscience, 20*, 3936–3945.

Meaney, M.J., Ferguson-Smith, A.C. (2010). Epigenetic regulation of the neural transcriptome: the meaning of the marks. *Nature Neuroscience, 13*(11),1313–8.

Meaney, M. J., & Szyf, M. (2005). Maternal effects as a model for environmentally-dependent chromatin plasticity. *Trends in Neuroscience, 28*, 456–463.

Menard, J., Champagne, D., & Meaney, M. J. (2004). Maternal care alters behavioral and neural activity patterns in the defensive burying paradigm. *Neuroscience, 129*, 297–308.

Meyer-Lindenberg, A., & Weinberger, D. R. (2006). Intermediate phenotypes and genetic mechanisms of psychiatric disorders. *Nature Reviews Neuroscience, 7*, 818–827.

Mitchell, J. B., Betito, K., Rowe, W., Boksa, P., & Meaney, M. J. (1992). Serotonergic regulation of type II corticosteroid receptor binding in cultured hippocampal cells: The role of serotonin-induced increases in cAMP levels. *Neuroscience, 48*, 631–639.

Mohandas, T., Sparkes, R. S., & Shapiro, L. J. (1981). Reactivation of an inactive human X chromosome: Evidence for X inactivation by DNA methylation. *Science, 211*, 393–396.

Moretti, P., Levenson, J. M., Battaglia, F., Atkinson, R., Teague, R., Antalffy, B., . . . Zoghbi, H. Y. (2006). Learning and memory and synaptic plasticity are impaired in a mouse model of Rett syndrome. *Journal of Neuroscience, 26*, 319–327.

Morris, R. G., & Frey, U. (1997). Hippocampal synaptic plasticity: Role in spatial learning or the automatic recording of attended experience? *Philosophical Transactions of the Royal Society of London—Series B: Biological Sciences, 352*, 1489–1503.

Morris, R. G. M., Moser, E. I., Riedel, G., Martin, S. J., Sandin, J., Day, M., & O'Carroll, C. (2003). Elements of a neurobiological theory of the hippocampus: The role of activity-dependent synaptic plasticity in memory. *Philosophical Transactions of the Royal Society of London: Series B: Biological Sciences, 358*, 773–786.

Murayama, A., Sakura, K., Nakama, M., Yasuzawa-Tanaka, K., Fujita, E., Tateishi, Y., . . . Yanagisawa, J. (2006). A specific CpG site demethylation in the human interleukin 2 gene promoter is an epigenetic memory. *EMBO Journal, 25*, 1081–1092.

Murgatroyd, C., Patchev, A. V., Wu, Y., Micale, V., Bockmühl, Y., Fischer, D., . . . Almeida, O. F. (2009). Dynamic DNA methylation programs persistent adverse effects of early-life stress. *Nature Neuroscience, 12*, 1559–1566.

Neigh, G. N., & Nemeroff, C. B. (2006). Reduced glucocorticoid receptors: Consequence or cause of depression? *Trends in Endocrinology and Metabolism, 17*, 124–125.

Nestler, E. J. (2009). Epigenetic mechanisms in psychiatry. *Biological Psychiatry, 65*, 189–190.

O'Donovan, K. J., Tourtellotte, W. G., Millbrandt, J., & Baraban, J. M. (1999). The EGR family of transcription-regulatory factors: Progress at the interface of molecular and systems neuroscience. *Trends in Neurosciences, 22*(4), 167–173.

Petronis, A. (2006). Epigenetics and twins: Three variations on the theme. *Trends in Genetics, 22*(7), 347–350.

Plomin, R., & Rutter, M. (1998). Child development, molecular genetics, and what to do with genes once they are found. *Child Development, 69*, 1223–1242.

Plotsky, P. M., Cunningham, E. T., Jr., & Widmaier, E. P. (1989). Catecholaminergic modulation of corticotropin-releasing factor and adrenocorticotropin secretion. *Endocrine Reviews, 10*, 437–458.

Plotsky, P. M., Thrivikraman, K. V., Nemeroff, C. B., Caldji, C., Sharma, S., & Meaney, M. J. (2005). Long-term consequences of neonatal rearing on central corticotropin releasing factor systems in adult male rat offspring. *Neuropsychopharmacology, 30*, 2192–2204.

Razin, A. (1998). CpG methylation, chromatin structure and gene silencing—a three-way connection. *EMBO Journal, 17*, 4905–4908.

Razin, A., & Cedar, H. (1993). DNA methylation and embryogenesis. In J. P. Jost & H. P. Saluz (Eds.), *DNA methylation: Molecular biology and biological significance* (pp. 343–359). Basel: Birkhäuser Verlag.

Razin, A., & Riggs, A. D. (1980). DNA methylation and gene function. *Science, 210*, 604–610.

Reik, W., & Walter, J. (2001). Genomic imprinting: Parental influence on the genome. *Nature Review Genetics, 2*, 21–32.

Renthal, W., & Nestler, E. J. (2008). Epigenetic mechanisms in drug addiction. *Trends in Molecular Medicine, 14*, 341–350.

Renthal, W., & Nestler, E. J. (2009). Histone acetylation in drug addiction. *Seminal Cell Developmental Biology, 20*(4), 387–394.

Riggs, A. D., & Pfeifer, G. P. (1992). X-chromosome inactivation and cell memory. *Trends in Genetics, 8*, 169–174.

Roceri, M., Cirulli, F., Pessina, C., Peretto, P., Racagni, G., & Riva, M. A. (2004). Postnatal repeated maternal deprivation produces age-dependent changes of brain-derived neurotrophic factor expression in selected rat brain regions. *Biological Psychiatry, 55*, 708–714.

Roceri, M., Hendriks, W., Racagni, G., Ellenbroek, B. A., & Riva, M. A. (2002). Early maternal deprivation reduces the expression of BDNF and NMDA receptor subunits in rat hippocampus. *Molecular Psychiatry, 7*, 609–616.

Roth, T. L., Lubin, F. D., Funk, A. J., & Sweatt, J. D. (2009). Lasting epigenetic influence of early-life adversity on the BDNF gene. *Biological Psychiatry, 65*, 760–769.

Rutter, M. (2007). Gene-environment interdependence. *Developmental Science, 10*, 12–18.

Schanberg, S. M., Evoniuk, G., & Kuhn, C. M. (1984). Tactile and nutritional aspects of maternal care: Specific regulators of neuroendocrine function and cellular development. *Proceedings of the Society for Experimental Biology and Medicine, 175*, 135–146.

Schatzberg, A. F., Rothschild, A. J., Langlais, P. J., Bird, E. D., & Cole, J. O. (1985). A corticosteroid/dopamine hypothesis for psychotic depression and related states. *Journal of Psychiatric Research, 19*, 57–64.

Sokolowski, M. B. (2001). Drosophila: Genetics meets behaviour. *Nature Reviews Genetics, 2*(11), 879–890.

Sokolowski, M. B., & Wahlsten, D. (2001). Gene-environment interaction and complex behavior. In S. O. Moldin (Ed.), *Methods in genomic neuroscience* (pp. 3–27). Boca Raton, FL: CRC Press.

Straub, R. E., Lipska, B. K., Egan, M. F., Goldberg, T. E., & Kleinman, J. E. (2007). Allelic variation in GAD1 (GAD67) is associated with schizophrenia and influences cortical function and gene expression. *Molecular Psychiatry, 10*, 1038.

Sweatt, J. D. (2009). Experience-dependent epigenetic modifications in the central nervous system. *Biological Psychiatry, 65*, 191–197.

Szyf, M., Weaver, I. C., Champagne, F. A., Diorio, J., & Meaney, M. J. (2005). Maternal programming of steroid receptor expression and phenotype through DNA methylation in the rat. *Frontiers in Neuroendocrinology, 26*, 139–162.

Timmusk, T., Palm, K., Metsis, M., Reintam, T., Paalme, V., Saarma, M., & Persson, H. (1993). Multiple promoters direct tissue-specific expression of the rat BDNF gene. *Neuron, 10*, 475–479.

Toki, S., Morinobu, S., Imanaka, A., Yamamoto, S., Yamawaki, S., & Honma, K. (2007). Importance of early lighting conditions in maternal care by dam as well as anxiety and memory later in life of offspring. *European Journal of Neuroscience, 25*, 815–829.

Tsankova, N., Renthal, W., Kumar, A., & Nestler, E. J. (2007). Epigenetic regulation in psychiatric disorders. *Nature Reviews Neuroscience, 8*, 355–367.

Turner, B. (2001). *Chromatin structure and the regulation of gene expression.* Oxford: Blackwell Science.

Turner, J. D., & Muller, C. P. (2005). Structure of the glucocorticoid receptor (NR3C1) gene 5'untranslated region: Identification and tissue distribution of multiple new human exon 1. *Journal of Molecular Endocrinology, 35*, 283–292.

Van Hasselt, F. N., Cornelisse, S., Zhang, T-Y., Meaney, M. J., Krugers, H. J., & Joëls, M. (2012). Adult hippocampal glucocorticoid receptor expression and dentate synaptic plasticity correlate with maternal care received by individuals early in life. *Hippocampus, 22*(2), 255-266.

Vecsey, C. G., Hawk, J. D., Lattal, K. M., Stein, J. M., Fabian, S. A., Attner, M. A., ... Wood, M. A. (2007). Histone deacetylase inhibitors enhance memory and synaptic plasticity via CREB: CBP-dependent transcriptional activation. *Journal of Neuroscience, 27*, 6128–6140.

Veldic, M., Caruncho, H. J., Liu, S., Davis, J., Satta, R., Grayson, D. R.,...Costa, E. (2004). DNA-methyltransferase 1 mRNA is selectively overexpressed in telencephalic GABAergic interneurons of schizophrenia brains. *Proceedings of the National Academy of Sciences USA, 101*, 348–353.

Waddington, C. H. (1957). *The strategy of the genes.* New York, NY: MacMillan.

Waterland, R. A., & Jirtle, R. L. (2003). Transposable elements: Targets for early nutritional effects on epigenetic gene regulation. *Molecular Cell Biology, 23*, 5293–5300.

Waterland, R. A., Lin, J. R., Smith, C. A., & Jirtle, R. L. (2006). Post-weaning diet affects genomic imprinting at the insulin-like growth factor 2 (Igf2) locus. *Human Molecular Genetics, 15*, 705–716.

Weaver, I. C. G., Cervoni, N., D'Alessio, A. C., Champagne, F. A., Seckl, J. R., Szyf, M., & Meaney, M. J. (2004). Epigenetic programming through maternal behavior. *Nature Neuroscience, 7*, 847–854.

Weaver, I. C. G., Champagne, F. A., Brown, S. E., Dymov, S., Sharma, S., Meaney, M. J., & Szyf, M. (2005). Reversal of maternal programming of stress responses in adult offspring through methyl supplementation: Altering epigenetic marking later in life. *Journal of Neuroscience, 25*, 11045–11054.

Weaver, I. C. G., DiAlessio, A. C., Brown, S. E., Hellstrom, I. C., Dymov, S., Diorio, J.,...Meaney, M. J. (2007). The transcription factor NGFI-A mediates epigenetic programming: Altering epigenetic marking through immediate early genes. *Journal of Neuroscience, 27*, 1756–1768.

Weaver, I. C. G., Meaney, M. J., & Szyf, M. (2006). Maternal care effects on the hippocampal transcriptome and anxiety-mediated behaviors in the offspring that are reversible in adulthood. *Proceedings of the National Academy of Sciences USA, 103*(9), 3480–3485.

Weber, M., Hellmann, I., Stadler, M. B., Ramos, L., Paabo, S., Rebhan, M., & Schubeler, D. (2007). Distribution, silencing potential and evolutionary impact of promoter DNA methylation in the human genome. *Nature Genetics, 39*, 457–466.

Weksberg, R., Shuman, C., Caluseriu, O., Smith, A. C., Fei, Y. L., Nishikawa, J.,...Squire, J. (2002). Discordant KCNQ1OT1 imprinting in sets of monozygotic twins discordant for Beckwith-Wiedemann syndrome. *Human Molecular Genetics, 11*, 1317–1325.

West, A. E., Chen, W. G., Dalva, M. B., Dolmetsch, R. E., Kornhauser, J. M., Shaywitz, A. J.,...Greenberg, M. E. (2001). Calcium regulation of neuronal gene expression. *Proceedings of the National Academy of Sciences USA, 98*, 11024–11031.

Whitelaw, N. C., & Whitelaw, E. (2006). How lifetimes shape epigeneotype within and across generations. *Human Molecular Genetics, 15*, R131–R137.

Wood, M. A., Attner, M. A., Oliveira, A. M., Brindle, P. K., & Abel, T. (2006). A transcription factor-binding domain of the coactivator CBP is essential for long-term memory and the expression of specific target genes. *Learning and Memory, 13*, 609–617.

Yeh, S. H., Lin, C. H., & Gean, P. W. (2004). Acetylation of nuclear factor-κB in rat amygdala improves long-term but not short-term retention of fear memory. *Molecular Pharmacology, 65*, 1286–1292.

Zhang, T. Y., Hellstrom, I. C., Bagot, R. C., Wen, X., Diorio, J., & Meaney, M. J. (2010). Maternal care and DNA methylation of a glutamic acid decarboxylase 1 promoter in rat hippocampus. *Journal of Neuroscience, 30*(39), 13130–13137.

Zhou, Z., Hong, E. J., Cohen, S., Zhao, W. N., Ho, H. Y., Schmidt, L.,...Greenberg, M. E. (2006). Brain-specific phosphorylation of MeCP2 regulates activity-dependent Bdnf transcription, dendritic growth, and spine maturation. *Neuron, 52*, 255–269.

Zoghbi, H. Y. (2003). Postnatal neurodevelopmental disorders: Meeting at the synapse? *Science, 302*, 826–830.

{ Commentary }

The Messages of Epigenetic Research
Jerome Kagan

Jean Baptiste Lamarck, who died in 1829, would have smiled had he read Michael Meaney's outstanding summary of the last two decades of research on epigenetic alterations of genes. This evidence, which affirms the influences of select experiences on genomes, has at least three important implications for psychologists.

First, this work invites a serious questioning of the assumptions and conclusions of traditional behavioral geneticists who assumed that the variance assigned to genes and experience was additive and that monozygotic twin pairs had identical genomes. Because experiences can alter the expressiveness of select genes via epigenetic mechanisms, identical twins may not possess the same genomes. That fact helps to explain why less than 50% of twin pairs are concordant for a psychosis.

A second, more important, implication is the need for a skeptical view of the popular belief that the biological and psychological effects of early experience—stressors, abuse, neglect—are likely to be permanent or preserved for a long time. If the effect of a methylated cytosine in CpG islands or a deacetylated lysine in a molecule of histone protein is subject to reversal, which is even true in some cancers in which a silenced tumor suppressor gene is reactivated, then surely it is likely that the emotions and beliefs generated by early experiences are also plastic. And there is substantial empirical support for this claim (Kagan, 1998). How paradoxical that study of the material entities of biology provided the most persuasive evidence for dynamic changes in psychological development. These observations require a re-examination of Bowlby's assertion that the consequences of a secure or insecure attachment during the first year were, in most cases, preserved indefinitely (Bowlby, 1969).

Third, the extraordinary specificity of epigenetic phenomena implies that an equivalent level of specificity applies to psychological events. Not only are the effects of maternal licking of the infant rat pup restricted to the first week of postnatal life, but also the effects are restricted to a very precise location in the genome, which, in turn, affects a precise brain site. This evidence should motivate psychologists to reflect on the utility of many popular abstract concepts that fail to specify the agent, the incentive, and the target of a reaction.

Compare Meaney's statement that rat pups in the first week of life who were reared by high-licking mothers showed very modest levels of methylation at the 5′ CpG site of the nerve growth factor–inducible factor A sequence with statements often found in a typical psychological paper. For example, one frequent conclusion with human subjects assumes the following form. Stress during childhood (no specification of the type of stress or the child's age) produces anxiety later in life (no specification of the form the anxiety assumes or the age when it develops). If biology is a useful model for psychology, and I believe it is, it is fair to argue that current psychological prose is far too general and insufficiently concerned with the class of agent, the nature of the incentive, and the exact properties of the outcome.

Other constructs, such as reward, regulation, well-being, executive processes, neuroticism, and fear, are also guilty of an extreme level of permissiveness. The epigenetic data also cast doubt on the utility of concepts for brain functioning, such as arousal or inhibition, which do not locate the state in a particular setting. Furthermore, it is likely that varied strains within an animal species, as well as varied human populations, differ in their susceptibility to epigenetic alterations (Kagan, 2011). This possibility means that the epigenetic consequences of some salient experiences may be dissimilar among Europeans, Africans, Asians, and Latin Americans.

Psychologists are discovering many instances of extreme specificity in measures of behavior and biology. A person's heart rate and blood pressure in a laboratory are lower if a favorite pet is present (Allen, Blascovich, & Mendes, 2002). The size of the room influences the probability that 2-year-olds will or will not use a landmark to find a hidden toy (Learmonth, Newcombe, & Huttenlocher, 2001). The heritability of cortisol levels in twins varies with the time of day and the place where the salivary source of cortisol was gathered (Franz et al., 2010). Rather than treat these restricted relations as exceptions, psychologists should anticipate them because an equivalent degree of specificity is apparent in the evidence on epigenetic alterations. Nature attends closely to the details.

The history of the natural sciences is marked by unexpected discoveries that demand a serious revision in current theory. Such a change occurred when Howard Temin and David Baltimore discovered that in some viruses RNA could be converted into DNA. No biologist working 50 years ago would have considered questioning the dogmatic belief that the sequence always goes one way, namely, from DNA to RNA.

The new epigenetic discoveries are having an equally profound effect on the investigators trying to find links between genetics, on the one hand, and physiology and behavior on the other. These are exciting times because there are early signs of a revolutionary shift in the properties of concepts and mechanisms. Psychology needs a new set of constructs to represent the plasticity of traits, emotions, and competences. Popular terms, such as extroversion, concept of number, secure attachment, and social phobia, will have to be replaced with terms that specify the likelihood of alteration in the property, the events responsible for the alteration, and always the source of evidence (Kagan, 2011). Because experience and genes appear to be engaged in a ballet in which each is continually affecting the other, psychologists must invent concepts that capture this dynamic process. Few if any candidates are to be found in our current journals.

References

Allen, K., Blascovich, J., & Mendes, W. V. (2002). Cardiovascular reactivity and the presence of pets, friends, and spouses. *Psychological Medicine, 64*, 727–739.

Bowlby, J. (1969). *Attachment and loss.* New York, NY: Basic Books.

Franz, C. E., York, T. P., Eaves, L. J., Mendoza, S. P., Hauger, R. L., Hellhammer, D. H., et al. (2010). Genetic and environmental influences on cortisol regulation across days and contexts in middle-aged men. *Behavior Genetics, 40*, 467–479.

Kagan, J. (1998). *Three seductive ideas.* Cambridge, MA: Harvard University Press.

Kagan, J. (2011). Three lessons learned. *Perspectives on Psychological Science, 6*, 107–113.

Learmonth, A. E., Newcombe, N. S., & Huttenlocher, J. (2001). Toddlers' use of metric information and landmarks to reorient. *Journal of Experimental Child Psychology, 80*, 225–244.

5

Neurobiology and the Evolution of Mammalian Social Behavior
C. Sue Carter and Stephen W. Porges

Humans are social mammals with highly variable behavioral patterns. Mechanisms that permit social behavior and the development of selective social bonds are assumed to be based on neural circuits and endocrine processes that evolved long before modern humans. Current research directed at understanding the ultimate (evolutionary) and proximate (ontogenetic, epigenetic, and physiological) causes of sociality offers new insights into the social and emotional features of human behavior across the life span. Based on new findings, it is becoming increasingly clear that humans are motivated to establish social bonds and require social behaviors and emotional support for normal development and optimal mental and physical health.

The physiological substrates for social behavior and social bonds are shared with the biobehavioral processes involved in reproduction and parturition. These systems also regulate emotion and behavioral and physiological reactivity to stressors throughout the life span. Thus, positive social relationships are translated by our nervous system from the physical features of the behavioral interaction into both a psychological experience related to a sense of safety and a physiological response strategy related to an improved capacity to cope with uncertainty. Awareness of the shared physiology of sociality and emotion regulation with other primary adaptive mechanisms (e.g., birth, nursing) provides a better understanding of how mental illness may be related to periods of vulnerability observed during early development and how mental illness is often expressed as atypical socioemotional reactions and compromised social behaviors.

Two mammalian neuropeptides, oxytocin (OT) and arginine vasopressin (AVP), have been shown to be central to social behavior. Here we will focus on the actions of these neuropeptides and mechanisms through which they may affect social and emotional behaviors.

Social Behavior and Definitions of Attachment and Bonding

Approach, social recognition, and social engagement are necessary first steps in social interactions. Social behaviors, including both positive and negative interactions, may be either selective or nonselective. Selective social behaviors and emotional responses are critical to the establishment of appropriate social attachments and strong social bonds. These patterns of behavior can be influenced by the physiological state of the individual and by gender. For example, in males, stressful experiences can facilitate pair-bond formation with a partner of the opposite sex, while in females, it may have the opposite effect (DeVries, DeVries, Taymans, & Carter, 1996).

Concepts such as "attachment" and "bonding" are based on selective social behaviors or feelings toward another individual. However, it is important to understand that these terms have acquired different and somewhat colloquial meanings within different disciplines. Based on the work of John Bowlby (1988), developmental psychologists have defined attachment as a phylogenetically programmed propensity of one person (usually a child) to bond to another, who is viewed as stronger and wiser. In the terminology of attachment theory, bonds are relatively long-lived ties to unique individuals. Also, according to the convention of attachment theory, a child forms one primary attachment to a caretaker (usually the mother) but may have many affectional bonds, including bonds formed with the other parent (or other caretakers).

Within biological disciplines, the terms *social bonds* and *social attachments* are often used interchangeably. Selective and long-lasting social relationships are not limited to humans or the caretaker–child dyad. However, the capacity to form selective social bonds between adults (i.e., pair bonds) may be used as one of the definitions of a social system called social monogamy (Carter, DeVries, & Getz, 1995). Sexual monogamy is rare even in species in which pair bonds appear to be lifelong, supporting the hypothesis that social bonds have benefits that extend beyond genetic monogamy. Both survival and reproduction fitness (genetic survival) may be facilitated by the presence of one or more partners, who provide support to the mother and offspring.

Biological Background to Understanding the Neurobiology of Social Behavior

Human infants are at the mercy of the environment. The young infant must be fed, requires aid in maintaining body temperature, and needs to be protected from potential predators. Infants are initially dependent on their biological mother for gestation and later for human milk (or a comparable substitute). Most typically, the primary caregiver for human infants is the biological mother, although individuals other than the mother may help to care for offspring (Hrdy, 2009). The discovery of the substrates of social behavior and bonding has been guided by the analysis of factors responsible for the responses of a mother toward her newborn infant. The original experimental data implicating OT in the biology of social behavior came from studies of maternal behavior in rats and precocial ungulates, such as sheep.

Studies of the mother–infant interaction formed a biological prototype for understanding the neurobiology of other forms of sociality. Accumulating evidence suggests that mammalian sociality relies on the same basic processes that regulate birth
and breastfeeding (Carter, 1998).

In humans, the capacity to form social bonds is considered a species-typical
trait. However, only a few species of mammals show selective and long-lasting
pair bonding. Species that show pair bonds, such as prairie voles, and those that
show selective maternal–infant bonds, such as sheep and guinea pigs, have been
the sources of much of what is known regarding the neurobiology of social
bonds.

Because the specific biochemical pathways and brain regions that are implicated in social behavior are well conserved, basic findings in rodents or sheep
may have relevance for human behavior. However, the proximate processes
involved in sociality tend to be species typical and gender specific, and also
shaped by experience and the individual's history (Carter, 2007; Carter, Boone,
Pournajafi-Nazarloo, & Bales, 2009). Within the life span of the individual,
and especially in early life, ontogenetic and epigenetic processes are sources of
individual variation in social behavior and emotion regulation. Oxytocin and
AVP play central roles in sociality and emotion regulation. Adaptive variations
in these same systems also permit species and individual differences in behavior.
Within the body, the actions of these peptides are played out in relation to each
other and to other hormones and neurotransmitters. The immediate physiology
of the individual, including the central and autonomic nervous systems and
other endocrine systems, such as the hypothalamic–pituitary–adrenal (HPA)
axis, provides a physiological context for sociality. For example, the actions of
OT are seen in the biological context of other hormones including AVP, as well
as other neuropeptides (e.g., corticotropin-releasing factor [CRF]), neurotransmitters (e.g., catecholamines and serotonin), and steroid hormones (e.g., glucocorticoids, estrogen, progesterone, and androgens). In turn, these chemicals act
on neural substrates, including the central and peripheral nervous systems.

Mammalian reproductive and coping strategies can involve either active
forms of response (including approach or avoidance) or passive responses
(including freezing or immobilization). Although there are many exceptions,
males tend to show more active behaviors, while the response of females tends
to be more passive (Palanza, Gioiosa, & Parmigiani, 2001). These patterns are
consistent with sex differences in reproductive functions, including the necessity for female mammals to assume immobile postures during sexual behavior,
birth, and nursing. Such patterns also are consistent with the actions of neuropeptides, including OT. In addition, females sometimes need to be able to
defend themselves or their young. Defensive patterns in females may rely on
AVP, which also may allow females to mobilize in the face of threat (Bosch &
Neumann, 2010).

Oxytocin and Vasopressin

The OT molecule consists of nine amino acids, configured as a ring and tail. Oxytocin is a small neuropeptide, primarily of brain origin. Two hypothalamic nuclei, the paraventricular nucleus (PVN) and supraoptic nucleus (SON), are the main sources of OT. Oxytocin from the PVN and SON is transported to the posterior pituitary (outside of the blood-brain barrier), where it is released into the general circulation. Significant amounts of OT from the PVN are released into and act directly on the brain. In addition, smaller amounts of OT are synthesized in other tissues, including the reproductive organs and immune system. Oxytocin induces uterine contractions and the contractions of smooth muscle necessary for milk ejection.

Arginine vasopressin is similar in structure to OT, consisting of nine amino acids, of which seven are shared with OT and two differ. The structural similarities and differences between AVP and OT allow each hormone to interact with the other's receptors. Both molecules can influence behavior, although in some cases the functional effects are in opposite directions, possibly in part because these neuropeptides may be natural antagonists for each other. Arginine vasopressin also is primarily of hypothalamic origin, although it may be synthesized in other brain regions. Arginine vasopressin usually is not made in the same cells that synthesize OT. As with OT, one of the basic actions of AVP may be to allow individuals to interact without fear. However, in contrast to the immobilizing actions of OT, centrally active AVP is generally associated with mobility and the activation of the sympathoadrenal systems that support active motor behavior. Moderate levels of AVP may reduce anxiety, permitting animals to engage in social behavior with unfamiliar conspecifics. However, it is also possible—especially at higher doses—that AVP might increase defensive aggression (De Vries & Panzica, 2006).

Receptors for both OT and AVP are localized in areas of the nervous system, and especially in brainstem regions, that play a role in reproductive, social, and adaptive behaviors (Gimpl & Fahrenholz, 2001) and in the regulation of the HPA axis and autonomic nervous system (Landgraf & Neumann, 2004). The OT receptor (OTR) belongs to the G-protein-coupled seven-transmembrane (GPCR) superfamily. There is only one known form of the OTR. Oxytocin receptors are found throughout brain regions that have been implicated in social behavior and reactions to stressors, as well as in many other tissues, including the uterus and breast. Oxytocin binds preferentially to the OTR. The expression of the OTR is increased by other reproductive hormones, including estrogen. Expression of or binding to the OTR also can be influenced by many factors, including androgens, which could in turn have direct consequences for expressing active social and defensive behaviors. Arginine vasopressin has at least three receptor subtypes and can bind to the OTR. Among the AVP receptors, the V1a receptor (V1aR), also a GPCR, is found in greatest abundance in the brain and other neural tissue. The V1aR is associated with cardiovascular functions as well as behavior.

What Conditions Lead to the Formation of Social Bonds?

The capacity to form a social bond is species specific and varies as a function of social experience and the physiological and emotional state of the individual. The conditions that lead to social bonding also may differ between males and females (DeVries et al., 1996). For a social preference or bond to form, it is first necessary for individuals to be in a state of readiness for interaction, including social approach and engagement. Social recognition, approach, and engagement require overcoming a sense of threat or fear.

Oxytocin and AVP play a central role in the formation of social bonds. Among the short-term processes affected by these neuropeptides are approach behaviors and appropriate reactions to novelty that are necessary to permit interactions with a social partner. Social recognition (Winslow & Insel, 2004) and social engagement (Porges, 2003a) are initial steps in social behavior and required for social bond formation; both are affected by OT and AVP.

Oxytocin also may overcome anxiety and thus modulate reactions toward either novel adults or infants (Carter, 1998). For example, at moderate levels AVP may be anxiolytic. The capacity to maintain contact with another individual is a component of affiliative behaviors, including lordosis or kyphosis. The ability to immobilize without eliciting autonomic reflexes (such as syncope and fainting) can be facilitated by AVP (Porges, 2003b).

Arginine vasopressin, acting at the V1aR, plays a central role in modulating social bonding (Winslow, Hastings, Carter, Harbaugh, & Insel, 1993) and facilitating positive social behaviors (Cho, DeVries, Williams, & Carter, 1999). Arginine vasopressin also has a role in modulating nonsocial behaviors such as emotionality. Stress-induced increases in AVP may act to amplify the actions of CRF, thus activating the HPA axis. Arginine vasopressin also is capable of increasing certain forms of repetitive and defensive behaviors (Winslow et al., 1993).

Centrally active AVP is generally associated with mobility and the activation of the sympathoadrenal systems that support motor behavior. Furthermore, because portions of the AVP system are androgen dependent and some aspects of OT's functions are estrogen dependent, knowledge of OT and AVP has begun to suggest insight into the nature of sex differences in social behavior and social bond formation (DeVries et al., 1996). It is unlikely that OT and AVP have identical effects on either the organization or expression of social behaviors, although their differential and interacting properties remain poorly understood.

The availability of the V1aR may have profound behavioral and emotional consequences. V1aR knockout (V1aRKO) male (but not female) mice show impaired social recognition. Increasing the V1aR, via site-specific injections of V1aR viral vectors, resulted in a marked increase in V1aR-related functions even in socially promiscuous mammals (Lim, Hammock, & Young, 2004). Polymorphisms within the 5' promoter region of the V1aR, in the form of tandem repeats, are associated in prairie voles with increased levels of V1aR binding in neural areas critical to male pair-bonding behavior. However, a comparative study of a number of mammalian species found that these tandem repeats were not unique to monogamous species (Heckel & Fink, 2008). Thus, different mechanisms may exist in different taxonomic groups to produce the convergent occurrence of the traits associated with social monogamy.

Both OT and AVP are capable of affecting neural systems implicated in initial neural social interactions as well as social bonding, including the olfactory bulb, medial preoptic area, amygdala, bed nucleus of the stria terminalis, and lateral septum. Receptors in this system in turn may regulate brainstem and autonomic areas that permit approach and avoidance even in the face of novelty (Viviani & Stoop, 2008).

The tendency to selectively prefer a partner, to seek contact with the partner, and in some cases to show distress in the absence of the preferred partner are all considered indicative of a social bond. Particularly useful in these studies have been socially monogamous rodents, including the prairie vole (Carter et al., 1995). Recent studies of the neurobiology of social bonds have focused on pair bonds between heterosexual partners. In prairie voles, sexual activity is not essential for selective social bonds to emerge; however, mating can facilitate the onset of a partner preference. Sexual interactions and mating provide a particularly powerful stimulus for the release of oxytocin (Carter, 1992). Oxytocin, in turn (even in the absence of sexual behavior or prolonged cohabitation), is capable of hastening the onset of partner preferences (Williams, Insel, Harbaugh, & Carter, 1994).

There is also evidence that the response to neuropeptides can be altered by the context in which they are experienced, such as social living versus isolation (Grippo, Trahanas, Zimmerman, Porges, & Carter, 2009). Stressful experiences, mediated through hormones of the HPA axis, modulate social bonding (DeVries et al., 1996; DeVries, Guptaa, Cardillo, Cho, & Carter, 2002). The effects of stress on pair-bond formation also differ in males and females. In females, exposure to a stressor inhibited female–male pair bonding (DeVries et al., 1996). However, in males exposed to a brief stressor or treated with stress hormones, pair-bond formation was facilitated. Centrally administered CRF, which stimulates the HPA axis, also increased pair bonding in male prairie voles (DeVries et al., 2002). However, the relationship between these hormones and behavior is complex and may differ according to the amount or duration of exposure to hormones of the HPA axis. Moderate amounts of activation and "stress" hormones might drive a tendency toward increased affiliation, while very high levels of these same factors might inhibit sociality or increase defensive aggression. Thus, once again, biological and behavioral context is critical to understanding the consequences of different hormonal experiences.

The physiology of social bonding is also regulated by systems responsible for rewarding experiences. For example, in socially naïve prairie voles, new pair bonds may form more readily when the partner is unfamiliar (i.e., not a member of the family), which reduces the potential for inbreeding and incest. In this context, pair bonds are reinforced by neural mechanisms that are shared with reward and pleasure. The dopamine system and, specifically, dopamine receptors in the nucleus accumbens have been implicated in pair bonding in prairie voles (Aragona & Wang, 2009). Dopamine-2 receptors appear to be important to the formation of pair bonds, while dopamine-1 receptors (activated by mating) may help to prevent the formation of a new pair bond while allowing the maintenance of previously formed social preferences. Oxytocin receptors are abundant in the nucleus accumbens, and interactions between OT and dopamine in this brain region may help to cement social bonds.

A Work in Progress: The Human Nervous System

We receive genes from our ancestors, and over this we have little control. However, the nervous system and body that each mammal inherits is a work in progress. Individual life experiences starting from the time of maternal egg development— while the mother herself is still a fetus—are capable of modifying the expression of those genes. This may be particularly true of genes that translate into neural systems regulating social and emotional behaviors.

Full-term human infants are capable of exhibiting and eliciting social interactions as early as the first day of life. From birth onward, appropriate social experiences are essential for normal development. It is increasingly clear that the social world of the infant is a factor in the prediction of behavior across the life span. Biological processes are in place to permit early experiences to have lifelong behavioral consequences.

Human research on the causes and consequences of early experience was strongly influenced by the work of Spitz (1945) and Bowlby (1988), who had described the behavior of children separated from their parents by war or other circumstances. During both early development and later life, these children were particularly sensitive to stressful experiences. The study of children who have had inadequate care or multiple caregivers offers support for the importance of caretaker consistency. Children raised in orphanages under conditions of severe emotional deprivation have provided some of the most extreme examples. Early adversity has been associated in later life with anxiety and also a vulnerability to severe depression and emotional "shutdown."

Particularly influential in the development of theories of early experience has been the studies done by Harlow (1958), Suomi (Suomi, van der Horst, & van der Veer, 2008), and their colleagues, who reared young monkeys with peers or inanimate surrogates rather than the mother. The atypical behaviors of surrogate-reared monkeys and motherless children are among the most potent pieces of experimental evidence that early experience played a critical role in later social behaviors. Among recent examples of the impact of early experience on physiology are studies suggesting that children who were orphaned in early life responded to social interactions with their caregivers with lower levels of OT, measured in urine, than those in children with a more typical childhood. Arginine vasopressin also was lower in these children (Fries, Ziegler, Kurian, Jacoris, & Pollak, 2005). Combined deficits in systems that rely on OT and AVP may partially explain the atypical social behaviors that have been reported in these children.

Early Experience Programs the Nervous System and Modulates Later Social and Emotional Reactivity

Genetic differences are another source of variance in sociality (Lim, Wang, et al., 2004). There also is increasing evidence that social experiences, especially in early life, may contribute to enduring changes in behavioral patterns, possibly including alterations in the capacity to exhibit social bonds (Bales & Carter, 2003a, 2003b; Bales, Lewis-Reese, Pfeiffer, Kramer, & Carter, 2007; Bales, Pfeifer, & Carter, 2004) or other forms of social behavior (Levine, 2001; Weaver et al., 2006). For example, when prairie voles are deliberately not disturbed during the preweaning period, subsequent tendencies to explore or form social bonds are reduced (Bales, Plotsky, et al., 2007).

Manipulations of the OT or AVP system in early life also can have long-lasting consequences. For example, even brief neonatal exposure to an oxytocin receptor antagonist (OTA) may disrupt subsequent social behaviors, including the tendency to form social bonds, to exhibit parental behaviors, and to manage anxiety or stress. Many of the consequences of early peptide manipulations are sexually dimorphic and map to sex differences in behavior. In males, although less sensitive in females, a single exposure to an OTA on the first day of life produced a long-lasting reduction in vasopressin (V1a) receptor binding in the extended amygdala and reductions in vasopressin synthesis in the paraventricular nucleus (Yamamoto et al., 2004). The androgen dependence of hypothalamic AVP (De Vries & Panzica, 2006) and the sexually dimorphic capacity of an OTA to down-regulate both the AVP V1aR and AVP peptide may help to explain the fact that OTA exposure was especially disruptive to male behavior. In contrast, in females, but not in males, a single treatment with exogenous OT up-regulated V1aRs in the ventral pallidum (Bales, Plotsky, et al., 2007). There are also recent data relating the effects of AVP in the ventral pallidum to an increased tendency to form pair bonds (Lim, Wang, et al., 2004). The changes observed in receptor binding are consistent with behavioral changes seen in these animals. Postnatal exposure to either AVP or an AVP V1aR antagonist did not disrupt the capacity of prairie voles to form pair bonds. However, animals exposed to neonatal AVP, especially males, tended to become more aggressive, while aggression was very low in animals exposed prenatally to either control treatments or an AVP V1aR antagonist (Stribley & Carter, 1999).

During early development, the same peptides that are implicated in adult social behaviors appear to be capable of programming individual differences in sociality (Carter, 2003; Carter et al., 2009). The capacity of these neuroendocrine systems to undergo long-lasting functional modifications presents an epigenetic model that may help to explain the origins of traits that have been called personality or temperament.

The effects of early experience may also, in later life, be affected by exposure to neuropeptides (Carter et al., 2009). For example, developmentally induced deficits, such as those associated with prenatal stressors including undernutrition, certain drug treatments, or blocking the negative effects of postnatal OTA, can be reduced or reversed by later treatments with OT.

Human Hormonal Experience in Early Life: Do They Matter?

In humans and other mammals, the emotional systems underlying social behavior are highly adaptive and can be influenced by the past history of the individual. In general, positive social experiences and appropriate levels of stimulation are associated with long-lasting social buffering, while neglect, abuse, or early life trauma may increase later vulnerability (Fries et al., 2005; Teicher et al., 2003). However, the effects of early experience can differ between males and females (Carter et al., 2009) and may be transmitted from one generation to another (Champagne & Meaney, 2007). Mechanisms for this form of developmental programming are only now becoming apparent. In many species of mammal, the primary caregiver(s) play an important role in determining the physiological state of offspring in later life. As described here, among the endocrine systems that can be influenced by early experiences, as well as exposure to exogenous hormones, are those that include OT, AVP, and their receptors.

The degree to which these findings might generalize to human behavior is not known. However, there is growing evidence that early experiences, including physiological and behavioral changes associated with pregnancy, birth, lactation, and the management of infants during the postpartum period, have the capacity to produce long-lasting changes in behavior. Routine endocrine manipulations, including the use of exogenous OT (in the synthetic form known as Pitocin) during labor and more recently the use of OT antagonists, also hold the potential to influence the parent and offspring in ways that have not been investigated in humans. Even apparently simple decisions, such as the amount of time that an infant is touched or receives other forms of social stimulation, hold the potential to retune the nervous system. For both practical and theoretical reasons, it is important to realize that the mechanisms underlying traits, such as the capacity to form affiliative bonds, are dynamic and capable of being influenced by early experience, often through effects on the same systems that regulate sociality in adulthood. It also is likely that experiences in later life may continue to modify the expression of social behaviors throughout the life span.

Symbiotic Regulation and Reciprocity

Most mammals, including humans and rodents, are altricial at birth. Care from an older individual is required to compensate for the infant's undeveloped motor and autonomic nervous systems. Due to an immature corticospinal motor system, the infant is incapable of independently obtaining food or protecting itself. Due to an immature autonomic nervous system, the infant is incapable of independently thermoregulating or ingesting and digesting certain foods. Thus, the mature nervous system of the infant becomes intertwined with the undeveloped nervous system of the infant to create a model of "symbiotic regulation." Infant behavior also triggers specific physiological processes (e.g., autonomic and endocrine feedback circuits) that help establish strong bonds, provide emotional comfort for the caregiver, and stimulate neural systems that support the health of the caregiver as well as the infant.

Social interactions may or may not be reciprocal. However, reciprocity and the spontaneous reversal of the roles of giving and receiving are positive features of strong relationships and are the optimal features of "symbiotic regulation." The inability of an individual to enter and maintain reciprocal social relations is a feature of several psychiatric disorders (Teicher et al., 2003). Conversely, reciprocity is a feature of healthy social behaviors.

When a mammalian mother initially interacts with her offspring, usually she has just given birth and must provide milk to nurture the newborn. The onset of maternal caregiving is normally closely associated with birth and lactation. The physical events of birth and lactation provide endocrine windows of opportunity for the establishment of strong social bonds. As described earlier, the hormones of birth and lactation are plausible candidates to explain the causes and beneficial effects of the interactions between children and adults (Carter, 1998).

The Evolution and Phylogeny of Mammalian Social Behavior

Most behaviors associated with prosociality in humans are seen in other mammals, but they are not evident in reptiles. In part, the phylogenetic transition from reptiles to mammals appears to be a shift from an organism capable of "self-regulation" to an organism that is dependent at certain points in development on "other regulation." It is within this phylogenetic transition, in which regulation by "other" becomes adaptive, that the neurobiology of sociality emerges. In most mammals, and especially humans, a developmental increase in self-regulation capacity parallels the development of specific features of the nervous system. Neural pathways from the cortex to the brainstem exhibit a maturational shift to greater efficiency in regulating the autonomic nervous system. This shift enables the maintenance of physiological homeostasis in both safe and dangerous situations (Porges, 2011).

The phylogeny of the mammalian nervous system offers important clues to the evolution of social behavior. In the transition from aquatic to terrestrial life, ancient gill (branchial) arches were co-opted to form the substrate for the face and head. The evolution of the mammalian head and face has implications for how and why features of the central nervous system are inextricably linked to the cranial functions. Taken together in modern mammals, including humans, these interconnections permit social engagement and social communication, including sucking, swallowing, facial expressions, and the production and receipt of airborne vocalizations (Porges, 2001, 2011; Porges & Lewis, 2009). Insights from phylogeny help explain how and why positive social behaviors are connected to the regulation of autonomic states.

The Polyvagal Theory

Mammalian social behavior relies on a neural platform that includes the autonomic nervous system (Porges, 2011). The mammalian nervous system cannot function without the support of visceral organs supplying oxygen and energy. The autonomic nervous system, via bidirectional pathways, regulates the viscera and conveys information upward to the hypothalamus, amygdala, and neocortex. Sensory information from the viscera contributes to what humans experience as "emotion" or "emotional states." These emotional states, in turn, are components of the "motivational" systems that stimulate social engagement and allow sociality to be experienced as reinforcing.

Traditional views of the mammalian autonomic nervous system have divided the system into two neural circuits including a sympathetic response that involves mobilizing energy or arousal for task demands (e.g., the fight-or-flight stress response) and a parasympathetic response that directs energy for use in restorative physiological functions. The polyvagal theory challenges this view by suggesting that the mammalian autonomic nervous system actually retains three (and not two) neural circuits that are hierarchically organized (Figure 5.1; Porges, 1998, 2001, 2011). These three circuits include the sympathetic fight-or-flight response, but parasympathetic activation is subdivided into (1) a vagal circuit that coordinates activity in the face and head while also promoting the regulation of restorative autonomic states above the diaphragm and (2) an evolutionarily ancient vagal circuit that regulates autonomic states below the diaphragm and permits an immobilization response to cues that the organism is in mortal danger. These three neural circuits are expressed in a phylogenetically organized *hierarchy* (Table 5.1). The newest circuit is the branch of the parasympathetic nervous system that coordinates activity in the face and head, permitting social communication. This newer circuit is used first in response to challenges to the organism. If the newest circuit fails to provide safety, older survival-oriented circuits are recruited sequentially, with the defensive fight-or-flight response preceding the use of an immobilization response. It is

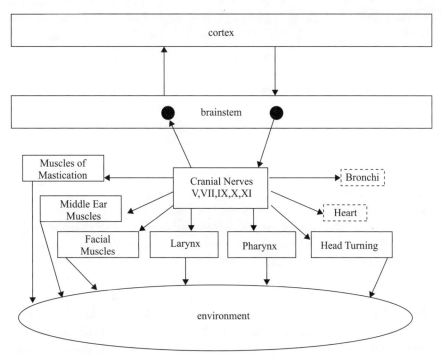

FIGURE 5.1 *The polyvagal theory: Efferent pathways of the mammalian social engagement system.*

important to note that social behavior, social communication, and visceral homeostasis, as promoted by the newest circuit, are largely incompatible with neurophysiological states and behaviors that are regulated by circuits that support the defense strategies of both "flight and fight" and immobilization. Inhibition of systems that are in general defensive or protective is necessary to initiate social engagement and to allow positive social behaviors. Conversely, positive social behaviors may be inhibited during prolonged periods of adversity. However, systems that support sociality, because they are intertwined with restorative physiological states, also may be protective against the destructive effects of *chronic* fear or stress.

TABLE 5.1 Phylogenetic Stages of the Polyvagal Theory

Stage	ANS Component	Behavioral Function	Lower Motor Neurons
III	Myelinated vagus *(ventral vagal complex)*	Social communication, self-soothing and calming, inhibition of "arousal"	Nucleus ambiguus
II	Sympathetic-adrenal system	Mobilization (active avoidance)	Spinal cord
I	Unmyelinated vagus *(dorsal vagal complex)*	Immobilization (death feigning, passive avoidance)	Dorsal motor nucleus of the vagus

ANS = autonomic nervous system.

The efferent component consists of two branches that influence the activities of these organs. The *unmyelinated* vagus primarily regulates organs below the diaphragm (e.g., gut), while the *myelinated* vagus regulates organs located above the diaphragm (e.g., heart and lungs). However, both branches *of the vagus influence the heart*, although the pacemaker (i.e., sinoatrial node) is predominantly regulated by the myelinated vagus. The unmyelinated component of the vagus, which permits slowing of the heart (*bradycardia*), originates in the dorsal motor nucleus of the vagus (also known as the dorsal vagal complex [DVC]). The unmyelinated vagus is shared by mammals with other vertebrates (i.e., reptiles, amphibia, and fish). The phylogenetically more recent myelinated branch originates in the nucleus ambiguus of the ventral vagal complex, allowing rapid interaction between the brain and viscera. The myelinated vagus stabilizes cardiovascular function and is responsible for *respiratory sinus arrhythmia* (RSA), a rise and fall in heart rate associated with phases of breathing: Usually heart rate increases with inspiration and decreases with expiration.

Respiratory sinus arrhythmia, sometimes called *vagal tone* or *cardiac vagal tone*, is an index of the dynamic influence of the myelinated vagus on the heart. The term *vagal tone* might be misleading, because there may be vagal influences to the heart via the unmyelinated vagus that would not be reflected in RSA. When RSA is depressed, because it reflects reduced influences of "myelinated" vagus on the heart, heart rate quickly accelerates. Recovery of RSA reflects the re-establishment of influence of the "myelinated" vagus on the heart (Porges, 2011) and reflects a physiological state that would promote social behavior. Respiratory sinus arrhythmia, reflecting the dynamic influence of the myelinated vagus, is cardioprotective and directly implicated in cortical oxygenation.

Of particular importance to mammalian social behavior, the myelinated vagus is associated in the brainstem with cranial nerves that innervate the face and head. Thus, the myelinated vagal functions are coordinated with the neural regulation of the larynx and pharynx to coordinate sucking, swallowing, and breathing with vocalizations. The muscles of the human face, especially of the upper face involved in subtle emotional expressions, have projections from this system, which may be particularly important in social communication during face-to-face interactions.

Neuroanatomical Evolution and Social Cognition

The comparatively modern processes that supplied oxygen to the large primate cortex coevolved with the emergence of higher levels of cognitive functions (Porges, 2001, 2007). The expanding mammalian cortex in general, and specific sensory and neuroanatomical changes in particular, set the stage for human cognition, speech, and more elaborate forms of caregiving beyond the maternal–infant interaction. For example, in contrast to their reptilian ancestors, mammals evolved auditory systems that enabled them to respond to airborne acoustic signals, an important requisite for increasingly complex modes of social interaction. Phylogenetic transitions in brainstem areas that regulate the vagus intertwined with areas that regulate the striated muscles of the face and head. The result of this transition from reptiles to mammals was the emergence of a capability for a dynamic social engagement system with social communication features (e.g., head movements, production of vocalizations, and a selective ability to hear conspecific [same species] vocal communication; Porges & Lewis, 2009).

Concurrently and in support of these anatomical changes, the new mammalian myelinated vagus emerged. The myelinated vagus could inhibit the sympathetic nervous system and the HPA axis, effectively making it possible to inhibit mobilization (fight-or-flight) responses. This inhibitory feature of the autonomic nervous system allowed animals to engage in high levels of social interaction, including nurturance of the young and an ability to engage other conspecifics in a prosocial manner without triggering defensive behaviors, while maintaining a calm physiological and behavioral state.

The phylogenetic transition from reptiles to mammals also resulted in a face–heart connection, in which the striated muscles of the face and head were regulated in the same brainstem areas that evoked the calming influence of the myelinated vagus. The striated muscles of the face and head are involved in social cueing (e.g., facial expressions, vocalizations, listening, head gesture, etc.). These systems serve as "trigger" stimuli to the feature detectors in the nervous system that detect risk and safety in the environment (see section on neuroception next). The expanded mammalian cortex also demands high levels of oxygen. Oxygenation of the cortex in mammals is accomplished in part through the same adaptations of the autonomic nervous system that permit elaborate forms of reciprocal sociality. These systems, including terrestrial lungs and a four-chamber heart, which support the oxygenation of the neocortex, also are regulated in part by the myelinated branch of the vagus nerve.

This synergism of neural mechanisms in mammals down-regulated defensive systems and promoted proximity by providing social cues (e.g., intonation of vocalization, facial expressivity, posture, and head gesture) that the organism was not in a physiological state that promoted aggressive and dangerous behaviors. Detection of these social cues allowed for symbiotic regulation of behavior and the elaboration of reciprocal caregiving. These same systems provided setting conditions under which social behaviors could have a significant impact on cognition and health. In the human nervous system, specific features of person-to-person interactions are innate triggers of adaptive biobehavioral systems, which in turn can support health and healing. In the absence of social interactions, or under conditions of social adversity, various forms of maladaptive behaviors and illness may be expressed.

Neuroception and the Social Management of Threat and Danger

The integrated functions of the myelinated vagus permit the expression of positive emotions and social communication. However, the nervous system also is constantly assessing the environment as safe, dangerous, or life threatening. For example, components of the autonomic nervous system also regulate the muscles of the middle ear, permitting the extraction of human voice from background noises that may include the very high or very low frequency sounds that signal danger. Under conditions of threat or fear, RSA is reduced, heart rate increases, and social communication is compromised. Through a process of "neuroception," specific neural circuits are triggered that may support defensive strategies.

As we discussed earlier, defensive strategies may involve either active coping (i.e., "fight-or-flight" responses) or passive coping (i.e., "immobilization" responses). The fight-or-flight system allows mobilization and permits the organism to engage in active or instrumental behaviors that facilitate coping. This system is supported by the sympathoadrenal systems, including the release of catecholamines and glucocorticoids, which increase available energy. Under some conditions, such as inescapable danger or other forms of extreme stress, mobilization strategies may be inhibited. These defensive strategies are characterized by passive coping, including immobility. Under more severe conditions, many systems may be shut down, including those dependent on the neocortex. In these circumstances, animals may show death-feigning or "helplessness" behaviors.

The unmyelinated vagus tends to slow the heart, consistent with a reptilian adaptive strategy of freezing and conserving energy in the face of danger. However, mammals, with their large cortex, cannot maintain clear cognition and consciousness without relatively high concentrations of oxygen. Thus, prolonged decelerations of the heart can lead to unconsciousness and eventually death. Mechanisms exist for protecting the heart and brain from "shutting down" at several levels within the body. As described earlier, among these are the neural and interactive effects of peptide hormones, such as OT and AVP.

Evolution and the Substrates for Mammalian Sociality and Emotion

As a species, humans are highly social mammals, capable of forming social bonds and dependent on others for survival and reproduction. The evolved neural, autonomic, and endocrine underpinnings of this sociality are shared with other mammalian species. Thus, the cross-species analysis of neurobiological processes responsible for sociality has relevance for understanding human behavior. Human concepts, such as social bonding and social support, rely on evolved neural and endocrine systems that are integrated throughout the body. Of particular importance are evolved changes in the mammalian brain, including changes at the level of the brainstem. Projections to and from these ancient systems are experienced by more modern brain structures, including the cortex, as diffuse and sometimes powerful feelings or emotions. The same neuroendocrine and autonomic systems that permit high levels of social behavior and social bonds regulate the management of stressful experiences and the capacity of the mammalian body to adapt in the context of individual differences in experience. The activities of the brainstem and autonomic systems are context dependent. In a context of safety or comparatively mild or acute stressors, the release of OT and the involvement of the myelinated vagus may down-regulate defensive systems and allow a "feed-forward" up-regulation of OT. These changes permit and promote reciprocal social interactions with the consequence of enhanced opportunities for symbiotic regulation to support health and restorative processes. In the context of chronic stress or fear, the actions of these same adaptive systems can interfere with both the establishment and expression of social behavior (Figure 5.2).

The neuropeptide profile of the reptilian ancestors of mammals transitioned into the distinctly mammalian neuropeptides, OT and AVP. These peptides have selective receptors and unique adaptive functions. Oxytocin supports prosocial behaviors and passive coping styles, including the capacity to remain immobile without fear. In contrast, the functions of AVP within the central nervous system are generally associated with mobilization and can support defensive or even aggressive behaviors. During the transition from reptiles to mammals, the myelinated component of the vagal system also emerged. This myelinated vagal "brake" was capable of overriding the defensive functions of the sympathetic nervous system and also

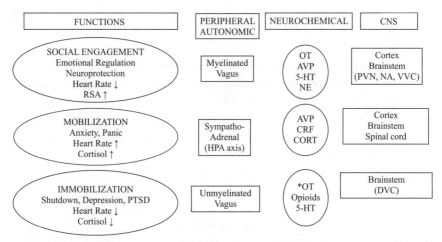

FIGURE 5.2 *Hierarchal organization of neuroendocrine and autonomic processes implicated in social behavior and the adaptive management of stressful experiences. Neuropeptides, including oxytocin (OT), arginine vasopressin (AVP), corticotropin-releasing factor (CRF), and endogenous opioids, as well as neurotransmitters such as serotonin (5-HT) and norepinephrine (NE), influence behavior and emotions through direct actions on the brain, as well as indirect effects on different components of the autonomic nervous system and the hypothalamic–pituitary–adrenal (HPA) axis. Oxytocin, 5-HT, and endogenous opioids, acting in the brainstem, may be protective during or against shutting down and immobilization. RSA = respiratory sinus arrhythmia; CORT = cortisol; CNS = central nervous system; PVN = paraventricular nucleus; NA = nucleus ambiguus; VVC = ventral vagal complex; DVC = dorsal vagal complex.*

protecting against shutdown functions characteristic of the older, unmyelinated functions of the vagus. These uniquely mammalian systems actively oppose and inhibit neural circuits such as the HPA axis and the sympathetic nervous system and serve defensive behaviors necessary for survival.

Summary

In this chapter we describe two complementary neurophysiological systems that—in the context of safety—allow mammals to rapidly regulate integrative states, functionally turning off defense systems while at the same time promoting behaviors that characterize mammalian sociality, including physical contact, nurturance, and face-to-face social communication. Phylogenetic transitions provided the neurophysiological resources and substrates needed to support maternal nurturance and high levels of prosocial behaviors that are typical of mammals. The emergence of these systems also provided the functional ability to shift rapidly between states of defense and states that promote prosocial behaviors. The functions of the autonomic nervous system and especially the myelinated vagus, regulated in part by neuropeptides, allow these rapid behavioral shifts.

Neuroanatomical and neuroendocrine transitions across the course of evolution provided mammals with a neural platform permissive for the expanded range of adaptive and flexible behaviors that allowed mammals to survive and to reproduce in a changing environment. Survival of our ancestors in the "environment of evolutionary adaptiveness" was dependent on the recruitment of these novel mammalian systems and their ability to rapidly transition between prosocial and defensive behavioral strategies. Knowledge of the evolutionary origins and neurobiology of sociality provides a neurophysiological perspective for a deeper understanding of both the causes and consequences of the complex social behaviors that differentiate mammals, and especially modern humans, from their ancestors.

Acknowledgments

Much of the research described here was supported by the National Institutes of Health. We also are grateful for the hard work of many colleagues who provided the original research upon which this chapter is based. Portions of the material covered here are also described in earlier chapters from our laboratories.

References

Aragona, B. J., & Wang, Z. (2009). Dopamine regulation of social choice in a monogamous rodent species. *Frontiers in Behavioral Neuroscience, 3*, 15.

Bales, K. L., & Carter, C. S. (2003a). Developmental exposure to oxytocin facilitates partner preferences in male prairie voles (*Microtus ochrogaster*). *Behavioral Neuroscience, 117*, 854–859.

Bales, K. L., & Carter, C. S. (2003b). Sex differences and developmental effects of oxytocin on aggression and social behavior in prairie voles (*Microtus ochrogaster*). *Hormones and Behavior, 44*, 178–184.

Bales, K. L., Lewis-Reese, A., Pfeiffer, L. A., Karmer, K. M., & Carter, C. S. (2007). Early experience affects the traits of monogamy in a sexually dimorphic manner. *Developmental Psychobiology, 49*, 335–342.

Bales, K. L., Pfeifer, L. A., & Carter, C. S. (2004). Sex differences and developmental effects of manipulations of oxytocin on alloparenting and anxiety in prairie voles. *Developmental Psychobiology, 44*, 123–131.

Bales, K. L., Plotsky, P. M., Young, L. J., Lim, M. M., Grotte, N., Ferrer, E., & Carter, C. S. (2007). Neonatal oxytocin manipulations have long-lasting, sexually dimorphic effects on vasopressin receptors. *Neuroscience, 144*, 38–45.

Bosch, O. J, & Neumann, I. D. (2010). Vasopressin released within the central amygdala promotes maternal aggression. *European Journal of Neuroscience, 31*, 883–891.

Bowlby, J. (1988). *A secure base: Parent-child attachment and healthy human development.* New York, NY: Basic Books.

Carter, C. S. (1992). Oxytocin and sexual behavior. *Neuroscience and Biobehavioral Reviews, 16*, 131–144.

Carter, C. S. (1998). Neuroendocrine perspectives on social attachment and love. *Psychoneuroendocrinology, 23*, 779–818.

Carter, C. S. (2003). Developmental consequences of oxytocin. *Physiology and Behavior, 79*, 383–397.

Carter, C. S. (2007). Sex differences in oxytocin and vasopressin: Implications for autism spectrum disorders? *Behavioural Brain Research, 176*, 170–186.

Carter, C. S., Boone, E. M., Pournajafi-Nazarloo, H., & Bales, K. L. (2009). The consequences of early experiences and exposure to oxytocin and vasopressin are sexually-dimorphic. *Developmental Neuroscience, 31*, 332–341.

Carter, C. S., DeVries, A. C., & Getz, L. L. (1995). Physiological substrates of mammalian monogamy: The prairie vole model. *Neuroscience and Biobehavioral Reviews, 19*, 303–314.

Champagne, F. A., & Meaney, M. J. (2007). Transgenerational effects of social environment on variations in maternal care and behavioral response to novelty. *Behavioral Neuroscience, 121*, 1353–1363.

Cho, M. M., DeVries, A. C., Williams, J. R., & Carter, C. S. (1999). The effects of oxytocin and vasopressin on partner preferences in male and female prairie voles (*Microtus ochrogaster*). *Behavioral Neuroscience, 113*, 1071–1080.

De Vries, G. J., & Panzica, G. C. (2006). Sexual differentiation of central vasopressin and vasotocin systems in vertebrates: Different mechanisms, similar endpoints. *Neuroscience, 138*, 947–955.

DeVries, A. C., DeVries, M. B., Taymans, S. E., & Carter, C. S. (1996). The effects of stress on social preferences are sexually dimorphic in prairie voles. *Proceedings of the National Academy of Sciences USA, 93*, 11980–11984.

DeVries, C. A., Guptaa, T, Cardillo, S., Cho, M. M., & Carter, C. S. (2002). Corticotropin-releasing factor induced social preferences in male prairie voles. *Psychoneuroendocrinology, 27*, 705–714.

Fries, A. B. W., Ziegler, T. E., Kurian, J. R., Jacoris, S., & Pollak, S. D. (2005). Early experience in humans is associated with changes in neuropeptides critical for regulating social behavior. *Proceedings of the National Academy of Sciences USA, 102*, 17237–17240.

Gimpl, G., & Fahrenholz, F. (2001). The oxytocin receptor system: Structure, function and regulation. *Physiological Reviews, 81*, 629–683.

Grippo, A. J., Trahanas, D. M., Zimmerman II, R. R., Porges, S. W., & Carter, C. S. (2009). Oxytocin protects against isolation-induced autonomic dysfunction and behavioral indices of depression. *Psychoneuroendocrinology, 34*, 1542–1553.

Harlow, H. (1958). The nature of love. *American Psychologist, 13*, 673–685.

Heckel, G., & Fink, S. (2008). Evolution of the arginine vasopressin 1a receptor and implications for mammalian social behaviour. *Progress in Brain Research, 170*, 321–330.

Hrdy, S. B. (2009). *Mothers and others: The evolutionary origins of mutual understanding.* Cambridge, MA: Belknap Press, Harvard University.

Landgraf, R., & Neumann, I. D. (2004). Vasopressin and oxytocin release within the brain: A dynamic concept of multiple and variable modes of neuropeptide communication. *Frontiers in Neuroendocrinology, 25*, 50–176.

Levine, S. (2001). Primary social relationships influence the development of the hypothalamic-pituitary-adrenal axis in the rat. *Physiology and Behavior, 73*, 255–260.

Lim, M. M., Hammock, E. A. D., & Young, L. J. (2004). The role of vasopressin in the genetic and neural basis of monogamy. *Journal of Neuroendocrinology, 16*, 325–332.

Lim, M. M., Wang, Z. X., Olazabal, D. E., Ren, X. H., Terwilliger, E. F., & Young, L. J. (2004). Enhanced partner preference in a promiscuous species by manipulating the expression of a single gene. *Nature, 429*, 754–757.

Palanza, P., Gioiosa, L., & Parmigiani, S. (2001). Social stress in mice: Gender differences and effects of estrous cycle and social dominance. *Physiology and Behavior, 73*, 411–420.

Porges, S. W. (1998). Love: An emergent property of the mammalian autonomic nervous system. *Psychoneuroendocrinology, 23*, 837–861.

Porges, S. W. (2003a). The polyvagal theory: Phylogenetic contributions to social behavior. *Physiology and Behavior, 79*, 503–513.

Porges, S. W. (2003b). Social engagement and attachment: A phylogenetic perspective. *Annals of the New York Academy of Sciences, 1008*, 31–47.

Porges, S. W. (2011). *The polyvagal theory: Neurophysiological foundations of emotions, attachment, communication, and self-regulation.* New York, NY: W. W. Norton and Co.

Porges, S. W., & Lewis, G. F. (2009). The polyvagal hypothesis: Common mechanisms mediating autonomic regulation, vocalizations, and listening. In S. M. Brudzynsk (Ed.), *Handbook of mammalian vocalizations: An integrative neuroscience approach* (pp. 255–264). Amsterdam: Academic Press.

Spitz, R. (1945). Hospitalism: An inquiry into the genesis of psychiatric conditions in early childhood. *Psychoanalytic Study of the Child, 1*, 53–75.

Stribley, J. M., & Carter, C. S. (1999). Developmental exposure to vasopressin increases aggression in adult prairie voles. *Proceedings of the National Academy of Sciences USA, 96*, 12601–12604.

Suomi, S. J., van der Horst, F. C., & van der Veer, R. (2008). Rigorous experiments on monkey love: An account of Harry F. Harlow's role in the history of attachment theory. *Integrative Psychology and Behavioral Science, 42*, 354–369.

Teicher, M. H., Andersen, S. L., Polcari, A., Anderson, C. M., Navalta, C. P., & Kim, D. M. (2003). The neurobiological consequences of childhood maltreatment. *Neuroscience and Biobehavioral Reviews, 27,* 33–44.

Viviani, D., & Stoop, R. (2008). Opposite effects of oxytocin and vasopressin on the emotional expression of the fear response. *Progress in Brain Research, 170,* 207–218.

Weaver, I. C., Champagne, F. A., Brown, S. E., Dymov, S., Sharma, S., Meaney, M. J., & Szyf, M. (2006). Reversal of maternal programming of stress responses in adult offspring through methyl supplementation: Altering epigenetic marking later in life. *Journal of Neuroscience, 25,* 11045–11054.

Williams, J. R., Insel, T. R., Harbaugh, C. R., & Carter, C. S. (1994). Oxytocin administered centrally facilitates formation of a partner preference in female prairie voles. *Journal of Neuroendocrinology, 6,* 247–250.

Winslow, J. T., Hastings, N., Carter, C. S., Harbaugh, C. R., & Insel, T. R. (1993). A role for vasopressin pair bonding in monogamous prairie voles. *Nature, 365,* 545–548.

Winslow, J. T., & Insel, T. R. (2004). Neuroendocrine basis of social recognition. *Current Opinion in Neurobiology, 14,* 248–253.

Yamamoto, Y., Cushing, B. S., Kramer, K. M., Epperson, P. D., Hoffman, G. E., & Carter, C. S. (2004). Neonatal manipulations of oxytocin alter oxytocin and vasopressin in the paraventricular nucleus of the hypothalamus in a gender-specific manner. *Neuroscience, 125,* 947–955.

6

Dopamine: Another "Magic Bullet" for Caregiver Responsiveness?

Viara Mileva-Seitz, Veronica M. Afonso, and
Alison S. Fleming

Introduction

Since the early 20th century, the study of mothering has looked for a "magic bullet" that transforms a female from being neutral or totally disinterested in her young to compulsively attending to the needs of her young—even to the extent that puts her life in jeopardy to protect those young (Numan, Fleming, & Levy, 2006; Numan & Insel, 2003; Rosenblatt & Lehrman, 1963; Wiesner & Sheard, 1933). The magic-bullet search was often a search for a primary hormone, neurotransmitter, or brain site that could explain the radical change new mothers undergo within hours or days after birthing. The early candidates included the hormones prolactin, estrogen, and oxytocin, whose action on the medial preoptic area (MPOA) in the brain could induce a rapid onset of pup retrieval in the new mother rat (reviewed in Numan et al., 2006). In contrast to a unitary mechanism that has trigger-like effects on a single stereotypical maternal response, our present-day understanding is that there exists a complex sequence of hormonal, neurochemical, and brain changes occurring at the time of birth that are associated with an equally complex set of changes in mothers' emotional affect, perceptions, plasticity, "reward," attention, and motor behavior. These changes enhance mothers' motivation to mother and their ability to do so. While the details and behavioral phenotypes differ across species and cultures, this approach to understanding mothering is equally valuable in the analysis of mothering in nonhumans and humans alike. To understand this complexity constitutes the goal of this chapter.

In the present chapter, we focus on the factors that influence a mother's desire to provide care for her offspring. We believe that these changes likely occur in most mammalian species, including humans. The extent of their occurrence, quality of behavior exhibited, and outcomes for the young, of course, vary considerably depending on the species, context (culture), and individual life experiences of the individual mother. We discuss the psychological systems or processes that are activated when a mother gives birth for the first time and enhance her motivation to be nurturant. Discussions of maternal behavior are followed by a description of the primary hormonal, neurochemical, and neural changes that occur in pregnancy, at parturition, and during the following postpartum period that underlie these psychological processes. The neurochemical that we focus on—our most recent magic bullet—is the dopamine system. This system can be viewed as a node that interconnects with a complex network of neural, neurochemical, and endocrine systems that together affect mothering. Attention will then shift to dopamine-related genetic influences that assist in explaining the vast individual differences characteristic of human mothering. We briefly touch on how this entire system develops and how genes and early postnatal experiences may act and interact to influence the motivation and expression of mothering in adulthood. Given the vast nature of the mothering literature, we are unable to do an exhaustive review. Of necessity, we focus on our own numerous recent studies. However, the work described herein could not have happened without the prior and concurrent work of hundreds of excellent parenting scientists (for excellent reviews, see Bridges, 2008; Carter et al., 2005; Hrdy, 1999, 2009; Numan & Insel, 2003).

Stereotypy, Individual Differences, and the Maternal Phenotype

RAT MOTHERS

As with most mammals, a new first-time (primiparous) mother rat is very responsive to her offspring. Without explicit "practice" or "learning," she shows the full range of stereotyped responses to the newborn pups. For example, she builds a nest prior to her birthing, eats the placenta, retrieves scattered pups into her nest, licks pups, and adopts a nursing posture over pups to allow suckling for milk (see Numan et al., 2006; Rosenblatt & Lehrman, 1963; Wiesner & Sheard, 1933). These behaviors are exhibited in an efficient sequence, and even in the absence of explicit maternal experience the mother responds adequately enough to her young so that they can survive. This efficiency increases after practice. In the face of this apparent stereotypy, it would seem that maternal behavior is quite simple in its organization and regulation. However, psychologically the mother undergoes many changes when she gives birth that enhances the likelihood she will be motivated to respond to pups during this inexperienced postparturient period. Once motivated with some pup experience, the mother will show an adequate behavioral pattern that becomes synchronized with pup development and lactation (Rosenblatt & Lehrman, 1963).

Hedonics, Affect, and Motivation

Perhaps the primary change seen in the new mother is her development of an attraction to pups and their cues, an attraction that ensures approach behavior of mother to pups. Approach behavior facilitates physical mother–pup interactions and pro-motes assignment of a positive valence or salience to pups such that they become conditioned stimuli to facilitate further interactions. These changes occur under the influence of pregnancy and parturitional hormones.

First, hormones appear to facilitate changes in the new mothers' fear and with-drawal tendencies; new mothers or hormonally primed animals are more inclined to approach novel stimuli and ambulate in a novel environment, independent of pups (Fleming, Cheung, Myhal, & Kessler, 1989; Fleming, Vaccarino, & Luebke, 1980). This reduced fearfulness (or anxiety) is expressed along with enhanced aggression, where the mother will attack intruders that approach the nest site or the young (Lonstein, 2005, 2007; Lonstein & Gammie, 2002; Numan et al., 2006). In contrast, on exposure to pups, the virgin nonmother withdraws from or buries pups and may even cannibalize them (Fleming & Li, 2002; Fleming & Luebke, 1981). If the maternal nest with pups is placed into the quadrant of the cage where the female normally sleeps, the virgin animal will change her preferred sleeping site. In fact, always placing pups into the daily preferred resting quadrant will lead to the female being chased around the cage with the ever-present objective of avoiding pups.

Second, hormones appear to facilitate maternal preference for pup-related cues. For instance, mothers develop a preference for pups and their nest odor over adult females and their nest odor (Fleming & Li, 2002; Fleming, Vaccarino, Tambosso, & Chee, 1979). This olfactory preference also enhances the differential responses shown by virgins and postpartum animals to pup vocalizations (Farrell & Alberts, 2002). The natural preference for pup-related cues shown by the new mother can be induced in virgins by administering a parturient-like hormone regimen (reviewed in Fleming & Li, 2002). This indicates that the initial preference for pups can occur in the absence of specific experience with that odor in adult life, although it is affected by previous preweaning nest experiences (Shah, Oxley, Lovic, & Fleming, 2002). By using operant reward tasks, one can show the rewarding properties of pups to mothers. Mothers will work to attain contact with pups (Lee, Clancy, & Fleming, 2000) and develop a preference for an environment previously paired with pups over an environment associated with cocaine (Mattson, Williams, Rosenblatt, & Morrell, 2001). These examples demonstrate the ability of pups to take on a posi-tive valence.

Individual differences exist among females in terms of both maternal moti-vation and maternal behavior. In the first place, virgin animals that are normally unresponsive to pups become pup responsive if provided with continuous contact with foster pups—a process called "sensitization" (Fleming & Rosenblatt, 1974a) or "pup induction" (Numan et al., 2006). This process occurs in the absence of any apparent change in the animals' hormonal state, but rather involves sensory input (e.g., olfactory, somatosensory). One feature of sensitization is that different rats require different amounts of stimulation to begin to show maternal behavior; some respond within a day of exposure to foster pups, and others take up to 10 or more days of continuous contact (with pups rotated daily and returned daily to the mother for feeding). Hence, females differ in their underlying "maternal responsiveness" or maternal motivation as reflected in their latencies to become maternal.

Maternal motivation is affected by the animals' emotional state. Virgins that are rendered less anxious through administration of anxiolytics or previously exposed to pups and their odors in the colony—or rendered anosmic and unable to smell pups altogether—become maternal more quickly than more anxious animals (Fleming & Li, 2002; Fleming & Rosenblatt, 1974b, 1974c; Numan et al., 2006; see also Lonstein, 2005, 2007).

Attention and Quality of Behavior

Once mothers have become motivated to respond to the young, the intensity of their responses varies considerably. Within rat strains and across strains, some mothers intensely lick and crouch over their young, while others seldom exhibit these behaviors. This distinction between the high–licking and grooming (LG) mothers and low-LG mothers has become the fulcrum of an extensive series of very elegant and provocative studies by Michael Meaney, Francis Champagne, and their colleagues (e.g., Cameron et al., 2005; Cameron et al., 2008; Shahrokh, Zhang, Diorio, Gratton, & Meaney, 2010) and will be discussed in greater detail in later sections.

Whereas maternal motivation is affected by the animal's emotional state, individual differences in licking and grooming, as described by Meaney and colleagues, are affected by the animal's level of attention, impulsivity, and executive function. The relation between licking intensity and both motor impulsivity and errors in an attention set-shifting task is inverse and quite linear. The greater the animal's impulsivity or inattention, the lower the mother's licking intensity was during its previous preweaning period (Lovic & Fleming, 2004; Lovic, Palombo, & Fleming, 2010). When mothers have attention problems or when they exhibit a high level of action impulsivity, they are easily distracted when with their pups, frequently going into and out of the nest and showing erratic retrieval patterns.

Human Mothers

How do maternal phenotypes so well understood in rats (and in other nonhuman mammals) map onto maternal phenotypes in humans? In their many details, of course, not well; however, in their overall functions, considerably. Human mothers transport, protect, nurse, and clean the young. For example, the young can be transported on mothers' backs, on their ventrums, in side slings, in strollers, or in perambulators. The mode of carrying may differ in cultures, but the function is the same: to keep the baby close to the mother, protected from danger, and in an environment that enhances the infant's physiological and behavioral development. Mothers across cultures also vary in how much they hold their babies and stimulate them through movement and skin contact, whether they co-sleep with, talk to, or sing to them. Not surprisingly, in most cultures mothers also nurse their infants, although cross-cultural differences exist in how often and for how long this behavior occurs. And even when relatives and friends—the allomothers—also participate in childcare, the mother is normally the primary care provider in at least the first 3 months of the infant's life (Barrett & Fleming, in press; Corter & Fleming, 2002; Keller, 2002). The ancillary effect of the type of postnatal care varies from providing the baby with close physical contact, warmth, and somatosensory/kinesthetic stimulation, which functions to promote healthy growth, to a more removed form of distal interaction, which affords the baby access to the mother's face, contingent exchanges, and the development of a certain amount of autonomy.

Hedonics, Mood, and Maternal Responsiveness

During the early postpartum period, human mothers are attracted to infants and infant odors and respond sympathetically to infant vocalizations (Fleming, Steiner, & Corter, 1997; Stallings, Fleming, Corter, Worthman, & Steiner, 2001). In several studies on Canadian mothers, we presented new mothers and nonmothers with a series of odors including infant body and head odors (cotton t-shirts worn for 12 hours by a newborn infant and rubbed over infant's head) and infant urine, meconium, and/or fecal odors (collected from diapers). Among the control odors were tarragon brew, gorgonzola cheese odors, and axillary sweat odors. The odorants were presented in random order to subjects and without identification of the odors' source. In comparison with nonmothers, mothers gave higher hedonic or pleasantness ratings to the infant body and head odors and no differences in the extent of their negative ratings of cheese, infant urine, or axillary sweat. These differences existed on the first postpartum day in first-time mothers, suggesting mothers are in some sense primed to respond positively to infant cues. However, experience clearly contributes to the hedonic valence, because mothers who have spent more time with their infants immediately after birth and who nursed sooner after the birth also rated the infant body odors more positively. Consistent with reports by other investigators, these mothers were also better able to recognize their own infants' body odors when these were paired with another infant's odor (Corter & Fleming, 2002; Fleming et al., 1993; Fleming, Corter, Surbey, Franks, & Steiner, 1995; Fleming, Steiner, et al., 1997; Porter, Cernoch, & McLaughlin, 1983).

In addition to the preference for infant odors, new mothers respond more sympathetically to infant cries than nonmothers: Mothers have a pattern of elevated heart rate responses and levels of salivary cortisol related to the extent of their sympathy to those cries (Stallings et al., 2001). As in other animals, there is a role of prior experience and parity in these relations. For instance, first-time mothers show no differences in their responses to pain versus hunger cries; in contrast, multiparous mothers are much more sympathetic than primiparous mothers to the pain cry and somewhat less sympathetic to the hunger cry (Stallings et al., 2001). Moreover, among all mothers there is a correlation between levels of sympathy, heart rate responses, and circulating cortisol levels, which was strongest among multiparous mothers. In response to odors, a somewhat different situation occurs, where primiparous mothers are more attracted to the odors of babies and the relation between positive ratings and cortisol is stronger in primiparous mothers than in multiparous mothers (Fleming, Steiner, et al., 1997).

In addition to an enhanced "appreciation" of the young and attention to them, parturition often brings about changes in mothers' mood: Mothers become more labile, experiencing periods of elation alternating with tearfulness (O'Hara, Zekoski, Phillips, & Wright, 1990). Some experience a period of real postpartum blues, which is also characterized by lability but tends to involve more dysphoria, anxiety, and depression that is time limited and usually remits by the end of the first month (Cox, Murray, & Chapman, 1993). If the "blues" persist beyond this period and deepen, mothers are characterized as experiencing postpartum depression, which, like depression during other periods of life, involves sleep disorders, negative thoughts, sleeping and eating problems, anxiety, and often motor retardation. In short, new mothers often undergo large changes in affect with the birth of the baby that can enhance or retard mothers' attention and "bonding" with the baby (Field, Healy, Goldstein, & Guthertz, 1990; Fleming, Ruble, Flett, & Shaul, 1988). These changes may also alter mothers' actual perceptions of infant cues, which could then affect the salience of the infant to the mother and her competence to mother (Field et al., 1990; Fleming et al., 1988.

Many studies show that depressed mothers tend to be less responsive to the baby's cues (Milgrom, Westley, & Gemmill, 2004) and have reduced tactile interaction and a more negative affect in general (Herrera, Reissland, & Shepherd, 2004; Murray, Fiori-Cowley, Hooper, & Cooper, 1996; see meta-analysis by Lovejoy, Graczyk, O'Hare, & Neuman, 2000). In our studies of depressed mothers, we have not noted reduced feelings of attachment to the infant, although we have found that in comparison to nondepressed mothers, depressed mothers respond less contingently—vocalizing less predictably to the baby's vocalizations—as well as less contactfully (Fleming et al., 1988). In a recent study we presented new depressed and nondepressed mothers with tapes of infant pain and hunger cries and assessed their emotional, autonomic, and endocrine responses to these cries. We found that in comparison to nondepressed mothers, depressed mothers were particularly prone to feeling anxious when listening to infant cries and responded particularly strongly to the pain as opposed to the hunger cries. Depressed mothers also had higher overall cortisol levels than nondepressed mothers; however, the nondepressed mothers showed a hormonal response to the cries, whereas the depressed mothers did not (Gonzalez et al., in preparation). This indicates that the two groups are responding to the different stimuli differently. It seems that depressed mothers are more responsive to the high-intensity and aversive stimulus and that the normal level of signaling provided by the lower intensity hunger cries is not sufficient to activate a hormonal response in these depressed mothers. It is not surprising, therefore, that the infants of depressed mothers often come to show depressed symptomatology themselves (Tronick & Reck, 2009). Whether these affective changes found in mothers in many cultures relate at all to the reduced fearfulness and enhanced aggression shown by new rat mothers is an interesting question.

Attention and Maternal Sensitivity

Recently we have begun to explore the relation of cognitive functioning and mothering in human mothers. We compared 6-month postpartum mothers and age- and socioeconomic status–matched nonmothers on a variety of executive function tasks administered on a computer-based battery of tests called the Cambridge Neuropsychological Test Automated Battery (CANTAB). This is a series of computer-based tests presented on a touch-sensitive screen that assess cognitive functioning and is used extensively on clinical or elderly populations (Robbins et al., 1994; Singer, MacGregor, Cherkas, & Spector, 2006). Compared to nonmothers, adult mothers tended to do less well on tasks of working memory, while not differing as a group in attention, impulsivity, or simple associative learning tasks (Chico, Gonzalez, Ali, Steiner, & Fleming, in preparation).

Gonzalez, Jenkins, Steiner, and Fleming (in press) found that 6-month postpartum mothers who were evaluated as less sensitive to their babies (by Ainsworth sensitivity coding) also made more errors on a selective attention task. These mothers also experienced earlier neglect or adversity in family of origin. When adult and teenage mothers were compared, the teen mothers made considerably more errors in attention set-shifting, impulsivity, and working memory; and, in correlational analyses these deficits in executive function were associated with reduced maternal sensitivity and reduced attention to the baby. In coded observations of videotapes of mothers interacting with their babies, these teenage mothers showed reduced contingent responding, reduced talking to and playing with the baby, and reduced focus toward the baby.

Summary

The challenge for mothering in humans is no different than in other animals. What motivates the human mother to expend so much energy, often at terrific personal cost, to care for an infant? We suggest that the range of explanations of human maternal behavior overlaps considerably with what we have learned from other mammalian species and has a phylogenetic history (Hrdy, 1999, 2009): hormones and neurotransmitters prime the mother to respond positively to infant cues and enhance the saliency of those cues. Prior experiences—including experience with the infant, with previous infants, and in earlier life, as an infant with her own parents—further enhance the rewarding value of the infant (see Corter & Fleming, 2002; Gonzalez, Jenkins, Steiner, & Fleming, 2009). The combination of physiology and experience motivates the mother to care for her infant and also impacts other aspects of her behavior that affect her mothering. These likely include her ability to focus her attention and to shift her attention, as necessary; her ability to inhibit inappropriate responses (impulsivity); and her ability to learn as she mothers.

Role of Hormones in the Regulation of Mothering

There are a number of hormones that clearly play a role in the onset of maternal behavior and maternal "motivation" in the rat, sheep, monkeys, and humans. However, rather than review the extensive literature on the endocrine bases of maternal behavior in these different species, here we present only the broad strokes and highlight the cross-species similarities. For more details we also refer the reader to the many exhaustive reviews of this topic (see Numan & Insel, 2003; Numan et al., 2006).

What are the commonalities? Progesterone is of course "the" gestational hormone and is sustained at high levels throughout pregnancy in all these species. In some, but not all, progesterone begins to decline toward the end of gestation and the other steroid hormone, estrogen, is either also sustained at high levels (humans) or rises (rats) in the latter half of pregnancy. This shift in the ratio of the steroids sets the stage for parturition and mothers' subsequent attraction to infants and maternal responsiveness toward them. In rats, of course, these hormonal effects have been experimentally demonstrated and are well established (Numan et al., 2006). Among humans, who do not all show this same shift, those who do tend to experience greater postpartum nurturance toward their infants than those who do not (Fleming, Ruble, Krieger, & Wong, 1997). Although this correlation exists in humans, the causal relation between the estrogen/progesterone ratio and maternal motivation has of course not been established.

Associated with the estrogen/progesterone shift, in most species an increase occurs in the pituitary lactogen and prolactin, contributing to mothering behavior in the rat and monkey along with milk synthesis in all the mammalian species. Estrogen also prepares the brain and peripheral tissue for release of oxytocin, promoting uterine contractions at parturition, after which oxytocin is released in pulsatile fashion with suckling stimulation during nursing and lactation. Within the maternal context, in the rat, sheep, and monkey oxytocin has been implicated in activating the onset of maternal behavior but requires estrogen priming to do so (Numan et al., 2006). In humans, there is now good evidence to suggest that oxytocin levels measured in saliva are associated with affectionate mothering behavior (Gordon, Zagoory-Sharon, Leckman, & Feldman, 2010).

In animals, these hormonal changes definitely contribute to mothers' attraction to infants and maternal motivation, and they do so by acting on receptors in the brain. Although causal links have yet to be established, they likely also exert similar effects in humans. To understand just what the role of the brain is in this process and especially the role of the neurotransmitters, in the next section we describe the functional neuroanatomy of maternal and associated behaviors in the rat and in humans, with particular emphasis on the contribution to that neuroanatomy of the dopamine system. We argue that hormonally induced alterations of the dopamine system are essential to mothers' appreciation of the young as salient stimuli. Once the salience of infants is established, mothers become aroused and activated, and approach infants readily. This process is thought to be mediated by dopaminergic systems and related "neurochemical" systems (opioid, glutamate, nitric oxide synthetase) influencing the reward value of the young and recruiting behaviors necessary for adequate mothering.

Neuroanatomy and Dopamine in the Regulation of Mothering

NEUROANATOMY OF MOTHERING

Cross-species studies in rats, voles, sheep, and primates (reviewed in Numan et al., 2006; Numan & Insel, 2003) indicate a striking similarity in the neuroanatomy underlying mothering. The final common path for the expression of the behavior involves the medial preoptic area (MPOA) and its downstream projections into the midbrain (ventral tegmental area [VTA]) and hindbrain (periaqueductal gray). In addition, the MPOA interconnects with sensory, limbic, and cortical systems (see Figure 6.1). Most of these sites contain dense levels of hormone receptors allowing periparturitional hormone binding at these sites to influence behavioral changes at parturition (Numan et al., 2006).

Many of the neural sites implicated in the mothering of animals are similar to those associated with human mothering. To summarize a growing literature on the anatomy of mothering in humans (Barrett & Fleming, 2011), functional magnetic resonance imaging studies show increased blood oxygen level–dependent responses in many cortical and limbic brain sites of human mothers as they attended to

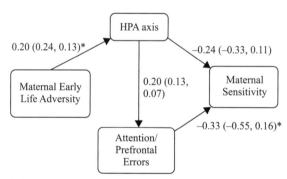

FIGURE 6.1 *Path diagram of model relationships between maternal early life adversity, hypothalamic–pituitary–adrenal (HPA) axis and lateral prefrontal cortex (LPFC) function (measured by cortisol area under the curve and CANTAB extra-dimensional [ED] shifting score, respectively), and maternal sensitivity toward infant during a 30-minute video-recorded interaction at 3 to 5 months postpartum. Numbers represent standardized coefficients (unstandardized coefficients and standard errors, respectively, in brackets). * p < .05. Modified from Gonzalez, A., Jenkins, J. M., Steiner, M., & Fleming, A. S. (in press). Maternal early life experiences and parenting: The mediating role of cortisol and executive function. Journal of the American Academy of Child and Adolescent Psychiatry.*

vocalizations (Lorberbaum et al., 2002; Sander, Frome, & Scheich, 2007; Seifritz et al., 2003), pictures (Barrett et al.,2011; Bartels & Zeki, 2004; Leibenluft, Gobbini, Harrison, & Haxby, 2004; Nitschke et al., 2004; Strathearn, Li, Fonagy, & Montague, 2008), or videos (Noriuchi, Kikuchi, & Senoo, 2008; Ranote et al., 2004) of their own or other infants. Activated regions are involved in behavioral changes related to the mother's affect (amygdala, prefrontal cortex), inhibition (ventral medial hypothalamus, bed nucleus of the stria terminalis), stimulus salience (mesocorticolimbic structures), and attention and memory (medial prefrontal cortex, nucleus accumbens [NAC]; see Figure 6.2). Other aspects of mothering involved in lactation and in stress responsiveness are also integrated into this system (supraoptic nucleus, paraventricular nucleus, hippocampus, amygdala).

NEUROANATOMY OF DOPAMINE

Although a number of neurotransmitter systems contribute to mothering, dopamine (DA) has received the most attention, and with the most payoff. Mothering is one of many motivated behaviors that depend on activation of the DA system to give meaning and salience to stimuli. For example, DA is activated in the male brain of many species when they are exposed to receptive females, palatable food, and rewarding drugs (see Berridge & Robinson, 1998). The DA hypothesis of motivation is well supported and provides a viable framework to understand both the mothering motivation and organization of mothering behavior.

Three distinct pathways make up the DA neurotransmitter system (see Berridge & Robinson, 1998; Robbins & Everitt, 1992; Salamone, 1992). The nigrostriatal pathway originates in neurons within the substantia nigra of the midbrain, and its

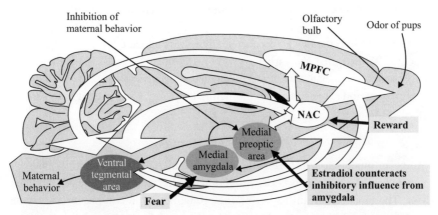

FIGURE 6.2 *Neuroanatomy of maternal behavior in the rat. Many of these brain regions are prolactin, estrogen, and oxytocin receptor–containing sites. White projections indicate recruitment of dopaminergic mechanisms important for maternal responsiveness. MPFC = medial prefrontal cortex; NAC = nucleus accumbens. Modified from Carlson, N. R. (2004). Physiology of behavior. New York, NY: Allyn and Bacon.*

axons project into the striatum region of the forebrain, in dorsal regions known as the caudate and putamen. This pathway is involved primarily in motor control. The second major DA pathway originates in the midbrain VTA. These cells synthesize DA and project primarily to the ventral part of the striatum or NAC, as well as in the amygdala and the hippocampus. This system is known as the mesolimbic DA system and has traditionally been associated with stimulus salience, behavioral activation, and "reward" prediction error. The third system, called the mesocortical system, projects from the midbrain into the forebrain and up to the frontal cortex. This system is particularly prominent in humans and is involved in "executive functions," including attention, planning, and working memory.

DOPAMINE AND MOTHERING

The mesolimbic and mesocortical DA systems are strongly implicated in the regulation of motivated and species-specific behaviors (see Berridge & Robinson, 1998) that in some cases are hormonally dependent. There is good evidence that activation of the mesolimbic DA system is necessary for the occurrence of maternal behavior (see Numan & Insel, 2003). For example, maternal retrieval behavior in mothers is disrupted when animals are infused with a DA receptor antagonist (D1 and/or D2) into the NAC (Keer & Stern, 1999; Li & Fleming, 2003a, 2003b; Lonstein et al., 2003; Numan et al., 2005) and enhanced when infused with a DA receptor agonist (D1; Numan, 2007; Numan et al., 2005). Maternal behavior is also blocked when the input from the VTA is altered by VTA electrolytic lesions (Numan & Smith, 1984) or with infusion into this region of the DA neurotoxin 6-hydroxydopamine (Hansen, Harthon, Wallin, Lofberg, & Svensson, 1991a, 1991b). Work by Hansen, Bergvall, and Nyiredi (1993) followed by Champagne et al. (2004) shows there is a release of DA into the NAC of mother rats when they engaged in maternal behavior.

Our entry into the DA arena started a few years ago and has proven quite productive. We extended the earlier work by exploring DA release and the role of (1) hormones associated with late pregnancy and parturition, (2) prior maternal experiences, and (3) variations in mothering behavior. These findings are summarized in Figure 6.3.

Dopamine and Hormones

We begin our discussion here with a series of microdialysis rat studies that illuminated a DA profile associated with mothering hormones, experience, and behavior. The most significant aspect of the profile is that in contrast to the cycling rat (Figure 6.4, black) postpartum females (Figure 6.4, red) have suppressed basal DA levels, which increase significantly above basal concentrations for the duration of pup availability (also see Afonso, King, Chatterjee, & Fleming, 2009). Like the intact postpartum mother, ovariectomized rats treated with progesterone and estradiol (to induce maternal rapid responsiveness to foster pups) display a reduced

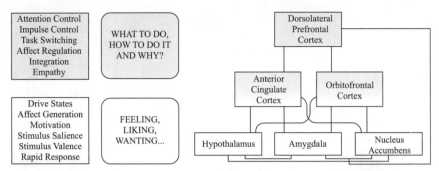

FIGURE 6.3 *Neuroanatomy of decision making and motivation in humans. Gray shading indicates attentional mechanisms and white shading indicates motivational mechanisms needed for mothering infants. Modified from Barrett, J., & Fleming, A. S. (in press). All mothers are not created equal: Neural and psychobiological perspectives on mothering and the importance of individual differences. Journal of Child Psychology and Psychiatry.*

basal DA level and an increased pup-evoked DA response even in the absence of any prior pup experience (Figure 6.4, pink). Furthermore, the lower the basal DA assessment is prior to pup exposure, the more rapidly this pup-naïve rat becomes maternal under the influence of hormones (Afonso et al., 2009). Thus, hormones that facilitate maternal responsiveness in the absence of previous maternal experience have the same effects on NAC DAdopamine functioning as in the intact postpartum experienced female, and this hormone-induced basal suppression is related to heightened maternal responsiveness.

Next, cycling females that have had prior maternal experience after an earlier pregnancy do not show a reduced baseline DA, but they do show an acute, but not sustained, rise in DA with presentation of pups (Figure 6.4, blue; also see Afonso, Grella, Chatterjee, & Fleming, 2008). This demonstrates that the DA response to pups is not dependent on a reduced baseline, although these responses are different from that of the hormonally primed female rat.

Prior experience with pups affects the DA response to subsequent pup exposure. In fact, there are additive effects of maternal experiences. Multiparous females reinduced to be maternal through continuous exposure to pups immediately prior to testing show greater pup-evoked DA responses than multiparous females with no recent pup exposure or virgin pup-sensitized females (see Afonso et al., 2008). All three experienced groups show greater pup-induced DA responses compared to virgin pup-naïve females (Afonso et al., 2008).

In summary, our studies suggest that the hormonally induced reduction of basal DA transmission is related to the rapid expression of maternal behavior in the postpartum rat. The females that demonstrate robust DA responses to pups also have a robust suppression in basal DA release (Figure 6.4). It can be argued that basal DA suppression aids the rapid expression of maternal behavior through a reduction in the DA noise in the absence of other stimuli. In this way, it might serve as

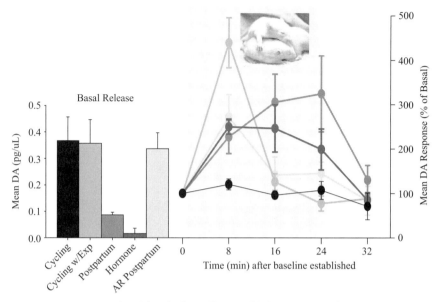

FIGURE 6.4 *Dopamine (DA) basal release (bar graph) data represent the average DA concentration of three samples prior to the 24-minute period of pup stimuli exposure (shaded area on x-axis). Line graph data represent mean (+ SEM) percent of basal DA release during and after removal of pup stimuli. Postpartum females sustain increased DA responses for the duration of pup stimuli. Cycling females, even after pup experience (Exp) in the home cage, have increased responses only to the initial presentation of pup stimuli. Artificially reared (AR) postpartum rats show a blunted DA response to pup stimuli that was reflected in their maternal responses to pups.*

a mechanism for sharpening the DA signal in response to pup stimuli and enhance the initial pup experience such that saliency develops. Impairments to this basal suppression (e.g., by manipulations of the early environment; see later) would be expected to result in subsequent DA signal reduction accompanied by reduced pup saliency, culminating in impaired mother–pup interaction.

Dopamine and Stimulus Specificity

Next we asked: Does this signal-to-noise mechanism result in sharpened DA signals to all stimuli, or only to pup stimuli, in postpartum females? In subsequent studies, we compared female rats' behavioral and DA profiles when exposed to (1) pups and (2) palatable food (sweet cereal). Both nulliparous and parous females showed increased DA responses when ingesting the sweet treat. However, only postpartum females showed pup-evoked DA responses greater than the food-evoked DA responses—a finding not observed in cycling females even after pup experience. The enhanced DA responsiveness to pups in postpartum females is sustained even when the dams are exposed to pups in a perforated box at a distance and cannot interact with them (see Figure 6.5). This suggests a conditioned DA response to pup-associated cues that is related to the postpartum experience. However, we tested ovariectomized pup-naïve hormone-treated rats, and this DA response to boxed pups is like that in the postpartum rat (Afonso, Shams, Jin, & Fleming, 2012), suggesting that the hormonally induced suppression of basal DA provides a very important mechanism for the rapid response to pups.

In summary, our microdialysis work suggests that with suppressed basal DA, pups take on robust saliency to hormonally primed postpartum females. This is reflected in significantly increased pup-evoked DA release, even in the absence of actual interactions with the pups.

DOPAMINE, EARLY EXPERIENCE, AND MATERNAL RESPONSIVENESS

Finally, we were interested in how early maternal deprivation designed as a model of maternal neglect would affect later variations in mothering and DA responsiveness. We raised female rat pups without their mothers and siblings through artificial rearing. This procedure involves raising pups in an artificial brooder, without mother and siblings but with regulated access to food and warmth. Artificially reared (AR) animals were also stroked to facilitate the urinary/defecation process. Like mother-reared animals, AR adults become pregnant, give birth, and engage in maternal behavior (Gonzalez et al., 2001). However, the quality of their maternal behavior is disrupted. In comparison to mother-reared animals, AR animals show less licking, grooming, and crouching over their pups. Artificially reared animals

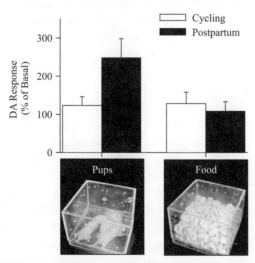

FIGURE 6.5 *Mean dopamine (DA) response (% of basal release) of postpartum and cycling female rats when presented with boxed (restricted) pup (left) and food (right) stimuli. Postpartum females display an increased DA response when presented with restricted access to pup stimuli in comparison to cycling females and restricted access to food stimuli. p < .05 parity differences.*

given additional somatosensory stimulation during the first 20 days of life are behaviorally more similar to mother-reared animals (Gonzalez et al., 2001; Lovic & Fleming, 2004; Melo et al., 2006). This indicates that the detrimental effects on maternal behavior can be partially reversed in the artificial group by additional stimulation. Artificially reared rats also showed impairment to the hormonally induced suppression of basal DA and a reduction in the DA response to pups when compared with the mother-reared rats (Figure 6.4, green; Afonso, King, Novakov, & Fleming, 2011).

When tested on a pup versus food preference test, maternally reared postpartum females ignore the food and only engage in pup-related behaviors (Afonso et al., 2009). Cycling females, regardless of pup experience, ignore pups and only engage in food consumption. ARrtificially reared postpartum females engage in both behaviors when pups and food are made available simultaneously (Afonso et al., 2011). Thus, AR mothers show impairment to ongoing maternal behavior that is reflected in the ability of unrelated stimuli to greatly distract the AR rat. They also have an altered DA baseline and an impaired pup-evoked DA response.

Dopamine Genetics in the Regulation of Human Mothering

DOPAMINE GENE POLYMORPHISMS AND MATERNAL RESPONSIVENESS

We do not possess the technology at present to noninvasively measure neurotransmitter release during ongoing behavior in humans. However, with new imaging and genetic techniques, we can begin to understand possible brain mechanisms involved in human mothering. Studies in humans that employ functional magnetic resonance imaging link the mesocorticolimbic DA system with parenting. These studies suggest that activity along DA pathways, including the NAC, may be associated with individual differences in human maternal responsivity to infant-related stimuli (Barrett et al, 2011). Similarly, individual genetic markers in DA-related genes predict differences in maternal behavior related to the regulation of maternal mood, attention, and reward. Therefore, an examination of genetic factors associated with dopaminergic function might be useful in predicting differences in human maternal behavior. This in itself is a broad endeavor. Numerous genetic components regulate DA transmission, at the level of DA synthesis, release, binding, and clearance. Theoretically, polymorphic variation in any of these DA-regulating genes could influence maternal behavior directly or indirectly (e.g., through influences on maternal mood, attention, and reward processing). Furthermore, experiential or environmental factors such as recent stress or early life adversity are bound to moderate the influence of these genetic factors.

Before we proceed, we would like to offer a cautionary note. As will become evident in the following paragraphs, different dopamine genes relate differently to measures of mothering—if related at all, making interpretation sometimes challenging. Moreover, a statistically significant association between a gene polymorphism and a behavioral outcome does not reveal anything about the expression levels of that gene, which can differ with experience and brain region. Indeed, we do not yet understand the relation between genetic sequence and mechanism (as in epigenesis) for most complex phenotypes in both humans and nonhuman animals. However, we have a beginning.

The genetic analysis of mothering has been most fruitful in the studies of human mothering. There is direct evidence of an association between polymorphic variation in human DA genes and individual differences in maternal behavior. Van Ijzendoorn, Bakermans-Kranenburg, and Mesman (2008) report that polymorphisms in two DA-related genes, the DRD4 (a DA receptor gene) and catechol-O-methyl transferase (COMT, encoding for an enzyme that degrades DA) genes, in mothers interact to predict mothers' maternal sensitivity at 23 months postpartum, an interaction that is moderated by the levels of current stress (daily hassles) experienced by the mothers. Human DRD4 receptors are found predominantly in the prefrontal cortex (reviewed in Oak, Oldenhof, & Van Tol, 2000), which is involved in the regulation and response to cognitive demands, including attention. Genetic variation in DRD4 has been consistently associated with both childhood and adult attention deficit disorder (Monuteaux et al., 2008; Thapar, O'Donovan, & Owen, 2005), but in fact, it also influences attentional processes in healthy children (Schmidt, Fox, Perez-Edgar, Hu, & Hamer, 2001) and adults (Wilkość et al., 2010). The COMT gene in turn has been associated with differences in cognitive function and prefrontal activation (e.g., Caldu et al., 2007). There appears to be some overlap between maternal sensitivity—mothers' ability to perceive and respond to children's cues promptly and appropriately—and executive function (Gonzalez et al., personal communication, outlined later), and this could potentially explain the findings by van IJzendoorn et al. (2008). However, Mill-Koonce et al. (2007) failed to find an association between maternal genotype at a genetic marker close to DRD2 (another DA receptor) and maternal sensitivity. Finally, a recent study showed that polymorphic variation at the DA transporter (DAT1) gene in mothers was associated with more negative maternal behaviors and commands in response to their 5-year-old children during a structured mother–child interaction task (Lee et al., 2010).

In our own research, we are exploring associations between DA polymorphisms, environment, and mothering in new mothers, as part of a larger study on maternal adversity, vulnerability, and neurodevelopment (MAVAN). The entire study follows a longitudinal sample of over 500 women from Hamilton, Ontario, and Montreal, Quebec, recruited at pregnancy and followed until at least 6 years postpartum. This report describes analyses on 250 of these women recruited from our Hamilton cohort. We selected several polymorphisms on candidate genes in the DA family, chosen because these genes are important for mothering in rats (e.g., DRD1, DRD2) or are related to mothering and factors affecting mothering in humans (DRD3, DRD4, DAT1, COMT). As part of the protocol, at 6 months postpartum, mothers filled out Likert-scale questionnaires to assess their maternal feelings and attitudes. Mothers also interacted with their infants for 30 minutes on camera, and we later coded the videotaped interactions for frequency and duration of many maternal and infant behaviors, including different kinds of touching, vocalizing to the baby, looking at and away from the baby, smiling at the baby, playing with the baby, and infant smiles, coos, cries, arm and feet movements, and so on. As well, videotapes were coded for maternal sensitivity using the Ainsworth scale (Ainsworth, Blehar, Waters, & Wall, 1978) to assess the level of maternal contingent and appropriate responsiveness, among other things.

We found that a single nucleotide polymorphism on the DRD1 receptor predicted significant differences in both the frequency and duration of time with which mothers looked away from their infants during the recorded interaction at 6 months (Figure 6.5A). Mothers possessing the G allele of the DRD1 gene (polymorphic region rs4325) looked away from their babies less than did mothers without this allele. Moreover, mothers who looked away less tended to be more sensitive, both in this cohort and in a number of our previous datasets. Additionally, mothers who looked away less also tended to be more attentive as assessed by the Cambridge Neuropsychological Test Battery (CANTAB) (A. Gonzalez, personal communication), suggesting a potential relation to attentional mechanisms.

Finally, when mothers who had had prior children were compared with first-time mothers on the genetic association between DRD1 and looking away, we found that inexperienced mothers spent less time looking away from their babies than experienced mothers. Furthermore, in the experienced mothers the genetic effect appears to be important in predicting the duration of looking away.

DOPAMINE GENES AND MATERNAL MOOD

As previously described, depressed mothers exhibit differences in maternal behaviors compared with nondepressed mothers. These include increased negativity and reduced contingency toward the infant. To our knowledge, studies of associations between genetic polymorphisms and postpartum depression do not exist. However, there is substantial literature implicating DA dysregulation in the etiology of major depression. For example, there is decreased DA turnover in depressed patients (reviewed in Cannon et al., 2009). A positron emission tomography study showed that depressed patients exhibit reduced binding potential at the DRD1 receptor in the striatum, which includes the NAC (Cannon et al., 2009). Given that postpartum depression is clinically very similar to major depression and the underlying DA dysregulations are likely to be the same, the literature on the dopaminergic involvement in major depression might inform the maternal literature.

Evidence from mice knockouts suggests that DA receptors 1, 2, and 3 (DRD1, DRD2, and DRD3) are involved in the DA-regulated reward and emotional processing (reviewed in Cannon et al., 2009). Individual variation in reward and emotional processing might be useful in predicting the development of affective disorders and may predict natural variation in the extent to which mothers find their own infants to be salient and rewarding. In fact, the animal literature has shown that DA dysregulations influence the salience of offspring-related cues (see section on "Dopamine and Mothering" earlier). In humans, genetic association studies tend to focus on genetic predictors of psychopathology in the reward system. Much of the DA literature has attempted to relate polymorphisms in the DA system genes to impulsivity, addiction, and gambling. In a study of genetic variation on nonpathological reward system function, Dreher, Kohn, Kolachana, Weinberger, and Berman (2009) found that polymorphisms in two DA-system genes, DAT1 and COMT, were associated with interindividual differences in activation of brain regions involved in reward processing and anticipation, including the ventral striatum and prefrontal cortex.

In our studies, we wanted to assess (1) whether differences in maternal affect relate to maternal outcomes involving the rewarding value of the infant to the mother and (2) the extent DA-related genetic differences may influence these effects of mood on mothering. We assessed mothers' depressive symptoms at 6 months through the Edinburgh Postpartum Depression Scale (EPDS; Cox, Holden, & Sagovsky, 1987). Because we did not measure directly the rewarding value of infants to the mothers, we used the Childbearing Attitudes Questionnaire (CAQ; Ruble et al., 1990). This large questionnaire assesses maternal attitudes along 18 factors relating to social relationships, self-concept, parenting, and the infant. Although the EPDS score was strongly negatively correlated with a number of the social relationships and self-concept factors, we chose to focus on the following items, as we thought they were most related to the rewarding value of infants: "feelings about children," "feelings about caretaking," and "feelings of perceived attachment to the infant."

Mothers who scored as more depressed on the EPDS also expressed more negative attitudes about caretaking, infant-related feelings, and perceived attachment. Moreover, there was a significant effect of DRD4 genotype on "perceived attachment" and a significant gene–environment interaction between this genotype and the EPDS on all three components. Mothers who had a copy of the seven-repeat allele at the exon III repeat polymorphism on DRD4 and who also reported higher depressive symptoms on the EPDS at 6 months reported feeling significantly less attached to their infants, had more negative feelings about caretaking, and had more negative feelings about children in general. Strikingly, this relationship persisted even when we controlled for maternal early life experiences (see later). This suggests that although the DRD4 genotype does not predict differences across multiple dimensions of maternal attitudes by itself, it significantly moderates the effects of depressive symptoms on maternal attitudes. Furthermore, when we took parity into account, we found that the interaction between the EPDS and DRD4 genotype was highly significant for experienced mothers, whereas it disappeared for first-time mothers, where the most important predictor in the regression was the EPDS depression score alone.

DOPAMINE GENES, EARLY EXPERIENCES, AND MOTHERING: GENES × ENVIRONMENT INTERACTIONS

As with all living organisms, humans are shaped by the environments in which they develop. Environmental and contextual variables have numerous influences on the developing organism, and they act to shape neurotransmitter pathways that later influence adult behaviors. Moreover, the dopaminergic system is open to a number of influences from ongoing experiences, including experiences with children and caregiving. For these reasons, we wanted to explore the moderating effects of experience and environment on the DA genetic associations with mothering. There is some evidence of gene–environment moderation (interaction) in humans. For instance, DAT1 interacts with psychosocial adversity to affect attentional outcomes in adolescents (Laucht et al., 2007). In children, DRD2 polymorphisms have also been shown to interact with alcoholism in the childhood home and with present stress, to predict differences in personality, including extroversion and neuroticism (reviewed in Rutter, Moffit, & Caspi, 2006). These personality differences, evident in childhood, may also relate to persisting differences in adulthood temperament, behavior, and mothering.

In our studies, we found that variation along DRD1 (which we know predicts differences in the frequency that mothers look away from their infants during a 20-minute interaction; Figure 6.6) is also moderated by women's early experiences with their own parents, especially their experiences of family instability, early abuse, or neglect. Mothers who have the GG genotype at one DRD1 polymorphic region (rs686) looked away from their infants significantly more often than mothers of alternate genotypes, but only if they also reported having experienced higher levels of early life adversity (Figure 6.6). Parity, or the prior experience with one's own children, had only a slight effect on this relationship. In addition to early experiences, we also found that recent experiences could moderate the influences of DA polymorphisms on maternal outcomes. In fact, we see that both recent "chronic stress" and current "life events" significantly moderate the effects of DRD1 genotype on maternal looking away. Mothers with the GG genotype at the locus are more susceptible to environmental moderation, and they look away far more than mothers with the other genotypes if they have experienced a high level of early adversity or current stress (Figure 6.6A, B). This gene–environment interaction is not present when we tested other maternal outcomes, including maternal sensitivity to the infant, maternal vocalizations, and a number of maternal attitudes about parenting the infant, including perceived attachment to the infant. Furthermore, parity did not affect the relationship between DA genotype and recent stress. There is no reason why early and recent experiences do not act in chorus, additively or synergistically. Given a greater sample size, we may be able to test these higher order interactions with statistical rigor.

These human genetic association studies suggest that there are complex interactions between genetics, environment (both early and more recent experiences, which

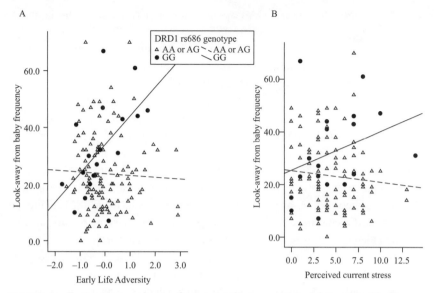

FIGURE 6.6 *Environment moderates the genetic effects on maternal frequency of looking away from the infant. (A) Mothers with the GG genotype on the DRD1 (rs686) marker look away more frequently from their infants when they experience higher levels of early adversity. (B) Mothers with the GG genotype of the DRD1 (rs686) marker look away more frequently from their infants when they report having greater current stress in their lives.*

may be infant related or not), and dimensions of mothering. Future studies can better elucidate these by studying the underlying systems that may be interrelated with each of these mothering dimensions.

Summary and Conclusions

Over the past 10 years, we have developed a much clearer picture of the parturitional changes in the maternal brain that alter a female's responsiveness to newborn young. No single hormone, brain site, or neurotransmitter accomplishes this motivational shift on its own. Instead, a suite of hormones affect multiple neuropeptides and neurotransmitters to alter the brain's responsivity to infants and their cues. In this chapter, we focus on one of these mediators, the DA system. New research indicates that in rats, dramatic hormonal fluctuations occurring with parturition have dramatic effects on neurotransmission of DA, which in turn is associated with heightened responsiveness to the young. This heightened responsiveness is also associated with changes in the mother's emotionality, attention, cognition and the valence she attaches to stimuli in her environment. In the rat, some of these behavioral changes are also dopaminergically mediated. Whether a similar hormonally induced DA responsiveness underlies human mothering we do not know.

The development of larger brains in humans has, to some extent, released decision making from hormonal determinants. Mother–infant bonding is neither restricted by the hormones of pregnancy nor limited to the postpartum period. The evolutionary relevance of maternal behavior has ensured a number of stereotyped physiological and behavioral systems in mothers across mammalian species. Nonetheless, experiences in early life and adulthood play a role in the intensity and quality of maternal behavior in all species that have been studied, leading to vast individual variation, both in the "simple" laboratory rat model and the "complex" human. Although part of the variation is a result of individual life experiences, part of it is unexplained. The unexplained portion of the variance in maternal behavior is just beginning to be explored. For instance, there may be a genetic basis for some of this maternal variance. Genetic variants in diverse genes may affect the expression and signaling of proteins and neuropeptides important to mothering. As we have described in this chapter, polymorphisms in DA genes are proving important predictors, but even they are limited. The future of maternal research will necessarily include a complex analysis of the dynamic regulation of mothering. Early environmental experiences (both prenatal and postnatal), genetics, epigenetics, recent experiences, and contextual and stochastic factors will all likely have a place in this future.

References

Afonso, V. M., Grella, S. L., Chatterjee, D., & Fleming, A. S. (2008). Previous maternal experience affects accumbal dopaminergic responses to pup-stimuli. *Brain Research, 1198*, 115–123.

Afonso, V. M., King, S. M., Chatterjee, D., & Fleming, A. S. (2009). Hormones that increase maternal responsiveness affect accumbal dopaminergic responses to pup- and food-stimuli in the female rat. *Hormones and Behavior, 56*, 11–23.

Afonso, V. M., King, S. M., Novakov, M., & Fleming, A. S. (2011). The effects of complete maternal deprivation on hormonally-induced dopaminergic responses to pup-stimuli. *Hormones and Behavior, 60*, 632–643.

Afonso, V. M., Shams, W. M., Jin, D., & Fleming, A. S. (2012). Distal pup cues evoke DA responses in hormonally-primed rats in the absence of pup-experience or ongoing maternal behavior. Manuscript submitted for publication.

Ainsworth, M. D. S., Blehar, M. C., Waters, E., & Wall, S. (1978). *Patterns of attachment: A psychological study of the strange situation.* Hillsdale, NJ: Lawrence Erlbaum.

Barrett, J., & Fleming, A. S. (2011). Annual Research Review: All mothers are not created equal: neural and psychobiological perspectives on mothering and the importance of individual differences. *Journal of Child Psychology and Psychiatry, 52*, 368–397.

Barrett, J., Wonch, K. E., Gonzalez, A., Ali, N., Steiner, M., Hall, G. B., & Fleming, A. S. (2011). Maternal affect and quality of parenting experiences are related to amygdala response to infant faces. *Social Neuroscience*, 37–41.

Bartels, A., & Zeki, S. (2004). The neural correlates of maternal and romantic love. *Neuroimage, 21*, 1155–1166.

Berridge, K. C., & Robinson, T. E. (1998). What is the role of dopamine in reward: Hedonic impact, reward learning, or incentive salience. *Brain Research Reviews, 28*(3), 309–369.

Bridges, R. S. (Ed.). (2008). *Neurobiology of the parental brain*. San Diego, CA: Academic Press.

Caldu, X., Vandrell, P., Bartrés-Faz, D., Clemente, I., Bargalló, N., Clemente, I., ... Junque, C. (2007). Impact of the COMT Val108/158Met and DAT genotypes on prefrontal function in healthy subjects. *NeuroImage, 37*, 1437–1444.

Cameron, N. M., Champagne, F. A., Parent, C., Fish, E. W., Osaki-Kuroda, K., & Meaney, M. J. (2005). The programming of individual differences in defensive responses and reproductive strategies in the rat through variations in maternal care. *Neuroscience and Biobehavioral Reviews, 29*, 843–865.

Cameron, N. M., Shahrokh, D., Del Corpo, A., Dhir, S. K., Szyf, M., Champagne, F. A., & Meaney, M. J. (2008). Epigenetic programming of phenotypic variations in reproductive strategies in the rat through maternal care. *Journal of Neuroendocrinology, 20*, 795–801.

Cannon, D. M., Klaver, J. M., Peck, S. A., Rallis-Voak, D., Erickson, K., & Drevets, W, C. (2009). Dopamine type-1 receptor binding in major depressive disorder assessed using positron emission tomography and [11C]NNC-112. *Neuropsychopharmacology, 34*, 1277–1287.

Carter, C. S., Ahnert, L., Grossman, K. E., Hrdy, S. B., Lamb, M. E., Porges, S. W., & Sachser, N. (2005). *Attachment and bonding: A new synthesis.* Dahlem Workshop Report 92. Cambridge, MA: MIT Press.

Champagne, F. A., Chretien, P., Stevenson, C. W., Zhang, T. Y., Gratton, A., & Meaney, M. (2004). Variations in nucleus accumbens dopamine associated with individual differences in maternal behavior in the rat. *Journal of Neuroscience, 24*, 4113–4123.

Chico, E., Gonzalez, A., Ali, N., Steiner, M., & Fleming, A. S. (in preparation). Early experience is related to executive function and mothering: Challenges faced by teenage mothers.

Corter, C., & Fleming, A. S. (2002). Psychobiology of maternal behavior in human beings. In M. Bornstein (Ed.), Handbook of parenting (2nd ed., Vol. 2, pp. 141–181). Hillsdale, NJ: L. Erlbaum Associates.

Cox, J. L., Holden, J. M., & Sagovsky, R. (1987). Detection of postnatal depression: Development of the 10-item Edinburgh Postnatal Depression Scale. *British Journal of Psychiatry, 150*, 782–786.

Cox, J. L., Murray, D., & Chapman, G. (1993). A controlled study of the onset, duration and prevalence of postnatal depression. *British Journal of Psychiatry, 163*, 27–31.

Dreher, J-C., Kohn, P., Kolachana, B., Weinberger, D. R., & Berman, K. F. (2009). Variation in dopamine genes influences responsivity of the human reward system. *Proceedings of the National Academy of Sciences U S A, 106*, 617–622.

Farrell, W. J., & Alberts, J. R. (2002). Maternal responsiveness to infant Norway rat (Rattus norvegicus) ultrasonic vocalizations during the maternal behavior cycle and after steroid and experiential induction regimens. *Journal of Comparative Psychology, 116*(3), 286–296.

Field, T., Healy, B. T., Goldstein, S., & Guthertz, M. (1990). Behavior-state matching and synchrony in mother-infant interactions of nondepressed versus depressed dyads. *Developmental Psychology, 26*(1), 7–14.

Fleming, A. S., Cheung, U., Myhal, N., & Kessler, Z. (1989). Effects of maternal hormones on 'timidity' and attraction to pup-related odors in female rats. *Physiology and Behavior, 46*, 449–453.

Fleming, A. S., Corter, C., Franks, P., Surbey, M., Schneider, B., & Steiner, M. (1993). Postpartum factors related to mother's attraction to newborn infant odors. *Developmental Psychobiology, 26*(2), 115–132.

Fleming, A. S., Corter, C., Surbey, M., Franks, P., & Steiner, M. (1995). Postpartum factors related to mother's recognition of newborn infant odors. *Journal of Reproductive and Infant Psychology, 13*, 197–210.

Fleming, A. S., & Li, M. (2002). Psychobiology of maternal behavior and its early determinants in nonhuman animals. In M. H. Bornstein (Ed.), *Handbook of parenting: Biology and ecology of parenting* (Vol. 2, pp. 141–182). Hillsdale, NJ: Lawrence Erlbaum Associates.

Fleming, A. S., & Luebke, C. (1981). Timidity prevents the virgin female rat from being a good mother: Emotionality differences between nulliparous and parturient females. *Physiology and Behavior, 27*(5), 863–868.

Fleming, A. S., & Rosenblatt, J. S. (1974a). Maternal behavior in the virgin and lactating rat. *Journal of Comparative and Physiological Psychology, 86*, 957–972.

Fleming, A. S., & Rosenblatt, J. S. (1974b). Olfactory regulation of maternal behavior in rats. I. Effects of olfactory bulb removal in experienced and inexperienced lactating and cycling females. *Journal of Comparative and Physiological Psychology, 86*, 221–232.

Fleming, A. S., & Rosenblatt, J. S. (1974c). Olfactory regulation of maternal behavior in rats. II. Effects of peripherally induced anosmia and lesions of the lateral olfactory tract in pup-induced virgins. *Journal of Comparative and Physiological Psychology, 86*, 233–246.

Fleming, A. S., Ruble, D. N., Flett, G. L., & Shaul, D. L. (1988). Postpartum adjustment in first-time mothers: Relations between mood, maternal attitudes, and mother-infant interactions. *Developmental Psychology, 24*(1), 71–81.

Fleming, A. S., Ruble, D., Krieger, H., & Wong, P. Y. (1997). Hormonal and experiential correlates of maternal responsiveness during the pregnancy and the puerperium in human mothers. *Hormones and Behavior, 31*, 145–158.

Fleming, A. S., Steiner, M., & Corter, C. (1997). Cortisol, hedonics, and maternal responsiveness in human mothers. *Hormones and Behavior, 32*, 85–98.

Fleming, A. S., Vaccarino, F., & Luebke, C. (1980). Amygdaloid inhibition of maternal behavior in the nulliparous female rat. *Physiology and Behavior, 25*, 731–743.

Fleming, A. S., Vaccarino, F., Tambosso, L., & Chee, P. (1979). Vomeronasal and olfactory system modulation of maternal behavior in the rat. *Science, 203*, 372–374.

Gonzalez, A., Jenkins, J. M., Steiner, M., & Fleming, A. S. (2009). The relation between early life adversity, cortisol awakening response and diurnal salivary cortisol levels in postpartum women. *Psychoneuroendocrinology, 34*(1), 76–86.

Gonzalez, A., Jenkins, J. M., Steiner, M., & Fleming, A. S. (in press). Maternal early life experiences and parenting: The mediating role of cortisol and executive function. *Journal of the American Academy of Child and Adolescent Psychiatry.*

Gonzalez, A., Lovic, V., Ward, G. R., Wainwright, P. E., & Fleming, A. S. (2001). Intergenerational effects of complete maternal deprivation and replacement stimulation on maternal behavior and emotionality in female rats. *Developmental Psychobiology, 38*, 11–32.

Gordon, I., Zagoory-Sharon, O., Leckman, J. F., & Feldman, R. (2010). Oxytocin and the development of parenting in humans. *Biological Psychiatry, 68*(4), 377–382.

Hansen, S., Bergvall, A. H., & Nyiredi, S. (1993). Interaction with pups enhances dopamine release in the ventral striatum of maternal rats: A microdialysis study. *Pharmacology Biochemistry and Behavior, 45*, 673–676.

Hansen, S., Harthon, C., Wallin, E., Lofberg, L., & Svensson, K. (1991a). The effects of 6-OH-DA-induced dopamine depletions in the ventral and dorsal striatum on maternal and sexual behavior in the female rat. *Pharmacology Biochemistry and Behavior, 39*, 71–77.

Hansen, S., Harthon, C., Wallin, E., Lofberg, L., & Svensson, K. (1991b). Mesotelencephalic dopamine system and reproductive behavior in the female rat: Effects of ventral tegmental 6-hydroxydopamine lesions on maternal and sexual responsiveness. *Behavioral Neuroscience, 105*, 588–598.

Herrera, E., Reissland, N., & Shepherd, J. (2004). Maternal touch and maternal child-directed speech: Effects of depressed mood in the postnatal period. *Journal of Affective Disorders, 81*, 29–39.

Hrdy, S. B. (1999). *Mother Nature: A history of mothers, infants and natural selection.* New York, NY: Pantheon.

Hrdy, S. B. (2009). *Mothers and others: The evolutionary origins of mutual understanding.* Cambridge, MA: Harvard University Press.

Keer, S. E., & Stern, J. M. (1999). Dopamine receptor blockade in the nucleus accumbens inhibits maternal retrieval and licking, but enhances nursing behavior in lactating rats. *Physiology and Behavior, 67*, 659–669.

Keller, H. (2002). Development as the interface between biology and culture: A conceptualization of early ontogenic experiences. In H. Keller, Y. H. Poortinga, & A. Schölmerich (Eds.), *Between culture and biology* (pp. 215–240). Cambridge: Cambridge University Press.

Laucht, M., Skowronek, M. H., Becker, K., Schmidt, M. H., Esser, G., Schulze, T. G., & Rietschel, M. (2007). Interacting effects of the dopamine transporter gene and psychosocial adversity on attention-deficit/hyperactivity disorder symptoms among 15-year-olds form a high-risk community sample. *Archives of General Psychiatry, 64*, 585–590.

Lee, A., Clancy, S., & Fleming, A. S. (2000). Mother rats bar-press for pups: Effects of lesions of the mpoa and limbic sites on maternal behavior and operant responding for pup-reinforcement. *Behavioural Brain Research, 100*(1–2), 15–31.

Lee, S. S., Chronis-Tuscano, A., Keenan, K., Pelham, W. E., Loney, J., Van Hulle, C. A., . . . Lahey, B. B. (2010). Association of maternal dopamine transporter genotype with negative parenting: Evidence for gene x environment interaction with child disruptive behavior. *Molecular Psychiatry, 15*, 548–558.

Leibenluft, E., Gobbini, M. I., Harrison, T., & Haxby, J. V. (2004). Mothers' neural activation in response to pictures of their children and other children. *Biological Psychiatry, 56*(4), 225–232.

Li, M., & Fleming, A. S. (2003a). Differential involvement of nucleus accumbens shell and core subregions in maternal memory in postpartum female rats. *Behavioral Neuroscience, 117*, 426–445.

Li, M., & Fleming, A. S. (2003b). The nucleus accumbens shell is critical for normal expression of pup-retrieval in postpartum female rats. *Behavioral Brain Research, 145*, 99–111.

Lonstein, J. S. (2005). Reduced anxiety in postpartum rats requires recent physical interactions with pups, but is independent of suckling and peripheral sources of hormones. *Hormones and Behavior, 47,* 241–255.

Lonstein, J. S. (2007). Regulation of anxiety during the postpartum period. *Frontiers in Neuroendocrinology, 28,* 115–141.

Lonstein, J. S., Dominguez, J. M., Putnamb, S. K., De Vries, G. J., & Hull, E. M. (2003). Intracellular preoptic and striatal monoamines in pregnant and lactating rats: Possible role in maternal behavior. *Brain Research, 970,* 149–158.

Lonstein, J. S., & Gammie, S. C. (2002). Sensory, hormonal, and neural control of maternal aggression in laboratory rodents. *Neuroscience and Biobehavioral Reviews, 26,* 869–888.

Lorberbaum, J. P., Newman, J. D., Horwitz, A. R., Dubno, J. R., Lydiard, R. B., Hamner, M. B.,...George, M. S. (2002). A role for thalamocingulate circuitry in human maternal behavior. *Biological Psychiatry, 51*(6), 431–445.

Lovejoy, M. C., Graczyk, P. A., O'Hare, E., & Neuman, G. (2000). Maternal depression and parenting behavior: A meta-analytic review. *Clinical Psychology Review, 20*(5), 561–592.

Lovic, V., & Fleming, A. S. (2004). Artificially reared female rats show reduced prepulse inhibition and deficits in the attentional set shifting task-reversal of effects with maternal-like licking stimulation. *Behavioral Brain Research, 148,* 209–219.

Lovic, V., Palombo, D. J., & Fleming, A. S. (2011). Impulsive rats are less maternal. *Developmental Psychobiology. 53(1),* 13–22.

Mattson, B. J., Williams, S., Rosenblatt, J. S., & Morrell, J. I. (2001). Comparison of two positive reinforcing stimuli: Pups and cocaine throughout the postpartum period. *Behavioral Neuroscience, 115,* 683–694.

Melo, A. I., Lovic, V., Gonzalez, A., Madden, M., Sinopoli, K., & Fleming, A. S. (2006). Maternal and littermate deprivation disrupts maternal behavior and social-learning of food preferences in adulthood: Tactile stimulation, nest odor, and social rearing prevent these effects. *Developmental Psychobiology, 48*(3), 209–219.

Milgrom, J., Westley, D. T., & Gemmill, A. W. (2004). The mediating role of maternal responsiveness in some longer term effects of postnatal depression on infant development. *Infant Behavior and Development, 27,* 443–454.

Mills-Koonce, W. R., Propper, C. B., Gariepy, J.-L., Blair, C., Garrett-Peters, P., & Cox, M. J. (2007). Bidirectional genetic and environmental influences on mother and child behavior: The family system as the unit of analyses. *Development and Psychopathology, 19,* 1073–1087.

Monuteaux, M. C., Seidman, L. J., Faraone, S. V., Makris, N., Spencer, T., Valera, E.,...Biederman, J. (2008). A preliminary study of dopamine D4 receptor genotype and structural brain alterations in adults with ADHD. *American Journal of Medical Genetics Part B (Neuropsychiatric Genetics), 147B,* 1436–1441.

Murray, L., Fiori-Cowley, A., Hooper, R., & Cooper, P. (1996). The impact of postnatal depression and associated adversity on early mother-infant interactions and later infant outcome. *Child Development, 67*(5), 2512–2526.

Nitschke, J. B., Nelson, E. E., Rusch, B. D., Fox, A. S., Oakes, T. R., & Davidson, R. J. (2004). Orbitofrontal cortex tracks positive mood in mothers viewing pictures of their newborn infants. *Neuroimage, 21,* 583–592.

Noriuchi, M., Kikuchi, Y., & Senoo, A. (2008). The functional neuroanatomy of maternal love: Mother's response to infant's attachment behaviors. *Biological Psychiatry, 63(4)*, 415–423.

Numan, M. (2007). Motivational systems and the neural circuitry of maternal behavior in the rat. *Developmental Psychobiology, 49*, 12–21.

Numan, M., Fleming, A. S., & Levy, F. (2006). Maternal behavior. In J. D. Neill (Ed.), *Knobil and Neill's physiology of reproduction* (pp. 1921–1993). San Diego, CA: Elsevier.

Numan, M., & Insel, T. R. (2003). *The neurobiology of parental behavior*. New York, NY: Springer.

Numan, M., Numan, M. J., Pliakou, N., Stolzenberg, D. S., Mullins, O. J., Murphy, J. M., ...Smith, C. D. (2005). The effects of D1 or D2 dopamine receptor antagonism in the medial preoptic area, ventral pallidum, or nucleus accumbens on the maternal retrieval response and other aspects of maternal behavior in rats. *Behavioral Neuroscience, 199*, 1588–1604.

Numan, M., & Smith, H. G. (1984). Maternal behavior in rats: Evidence for the involvement of preoptic projections to the ventral tegmental area. *Behavioral Neuroscience, 98*, 712–727.

Oak, J. N., Oldenhof, J., & Van Tol, H. H. M. (2000). The dopamine D4 receptor: One decade of research. *European Journal of Pharmacology, 405*, 303–327.

O'Hara, M. W., Zekoski, E. M., Phillips, L. H., & Wright, E. J. (1990). Controlled prospective study of postpartum mood disorders: Comparison of childbearing and nonchildbearing women. *Journal of Abnormal Psychology, 99*, 3–15.

Porter, R. H., Cernoch, J. M., & McLaughlin, F. J. (1983). Maternal recognition of neonates through olfactory cues. *Physiology and Behavior, 30*(1), 151–154.

Ranote, S., Elliott, R., Abel, K. M., Mitchell, R., Deakin, J. F., & Appleby, L. (2004). The neural basis of maternal responsiveness to infants: An fMRI study. *Neuroreport, 15*, 1825–1829.

Robbins, T. W., & Everitt, B. J. (1992). Functions of dopamine in the dorsal and ventral striatum. *Seminars in Neuroscience, 4*, 119–128.

Robbins, T. W., James, M., Owen, A. M., Sahakian, B. J., McInnes, L., & Rabbitt, P. M. A. (1994). Cambridge Neuropsychological Test Automated Battery (CANTAB): A factor analytic study of a large sample of normal elderly volunteers. *Dementia, 5*, 266–281.

Rosenblatt, J. S., & Lehrman, D. S. (1963). Maternal behavior in the laboratory rat. In H. L. Rheingold (Ed.), *Maternal behavior in mammals* (pp. 8–57). New York, NY: John Wiley & Sons.

Ruble, D. D., Brooks-Gunn, J., Fleming, A. S., Fitzmaurice, G., Stangor S., & Deutsch, F. (1990). Transition to motherhood and the self: Measurement, stability, and change. *Journal of Personal and Social Psychology, 58*, 450–463.

Rutter, M., Moffit, T. E., & Caspi, A. (2006). Gene-environment interplay and psychopathology: Multiple varieties but real effects. *Journal of Child Psychology and Psychiatry, 47*, 226–261.

Salamone, J. D. (1992). Complex motor and sensorimotor functions of striatal and accumbens dopamine: Involvement in instrumental behavior processes. *Psychopharmacology, 107*, 160–174.

Sander, K., Frome, Y., & Scheich, H. (2007). FMRI activations of amygdala, cingulate cortex, and auditory cortex by infant laughing and crying. *Human Brain Mapping, 28*, 1007–1022.

Schmidt, L. A., Fox, N. A., Perez-Edgar, K., Hu, S., & Hamer, D. H. (2001). Association of DRD4 with attention problems in normal childhood development. *Psychiatric Genetics, 11*, 25–29.

Seifritz, E., Esposito, F., Neuhoff, J. G., Lüthi, A., Mustovic, H., Dammann, G.,... Di Salle, F. (2003). Differential sex-independent amygdala response to infant crying and laughing in parents versus nonparents. *Biological Psychiatry, 54*(12), 1367–1375.

Shah, A., Oxley, G., Lovic, V., & Fleming, A. S. (2002). Effects of preweaning exposure to novel maternal odors on maternal responsiveness and selectivity in adulthood. *Developmental Psychobiology, 41*(3), 187–196.

Shahrokh, D. K., Zhang, T. Y., Diorio, J., Gratton, A., & Meaney, M. J. (2010). Oxytocin-dopamine interactions mediate variations in maternal behavior in the rat. *Endocrinology, 151*, 2276–2286.

Singer, J. J., MacGregor, A. J., Cherkas, L. F., & Spector, T. D. (2006). Genetic influences on cognitive function using the Cambridge Neuropsychological Test Automated Battery. *Intelligence, 34*, 421–428.

Stallings, J., Fleming, A. S., Corter, C., Worthman, C., & Steiner, M. (2001). The effects of infant cries and odors on sympathy, cortisol, and autonomic responses in new mothers and nonpostpartum women. *Parenting: Science and Practice, 1*(1 & 2), 71–100.

Strathearn, L., Li, J., Fonagy, P., & Montague, P. R. (2008). What's in a smile? Maternal brain responses to infant facial cues. *Pediatrics, 122*, 40–51.

Thapar, A., O'Donovan, M., & Owen, M. J. (2005). The genetics of attention deficit hyper-activity disorder. *Human Molecular Genetics, 14*(Spec No. 2), R275–R282.

Tronick, E., & Reck, C. (2009). Infants of depressed mothers. *Harvard Review of Psychiatry, 17*, 147–156.

Van IJzendoorn, M. H., Bakermans-Kranenburg, M. J., & Mesman, J. (2008). Dopamine system genes associated with parenting in the context of daily hassles. *Genes, Brain, and Behavior, 7*, 403–410.

Wiesner, B. P., & Sheard, N. M. (1933). *Maternal behaviour in the rat*. Edinburgh: Oliver & Boyd.

Wilkość, M., Hauser, J., Tomaszewska, M., Dmitrzak-Węglarz, M., Skibńiska, M., Szczepankiewicz, A., & Borkowska, A. (2010). Influence of dopaminergic and seroto-nergic genes on working memory in healthy subjects. *Acta Neurobioligiae Experimentalis, 70*, 86–94.

7

The Neurobiological Basis of Empathy and Its Development in the Context of Our Evolutionary Heritage

Eric E. Nelson

Introduction

As has been emphasized throughout this volume, dramatic differences in social structure have emerged in the short time between the current state and our species' evolutionary heritage (EH). This shift is evident not just in the infant–mother relationship but also throughout development. For example, in the modern industrial society much social contact occurs in structured environments such as school and extracurricular classes. Furthermore, increasingly social interaction with peers takes place with or even via electronic media such as computers, television, and video games. Such environments are quite different from the extended periods of free play with multiple generations of extended kin that likely characterized the social life of the hunter-gatherer small band (HGSB) societies that made up the majority of our species' evolutionary history (Konner, 2010; Pinker, 2002).

Thus, the brain networks that guide various aspects of social behavior, from affective responding to cognitive decision making, evolved in a very different context during the HGSB era. The consequences of this mismatch for both behavioral and brain development are unclear though clearly worthy of consideration. In this chapter, I will review the current understanding of the brain systems that mediate one specific aspect of social behavior—empathy—and speculate as to how this may be impacted by the contextual changes that have taken place in modern social structure.

Empathy is generally defined as an affective response in one individual that is triggered by the observed or imagined feeling state of another individual (Blair, 2005; Singer & Lamm, 2009). To distinguish empathy from similar emotions like sympathy or compassion, the importance that the feeling states be shared or isomorphic between observer and observed is often emphasized (Singer & Lamm, 2009). Empathy plays a fundamental role in human interaction and is at the heart of many facets of our social structure, from pair bonding to construction of legal rules for acceptable behavior. Empathic responses not only serve group social cohesiveness but also benefit the individual by facilitating social learning and effective dyadic interactions, such as parental care, and promoting group-level behavior, such as antipredator signals (Chen, Panksepp, & Lahvis, 2009; Preston & de Waal, 2002).

At a neurobiological level, empathy is a complex phenomenon that subsumes many subprocesses ranging from perception and emotion to higher level cognitive representation of alternate experiences in other individuals (i.e., theory of mind). From the neuroscience perspective, therefore, empathy is not a unitary phenomenon but rather a linguistic category that is a reflection of several core neurobiological networks often, though not necessarily, acting in synchrony (Blair, 2005; Derntl et al., 2009). Nor from a neuroscience perspective is empathy a uniquely human experience, as elements of empathy have been observed in other social animals. For example, distress signals from a conspecific are aversive for animals ranging from birds to mice to monkeys (Chen et al., 2009; Langford et al., 2006; Preston & de Waal, 2002), and animals will work and even put themselves in danger to avoid experiencing those signals.

Some of the subcomponents of empathy are evident at a very early age in humans. Human infants imitate facial expressions of others (Meltzoff & Decety, 2003) and display a distress response to the sound of other infants' cries (Sagi & Hoffman, 1976), and by the time of toddlerhood, children direct prosocial behaviors to peers that they perceive to be in distress (Zahn-Waxler, Radke-Yarrow, Wagner, & Chapman, 1992). However, other studies have shown that developmental changes in empathic responses continue to emerge through adolescence and into early adulthood (Burnett, Bird, Moll, Frith, & Blakemore, 2009; Dumontheil, Apperly, & Blakemore, 2010). Thus, like many complex social behaviors, although elemental components of empathy appear early in life, a fully mature empathic response does not coalesce until much later in development. Furthermore, the trajectory of the empathic response can be influenced by social experiences encountered during development.

In this chapter, I will selectively review the literature on empathic networks in the brain and provide some speculation on how empathic emotions emerge and change across development. Because empathy is fundamentally a social emotion, I will begin with a brief overview of the neural systems that are involved in social behavior more generally and then discuss the specific systems that are thought to be involved in empathic responding. Finally, I will integrate this with what is known about neural development and speculate on how empathy emerges and changes across development and how this process may be impacted by the dramatic shift in social environment that has occurred since the time of our EH.

Elements of the Social Brain

Social behavior, like any other complex action, requires coordination of multiple brain systems. Social behavior is the end product of the interplay of brain circuits that mediate sensation, perception, affect, and executive functions with motor output (Adolphs, 2009; Nelson, Leibenluft, McClure, & Pine, 2005). However, unlike most other complex processes, social behavior requires additional layers of complexity because the target of behavior is an animate and dynamic entity that generates a multitude of different signals that are often quite subtle (Nelson & Guyer, 2011). For example, different facial expressions or even changes in eye contact that convey important information can occur during a relatively short window of time without any other overt signals and fundamentally change the nature of the signal (Frith & Frith, 2007). Furthermore, the context in which social signals are emitted and perceived can dramatically alter their meaning and salience. Attention from an authority figure is generally desired, but not if it happens when you are in the act of cheating, for example. Finally, to make things even more complex, animals such as primates who live in complex social environments often emit deceptive signals to manipulate the perceiver, or are responding as part of an alliance with another animal with some larger alternate goal in mind. Therefore, competent social behavior requires perception of small changes in signal, attention to context, knowledge of individual history, and integration with one's own goals and states (Frith & Frith, 2007). Clearly, social perception and social cognition are more complex than most processes and in highly social species such as humans and many nonhuman primates necessitate recruitment of a variety of neural networks to perceive, decode, interpret, and convey signals (Adolphs, 2009; Dunbar & Shultz, 2007; Frith & Frith, 2007; Preston & de Waal, 2002). Moreover, these neural networks are constantly interacting with each other such that changes in one domain can lead to updating in other networks. For example, an audible scream may result in salience signals from the amygdala back-projecting onto ventral visual stream systems and a decreasing of the detection threshold for aggressive displays or engaging systems that will put the scream in context (Cheney & Seyfarth, 2007).

In most species, sensory and perceptual processing of social signals occurs in systems that are specialized for that purpose (Adolphs, 2009; Insel & Fernald, 2004). For olfactory-based animals, social signals are often processed in the vomeronasal organ within the accessory olfactory system (Mucignat-Caretta, 2009). The vomeronasal organ detects chemosensory signals and pheromones from conspecifics and can detect everything from the individual identity of an animal to signals conveying reproductive status or emotional state (Mucignat-Caretta, 2009). In humans and nonhuman primates whose sensory systems are visually dominated, areas within the visual stream such as the fusiform face area, the superior temporal sulcus, and the inferior temporal area are uniquely dedicated to processing social signals such as facial identity and biological motion (Haxby, Hoffman, & Gobbini, 2002; Puce & Perrett, 2003). In addition, some studies have suggested that chemosensory signals may also convey important social signals for humans as well (Prehn-Kristensen et al., 2009; Savic, Berglund, Gulyas, & Roland, 2001).

The sensory domain is one area in which recent social behavior has diverged quite markedly from the EH. In the modern era of electronic communication with telephones, e-mail, and online communication, ease of communication has clearly increased, which may have made it easier to maintain wider social networks and more frequent social contact, but the sensory experience of those social contacts is clearly not as rich as live personal contact. The impact this change may have on the neural basis of social interaction is unclear, but because sensory elements of social interaction form a core of the neural basis of sociality, it is likely to be relevant at some level.

Highly processed sensory signals intermingle with regions involved in more general emotional and cognitive processes in limbic regions such as the amygdala, hypothalamus, and striatum. Here, social signals are integrated with more general emotional action systems of the brain such as the hypothalamic–pituitary–adrenal axis or striatal motor approach systems. Some limbic regions such as the medial preoptic area of the hypothalamus may have specific social functions such as maternal or reproductive behavior (Hull, Du, Lorrain, & Matuszewich, 1997; Numan, 2006), and many receive innervations from socially specific neuropeptides such as oxytocin, vasopressin, and endogenous opioids (Insel, 2010; Nelson & Panksepp, 1998; Panksepp, 2005; Way, Taylor, & Eisenberger, 2009). But in general limbic regions are not dedicated to processing social signals per se in the same way that sensory systems are, and the neural processing in limbic networks serves to add a general affective tone of the social percepts.

Finally, social signals interface with executive control systems in the anterior cingulate, medial prefrontal, and orbitofrontal cortex. Here, social signals are processed in networks dedicated to functions such as reward and punishment expectancies, systems that monitor and update responses, and systems that exert inhibitory control, and even a reversal of response tendencies (Amodio & Frith, 2006; Decety & Lamm, 2006). As discussed later, two aspects of the executive system are particularly important for understanding empathy. The first is the so-called theory-of-mind network. This system is engaged when individuals reflect on the mental states, perceptions, and belief systems of other individuals. Theory-of-mind tasks often involve understanding that another individual holds different beliefs (often false beliefs) from the subject himself or herself (Chakrabarti & Baron-Cohen, 2006; Frith & Frith, 1999). The second executive system that is likely to play a particularly important role in empathic responses is the so-called mirror neuron system. The mirror neuron system generates neural representations of passively viewed experiences and actions that occur in other individuals and creates a virtual experiential mirror in the observer (Gallese, Keysers, & Rizzolatti, 2004).

Brain Basis of Empathy

Neuroscientists view empathy as a culmination of the cognitive and affective response generated from the coordinated activity of a variety of dissociable subcomponents (Blair, 2005; Decety & Lamm, 2006; Hooker, Verosky, Germine,

Knight, & D'Esposito, 2010; Preston & de Waal, 2002; Singer & Lamm, 2009). These different subcomponents include motor systems, emotional systems, and cognitive or executive systems. The motor component of empathy can be seen in the tendency, often automatic and likely innate, of individuals to adopt the posture, movement patterns, or facial expressions they observe in others. This is referred to as mimicry and is more likely to occur when observing someone who is both familiar and liked (Meltzoff & Decety, 2003; Preston & de Waal, 2002; Singer & Lamm, 2009). A number of recent functional neuroimaging studies have now shown that the simple act of observing an action in another individual generates a pattern of neural activity in the observer that resembles the motor pattern generated when executing that same action. This phenomenon is thought to be driven by a network of neural circuits called mirror neurons. The mirror neuron system includes the inferior frontal gyrus, the inferior parietal lobule, and the premotor and supplementary motor cortices (Gallese et al., 2004). Mimicry of the movement patterns of another is clearly relevant for empathy as it creates a shared experience between observer and observed, and it may be a key building block for empathic responding early in development (Kuhl, 2010; Meltzoff & Decety, 2003).

However, motor mimicry lacks an emotional link between individuals, which is a critical aspect of what is typically thought of as empathy (Blair, 2005; Chakrabarti & Baron-Cohen, 2006; Singer & Lamm, 2009). A number of recent studies have found a similar pattern of shared neural activity in emotional circuits as in motor circuits. For example, people who either experience a painful event like an electric shock or a needle prick or observe that same event happen to someone else have been found to have a very similar pattern of neuronal activity (Decety & Lamm, 2006; Singer & Lamm, 2009). In both situations, activation was observed in the anterior cingulate cortex, the anterior insula, the brainstem, and the cerebellum. Importantly, this network is thought to reflect the emotional and somatic experience of pain. The fact that this same network was activated in both receivers and observers of the painful event indicates that this likely represents a shared emotional experience like the mirror motor pattern, which is the core of empathy. Subsequent study demonstrated that although the vicarious observation of a painful event generates a similar pattern of neural activation, it is not identical. Experienced events generate patterns that are more rostral and ventral in the anterior cingulate cortex and anterior insula, for example (Decety & Lamm, 2006; Singer & Lamm, 2009), than those that are observed. Singer and Lamm (2009) have speculated that somatosensory (and possibly other emotional) events generate a visceral signature and a *representation* of the visceral signature. The representation of the signature is useful for generating expectancies and is also a critical component of empathic experience.

The final major component of empathy is the executive or cognitive aspect, which enables an individual to take the perspective of another individual and understand that an observed individual has a different experience from the observer. This so-called mentalizing or theory of mind (TOM) ability enables the observer to take both concrete (e.g., his knife is sharper than mine) and abstract (e.g., it must be difficult for a mother to take a child to kindergarten) perspectives of other individuals even if they are different from the direct experience of the observer (Dumontheil et al., 2010; Frith & Frith, 1999; Gallagher et al., 2000; Saxe, 2006). Theory-of-mind capability is generally thought to depend on the medial prefrontal cortex (sometimes referred to as the paracingulate cortex) and the tempo-parietal junction at the caudal end of the superior temporal sulcus (Dumontheil et al., 2010; Frith & Frith, 1999; Gallagher et al., 2000; Saxe, 2006). These executive systems will generally interact with limbic structures such as the amygdala to generate both cognitive and emotional components of alternate experiences, although joint activations of these systems does not always occur (Blair, 2005).

Social Development

In general, social development can be divided into three gross periods: the infancy period between birth and weaning; the juvenile period between weaning and the prepubertal phase; and the adolescent period between early puberty and full maturation. In infancy, socialization occurs primarily with the mother; in the juvenile period, social behavior consists mainly of play with conspecifics while using the mother as a safe base; in the adolescent period, socialization takes the form of transition from the home environment into peer groups (even though active play is reduced) and searching for potential mates; and in the mature period, socialization is primarily focused on reproduction and maintaining social status within the group (Nelson et al., 2005). In each of these periods, distinct social information is likely to be obtained that informs the construction of specific social networks within the maturing brain.

There are two meanings of the term *social development*. The first is the time at which new patterns of social behavior first emerge. For example, human infants often begin talking by age 1 year, display theory-of-mind capabilities by age 4 years, display romantic interest in early adolescence, and so on. The second meaning of social development is the effects that various social experiences exert on the trajectory of maturation and influence the ultimate form of the mature brain. These two are likely interrelated because the social experiences an organism seeks out at different points of development are likely to provide information to the systems that are undergoing developmental change.

In our EH, the interplay between the maturing child and the social context was quite different than it is today. Infants maintained intensive contact with the mother for a longer period of development; social groups were smaller, more interconnected, and mobile; and social interaction was unstructured, especially during the juvenile period. Although the social context did differ from the present, the basic organizational blueprint for brain development was probably very similar to what it is currently (Konner, 2010; Pinker, 2002). One can only speculate about the development of social behavior during our EH, but because development is generally considered to occur as an interplay between genetic blueprints and environmental context (Meaney, 2010), one can assume that it did differ in meaningful ways.

One way in which different information is obtained across development is through attention. Attentional shifts to different details of the social environment clearly occur across development. Infants attend to the linguistic characteristics of the mother, while adolescents attend to the clothing styles of peers, for example. In adulthood, control of attention becomes more willful and may depend on maturation of regions of the prefrontal cortex, while emotional content of the stimulus may drive attention orienting in immature individuals (Monk et al., 2003). Shifting emotional salience across development may be mediated by an interaction between changes in subcortical structures such as the amygdala, striatum, and hypothalamus and maturation of prefrontal regions that can exert regulatory control on attention and behavioral responses (Burnett et al., 2009; Casey, Duhoux, & Cohen, 2010; Dumontheil et al., 2010; Ernst et al., 2005; Forbes & Dahl, 2010; Monk et al., 2003; Nelson et al., 2005; Pine, Helfinstein, Bar-Haim, Nelson, & Fox, 2009). Importantly, the experiences that occur during these attention-focused organizational periods are likely to influence the construction of the nervous system and affect the trajectory of development.

There are many examples of how attentional focus and sensitive periods of brain organization coincide. In humans and some nonhuman primates, a great deal of time is spent with up-close face-to-face interaction between the infant and mother (Ferrari, Paukner, Ionica, & Suomi, 2009; Ferrari et al., 2006; Paukner, Suomi, Visalberghi, & Ferrari, 2009; Van Egeren, Barratt, & Roach, 2001), and this corresponds to the same period of time that appears to be a sensitive period for the development of face perceptual systems in the brain (Moulson, Westerlund, Fox, Zeanah, & Nelson, 2009; Pascalis, de Haan, & Nelson, 2002; Sugita, 2008). This pattern of data suggests that what is most salient for the infant at a behavioral level corresponds to the functional systems that are undergoing construction in the nervous system and the information that is obtained behaviorally is integrated into the structure of the brain. Similar regulatory symbiosis between attention and sensitive developmental periods appear to occur for development of language systems (Kuhl, 2010), stress and coping systems (Coplan et al., 2005; Levine, 2001), and a variety of other regulated physiological processes (Hofer, 1994a, 1994b). In other words, the infant appears to be seeking out "information" from the environment on how to construct the nervous system consistent with when that functional capacity of the nervous system is maturing.

If this is a general principle of development, then the varied social behaviors and experiences that occur at different periods of development can serve as a marker for different aspects of the social brain that are undergoing maturation at different points in development. Recent neuroimaging and cellular studies clearly demonstrate that programmed neural development continues into the third decade of life in humans (Gogtay et al., 2004; Huttenlocher & Dabholkar, 1997), and the patterns of social behavior also continue to change markedly from early life across adolescence and into the early adult period (Forbes & Dahl, 2010; Nelson et al., 2005; Rutter, 1989; Steinberg & Morris, 2001; Spear, 2000). Recent neuroimaging studies have also suggested that changes in brain response to social cognition occur not only during early life but also across the adolescent period (Burnett et al., 2009; Choudhury, Blakemore, & Charman, 2006; Dumontheil et al., 2010; Guyer, McClure-Tone, Shiffrin, Pine, & Nelson, 2009). This suggests that brain systems that generate the mature empathic response continue to mature through the adolescent period.

Social Development as Environmental Adaptation

In general, the structural modifications that are made in the nervous system as it unfolds across development are adaptive for the organism and direct the resources involved in growth and maturation toward those areas that are most likely to be useful for the organism (Coplan et al., 2005; Hofer, 1994b; Meaney, 2010; see also Belsky, this volume). From a psychological perspective, therefore, development is similar in many ways to learning. Learning and development both involve altering the existing structure of the nervous system as a consequence of environmental context, and both use similar mechanisms of generating structural change. For example, synaptic strengthening and weakening, alterations of gene regulatory processes, and use of neurochemical factors such as brain-derived neurotrophic factor are mechanisms that alter neurobiological processes for both learning and development (Knudsen, 2004; McClung & Nestler, 2008; Meaney, 2010).

There are, however, some important differences between learning and development. Whereas learning takes place equipotentially across the life span as a consequence of environmental experience, development occurs on its own preprogrammed schedule and uses whatever environmental resources are available at the time to guide structural development. This is a critical point because it brings to the equation an additional factor—not only what but when something occurs—and highlights the importance of particular periods of time when specific circuits are being established or strengthened. Therefore, the timing of shifts in social structures like breastfeeding, caregiver separation, and puberty may have important implications for the formation of networks in the developing brain. While the change itself from breastfeeding to weaning, for example, is likely to produce large-scale changes in brain network dynamics, the timing of the change will likely affect the degree to which other networks are affected by this change. For example, rodent models have demonstrated that extending the presence of the mother or the nursing experience can delay the ability of infant rats to form odor aversion associations (Melcer, Alberts, & Gubernick, 1985; Moriceau, Roth, & Sullivan, 2010).

A second major difference between development and learning is that developmental changes tend to occur hierarchically in time (Fox, Levitt, & Nelson, 2010).

Developmental changes are typically modifications and elaborations of existing structures and circuits so that directions taken early in development are more consequential than are elaborations made later in development. In this context, it is noteworthy therefore that Narvaez (Narvaez, 2008; see also Narvaez & Gleason, this volume) has reported a relationship between both breastfeeding and maternal care in infancy and the expression of empathy in toddlers. This suggests not only that brain networks involved in empathic responding are undergoing developmental change in infancy but also that variation in maternal behavior can affect the course of that development (Narvaez, 2008).

Empathy Development

From a phenomenological perspective, some aspects of empathy are evident very early in life. In a classic study, Meltzoff and Moore (Meltzoff & Moore, 1977) demonstrated that within hours of birth, infants will imitate basic facial expressions directed at them by an adult. Recently, a similar capacity has been reported in infant rhesus monkeys as well (Ferrari et al., 2006). Therefore, motor mimicry appears to be an innate capacity of the primate nervous system and may play an important role in developing dynamic interactions and forming emotional bonds with caretakers (Meltzoff & Decety, 2003; Paukner et al., 2009). Many years ago Sagi and Hoffman (Sagi & Hoffman, 1976) demonstrated that within 48 hours of birth, infants respond to the sound of another infant's cry with their own cry, and this response is not elicited by an auditory stimulus that is matched in intensity and other phonological characteristics. By 3 to 4 months of age, infants are reliably imitating their mother's vocalization patterns, and this forms an important part of the dynamic interplay between them (Van Egeren et al., 2001).

However, not all motor mimicry is evident at birth. Studies of the development of contagious yawning have found that this form of mimicry doesn't emerge until 4 to 5 years of age and may require engagement of systems involved in TOM mechanisms (Anderson & Meno, 2003; Senju, 2010; Senju et al., 2007). It may be that during the first years of life, mimicry primarily occurs in face-to-face interactions when the infant is most likely to be interacting with the caretaker. In the juvenile period, mimicry is therefore likely to be focused on patterns of play behavior, and in adolescence, mimicry should be more focused on cultural patterns of peer group behavior. In other words, empathic interchanges may serve development of specific networks involved in dyadic or social interactions, whereas other motor systems experienced by infants are not developmentally relevant and therefore not mimicked.

One major developmental change that occurs in empathic responding is the ability of an emotional provocation to elicit a prosocial behavioral response. Although this is occasionally evident prior to age 2 years, this is consistently seen during the second year of life (Zahn-Waxler et al., 1992). Another developmental transition that occurs across early to middle childhood is the degree to which observing a negative event triggers personal distress versus a sympathetic (other-focused) emotional response (Eisenberg, 2005). This transition probably involves activation of the TOM network, and although this is functional in early childhood, the facility with which the other-focused cognitive engagement occurs increases through mid- to late adolescence (Dumontheil et al., 2010). Although generating an other-focused behavioral response to the observation of an empathy-inducing event likely coalesces across development, Eisenberg has argued that individuals who express a strong tendency for prosocial behaviors can be identified relatively early in life (by age 4 to 5) by a tendency to share with others (Eisenberg, 2005). Thus, there may be some temperamental or other early emerging properties of the nervous system that facilitate empathic responding once it reaches maturity.

Another important developmental aspect of empathy has less to do with programmed maturation of circuits than it does with life experience that is gained with age. To the extent that empathy involves induction of a virtual experience in an observer (Singer & Lamm, 2009), having past experience with a variety of emotional events will facilitate this virtual experience. For example, it is likely to be much easier for a young child to empathize with someone who is in distress because of a skinned knee than it is to empathize with someone who is in distress because of a broken romantic relationship.

The empathic response can also be strongly modulated by the nature of the relationship between the observer and the observed (Singer & Lamm, 2009). Not only is a stronger empathic response likely to be triggered by observing someone emotionally close than someone emotionally distant to the observer, but factors such as competition and whether or not the target deserved the action he or she received can also strongly modulate the empathic response. It is likely that subtle changes like this impact the empathic response during the late childhood and adolescent period. For example, during the infancy and juvenile period, strong empathic responses may be reserved for immediate family members, while in adolescence and adulthood, strong empathy may occur within a wider social network, but other mediating factors may also begin to impinge on empathic responding during later periods of development as well.

In summary, shared emotional experiences between individuals are evident in infancy, and this is the most elemental aspect of empathy. As the brain matures, this elemental empathic response becomes integrated with systems involved in behavioral regulation and the ability to understand different perspectives. The nature of the empathic response itself also expands with both experience and further maturation and integration of the brain systems that mediate the elemental response. The social experiences we encounter throughout development in modern society are likely largely similar to those in our EH but differ in their variability, timing, and extent. These things are likely to have had an impact on the development of the empathic response.

Empathy Development in Atypical Contexts

Given that empathy is an emergent process of social development, it follows that empathic development is compromised in atypical social environments. One of the most austere social environments during early life is institutionalized care that some orphanages routinely provide. Although the empathic response has not been systematically investigated in institutionalized children, a number of abnormalities in social behavior have been noted in this population that are both directly and indirectly related to empathy development. Institutionalized children pay less attention to pantomimed displays of dyadic emotional interaction in puppet shows (Ghera et al., 2009) and have difficulty with attention more generally (Pollak et al., 2010). Institutionalized children have an attenuated event-related potential response to faces (Moulson et al., 2009), have difficulties with attachment formation (Smyke, Zeanah, Fox, Nelson, & Guthrie, 2010), have language delays (Loman, Wiik, Frenn, Pollak, & Gunnar, 2009), and have more internalizing and externalizing disorders (Wiik et al., 2010; Zeanah et al., 2009). All of these would tend to reduce the ability of individuals to have shared experiences with others and foster empathic capabilities, and many may also be the result of not being exposed to experiences of others during critical developmental periods. Many of these social problems may tend to be progressive because poor social development in one stage will likely reduce social exposure in subsequent stages. In general, these deficiencies are ameliorated though not eliminated when children are moved from the institutionalized setting to foster care within the first few years of life, but placement in this environment later, during early childhood, is often largely ineffective (Kreppner et al., 2007; Vanderwert, Marshall, Nelson, Zeanah, & Fox, 2010).

Institutionalized children also show physiological abnormalities that may relate to empathic difficulties. For example, postinstitutionalized children have reduced peripheral levels of oxytocin and vasopressin both tonically and after a period of affiliative interaction with a caregiver (Fries, Ziegler, Kurian, Jacoris, & Pollak, 2005). Structural magnetic resonance images have also revealed increases in the volume of the amygdala (Tottenham et al., 2010) and reduction in the volume of the cerebellum in children who spent early infancy and childhood in an institutional setting (Bauer, Hanson, Pierson, Davidson, & Pollak, 2009). A variety of differences in brain structure have been found in children who were reared in an abusive environment; perhaps most important among these is a reduced volume in the lateral orbitofrontal cortex, which also related to psychiatric symptoms in this population (Hanson et al., 2010). Similar changes have also been found in monkeys who were subject to peer rearing and deprived of an adult caregiver for the first 6 months of life (Spinelli et al., 2009; Winslow, Noble, Lyons, Sterk, & Insel, 2003). It is not clear the extent to which these institutionalized findings represent the extreme end of a continuum, with optimal rearing practices marking the other end of the spectrum, or if these findings represent a qualitative difference due to extreme deprivation conditions. They do, however, point to the importance of early life social interactions in social development.

Other atypical rearing environments may also affect the development of empathic skills. Recently, it has been shown that infants of depressed mothers are less attentive and less emotionally responsive to adult faces and to cries of other infants (Field, Diego, & Hernandez-Reif, 2009; Field, Diego, Hernandez-Reif, & Fernandez, 2007), suggesting that reduced dynamic face-to-face interactions with the mother may have impacted their ability to form rudimentary empathic responses. Similarly, children who were reared in an abusive environment show increased perceptual sensitivity to displays of anger (Pollak, Messner, Kistler, & Cohn, 2009; Pollak & Sinha, 2002). While technically this is not the same as empathy because anger perception is not the same as anger experience and therefore not necessarily an isomorphic response (Singer & Lamm, 2009), it does suggest that exposure to emotional experiences during the period of early social development can influence low-level perceptual processes that have a direct impact on empathic skills.

In addition to effects of rearing environments, the emergence of empathy can be affected by factors endogenous to brain structure. People with autism spectrum disorders are noted for having an impoverished ability to relate to others. Clear deficits have been shown in autistic individuals with regard to theory-of-mind abilities (Frith, 1996); however, a recent study reported normal responses on a shared emotions task (Bird et al., 2010). This suggests that the interpersonal deficits of autism may primarily be a reflection of difficulties with theory of mind and other executive functions related to social interaction rather than with the emotional component of empathy per se.

Another disorder that is noted for a distinct lack of empathic response is psychopathy (Lynam & Gudonis, 2005). Although few studies have been conducted on psychopathy in very young children, studies that have focused on midchildhood, adolescence, and adulthood have found a very high degree of stability across development, and many feel that psychopathic tendencies are likely either innate or are present very early in life and largely sustained through development (Blair, Peschardt, Budhani, Mitchell, & Pine, 2006; Lynam & Gudonis, 2005). Several theorists have argued that psychopathy is a result of dysfunctional social learning systems that fail to integrate emotional responses into behavioral decisions (Blair, 2008; Lynam & Gudonis, 2005). Interestingly, Blair has argued that while aggressive behavioral tendencies are often more frequent in individuals after early childhood traumatic experiences, this is distinctly different from psychopathic aggressive behavior that is typically used only instrumentally—to further their own goals—and not in response to any type of emotional provocation. Therefore, early childhood traumatic experiences, although they may increase aggressive behavior, are not likely to lead to increases in psychopathy (Blair et al., 2006).

Finally, several studies have noted a marked and persistent deficit in socioemotional behavior, including expression of empathy, in individuals who experienced damage to the prefrontal cortex in early life (Anderson, Bechara, Damasio, Tranel,

& Damasio, 1999; Anderson, Wisnowski, Barrash, Damasio, & Tranel, 2009; Tonks et al., 2009). Sometimes the deficit is not apparent immediately after injury but becomes apparent later in development when social demands change (Tonks et al., 2009). This persistent functional impairment in social behavior following early brain injury is in contrast to many functions such as language that show remarkable flexibility and resiliency following early brain injury. This observation in some ways resembles observations in nonhuman primates of fundamentally different consequences to social behavior as a result of amygdala lesions received either neonatally or during the juvenile or adult period. While the latter results in a marked decrease in social fear, the former results in an increase in social fear (Kalin, Shelton, Davidson, & Kelley, 2001; Prather et al., 2001). These studies suggest that while other neural systems can generate flexible behavioral response patterns following a lesion, this flexibility may depend critically on having *some* foundation to work with. Because social development begins in infancy and continues throughout life, early lesions to key circuits in social functioning may make it impossible to generate flexible response patterns using other neural circuits.

Social Structure in the Environment of Evolutionary Adaptedness

As has been discussed throughout this volume, the social structure of modern human societies has undergone dramatic change over the last several centuries. In contrast to the HGSB structure, which made up the majority of our species' evolutionary history and remains the predominant structure for many of our primate cousins, modern human society has become markedly less social in many ways. The infancy period now typically involves a shorter period of breastfeeding and separation of caregiver–offspring sleeping arrangements, and parents are often discouraged from responding to infants' protestations to encourage resiliency (Narvaez, 2008). In addition, we have largely lost the "extended family" cohabitation structure that typically occurs in hunter-gatherer cultures. The juvenile and adolescent periods are largely spent in age- and occasionally sex-segregated classrooms where free social interaction is discouraged, adolescents spend large amounts of time socializing online, and adult work life is increasingly spent in isolated offices with relatively limited social contact with peers.

All of these changes are likely to have an impact on the development of neural networks that regulate social behavior more generally and empathy in particular. Yet we are clearly not a species that is devoid of empathic capabilities. Indeed, modern humans spend a great deal of time and effort engaged in multimedia activities such as films, television, music, and even video games that induce empathic responding. This attentional hunger for empathic experiences may in part be mediated by the impoverished experience of empathy created by our modern natural world. On the other hand, one potentially positive change in our social environment that may impact empathic responding is the relative openness of our group networks.

Research has clearly shown a greater empathic response toward individuals considered inside rather than outside the group (Hein, Silani, Preuschoff, Batson, & Singer, 2010), and in modern times the size of the inside group has likely expanded tremendously relative to that in our EH. Ultimately, however, whether our experience of empathy is qualitatively or quantitatively different from that of our human forebears in our EH is something we will never know.

What we do know is that evolution crafted a social brain that does not mature for many years after birth. The mature brain is the product of interaction between a general organizational blueprint and life experiences encountered along the way. Life experiences clearly differ from the time of our EH, and some of the differences have been linked to changes in empathic behavior (Narvaez, 2008). As specific networks have now been implicated in empathic social experiences, a puzzle piece that is clearly missing is the ways in which development in contexts that vary in the degree of relatedness to our EH may impact the maturation of these circuits.

In some ways, interaction between infant and mother may be one of the most important developmental time frames because of both the importance of brain systems that are forming connections during the infantile period and the foundational nature of development during this early time. Recent research on empathy suggests that such infant–mother interactions as enface, emotional mimicry, tactile contact, and shared experiences are likely to play an important role in the development of empathic abilities. Research has also shown that infants reared under conditions of extreme social impoverishment or neglect have atypical development of both behavioral and neuronal systems related to empathy. This suggests that the changed environment that is typical of the modern mother–infant relationship may have an impact on the emergence of empathic responding. However, as with many behaviors, it is now recognized that social development at both the behavioral and neural levels continues to undergo programmed developmental changes into puberty and beyond. Social experiences encountered during these periods are also quite different in modern society than in our EH. These changes may affect the developmental trajectory of brain systems involved in empathic responding.

The modern neuroimaging era has provided a framework for understanding the physiological networks that underlie empathy. This in turn will enable more specific and testable hypotheses about what impact different social contexts might have on the development of specific networks underlying social perception, social affect, and social cognition that work together for complex processes like empathy. It seems highly likely that the dramatic shift in social environment since our EH, many of the most dramatic occurring in just the last several generations, has impacted the development of the social brain. Some of these changes may be adaptive in the sense that the brain is learning to function optimally in the present environment, but conversely, some of the changes in brain development may also be driving wide-scale changes in social structure itself. It is important that this process be better understood by professionals in public policy, health care, and education as well as by parents. More research in this area is clearly needed.

References

Adolphs, R. (2009). The social brain: Neural basis of social knowledge. *Annual Review of Psychology, 60*, 693–716.

Amodio, D. M., & Frith, C. D. (2006). Meeting of minds: The medial frontal cortex and social cognition. *Nature Reviews Neuroscience, 7*(4), 268–277.

Anderson, J. R., & Meno, P. (2003). Psychological influences on yawning in children. *Current Psychology Letters, 11*(2), 1–6.

Anderson, S. W., Bechara, A., Damasio, H., Tranel, D., & Damasio, A. R. (1999). Impairment of social and moral behavior related to early damage in human prefrontal cortex. *Nature Neuroscience, 2*(11), 1032–1037.

Anderson, S. W., Wisnowski, J. L., Barrash, J., Damasio, H., & Tranel, D. (2009). Consistency of neuropsychological outcome following damage to prefrontal cortex in the first years of life. *Journal of Clinical and Experimental Neuropsychology 31*(2), 170–179.

Bauer, P. M., Hanson, J. L., Pierson, R. K., Davidson, R. J., & Pollak, S. D. (2009). Cerebellar volume and cognitive functioning in children who experienced early deprivation. *Biological Psychiatry, 66*(12), 1100–1106.

Bird, G., Silani, G., Brindley, R., White, S., Frith, U., & Singer, T. (2010). Empathic brain responses in insula are modulated by levels of alexithymia but not autism. *Brain, 133* (Pt 5), 1515–1525.

Blair, R. J. (2005). Responding to the emotions of others: Dissociating forms of empathy through the study of typical and psychiatric populations. *Conscious Cognition, 14*(4), 698–718.

Blair, R. J. (2008). The amygdala and ventromedial prefrontal cortex: Functional contributions and dysfunction in psychopathy. *Philosophical Transactions of the Royal Society of London B: Biological Sciences, 363*(1503), 2557–2565.

Blair, R. J., Peschardt, K. S., Budhani, S., Mitchell, D. G., & Pine, D. S. (2006). The development of psychopathy. *Journal of Child Psychology and Psychiatry, 47*(3–4), 262–276.

Burnett, S., Bird, G., Moll, J., Frith, C., & Blakemore, S. J. (2009). Development during adolescence of the neural processing of social emotion. *Journal of Cognitive Neuroscience, 21*(9), 1736–1750.

Casey, B. J., Duhoux, S., & Cohen, M. M. (2010). Adolescence: What do transmission, transition, and translation have to do with it? *Neuron, 67*(5), 749–760.

Chakrabarti, B., & Baron-Cohen, S. (2006). Empathizing: Neurocognitive developmental mechanisms and individual differences." *Progress in Brain Research, 156*, 403–417.

Chen, Q., Panksepp, J. B., & Lahvis, G. P. (2009). Empathy is moderated by genetic background in mice. *PLoS One, 4*(2), e4387.

Cheney, D. L., & Seyfarth, R. M. (2007). *Baboon metaphysics*. Chicago, IL: University of Chicago Press.

Choudhury, S., Blakemore, S. J., & Charman, T. (2006). Social cognitive development during adolescence. *Social and Cognitive Affect Neuroscience, 1*(3), 165–174.

Coplan, J. D., Altemus, M., Mathew, S. J., Smith, E. L., Sharf, B., Coplan, P. M., . . . Rosenblum, L. A.(2005). Synchronized maternal-infant elevations of primate CSF CRF concentrations in response to variable foraging demand. *CNS Spectrum, 10*(7), 530–536.

Decety, J., & Lamm, C. (2006). Human empathy through the lens of social neuroscience. *Scientific World Journal, 6*, 1146–1163.

Derntl, B., Finkelmeyer, A., Toygar, T. K., Hulsmann, A., Schneider, F., Falkenberg, D. I., & Habel, U. (2009). Generalized deficit in all core components of empathy in schizophrenia. *Schizophrenia Research, 108*(1–3), 197–206.

Dumontheil, I., Apperly, I. A., & Blakemore, S. J. (2010). Online usage of theory of mind continues to develop in late adolescence. *Developmental Science, 13*(2), 331–338.

Dunbar, R. I., & Shultz, S. (2007). Evolution in the social brain. *Science, 317*(5843), 1344–1347.

Eisenberg, N. (2005). The development of empathy-related responding. *Nebraska Symposium on Motivation, 51*, 73–117.

Ernst, M., Nelson, E. E., Jazbec, S., McClure, E. B., Monk, C. S., Leibenluft, E.,... Pine, D. S. (2005). Amygdala and nucleus accumbens in responses to receipt and omission of gains in adults and adolescents. *Neuroimage, 25*(4), 1279–1291.

Ferrari, P. F., Paukner, A., Ionica, C., & Suomi, S. J. (2009). Reciprocal face-to-face communication between rhesus macaque mothers and their newborn infants. *Current Biology, 19*(20), 1768–1772.

Ferrari, P. F., Visalberghi, E., Paukner, A., Fogassi, L., Ruggiero, A., & Suomi, S. J. (2006). Neonatal imitation in rhesus macaques. *PLoS Biology, 4*(9), e302.

Field, T., Diego, M., & Hernandez-Reif, M. (2009). Depressed mothers' infants are less responsive to faces and voices. *Infant Behavioral Development, 32*(3), 239–244.

Field, T., Diego, M., Hernandez-Reif, M., & Fernandez, M. (2007). Depressed mothers' newborns show less discrimination of other newborns' cry sounds. *Infant Behavioral Development, 30*(3), 431–435.

Forbes, E. E., & Dahl, R. E. (2010). Pubertal development and behavior: Hormonal activation of social and motivational tendencies. *Brain Cognition, 72*(1), 66–72.

Fox, S. E., Levitt, P., & Nelson, C. A., 3rd. (2010). How the timing and quality of early experiences influence the development of brain architecture. *Child Development, 81*(1), 28–40.

Fries, A. B., Ziegler, T. E., Kurian, J. R., Jacoris, S., & Pollak, S. D. (2005). Early experience in humans is associated with changes in neuropeptides critical for regulating social behavior. *Proceedings of the National Academy of Sciences U S A, 102*(47), 17237–17240.

Frith, C. D., & Frith, U. (1999). Interacting minds—a biological basis. *Science, 286*(5445), 1692–1695.

Frith, C. D., & Frith, U. (2007). Social cognition in humans. *Current Biology, 17*(16), R724–R732.

Frith, U. (1996). Cognitive explanations of autism. *Acta Paediatrica Supplementum, 416*, 63–68.

Gallagher, H. L., Happe, F., Brunswick, N., Fletcher, P. C., Frith, U., & Frith, C. D. (2000). Reading the mind in cartoons and stories: An fMRI study of 'theory of mind' in verbal and nonverbal tasks. *Neuropsychologia, 38*(1), 11–21.

Gallese, V., Keysers, C., & Rizzolatti, G. (2004). A unifying view of the basis of social cognition. *Trends in Cognitive Science, 8*(9), 396–403.

Ghera, M. M., Marshall, P. J., Fox, N. A., Zeanah, C. H., Nelson, C. A., Smyke, A. T., & Guthrie D. (2009). The effects of foster care intervention on socially deprived institutionalized children's attention and positive affect: Results from the BEIP study. *Journal of Child Psychology and Psychiatry, 50*(3), 246–253.

Gogtay, N., Giedd, J. N., Lusk, L., Hayashi, K. M., Greenstein, D., Vaituzis, A. C.,...Tompson, P. M. (2004). Dynamic mapping of human cortical development during childhood through early adulthood. *Proceedings of the National Academy of Sciences U S A, 101*(21), 8174–8179.

Guyer, A. E., McClure-Tone, E. B., Shiffrin, N. D., Pine, D. S., & Nelson, E. E. (2009). Probing the neural correlates of anticipated peer evaluation in adolescence. *Child Development, 80*(4), 1000–1015.

Hanson, J. L., Chung, M. K., Avants, B. B., Shirtcliff, E. A., Gee, J. C., Davidson, R. J., & Pollak, S. D. (2010). Early stress is associated with alterations in the orbitofrontal cortex: A tensor-based morphometry investigation of brain structure and behavioral risk. *Journal of Neuroscience, 30*(22), 7466–7472.

Haxby, J. V., Hoffman, E. A., & Gobbini, M. I. (2002). Human neural systems for face recognition and social communication. *Biological Psychiatry, 51*(1), 59–67.

Hein, G., Silani, G., Preuschoff, K., Batson, C. D., & Singer, T. (2010). Neural responses to ingroup and outgroup members' suffering predict individual differences in costly helping. *Neuron, 68*(1), 149–160.

Hofer, M. A. (1994a). Early relationships as regulators of infant physiology and behavior. *Acta Paediatrica Supplementum, 397*, 9–18.

Hofer, M. A. (1994b). Hidden regulators in attachment, separation, and loss. *Monographs of the Society of Research on Child Development, 59*(2–3), 192–207.

Hooker, C. I., Verosky, S. C., Germine, L. T., Knight, R. T., & D'Esposito, M. (2010). Neural activity during social signal perception correlates with self-reported empathy. *Brain Research, 1308*, 100–113.

Hull, E. M., Du, J., Lorrain, D. S., & Matuszewich, L. (1997). Testosterone, preoptic dopamine, and copulation in male rats. *Brain Research Bulletin, 44*(4), 327–333.

Huttenlocher, P. R., & Dabholkar, A. S. (1997). Regional differences in synaptogenesis in human cerebral cortex. *Journal of Comparative Neurology, 387*(2), 167–178.

Insel, T. R. (2010). The challenge of translation in social neuroscience: A review of oxytocin, vasopressin, and affiliative behavior. *Neuron, 65*(6), 768–779.

Insel, T. R., & Fernald, R. D. (2004). How the brain processes social information: Searching for the social brain. *Annual Review of Neuroscience, 27*, 697–722.

Kalin, N. H., Shelton, S. E., Davidson, R. J., & Kelley, A. E. (2001). The primate amygdala mediates acute fear but not the behavioral and physiological components of anxious temperament. *Journal of Neuroscience, 21*(6), 2067–2074.

Knudsen, E. I. (2004). Sensitive periods in the development of the brain and behavior. *Journal of Cognitive Neuroscience, 16*(8), 1412–1425.

Konner, M. (2010). *The evolution of childhood. Relationships, emotion, mind.* Cambridge, MA: Belknap Press.

Kreppner, J. M., Rutter, M., Beckett, C., Castle, J., Colvert, E., Groothues, C.,...Sonuga-Barke, E. J. (2007). Normality and impairment following profound early institutional deprivation: A longitudinal follow-up into early adolescence. *Developmental Psychology, 43*(4), 931–946.

Kuhl, P. K. (2010). Brain mechanisms in early language acquisition. *Neuron, 67*(5), 713–727.

Langford, D. J., Crager, S. E., Shehzad, Z., Smith, S. B., Sotocinal, S. G., Levenstadt, J. S., ...Mogil, J. S. (2006). Social modulation of pain as evidence for empathy in mice. *Science, 312*(5782), 1967–1970.

Levine, S. (2001). Primary social relationships influence the development of the hypotha-lamic–pituitary–adrenal axis in the rat. *Physiology and Behavior, 73*(3), 255–260.

Loman, M. M., Wiik, K. L., Frenn, K. A., Pollak, S. D., & Gunnar, M. R. (2009). Postinstitutionalized children's development: Growth, cognitive, and language out-comes. *Journal of Development and Behavior in Pediatrics, 30*(5), 426–434.

Lynam, D. R., & Gudonis, L. (2005). The development of psychopathy. *Annual Review of Clinical Psychology, 1*, 381–407.

McClung, C. A., & Nestler, E. J. (2008). Neuroplasticity mediated by altered gene expres-sion. *Neuropsychopharmacology, 33*(1), 3–17.

Meaney, M. J. (2010). Epigenetics and the biological definition of gene x environment inter-actions. *Child Development, 81*(1), 41–79.

Melcer, T., Alberts, J. R., & Gubernick, D. J. (1985). Early weaning does not accelerate the expression of nursing-related taste aversions. *Developmental Psychobiology, 18*(5), 375–381.

Meltzoff, A. N., & Decety, J. (2003). What imitation tells us about social cognition: A rapprochement between developmental psychology and cognitive neuroscience. *Philosophical Transactions of the Royal Society of London B: Biological Sciences 358*(1431), 491–500.

Meltzoff, A. N., & Moore, M. K. (1977). Imitation of facial and manual gestures by human neonates. *Science, 198*(4312), 75–78.

Monk, C. S., McClure, E. B., Nelson, E. E., Zarahn, E., Bilder, R. M., Leibenluft, E., . . . Pine, D. S. (2003). Adolescent immaturity in attention-related brain engagement to emotional facial expressions. *Neuroimage, 20*(1), 420–428.

Moriceau, S., Roth, T. L., & Sullivan, R. M. (2010). Rodent model of infant attachment learning and stress. *Developmental Psychobiology, 52*(7), 651–660.

Moulson, M. C., Fox, N. A., Zeanah, C. H., & Nelson, C. A. (2009). Early adverse experi-ences and the neurobiology of facial emotion processing. *Developmental Psychology, 45*(1), 17–30.

Moulson, M. C., Westerlund, A., Fox, N. A., Zeanah, C. H., & Nelson, C. A. (2009). The effects of early experience on face recognition: An event-related potential study of insti-tutionalized children in Romania. *Child Development, 80*(4), 1039–1056.

Mucignat-Caretta, C. (2009). The rodent accessory olfactory system. *Journal of Comparative Physiology A: Neuroethology, Sensory, Neural, and Behavioral Physiology, 196*(10), 767–777.

Narvaez, D. (2008). Triune ethics: The neurobiological roots of our multiple moralities. *New Ideas in Psychology, 26*, 95–119.

Nelson, E. E., & Guyer, A. E. (2011). The development of the ventral prefrontal cortex and social flexibility. *Developmental Cognitive Neuroscience, 1*(3), 233–245.

Nelson, E. E., Leibenluft, E., McClure, E. B., & Pine, D. S. (2005). The social re-orientation of adolescence: A neuroscience perspective on the process and its relation to psychopa-thology. *Psychological Medicine, 35*(2), 163–174.

Nelson, E. E., & Panksepp, J. (1998). Brain substrates of infant-mother attachment: Contributions of opioids, oxytocin, and norepinephrine. *Neuroscience and Biobehavioral Reviews, 22*(3), 437–452.

Numan, M. (1994). A neural circuitry analysis of maternal behavior in the rat. *Acta Paediatrica Supplementum, 397*, 19–28.

Panksepp, J. (2005). Why does separation distress hurt? Comment on MacDonald and Leary (2005). *Psychology Bulletin, 131*(2): 224–230; author reply 237–240.

Pascalis, O., Scott, L. S., Kelly, D. J., Shannon, R. W., Nicholson, E., Coleman, M., & Nelson, C. A. (2005). Plasticity of face processing in infancy. *Proceedings of the National Academy of Sciences U S A, 102*(14), 5297–5300.

Paukner, A., Suomi, S. J., Visalberghi, E., & Ferrari, P. F. (2009). Capuchin monkeys display affiliation toward humans who imitate them. *Science, 325*(5942), 880–883.

Pine, D. S., Helfinstein, S. M., Bar-Haim, Y., Nelson, E., & Fox, N. A. (2009). Challenges in developing novel treatments for childhood disorders: Lessons from research on anxiety. *Neuropsychopharmacology, 34*(1), 213–228.

Pinker, S. (2002). *The blank slate: The modern denial of human nature.* New York, NY: Penguin.

Pollak, S. D., Messner, M., Kistler, D. J., & Cohn, J. F. (2009). Development of perceptual expertise in emotion recognition. *Cognition, 110*(2), 242–247.

Pollak, S. D., Nelson, C. A., Schlaak, M. F., Roeber, B. J., Wewerka, S. S., Wiik, K. L., ... Gunnar, M. R. (2010). Neurodevelopmental effects of early deprivation in postinstitutionalized children. *Child Development, 81*(1), 224–236.

Pollak, S. D., & Sinha, P. (2002). Effects of early experience on children's recognition of facial displays of emotion. *Developmental Psychology, 38*(5), 784–791.

Prather, M. D., Lavenex, P., Mauldin-Jourdain, M. L., Mason, W. A., Capitanio, J. P., Mendoza, S. P., & Amaral, D. G. (2001). Increased social fear and decreased fear of objects in monkeys with neonatal amygdala lesions. *Neuroscience, 106*(4), 653–658.

Prehn-Kristensen, A., Wiesner, C., Bergmann, T. O., Wolff, S., Jansen, O., Mehdorn, H. M., ... Pause, B. M. (2009). Induction of empathy by the smell of anxiety. *PLoS One, 4*(6), e5987.

Preston, S. D., & de Waal, F. B. (2002). Empathy: Its ultimate and proximate bases. *Behavioral and Brain Sciences, 25*(1), 1–20; discussion 20–71.

Puce, A., & Perrett, D. (2003). Electrophysiology and brain imaging of biological motion. *Philosophical Transactions of the Royal Society of London B: Biological Sciences, 358*(1431), 435–445.

Rutter, M. (1989). Pathways from childhood to adult life. *Journal of Child Psychology and Psychiatry, 30*(1), 23–51.

Sagi, A., & Hoffman, M. L. (1976). Empathic distress in the newborn. *Developmental Psychology, 12*, 175–176.

Savic, I., Berglund, H., Gulyas, B., & Roland, P. (2001). Smelling of odorous sex hormone-like compounds causes sex-differentiated hypothalamic activations in humans. *Neuron, 31*(4), 661–668.

Saxe, R. (2006). Four regions for one theory of mind? In J. T. Cacioppo, P. S. Vissser, & C. L. Pickett (Eds.), *Social neuroscience.* Cambridge, MA: MIT Press.

Senju, A. (2010). Developmental and comparative perspectives of contagious yawning. *Frontal Neurology and Neuroscience, 28*, 113–119.

Senju, A., Maeda, M., Kikuchi, Y., Hasegawa, T., Tojo, Y., & Osanai, H. (2007). Absence of contagious yawning in children with autism spectrum disorder. *Biological Letters, 3*(6), 706–708.

Singer, T., & Lamm, C. (2009). The social neuroscience of empathy. *Annals of the New York Academy of Sciences, 1156*, 81–96.

Smyke, A. T., Zeanah, C. H., Fox, N. A., Nelson, C. A., & Guthrie, D. (2010). Placement in foster care enhances quality of attachment among young institutionalized children. *Child Development, 81*(1), 212–223.

Spear, L. P. (2000). The adolescent brain and age-related behavioral manifestations. *Neuroscience Biobehavioral Reviews, 24*(4), 417–463.

Spinelli, S., Chefer, S., Suomi, S. J., Higley, J. D., Barr, C. S., & Stein, E. (2009). Early-life stress induces long-term morphologic changes in primate brain. *Archives of General Psychiatry, 66*(6), 658–665.

Steinberg, L., & Morris, A. S. (2001). Adolescent development. *Annual Review of Psychology, 52*, 83–110.

Sugita, Y. (2008). Face perception in monkeys reared with no exposure to faces. *Proceedings of the National Academy of Sciences U S A, 105*(1), 394–398.

Tonks, J., Slater, A., Frampton, I., Wall, S. E., Yates, P., & Williams, W. H. (2009). The development of emotion and empathy skills after childhood brain injury. *Developmental Medicine and Child Neurology, 51*(1), 8–16.

Tottenham, N., Hare, T. A., Quinn, B. T., McCarry, T. W., Nurse, M., Gilhooly, T., . . . Casey, B. J. (2010). Prolonged institutional rearing is associated with atypically large amygdala volume and difficulties in emotion regulation. *Developmental Science, 13*(1), 46–61.

Van Egeren, L. A., Barratt, M. S., & Roach, M. A. (2001). Mother-infant responsiveness: Timing, mutual regulation, and interactional context. *Developmental Psychology, 37*(5), 684–697.

Vanderwert, R. E., Marshall, P. J., Nelson, C. A., 3rd, Zeanah, C. H., & Fox, N. A. (2010). Timing of intervention affects brain electrical activity in children exposed to severe psychosocial neglect. *PLoS One, 5*, e11415.

Way, B. M., Taylor, S. E., & Eisenberger, N. I. (2009). Variation in the mu-opioid receptor gene (OPRM1) is associated with dispositional and neural sensitivity to social rejection. *Proceedings of the National Academy of Sciences U S A, 106*(35), 15079–15084.

Wiik, K. L., Loman, M. M., Van Ryzin, M. J., Armstrong, J. M., Essex, M. J., Pollak, S., & Gunnar, M. R. D. (2010). Behavioral and emotional symptoms of post-institutionalized children in middle childhood. *Journal of Child Psychology and Psychiatry, 52*(1), 56–63.

Winslow, J. T., Noble, P. L., Lyons, C. K., Sterk, S. M., & Insel, T. R. (1992). Development of concern for others. *Developmental Psychology, 28*(1), 126–136.

Winslow, J. T., Noble, P. L., Lyons, C. K., Sterk, S. M., & Insel, T. R. (2003). Rearing effects on cerebrospinal fluid oxytocin concentration and social buffering in rhesus monkeys. *Neuropsychopharmacology, 28*(5), 910–918.

Zeanah, C. H., Egger, H. L., Smyke, A. T., Nelson, C. A., Fox, N. A., Marshall, P. J., & Guthrie, D. (2009). Institutional rearing and psychiatric disorders in Romanian preschool children. *American Journal of Psychiatry, 166*(7), 777–785.

{ Commentary }

The Death of Empathy?
Bruce D. Perry

Humankind is a social species. We are born completely dependent on others and as we mature remain interdependent. We need each other to survive and thrive. The capacity to form and maintain relationships is essential to our health, productivity, and creativity and is the key to our survival as a species. Our individual physiology—including the neurophysiology that mediates our cognitive, motor, social, and emotional functioning—is profoundly impacted by the presence, behaviors, and emotions of those around us. Central to this remarkable social capacity (and contagion) is empathy.

In his excellent overview of empathy, Dr. Nelson highlights the complex developmental and neurobiological factors involved in empathy. But most fascinating, Dr. Nelson views the brain-mediated capacity for empathy through the lens of evolution. He makes several key points: Empathy is a component of human social behavior; the functional capacity for empathy is mediated by a set of interacting neural networks spanning multiple systems in the brain; the development of empathy is influenced by developmental experiences—both the nature of these experiences and the timing; and, finally, changes in the social and developmental environments of human living groups over the modern era are likely to have an impact on the development of empathy. As Dr. Nelson points out, "The brain networks that guide various aspects of social behavior, from affective responding to cognitive decision making, evolved in a very different context during the HGSB [hunter-gatherer small band] era."

Simply stated, the human brain is not designed for the modern world—despite the fact that the modern world is a "product" of the human brain's remarkable capacities for invention, communication, and adaptation. We are now living in a world that is disconnected from the rhythms of nature (i.e., climate controlled, light–dark manipulated, overstimulating to our auditory and visual senses); we raise and educate our children in social environments at once more complex and demanding on our social neurobiology (e.g., hundreds of day-by-day interactions with acquaintances or strangers) yet oddly impoverished of complex somatosensory-rich, relational interactions (i.e., touch, holding, rocking, conversation, or intergenerational interactions).

The relational environment of the typical American child has changed dramatically in the last 50 years (Szalavitz & Perry, 2010). Our society is more mobile; approximately one-third of the students in any given school year are new to the community and class. We move away from our extended families. We eat fewer meals together as families. We have smaller families. The ratio of developmentally mature individuals capable of modeling for, enriching, educating, nurturing, and protecting a young child in an HGSB group (at population equilibrium) was 4:1; we now—in our "advanced" Western societies—think it is an "enriched" ratio to have one caregiver for four children in a preschool setting. This is one-sixteenth the relational ratio of the HGSB. It is not unusual to have a ratio of 1:30 for 6-year-old children in an "educational" setting. Six or more hours a day of "screen" time is not uncommon for a typical child in the United States. This dilution of the relational milieu in the Western world has created a poverty of relationships for millions of children—a form of poverty, I would argue, far more destructive than economic poverty. Many of the choices we make about owning our own homes with our own rooms with their own TVs, structuring education in a hierarchical fashion, compartmentalizing work/home, and childrearing (e.g., "Don't sleep with your baby," "Stimulate your toddler's brain with Baby Einstein videos," "Use this electric rocking machine," "My third grader needs a cell phone for safety") contribute to a relational poverty unknown to any other generation of humankind.

The consequences of this poverty of relationships are not well understood. But in light of the key points made by Dr. Nelson, it is worth considering that we may have invented ourselves into a corner. The very capacity that binds us together appears to be vulnerable to the changes in demographics, technology, and child-rearing practices we have created. Consider for a moment the remarkable malleability of neural networks in the brain—recognizing that while these networks develop and are modified by genetic and epigenetic factors, a primary factor in the ultimate functional capacity of these networks is based on the timing, pattern, and nature of activity (i.e., "experience"). Again, simply stated, key capacities for social functioning are expressed in a "use-dependent" fashion. This includes the capacity for empathy. Considering the central role of empathy in health—in all domains, cognitive, social, emotional, and physiological—it is sobering to consider the impact of experience-dependent shifts in the capacity for empathy that would result from relationally impoverished childhoods. The combination of the relational poverty of our modern world and the sensitivity of the developing brain to experience suggests that these changes cannot be ideal to fully express our capacity for empathy.

The full expression of our capacity to be humane is a product of our genetic potential and how that potential is expressed as a function of the timing, nature, and pattern of experience. To become humane, therefore, a child has to be treated in humane ways; to be capable of loving, a child has to be loved; to be capable of sharing, someone had to share with that child. A key question raised by Dr. Nelson's chapter is whether, given the neurodevelopmental factors he outlines, our current childrearing, educational, and social practices are sufficient to express a child's capacity for empathy. Many of us who work with children and families in the child welfare, mental health, educational, juvenile justice, and criminal justice systems see every day the multidimensional and destructive effects of growing up in relational poverty, chaos, fear, and violence. And we often see how relational health and stability can contribute to resilience in the face of the same chaos, violence, and trauma. Have we created a society that will lead to the death of empathy? Or can we self-correct—can we invent our way to a more humane future? I, for one, am confident that we can. The first step to intentional positive change is insight. And the insights regarding the neurodevelopmental factors involved in empathy outlined by Dr. Nelson will be essential in this reinventing process.

Reference

Szalavitz, M., & Perry, B. D. (2010). *Born for love: Why empathy is essential and endangered.* New York, NY: Harper Collins.

Born for Art, and the Joyful Companionship of Fiction

Colwyn Trevarthen

My aim is to shew, although this is not generally attended to, that the roots of all sciences and arts in every instance arise as early as in the tender age, and that on these foundations it is neither impossible nor difficult for the whole superstructure to be laid; provided always that we act reasonably with a reasonable creature.

—John Amos Comenius (1592–1671) in *The School of Infancy*, Chapter viii, Section 6, on the education of rhetoric. Translated by D. Benham. London, 1858. Quoted by Quick, 1894, pp. 144–145.

Playful Human Nature and the Creation of Culture

All human communities take pleasure in fictional, poetic worlds, inventing arts and techniques that go far beyond immediate vital needs and facts. Often fantasy seems more important to us than informative language or logic, especially if we are a young child, a performer, an artist—or, as both Albert Einstein and Alfred North Whitehead have said, a scientist seeking inspiration, aiming to think free of conventional "truths." We may become obedient to the most arcane procedures or complicated explanations, arguments, and laws (Bruner, 2003). A sense of humor brings relief from oppressive rules.

Why does it matter so much that our recreations, beliefs, and invented ways of making things should be done "properly," and why are we so ambitious to invent new, more complex twists of logic to "justify" our case? Why do we judge our companions by their abilities to share their thoughts inventively, calling the differences "personality?" No other mammal has so much invention to cope with. The strange human urge to shape and share fantasies of action and experience is with us from birth. It is innate, not acquired, but must grow in company (Trevarthen, 2001a, 2005, 2009a, 2011).

A mother loves to test her infant's invention. While breastfeeding, washing, or dressing, she will interrupt the task to touch invitingly and speak musically to her infant, watching for a "thoughtful" reaction. Her infant's knowing response comes and makes her smile, then exclaim with joy. Why is the infant so alert to how she acts in this provocative way, which does not meet needs for comfort and care? Why does the baby turn to hear and see her? Sometimes an expectant mother addresses her unborn infant, imagining the baby is attentive to her talk. After birth she is rewarded—the infant immediately knows and prefers her voice (DeCasper & Prescott, 2009). And the communication of fanciful notions grows quickly. What other use does the sense of fun in absurd jokes and mannerisms that even a 6-month-old can display have, which can be used cunningly to tease loved ones and provoke joy in them (Reddy, 2008)? The inventive instinct becomes the fantasy play of toddlers.

The idea that this is the true and original story of uniquely human inherent needs and skills for adaptation to a culture receives support from a report of how infants are played with and spoken to in a hunter-gatherer society that has managed to keep legendary social ways and ancient language (Takada, 2005). It carries a clear message about the best environment for our modern infants and young children. Mothers, fathers, and others of the family are to be an infant's companions in the fun of human fantastic story making.

I agree with Dan Hughes and Bruce Perry that in health the human brain grows to build creative relationships (Hughes, 2006; Perry & Szalavitz, 2010). That is what love is about and why it is cruel to treat an infant without joy and imagination, even if the child's love of life is not actually terrified and wounded by violence in the family (Trevarthen, 2001a).

How the Human Past Might Have Led to Our Fantastic Present

The emergence of modern human beings is signaled by what remains of their imaginative art, not by their skills of technical manipulation. The Neanderthals, who they replaced, made exquisitely crafted stone tools and weapons but appear to have had no pictorial artistry or instrumental music. *Homo sapiens sapiens* were creating both of these to satisfy delicate aesthetic appreciation 35,000 years ago (Clottes, 2010; Conard, Malina, & Münzel, 2009).

Anthropological research encourages an idea that the first modern humans had imaginative parenting. Along with frequent breastfeeding and cosleeping with enjoyment of the special comfort of human fine-haired skin, the shared care of alloparents, and the companionship of family groups (Hrdy, 2009), early human adults must have been playful with infants. The whole family surely took joy in the experimental and humorous actions of their babies. They would have followed each infant's growing curiosity about how to deal with objects playfully and cooperatively, joining them in learning by "intent participation" how to make and use toys and tools and how to deal with plants and animals, friends, and strangers (Bakeman, Adamson, Konner, & Barr, 1990; Rogoff, 2003).

I am sure that in the evolutionary past of humans, the infant's affectionate ingenuity, beginning first in an intimate motherly attachment, was responded to happily and provocatively by fathers, siblings, uncles, aunts, and grandparents, helping to make a community culture that could pass on the rituals of art, technique, and understanding of ancestors. Busy modern families do the same when happily at home in a peaceful village subcommunity, away from the "services" of a demanding urban society—distanced for a time from employment by the "system," fancy technology, artificial mobility and means of global communication with all manner of human contrivance, and competition for commodities and status in the system (Habermas, 1987; McGilchrist, 2009; Smyth & Dewar, 2009).

The Growth of Meaning in Company, With a Multiplex, Polyrhythmic Body and Mind

Bjorn Merker (2009), comparing us with other primates, concludes that the first step to humanness was the evolution of "ritual culture," going beyond the shared learning of "instrumental" skills for getting food, such as apes show, or finding a place in a rivalrous society of smart status-conscious companions by appropriate use of deference in tone and manner of communication, by which many social species regulate their "politics." Research on infant action games and baby songs, such as are found in every existing human group, supports his thesis (Ekerdal & Merker, 2009).

Stephen Malloch and I have made an acoustic exploration of the infant's vocal and gestural talents for what we call "communicative musicality," which has "pulse," affective "quality," and the persuasive time sense of "narrative" (Malloch, 1999; Trevarthen, 1999, 2008a, 2008b, 2009b; Trevarthen, Delafield-Butt, & Schögler, 2011). This artful moving and thinking, which elaborates an early human talent for fantasy in "mimesis" (Donald, 2001), is dependent on the sympathy of companions. It has aesthetic and moral emotions, which may be cultivated and refined with learned social rules, but which are part of its sociable human emotional nature.

On the "aesthetics of childhood," Pauline von Bonsdorff (2009, p. 98) has this to say: "The aesthetics of childhood is not just about children, but about the human situation. We were all children once, and childhood is on the whole a permanent structure of individual lives, of culture and society."

Ellen Dissanayake, who has studied prehistoric creations and the values given to art in many cultures, concludes that art begins in the intimacy of mother–infant play (Dissanayake, 2009a), agreeing with Merker that the temporal arts give energy to the development of a collaborative spirit in a community, encouraging cultural invention (Dissanayake, 2009b).

Before language is mastered, there are growth-regulated steps of brain and body in motives and control of movement by which an infant becomes a collaborator in human meaning and human feeling (Reddy, Hay, Murray, & Trevarthen, 1997; Trevarthen, 1998, 2011; Trevarthen & Aitken, 2003; Trevarthen & Reddy, 2007). The development of each individual's well-being and self-confidence in society and the process by which a culture is passed on depend on a developing ability in the child to "learn how to mean" (Halliday, 1975) and to learn the narratives of culture (Bruner, 1990, 2003). The steps archaeologists trace from the first small settlements to organized agriculture, the making of cities, and the invention of writing appear to depend on such motives (Renfrew, 2006) and on the acceptance by the community of artificial "institutional facts" (Searle, 1995), which are not the same as what a rational philosopher takes to be "real facts."

We come to a new view of the expanding consciousness of a young child as a life story created with love in companionship, a "narration" or communicative "project" that is guided by specifically human social feelings, by a "sociocultural brain" actively using its body in expressive, imaginative, and person-sensitive ways. These new sympathies extend the heritage of mammalian emotions for regulating individual and social enterprises and the imitative skills of other primates (Trevarthen, 2009b, 2011).

Epigenetics, Developmental Ingenuity, and "Resilience"

We can learn about the biology of humanity and its cultures from three generations of Batesons. Grandfather William (1894) discovered the principle of homeosis or regulation of gene expression by epigenetic factors, making a common theory of phylogenesis, embryology, and genetics. His theory is the foundation of modern epigenetics (Lewis, 1994; Stern, 2000).

William's son, Gregory, pioneered systems theory and cybernetics and stressed the two sides of an organism's adaptation to the world, the time-tested instincts and the special abilities to be modified in "use." Gregory said,

> No animal or plant can ever be "ready made." The internal recipe insists upon compatibility but is never sufficient for the development and life of the organism.... It must acquire certain somatic characteristics by use, by disuse, by habit, by hardship, and by nurture.... [[And]] the acquisition of bad habits, at a social level, surely sets the context for selection of ultimately lethal genetic propensities. (G. Bateson, 1979, pp. 234–235)

Gregory's daughter, Mary Catherine, studied a "proto-conversation" between a mother and her 9-week-old infant, marking the subtle rhythms of the dialogic "system"—how the two sides of an adaptive action were played out between mother and child in what may be called "four-part harmony," each person giving and receiving sympathetic affection. She identified this as the foundation for language and the "healing practices" of diverse cultures, which her mother, Margaret Mead, and her father had investigated. She gave the first clear description of infant "intersubjectivity":

> These interactions were characterized by a sort of delighted, ritualized courtesy and more or less sustained attention and mutual gaze. Many of the vocalizations were of types not described in the acoustic literature on infancy,

since they were very brief and faint, and yet were crucial parts of the jointly sustained performances. (M. C. Bateson, 1979, p. 65)

Creating the Life Story of a People

Endel Tulving (2002) proposes that an "episodic memory," recalling key moments of experience for future reference, is a special human talent. It seems to be what makes "processual," problem-thinking, inventive intelligence possible. It builds each individual's personal history, an "autonoesis" that links emotion-charged moments of action and awareness in the "phenomenological present" recalled as specially significant in a fictional plan of life's ambitions and achievements. Stern has given us an account of how "vitality dynamics" seen in communication with infants or psychiatric patients are cultivated in the arts as "layered composite narratives" (Stern, 2010, p. 131). A healthy mind builds proud memories in loving company with specially trusted family and friends, making a good story. Loneliness, shame, depression, and sadness are the emotions that identify loss of this collective story making, which can be called "socionoesis" (Trevarthen, 2007). The developing human psyche and brain have needs for company, and human psychopathology is identified by a deep confusion in self-awareness as well as an incapacity to communicate sympathetically with other human imaginations and purposes (Northoff, 2011) and to contribute to work in society (Heckman, 2007).

Growth of a Human Brain Expectant for Culture

Our knowledge of human evolution (Renfrew, 2006) makes clear that the evolution of human cultural understanding has been made possible by growth of a larger brain that first appeared in our ancestors more than 2,000,000 years ago and that made a great advance only 200,000 years ago with the appearance of *Homo sapiens sapiens*. A new kind of epigenetics in brain tissues motivates new ways of using the body to engage with what is discovered, done, and made.

Learning culture, according to the science of neuroanthropology, changes the shape of the parts of the brain undergoing development in individuals as they seek to communicate and cooperate in a "meaning-sustaining" community (Domínguez Duque, Turner, Lewis, & Egan, 2010; Han & Northoff, 2008). The human brain has an extended ontogenesis, one that transforms shared biological regulations of vital states between the *bodies* of the developing fetus and mother to a psychological coregulation of intentions, interests, and inner feelings of *minds* by movements of intersubjective communication. We have called the first *amphoteronomic* ("together" regulation of bodies, in contrast to autonomic "self"-regulation) and the second *synrhythmic* (dependent on close temporal engagement of rhythms of movement that express mind states; Trevarthen, Aitken, Vandekerckhove, Delafield-Butt, & Nagy, 2006).

At birth, the infant has special expressive and receptive organs adapted to monitor mental processes in the self and in others by keeping track of the prospective awareness made manifest in the shape and timing of movements (Trevarthen, 2001b). A key ingredient is a polyrhythmic time generator in the brain built to track and make productive use of proprioceptive and visceral dynamics throughout the body (Meissner & Wittmann, 2011). This time sense, a hierarchical biochronology of rhythms, is innate and matching between the infant and an attentive adult, enabling them to attune in agile jazzlike synchrony and alternation, leading and following one another in a way that generates pleasure and makes learning of new creations easy (Gratier, 2008; Gratier & Trevarthen, 2008). The life dynamics that flow within one human brain and body, involving subtle new variations of the affective systems of the brain that have regulated activities and social cooperation in mammals for millennia, make engaging melodies, helping that person make "good time" with others, getting "in the groove" emotionally (Panksepp & Trevarthen, 2009). They direct and organize intentions and awareness in the brain and give value to memories and imaginings. They motivate learning in an intimacy that changes what the brain perceives, can do, plans to do, and remembers.

Advances in the Psychobiology of Attachment and Human Needs

In response to the remarkable presentations in this section on the psychobiology of early stages of human vitality with maternal support, I try to relate scientific inspection of the details of the organism at the sub-subject, subpersonal level so I can begin to comprehend the rich intersubjective and interpersonal level of human presence and its special epigenetics. We need the evidence for mechanisms of neural, neurochemical, hormonal, and molecular (genetic and epigenetic) regulation of mind functions. Charles Sherrington (1906) distinguished these as "projicience," for identifying by "distance reception" the shape and substance of objects to serve prospective control of purposes and projects, and "affective appraisals" of tastes and odors that protect well-being of the body. But there are advantages of going back to how Darwin observed human nature and its emotions before any of these wonders of animal and human biology were accessible, or indeed to the rich philosophical picture Adam Smith gave of human commercial enterprise and its moral foundations a century before Darwin.

If we are to protect young children, their bodies and their brains, from harm in the complex, busy, and sometimes cruel world they come to live in, a world that has to satisfy artificial rituals and beliefs of an adult industrial and e-literate society, we will have to value more and give response to what children bring to human life—the eager spirit of their joyful projects beyond their seeking to survive as organisms, and especially what kind of company they expect from us, their parents, brothers and sisters, teachers, and professional caregivers. It turns out that a newborn infant has clear expectations of human sense and is active in starting a personal quest for meaningful stories in good company:

> The old model of thinking of the newborn infant as helpless and ready to be shaped by his environment prevented us from seeing his power as a communicant in the early mother-father-infant interaction. To see the neonate as chaotic or insensitive provided us with the capacity to see ourselves as acting "on" rather than "with" him. (Brazelton, 1979, p. 79)

Primary-Process Emotional Systems and Child Development

Panksepp gives us a rich account of ancestral neural systems of emotion in mammals. He believes these same systems constitute the "affective consciousness" of infants, which is "anoetic" or "unknowing," comparable with that of anencephalic children. Affectionate parents guide the infant's immature embodied impulses toward more cultivated "secondary-process" forms of feeling-with-knowledge. He employs Tulving's concept of autonoesis or "self-knowing" in human beings, reliant on "tertiary-process higher order cognitive mechanisms" and an "episodic memory," concluding that a mother's intimate loving, first protective against fear and sadness, and a father's more physical playfulness, later encouraging mastery of anger, are required for the maturation of "higher" emotions and a responsible and self-confident "personal history" in society. For development of understanding of intimate sensuous affection, he believes that for a young child it is best "to educate by empathic example rather than cognitive instruction." A child's temperament and emotional health depend on both "inbuilt" and "developmentally emergent" sources, the latter depending on greatly expanded learning powers of the human cerebral cortex, which is proposed to function like the programmable RAM of a computer, a "cognitive information-processing device."

The discovery that rat pups "laugh" as they "tease" one another inspires a generous interpretation of the biology of joy in companionship. Aesthetic and moral sensibilities have a foundation in more elaborate human "dynamic affects" (Stern, 2010), which are adapted to create and retain imaginative narratives of life in movement for the self and in community with others. Surely the evolutionary expansion of the human cortex, with its somatotopic mapping of circuits of agency and experience (Trevarthen, 1985), was accompanied by a rapid evolution of new emotional and motivational powers in the subcortex. Basic complex emotions are evident in accurate descriptions of how infants know our minds (Reddy, 2008). Panksepp concludes, "We will have to have integrated scientific views of higher and lower BrainMind functions that do not yet exist in mature forms either in our scientific research, in our academic discussion, or in our educational endeavors." His research is a clarion call to find these views.

Neurobiology and the Evolution of Mammalian Social Behavior

The research of Carter and Porges explores the evolutionary elaboration of hormonal systems that link the vital functions of one mammalian body to those of a social partner, especially between sex partners and between mothers and their young, but in other cooperative affiliations, too. Two hormones, oxytocin (OT) and arginine vasopressin (AVP), play key roles in development of social bonds and in mental health. They motivate female nurturance and more masculine active resistance to danger and uncertainty. Human young have an exceptionally long dependence on physical and physiological support and protection, and attachment between children and parents is strong and usually lifelong. These emotional regulations are elaborated in the cultural celebrations of community in art and technique, and the hormonal mediations are modified by the context of behavior and experience. "The capacity of these neuroendocrine systems to undergo long-lasting functional modifications presents an epigenetic model that may help to explain the origins of traits that have been called personality or temperament." Clearly the biological regulations, and differences between male and female reactions, are not just subservient to cognitive or rational deliberations and instruction. A young nervous system is sensitive to the quantity and quality of intimate contact with a caregiver and the sharing of playful enjoyments in "symbiotic regulation," which benefits both the caregiver and infant. Psychiatric disorders consequent on early stress or neglect affect both individual experience and the capacity to benefit from relationships.

Porges has charted evolutionary transformations in the neural systems that link the brain with autonomic regulations of the body that enable intimate collaborations between the vital states and intelligence of individuals. His "polyvagal theory" of mammalian social behavior explains how reptilian "self-regulations" became mammalian "other regulations" serving more elaborate social life. All of the movements that mediate in the proto-conversation between an infant and a mother described by M. C. Bateson (1979)—the shifting contact between the eyes with their white sclerae; the subtle modulations of upper and lower face expressions; the changes of pitch and melody of vocalizations by actions of muscles in the throat, jaws, tongue, and lips; and the listening to the tones of speech—are directed by visceral motor neurons that were originally evolved for vital self-regulations of breathing, heartbeat, and prospective awareness of the environment seen and heard. All are uniquely elaborated in humans for a new kind of intersubjective awareness that leads to transmission of ideas and descriptions of experience in language.

We need, I believe, to add hands to this theory of human self-regulating, creative, communicative, and therapeutic motor control. In primates, the forelimbs become involved in new self-regulations of the body's comfort, as well as in foraging for food and its transport to the mouth, and they evolve in humans into organs of gesture. Besides transmitting intimate messages of comfort, using resonant objects to make music that imitates song, and making all manner of tools and mechanical contrivances, human hands can acquire a full language capacity. And they are highly expressive in dramatic and artful intersubjective ways in infancy (Trevarthen et al., 2011).

Dopamine and Caregiver Responsiveness

Mileva-Seitz, Afonso, and Fleming add an account of dopamine (DA) to the exploration of the biology of affectionate behavior and infant care. In mammals, this catecholamine neurotransmitter motivates intense affectionate maternal care of offspring, changing the responses and actions of the mother's brain around birth. There are individual differences in this maternal responsiveness, which may have consequences for the development of the young.

Human mothers both engage in intimate bodily contact with their infants, holding, caressing, and breastfeeding them, and communicate by the subtle expressions of eyes, face, and voice described earlier. Their sensibility to the odor and touch of their infants is enhanced around birth, and both mother and infant rapidly acquire greater sensibility for one another with early experience. The loving mother's sense of comfort and resistance to stress is correlated with her level of sympathy and perception of distress in her infant. The mood of new mothers becomes more labile. In some this leads to a brief period of postnatal depression, which can, if severe, have consequences for the infant's responses to her and for socioemotional development and learning.

These authors give consideration to evidence for variability in human mothers' responses to their infants, concluding, "There is direct evidence of an association between polymorphic variation in human DA genes and individual differences in maternal behavior." It appears that maternal sensitivity of new mothers is inversely correlated with their capacity to engage in abstract reasoning or "executive function," which may explain the stress modern mothers have in juggling the demands of employment and infant care. The development of larger brains in humans may get in the way of warm mothering. This recalls the concerns of McGilchrist (2009) about the effects of modern "environment detached" cultivation of the human brain and mind.

Epigenetics and the Environmental Regulation of the Genome and Its Function

Meaney takes us to a detailed consideration of molecular events around gene transcription, addressing the question of epigenetic regulation of human behavior and experience, and how experience can affect "reading" of the genome, changing or "remodeling" neural function and learning, thereby affecting personality, stress response, vulnerability, and resistance to a wide range of chronic illnesses and risk for psychopathology.

Research with rats demonstrates effects of maternal care on adult behavior of the offspring, including their parenting behavior. The neurotransmitter serotonin is associated with feelings of pleasure and regulation of digestion and well-being in relation to environmental events, and also regulates glucocorticoid receptor gene transcription in hippocampal neurons, thus affecting memory and learning. Meaney presents evidence that "variations in parental care can modify the epigenetic state of selected sites of the human genome," changing "activity-dependent" intercellular signaling in the brain. Indeed, monozygotic twins are always increasingly different in agency, temperament, and stress resistance (Piontelli, 2002). But the genomic sequence is not just a passive player in the processes of expression, and moreover, "specific epigenetic modifications, once established, might be actively maintained," and may even be transmitted across generations. Meaney's work gives new life to William Bateson's ideas of more than a century ago.

Human Nature and Early Experience

Suomi extends the pioneering work of Harlow, which gave inspiration and solid scientific support to Bowlby's theory of the effects of maternal deprivation. In remarkable ways, rhesus monkeys resemble human beings at all stages of life, in their vital self-regulations, brain functions, and social development. After birth their "infancy" leads to physical and social maturity, stage by stage, at four times the human rate. It begins with the same strong emotional bond between the mother and her offspring, then leads to more independent adventures in a school of peers, but with the benefit of the mother's continued affectionate concern as a "stable base." Indeed, the neurophysiological foundation of our capacity to be part of or "mirror" one another's intentions and feelings was (accidentally) discovered in a monkey before it was imagined in a human being.

Now the fate of monkey offspring in controlled circumstances with or without maternal support is studied by the most sophisticated techniques of biochemistry, molecular genetics, and functional brain science, and the harvest of data is rich. We can understand better how timidity and cautious fear or careless risk taking and aggression are mediated in the brain; how genes have variable responsibility for personality depending on circumstances, including maternal care; and how subtle modulation of gene ordering and expression can enhance or diminish the effects in the body and in behavior.

I am delighted to see that close and "respectful" observation at the early newborn stage reveals a hitherto unimagined ability of a monkey mother and offspring to engage in intense face-to-face communication by means of explicit face expressions.

But two things appear to be missing or very limited in this monkey talk: There is no vocal protoconversation, and the hand gestures made by monkeys, young or old, have less "narrative" attraction. Nevertheless, the passion of intimate attachment is there, and in humans similar face-to-face communication remains the arena for conversation and the growth of language.

The research is providing a cornucopia of evidence of the importance of maternal affection for neurohumoral regulation of the growing body and brain, for epigenetic regulation, and for "developmental programming" of expression of the genome. Temperamental differences between young monkeys are revealed to play a key part in the dynamic regulation of roles in a highly stratified society where individual differences count, not just as forms of pathology, but as ways of collaborating and adapting to changing circumstances. The evidence helps dispel the medical impulse to call every behavior that is "abnormal" a disorder or disease. The fact that a young monkey with a certain allele can become timid or aggressive, or both, and too fond of alcohol with poor mothering, yet be perfectly well behaved and sober with good affectionate attachment to a mother, underlines the importance of the evolution of human maternal care for epigenetic regulation of gene effects in development of the child.

The Neurobiological Basis of Empathy and Its Development

Since that discovery of "mirror neurons" in monkeys, the psychology of behavioral sharing has been radically changed. It is now fashionable to believe that intentions can transfer between brains by a direct mapping of the form of movement done to what is seen to be done. However, the findings from research using functional brain imaging with human subjects are complex, especially for the communication of emotional states by movements that have no instrumental purpose in the objective world.

Nelson accepts the definition of empathy as "an affective response in one individual that is triggered by the observed or imagined feeling state of another individual," and he distinguishes empathy from "sympathy" or "compassion" because states shared empathically are to be "isomorphic." This rules out "complementary" states of emotion "shared with" another (the original meaning of the Greek word *sympatheia*) to attain a new state of relationship. Such a mutual assistance in emotion would appear to be essential in freely creative interpersonal contacts, with dynamic shifts of different feelings and expectations. Empathy is an "estimation" (in Greek a "projection into," or "taking in") of an other person's feelings, a somewhat detached trying to have the same feelings.

He divides the development of the human social brain into three periods: *infancy*, where the mother is the socializing agent; *juvenile*, where experience of play with peers promotes development of empathy while the mother acts as a safe base; and *adolescence,* occupied with transition from home to the adult groups and becoming concerned with reproduction and maintaining social status in the group.

He hypothesizes, "Shifting emotional salience across development may be mediated by an interaction between changes in subcortical structures such as the amygdala, striatum, and hypothalamus and maturation of prefrontal regions that can exert regulatory control on attention and behavioral responses."

Emotional development is seen to be a slow acquisition of systematic explanatory awareness.

Familiar provocative behaviors of infants' and parents' joking and teasing, and the soliciting of prosocial response, described by Reddy (2008) give evidence of an early appearance of awareness of others' actual and potential states of mind. The damaging effects of institutionalization and the consequences of abnormal development in autism receive clearer explanation if it is taken that innate motive systems normally act as epigenetic regulators of the expression of sympathetic emotions seeking social response. They are injured by neglect or abuse, and they may be distorted by abnormal prenatal development that closes down important avenues of development.

The Interpersonal Neurobiology of Attachment and Emotional Development

Schore gives us conclusive evidence, from many sources, that both the self-sustaining vital functions and the affectionate love-regulated interpersonal neurobiology are mediated more in the right hemisphere of the human brains of infant and mother, and later in the right brains of infant and father. This side of the MindBrain is most active and growing in infancy, preparing the growing body and its functions and activities for survival first, then for a life of learning in human company. Schore proposes that Bowlby's environment of evolutionary adaptedness (EEA) can be identified with how the mother as the primary caregiver "shapes, for better or worse, the experience-dependent maturation of the brain systems involved in attachment." This puts great responsibility on a mother's affectionate care "at implicit nonverbal levels" and the support she gives to the "right lateralized self-regulatory systems" of her child, including those mediated by the vagus that promote oxygenation of the expanding neocortical tissues by parasympathetic regulation of cardiac function, as Porges describes.

Schore concludes that in late gestation and the early months of infancy, a mother's intimate care and concern promote development of a posterior parietotemporal corticolimbic sensory system of the right hemisphere, supporting the child's capacity to overcome hunger and fatigue and to calm distress. When both mother and infant are active in a more "playful" exchange of expressions of their emotions, midfrontal limbic circuits of their right hemispheres are engaged. Development of this expressive right fronto-limbic system in the later months of infancy engages with paternal feelings of affection for the toddler, which are important in shaping the child's regulation of more proactive emotional states of anger and resistance—in a word, for "moral" development and listening to the voice of conscience. This recalls Freud's "superego," but with the benefit of the shared fun of vigorous play rather than just stern discipline. In the EEA, the father would surely have collaborated with the mother in enjoyment of the infant's vitality, complementing her signs of emotion by which "she smiles approval and thus encourages her child on the right path, or frowns disapproval" (Darwin, 1873, p. 365).

It is important to note that territories of *both* hemispheres are already adapted for their different interpersonal purposes in a young infant long before the left hemisphere growth spurt (Tzourio-Mazoyer et al., 2002). Gestural asymmetry is evident in neonatal imitation (Nagy, 2006), and early postnatal development of these gestures reveals that the two hemispheres of the infant, and of the mother, have complementary emotional functions: Protective self-related actions of the left hand indicate greater activity of the right hemisphere, while expressive or "assertive" actions are right-handed and presumably guided from the left hemisphere (Murray & Trevarthen, 1985; Trevarthen, 1996).

With Panksepp, Schore emphasizes that perinatal and postnatal development depend on developments in emotional systems. Growth of the infant's body and mind guides the optimal developmental path, as well as the support and help it requires in what Vygotsky (1978) called the "zone of proximal development" of the child. Responsive guidance of emotional impulses is important for maturation of internal well-being or physiological health, for psychological creativity, and especially for socioemotional cooperation in a work-oriented world.

Since Spitz's description of "anaclitic depression" following loss of support of an affectionate mother, which he called "hospitalism," and Bowlby's definition of "maternal deprivation," hospitals and orphanages have improved care of infants. There is still shocking evidence of the effects of loss of parental care—withdrawal of infants from engagement with other persons; loss of vitality; poor regulation of anxiety, fear, and anger through childhood; and lifelong incapacity to cope in relationships and in society. This leads to a massive social and economic cost (Heckman, 2007). Research abundantly confirms that lack of warm maternal support and companionship can have lasting effects on brain growth and function, which may or may not be alleviated by subsequent therapeutic attention (Perry & Szalavitz, 2010). Long periods of daycare in the first year are clearly detrimental.

In conclusion, our attention is drawn to a key topic for this volume, the mounting evidence that the United States, an "advanced" culture in terms of population, organized structure, productivity, and material wealth, offers less social or community support to families than other "advanced" cultures. The evidence shows the United States, with its poor maternal and paternal leave policies, is "providing a growth-inhibiting EEA" for many families, including prosperous ones. Schore notes, "Developmental neuropsychological studies of infants before, during, and after early day care are now essential."

References

Bakeman, R., Adamson, L. B., Konner, M., & Barr, R. G. (1990). !!Kung infancy: The social context of object exploration. *Child Development, 61*(3), 749–809.

Bateson, G. (1979). *Mind and nature: A necessary unity*. London: Wildwood House.

Bateson, M. C. (1979). The epigenesis of conversational interaction: A personal account of research development. In M. Bullowa (Ed.), *Before speech: The beginning of human communication* (pp. 63–77). London: Cambridge University Press.

Bateson, W. (1894). *Materials for the study of variation treated with especial regard to discontinuity in the origin of species*. Baltimore, MD, and London: Johns Hopkins University Press.

Brazelton, T. B. (1979). Evidence of communication during neonatal assessment. In M. Bullowa (Ed.), *Before speech: The beginning of human communication* (pp. 79–88). London: Cambridge University Press.

Bruner, J. S. (1990). *Acts of meaning*. Cambridge, MA: Harvard University Press.

Bruner, J. S. (2003). *Making stories: Law, literature, life*. New York, NY: Farrar, Strauss, and Giroux.

Clottes, J. (2010). *Cave art*. London: Phaidon Press.

Conard, N. J., Malina, M., & Münzel, S. C. (2009). New flutes document the earliest musical tradition in southwestern Germany. *Nature, 460*, 737–740.

Darwin, C. (1873). *The expression of emotion in man and animals*. New York, NY: D. Appleton and Co.

DeCasper, A. J., & Prescott, P. (2009). Lateralized processes constrain auditory reinforcement in human newborns. *Hearing Research, 255*, 135–141.

Dissanayake, E. (2009a). Root, leaf, blossom, or bole: Concerning the origin and adaptive function of music. In S. Malloch & C. Trevarthen (Eds.), *Communicative musicality: Exploring the basis of human companionship* (pp. 17–30). Oxford: Oxford University Press.

Dissanayake, E. (2009b). Bodies swayed to music: The temporal arts as integral to ceremonial ritual. In S. Malloch & C. Trevarthen (Eds.), *Communicative musicality: Exploring the basis of human companionship* (pp. 533–544). Oxford: Oxford University Press.

Domínguez Duque, J. F., Turner, R., Lewis, E. D., & Egan, G. (2010). Neuroanthropology: A humanistic science for the study of the culture–brain nexus. *Social Cognitive and Affective Neuroscience, 5*(2–3), 138–147.

Donald, M. (2001). *A mind so rare: The evolution of human consciousness*. New York, NY, and London: Norton.

Eckerdal, P., & Merker, B. (2009). 'Music' and the 'action song' in infant development: An interpretation. In S. Malloch & C. Trevarthen (Eds.), *Communicative musicality: Exploring the basis of human companionship* (pp. 241–262). Oxford: Oxford University Press.

Gratier, M. (2008). Grounding in musical interaction: Evidence from jazz performances. M. Imberty & M. Gratier (Eds.). [[Special Issue: Narrative in Music and Interaction.]] *Musicae Scientiae.*

Gratier, M., & Trevarthen, C. (2008). Musical narrative and motives for culture in mother-infant vocal interaction. *Journal of Consciousness Studies, 15*(10–11), 122–158.

Habermas, J. (1987). *The theory of communicative action. Vol. 2: Lifeworld and system: A critique of functionalist reason.* Boston, MA: Beacon Press.

Halliday, M. A. K. (1975). *Learning how to mean: Explorations in the development of language.* London: Edward Arnold.

Han, S., & Northoff, G. (2008). Culture-sensitive neural substrates of human cognition: A transcultural neuroimaging approach. *Nature Reviews Neuroscience, 9,* 646–654.

Heckman, J. J. (2007). The economics, technology and neuroscience of human capability formation. *Proceedings of the National Academy of Sciences USA, 104*(33), 13250–13255.

Hrdy, S. B. (2009). *Mothers and others: The evolutionary origins of mutual understanding.* Cambridge, MA: Harvard University Press.

Hughes, D. (2006). *Building the bonds of attachment: Awakening love in deeply traumatized children* (2nd ed.). Lanham, MD: Rowman and Littlefield.

Lewis, E. B. (1994). Homeosis: The first 100 years. *Trends in Genetics, 10*(10), 341–343.

Malloch, S. (1999). Mothers and infants and communicative musicality. *Musicae Scientiae (Special Issue, 1999–2000),* 29–57.

McGilchrist, I. (2009). *The master and his emissary: The divided brain and the making of the western world.* New Haven, CT, and London: Yale University Press.

Meissner, K., & Wittmann, M. (2011). Body signals, cardiac awareness, and the perception of time. *Biological Psychology, 86*(3), 289–297.

Merker, B. (2009). Ritual foundations of human uniqueness. In S. Malloch & C. Trevarthen (Eds.), *Communicative musicality: Exploring the basis of human companionship* (pp. 45–60). Oxford: Oxford University Press.

Murray, L., & Trevarthen, C. (1985). Emotional regulation of interactions between two-month-olds and their mothers. In T. M. Field & N. A. Fox (Eds.), *Social perception in infants* (pp. 177–197). Norwood, NJ: Ablex.

Nagy, E. (2006). From imitation to conversation: The first dialogues with human neonates. *Infant and Child Development, 15,* 223–232.

Northoff, G. (2011). Self and brain: What is self-related processing? *Trends in Cognitive Science, 15,* 186–187.

Panksepp, J., & Trevarthen, C. (2009). The neuroscience of emotion in music. In S. Malloch & C. Trevarthen (Eds.), *Communicative musicality: Exploring the basis of human companionship* (pp. 105–146). Oxford: Oxford University Press.

Perry, B., & Szalavitz, M. (2010). *Born for love: Why empathy is essential—and endangered.* New York, NY: Harper Collins.

Piontelli, A. (2002). *Twins: From fetus to child.* London: Routledge.

Quick, R. H. (1894). *Essays on educational reformers.* London: Longmans, Green and Co.

Reddy, V. (2008). *How infants know minds.* Cambridge, MA: Harvard University Press.

Reddy, V., Hay, D., Murray, L., & Trevarthen, C. (1997). Communication in infancy: Mutual regulation of affect and attention. In G. Bremner, A. Slater, & G. Butterworth (Eds.), *Infant development: Recent advances* (pp. 247–274). Hove, East Sussex: Psychology Press.

Renfrew, C. (2006). Becoming human: The archaeological challenge. *Proceedings of the British Academy, 139,* 217–238.

Rogoff, B. (2003). *The cultural nature of human development.* Oxford: Oxford University Press.

Searle, J. (1995). *The construction of social reality.* New York, NY: The Free Press.

Sherrington, C. S. (1906). *The integrative action of the nervous system.* New Haven, CT: Yale University Press.

Smyth, T., & Dewar, T. (2009). *Raising the village: How individuals and communities can work together to give our children a stronger start in life* (C. Hertzman, Foreword). Toronto and New York, NY: BPS Books.

Stern, D. L. (2000). Evolutionary developmental biology and the problem of variation. *Evolution, 54*, 1079–1091.

Stern, D. N. (2010). *Forms of vitality: Exploring dynamic experience in psychology, the arts, psychotherapy and development.* Oxford: Oxford University Press.

Takada, A. (2005). Early vocal communication and social institution: Appellation and infant verse addressing among the Central Kalahari San. *Crossroads of Language, Interaction, and Culture, 6*, 80–108.

Trevarthen, C. (1985). Neuroembryology and the development of perceptual mechanisms. In F. Falkner & J. M. Tanner (Eds.), *Human growth* (2nd ed., pp. 301–383). New York, NY: Plenum.

Trevarthen, C. (1996). Lateral asymmetries in infancy: Implications for the development of the hemispheres. *Neuroscience and Biobehavioral Reviews, 20*(4), 571–586.

Trevarthen, C. (1998). The concept and foundations of infant intersubjectivity. In S. Bråten (Ed.), *Intersubjective communication and emotion in early ontogeny* (pp. 15–46). Cambridge: Cambridge University Press.

Trevarthen, C. (1999). Musicality and the intrinsic motive pulse: Evidence from human psychobiology and infant communication. [[Special Issue: Rhythms, Musical Narrative, and the Origins of Human Communication.]] *Musicae Scientiae, 1999–2000*, 157–213.

Trevarthen, C. (2001a). Intrinsic motives for companionship in understanding: Their origin, development and significance for infant mental health. *Infant Mental Health Journal, 22*(1–2), 95–131.

Trevarthen, C. (2001b). The neurobiology of early communication: Intersubjective regulations in human brain development. In A. F. Kalverboer & A. Gramsbergen (Eds.), *Handbook on brain and behavior in human development* (pp. 841–882). Dordrecht, The Netherlands: Kluwer.

Trevarthen, C. (2005). Stepping away from the mirror: Pride and shame in adventures of companionship: Reflections on the nature and emotional needs of infant intersubjectivity. In C. S. Carter, L. Ahnert, K. E. Grossman, S. B. Hrdy, M. E. Lamb, S. W. Porges, & N. Sachser (Eds.), *Attachment and bonding: A new synthesis. Dahlem Workshop Report 92* (pp. 55–84). Cambridge, MA: MIT Press.

Trevarthen, C. (2007). Wer schreibt die Autobiographie eines Kindes? [[Who writes the autobiography of an infant?]] In H. Welzer & H. J. Markowitsch (Eds.), *Warum Menschen sich erinnern können. Fortschritte der interdisziplinaeren Gedaechtnisforschung* (pp. 225–255). Stuttgart: Klett-Cott.

Trevarthen, C. (2008a). The musical art of infant conversation: Narrating in the time of sympathetic experience, without rational interpretation, before words. [[Special Issue: Narrative in Music and Interaction.]] *Musicae Scientiae, March 20, 2008*, 15–46.

Trevarthen, C. (2008b). Foreword. Shared minds and the science of fiction: Why theories will differ. In J. Zlatev, T. P. Racine, C. Sinha, & E. Itkonen (Eds.), *The shared mind: Perspectives on intersubjectivity* (pp. vii–xiii). Amsterdam: Benjamins.

Trevarthen, C. (2009a). The intersubjective psychobiology of human meaning: Learning of culture depends on interest for co-operative practical work and affection for the joyful art of good company. *Psychoanalytic Dialogues, 19*(5), 507–518.

Trevarthen, C. (2009b). The functions of emotion in infancy: The regulation and communication of rhythm, sympathy, and meaning in human development. In D. Fosha, D. J. Siegel, & M. F. Solomon (Eds.), *The healing power of emotion: Affective neuroscience, development, and clinical practice* (pp. 55 85). New York, NY: Norton.

Trevarthen, C. (2011). What young children give to their learning, making education work to sustain a community and its culture. *European Early Childhood Education Research Journal, 19*(2), 173–193.

Trevarthen, C., & Aitken, K. J. (2003). Regulation of brain development and age-related changes in infants' motives: The developmental function of "regressive" periods. In M. Heimann (Ed.), *Regression periods in human infancy* (pp. 107–184). Mahwah, NJ: Erlbaum.

Trevarthen, C., Aitken, K. J., Vandekerckhove, M., Delafield-Butt, J., & Nagy, E. (2006). Collaborative regulations of vitality in early childhood: Stress in intimate relationships and postnatal psychopathology. In D. Cicchetti & D. J. Cohen (Eds.), *Developmental psychopathology. Vol. 2: Developmental neuroscience* (2nd ed., pp. 65–126). New York, NY: Wiley.

Trevarthen, C., Delafield-Butt, J., & Schögler, B. (2011). Psychobiology of musical gesture: Innate rhythm, harmony and melody in movements of narration. In A. Gritten & E. King (Eds.), *New perspectives on music and gesture* (SEMPRE studies in the psychology of music, pp. 11–43). Farnham, Surrey, and Burlington, VT: Ashgate.

Trevarthen, C., & Reddy, V. (2007). Consciousness in infants. In M. Velman & S. Schneider (Eds.), *A companion to consciousness* (pp. 41–57). Oxford: Blackwell.

Tulving, E. (2002). Episodic memory: From mind to brain. *Annual Review of Psychology, 253*, 1–25.

Tzourio-Mazoyer, N., De Schonen, S., Crivello, F., Reutter, B., et al. (2002). Neural correlates of woman face processing by 2-month-old infants. *Neuroimage, 15*, 454–461.

Von Bonsdorff, P. (2009). Aesthetic of childhood: Phenomenology and beyond. *Proceedings of the European Society for Aesthetics, 1*, 84–100.

Vygotsky, L. S. (1978). *Mind in society: The development of higher psychological processes* (M. Cole, V. Steiner, S. Scribner, & E. Souberman, Eds.). Cambridge, MA: Harvard University Press.

Early Experience: The Effects of Cultural Practice

8

Birth and the First Postnatal Hour
Wenda R. Trevathan

Morbidity and mortality related to childbirth remain among the top health concerns in much of the world today, and birth complications were probably the major causes of death of women in their reproductive years for most of human history. Hence, to argue for a return to the ancestral ways of giving birth would also argue for an increase in maternal and neonatal mortality and morbidity attributable to birth complications. I doubt that anyone considering the beneficial traits from ancestral birth environments would advocate for something like this. But that is not to say that there are not ancestral practices at birth that would benefit both mothers and infants if they could be incorporated into the ways we approach healthy motherhood and infant development in the 21st century.

In this chapter, I will discuss five aspects of childbirth with regard to their manifestation in ancestral environments (based on reasonable conjecture), compare them very generally with the way in which birth occurs in contemporary settings, and propose ancestral behaviors that are or could be safely incorporated into "natural childbirth" practices today with potentially better outcomes for maternal and infant health and development. The potentially beneficial practices include emotional support from a doula, delivery in the upright position, delayed clamping of the umbilical cord, little or no separation of the mother and infant during the first postnatal hour, and initiation of breastfeeding soon after birth. In addition to the beneficial ancestral practices, I will also discuss contemporary practices that are potentially harmful and should probably be avoided whenever possible, the most egregious of which may be elective cesarean section.

It is common for women in contemporary Western societies to talk about maternal satisfaction at birth with hopes of having a "good experience" in labor and delivery. Too often these concerns are dismissed as passing fads with an argument that what is most important is having a healthy baby, and if that means a "good birth experience," all the better, but the experience is far less important than the outcome. I will argue, however, that there is more to it than that. A woman's experience at birth may have an impact on her confidence in parenting, stress levels in herself and her infant, whether or not she breastfeeds and for how long, and her long-term relationship with her infant. Furthermore, there is evidence of a long-term impact of birth on development of the infant itself. In a commentary on a paper reporting evidence of epigenetic changes associated with mode of delivery (cesarean section or vaginal), Moshe Szyf noted that we are beginning to see evidence of "the dramatic impact that altered environments, commonly encountered during birth, could have on our epigenomes" (Szyf, 2009, p. 1084).

First, try to imagine a birth in the distant past. If we could have filmed a normal, uncomplicated birth in the Pleistocene, what would we have seen?

A Possible Scenario for Ancestral Birth

For the first several hours of labor the woman shows signs of mild discomfort and restlessness, but she continues to forage with the rest of the group, moving only slightly slower with occasional stops to breathe deeply and clutch her abdomen, exhibiting slight grimaces suggestive of pain. About an hour before birth she begins to show more signs of discomfort and more intense pain as the contractions become more powerful. Showing evidence of mild anxiety, she moves in closer to her female companions who have begun to watch her behavior more closely.

As dusk arrives, her contractions become more frequent and more powerful, so that by the time she is unable to keep up with the group, everyone has stopped to settle down for the evening. The women in the group gather around the woman in labor, holding her and making reassuring noises. Between contractions she walks and talks with her companions. As contractions intensify even further, she vocalizes, clenches her fists, holds onto her companions, and even whimpers and cries. When it comes time to deliver the baby, she squats and is supported by two of the stronger women in the group. Another woman stands behind her, ready to guide the baby out when the head appears. Contractions are expulsive and the laboring woman bears down to help push the baby out. She does not seem to be experiencing much pain, but this is the stage at which the word *labor* in its sense of work is most evident. It appears that all muscles of her body are engaged in pushing the baby out.

The baby's head emerges facing the mother's anus and then rotates to the side. An attendant feels around the baby's neck, checking to see if the umbilical cord is wrapped too tightly. She also wipes the mucus and birth fluids from the baby's mouth and nose so that it can breathe more easily. At this stage the mother is no longer pushing and the contractions alone serve to complete the delivery. The baby's body rotates again and the shoulders are born, followed by the rest of the body as the baby emerges quickly with a gush of amniotic fluid into the arms of the waiting attendant. She grasps the baby to keep it from falling to the ground and the mother reaches through her legs to take the infant from her companion. The attendant guides the baby to her to minimize traction on the umbilical cord before it has detached from the uterine wall. (In some cases, the mother herself may complete the final delivery of her infant after the shoulders are born.)

The mother lies back exhausted and takes her infant into her arms. The baby breathes on his own and cries as the air passes over the vocal cords for the first time, but the crying does not persist. As he lies upon his mother's abdomen, he begins to make crawling movements up toward her breasts. When he reaches the breast, the baby nuzzles and roots around the nipple, not fully latching on but clearly showing interest in the breasts. The cord stops pulsing 2 to 3 minutes after birth and is cut by one of the attendants, allowing the mother to pull the baby up toward her breasts on the left side of her body, fully encompassing him. After cradling the infant against her chest for a few minutes, she gazes into the baby's eyes, speaks to him in a high-pitched voice, and massages him with her palms. She seems fully attentive to her infant, paying very little attention to her companions or her own body, even when she has another contraction and delivers the placenta. The infant seems equally interested in her and gazes into her eyes, while continuing to root at the breast. He seems especially alert as he focuses attention on his mother. Eventually he latches on to the nipple and begins suckling. Finally, about an hour after birth, both mother and baby fall asleep.

This scenario is based on my observations of more than 250 out-of-hospital births that were attended by empirical ("lay") midwives. A subset of 110 of these births formed an ethological study that was the basis of my doctoral dissertation (reviewed in Trevathan, 1987), the details of which form this description. I will now take specific aspects of this scenario and discuss their significance and possible functions in ancestral settings.

Others Are Usually Present at Human Births When the Norm for Most Mammals Is Solitary Birth

Although normal childbirth has become more complicated and perhaps more stressful with medicalization and modern technological interventions, it has probably been a challenging process for humans since the origin of bipedalism and perhaps even earlier. Primates, including humans, are notable for being highly encephalized, that is, having large brains relative to their bodies. With large heads and small bodies, the passage of the neonatal primate head through the birth canal provides a challenge that is unusual among mammals (Figure 8.1). Birth in the earliest hominins was likely marked by a close fit between the neonatal head and the maternal birth canal, so challenging birth probably preceded the ape–human divergence. From that point on, birth probably became easier for great apes as their bodies increased in size, but more difficult for humans and their immediate ancestors because of bipedalism. For the first 2 to 3 million years of evolution of hominins, the birth process was probably similar to what is described for large monkeys. With the origin of the genus *Homo* about 2 million years ago, brain size began its evolutionary trajectory toward a doubling in size with very little increase in the size of the birth canal. Rather than sacrifice efficiency in locomotion, the human adaptation appears to have been selection for most of brain growth to occur after birth. Associated with this was a greater degree of altriciality in the human infant and greater dependence on direct postpartum care from (most likely) the mother.

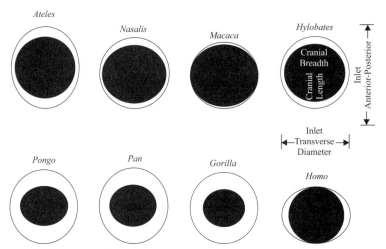

FIGURE 8.1 *Pelvic openings (outer circles) and newborn infant heads (solid inner circles)*
in selected primate species illustrating the tight squeeze for monkeys and humans. From
Schultz, A. H. (1949). Sex differences in the pelves of primates. American Journal of
Physical Anthropology, 7, 401–424; Jolly, A. (1985). The evolution of primate behavior.
New York, NY: Macmillan; and Trevathan, W. R. (2010). Ancient bodies, modern lives:
How evolution has shaped women's health. New York, NY: Oxford University Press.

The hominin female of the Pleistocene inherited from her ancestors challenging births and somewhat helpless neonates, due in part to the opposing forces of
encephalization and bipedalism. In medical terminology, when the neonatal head is
too large to fit through the mother's pelvis, the situation is referred to as cephalopel-
vic disproportion, or CPD. This is one of the most frequently cited reasons for
performing cesarean section today, but before modern technology and the availability of surgical deliveries, true CPD would probably have resulted in death of both
mother and infant.

The close fit between the neonatal head and the birth canal typically means that
the large neonatal occiput (back of the head) must rotate to exit against the anterior
part of the birth canal in the pelvic outlet (presentation is OA in obstetric terminology). This means that the infant emerges from the birth canal facing away from
the mother, in contrast to the more typical monkey delivery in which the infant
emerges facing the mother. When the monkey infant is born, the mother can reach
down and grasp the emerging body with her hands to guide it from the birth canal
and up toward her chest (Figure 8.2). Using her hands to complete the birth is
important for a species that often gives birth in the trees. A baby emerging facing
away from her provides a challenge to the human mother who tries to guide it out or
provide other assistance such as checking for a wrapped umbilical cord or cleaning
away mucus that interferes with breathing. An adaptation to this difficulty is to seek
assistance at delivery (Figure 8.3).

FIGURE 8.2 *A monkey delivery showing the mother's response. Redrawn from Trevathan, W. R. (1987). Human birth: An evolutionary perspective. New York, NY: Aldine de Gruyter, and Trevathan, W. R. (2010). Ancient bodies, modern lives: How evolution has shaped women's health. New York, NY: Oxford University Press.*

In summary, one of the major differences between birth in humans and most mammals is that it takes place in the presence of other people, usually people known to the woman giving birth. For social-living monkeys, births often take place in the presence of other members of the troop (Turner et al., 2010), but there is little evidence that assistance is routinely provided. For humans, emotional support is probably the most important aid provided by birth attendants, but physical or mechanical assistance is probably important as well. Although human mothers have delivered their babies alone for millennia, turning to another person for help at the time of delivery may have increased infant survival to the extent that it is almost universally distributed in our species today. Women can raise children completely on their own, and people can hunt successfully alone and build houses on their own, but in most cases, these activities—and the birth of a child—benefit from the presence of others.

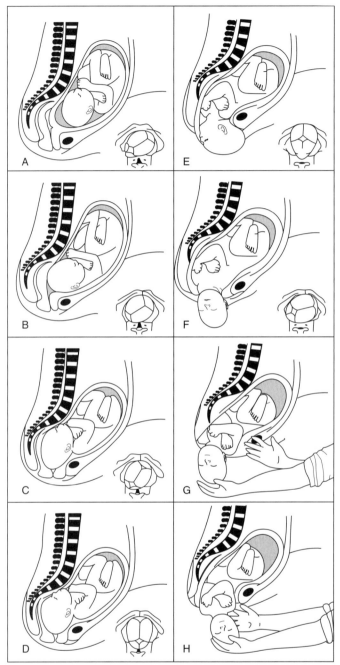

FIGURE 8.3 *Human birth showing the series of rotations and the benefit of having assistance at delivery. From Rosenberg, K. R., & Trevathan, W. R. (1996). Bipedalism and human birth: The obstetrical dilemma revisited. Evolutionary Anthropology, 4, 161–168; and Trevathan, W. R. (2010). Ancient bodies, modern lives: How evolution has shaped women's health. New York, NY: Oxford University Press.*

I have argued that seeking companionship for emotional support at the time of birth may have been the proximate reason for delivering with the assistance of others that translated into the ultimate benefit of lowering mortality. If this is true, the legacy that human females have inherited from their ancestors may be a healthful level of apprehension and anxiety that can become harmful in the absence of supportive companions. In the language of evolutionary medicine, a certain level of anxiety at the time of birth may be a "defense" rather than a "defect" in need of medical attention (Nesse & Williams, 1994). The defensive benefits of birth anxiety led to greater infant survival in the past, but today in some hospital settings, the anxiety is often not met with emotional support and becomes so great that it must be treated with analgesics or more powerful drugs. Providing emotional support from trusted friends and family members or doulas is a response to the normal anxiety felt by women in labor that reflects our evolutionary heritage.

The Greek term *doula* was introduced into contemporary usage by Dana Rafael, who used it to describe a person who assists a new mother in establishing breastfeeding (Rafael, 1973). Marshall Klaus, John Kennell, and their colleagues adopted the word to describe the supportive companions who attended births in several of the settings in which they explored mother–infant bonding. They found that doula support was associated with shorter labors and a reduction in birth complications including cesarean section (Klaus & Kennell, 1982). Randomized controlled trials have confirmed that births that are attended by doulas have fewer cesarean sections, lower use of epidurals, and higher reported levels of confidence and satisfaction (Kashanian, Javadi, & Haghighi, 2010; McGrath & Kennell, 2008; Pascali-Bonaro & Kroeger, 2004). Several studies have also shown increased breastfeeding success following doula-supported births (Mottl-Santiago et al., 2008; Nommsen-Rivers, Mastergeorge, Hansen, Cullum, & Dewey, 2009). These findings were confirmed in a Cochrane Library review of 16 trials with more than 13,000 women participants; there was no evidence of adverse effects of continuous labor support (Hodnett, Gates, Hofmeyr, & Sakala, 2007). In another review of evidence-based labor and delivery practices based on searches of MEDLINE, PubMed, and COCHRANE, it was concluded that doula support was one of five practices associated with positive delivery outcomes based on high-quality data and that doulas should become a routine part of labor and delivery management (Berghella, Baxter, & Chauhan, 2008). This last review was published in the *American Journal of Obstetrics and Gynecology* as an "editors' choice," indicating some level of acceptance by the somewhat conservative American College of Obstetrics and Gynecology.

In Ancestral Environments, the Mother Delivered in an Upright Position

There are a few other behaviors from our evolutionary heritage that could be incorporated into modern childbirth practices without harm and with potential benefits. One is the upright posture in the second stage. There is evidence that the upright position is associated with shorter second stage labor, less pain, and lower use of fetal heart monitors, forceps, and vacuum extractors (Berghella et al., 2008). In the upright position, the woman's efforts to push the baby out work with gravity and the force of the uterine contractions is born by the back of the baby's head (the occiput) in a normal head-first position (Trevathan, 1988). The occiput is the most developed of the fetal cranial bones and is the best for withstanding the intense pressure of the contractions. In the flat-on-the-back or lithotomy position, the baby's fragile frontal bones have to bear the force against the mother's sacrum. The upright position, especially squatting, also widens the birth canal in several dimensions (Michel et al., 2002). Unfortunately, if a woman has not spent a lot of time squatting in her everyday life, trying to give birth while squatting may prove difficult. If someone is available to support her, however, even a woman who does not routinely squat can deliver in that, potentially more optimal, position (Simkin, 2003), thus incorporating a beneficial practice from the past into contemporary birth.

In Ancestral Environments, the Umbilical Cord Was Cut After It Had Stopped Pulsating

During pregnancy, the placenta serves as the organ of respiration, digestion, and excretion. At birth, these functions are taken over by various organs of the infant itself. In particular, the lungs rather than the placenta become the source of oxygen, but for a few minutes after birth, the placenta continues to provide oxygen to the infant. Even a few minutes without oxygen can cause brain damage, so among our adaptations to birth is a brief period of time, perhaps only 2 to 3 minutes, when oxygen is supplied by both the placenta and the lungs. This adaptation was probably particularly important in the past when other sources of oxygen were not available and delays in respiration may have occurred.

In most hospital births, the umbilical cord is usually cut immediately after birth, based on the argument that an excess of blood transfusion from the placenta will put stress on the neonatal circulatory system, which is already stressed to its limits. Excess blood may also result in a higher than normal hematocrit, which could lead to polycythemia (excess red blood cells), a condition that in turn can result in respiratory and neurological problems. There is concern that delayed clamping could result in transfer of higher than normal levels of placental steroids that could impact the newborn at this critical time. Early cord clamping has also been used as a way of preventing postpartum hemorrhage, although the evidence for this is sparse (Chaparro et al., 2006).

There are several arguments for delaying cord clamping, the most significant of which is that it increases infant blood volume by as much as 30% (Wiberg, Källén, & Olofsson, 2008). This is especially important if the mother's hemoglobin has been low during pregnancy, a phenomenon that characterizes most pregnancies in the world. (A recent World Health Organization [WHO] report noted that the global prevalence of anemia in pregnant women was almost 42%; a far higher percent have low iron levels.) And as noted, delayed clamping also provides the infant with a backup supply of oxygen while respiration is being established.

Under conditions of the past, waiting until the cord stopped pulsing may have given babies a head start in both oxygen and iron retention. Today, in many parts of the world, delayed cord clamping could enhance infant health, especially in malarial areas where it serves to increase red blood cells and iron storage for up to 4 months (van Rheenen, de Moor, Eschbach, de Grooth, & Brabin, 2007). Under conditions of maternal iron deficiency and anemia, delayed cord clamping can increase infant iron stores for as long as 6 months (Chaparro, Neufeld, Tena Avarez, Eguia-Liz Cedillo, & Dewey, 2006). Even in the United States, delayed cord clamping has been shown to reduce infant anemia.

Preterm infants also benefit from delayed cord clamping, which has been shown to be associated with higher hematocrits, reduced need for blood transfusions, better blood pressure, and higher circulating blood volume (Rabe, Reynolds, & Diaz-Rossello, 2008). For vulnerable infants, the higher stem cell transfer afforded by delayed cord clamping may have numerous benefits. It appears that the simple practice of delaying cord clamping for 1 to 3 minutes after birth can enhance infant health without serious negative effects. Even in cases of infant distress caused by a cord wrapped too tightly around the neck or need for resuscitation, delayed clamping may provide benefits (Coggins & Mercer, 2009). Despite the evidence for positive benefits, the practice remains controversial (Wiberg et al., 2008). The International Confederation of Midwives and the International Federation of Gynaecology and Obstetrics have advocated for clamping the cord when it stops pulsating, but the American College of Obstetricians and Gynecologists does not state an opinion (Coggins & Mercer, 2009).

In Ancestral Environments, Mothers and Infants Remained Together After Birth

For the past 20 to 30 years there has been a great deal of controversy about the significance of the immediate postpartum period for optimal infant development and for the mother–infant bond (Stern, 1996). In their early works, Klaus and Kennell extended Bowlby's ideas of attachment formation to the immediate postpartum period and suggested that the first hour after birth is a "sensitive period" for mother–infant bonding. They also argued that if mothers and infants are separated immediately after birth for several hours, they may have more difficulty forming attachments than if they are together in that period. Furthermore, they argued that the mother engages in a series of "species specific" behaviors during this early postpartum period that enhance optimal bond formation. I first heard about the Klaus and Kennell research at a meeting of the American

Anthropological Association in San Francisco in 1976. In pursuit of a doctoral research project, I was inspired to replicate their studies in a population where births occurred out of the hospital in nonmedical settings. I was fascinated by the concept of species-specific behaviors in new mothers, but I was also skeptical that one could propose them based on a small sample of hospital births. In short, we needed more observations.

I enrolled in a midwifery training program where births were attended in private homes or homelike settings with lay or empirical midwives and where mothers and infants remained together from birth on. In observations of more than 100 deliveries, I was able to support the proposals for species-specific behaviors, but with a few modifications. The behaviors I focused on were patterns of maternal touch, lateral preferences for holding the infant, eye contact, voice pitch, and timing of initial breastfeeding.

THE IMPORTANCE OF TOUCH IN THE FIRST POSTNATAL HOURS

Most mammalian mothers lick their infants following birth. The licking appears to serve a number of functions, including removing birth fluids, drying the infant, removing odors, orienting the infant to the nipple, and facilitating attachment. Of more immediate importance, perhaps, the licking serves to stimulate breathing, digestion, and elimination, and infants who are not licked often have difficulty establishing these functions. In rats, licking regulates cardiovascular and endocrine function (Hofer, 2005). Exceptions to this near-universal mammalian behavior are water-living mammals and humans. Perhaps as a substitute, human mothers use their hands in interacting with their infants in the first hour after birth. Tactile contact was reported by Klaus and Kennell, who also proposed that the sequence used by the mother interacting with her infant followed a species-specific pattern that began with fingertip contact with the extremities and proceeded to fully encompassing the infant's body. The mothers in their study were separated from their infants for up to 15 minutes after delivery while they were bathed and examined. The mothers in my sample received their messy, greasy infants immediately, some even completing the delivery themselves following emergence of the head and shoulders. The tactile sequence I observed began with fully encompassing the infant, and only toward the end of the first hour after birth did the mothers explore their infants' fingers and toes. I concluded that tactile contact including rubbing and massaging was a ubiquitous response to birth but that the specific pattern varied by circumstance. Furthermore, I suggested that the pattern I observed was more likely to have been the one followed in the ancestral past when the infants were probably not removed from their mothers.

Licking or touch thus appears to serve a number of functions in helping the newborn infant adjust to life outside the womb, but there is increasing evidence that the effects of these behaviors may be long-lasting. A number of recent studies suggest that maternal licking of infant mammals also plays a role in neuroendocrine development through an effect on epigenetic processes (Weaver et al., 2004). For example, licking of infants by rat mothers is inversely correlated with neuroendocrine responses to stress in the pups when they reach adulthood—the more licking they had in infancy, the less fearfulness they showed in adulthood (Caldji et al., 1998; Liu & Diorio, 1997; Zhang & Meaney, 2010). This provides evidence that maternal licking programs the stress response by altering neuroendocrine function. Furthermore, maternal licking patterns are transmitted to daughters, providing a mechanism for nongenomic behavioral transmission of stress reactivity (Francis, Diorio, Liu, & Meaney, 1999; Matthews & Phillips, 2010).

Although the research into effects of maternal licking on infant development has not focused specifically on the immediate postpartum period, it is possible that the drive to engage in this behavior is first triggered by the birth process and that the first interaction with the offspring is crucial. Furthermore, maternal separation has been shown to have a number of negative effects on neuroendocrine development in rats (Litvin et al., 2010). Humans are not rats, of course, but I am not the first to suggest that some of the same processes and behaviors seen in rat mothers and infants may occur in humans.

Other behaviors in the first postnatal hour that were described by Klaus and Kennell and that I observed in my sample included a preference for holding the infants on the left side of the body regardless of maternal handedness, talking to the infant in a high-pitched voice, looking at the infant in the *en face* position, and initiating breastfeeding within the first hour of life. These behaviors have all been discussed as contributors to mother–infant bonding, but if they are recast into the context of ancestral environments, it can be seen that they also had survival value.

For example, as the mother takes her infant from the arms of her birth attendant, she fully wraps her arms around him, encompassing him on her chest in what pediatrician Jan Winberg has called the "maternal nest" (Winberg, 2005). One of the consequences of altriciality for the human infant is that he has trouble maintaining a stable body temperature for the first few days of life, but being encompassed in his mother's arms provides him with more warmth than artificially warmed cots. When Winberg and his team compared skin-to-skin contact with cot babies, they found that the babies held in their mothers' arms were able not only to reach a stable body temperature but also to maintain better blood glucose levels, something that is important very early in life before milk production begins. In the past, anything the mother could do to help her infant conserve heat and energy would have enhanced survival. Thus, one could conclude that encompassing the infant was important, perhaps critical, for survival regardless of its role in enhancing bond formation. When mothers hold their infants close to their chests, fully encompassing them, they may be reflecting a behavioral legacy from the past

After fully encompassing the infant for a few minutes, the mother may begin massaging him with broad palmar strokes along his trunk. This behavior seems to enhance respiration and gastrointestinal development in the way that maternal licking does for most mammalian infants. It also helps to warm him. A further benefit of massaging the infant immediately after birth is that it serves to rub the *vernix caseosa* into the baby's skin, which protects it from drying out and heat loss. The vernix is a cold cream–like substance that has the remarkable ability to both protect the skin from excess moisture in utero and prevent dehydration upon exposure to air after birth. The vernix also has antimicrobial properties that protect the infant before and after birth. These anti-infective properties may also protect the mother from infections that could result from the nicks and abrasions that occur in the perineal area during birth. In short, it is an amazing substance that serves as a moisturizer, cleanser, anti-infective, and antioxidant, but today it is most commonly removed soon after birth in an effort to clean the unsightly birth fluids from the infant's body and make it more attractive when returned to the mother. The numerous functions of vernix probably enhanced maternal and infant health in the past when it was not likely removed until several minutes or hours after birth. It remains important in health-poor regions of the world, and the WHO recommends that bathing infants should be delayed for several hours after birth to minimize heat loss and other functions that would be lost (Singh & Archana, 2008; WHO, 2006). Even in hospital births in health-rich regions, the vernix may protect infants from hospital-acquired infections. The value of vernix is another lesson that can be learned from examining birth in ancestral environments, and there is no evidence that leaving it on for a few minutes causes harm.

THE IMPORTANCE OF SOOTHING NEWBORN INFANTS

In addition to cradling and massaging the infant, mothers engage in a number of behaviors that serve to soothe the infant. These include the tendency to hold the infant on the left side of the body over the heartbeat; the apparent drive to look into the infant's eyes, often in the *en face* position; and the inclination to vocalize to the infant in a high-pitched voice. Birth is obviously a disruptive experience for infants, and although the "stress of being born" (Lagercrantz & Slotkin, 1986) has numerous positive effects, efforts to calm a newborn infant serve to conserve energy at a potentially vulnerable time. Furthermore, in the ancestral past, a crying infant was likely very attractive to predators and extremely annoying to other members of the social group. It was probably best for the mother–infant dyad to remain quiet and not attract unwelcomed attention.

In addition to the soothing properties of the maternal behaviors discussed, mother–infant interactions in the first hour after birth serve to enhance breastfeeding, certainly one of the most significant maternal investments in the past, as it is today. When an infant is placed on his mother's abdomen immediately after birth, he orients toward the mother's breast and makes efforts, including rudimentary crawling, to move toward it. Smell seems to play a role in this orienting process so that when the breasts are washed, the baby's efforts are not as directed (Varendi,

Porter, & Winberg, 1994). The initial efforts at latching onto the breast may not serve nutritional purposes in that the milk will not be produced for 2 to 3 more days and most infants that are well nourished in utero are not likely hungry for a few hours after birth. There is evidence, however, that early initiation of breastfeeding, regardless of the nutritional benefits, contributes to greater success of breastfeeding over the long term.

The baby's initial efforts at nipple contact also trigger oxytocin release. Oxytocin has numerous effects at this time, but one of the most immediate and perhaps most significant in the past is that it stimulates contractions that result in expulsion of the placenta and reduction in maternal uterine bleeding. Thus, the early efforts at nursing may not benefit the infant directly, but they may save the mother's life by preventing postpartum hemorrhage. Postpartum hemorrhage is the most common cause of maternal death worldwide, causing almost one-fourth of all deaths annually (http://www.pphprevention.org/pph.php). We usually think of events of the postpartum period as part of maternal efforts to help infants, but in this case, the infant is contributing to his mother's survival. One of the UN Millennium Development Goals is the reduction of maternal mortality worldwide. Simply adopting the common ancestral practice of allowing the newborn infant to have access to his mother's breast would go a long way toward achieving that goal. The recent "WHO Guidelines for the Management of Postpartum Haemorrhage and Retained Placenta" (WHO, 2009) have no mention of this as a way of slowing or stopping excessive bleeding postpartum, although nipple stimulation is mentioned in an earlier WHO report as a way of hastening placenta delivery (WHO, 2007).

As noted earlier, one effect of labor, delivery, and skin-to-skin and nipple contact is the release of oxytocin in both the mother and infant. This hormone appears to play important roles in affiliation, stress reduction, and infant development and is reviewed thoroughly by Carter (Carter & Porges, this volume). A number of known or possible effects of oxytocin that may have their inception during birth and the immediate postnatal period include stress reduction; growth promotion; energy conservation; gut maturation; milk production and ejection; heat production, especially in the mother's chest and breasts; mobilization of nutrients such as glucose and glucagon; calming; and bonding (reviewed in Uvnäs-Moberg, 1996). All of these effects are continued with ongoing skin-to-skin contact and breastfeeding. Given the evidence that oxytocin plays a role in mother–infant bonding and the fact that this hormone is elevated in the immediate postpartum period (Nissen, Lilja, Widström, & Uvnäs-Moberg, 1995), there are grounds for proposing that the first hour after birth is, indeed, a "maternal sensitive period" as proposed by Klaus and Kennell more than 25 years ago (1976). Furthermore, there is evidence that oxytocin levels in mothers are directly correlated with length of breastfeeding (Silber, Larsson, & Uvnäs-Moberg, 1991). Unfortunately, many of the effects of oxytocin are lessened or inhibited with surgical deliveries, as will be discussed later. Uvnäs-Moberg refers to the effects of oxytocin as "biological messages" (from the past?) that have, unfortunately, been disregarded in modern cultures (1996, p. 129).

THE SIGNIFICANCE OF BREASTFEEDING SOON AFTER BIRTH

There are several other chapters in this book that address breastfeeding (see Ball & Russell, this volume; Sulaiman, Amir, & Liamputtong, this volume), so I will limit my comments here to events and behaviors at birth and the immediate postpartum period that seem to influence subsequent breastfeeding experiences. As noted earlier, there is evidence that early breastfeeding contributes to longer and more successful breastfeeding. One of the steps to successful breastfeeding in the WHO/UNICEF Baby-Friendly Hospital Initiative is encouraging mothers to initiate breastfeeding within the first hour after birth because of the evidence that early initiation is associated with more successful and longer breastfeeding (DiGirolamo, Grummer-Strawn, & Fein, 2008). Skin-to-skin contact within the first hour has also been shown to be associated with breastfeeding duration (Mikiel-Kostyra, Mazur, & Bołtruszko, 2002), as is doula assistance, as noted earlier. Breastfeeding initiation in the first hour after birth has been shown to be significantly associated with a lower rate of under-5 mortality in Africa and Asia (Boschi-Pinto, Bahl, & Martines, 2009). On the other hand, epidural anesthesia, cesarean section, forceps, and vacuum extraction all have negative effects on early initiation and later success of breastfeeding (Smith, 2007).

Contemporary Practices That Were Not Part of Birth in Ancestral Environments

So far I've reviewed a possible scenario for birth and the immediate postpartum period in ancestral environments. I've suggested some practices and legacies from the past that may benefit mothers and infants today and may contribute to more optimal infant and child development. In addition to the absence of some of these beneficial practices at contemporary births, there are a number of existing birth practices that may have negative effects on the development of the mother–infant relationship and ongoing child development. The lithotomy position and immediate cord clamping were described previously, but perhaps the most disturbing of the potentially negative contemporary practices and the one furthest removed from ancestral environments is surgical delivery by cesarean section. I recognize, of course, that millions of mothers and infants would not be alive today had they not had the option of safe surgical delivery. On the other hand, it appears that many of the millions of cesarean sections that are performed each year may not be medically necessary. This begs the question of whether or not something is lost when a woman and her physician choose surgical delivery in the absence of other indicators of its necessity. In other words, is birth "good for" mothers and infants, and are there good medical and humanitarian reasons to be concerned about the spiraling rates of c-sections throughout the world?

Most investigators suggest an "expected" rate of 10–15% for c-sections, and this is the rate recommended by the WHO. Rates around the world are highly variable: 30% in the United States; 22–23% in the United Kingdom, Canada, and Australia; up to 70% in Brazil; and 35% in Italy and Taiwan. It is estimated that between 2% and 3% of cesarean section births in the United States are due to maternal request in the absence of any medical indications (Lee & D'Alton, 2008). Despite the fact that many lives have been saved because of safe surgical delivery, there are still risks associated with it, including hemorrhage, pulmonary embolism, sepsis, anesthesia complications, and even death (Liston, 2003). Recovery time is longer and breastfeeding and mother–infant bonding are often compromised. Additionally, cesarean section may compromise a woman's future fertility, and it is common for women who have one cesarean section delivery to have all future children this way, whether indicated or not. A recent recommendation from the National Institutes of Health and American College of Obstetrics and Gynecology is that women be advised against elective cesarean if they desire to have more children (Lee & D'Alton, 2008).

Cesarean section also presents problems for infants, including higher incidence of respiratory distress, disrupted sleep rhythm in the early postnatal days, and greater challenges to self-regulation, the process by which the infant begins to maintain behavioral and physiological balance following the disruptions caused by birth. The mother has experienced major surgery, so she may not be in a position to help her infant achieve self-regulation through the usual interactive processes of holding, stroking, skin-to-skin contact, and vocal and visual engagement. In one study conducted 2 to 4 weeks after delivery, the brains of mothers who delivered vaginally were significantly more responsive to their babies' cries than those who delivered by c-section as shown in functional magnetic resonance imaging (Swain et al., 2008).

Ashley Montagu was one of the first to suggest that relatively long labors were "good for" human infants (Montagu, 1978). In fact, he argued that the stroking and massaging provided by the uterine contractions replace the functional significance of licking the young seen in virtually all other mammalian species. In support of this, there is evidence that infants born by cesarean after a trial of labor have better functioning systems than those born without the benefit of contractions (Doherty & Eichenwald, 2004).

Another reason that labor might be good for babies is that the stress hormones that both the mother and fetus produce during labor trigger the production of catecholamines (e.g., adrenalin/epinephrine and dopamine) in the infant that help him cope with life outside the womb. These "stress hormones" increase lung maturation and fetal blood flow, especially to the brain, and increase white blood cells for immune protection (Lagercrantz & Slotkin, 1986). Further, catecholamines help the fetus withstand hypoxia during delivery, and those who are born by elective cesarean section without labor often have breathing problems. Catecholamines also increase availability of calories to the baby, which may have been particularly important for infant survival in the first few days after birth in the past and in contemporary cultures where colostrum is withheld and breastfeeding does not begin until the milk comes in.

There are also arguments that the stress hormones play a positive role in mother–infant bonding (Lagercrantz & Slotkin, 1986) by increasing alertness in the infants. This alertness and ability to respond to stimuli play a role in initiation of mother–infant interaction. Babies who were born after normal labor and delivery showed enhanced learning of odors to which they were exposed immediately after birth compared with infants born by cesarean section (Winberg, 2005). Additionally, babies who experienced labor contractions before surgical delivery showed better olfactory learning than those who were delivered before labor began (Varendi, Porter, & Winberg, 2002). This suggests that infants can more readily recognize their mothers' odors if they have been through the contractions of labor, which may contribute to maturation of the olfactory system.

The view of cesarean sections from our ancestral heritage argues that it may be possible to have the benefits of labor and the benefits of cesarean section when necessary. Babies who are delivered surgically after labor has been initiated show a reduced risk of respiratory problems (Doherty & Eichenwald, 2004). Similarly, babies who have experienced labor show higher levels of catecholamines even if delivered by c-section compared with those who did not experience labor. Thus, allowing labor to begin before performing a medically necessary cesarean section may enable the mother and baby to have the advantages of both.

Finally, there is evidence that mode of birth may have epigenetic effects. A Swedish team examined DNA methylation in leucocytes in infants born by elective cesarean section and vaginally. Infants born by cesarean section had higher DNA methylation in white blood cells than those born vaginally (Schlinzig et al., 2009). This appears to be the first evidence of epigenetic modulation associated with mode of birth, but it suggests new avenues of research related to the issues of concern in this volume. It also suggests molecular mechanisms for negative later life health consequences of c-section delivery. Considering the profound changes that occur at birth, especially for the infant, it would not be surprising to find many more significant epigenetic effects of mode of delivery. The authors of the Swedish study conclude that their research demonstrates that DNA methylation is "more dynamic around birth than previously known" (Schlinzig, Johansson, Gunnar, Ekström, & Norman, 2009, p. 1098; see also Weaver, 2009). This research suggests that the parallel increases in c-section rates and later life diseases like obesity, diabetes, and asthma may be more than coincidence. It also suggests a place to look for the origins of many of the developmental disorders that we are considering in this volume.

Conclusion

In summary, there is a mismatch between the way birth occurred in ancestral environments and the way it occurs in many hospital settings today. The consequences of this mismatch range from maternal dissatisfaction with the birth experience to alterations in maternal–infant interaction behaviors that may modify epigenetic processes and have lifelong impact on mental and physical health. On the other hand, humans are incredibly flexible organisms, and there is increasing evidence that some of the deleterious epigenetic patterns established in utero and in the early postpartum period may be reversible (Ellison, 2010; Weaver, 2009). We have little doubt that early experiences have long-term effects and are just beginning to consider that events of birth and the immediate postpartum period may also play a role in subsequent mental and physical development. We've argued for more than 30 years over whether or not the immediate postpartum period is a sensitive period for bonding, but there may be more to it than that. The rapidly expanding field of epigenetics has proposed a number of mechanisms by which genes and environments interact to produce child and adult phenotypes, and some of these mechanisms may have their origin not only in prenatal processes but also in perinatal experiences. I urge attention to what may well be the most important single hour in a person's life: the first hour after birth.

References

Berghella, V., Baxter, J. K., & Chauhan, S. P. (2008). Evidence-based labor and delivery management. *American Journal of Obstetrics and Gynecology, 199*(5), 445–454.

Boschi-Pinto, C., Bahl, R., & Martines, J. (2009). Limited progress in increasing coverage of neonatal and child-health interventions in Africa and Asia. *Journal of Health, Population, and Nutrition, 27*(6), 755–762.

Caldji, C., Tannenbaum, B., Sharma, S., Francis, D. D., Plotsky, P. M., & Meaney, M. J. (1998). Maternal care during infancy regulates the development of neural systems mediating the expression of behavioral fearfulness in adulthood in the rat. *Proceedings of the National Academies of Science USA, 95*, 5335–5340.

Chaparro, C. M., Neufeld, L. M., Tena Avarez, G., Eguia-Liz Cedillo R., & Dewey, K. G. (2006). Effect of timing of umbilical cord clamping on iron status in Mexican infants: A randomized controlled trial. *Lancet, 367*, 1997–2004.

Coggins, M., & Mercer, J. (2009). Delayed cord clamping: Advantages for infants. *Nursing for Women's Health, 13*(2), 132–139.

DiGirolamo, A. M., Grummer-Strawn, L. M., & Fein, S. B. (2008). Effect of maternity-care practices on breastfeeding. *Pediatrics, 122*, S43–S49.

Doherty, E. G., & Eichenwald, E. C. (2004). Cesearean delivery: Emphasis on the neonate. *Clinical Obstetrics and Gynecology, 47*(2), 332–341.

Ellison, P. T. (2010). Fetal programming and fetal psychology. *Infant and Child Development, 19*, 6–20.

Francis, D., Diorio, J., Liu, D., & Meaney, M. J. (1999). Nongenomic transmission across generations of maternal behavior and stress responses in the rat. *Science, 286* (5442), 1155.

Hodnett, E. D., Gates, S., Hofmeyr, G. J., & Sakala, C. (2007). Continuous support for women during childbirth. *The Cochrane Library, 3*.

Hofer, M. A. (2005). The psychobiology of early attachment. *Clinical Neuroscience Research, 4*, 291–300.

Kashanian, M., Javadi, F., & Haghighi, M. M. (2010). Effect of continuous support during labor on duration of labor and rate of cesarean delivery. *International Journal of Gynaecology and Obstetrics, 109*(3), 198–200.

Klaus, M. H., & Kennell, J. H. (1976). *Mother-infant bonding*. St. Louis, MO: Mosby.

Klaus, M. H., & Kennell, J. H. (1982). *Parent-infant bonding*. St. Louis, MO: Mosby.

Lagercrantz, H., & Slotkin, T. A. (1986). The "stress" of being born. *Scientific American, 254*, 100–107.

Lee, Y. M., & D'Alton, M. E. (2008). Cesarean delivery on maternal request: Maternal and neonatal complications. *Current Opinion in Obstetrics and Gynecology, 20*, 597–601.

Liston, W. A. (2003). Rising caesarean section rates: Can evolution and ecology explain some of the difficulties of modern childbirth? *Journal of the Royal Society of Medicine, 96*, 559–561.

Litvin, Y., Tovote, P., Pentkowski, N. S., Zeyda, T., King, L. B., Vasconcellos, A. J., …Blanchard, R. J. (2010). Maternal separation modulates short-term behavioral and physiological indices of the stress response. *Hormones and Behavior, 58*, 241–249.

Liu, D., & Diorio, J. (1997). Maternal care, hippocampal glucocorticoid receptors, and hypothalamic-pituitary-adrenal responses to stress. *Science, 277*(5332), 1659.

Matthews, S. G., & Phillips, D. I. W. (2010). Minireview: Transgenerational inheritance of the stress response: A new frontier in stress research. *Endocrinology, 151*, 7–13.

McGrath, S. K., & Kennell, J. H. (2008). A randomized controlled trial of continuous labor support for middle-class couples: Effect on cesarean delivery rates. *Birth, 35*, 92–97.

Michel, S. C. A., Rake, A., Treiber, K., Seifert, B., Chaoui, R., Huch, R.,…Kubik-Huch, R. (2002). MR obstetric pelvimetry: Effect of birthing position on pelvic bony dimensions. *American Journal of Roentgenology, 179*, 1063–1067.

Mikiel-Kostyra, K., Mazur, J., & Bołtruszko, I. (2002). Effect of early skin-to-skin contact after delivery on duration of breastfeeding: A prospective study. *Acta Paediatrica, 91*, 1301–1306.

Montagu, A. (1978). *Touching: The human significance of the skin* (2nd ed.) New York, NY: Harper and Row.

Mottl-Santiago, J., Walker, C., Ewan, J., Vragovic, O., Winder, S., & Stubblefield, P. (2008). A hospital-based doula program and childbirth outcomes in an urban, multicultural setting. *Maternal & Child Health Journal, 12*(3), 372–377.

Nesse, R. M., & Williams, G. C. (1994). *Why we get sick—The new science of Darwinian medicine*. New York, NY: Times Books.

Nissen, E., Lilja, G., Widström, A. M., & Uvnäs-Moberg, K. (1995). Elevation of oxytocin levels early post partum in women. *Acta Obstetricia et Gynecologica Scandinavica, 74*(7), 530–533.

Nommsen-Rivers, L. A., Mastergeorge, A. M., Hansen, R. L., Cullum, A. S., & Dewey, K. G. (2009). Doula care, early breastfeeding outcomes, and breastfeeding status at 6 weeks postpartum among low-income primiparae. *Journal of Obstetric, Gynecologic, and Neonatal Nursing: JOGNN/NAACOG, 38*(2), 157–173.

Pascali-Bonaro, D., & Kroeger, M. (2004). Continuous female companionship during childbirth: A crucial resource in times of stress or calm. *Journal of Midwifery and Women's Health, 49*, 19–27.

Rabe, H., Reynolds, G., & Diaz-Rossello, J. (2008). A systematic review and meta-analysis of a brief delay in clamping the umbilical cord of preterm infants. *Neonatology, 93*(2), 138–144.

Rafael, D. (1973). *The tender gift: Breastfeeding.* New York, NY: Schocken Books.

Schlinzig, T., Johansson, S., Gunnar, A., Ekström, T., & Norman, M. (2009). Epigenetic modulation at birth—altered DNA-methylation in white blood cells after caesarean section. *Acta Paediatrica, 98,* 1096–1099.

Silber, M., Larsson, B., & Uvnäs-Moberg, K. (1991). Oxytocin, somatostatin, insulin and gastrin concentrations vis-à-vis late pregnancy, breastfeeding and oral contraceptives. *Acta Obstetrica Gyencologica Scandinavia, 70,* 283–289.

Simkin, P. (2003). Maternal positions and pelves revisited. *Birth, 30*(2), 130–132.

Singh, G., & Archana, G. (2008). Unraveling the mystery of vernix caseosa. *Indian Journal of Dermatology, 53*(2), 54–60.

Smith, L. J. (2007). Impact of birthing practices on the breastfeeding dyad. *Journal of Midwifery and Women's Health, 52,* 621–630.

Stern, J. M. (1996). Offspring-induced nurturance: Animal–human parallels. *Developmental Psychobiology, 31,* 19–37.

Swain, J. E., Tasgin, E., Mayes, L. C., Feldman, R., Constable, R. T., & Leckman, J. F. (2008). Maternal brain response to own baby-cry is affected by cesarean section delivery. *Child Psychology and Psychiatry, 49*(10), 1042–1052.

Szyf, M. (2009). Early life, the epigenome and human health. *Acta Paediatrica, 98,* 1082–1084.

Trevathan, W. R. (1987). *Human birth: An evolutionary perspective.* New York, NY: Aldine de Gruyter.

Trevathan, W. R. (1988). Fetal emergence patterns in evolutionary perspective. *American Anthropologist, 90,* 19–26.

Turner, S. E., Fedigan, L. M., Nakamichi, M., Matthews, H. D., McKenna, K., Nobuhara, H.,…Shimizu, K. (2010). Birth in free-ranging *Macaca fuscata. International Journal of Primatology, 31,* 15–37.

Uvnäs-Moberg, K. (1996). Neuroendocrinology of the mother-child interaction. *Trends in Endocrinology and Metabolism, 7*(4), 126–131.

Van Rheenen, P., de Moor, L., Eschbach, S., de Grooth, H., & Brabin, B. (2007). Delayed cord clamping and haemoglobin levels in infancy: A randomised controlled trial in term babies. *Tropical Medicine and International Health, 12*(5), 603–616.

Varendi, H., Porter, R. H., & Winberg, J. (1994). Does the newborn baby find the nipple by smell? *Lancet, 344,* 989–990.

Varendi, H., Porter, R. H., & Winberg, J. (2002). The effect of labor on olfactory exposure learning within the first postnatal hour. *Behavioral Neuroscience, 116,* 206–211.

Weaver, I. C., Cervoni, N., Champagne, F. A., D'Alessio, A. C., Sharma, S., Seckl, J. R., …Meaney, M. J. (2004). Epigenetic programming by maternal behavior. *Nature Neuroscience, 7*(8), 847–854.

Weaver, I. C. G. (2009). Shaping adult phenotypes through early life environments. *Birth Defects Research (Part C), 87,* 314–326.

Wiberg, N., Källén, K., & Olofsson, P. (2008). Delayed umbilical cord clamping at birth has effects on arterial and venous blood gases and lactate concentrations. *BJOG, 115,* 697–703.

Winberg, J. (2005). Mother and newborn baby: Mutual regulation of physiology and behavior—a selective review. *Developmental Psychobiology, 47*, 217–229.

World Health Organization. (2006). *Pregnancy, childbirth, postpartum and newborn care: A guide for essential practice.* Geneva: Author.

World Health Organization. (2007). *WHO recommendations for the prevention of postpartum haemorrhage.* Geneva: Author.

World Health Organization. (2009). *WHO guidelines for the management of postpartum haemorrhage and retained placenta.* Geneva: Author.

Zhang, T-Y., & Meaney, M. J. (2010). Epigenetics and the environmental regulation of the genome and its function. *Annual Review of Psychology, 61*, 439–466.

9

Nighttime Nurturing: An Evolutionary Perspective on Breastfeeding and Sleep

Helen L. Ball and Charlotte K. Russell

Introduction

When considering the nighttime needs of mothers and babies, an anthropological vantage point provides a unique perspective on "human nature" by employing both phylogenetic depth and cross-cultural breadth to expose a variety of tensions between contemporary infant care and maternal and infant evolved biology. This chapter examines mothers' and babies' needs with regards to feeding, sleeping, and nighttime care and begins by drawing comparisons in infant care across humans and other mammals. This comparative phylogenetic perspective defines three things: (1) those traits of human mothers and infants that are common to all mammals, (2) those that are shared only with our closest primate relatives, and (3) those that are unique to the evolution of our species. A comparative historical and cross-cultural perspective can then help identify infant care practices that are adaptations to more recent ancestral environments and those that are historically novel cultural developments within particular societies. Cultural adaptations to recent ancestral environments would be infant care practices such as the use of the cradleboard or Peruvian manta pouch for transporting and securing infants in cold environments, compared with the use of carrying slings and bags in tropical environments.

The comparative phylogenetic approach also reminds us that when contemplating aspects of human nature with deep evolutionary roots, a single ancestral environment (AE) does not exist; in framing our potential AEs we must consider both shifting selection pressure over time and intersection with ancestral cultural adaptations (ACAs). The first relevant AE in this example (AE-1) relates to the fundamental biology and behavior of humans as placental mammals involving the production of relatively well-developed live-born young who require postnatal maternal care and lactation (the defining characteristic of the Mammalia; Pond, 1977).

Length of gestation period and developmental state at birth vary among mammals, with infants generally categorized into two well-known types. Altricial newborns are poorly developed, sequestered in nests, and fed infrequently with high-fat milk. Precocial newborns are well developed, able to follow or cling to their mothers, and suckle frequently and at will on milk that is relatively low in fat but high in calories (lactose), providing energy in a quickly digested form (Small, 1998). Among the primates, monkey and ape infants are precocial; human infants conform, by consequence of evolutionary relatedness, to this precocial primate pattern (AE-2).

Yet human infants also display "secondarily altricial" characteristics— primarily lack of neuromuscular control—a consequence of the limits imposed on gestational brain development by the evolution of the human pelvis. Human newborn brains are 25% of their adult volume (compared to 50% for infant chimpanzees and gorillas) due to the constraints of a birth canal that was modified for bipedal walking. Although displaying many precocial traits, therefore, human infants are unable to independently locomote or cling, and therefore maintain proximity with their mothers, or to effectively regulate temperature and breathing during the first few months of rapid brain growth and development (AE-3; Hrdy, 1999; Small, 1998).

Human milk has a similar composition to that of other precocial primates, being relatively low in fat and protein but high in sugar (Jelliffe & Jelliffe, 1978). It is milk produced for infants (AE-1) who suckle frequently and of their own volition day and night (AE-2), and the high sugar content in the case of humans provides the energy needed for rapid brain growth. Due to poor neuromuscular control, however, human neonates require their mothers to ensure that proximity is maintained, frequent feeding facilitated, and physiology regulated (AE-3). Ethnographic data from societies around the world confirm that mothers in traditional human societies are in almost constant contact with their infants, carrying them strapped to their bodies by day, sleeping beside them at night (Ball, 2007), and breastfeeding at will. Consideration of the human neonate from an evolutionary perspective therefore highlights the fact that many aspects of what is considered to be "normal infant care" in contemporary Western societies are historically recent culturally adopted practices (Crawford, 1994).

Since the mid-1930s, for instance, prolonged and independent nighttime sleep has been the hallmark of a "good baby" in many Western societies; early infant independence has been viewed as a developmental goal, and its achievement as a measure of effective parenting (e.g., Javo, Ronning, & Hyerdahl, 2004; Valentin, 2005). Yet for the majority of the world's cultures, separation of an infant from its mother for sleep is considered abusive or neglectful treatment (Jenni & O'Connor, 2005; Morelli, Rogoff, Oppenheim, & Goldsmith, 1992), for which Westerners are criticized. In the United States and United Kingdom, separate sleep locations for parents and infants in the household are historically recent—less than two centuries ago mother–baby sleep contact was the norm (Hardyment, 1993). Two particularly influential new cultural environments (NCEs) emerging during the 19th and 20th centuries gave rise to rapid and dramatic introduction of novel infant care practices (NICPs): the medicalization of childbirth and the emergence of "scientific motherhood" (Hardyment, 1993; Hulbert, 2003); principal among the novel practices introduced in response to these NCEs was the decoupling of infant feeding and sleeping from the mother's body (Hardyment, 1993; see Figure 9.1).

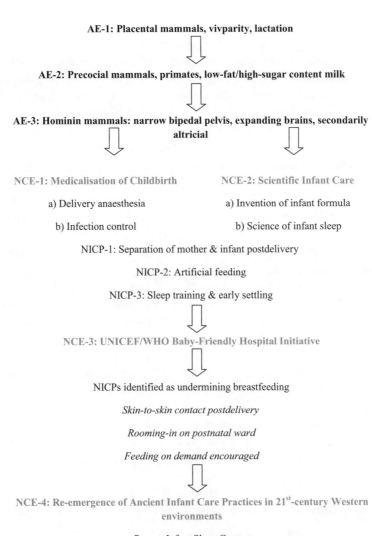

AE-1: Placental mammals, vivparity, lactation

AE-2: Precocial mammals, primates, low-fat/high-sugar content milk

AE-3: Hominin mammals: narrow bipedal pelvis, expanding brains, secondarily altricial

NCE-1: Medicalisation of Childbirth   NCE-2: Scientific Infant Care

a) Delivery anaesthesia   a) Invention of infant formula

b) Infection control   b) Science of infant sleep

NICP-1: Separation of mother & infant postdelivery

NICP-2: Artificial feeding

NICP-3: Sleep training & early settling

NCE-3: UNICEF/WHO Baby-Friendly Hospital Initiative

NICPs identified as undermining breastfeeding

Skin-to-skin contact postdelivery

Rooming-in on postnatal ward

Feeding on demand encouraged

NCE-4: Re-emergence of Ancient Infant Care Practices in 21st-century Western environments

Parent–Infant Sleep Contact

Prolonged breastfeeding

FIGURE 9.1 *Ancestral environments (AEs) and new cultural environments (NCEs) affecting mother–infant relationships and nighttime care. NICP = novel infant care practice.*

Medicalization of Childbirth (New Cultural Environment-1)

One consequence of AE-3, when brain size increased following pelvic constriction, was that childbirth became a hazardous and liminal activity with unavoidably high rates of maternal and infant deaths associated with the birth process throughout human history (Loudon, 1993). By the Victorian era, interventions to ease the fear of pain and death in childbirth were becoming popular (Loudon, 1993; Tew 1995). The use of chloroform, the anesthetic of the day, was restricted to hospital settings; women increasingly chose to deliver their babies in hospitals to avail themselves of anesthesia, even though chloroformed mothers were unable to care for their babies while recovering from the effects of the gas. Due to maternal incapacitation, nurseries were established in hospitals and babies were cared for by nursing staff (Tew, 1995). Efforts to improve the experience of childbirth for women (NCE-1a) therefore had serious and unanticipated repercussions for early infant care and mother–infant relationships, leading to popular acceptance of mother–newborn separation as normative behavior (NICP-1). Subsequent generations of anesthetics such as twilight sleep and intravenous barbiturates (Pitcock & Clark, 1992; Tew, 1995) also incapacitated women during and following delivery; recovery was a long process and infant care was impossible. Twilight sleep and barbiturates also affected infants, who were born sleepy and unable to respond or suck, many being force-fed in the first days after birth. Even respiratory movements were suppressed, and babies in the nurseries had to be monitored carefully (Feldhusen, 2006). From the 1940s, when aseptic practices and sulphur antibiotics were introduced into clinical practice and hospital birth mortality rates declined, the proportion of hospital births increased exponentially, reaching a zenith in 1973 when 99% of all US births took place in a hospital under the control of a physician (Nusche, 2002). The separation of mothers and infants following birth (NICP-1) was now routine. Campaigns to reduce medicated childbirth, such as those spear-headed by Grantley Dick-Reed and Fernand Lamaze, reduced narcotic use in labor throughout the 1950s and 1960s (Feldhusen, 2006; Nusche, 2002; Tew, 1995); however, the continued transfer of neonates to the hospital nursery was now justified with reference to infection control (NCE-1b). Although mothers were no longer incapacitated, babies were "removed to a safe place" for observation, and mothers were encouraged to rest following delivery—viewing their infants through glass partitions and meeting them only at scheduled feeding times (Hock, McBride, & Gnezda, 1989).

The Application of Science to Infant Care (New Cultural Environment-2)

While the medicalization of childbirth created one new cultural environment in which novel infant care practices arose, the application of science to infant care created another (NCE-2). The legacies of "experts" such as Holt, Watson, Freud, and Skinner in persuading parents that infant care should conform to rigid schedules, involve minimal touching and cuddling, eschew breastfeeding as an inappropriately sexualized activity, and promote independence by refusal to respond to crying had consequences reaching into the present day (Apple, 1995; Hardyment, 1983; Hulbert, 2003). The development and promotion of "scientifically formulated" infant food (NCE-2a) have been well documented (Apple, 1995; Hulbert, 2003) and played an important role in keeping infants alive during their mothers' "absence" in the context of the NCE-1a. However, even once the after-effects of labor and delivery anesthesia had subsided, physicians advocated feeding infants via artificial formula so that their food intake could be "scientifically managed." Arguably the most negative outcome of the near-universal uptake of hospital births, medicated deliveries, and mother–newborn separation was the fall in the proportion of mothers initiating breastfeeding. In the United States and Western Europe, breastfeeding rates (which had once been almost universal) fell dramatically to a nadir of 20–22% initiation rate in the United States between 1956 and 1972 (Wright, 2001). The acceptance of "scientific motherhood," combined with the influx of women into the industrial workforce in the era of World War II, led to the massive popularity of artificial formula for infants in the mid-20th century and cemented a second cultural shift in infant care (NICP-2) with further unforeseen ramifications.

In the 1940s, when sleep researchers Moore and Ucko (1957) began systematically documenting the developmental pattern of infant sleep, tables enumerating an infant's month-by-month sleep requirements were de rigueur (Good Housekeeping, 1956; Hardyment, 1983). Moore and Ucko's data became regarded as the yardstick against which infant sleep development should be assessed. Seventy percent of the 160 babies they studied commenced settling by 3 months of age—and it soon became the advice of pediatricians and the goal of parents that infants should "settle" (begin sleeping through the night, defined as midnight to 5 a.m.) by 3 months of age (NCE-2b; e.g., Better Homes and Gardens, 1965). Although Moore and Ucko recognized that feeding type (breast milk or formula) had an impact on infant sleep behavior, the establishment of prolonged and early sleep habits were their principal priority: "Unsatisfactory feeding is generally the first thing to be looked for in a wakeful baby.... Where breast feeding proved unsatisfactory, weaning to a bottle or complementary feeds sometimes had an immediate beneficial effect on sleep; in other cases, strengthening the formula or introducing solids settled the child" (p. 338). As decades passed the pursuit of early and unbroken sleep in young infants became a parental priority, and expectations regarding the normal pattern of infant sleep development were culturally codified in pediatric and parenting manuals; the second sentence of the American Academy of Pediatrics' Guide to Your Child's Sleep (Cohen, 1999) states, "In early infancy, the first task is to help your baby learn to sleep longer at night ... " (p. 1). Hundreds of books, magazine articles, and Internet sites extol myriad techniques for achieving a somnolent baby. However, it is now apparent that Moore and Ucko's infant population was predominantly composed of formula-fed infants and that they recorded artificially premature settling (consolidation of nighttime sleep) of their subjects, in part due to the soporific effects of cow's milk and in part due to the separation of infants at night from their mothers, who underestimated their infant's night waking (Anders, 1979). However, the notion of these developmental milestones for infant sleep are now cemented in parenting folklore as targets to be attained and consequently give rise to conflict between parental efforts to ensure that infants sleep through the night at as early an age as possible (NICP-3) and the biological requirement for breastfed infants to wake and feed frequently throughout the day and night (Carey, 1975; Quillin & Glenn, 2004; Wright, MacLeod, & Cooper, 1983; Zuckerman, Stevenson, & Bailey, 1987).

The differences in sleep patterns between breastfed and formula-fed infants arise largely as a consequence of the human infant's inability to easily digest cow's milk (Raphael, 1976), which can cause formula-fed infants to sleep more deeply and for longer periods at an earlier age than breastfed infants (Butte & Jensen, 1992; although see Doan, Gardiner, Gay, & Lee, 2007). Infant sleep bouts gradually con-solidate into a diurnal rhythm over the course of the first year of life, but breastfed infants—particularly those who are exclusively breastfed for at least 6 months in accordance with current health guidelines (World Health Organization, 2003)—do not experience consolidation of nighttime sleep as early as their formula-fed coun-terparts (Carey, 1975). Additionally, infants fed artificial formula exhibit signifi-cantly different sleep patterns compared with breastfed infants in terms of shorter sleep latency (time taken to fall asleep), longer duration of rapid eye movement (REM; active) sleep, and a larger percentage of REM, while breastfed infants experience significantly more sleep interruptions during the night, are fed more fre-quently, and consequently have significantly more night feedings (Elias, Nicolson, Bora, & Johnston, 1986). The "... development of a long unbroken night's sleep by the early age of 4 months is surprising when considered from an evolutionary view-point, because human infants, like other primates, are physiologically adapted for frequent suckling and close physical contact with their mothers" (Elias et al., 1986 p. 322). Unrealistic ideals for infant sleep continue to undermine the confidence of new parents regarding their infants' normal development. For those committed to breastfeeding, sleeping with their babies (i.e., conforming to the "precocial mam-malian pattern" of the AE-2) is one of the means by which mothers ameliorate fre-quent nighttime feeding and later settling (Ball, 2002; McCoy et al., 2004; Morgan, Groer, & Smith, 2006).

Consequences of Novel Infant Care Practices on Breastfeeding, Lactation, and Sleep

BREASTFEEDING

Postpartum separation of mothers and babies (NICP-1) and artificial infant feed-ing (NICP-2) were unprecedented and untested interventions in human reproduc-tive biology and behavior. They subjected Euro-American mothers and infants to experiences that contrast markedly with the close and prolonged postnatal contact of mothers and infants across the anthropoid primates, and across human societies worldwide (Barry & Paxson, 1971; Small, 1998). The results of Harlow's research with infant monkeys dramatically demonstrate the importance for infants of 24-hour physical contact with their mothers' bodies—even when the mother is an inanimate cloth-covered surrogate (Blum, 2002; Harlow, 1959). Subsequent clinical studies regarding the effects on infants of separation from their mothers confirms the importance of close physical contact—not just in terms of psychological development, but also in terms of basic physiological functioning (Anderson, Moore, Hepworth, & Bergman, 2003; De Chateau & Wiberg, 1977; Righard & Alade, 1990; Varendi & Porter, 2001) for both infant and mother (Uvnas-Moberg, 2003).

When, in the 1980s, research began to demonstrate the detrimental consequences to both maternal and infant health of feeding babies with artificial formula (Cunningham, Jellife, & Jellife, 1991; Dewey, Heinig, & Nommsen-Rivers, 1995; Howie, Forsyth, Ogston, Clark, & Florey, 1990), mechanisms were sought to reverse the breastfeeding decline, and it soon became apparent that mother–infant separation in the postbirth period undermined both breastfeeding and lactation (Anderson et al., 2003). As a consequence, the past two decades have witnessed a renewed recognition of the importance of close contact for mothers and babies and increasing rejection of NICP-1 and NICP-2.

In the immediate postnatal period, human infants born following an unmedicated labor and placed directly onto their mothers' abdomens exhibit innate nipple-seeking behavior (Righard & Alade, 1990), during which they crawl and squirm up their mothers' bodies, guided to the nipple by smell (Nissen et al, 1995; Varendi & Porter, 2001; Varendi, Porter, & Winberg, 1994); locate the nipple by head bobbing; and spontaneously latch and suckle without assistance (Varendi et al., 1994) over the first hour of life. Infants delivered following a medicated labor involving opioid analgesics make little or no attempt to crawl, and those that try are disorganized, uncoordinated, and unsuccessful in gaining the nipple (Ransjo-Arvidson et al., 2001; Righard & Alade, 1990). Unmedicated infants perform an instinctive pattern of hand movements during nipple seeking that is associated with an increase in maternal oxytocin levels and is similar to those observed in other mammals where massage of the mammary tissue facilitates milk let-down (Matthiesen, Ransjo-Arvidson, Nissen, & Uvnas-Moberg, 2001). Mothers and babies who experience unhurried skin-to-skin contact immediately following delivery, during which time these behaviors can unfold, have a far greater chance of both establishing successful breastfeeding and having prolonged breastfeeding duration (Andersen et al., 2003; Johnston & Amico, 1986; Uvnas-Moberg, Widstrom, Werner, Matthiesen, & Winberg, 1990).

MOTHER–INFANT SLEEP CONTACT

By the end of the 20th century, recognition of the importance of breastfeeding to infant health, and the role of separation in preventing the effective establishment of breastfeeding, led to the closure of newborn nurseries in many European hospitals (e.g., Sweden, United Kingdom), although the United States still lags behind (Young, 2005). With the closure of nurseries came a shift to mothers and babies "rooming-in," with the baby located at the mother's bedside during the day but removed to a communal nursery at night or (more recently) 24-hour rooming-in with mothers performing all aspects of their infant's care. Comparison of the effects of rooming-in with nursery care found that separation of infants to neonatal nurseries resulted in less frequent breastfeeding (Yamauchi & Yamanouchi, 1990) and greater likelihood of breastfeeding failure (Uvnas-Moberg et al., 1990), but no increase in maternal sleep or alertness (Keefe, 1988; Waldenstrom & Swenson, 1991). Infants who spent their nights in nurseries were also found to sleep significantly less and to cry more than those at their mothers' bedside (Keefe, 1987). The evidence concerning the impact of mother–baby separation on breastfeeding drives the current cultural changes that emphasize skin-to-skin contact following delivery and rooming-in on the postnatal ward (NCE-3; DiGirolamo, Grummer-Strawn, & Fein, 2001; Perez-Escamilla, Pollitt, Lonnerdal, & Dewey, 1994; UNICEF UK, 2000; World Health Organization, 1999).

Given the importance of close contact in establishing breastfeeding and the need for frequent suckling to promote continued lactation, anthropologists consider mother–infant sleep contact to be a normal, species-typical parenting behavior for humans. Over the past two decades, research into infant sleep behavior in postindustrial contexts has revealed that, contrary to earlier assumptions (Davies, 1994), parent–baby sleep contact is a common form of nighttime care (see Figure 9.2). Bed-sharing prevalence in the United Kingdom (ever sleeping with baby in the same bed) is around 50% among 1-month-old infants, dropping to 25–29% at 3 months old (Ball, 2003; Blair & Ball, 2004; Bolling, Grant, Hamlyn, & Thornton, 2007; Greenslade, 1995), and a baseline bed-sharing prevalence of 40–50% among neonates has subsequently been replicated around the world, indicating that parent–infant sleep contact is common in a wide variety of Western countries. Repeatedly in these studies researchers have found a strong association between sleep contact and breastfeeding (Ball, 2003; McKenna, Mosko, & Richard, 1997), with mothers identifying "ease and convenience of breastfeeding" as their overwhelming reason for keeping their infants close at night.

In locations such as the United States and United Kingdom, where breastfeeding has not been the cultural norm for a generation or more and new mothers are often unprepared for the frequency with which their breastfed newborns need to feed or how long nighttime breastfeeding is likely to continue (Ball, 2003; Bolling et al., 2007, Greenslade, 1995), studies report that frequent night waking is a factor contributing to the introduction of artificial formula to babies, thereby undermining breastfeeding (Marchand & Morrow, 1994; Pinilla & Birch, 1993). In the United Kingdom, we observed that babies who bed-shared were twice as likely to be breastfeeding at 4 months of age, compared to babies who were initially breastfed

---

What is 'Bed-sharing' and 'Co-sleeping'?

It is important to note that researchers and healthcare practitioners have established different usage for the terms 'bed-sharing' and 'co-sleeping'. Among the anthropological and epidemiological research literature (including the majority of SIDS-risk case-control studies and parent-infant sleep studies) the term 'bed-sharing' has been restricted to encompass only 'adults and infants sharing the same surface for sleep'. Technically its use should be restricted to 'sharing the same bed' however sofa-sharing and other same-surface sleeping arrangements are subsumed into bed-sharing in some studies. In the more recent research literature, 'co-sleeping' refers to parents and infants sleeping in close proximity, but not necessarily on the same surface: this could therefore include room-sharing with the infant's crib near the bed, or parents and infants sleeping on adjacent mattresses. Under this definition bed-sharing is a sub-set of co-sleeping, but not all co-sleeping is bed-sharing. And bed sharing means sleeping for at least some of the night in the same bed as a parent or parents. Among health practitioners in various countries bed-sharing is sometimes taken to mean 'bringing a baby in to bed for a feed while the mother/caregiver is awake', while co-sleeping refers to 'sleeping in bed with a baby'. In this chapter, and in the majority of research articles cited here, the terms *bed-sharing* and *co-sleeping* are used according to the above research-based definitions.

FIGURE 9.2 *Definitions of bed-sharing and cosleeping.*

but did not bed-share (Ball, 2003). It was unclear, however, whether mothers with a commitment to long-term breastfeeding were predisposed to bed-sharing at the outset—or whether there was an underlying connection that linked bed-sharing with breastfeeding continuation. McKenna's previous research indicated that when babies bed-share they suckle more frequently at night than when sleeping alone (McKenna et al., 1997).

LACTATION

As frequent suckling is associated with the successful establishment of breastfeeding, we hypothesized that sleeping in close proximity following delivery (i.e., continuation of partial skin-to-skin contact for the duration of the postnatal ward stay) may have the potential to enhance breastfeeding establishment and continuation. To explore this we conducted a randomized controlled trial in a tertiary-level UK hospital (details of the trial protocol can be found in the clinical report; Ball, Ward-Platt, Heslop, Leech, & Brown, 2006). Overnight videos were made of mother–baby dyads randomized to three sleep locations for their postnatal ward stay: (1) baby in the standard bassinette at mother's bedside, (2) baby in a side-car crib attached to mother's bed, and (3) baby in mother's bed with rail attached to bedside—known as the bassinette, side-car, and bed conditions, respectively. We found that babies in the bed or side-car crib had more frequent attempted and successful feeds than those infants in the bassinette, with no significant differences found in feeding frequency measures between the bed and side-car conditions (Ball et al., 2006). Video data demonstrated that the stand-alone bassinette impeded breastfeeding by introducing a barrier between mother and baby, preventing contact; inhibited the baby's ability to effectively root and initiate suckling; obscured the baby's feeding cues from the mother; and by its height prevented mothers from retrieving their babies without either assistance or the need to get out of bed, thereby substantially hampering the ease and speed of maternal response (Ball et al., 2006; Ball, Ward-Platt, Howel, & Russell, 2011; Klingaman, 2010).

Prompt response to babies' feeding signals and frequent suckling in the early neonatal period are essential in ensuring successful milk production—a process controlled by prolactin (Johnston & Amico, 1986; Uvnas-Moberg et al., 1990). Babies trigger maternal prolactin surges with every feed attempt, so frequent attempts are key. Facilitating close contact at night is especially important because night feeds trigger greater prolactin release than day feeds (Tennekoon, Arulambalam, Karunanayake, & Seneviratne, 1994; Woolridge, 1995). The amount of prolactin released and the frequency of prolactin secretion following birth are associated with earlier lactogenesis II and increased milk production (Chapman & Perez-Escamilla, 1999; Neville, Morton, & Umemura, 2001; Sözmen, 1992).

Prolactin therefore links mother–infant sleep contact with improved breastfeeding initiation (Ball, 2008). Elevation of initial prolactin levels is also implicated in successful long-term lactation. The maintenance of lactation is dependent on the development of prolactin receptors in breast tissue (Riordan & Auerbach, 1993), which also result from frequent feeding in the early days after birth (Marasco & Barger, 1999) and are thought to be crucial in maintaining lactation following the switch from endocrine to autocrine control of milk production (Lawrence & Lawrence, 1999). We hypothesized, therefore, that frequency of early feeding attempts would be associated with breastfeeding duration. A common reason given by women for stopping breastfeeding is a perceived or real insufficiency in breast milk production (Bolling et al., 2007), suggesting inadequate prolactin receptor development in the initial phases of breastfeeding. As those infants sleeping in close proximity to their mothers on the postnatal ward in the trial described previously (bed or side-car crib) fed more frequently than infants randomly allocated to the stand-alone bassinette, we compared their long-term breastfeeding outcomes using data obtained via telephone interviews at 2, 4, 8, and 16 postnatal weeks. Although all mothers initiated breastfeeding on the postnatal ward, at 16 weeks 43% of babies who were in a separate bassinette on the postnatal ward were still breastfeeding, compared with 73% of the crib group and 79% of the bed group (Ball, 2008). Mother–infant sleep contact in the early neonatal period therefore promotes successful breastfeeding initiation and earlier lactogenesis II and may be associated with enhanced breastfeeding duration, signifying important benefits for both infant and maternal health.

INFANT PROTECTION

Several studies of mother–infant sleep behavior have now documented how routinely bed-sharing and breastfeeding dyads sleep in close proximity with a high degree of mutual orientation (facing one another) and arousal overlap (waking at the same time; see McKenna et al., 2007, for a comprehensive review). In recent years, these studies have been replicated in a variety of settings, and breastfeeding dyads have been observed displaying consistent bed-sharing behavior, regardless of whether they slept in a narrow hospital bed, in a full-size bed in a sleep lab, or at home in beds ranging from twin to king sized (Baddock, Galland, Bolton, Williams, & Taylor, 2006; Ball, 2006; Young, Fleming, Blair, & Pollard, 2001). Mothers sleep in a lateral position, facing their baby, and curled up around the baby. Babies, positioned level with their mothers' breasts, sleep in the space created between the mother's arm (positioned above her baby's head) and her knees (drawn up under her baby's feet; Baddock et al., 2006; Ball, 2006; Richard, Mosko, McKenna, & Drummond, 1996; Young et al., 2001). The cumulative results of these studies provide a robust understanding of breastfeeding-related bed-sharing behavior and suggest that mothers' characteristic sleep position represents an instinctive behavior on the part of a breastfeeding mother to protect her baby during sleep (Ball & Klingaman, 2007). Although this behavior would have evolved in a very different sleep context than one adorned with Western beds and bedding, the principle of infant protection is no less effective. When breastfeeding mothers sleep with their babies, they construct a safe space in which the baby can sleep constrained by their own body, protected from potentially dangerous environmental factors—be they predators, cold weather, the suffocation hazards of quilts and pillows, or the overlaying risk of bed partners. This could therefore be characterized as an ancient infant care practice that is being played out in a new cultural environment (the Western sleep environment).

HAZARDOUS SLEEP ENVIRONMENTS

The contemporary Western sleep environment in which mother–infant sleep contact occurs has been presumed to be hazardous to infants in terms of overheating and suffocation or rebreathing. Studies of the physiological effect on infants of sleep contact have been conducted by several researchers. Tuffnell, Petersen, and Wailoo (1996) reported that infants sleeping in contact with their mothers had an average core temperature 0.1°C higher than the average for lone-sleeping infants; other researchers have confirmed that while bed-sharing babies are generally warmer than cot-sleeping babies, they maintain a stable core temperature and are not overly heated (Baddock, Galland, Beckers, Taylor, & Bolton, 2004).

Physiological studies have also investigated the effects of airway covering during bed-sharing. In a study of 40 regularly bed-sharing parents and infants and 40 age- and season-matched cot-sleeping infants aged 0 to 6 months, Baddock, Galland,

Taylor, and Bolton (2007) found that 80% of infant head-covering episodes resulted from adult positional changes during sleep, and that 68% of uncovering of infant faces occurred by intentional and unintentional parental clearing of the covers, with infants clearing their own faces in 32% of cases (Baddock et al., 2007). In the Durham sleep lab, we also found that babies experienced more airway covering by bedding when bed-sharing than when sleeping in a cot, but that this airway covering did not compromise infants' ability to maintain normal levels of circulating oxygen, even when airway covering by bedding was prolonged (Ball, 2009). In the case of compromised oxygen supplies, it would be expected that infant heart rate would increase in order to more efficiently circulate available oxygen around the tissues. In the present study, airway covering was not associated with significantly lower oxygen saturation, nor with significantly increased infant heart rate, and although bed-sharing infants were frequently observed to have their airways covered, they also frequently got uncovered, sometimes as a consequence of the infant's own actions, but more commonly as a consequence of parental conscious or unconscious intervention. This study also found no evidence that sharing a bed with nonsmoking parents who were not under the influence of alcohol or drugs was a suffocation or compression hazard to a sleeping infant (Ball, 2009), and Sawcenko and Fleming (1996) reported that infants awoke or removed themselves from any potential rebreathing CO_2 situation encountered during bed-sharing. These studies indicate that Western adult sleep environments may not be as hazardous to bed-sharing babies as is sometimes presumed.

SLEEP ARCHITECTURE AND SUDDEN INFANT DEATH SYNDROME

In the 1980s, 2 to 4 infants per 1,000 died suddenly and with no explanation (classified as sudden infant death syndrome [SIDS]) in Western industrialized countries (Guntheroth, 1989). In many Asian societies, even in industrialized populations such as Hong Kong and Japan, SIDS deaths occurred at a fraction of the rate found in the West (Lee, Chan, Davies, Lau, & Yip, 1989; Watanabe et al., 1994). McKenna (1986) suggested that the Western NICP of solitary infant sleep meant that infants were in an environment for which they were not designed biologically, were lacking the physiological regulatory effects of the mother's body, and were therefore at increased risk for SIDS (see McKenna, Ball, & Gettler, 2007, for an overview). McKenna suggested that solitary sleeping infants were deprived of sensory stimuli that could induce infant arousals. Without them, he hypothesized, infants born with deficits may more easily experience a breathing control error during sleep such as the kind suspected to be involved in SIDS. One testable prediction from this hypothesis was the expectation that maternal sleep contact would affect infant sleep states by increasing arousal opportunities and preventing long periods of deep sleep. In examining the differences in sleep architecture between infants sleeping alone and in contact with their mothers, Mosko and McKenna found that when bed-sharing, both mothers and infants experienced significantly more light sleep and less deep sleep than when sleeping separately, and that infants experienced significantly more arousals per hour of sleep when bed-sharing than when sleeping alone. Mosko et al. (Mosko, Richard, & McKenna, 1997; Mosko, Richard, McKenna, & Drummond, 1996) have argued that these features of a shared sleep experience could serve to minimize the occurrence of long periods of consolidated sleep from which infants with deficient arousal mechanisms may have difficulties in terminating prolonged apneas. Mosko et al. (1996) also suggested that during the crucial period when infants are most vulnerable to SIDS, mother–infant sleep contact may assist in consolidating the integration of the neural mechanisms that underlie the arousal response. While further research is required in this area, the finding that transient arousal frequency was higher among routinely bed-sharing infants than among infants who routinely slept alone supports the notion that practice has a sustained impact on arousability. To date, however, epidemiological studies have only found a protective effect for SIDS and room sharing (cosleeping), and not bed-sharing. The novel infant care practice of encouraging long unbroken periods of sleep in young infants (e.g., sleep training) would therefore be a hazardous practice, particularly for infants with inbuilt arousal deficiencies.

Some authorities suggest that parent–infant sleep contact is a questionable practice that should be abandoned by parents and discouraged by health professionals due to concerns regarding risk of SIDS and/or accidental death (e.g., Ateah & Hamelin, 2008; Byard, 1994; Weale, 2003). Such recommendations acknowledge little or no value in mother–infant sleep contact and are based on case-control studies of SIDS or accidental infant deaths. Babies sleeping prone, parental smoking, poverty, and young maternal age are all well-known factors that are associated with an increased risk of unexpected infant death (Fleming, 1994), with many NICPs being implicated. However, estimates of the relative risk of SIDS in the context of bed-sharing vary widely. Assessments of the impact of bed-sharing on SIDS risk in the United Kingdom range from no increased risk to babies of nonsmoking parents to a 12-fold increase for infants sharing a sofa for sleep with a parent who smokes (Blair et al., 1999). The picture is obscured because studies use different criteria to define bed-sharing (e.g., Carpenter et al., 2004; Hauck et al., 2003; Tappin et al., 2005), have produced a confusing array of statistics that cannot easily be compared (see Côté, 2006; Horsley et al., 2007), and have conducted multivariate analyses in a nonsystematic manner (Matthews, McDonnell, McGarvey, Loftus, & O'Regan, 2004). These issues make it difficult to ascertain the truly risky elements of bed-sharing. Furthermore, SIDS case-control studies consistently ignore infant feeding type in calculating relative risks associated with bed-sharing. Until more appropriate data are collected, it is impossible to ascertain whether breastfeeding-related sleep contact between mothers and babies confers a reduction or an increase in SIDS risk. However, it is unlikely that any potential risk would be of great magnitude (see Leduc & Camfield, 2006) given that breastfeeding is associated with a reduced SIDS risk compared to formula feeding in several studies (e.g., Hauck et al., 2003; Hoffman, Damus, Hillman, & Kongrad, 1988; Vennemann et al., 2009).

With regard to other bed-sharing risks, babies of breastfeeding mothers appear to avoid the presumed hazards of sleeping in adult beds (e.g., suffocation, overlaying, wedging, entrapment; Nakamura, Wind, & Danello, 1999), due to the presence and behavior of their mothers and as a result of their own agency (see earlier). We have observed the "protective sleep position" among first-time mothers sleeping with their newborn on the first night of life (Ball & Klingaman, 2007), and we have documented differences in behavior between breastfeeding and nonbreastfeeding mothers when sleeping with their babies (Ball, 2006). In the latter video study, nonbreastfed infants were generally placed high in the bed, at parental face height, and positioned between, or on top of, parental pillows. In contrast, breastfed babies were always positioned flat on the mattress, below pillow height and level with the mother's chest. Nonbreastfeeding mothers spent significantly less time facing their baby and in mutual face-to-face orientation than did breastfeeding mother–baby pairs, and they did not adopt the "protective" sleep position with the same consistency (Ball, 2006).

The patterning of these differences is consistent with the physiological mechanisms mediating maternal and infant behavior, in that breastfeeding mothers experience a hormonal feedback cycle, which promotes close contact with, heightened responsiveness toward, and bonding with infants in a way that is different among mothers who do not breastfeed (Uvnas-Moberg, 2003). The implication here—that breastfeeding mothers and babies sleep together in qualitatively and significantly quantitatively different ways than do nonbreastfeeding mothers and babies—suggests that epidemiological studies of bed-sharing that have not considered feeding type as a variable for matching cases and controls may have drawn inappropriate conclusions in assessing risk factors associated with bed-sharing, and the criticisms of breastfeeding-related bed-sharing may be unfounded.

Over the past decade, recognition of the evolved needs of mothers and babies during childbirth and the immediate postpartum period have become incorporated into a new cultural environment, NCE-3, well established in European hospitals and emerging in the United States in the form of the UNICEF Baby-Friendly Hospital Initiative, that goes some way toward redressing some of the NICPs established in the contexts of NCE-1 and -2. Mother–infant skin-to-skin contact immediately following delivery, encouragement of breastfeeding, and 24-hour rooming-in provide conditions that are closer to those our evolved physiology might expect, but our research shows that this is just one step in the right direction, and there is still further progress to be made.

Conclusion

It would be unrealistic to believe that in the 21st century postindustrial world we can duplicate the conditions of our ancestral evolved environment; however, there is a growing recognition that elements of our ancestral environments that are crucial to the operation of our mammalian, primate, and hominin physiology can be emulated within a contemporary environment of cultural adaptation. Breastfeeding mothers do this instinctively when they sleep in close contact with their infants, encouraging them to feed at will, supporting their physiological development with their own bodies and behaviors, and allowing their infant's chronobiology to unfold according to the infant's individual schedule. It is also apparent as a result of our research that infants are not the only component of the dyad to be affected by environments of recent cultural change, with the impact of sleep contact on maternal physiology (lactation) also having profound effects.

References

Anders, T. (1979). Night-waking in infants during the first year of life. Pediatrics, 63, 860–864.

Anderson, G. C., Moore, E., Hepworth, J., & Bergman, N. (2003). Early skin-to-skin contact for mothers and their healthy newborn infants. Birth, 30, 206–207.

Apple, R. (1995). Constructing mothers: Scientific motherhood in the 19th and 20th centuries. Social History of Medicine, 8(2), 161–178.

Ateah, C. A., & Hamelin, A. J. (2008). Maternal bedsharing practices, experiences, and awareness of risks. Journal of Obstetric, Gynecologic and Neonatal Nursing, 37, 274–281.

Baddock, S. A., Galland, B. C., Beckers, M. G., Taylor, B. J., & Bolton, D. P. (2004). Bedsharing and the infant's thermal environment in the home setting. Archives of Disease in Childhood, 89(12), 1111–1116.

Baddock, S. A., Galland, B. C., Bolton, D. P. G., Williams, S. M., & Taylor, B. J. (2006). Differences in infant and parent behaviors during routine bed sharing compared with cot sleeping in the home setting. Pediatrics, 117, 1599–1607.

Baddock, S. A., Galland, B. C., Taylor, B. J., & Bolton, D. P. G. (2007). Sleep arrangements and behavior of bed-sharing families in the home setting. Pediatrics, 119(1), e200–e207.

Ball, H. L. (2002). Reasons to bed-share: Why parents sleep with their infants. Journal of Reproductive and Infant Psychology, 20(4), 207–222.

Ball, H. L. (2003). Breastfeeding, bed-sharing and infant sleep. Birth, 30(3), 181–188.

Ball, H. L. (2006). Parent-infant bed-sharing behavior: Effects of feeding type, and presence of father. Human Nature, 17(3), 301–318.

Ball, H. L. (2007). Night-time infant care: Cultural practice, evolution, and infant development. In P. Liamputtong (Ed.), Childrearing and infant care issues: A cross-cultural perspective (pp. 47–61). Melbourne, Australia: Nova.

Ball, H. L. (2008). Evolutionary paediatrics: A case study in applying Darwinian medicine. In S. Elton & P. O'Higgins (Eds.), Medicine and evolution: Current applications, future prospects (pp. 127–152). New York, NY: Taylor & Francis.

Ball, H. L. (2009). Airway covering during bed-sharing. Child: Care, Health and Development, 35(5), 728–737.

Ball, H. L., & Klingaman, K. P. (2007). Breastfeeding and mother-infant sleep proximity: Implications for infant care. In W. Trevathan, E. O. Smith, & J. J. McKenna (Eds.), Evolutionary medicine and health: New perspectives (pp. 226–241). New York, NY: Oxford University Press.

Ball, H. L., Ward-Platt, M. P., Heslop, E., Leech, S. J., & Brown, K. (2006). Randomised trial of mother-infant sleep proximity on the post-natal ward: Implications for breast-feeding initiation and infant safety. Archives of Disease in Childhood, 91, 1005–1010.

Ball, H. L., Ward-Platt, M. P., Howel, D., & Russell, C. K. (2011). Randomised trial of side-car crib use on breastfeeding duration (NECOT). Archives of Disease in Childhood, 96, 360–364.

Barry, H., & Paxson, L. M. (1971). Infancy and early childhood: Cross-cultural codes 2. Ethnology, 10, 466.

Better Homes and Gardens. (1965). Baby book. New York, NY: Bantam.

Blair, P. S., & Ball, H. L. (2004). The prevalence and characteristics associated with parent–infant bed-sharing in England. Archives of Disease in Childhood, 89, 1106–1110.

Blair, P. S., Fleming, P. J., Smith, I. J., Ward Platt, M., Young, J., Nadin, P., ...Golding, J. (1999). Babies sleeping with parents: Case-control study of factors influencing the risk of the sudden infant death syndrome. British Medical Journal, 319, 1457–1461.

Blum, D. (2002). Love at goon park: Harry Harlow and the science of affection. Cambridge, MA: Perseus.

Bolling, K., Grant, C., Hamlyn, B., & Thornton, A. (2007). Infant feeding survey 2005. London: The Information Centre.

Butte, N., & Jensen, C. (1992). Sleep organisation and energy expenditure of breast-fed and formula-fed infants. Pediatric Research, 32(5), 514–519.

Byard, R. W. (1994). Is co-sleeping in infancy a desirable or dangerous practice? Journal of Paediatric Child Health, 30, 198–199.

Carey, W. B. (1975). Breast feeding and night waking. Journal of Pediatrics, 87(2), 327.

Carpenter, R. G., Irgens, L. M., Blair, P. S., England, P. D., Fleming, P., Huber, J., ...Schreuder, P. (2004). Sudden unexplained infant death in 20 regions in Europe: Case control study. Lancet, 363, 185–191.

Chapman, D. J., & Perez-Escamilla, R. (1999). Identification of risk factors for delayed onset of lactation. Journal of the American Dietetic Association, 99(4), 450–454.

Cohen, G. J. (Ed.). (1999). American Academy of Pediatrics: Guide to your child's sleep. New York, NY: Villard.

Côté, A. (2006). Bed sharing and sudden infant death syndrome: Do we have a definition problem? Paediatrics and Child Health, 11(Suppl A), 34A–38A.

Crawford, C. (1994). Parenting practices in the Basque country: Implications of infant and childhood sleeping location for personality development. Ethos, 22(1), 42–82.

Cunningham, A. S., Jellife, D. B., & Jellife, E. E. P. (1991). Breastfeeding and health in the 1980's: A global epidemiologic review. Journal of Pediatrics, 118, 656.

Davies, D. P. (1994). Ethnicity and SIDS: What have we learnt? Early Human Development, 38(3), 215–220.

De Chateau, P., & Wiberg, B. (1977). Long-term effect on mother-infant behaviours of extra contact during the first hour post partum. II. A follow up at three months. Acta Paediatrica Scandinavia, 66, 145.

Dewey, K. G., Heinig, M., & Nommsen-Rivers, L. A. (1995). Differences in morbidity between breastfed and formula fed infants. Journal of Pediatrics, 126, 696.

DiGirolamo, A. M., Grummer-Strawn, L. M., & Fein, S. B. (2001). Maternity care practices: Implications for breastfeeding. Birth, 28, 94.

Doan, T., Gardiner, A., Gay, C. L., & Lee, K. A. (2007). Breast-feeding increases sleep duration of new parents. Journal of Perinatal and Neonatal Nursing, 21(3), 200–206.

Elias, M. F., Nicolson, N. A., Bora, C., & Johnston, J. (1986). Sleep/wake patterns of breast-fed infants in the first 2 years of life. Pediatrics, 77(3), 322–329.

Feldhusen, A. E. (2006). The history of midwifery and childbirth in America: A time line. Midwifery Today. Retrieved May 13, 2006, from www.midwiferytoday.com/Articles/Timeline.Asp

Fleming, P. J. (1994). Understanding and preventing sudden infant death syndrome. Current Opinion in Paediatrics, 6, 158–162.

Good Housekeeping. (1956). Baby book. London: National Magazine Company.

Greenslade, J. (1995). What's best about breastfeeding. Nursery World, January, 19–21.

Guntheroth, W. G. (1989). Crib death. New York, NY: Futura.

Hardyment, C. (1983). Dream babies: Child care from Locke to Spock. London: Jonathan Cape.

Harlow, H. F. (1959). Love in infant monkeys. Scientific American, 200, 68–74.

Hauck, F. R., Herman, S. M., Donovan, M., Iyasu, S., Merrick Moore, C., Donoghue, E., ...Willinger, M. (2003). Sleep environment and the risk of sudden infant death syndrome in an urban population: The Chicago infant mortality study. Pediatrics, 111(5), 1207–1214.

Hock, E., McBride, S., & Gnezda, M. T. (1989). Maternal separation anxiety: Mother-infant separation from the maternal perspective. Child Development, 60, 793.

Hoffman, H. J., Damus, K., Hillman, L., & Kongrad, E. (1988). Risk factors for SIDS: Results of the National Institute of Child Health and Human Development SIDS cooperative epidemiological study. Annals of the New York Academy of Science, 533, 13–31.

Horsley, T., Clifford, T., Barrowman, M., Bennett, S., Yazdi, F., Sampson, M., ...Côté, A. (2007). Benefits and harms associated with the practice of bed sharing. Archives of Pediatric and Adolescent Medicine, 161, 237–245.

Howie, P. W., Forsyth, J. S., Ogston, S. A, Clark, A., & Florey, C. D. (1990). Protective effect of breastfeeding against infection. British Medical Journal, 300, 11.

Hrdy, S. B. (1999). Mother Nature: A history of mothers, infants, and natural selection. New York, NY: Ballantine.

Hulbert, A. (2003). Raising America: Experts, parents and a century of advice about children. New York, NY: Knopf Publishing

Javo, C., Ronning, A. J., & Hyerdahl, S. (2004). Child-rearing in an indigenous Sami population in Norway: A cross-cultural comparison of parental attitudes and expectations. Scandinavian Journal of Psychology, 45, 67–78.

Jelliffe, D. B., & Jelliffe, E. F. P. (1978). Human milk in the modern world. Oxford: Oxford University Press.

Jenni, O., & O'Connor, B. (2005). Children's sleep: An interplay between culture and biology. Pediatrics, 115(Suppl), 204–216.

Johnston, J. M., & Amico, J. A. (1986). A prospective longitudinal study of the release of oxytocin and prolactin in response to infant suckling in long term lactation. Journal of Clinical Endocrinology and Metabolism, 62, 653.

Keefe, M. (1987). Comparison of neonatal night time sleep-wake patterns in nursery versus rooming environments. Nursing Research, 36, 140.

Keefe, M. R. (1988). The impact of infant rooming-in on maternal sleep at night. Journal of Obstetrics, Gynecology, and Neonatal Nursing, 17, 122.

Klingaman, K. P. (2010). *Breastfeeding after a caesarean section: Mother-infant health trade-offs.* Durham University PhD thesis 2010.

Lawrence, R. A., & Lawrence, R. M. (1999). Breastfeeding: A guide for the medical profession. St. Louis, MO: Mosby.

Leduc, D., & Camfield, C. (2006). Putting sudden infant death syndrome research into practice: Paediatricians' perspective. Paediatrics and Child Health, 11(Suppl A), 51A–52A.

Lee, N. Y., Chan, Y. F., Davies, D. P., Lau, E., & Yip, D. C. P. (1989). Sudden infant death syndrome in Hong Kong: Confirmation of low incidence. British Medical Journal, 298, 721.

Loudon, I. (1993). An international study of maternal care and maternal mortality 1800–1950. New York, NY: Oxford University Press.

Marasco, L., & Barger, J. (1999). Cue feeding: Wisdom and science. Breastfeeding Abstracts, 18(4), 28–29.

Marchand, L., & Morrow, M. H. (1994). Infant feeding practices: Understanding the decision-making process. Clinical Research and Methods, 26(5), 319–324.

Matthews, T., McDonnell, M., McGarvey, C., Loftus, G., & O'Regan, M. (2004). A multivariate "time based" analysis of SIDS risk factors Archives of Disease in Childhood, 89, 267–271.

Matthiesen, A., Ransjo-Arvidson, A., Nissen, E., & Uvnas-Moberg, K. (2001). Postpartum maternal oxytocin release by newborns: Effects of infant hand massage and sucking. Birth, 28, 13.

McCoy, R. C., Hunt, C. E., Lesco, S. M., Vezina, R., Corwin, M. J., Willinger, M., ... Mitchell, A. A. (2004). Frequency of bed sharing and its relationship to breastfeeding. Journal of Developmental and Behavioral Pediatrics, 25(3), 141–9.

McKenna, J. J. (1986). An anthropological perspective on the sudden infant death syndrome (SIDS): The role of parental breathing cues and speech breathing adaptations. Medical Anthropology, 10(1), 9–53.

McKenna, J. J., Ball, H. L., & Gettler, L. T. (2007). Mother–infant cosleeping, breastfeeding and sudden infant death syndrome: What biological anthropology has discovered about normal infant sleep and pediatric sleep medicine. Yearbook of Physical Anthropology, 50, 133–161.

McKenna, J. J., Mosko, S. S., & Richard, C. A. (1997). Bedsharing promotes breastfeeding. Pediatrics, 100, 214–219.

Moore, T., & Ucko, C. (1957). Night waking in early infancy. Archives of Disease in Childhood, 32, 333–342.

Morelli, G. A., Rogoff, B., Oppenheim, D., & Goldsmith, D. (1992). Cultural variations in infants' sleeping arrangements: Questions of independence. Developmental Psychology, 28(4), 604–613.

Morgan, K. H., Groer, M. W., & Smith, L. J. (2006). The controversy about what constitutes safe and nurturant infant sleep environments. Journal of Obstetric, Gynecologic, and Neonatal Nursing, 35, 684–691.

Mosko, S., Richard, C., & McKenna, J. (1997). Infant arousals during mother-infant bedsharing: Implications for infant sleep and SIDS research. Pediatrics, 100(5), 841–849.

Mosko, S., Richard, C., McKenna, J., & Drummond, S. (1996). Infant sleep architecture during bedsharing and possible implications for SIDS. Sleep, 19, 677–684.

Nakamura, S., Wind, M., & Danello, M. A. (1999). Review of hazards associated with children placed in adult beds. Archives of Pediatric and Adolescent Medicine, 153, 1019–1023.

Neville, M. C., Morton, J., & Umemura, S. (2001). Lactogenesis. The transition from pregnancy to lactation. Pediatric Clinics of North America, 48, 35–52.

Nissen, E., Lilja, G., Matthiesen, A. S., Ransjo-Arvidsson, A. B., Uvnas-Moberg, K., & Widstrom, A-M. (1995). Effects of maternal pethidine on infants' developing breast feeding behaviour. Acta Paedatrica, 84, 140.

Nusche, J. (2002). Lying in. Canadian Medical Association Journal, 167, 675.

Perez-Escamilla, R., Pollitt, E., Lonnerdal, B., & Dewey, K. (1994). Infant feeding policies in maternity wards and their effect on breast-feeding success: An analytical overview. American Journal of Public Health, 84, 8.

Pinilla, T., & Birch, L. L. (1993). Help me make it through the night: Behavioral entrainment of breast-fed infants' sleep patterns. Pediatrics, 91(2), 436–444.

Pitcock, C. D., & Clark, R. B. (1992). From Fanny to Fernand: The development of consumerism in pain control during the birth process. American Journal of Obstetrics and Gynecology, 167, 581.

Pond, C. M. (1977). The significance of lactation in the evolution of mammals. Evolution, 31, 177–199.

Quillin, S. I., & Glenn, L. (2004). Interaction between feeding method and co-sleeping on maternal-newborn sleep. Journal of Obstetric, Gynecologic, and Neonatal Nursing, 33(5), 580–588.

Ransjo-Arvidson, A. B, Matthiesen, A. S., Lilja, G., Nissen, E., Widstrom, A. M., & Uvnas-Moberg, K. (2001). Maternal analgesia during labor disturbs newborn behavior: Effects on breastfeeding, temperature, and crying. Birth, 28, 5.

Raphael, D. (1976). Night waking: A normal response? Journal of Pediatrics, 88(1), 169–170.

Richard, C., Mosko, S., McKenna, J., & Drummond, S. (1996). Sleeping position, orientation, and proximity in bedsharing infants and mothers. Sleep, 19(9), 685–690.

Righard, L., & Alade, M. O. (1990). Effect of delivery room routines on success of first breast-feed. Lancet, 336, 1105.

Riordan, J., & Auerbach, K. G. (Eds.). (1993). Breastfeeding and human lactation. Boston, MA: Jones and Bartlett.

Sawcenko, A., & Fleming, P. J. (1996). Thermal stress, sleeping position, and the sudden infant death syndrome. Sleep, 19(10), S267–S270.

Small, M. F. (1998). Our babies ourselves—how biology and culture shape the way we parent. New York, NY: Doubleday Dell Publishing Group.

Sözmen, M. (1992). Effects of early suckling of caesarean-born babies on lactation. Biology of the Neonate, 62, 67–68.

Tappin, D., et al. (2005). Bedsharing, roomsharing, and sudden infant death syndrome in Scotland: A case-control study. Journal of Pediatrics, 147, 32–37.

Tennekoon, K. H., Arulambalam, P. D., Karunanayake, E. H., & Seneviratne, H. R. (1994). Prolactin response to suckling in a group of fully breastfeeding women during the early postpartum period. Asia Oceania Journal of Obstetrics and Gynaecology, 20(3), 311–319.

Tew, M. (1995). Safer childbirth? A critical history of maternity care. London: Chapman and Hall.

Tuffnell, C. S., Petersen, S. A., & Wailoo, M. P. (1996). Higher rectal temperatures in co-sleeping infants. Archives of Disease in Childhood, 75, 249–250.

UNICEF UK. (2000). Implementing the Baby Friendly best practice standards. London: UNICEF UK Baby-Friendly Initiative.

Uvnas Moberg, K. (2003). The oxytocin factor. Cambridge, MA: Da Capo Press.

Uvnas-Moberg, K., Widstrom, A-M., Werner, S., Matthiesen, A-S., & Winberg, J. (1990). Oxytocin and prolactin levels in breast-feeding women. Correlation with milk yield and duration of breast-feeding. Acta Obstetrica Gynecologica Scandinavica, 69, 301.

Valentin, S. R. (2005). Sleep in German infants—the "cult" of independence. Pediatrics, 115(1), 269–271.

Varendi, H., & Porter, R. (2001). Breast odour as the only maternal stimulus elicits crawling towards the odour source. Acta Paediatrica, 90, 372–375.

Varendi, H., Porter, R. H., & Winberg, J. (1994). Does the newborn baby find the nipple by smell? Lancet, 8, 989.

Vennemann, M. M., Bajanowski, T., Brinkmann, B., Jorch, G., Yucesan, K., Sauerland, C., ... & the GeSID Study Group. (2009). Does breastfeeding reduce the risk of sudden infant death syndrome? Pediatrics, 123(3), e406–e410.

Waldenstrom, U., & Swenson, A. (1991). Rooming-in at night in the postpartum ward. Midwifery, 7, 82.

Watanabe, N., Yotsukura, M., Kadoi, N., Yashiro, K., Sakanoue, M., & Nishida, H. (1994). Epidemiology of sudden infant death syndrome in Japan. Acta Paediatrica Japan, 36, 329–332.

Weale, S. (2003). Too close for comfort? The Guardian, January 20. Retrieved August 24, 2009, from www.guardian.co.uk/medicine/story/0,11381,878280,00.html

Woolridge, M. W. (1995). Baby-controlled breastfeeding. In P. Stuart-Macadam & K. Dettwyler (Eds.), Breastfeeding: Biocultural perspectives (pp. 217–242). New York: Aldine de Gruyter.

World Health Organization. (1999). Postpartum care of the mother and newborn: A practical guide. Technical Working Group, World Health Organization. Birth, 26, 255.

World Health Organization. (2003). Global strategy for infant and young child feeding. Geneva: Author.

Wright, A. L. (2001). The rise of breastfeeding in the United States. In R. J. Schanler (Ed.), Breastfeeding 2001, Part 1: The evidence for breastfeeding. Philadelphia, PA: WB Saunders.

Wright, P., MacLeod, H., & Cooper, M. J. (1983). Waking at night: The effect of early feeding experience. Child: Care, Health and Development, 9, 309–319.

Yamauchi, Y., & Yamanouchi, I. (1990). The relationship between rooming-in/not rooming-in and breast-feeding variables. Acta Paediatrica Scandinavica, 79, 1017.

Young, D. (2005). Rooming-in at night for mothers and babies: Sweden shows the way. Birth, 32, 161.

Young, J., Fleming, P., Blair, P. S., & Pollard, K. (2001). Night-time infant care practices: A longitudinal study of the importance of close contact between mothers and
their babies. In S. Springer (Ed.), Stillmanagment und laktation; Deutscher still-und
laktationkongress, Bonn-Bad Godesberg (pp. 179–209). Leipzig, Germany: Leipziger
Universitatsverlag.

Zuckerman, B., Stevenson, J., & Bailey, V. (1987). Sleep problems in early childhood:
Continuities, predictive factors, and behavioral correlates. Pediatrics, 80, 664–671.

10

Touch and Pain Perception in Infants

Tiffany Field and Maria Hernandez-Reif

Touch

Touch is typically defined as stimulation of the skin by thermal, mechanical, chemical, and electrical stimuli (Field, 2001). These stimuli give us the sensations of pressure, warmth, and vibration. Understanding how stimulation signals are conveyed from the skin to the brain is important for understanding the various functions that touch serves. Touch has been called "the mother of the senses," perhaps because it was the first to develop in evolution. Touch is defined in the *Oxford English Dictionary* as "the most general of the bodily senses, diffused through all parts of the skin, but (in man) especially developed in the tips of the fingers and the lips." The fingers and lips have a disproportionately large number of neurons that travel to and from the brain. The fingers and the lips are the means by which the infant does most of its early learning, hence the need for "baby proofing" rooms and locales where the baby lives.

Touch is the earliest sensory system to develop in all species (Montagu, 1986). And, in Bowlby's (1951) environment of evolutionary adaptedness, nurturant touching by caregivers and others is necessary for infant growth and development in all species. For example, in the rat model, nurturant touch leads to the release of ornithine decarboxylase, which contributes to the growth of all organs including the brain (Schanberg & Field, 1987). The equivalent form of moderate-pressure touch releases insulinlike growth factor-1 in the human infant, which is an important growth hormone (Field et al., 2009). Conversely, touch deprivation leads to failure to thrive in both the rat and the human (Schanberg & Field, 1985). When a human embryo is less than an inch long and less than 2 months old, the skin is already highly developed. For example, when the palm is touched at 2 months' gestation, the fingers grasp the palm. The fingers and thumb will close at 3 months when the palm is touched. Touch can have strong effects on physiology. When the skin is touched, that stimulation is quickly transmitted to the brain, which in turn regulates physiology. Different types of touch lead to different responses. Light-pressure touch, for example, can lead to physiological arousal, and moderate-pressure touch can be calming (Diego et al., 2007).

The skin is the oldest, largest, and most sensitive of our organs and is critical for perceiving and processing the meaning of different touch stimuli. The receptors in the skin are named after their discoverers (Meissner corpuscles, Ruffini cylinders, Merkel discs, and Pacinian corpuscles) and are responsible for conveying the neural signals from thermal, mechanical, chemical, and electrical stimuli (Cholewiak & Collins, 1991). Meissner corpuscles are located between the epidermis and the dermis on the hairless parts of the body including the fingertips, the palms, the soles of the feet, and the tongue, and they respond to the lightest forms of stimulation. Pacinian corpuscles are near the joints and deep tissues and respond to pressure, vibrations, and high-frequency sounds. Merkel discs located just beneath the skin respond to constant pressure. Ruffini endings located deep below the skin can also register pressure and temperature.

The Nerve Fibers and the Cortex

Any stimulus that touches the skin is transmitted to the spinal cord on nerve fibers that are sometimes no longer than a meter. The nerve fibers that carry pain stimulation are small. Mechanical information such as pressure is carried by larger fibers up the spinal cord to the brain. Stimulation traveling to the brain ultimately crosses the sensory cortex to the opposite side of the brain where it is processed. To determine where the stimulation of the body gets processed in the brain, scientists have placed electrodes on the cortex and noted where the stimulation was received. Frequently, the extent of the brain area affected is depicted in a diagram called the homunculus. The homunculus illustrates how much space is needed on the cortex depending on how dense the nerves are in that body part. For example, areas with many nerve endings such as the fingertips and the lips require more space on the cortex than the back, which has fewer nerve endings, and therefore the fingers and lips are disproportionately large on the homunculus diagram. The nerve cells in the cortex are also sensitive to specific types of stimulation, so that some cells may be sensitive only to stroking the surface of a body part in a single direction or at a specific frequency. Different types of stimulation may alter the size of the cells in the cortex as well as the number of cells responding to different types of stimulation.

Sensory Thresholds

Researchers have used different stimuli including brush bristles and air puffs for pressure and vibration to determine individuals' thresholds to the intensity, frequency, and temperature of the tactile stimulus. One popular measure is how far apart two touch points must be for a person to perceive them as separate. One or two hairs (called an aesthesiometer) are touched to the skin, and the subject is asked to indicate the number of points felt. Thresholds are lower in the parts that have more nerve endings, for example, the fingertips and the lips. These are the most sensitive areas for perceiving texture, temperature, and pain. Another measure is the dolorimeter (a rod that exerts pressure) that is pushed against the skin to determine pain thresholds. Wide differences in individuals' sensory thresholds may explain the differences noted in pain tolerance. However, very little is known about these relationships.

Touch Perception in the Fetus and Neonate

Touch is the first sense to develop in utero and the most developed at birth. As early as 3 months' gestation, the fetus turns toward a tactile stimulus, much like a rooting reflex, and responds to electrical stimuli and puffs of air that are even difficult for adults to discriminate (Humphrey, 1972; Jacklin, Snow, & Maccoby, 1981). Neonatal perception research by our group suggests that touch discrimination by mouth (Hernandez-Reif, Field, & Diego, 2004) and by the hands (Hernandez-Reif, Field, Diego, & Shay, 2003) is evident as early as the newborn period. Different texture nipples (nubby versus smooth) can be discriminated by the newborn's mouth and hands. In the habituation/recovery paradigm we used, the newborns explored different texture nipples by their mouths and by their hands. After experience with one nipple, they habituated or stopped sucking. When the new texture nipple was presented, they started to suck again.

Texture perception has also been investigated in newborns using an habituation paradigm with a smooth or granular object (Molina & Jouen, 2004). After holding the object, the neonates were given either a familiar or a new textured object. Holding time was used to assess habituation as well as reaction to novelty, and hand pressure frequency exerted on the object was used to examine the neonates' ability to adjust their manipulation to the texture of new objects. Both measures revealed texture perception.

Weight perception has also been studied by our group (Hernandez-Reif, Field, Diego, & Shay, 2001). Lightweight (2 grams) or heavier weight (8 grams) objects (vials of cotton or pellets, respectively) were placed in the right hand of newborns of depressed and nondepressed mothers. After the infants habituated one weight by hand, they were tested with the opposite weight object. The infants of the depressed mothers did not respond to the novel weight, and only 15% of those infants showed hand movements that might have helped them perceive different weights (e.g., hand to mouth or hand to face, turning/moving of the wrist or hand). In contrast, 78% of the infants of nondepressed mothers showed hand activity that would facilitate weight perception, and they held the novel weight longer, suggesting that they had perceived the weight change (see Figure 10.1).

Cross-modal or intersensory perception also occurs at the newborn period. Based on an intersensory paired-preference procedure, newborns visually recognized the shape of an object that they had previously manipulated with their right

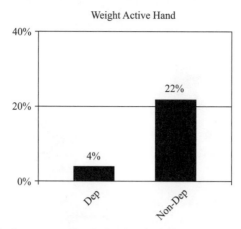

FIGURE 10.1 *Weight discriminated by the hand in the depressed (dep) and non-depressed groups of neonates.*

hand, when the object was out of sight (Streri, 2003). The newborns apparently extracted shape information in a tactual format and transformed it into a visual format before they had experienced pairings of visual and tactual stimuli. The same authors later showed that the newborns did not make this discrimination with their left hand (Streri & Gentaz, 2003).

Temperature Perception

Temperature perception by the newborn has also been studied by our group (Hernandez-Reif et al., 2003; Hernandez-Reif, et al., 2004). In a study on temperature perception by mouth, neonates of depressed and nondepressed mothers were given cold and warm nipples on alternating trials (Hernandez-Reif et al., 2004). The newborns of depressed mothers sucked twice as long as those of nondepressed mothers, suggesting the possibility that they were aroused, dysregulated, or overactive. The newborns did not show a preference for cold or warm nipples, but when they received the cold nipple on the first trial, they sucked more on the subsequent trials, suggesting that for some reason the cold nipple elicited more sucking, possibly to warm the nipple.

In our study on temperature perception by hand, newborns of depressed and nondepressed mothers were given tubes containing cold or warm water to hold with their hands (Hernandez-Reif et al., 2003). Both groups of infants habituated the warm and cold tubes, as indicated by a decrease in holding, and they showed dishabituation, suggested by increased holding of the novel temperature tube. The newborns of depressed mothers, however, spent twice the time habituating, possibly because they did not actively explore the tubes with their hands (see Figure 10.2). It is unclear from these studies whether these high-risk infants have limited perceptual abilities or limited performance due to inattentiveness and/or less exploratory

Temperature
Total Seconds to Habituation

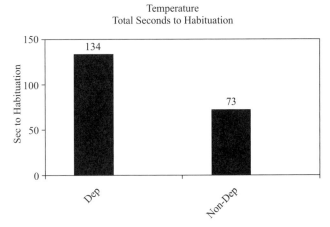

FIGURE 10.2 *Temperature: total seconds to habituation in depressed (dep) and non-depressed groups of neonates.*

behavior (Field, Hernandez-Reif, & Diego, 2010). Additional research is needed to explore these potential underlying mechanisms as well as other possibilities such as different arousal levels.

Pain Perception

Painful stimuli lead to a stress response as early as the newborn period. Preterm infants experience up to 60 invasive procedures before being discharged from the neonatal intensive care unit, with heelsticks being the most common procedure (Anand et al., 2005). Both animal and human research has shown that repetitive pain has adverse effects on neonatal development (Grunau, Oberlander, Whitfield, Morison, & Saul, 2001; Mitchell & Boss, 2002). Although some invasive procedures are still conducted without analgesia because they are not thought to be painful (see Anand et al., 2005), newborns clearly show physiological and behavioral distress during heelsticks and other invasive procedures (Holsti, Grunau, Oberlander, & Whitfield, 2005; Morison et al., 2003).

Behavioral Responses to Pain

Facial expressions and crying are the most widely studied behavioral responses to pain, although body movements have also been reported as distress behaviors in preterm infants experiencing heelsticks, including extension of the arms and legs (80%) and finger splays (70%; Holsti et al., 2005; Morison et al., 2003). The flexion reflex or limb withdrawal from a pain stimulus has also been reported (Andrews & Fitzgerald, 1994; Fitzgerald & McIntosh, 1989; Franck, 1987). This limb withdrawal is similar to the adult's response to pain.

Facial expressions following invasive procedures include a brow bulge, eye squeeze, lip purse, stretched mouth (horizontal or vertical), and chin quiver (Franck, Greenberg, & Stevens, 2000; Grunau & Craig, 1987; Izard, Huebner, Risser, McGinnes, & Dougherty, 1980). In a study on cry sounds and cry faces in response to pain, female infants cried louder than males, and their cries were higher pitched than those of males (Fuller, 2002), although they did not differ on facial expression responses (Wolf, 1996). Age differences have also been noted, with younger infants displaying fewer facial expressions and fussing and spending more time sleeping. Going into deep sleep following pain, for example, after a circumcision, is called the conservation withdrawal response.

Experience with invasive procedures also has its effects. In one study, infants who experienced the most invasive procedures since birth showed fewer facial reactions to heelsticks (Johnston & Stevens, 2009). In another study, for example, a greater number of invasive procedures since birth were associated with dampened facial and heart rate reactions to a fingerprick, and changes in the brain and spinal cord occurred with repeated painful experiences (Puchalski & Hummel, 2002). In one study, preterm infants who experienced more frequent invasive procedures showed more motor stress behaviors after the heelstick (Morison et al., 2003). Surprisingly, another group found no relation between the number of invasive procedures that the preterm infants had experienced and their responses to heelsticks (Gibbins et al., 2002). And although infant crying may be the most obvious response to invasive procedures, some preterm infants did not cry, perhaps because of their weakness or shutting-down responses (Anand et al., 2005; Mitchell, Brooks, & Roane, 2000).

In still another study, the experienced infants appeared to anticipate the painful stimulus, but no change in reactivity was noted over days for most preterm infants observed (Goubet, Clifton, & Shah, 2001). These mixed data may relate to the timing of data collection. Some researchers conducted observations during and immediately after heelsticks, while others waited as long as 2 minutes after the heelstick to code the behaviors (Evans, McCartney, Lawhon, & Galloway, 2005).

Physiological Responses to Pain

Pain has been measured not only by facial expressions and body movements but also by physiological responses including heart rate and transcutaneous oxygen tension. These disorganized physiological responses during and following invasive procedures include increased heart rate, respiratory rate, and blood pressure and decreased transcutaneous oxygen levels. In studies on preterm and full-term neonates experiencing heelsticks (Field & Goldson, 1984; Franck & Miaskowski, 1997) and following circumcision (Brady-Fryer, Wiebe, & Lander, 2004), increased heart rate and blood pressure were noted both during and after the procedures. Heart rate elevations as high as 18% above baseline have been reported for preterm infants during heelsticks (Goubet et al., 2001; Harrison, Evans, Johnson, & Loughran, 2002). Brown (1987) reported a more complex response including increased heart rate, respiratory rate, and systolic blood pressure but unchanged diastolic blood pressure and decreased transcutaneous partial pressure of oxygen (TcPO2) levels. In one of our studies, TcPO2 dropped to a clinically low level during heelsticks (Morrow et al., 1990). This has more recently been reported by several investigators (Anand et al., 2005; Fazzi, Farinotti, Scelsa, Gerola, & Bollani, 1996; Morison et al., 2003). The physiological disorganization in response to repetitive heelsticks may redirect energy and oxygen, disturb sleep cycles, and increase morbidity and mortality (Mitchell et al., 2000; Morison et al., 2003).

Biochemical and Immune Responses to Pain

Not surprisingly, biochemical and immune changes accompany the behavioral and physiological responses to invasive procedures. More experience with painful procedures has led to a down-regulation of cortisol responses to subsequent neonatal intensive care unit stressors (Grunau et al., 2005), although a study by the same group suggested that infants who received numerous invasive procedures at birth had elevated cortisol levels later at 8 months of age (Grunau et al., 2001). The preterm infants' cortisol levels also showed the circadianlike pattern reported in the literature (Castro et al., 2000; Herrington, Olomu, & Geller, 2004). The pain that leads to increased cortisol has also led to decreased immune cells (Herrington et al, 2004). Recent animal research indicates that the toxic chemicals released during repetitive painful events in the neonatal rat have negative effects on the developing central nervous system (Mitchell & Boss, 2002). Thus, decreasing or preventing disorganized responses to invasive procedures is important for infant well-being and normal development.

Pain Interventions

Pain can be decreased by touching as, for example, pain was reduced in a study in which we gave pacifiers to preemies during heelsticks (Field & Goldson, 1984). Kangaroo care, or the holding of the infant skin to skin inside the parents' clothing, has effectively reduced pain during invasive procedures such as heelsticks and injections. This has been observed using different pain scales including the Neonatal Infant Pain Scale (Kashaninia, Sajedi, Rahgozar, & Noghabi, 2008) and the Premature Infant Pain Profile (Akcan, Yiğit, & Atici, 2009). In addition, kangaroo care has been more effective than glucose in lowering pain following heelsticks (a shorter duration of facial activity including brow bulge, eye squeeze, and nasolabial furrowing and a lower Premature Infant Pain Profile score; Freire, Garcia, & Lamy, 2008). And when rocking and singing by the mother was added to kangaroo care, it was not more effective than the kangaroo care alone (Johnston et al., 2009). Further, when kangaroo care was practiced by depressed mothers, the incidence of depression was reduced by approximately 50% (37% to 20%; de Alencar, Arraes, de Albuquerque, & Alves, 2009).

One of the theories for the effectiveness of touch in alleviating pain is that pressure receptors are longer and more myelinated (more insulated) and, therefore, they can transmit a signal to the brain faster than pain receptors because pain receptors are shorter and less insulated. The touch message reaches the brain first and "closes the gate" (a biochemical/electrical phenomenon) to the slower-to-reach-the-brain pain message. This "gate theory" has been illustrated by the common experience of rubbing your bumped "crazy bone." Other possible mechanisms underlying touch effects on pain include the increase in serotonin (antipain neurotransmitter) and the related decrease in substance P, a pain-related chemical that is released when one is deprived of deep (or restorative) sleep (Field et al., 2002).

Affectionate Touch

Surprisingly, affectionate touch has rarely been studied in both the home (Ferber, Feldman, & Makhoul, 2008) and in infant daycare (Field et al., 1994). Affectionate, stimulating, and instrumental types of touch have been observed during natural caregiving and mother–child play sessions in the home (Ferber et al., 2008). Maternal affection and stimulating touch decreased significantly during the second 6 months of life. This may relate to the infants' accelerated gross motor development during the second half of the first year, namely, crawling and walking, that would naturally move infants away from close physical contact with their mothers. Affectionate forms of touch such as hugging, kissing, and stroking also decreased in infant daycare in later infancy and the toddler years (Field et al., 1994; see Figure 10.3). However, reciprocal communication increased in the second half-year of life and was predicted by the frequency of affectionate touch that occurred in the first half-year of life.

Touch Deprivation

Infants and children in institutional care often receive minimal touching from caregivers, which is predictive of later cognitive (MacLean, 2003) and neurodevelopmental delays (Chugani et al., 2001; MacLean, 2003; Nelson, 2007). The deprived children are often below average on cognitive skills when compared to same-age children who are raised in families. Unfortunately, in at least one study, this deprivation and the associated developmental delays persisted for many years after adoption (Beckett et al., 2006).

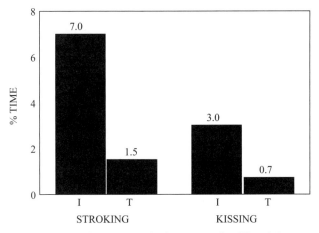

FIGURE 10.3 *Stroking/kissing by teachers of infants (I) and toddlers (T).*

Touch deprivation has also occurred in infants of depressed mothers (Field, 2001). For example, in one study, infants of depressed mothers versus those of nondepressed mothers spent more time touching themselves, which may have compensated for the less frequent positive touch from their mothers (Herrera, Reissland, & Shepherd, 2004). They also showed more aggressive types of self-touching (i.e., grabbing, patting, and pulling) than infants of nondepressed mothers during stressful situations, as if calming themselves (Moszkowski et al., 2009).

Massage Therapy

Massage therapy effects have been documented in many studies, especially for preterm infants who have gained significantly more weight and more bone density (see Field et al., 2010, for a review). In addition, following massage therapy, preterm infants have shown fewer stress behaviors (Hernandez-Reif, Field, & Diego, 2007), lower energy expenditure (Lahat, Mimouni, Ashbel, & Dollberg, 2007), and enhanced neurological, psychomotor, and sensorimotor development (Vaivre-Douret et al., 2009). A developmental follow-up at 2 years suggested that very preterm infants who received massage from their mothers had higher motor and mental development scores (Procianoy, Mendes, & Silveira, 2010). In studies we have conducted, we have shown increased vagal activity, gastric motility, and insulinlike growth factor-1 (growth hormone) levels following massage of preterm infants, suggesting that there may be underlying mechanisms for the weight gain and improved development of the infants (Field et al., 2010).

Mothers of low-birth-weight infants have also helped reduce their infants' developmental delays by massaging them (Weiss, Wilson, & Morrison, 2004), and high-risk mothers, for example, depressed mothers, who massaged their infants showed more affectionate touch, and their infants were more responsive (Field et al., 1996). The mothers benefited from massaging their infants by their depression decreasing, and their infants' growth and development also benefited (Goldstein-Ferber, 2004; O'Higgins, St James Roberts, & Glover, 2008). The mothers' sensitivity and responsivity during interactions with their infants and the infants' responsivity improved both in nondepressed and depressed mothers and their infants (Field et al., 1996; Lee, 2006). These data demonstrate positive effects for the massager simply from giving the massages. These data were not surprising given that pressure receptors are also stimulated in the hands of the person providing the massage, and it is the stimulation of pressure receptors that mediates the positive effects of massage (Field et al., 2010).

Another example of the reciprocal benefits is that premature infants had lower cortisol levels after being held by their mothers (Neu, Laudenslager, & Robinson, 2009), and during the holding period, the mothers' cortisol levels also decreased (Neu et al., 2009). Measuring the reciprocal effects of touch is complex, but this coregulation of cortisol paradigm is a good model for future studies. In the process of lowering cortisol, touching would also be expected to enhance immune function because cortisol kills immune cells.

POTENTIAL UNDERLYING MECHANISMS FOR MASSAGE THERAPY EFFECTS

Based on our comparisons between light and moderate-pressure massage, we have suggested that the stimulation of pressure receptors by moderate-pressure massage leads to enhanced vagal activity, which in turn "slows down" physiology (e.g., slows heart rate) and stress hormone production (Diego et al., 2007; Field et al., 2010). Other investigators have also reported touch effects on the cardiorespiratory system including a marker of vagal activity (increased low-frequency heart rate; Begum et al., 2008).

Future Directions

Although in the environment of evolutionary adaptedness nurturant touch is thought to be essential for the growth and development of all species, research on touch as one of the critical senses has been slow to develop, and particularly research on infant touch perception. Although the infant's early learning depends on exploration by mouth and then by the hands, very little is known about how the tactile world is perceived by the mouth and the hands. Skin-to-skin contact is thought to be critical for parent–infant relationships, but again, very little is known about how the infant perceives skin-to-skin contact. Perception of other touch modalities such as temperature and weight also need further research. Perception of pain by infants and interventions for pain have received considerable attention, but only recently. It wasn't a research issue reputedly because infants were thought to have no memory for pain. More research is needed on interventions to prevent the pain experience. Research is also needed on underlying mechanisms for touch perception and pain alleviation in order for interventions to be adopted into clinical practice.

Acknowledgments

We would like to thank those who participated in these studies and the research associates who assisted in data collection. This research was supported by a merit award (MH46586), NIH grants (AT00370 and HD056036) and Senior Research Scientist Awards (MH00331 and AT001585), and a March of Dimes Grant (12-FYO33-48) to Tiffany Field and funding from Johnson & Johnson Pediatric Institute to the Touch Research Institute. Correspondence should be sent to Tiffany Field, PhD, Touch Research Institute, University of Miami School of Medicine, PO Box 016820, Miami, Florida, 33101. Business phone number (305) 243–6781.

References

Akcan, E., Yiğit, R., & Atici, A. (2009). The effect of kangaroo care on pain in premature infants during invasive procedures. *The Turkish Journal of Pediatrics, 51*, 14–18.

Anand, K., Johnston, C., Oberlander, T., Taddio, A., Tutag Lehr, V., & Walco, G. (2005). Analgesia and local anesthesia during invasive procedures in the neonate. *Clinical Therapeutics, 27*, 844–876.

Andrews, K., & Fitzgerald, M. (1994). The cutaneous withdrawal reflex in human neonates: Sensitization, receptive fields and the effects of contralateral stimulation. *Pain, 56*, 95–101.

Beckett, C., Maughan, B., Rutter, M., Castle, J., Colvert, E., Groothues, C., et al. (2006). Do the effects of early severe deprivation on cognition persist into early adolescence? Findings from the English and Romanian adoptees study. *Child Development, 77*, 696–711.

Begum, E. A., Bonno, M., Yamashita, S., Tanaka, S., Yamamoto, H., Kawai, M., & Komada, Y. (2008). Cerebral oxygenation responses during kangaroo care in low birth weight infants. *BMC Pediatrics, 7*, 8–51.

Brady-Fryer, B., Wiebe, N., & Lander, J. A. (2004). Pain relief for neonatal circumcision. *Cochrane Database System Review, 4*, CD004217.

Brown, L. (1987). Physiologic responses to cutaneous pain in neonates. *Neonatal Network, 6*, 18–22.

Castro, M., Elias, P., Martinelli, C., Antonini, S., Santiago, L., & Moreira, A. (2000). Salivary cortisol as a tool for physiological studies and diagnostic strategies. *Brazilian Journal of Medical and Biological Research, 33*, 1171–1175.

Cholewiak, R. W., & Collins, A. A. (1991). Layers of the human skin. In M. A. Heller & W. Schiff (Eds.), *The psychology of touch.* Hillsdale, NJ: Lawrence Erlbaum Associates, 24.

Chugani, H. T., Behen, M. E., Muzik, O., Juhasz, C., Nagy, F., & Chugani, D. C. (2001). Local brain functional activity following early deprivation: A study of postinstitutionalized Romanian orphans. *Neuroimage, 14,* 1290–1301.

De Alencar, A. E., Arraes, L. C., de Albuquerque, E. C., & Alves, J. G. (2009). Effect of kangaroo mother care on postpartum depression. *Journal of Tropical Pediatrics, 55,* 36–38.

Diego, M., Field, T., Hernandez-Reif, M., Deeds, O., Ascencio, A., & Begert, G. (2007). Preterm infant massage elicits consistent increases in vagal activity and gastric motility that are associated with greater weight gain. *Acta Pediatrica, 96,* 1588–1591.

Evans, J., McCartney, E., Lawhon, G., & Galloway, K. (2005). Longitudinal comparison of preterm pain responses to repeated heelsticks. *Pediatric Nursing, 31,* 216–221.

Fazzi, E., Farinotti, L., Scelsa, B., Gerola, O., & Bollani, L. (1996). Response to pain in a group of healthy term newborns: Behavioral and physiological aspects. *Functional Neurology: New Trends in Adaptive and Behavioral Disorders, 11*(3), 5–43.

Ferber, S. G., Feldman, R., & Makhoul, I. R. (2008). The development of maternal touch across the first year of life. *Early Human Development, 84,* 363–370.

Freire, N. B., Garcia, J. B., & Lamy, Z. C. (2008). Evaluation of analgesic effect of skin-to-skin contact compared to oral glucose in preterm neonates. *Pain, 139,* 28–33.

Field, T. (2001). *Touch.* Cambridge, MA: MIT Press.

Field, T., Diego, M., Cullen, C., Hernandez-Reif, M., Sunshine, W., & Douglas, S. (2002). Fibromyalgia pain and substance P decrease and sleep improves after massage therapy. *Journal of Clinical Rheumatology, 8,* 72–76.

Field, T., Diego, M., & Hernandez-Reif, M. (2009). Preterm infant massage therapy research: A review. *Infant Behavior and Development, 33,* 115–124.

Field, T., & Goldson, E. (1984). Pacifying effects of nonnutritive sucking on term and preterm neonates during heelstick procedures. *Pediatrics, 74,* 1012–1015.

Field, T., Grizzle, N., Scafidi, F., Abrams, S., Richardson, S., Kuhn, C., & Schanberg, S. (1996). Massage therapy for infants of depressed mothers. *Infant Behavior and Development, 19,* 107–112.

Field, T., Harding, J., Soliday, B., Lasko, D., Gonzalez, N., & Valdeon, C. (1994). Touching in infant, toddler & preschool nurseries. *Early Child Development and Care, 98,* 113–120.

Field, T., Hernandez-Reif, M., & Diego, M. (2010). Depressed mothers' newborns are less responsive to animate and inanimate stimuli. *Infant Behavior and Development, 20,* 94–105.

Fitzgerald, M., & McIntosh, N. (1989). Pain and analgesia in the newborn. *Archives of Disease in Childhood, 64,* 441–443.

Franck, L. S. (1987). A national survey of the assessment and treatment of pain and agitation in the neonatal intensive care unit. *Journal of Obstetrics, Gynecology and Neonatal Nursing, 18,* 387–393.

Franck, L., Greenberg, C., & Stevens, B. (2000). Pain assessment in infants and children. *Pediatric Clinics of North America, 47,* 487–512.

Franck, L., & Miaskowski, C. (1997). Measurement of neonatal responses to painful stimuli: A research review. *Journal of Pain and Symptom Management, 14,* 343–378.

Fuller, B. F. (2002). Infant gender differences regarding acute established pain. *Clinical Nursing Research, 11,* 190–203.

Gibbins, S., Stevens, B., Hodnett, E., Pinelli, J., Ohlsson, A., & Darlington, G. (2002). Efficacy and safety of sucrose for procedural pain relief in preterm and term neonates. *Nursing Research, 51,* 375–382.

Goldstein-Ferber, S. (2004). Massage therapy and sleep-wake rhythms in the neonate. In T. Field (Ed.), *Touch and massage in early child development* (pp. 183–189). New Brunswick, NJ: Johnson & Johnson Pediatric Institute.

Goubet, N., Clifton, R., & Shah, B. (2001). Learning about pain in preterm newborns. *Journal of Developmental and Behavioral Pediatrics, 22,* 418–424.

Grunau, R. E., Holsti, L., Haley, D. W., Oberlander, T. F., Weinberg, J., Solimano, A., . . . Yu, W. (2005). Neonatal procedural pain exposure predicts lower cortisol and behavioral reactivity in preterm infants in the NICU. *Pain, 113,* 293–300.

Grunau, R. V. E., & Craig, K. D. (1987). Pain expression in neonates: Facial action and cry. *Pain, 28,* 395–410.

Grunau, R. V. E., Oberlander, T. F., Whitfield, M. F., Morison, J. S., & Saul, J. P. (2001). Pain reactivity in former extremely low birth weight infants at corrected age 8 months compared with term born controls. *Infant Behavior and Development, 24,* 41–55.

Harrison, D., Evans, C., Johnston, L., & Loughran, P. (2002). Bedside assessment of heel lance pain in the hospitalized infant. *Journal of Obstetric, Gynecological and Neonatal Nursing, 31,* 551–557.

Hernandez-Reif, M., Field, T., & Diego, M. (2004). Differential sucking by neonates of depressed versus non-depressed mothers. *Infant Behavior and Development, 27,* 465–476.

Hernandez-Reif, M., Field, T., & Diego, M. (2007). Preterm infants show reduced stress behaviors and activity after 5 days of massage therapy. *Infant Behavior and Development, 30,* 557–561.

Hernandez-Reif, M., Field, T., Diego, M., & Shay, L. (2001). Weight perception by newborns of depressed versus non-depressed mothers. *Infant Behavior and Development, 24,* 305–316.

Hernandez-Reif, M., Field, T., Diego, M., & Shay, L. (2003). Haptic habituation to temperature is slower in newborns of depressed mothers. *Infancy, 4,* 47–63.

Herrera, E., Reissland, N., & Shepherd, J. (2004). Maternal touch and maternal child-directed speech: Effects of depressed mood in the postnatal period. *Journal of Affective Disorders, 81,* 29–39.

Herrington, C., Olomu, L., & Geller, S. (2004). Salivary cortisol as indicators of pain in preterm infants. *Clinical Nursing Research, 13,* 53–68.

Holsti, L., Grunau, R., Oberlander, T., & Whitfield, M. (2005). Prior pain induces heightened motor responses during clustered care in preteen infants in the NICU. *Early Human Development, 81,* 293–302.

Humphrey, T. (1972). Central representation of the oral and facial areas of human fetuses. In J. F. Bosma (Ed.), *Third symposium on oral sensation and perception: The mouth of the infant.* Springfield, IL: Chas. C. Thomas.

Izard, C. E., Huebner, R. R., Risser, D., McGinnes, G. C., & Dougherty, L. M. (1980). The infant's ability to produce discrete emotional expressions. *Developmental Psychology, 16,* 132–140.

Jacklin, C. N., Snow, M. E., & Maccoby, E. E. (1981). Tactile sensitivity and muscle strength in newborn boys and girls. *Infant Behavior and Development, 4,* 261–268.

Johnston, C. C., Filion, F., Campbell-Yeo, M., Goulet, C., Bell, L., McNaughton, K., & Byron, J. (2009). Enhanced kangaroo mother care for heel lance in preterm neonates: A crossover trial. *Journal of Perinatology, 29*, 51–56.

Kashaninia, Z., Sajedi, F., Rahgozar, M., & Noghabi, F. A. (2008). The effect of kangaroo care on behavioral responses to pain of an intramuscular injection in neonates. *Journal for Specialists in Pediatric Nursing, 13*, 275–280.

Lahat, S., Mimouni, F. B., Ashbel, G., & Dollberg, S. (2007). Energy expenditure in growing preterm infants receiving massage therapy. *Journal of the American College of Nutrition, 26*, 356–359.

Lee, H. K. (2006). The effects of infant massage on weight, height, and mother-infant interaction. *Taehan Kanho Hakhoe Chi, 36*, 1331–1339.

MacLean, K. (2003). The impact of institutionalization on child development. *Development and Psychopathology, 15*, 853–884.

Mitchell, A., & Boss, B. (2002). Adverse effects of pain on the nervous systems of newborns and young children: A review of the literature. *Journal of Neuroscience Nursing, 34*, 228–236.

Mitchell, A., Brooks, S., & Roane, D. (2000). The premature infant and painful procedures. *Pain Management Nursing, 1*, 58–65.

Molina, M., & Jouen, F. (2004). Manual cyclical activity as an exploratory tool in neonates. *Infant Behavior and Development, 27*, 42–53.

Montagu, A. (1986). *Touching: The human significance of the skin*. New York, NY: Harper & Row.

Morison, S., Holsti, L., Grunau, R., Whitfield, M., Oberlander, T., Chan, H., & Williams, C. (2003). Are there developmentally distinct motor indicators of pain in preterm infants? *Early Human Development, 72*, 131–146.

Morrow, C., Field, T., Scafidi, F., Roberts, J., Eisen, L., Hogan, A. E., & Bandstra, E. S. (1990). Transcutaneous oxygen tension in preterm neonates during neonatal behavioral assessments and heelsticks. *Journal of Developmental and Behavioral Pediatrics, 11*, 312–316.

Moszkowski, R. J., Stack, D. M., Girouard, N., Field, T., Hernandez-Reif, M., & Diego, M. (2009). Touching behaviors of infants of depressed mothers during normal and perturbed interactions. *Infant Behavior and Development, 32*, 183–194.

Nelson, C. A. (2007). A neurobiological perspective on early human deprivation. *Child Development Perspectives, 1*, 13–18.

Neu, M., Laudenslager, M. L., & Robinson, J. (2009). Coregulation in salivary cortisol during maternal holding of premature infants. *Biological Research for Nursing, 10*, 226–240.

O'Higgins, M., St James Roberts, I., & Glover, V. (2008). Postnatal depression and mother and infant outcomes after infant massage. *Journal of Affective Disorders, 109*, 189–192.

Procianoy, R. S., Mendes, E. W., & Silveira, R. C. (2010). Massage improves neurodevelopment outcome at two years corrected age for very low birth weight infants. *Early Human Development, 86*, 7–11.

Puchalski, M., & Hummel, P. (2002). The reality of neonatal pain. *Advances in Neonatal Care, 2*, 233–244.

Schanberg, S. & Field, T. (1987). Sensory deprivation stress and supplemental stimulation in the rat pup and preterm human neonate. *Child Development, 58*, 1431–1447.

Streri, A. (2003). Cross-modal recognition of shape from hand to eyes in human newborns. *Somatosensory and Motor Research, 20,* 13–18.

Streri, A., & Gentaz, E. (2003). Cross-modal recognition of shape from hand to eyes and handedness in human newborns. *Neuropsychologia, 42,* 1365–1369.

Vaivre-Douret, L., Oriot, D., Blossier, P., Py, A., Kasolter-Pere, M., & Zwang, J. (2009). The effect of multimodal stimulation on cutaneous application of vegetable oils on neonatal development in preterm infants: A randomized controlled trial. *Child: Care, Health and Development, 35,* 96–105.

Weiss, W. J., Wilson, P. W., & Morrison, D. (2004). Maternal tactile stimulation and the neurodevelopment of low birth weight infants. *Infancy, 5,* 85–107.

Wolf, C. M. (1996). The development of behavioral response to pain in the human newborn. *Dissertation-Abstracts-International: Section B: The Sciences and Engineering, 57,* 1472.

11

Infant Feeding Practices

RATES, RISKS OF NOT BREASTFEEDING, AND FACTORS INFLUENCING BREASTFEEDING

Zaharah Sulaiman, Lisa H. Amir, and Pranee Liamputtong

Introduction

Breastfeeding is an interactive process between maternal biology and infant instinct (Small, 1998). The healthy newborn infant is born ready to latch on to the mother's breast and begin to breastfeed. The mother's body is also ready to move from pregnancy and childbirth into the next reproductive phase: lactation. Secretory differentiation (previously known as lactogenesis I) has begun in pregnancy, and following the delivery of the placenta and the rapid drop in progesterone, the hormone prolactin allows full milk production (secretory activation or lactogenesis II) to begin (Pang & Hartmann, 2007). Nipple stimulation leads to the release of oxytocin—the "love hormone"—from the mother's posterior pituitary gland (Newton, 1971). Oxytocin travels to the myoepithelial cells via the bloodstream and leads to the contraction of these cells and the milk ejection, or let-down, reflex. With time, just thinking about her baby can trigger a mother's let-down reflex. In response to the infant taking milk from the breast, milk production continues. This local or autocrine control of milk production explains "supply and demand": the emptier the breast, the faster milk is produced (Daly, Owens, & Hartmann, 1993).

Skin-to-skin contact between mother and infant after birth facilitates successful breastfeeding as discussed in chapter 9 by Ball and Russell. Furthermore, close contact with the mother's skin contributes to immune function development in several ways. Breastfed infants are colonized with commensal organisms from the mother's skin, thus protecting them from potential pathogenic organisms in the environment. The early milk, colostrum, has high levels of antibodies, which provide the baby's first immunization. The mother's body manufactures secretory IgA antibodies specifically against the microorganisms associated with the infant's surroundings, making each mother's milk unique (Hanson, 2004).

In the past, feeding newborn mammals with breast milk was never a choice but rather a natural way of feeding. Without the influence of culture and beliefs, babies would naturally continue to breastfeed until the age of 2.5 to 7 years (Dettwyler, 1995a). Wet nursing was the second best choice if for any reason a mother was unable to provide breast milk for her infant. Not until the early 19th century when mixtures of formulas based on animal milk became available did the prevalence of wet nursing start to decrease. Due to the vast availability and assumed convenience of infant formula women today appear to have a choice about infant feeding.

As science has recognized that breast milk is the natural way to feed infants, it is no longer appropriate to talk about the "benefits of breastfeeding" (Berry & Gribble, 2008). Instead, presenting the risks of not breastfeeding highlights how infants may be exposed to health risks when they are not given breast milk. Women respond more positively toward breastfeeding when the data are presented as risks of not breastfeeding rather than benefits of breastfeeding (Stuebe, 2009).

The World Health Organization (WHO) recommends that all infants be breastfed exclusively for 6 months, followed by the introduction of complementary foods and continued breastfeeding for up to 2 years of age or beyond (WHO, 2001). Not withstanding the established literature on the risks of formula feeding to infants, for most infants around the world, these WHO recommendations are not met. Infant feeding practices vary immensely in complex ways in response to individual, community, and societal factors.

This chapter presents the rates of breastfeeding around the world and risks of not breastfeeding and discusses the factors influencing infant feeding practices.

Breastfeeding Rates Around the World

Breastfeeding rates differ widely from country to country and also change over time. This section summarizes rates of breastfeeding in various continents. The data in this section are drawn from two main databases, namely, the Organization for Economic Cooperation and Development (OECD) Family database and the United Nation's International Children's Emergency Fund (UNICEF) database (Social Policy Division, 2009; UNICEF, 2009a, 2009b). Both databases have the most recent statistics on breastfeeding rates. Each study was conducted independently and various definitions have been used. Therefore, the methodologies in obtaining the rates differ, and reporting of results also differs. Rates are summarized for developed and developing countries (Table 11.1 and Table 11.2) and by region (Table 11.3).

BREASTFEEDING RATES IN DEVELOPED COUNTRIES

Data from developed countries are presented as rates of "ever breastfed" and "exclusive breastfeeding" at 3, 4, and 6 months (Table 11.1). Table 11.2 and

TABLE 11.1 Rates of Breastfeeding in Developed Countries

Country	Year Data Collected	Proportion of Children Who Were Ever Breastfed[a]	Year Data Collected	Proportion of Children Who Were Exclusively Breastfed at		
				3 Months	4 Months	6 Months
Norway	2006	99.0	2006	63.0	46.0	9.0
Denmark	2007	98.0	1999/2001	48.0	51.0	—
Sweden	2006/2007	97.6	2006	—	59.8	14.9
Slovenia	1999/2001	97.0	—	—	—	—
Iceland	2007	97.0	2000	69.0	46.0	—
Japan	2007	96.6	2005	38.0	36.8	34.7
Czech Republic	2007	95.6	2007	61.2	—	38.4
Finland	2007	93.0	2005	51.0	34.0	—
Romania	2006	92.2	2005	—	—	34.4
Australia	2006	92.0	2004	56.0	46.0	14.0
Portugal	2006	91.0	2003	54.7	—	34.1
Korea	—	—	2006	49.6	43.4	26.8
New Zealand	2005	87.8	2006/2007	56.0	39.0	8.0
Slovak Republic	2005	87.0	2007	63.0	55.0	41.0
Greece	2005	86.0	—	—	—	—
Canada	2005	84.5	2003	—	38.4	18.7
Italy	2005	81.1	2005	20.0	19.0	32.0
Netherlands	2005	79.0	2005	35.0	34.0	25.0
Spain	2003	77.2	2006	41.2	—	19.3

(continued)

Table 11.1 (Continued)

Country	Year Data Collected	Proportion of Children Who Were Ever Breastfed[a]	Year Data Collected	Proportion of Children Who Were Exclusively Breastfed at		
				3 Months	4 Months	6 Months
United Kingdom	2003	77.0	2005	13.0	7.0	—
United States	2003	74.2	2005	31.5	—	11.9
Malta	2000	69.0	—	—	—	—
Belgium	2007	65.9	—	35.4	—	—
France	2003	63.0	—	—	—	—
Ireland	2005	43.8	—	—	—	—

[a] "ever breastfed" = infants who have been put to breast at least once.

TABLE 11.2 Rates of Breastfeeding in Developing Countries

Developing Countries	Year Data Collected	Early Initiation of Breastfeeding (Within 1 Hour of Birth) (%)	Exclusively Breastfed[a] 0–5 Months (%)	Continue Breastfeeding for 12 Months (%)	24 Months (%)
Bangladesh	2007	43	43	95	91
Brazil	2006	43	40	50	25
Egypt	2008	56	53	78	35
Indonesia	2007	39	32	80	50
Kazakhstan	2006	62	17	57	16
Nepal	2006	35	53	98	95
Nigeria	2003	32	13	85	32
Pakistan	2006/2007	29	37	79	55
Rwanda	2005	41	88	96	77
Serbia	2005	17	15	22	8
Uzbekistan	2006	67	26	78	38
Zimbabwe	2005/2006	69	22	87	40

[a] "exclusively breastfed" = infants who have only received breast milk during a specified period of time.

Table 11.3 present regional data and data from developing countries, with rates of early initiation of breastfeeding within 1 hour of birth, exclusive rates between 0 and 5 months, and continuing breastfeeding until 12 months and 24 months.

The data presented in Table 11.1 for developed countries were collected around 2005. *Ever breastfed* is defined as infants who have been put to the breast at least once (Social Policy Division, 2009). The ever breastfed rate varied widely across nations, ranging from 44% in Ireland to 99% in Norway.

The OECD Family database defines exclusive breastfeeding as infants who have received only breast milk during a specified period of time (Social Policy Division, 2009). Despite intercounty variation, the exclusive rate decreases as the infant's age increases. At 3 months, the rate was about 50% on average, while by 6 months the rate decreased to approximately 20%. For example, in New Zealand in 2007, the exclusive rate was 56% at 3 months but decreased to only 8% at 6 months. The rate was even lower in the United Kingdom, with only 13% exclusively breastfeeding at 3 months and dropping to 7% at 4 months. The rates are low and far from achieving the WHO recommendation for 6 months of exclusive breastfeeding.

BREASTFEEDING RATES IN DEVELOPING COUNTRIES

Early initiation is defined by UNICEF as giving the infant the first breastfeed within the first hour of life (UNICEF, 2009a). In developing countries, early initiation

TABLE 11.3 Rates of Breastfeeding by Region

Regional Summary	Early Initiation of Breastfeeding (Within 1 Hour of Birth) (%)	Exclusively Breastfed 0–5 months (%)	Continue Breastfeeding for	
			12 Months (%)	24 Months (%)
Africa	47	32	85	49
Asia	31	41	73	53
Developing countries	39	37	75	50
Eastern and Southern Africa	59	42	87	61
East Asia and Pacific	46	—	54	26
Industrialized countries	—	—	—	—
Latin America and Caribbean	48	41	56	28
Least developed countries	49	39	91	67
Middle East and North Africa	47	30	73	34
South Asia	27	45	87	75
Sub-Saharan Africa	46	31	88	52
West and Central Africa	36	22	88	45

ranged from 17% in Serbia to 69% in Zimbabwe. Although exclusive breastfeeding rates were low in many countries, continuing to breastfeed to 12 and 24 months was high (Table 11.2; UNICEF, 2009b). For example, in Uzbekistan, only 26% of mothers exclusively breastfed their infant between 0 and 5 months, but 78% and 38% were continuing to breastfeed at 12 and 24 months, respectively.

BREASTFEEDING RATES BY REGION

Table 11.3 summarizes the rates by region as presented in the UNICEF database (UNICEF, 2009a, 2009b). Early initiation was lowest for South Asia (27%). There were no reported data from industrialized countries. Although the least developed countries had low exclusive rates at 0 to 5 months, 91% and 67% of infants were continuing to breastfeed at 12 and 24 months. This trend was similar for many regions.

Risks of Not Breastfeeding

It is well established that formula-fed infants have poorer health outcomes compared to breastfed infants (Stuebe, 2009). Infants who are not breastfed are at higher risks of developing infectious diseases and are more susceptible to certain chronic diseases in later life. It is less well known that maternal health is also affected by method of infant feeding. Mothers who do not breastfeed are more vulnerable to developing breast and ovarian cancers and chronic diseases such as rheumatoid arthritis (Allen & Hector, 2005; Ip et al., 2007; Leon-Cava,

Lutter, Ross, & Martin, 2002; Stuebe, 2009; van Rossum, Buchner, & Hoekstra, 2006).

This section gives an overview of the health risks of not breastfeeding. It summarizes the results of five reviews published in the last 8 years of the short- and long-term risks for preterm infants, term infants, and mothers (Allen & Hector, 2005; Horta, Bahl, Martines, & Victora, 2007; Ip et al., 2007; Leon-Cava et al., 2002; van Rossum et al., 2006). Only Ip et al. (2007) and Allen and Hector (2005) included preterm infants in their reviews, while Horta et al. (2007) focused on long-term health risks of formula feeding among term infants. Other reviewers looked at short- and long-term risks for term infants and mothers.

The findings in this section are drawn from more than 10,000 papers screened and reviewed, mainly in developed countries. In this section, we categorize the evidence of health risks as "convincing," "probable," and "possible" based on the strengths and weaknesses of the research methodology employed. The evidence is described as "convincing" when a significant relationship has been found in a meta-analysis or a systematic review; "probable" evidence is when there is evidence from many studies but confirmation is needed in better-designed studies; and "possible" evidence is used when only a few methodological sound studies have been conducted.

METHODS OF THE FIVE REVIEWS

Various methods were used by the five reviewer groups in their work. All reviewers extensively searched the literature using MEDLINE, OVID, and/or the Cochrane Library electronic databases. Each search was based on a list of keywords determined by the reviewers over a specified time frame as shown in Table 11.4. Most reviewers reported the evidence in a grading system. Allen and Hector (2005) and van Rossum et al. (2006) labeled the evidence as convincing, probable, or possible. Similarly, Ip et al. (2007) categorized their evidence as good, fair, or poor. Leon-Cava et al. (2002), however, either stated the evidence as convincing or suggested more studies are needed to confirm the findings. Only Horta et al. (2007) used statistical models to estimate the effects. Table 11.5 summarizes the results of the reviews.

RISKS FOR PRETERM INFANTS

All reviewers agreed that the risk of developing necrotizing enterocolitis (NEC), a severe gastrointestinal disease, was reduced among preterm infants with a history of breast milk feeding compared to those who were formula fed (Allen & Hector, 2005; Ip et al., 2007; Table 11.5). Although the absolute risk difference among formulafed infants was only 5% higher than for infants receiving breast milk, the clinical outcome is significant because the case fatality rate is high (Ip et al., 2007). The evidence for an effect of breast milk feeding on cognitive development was rated "possible" (Ip et al., 2007).

TABLE 11.4 Method of the Reviews

Authors, Year, and *Title*	Organization Name, Place, and Country	Method of Review	Review Groups	Review Risk
Allen & Hector (2005). "Benefits of Breastfeeding"	NSW Centre for Public Health Nutrition, University of Sydney, Australia	**Databases and time period:** Medline from 1996 to May 2005 OVID, CINAHL, and EMBASE (time was not specified) Cochrane Library database (time was not specified) **Keywords:** Breastfeeding or breast milk AND health or prevention or protection or reduced risk **Language:** Not specified **Evidence:** Mainly in developed countries **Reporting of evidence:** The strength of association between breastfeeding and a health benefit was classified as *convincing* (the findings were based on one or more cohort studies, with at least a measure of duration of breastfeeding, and/or showed a clear dose-response in relation to health outcomes), *probable* (the findings in most studies found an association, but confirmation is required in more, or better designed, studies), or *possible* (when evidence of an association was only found in few studies).	Preterm infants Term infants Mothers Mothers	Short-term Long-term Short-term Long-term
Horta, Bahl, Martines, & Victoria (2007). "Evidence on the Long-Term Effects of Breastfeeding: Systematic Reviews and Meta-Analysis"	The Department of Child and Adolescent Health and Development, World Health Organization	**Databases and time period:** MEDLINE from 1966 to March 2006 Scientific Citation Index databases (time was not specified) **Keywords:** breastfeeding, breastfed, breastfeed, bottle feeding, bottle fed, bottle feed, formula milk, formula fed, and formula feed were combined with these terms: blood pressure, obesity/overweight, total cholesterol, type-2 diabetes, and intellectual performance. **Languages:** English, French, Portuguese, and Spanish **Reporting of evidence:** Fixed and random-effects models were used to pool the effect estimates, and a random-effects regression was used to assess several potential sources of heterogeneity.	Term infants	Long-term

Study	Institution	Databases, keywords, evidence, and reporting	Population	Term
Ip et al. (2007), "Breastfeeding and Maternal and Infant Health Outcomes in Developed Countries"	Tufts-New England Medical Center Evidence-based Practice Center (EPC), under contract to the Agency of Healthcare Research and Quality (AHRQ) Rockville, MD, USA	**Databases and time period:** MEDLINE, CINAHL, and the Cochrane Library Databases from 1966 to May 2006 **Keywords:** Subject headings and text words relevant to breastfeeding and the different outcomes **Evidence:** Mainly in developed countries **Language:** English **Reporting of evidence:** A three grading category system was used to denote primary study methodological quality as **A (good):** least bias and results are valid; **B (fair/moderate):** susceptible to some bias, but not sufficient to invalidate the results; and **C (poor):** significant biases that may invalidate the results.	Preterm infants	Short-term
			Preterm infants	Short-term
			Term infants	Long-term
			Mothers	Short-term
			Mothers	Long-term
Leon-Cava, Lutter, Ross, & Martin (2002). "Quantifying the Benefits of Breastfeeding: A Summary of the Evidence"	Washington DC: Division of Health Promotion (HPP) of the Pan American Health Organization (PAHO), USA	**Databases and time period:** Medline and Popline from 1977 to January 2002 **Keywords:** Breastfeeding, lactation, infant mortality, cancer, intelligence, cognitive, motor development, obesity, diabetes, chronic disease, cardiovascular disease, maternal health, breast cancer, ovarian cancer **Evidence:** Mainly in "Western" populations **Language:** English **Reporting of evidence:** The results were reported as either convincing/better than formula feed or more research needed to confirm the findings.	Term infants	Short-term
			Term infants	Long-term
			Mothers	Long-term
Van Rossum, Buchner, & Hoekstra (2006). "Quantification of Health Effects of Breastfeeding: Review of the Literature and Model Simulation"	Ministry of Public Health, Welfare and Sports, BA, Bilthoven, The Netherlands	**Databases and time period:** Medline from 1980 to February 2005 **Keywords:** Breastfeeding, lactation, or human milk (primary search) Infections, otitis media, obesity (combination search) **Evidence:** Mainly in Western Europe, North America, Australia, and New Zealand **Language:** English and Dutch **Reporting of evidence:** The strength of association between breastfeeding and a health benefit was classified as *convincing, probable, possible, or insufficient*, based on WHO criteria for evidence.	Term infants	Short-term
			Term infants	Long-term
			Mothers	Short-term
			Mothers	Long-term

TABLE 11.5 The Short- and Long-Term Risk of Not Breastfeeding in Infants and Mothers, Based on Level of Evidence

Risk Groups	Risk Types	Convincing	Probable	Possible
			Level of Evidence	
Preterm infants	Short-term risks	Neonatal necrotizing enterocolitis (Allen & Hector, 2005; Ip et al., 2007)		Poorer cognitive development (Ip et al., 2007)
Term infants	Short-term risks	Gastrointestinal infection or diarrhea (Allen & Hector, 2005; Ip et al., 2007; Leon-Cava et al., 2002; van Rossum et al., 2006) Otitis media (Allen & Hector, 2005; Ip et al., 2007; Leon-Cava et al., 2002; van Rossum et al., 2006) Respiratory tract infection (Allen & Hector, 2005; Ip et al., 2007; Leon-Cava et al., 2002; van Rossum et al., 2006) Sudden infant death syndrome (SIDS) (Ip et al., 2007)	Asthma and allergy (Allen & Hector, 2005; Ip et al., 2007; van Rossum et al., 2006) Wheezing (van Rossum et al., 2006) Eczema (Ip et al., 2007; van Rossum et al., 2006) SIDS (Allen & Hector, 2005)	SIDS (van Rossum et al., 2006)
Term infants	Long-term risks	Childhood and adolescent obesity (van Rossum et al., 2006) Higher adult mean blood pressure (van Rossum et al., 2006)	Adult type 2 diabetes (Ip et al., 2007; Childhood leukemia (Allen & Hector, 2005; Childhood and adolescent obesity (Allen & Hector, 2005; Horta et al., 2007) Cognitive ability or intelligence level (Allen & Hector, 2005; Horta et al., 2007; Ip et al., 2007; Leon-Cava et al., 2002; van Rossum et al., 2006) Inflammatory bowel disease (Allen & Hector, 2005; Leon-Cava et al., 2002; van Rossum et al., 2006)	Childhood and adolescent type 1 diabetes (Allen & Hector, 2005; van Rossum et al., 2006) Adult type 2 diabetes (Allen & Hector, 2005; Horta et al., 2007; Leon-Cava et al., 2002; van Rossum et al., 2006) Childhood leukemia (Leon-Cava et al., 2002; van Rossum et al., 2006) Higher mean adult blood pressure (Horta et al., 2007; Leon-Cava et al., 2002) Higher mean adult blood cholesterol level (Horta et al., 2007; Ip et al., 2007)

Mothers and infants	Long-term risks			Reduced maternal–infant bonding (Allen & Hector, 2005; Leon-Cava et al., 2002)
Mothers	Short-term risks			Slow return to pre-pregnancy weight (Allen & Hector, 2005; Ip et al., 2007) Postpartum depression (Allen & Hector, 2005; Ip et al., 2007)
	Long-term risks	Premenopausal breast cancer (Allen & Hector, 2005; Ip et al., 2007; Leon-Cava et al., 2002) Postmenopausal breast cancer (Ip et al., 2007)	Postmenopausal breast cancer (Allen & Hector, 2005) Ovarian cancer (Allen & Hector, 2005; Ip et al., 2007; Leon-Cava et al., 2002; van Rossum et al., 2006) Rheumatoid arthritis (Allen & Hector, 2005; van Rossum et al., 2006)	Endometrial cancer (Allen & Hector, 2005) Osteoporosis (Allen & Hector, 2005; Ip et al., 2007) Premenopausal breast cancer (van Rossum et al., 2006)

RISKS FOR TERM INFANTS

The risks for term infants can be divided into short-term (infancy) and long-term (childhood and adolescence). There is convincing evidence for a range of infectious diseases in the first year of life: gastrointestinal tract, respiratory tract, and ear infections. The evidence for autoimmune health conditions was rated as "probable."

Looking at long-term health risks, chronic diseases were more prominent than infectious diseases, although the evidence was mostly rated as "probable" or "possible." In some instances, the reviewers rated the evidence differently. For example, the risk of developing adult type 2 diabetes was ranked as "probable" by Ip et al. (2007) and but only ranked as "possible" by Allen and Hector (2005) and Leon Cava et al., (2002).

RISKS FOR MOTHERS

The short-term health risks to mothers who do not breastfeed their babies were least convincing. All reviewers agreed that there was only possible evidence that mothers who did not breastfeed their babies were more likely to develop postpartum depression and late return to pre-pregnancy weight. For long-term risk, however, most reviewers found "convincing" evidence that mothers who did not breastfeed their babies were at higher risk of premenopausal breast cancer. However, for postmenopausal breast cancer and ovarian cancers, there were mostly probable evidence that mothers who did not breastfeed their babies were at higher risk compared to mothers who breastfed.

Factors Influencing Breastfeeding Practice

One way of conceptualizing the many factors that interact with infant feeding practices is to divide them into three levels as illustrated by Hector, King, Webb, and Heywood (2005), shown in Figure 11.1.

Individual-level factors deal directly with either the mother, infant, or mother–infant interaction. Group-level factors refer to the environment that has direct effects on mothers' and infants' ability to practice breastfeeding. The environments include hospital and health services, home or family, work, community, and public policy. Society-level factors have an influence on breastfeeding practices in the context of society, culture, and economy (Hector et al., 2005).

INDIVIDUAL-LEVEL FACTORS

Maternal Factors

Maternal breastfeeding intention has been shown to positively influence breastfeeding duration (Meedya, Fahy, & Kable, 2010). Prenatal intention to breastfeed has

A CONCEPTUAL FRAMEWORK OF FACTORS AFFECTING BREASTFEEDING PRACTICES

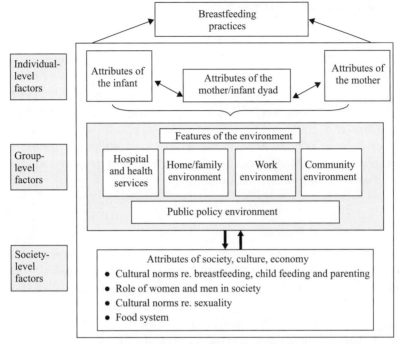

FIGURE 11.1 *A conceptual framework of factors affecting breastfeeding practices. Reproduced with permission from Hector, D., King, L., Webb, K., & Heywood, P. (2005). Factors affecting breastfeeding practices. Applying a conceptual framework. New South Wales Public Health Bulletin, 16(4), 52–55. doi:10.1071/NB05013. Copyright (2005) NSW Department of Health, CSIRO Publishing. http://www.publish.csiro.au/paper/ NB05013.htm*

been found to be a stronger predictor than the combination of other factors in determining the initiation and duration of breastfeeding (Donath & Amir, 2003). Among Western women, older maternal age and higher levels of education show strong and consistent association with longer duration of breastfeeding (Scott & Binns, 1999).

Similarly, women from higher socioeconomic status in Western countries are more likely to initiate breastfeeding and breastfeed for a longer duration compared to women with lower socioeconomic status (Gudnadottir, Gunnarsson, & Thorsdottir, 2006). In Australia, this gap between the most and least disadvantaged has been increasing over the last 15 years (Amir & Donath, 2008). Maternal smoking habits have been shown to be associated with lower rates of breastfeeding initiation and duration (Amir & Donath, 2002; Scott & Binns, 1999). A meta-analysis of 13 studies showed that smoking increased the likelihood of mothers ceasing breastfeeding by 3 months (Horta, Kramer, & Platt, 2001). Overweight and obese women are less likely to breastfeed, and if they breastfed, they do it for a shorter duration than normal-weight women (Amir & Donath, 2007).

Infant Factors

Prematurity and gestational age can have an impact on the initiation and duration of breastfeeding. In Australia, infants born at 35 to 36 weeks were less likely to be breastfed than infants born at 37 to 40 gestational weeks; even term infants born at 38 and 39 weeks were less likely to be breastfeeding at 6 months compared to infants born at 40 weeks or later, after adjusting for possible confounding factors (Donath & Amir, 2008). However, in Sweden, Flacking, Wallin, and Ewald (2007) found breastfeeding initiation and duration were influenced by socioeconomic status and not by the degree of prematurity.

Group-Level Factors

Hospital and Health Services

Following the Innocenti Declaration of 1990, the Baby-Friendly Hospital Initiative (BFHI) was launched by the WHO and UNICEF in 1991 as a global effort to implement practices that protect, promote, and support breastfeeding (WHO/UNICEF, 2009). In many countries, breastfeeding rates have increased significantly faster in hospitals that comply with the BFHI Ten Steps to Successful Breastfeeding (Table 11.6), as seen in the "Promotion of Breastfeeding Intervention Trial (PROBIT): A Randomized Trial in the Republic of Belarus" (Kramer et al., 2001) and observational reports from Scotland (Broadfoot, Britten, Tappin, & MacKenzie, 2005; Tappin, 2001).

Professional support by health care providers in hospitals has a beneficial effect on the duration of *any* breastfeeding, although the strength of its effect on the rate of *exclusive* breastfeeding is uncertain (Sikorski, Renfrew, Pindoria, & Wade, 2003). However, health professionals are only helpful if they have a positive attitude toward breastfeeding and appropriate knowledge and skills to help breastfeeding mothers, something that is often lacking in their training (Clifford & McIntyre, 2008).

HOME, FAMILY, AND COMMUNITY ENVIRONMENT

Fathers, other family members, and friends can have a significant impact on breastfeeding only if they are positive about, and have the skills to support, breastfeeding (Clifford & McIntyre, 2008). Galtry (2003) found that women who were regularly connected or visited by their relatives and friends had a positive attitude and were more confident about breastfeeding, and hence were more successful in maintaining breastfeeding while working. Fathers not only support but play the most important role in decision making regarding infant feeding choice and breastfeeding duration (Scott & Binns, 1999).

TABLE 11.6 The Ten Steps to Successful Breastfeeding

Every facility providing maternity services and care for newborn infants should

1. Have a written breastfeeding policy that is routinely communicated to all health care staff.
2. Train all health care staff in skills necessary to implement this policy.
3. Inform all pregnant women about the benefits and management of breastfeeding.
4. Place babies in skin-to-skin contact with their mothers immediately following birth for at least an hour and encourage mothers to recognize when their babies are ready to breastfeed, offering help if needed.
5. Show mothers how to breastfeed and how to maintain lactation even if they should be separated from their infants.
6. Give newborn infants no food or drink other than breast milk, unless medically Indicated.
7. Practice rooming-in, allowing mothers and infants to remain together 24 hours a day.
8. Encourage breastfeeding on demand.
9. Give no artificial teats or dummies to breastfeeding infants.
10. Foster the establishment of breastfeeding support and refer mothers on discharge from the facility.

From WHO/UNICEF (2009). *Baby-Friendly Hospital Initiative: Revised, updated and expanded for integrated care.* Retrieved from http://www.who.int/nutrition/publications/infantfeeding/9789241594950/en/index.html

WORK ENVIRONMENT

Mothers' return to work has been shown to affect the duration of breastfeeding (Cardenas & Major, 2005; Chuang et al., 2010; Jacknowitz, 2008). In America, about half of the women with children under the age of 3 contribute to the labor force (U.S Department of Labor, 2006). We will discuss mothers returning to work later in the chapter.

SOCIETY-LEVEL FACTORS

Traditional Beliefs and Culture

Traditional beliefs have been shown to influence breastfeeding practices in the United States (Dettwyler, 1995b), Australia (Sheehan & Schmied, 2010), Lebanon (Osman, Lama, & Wick, 2009), China (Raven, Chen, Tolhurst, & Garner, 2007), Thailand (Kaewsarn & Moyle, 2000; Liamputtong, 2011), and Israel (Bergman & Feinberg, 1981). Colostrum has been regarded by some cultural groups as unsuitable for newborns and is sometimes discarded (Ertem, 2011; Hizel, Ceyhun, Tanzer, & Sanli, 2006). For example, people in the Hmong community do not believe it is part of milk, but believe that true milk will be produced only after day 3 of the infant's life (Liamputtong Rice, 2000).

The decision to breastfeed is also influenced by cultural background; in the United States, Hispanic mothers tend to stop breastfeeding earlier than other non-Hispanic Black or White women, as a result of their perception that there is not enough milk for their infants (Li, Fein, Chen, & Grummer-Strawn, 2008). In Thailand, a study among working mothers showed that the cultural practice of family members supporting women after delivery has helped to increase breastfeeding duration (Liamputtong, 2011).

PUBLIC POLICY AND ECONOMY

The International Code of Marketing of Breast Milk Substitutes was developed in 1981 by the general assembly of the WHO, which recommended restrictions on the marketing of breast milk substitutes (infant formula) in order to ensure that mothers are not discouraged from breastfeeding and that substitutes are used safely if needed (WHO, 1981). Despite this, code violations by manufacturers continue to be reported in industrialized (Costello & Sachdev, 1998; Pisacane, 2000) and developing countries (Aguayo, Ross, Kanon, & Ouedraogo, 2003; Sokol, Thiagarajah, & Allain, 2001). A multicenter study in Thailand, Bangladesh, South Africa, and Poland showed that leading manufacturers were violating the code (Taylor, 1998).

THE INFLUENCE OF WORKING ON BREASTFEEDING PRACTICES

Working status has been shown to pose a barrier to breastfeeding as there is evidence that the timing of breastfeeding cessation often coincides with the mothers' return to work (Visness & Kennedy, 1997). The issue regarding infant feeding among working women is a public health concern as women with children who are less than 3 years old contribute to nearly 50% of the labor force in America (U.S Department of Labor, 2006). Breastfeeding practices need to be supported so that mothers do not resort to formula feeding, which potentially presents health risks to mothers and their infants.

In order to protect working mothers, the International Labor Organization (ILO) has outlined the basic needs that should be provided by employers to ensure that working mothers can continue giving breast milk to their infants. In general, there are seven key elements to maternity protection, which are scope, leave, benefits, health protection, job protection and nondiscrimination, breastfeeding breaks, and breastfeeding facilities at the workplace (WABA, 2003). The ILO convention on maternity protection is implemented in 120 countries, and each country sets its own national legislation, which tends to be narrow and excludes the informal work sector where nearly 80% of the workers are women (WABA, 2003).

Maternity Leave

Maternity leave is defined as "the number of weeks after childbirth when mothers were off work, without distinguishing whether it was a paid or unpaid leave, whether it was legally prescribed length, or whether there was a prolongation of maternity leave" (Staehelin, Bertea, & Stutz, 2007, p. 203). According to the ILO, working mothers are entitled to a minimum paid maternity leave of 14 weeks (WABA, 2003). Although it has been shown that a longer maternity leave produces health benefits for mothers and their infants, the length of leave varies from country to country (Staehelin et al., 2007). Women who are only entitled to a maternity leave of 6 weeks or less have been found to have more depressive symptoms than mothers who are entitled to 8 to 12 weeks' leave (Chatterji & Frick, 2004).

Workplace and Working Hours

Women who plan to work full-time outside the home are less likely to breast-feed than women working from home (Fein & Roe, 1998). Among women who work outside the home, those who can have access to their infants during working hours or can provide expressed breast milk are more likely to be successful in maintaining breastfeeding for longer than those who cannot (Ortiz, McGilligan, & Kelly, 2004).

Full-time shift workers with inflexible working hours have more difficulty maintaining breastfeeding; if women are denied breastfeeding breaks, they are unable to express breast milk, leading to reduced milk production and premature breastfeeding cessation (Avery, Duckett, Dodgson, Savik, & Henly, 1998).

Type of Work

Women in jobs that require them to attend at all times are less successful in breastfeeding than clerical workers who have greater flexibility to make time for breastfeeding breaks (Chuang et al., 2010). Usually, the lowest ranked workers have less autonomy in their work and many are not aware they have the right to breastfeeding breaks by legislation (Chen, Wu, & Chie, 2006). Even when there is a policy, many employers do not explicitly make it known to their workers. Workers in higher ranks have been shown to be more aware of their rights and have greater accessibility to the facilities in the workplace and greater empowerment to exercise their rights (Chen et al., 2006).

Working Conditions and Workplace Environment

Employers who are supportive of breastfeeding can help mothers of young children by providing flexibility in working hours, breastfeeding breaks and rooms, and equipment for milk expression. Workplaces are encouraged to provide crèches and allow mothers to take time for direct feeding of their infants (WABA, 2003).

The presence of co-workers who are also practicing breastfeeding instills a positive environment and gives encouragement to other mothers (Rojjanasrirat, 2004). On the other hand, working mothers find it difficult to express milk at the workplace when there are co-workers with negative attitudes toward breastfeeding (Brown, Poag, & Kasprzycki, 2001).

Conclusion

We have shown that there is high-level evidence that babies who do not receive breast milk are at a higher risk of developing infectious diseases and chronic diseases later in life. Mothers who do not breastfeed their infants are also at a higher risk of illnesses such as breast and ovarian cancer. Although it is a common practice for women worldwide to breastfeed their babies, it is not common for them to exclusively breastfeed their infants according to the recommendations of the World Health Organization.

Many factors influence infant feeding practices. Global initiatives, such as the Baby-Friendly Hospital Initiative, have targeted hospital services with great success (WHO/UNICEF, 2009). Another significant factor that deserves attention is maternal work. This is important because many women with young children are employed in formal and informal settings. Working by itself may not be a barrier, but it has been shown that the working conditions and long inflexible working hours are barriers to mothers maintaining breastfeeding.

We need to create working environments that are supportive and protective of breastfeeding. It is crucial to provide the basic needs, such as breastfeeding breaks and breastfeeding rooms, for mothers at the workplace so they can continue to provide the best nutrition for their infant while working. Women need to be empowered and well versed about their rights about infant feeding. The ILO convention and recommendations on maternity protection should be rectified in countries where it has not been implemented. Campaigns for adoption and implementation of maternity protection law should be encouraged for formal and informal sectors. Legislation must be accompanied by effective information, training, and monitoring systems to ensure that health care providers and manufacturers comply with evidence-based practice and the code (Holla-Bhar, 2006). We wish to conclude our chapter with the words of Beasley and Amir (2007, p. 5), who contend that:

> As individuals, women are powerless to counter the complexity of societal forces that interfere with exclusively breastfeeding their infants for six months. What is required are "structural changes...to society that will enable all mothers to breastfeed with assurance and safety", including full implementation of the ILO Maternity Protection Convention.

References

Aguayo, V. M., Ross, J. S., Kanon, S., & Ouedraogo, A. N. (2003). Monitoring compliance with The International Code of Marketing of Breastmilk Substitutes in West Africa: Multisite cross sectional survey in Togo and Burkina Faso. *British Medical Journal, 326*, 126.

Allen, J., & Hector, D. (2005). Benefits of breastfeeding. *NSW Public Health Bulletin, 16*(3–4), 42–46.

Amir, L. H., & Donath, S. M. (2002). Does maternal smoking have a negative physiological effect on breastfeeding? The epidemiological evidence. *Birth, 29*(2), 112–123.

Amir, L. H., & Donath, S. M. (2007). A systematic review of maternal obesity and breast-feeding intention, initiation and duration. *BMC Pregnancy Childbirth, 7*, 9.

Amir, L. H., & Donath, S. M. (2008). Socioeconomic status and rates of breastfeeding in Australia: Evidence from three recent national health surveys. *Medical Journal Australia, 189*(5), 254–256.

Avery, M. D., Duckett, L., Dodgson, J., Savik, K., & Henly, S. J. (1998). Factors associated with very early weaning among primiparas intending to breastfeed. *Maternal and Child Health Journal, 2*(3), 167–179.

Beasley, A., & Amir, L. H. (2007). Policy on infant formula industry funding, support or sponsorship of articles submitted for publication. *International Breastfeeding Journal, 2*, 5.

Bergman, R., & Feinberg, D. (1981). Working women and breastfeeding in Israel. *Journal of Advanced Nursing, 6*(4), 305–309.

Berry, N. J., & Gribble, K. D. (2008). Breast is no longer best: Promoting normal infant feeding. *Maternal and Child Nutrition, 4*(1), 74–79.

Broadfoot, M., Britten, J., Tappin, D. M., & MacKenzie, J. M. (2005). The Baby Friendly Hospital Initiative and breastfeeding rates in Scotland. *Archives of Disease in Childhood Fetal and Neonatal Edition, 90*, F114–F116.

Brown, C. A., Poag, S., & Kasprzycki, C. (2001). Exploring large employers' and small employers' knowledge, attitudes, and practices on breastfeeding support in the workplace. *Journal of Human Lactation, 17*, 39–46.

Cardenas, R. A., & Major, D. A. (2005). Combining employment and breastfeeding: Utilizing a work-family conflict framework to understand obstacles and solutions. *Journal of Business and Psychology, 20*(1), 31–51.

Chatterji, P., & Frick, K. D. (2004). Does returning to work after childbirth affect breastfeeding practices? *Review of Economics of the Household, 3*(3), 315–335.

Chen, Y. C., Wu, Y. C., & Chie, W. C. (2006). Effects of work-related factors on the breastfeeding behavior of working mothers in a Taiwanese semiconductor manufacturer: A cross-sectional survey. *BMC Public Health, 6*, 160.

Chuang, C., Chang, P., Chen, Y., Hsieh, W., Hurng, B., Lin, S., & Chen, P. (2010). Maternal return to work and breastfeeding: A population-based cohort study. *International Journal of Nursing Studies, 47*(4), 461–474.

Clifford, J., & McIntyre, E. (2008). Who supports breastfeeding? *Breastfeeding Review, 16*(2), 9–19.

Costello, A., & Sachdev, H. (1998). Protecting breastfeeding from breast milk substitutes. *British Medical Journal, 316*, 1103–1104.

Daly, S. E., Owens, R. A., & Hartmann, P. E. (1993). The short-term synthesis and infant-regulated removal of milk in lactating women. *Experimental Physiology, 78*(2), 209–220.

Dettwyler, K. A. (1995a). A time to wean: The hominid blueprint for the natural age of weaning in modern human populations In P. Stuart-Macadam & K. A. Dettwyler (Eds.), *Breastfeeding: Biocultural perspectives* (pp. 39–73). New York, NY: Aldine de Gruyter.

Dettwyler, K. A. (1995b). Beauty and the breast: The cultural context of feeding in the United States. In P. Stuart-Macadam & K. A. Dettwyler (Eds.), *Breastfeeding: Biocultural perspectives* (pp. 167–215). New York, NY: Aldine de Gruyter.

Donath, S. M., & Amir, L. H. (2003). Relationship between prenatal infant feeding intention and initiation and duration of breastfeeding: A cohort study. *Acta Paediatrica, 92*(3), 352–356.

Donath, S. M., & Amir, L. H. (2008). Effect of gestation on initiation and duration of breastfeeding. *Archives of Disease in Childhood Fetal and Neonatal Edition, 93*(6), F448–F450.

Ertem, M. (2011). Infant feeding beliefs and practices in Islamic societies: Focusing on rural Turkey. In P. Liamputtong (Ed.), *Infant feeding practices across cultural perspectives*. Dordrecht, Netherlands: Springer.

Fein, S. B., & Roe, B. (1998). The effect of work status on initiation and duration of breastfeeding. *American Journal of Public Health, 88*(7), 1042–1046.

Flacking, R., Wallin, L., & Ewald, U. (2007). Perinatal and socioeconomic determinants of breastfeeding duration in very preterm infants. *Acta Paediatrica, 96*(8), 1126–1130.

Galtry, J. (2003). The impact of breastfeeding on labour market policy and practice in Ireland, Sweden, and the USA. *Social Science and Medicine, 57*(1), 167–177.

Gudnadottir, M., Gunnarsson, B. S., & Thorsdottir, I. (2006). Effects of sociodemographic factors on adherence to breastfeeding and other important infant dietary recommendations. *Acta Paediatrica, 95*(4), 419–424.

Hanson, L. A. (2004). Mother's defense of the offspring via the milk. *Immunology of human milk: How breastfeeding protects babies* (pp. 77–121). Amarillo, TX: Pharmasoft Publishing.

Hector, D., King, L., Webb, K., & Heywood, P. (2005). Factors affecting breastfeeding practices. Applying a conceptual framework. *NSW Public Health Bulletin, 16*(3–4), 52–55.

Hizel, S., Ceyhun, G., Tanzer, F., & Sanli, C. (2006). Traditional beliefs as forgotten influencing factors on breastfeeding performance in Turkey. *Saudi Medical Journal, 27*(4), 511–518.

Holla-Bhar, R. (2006). *Against all odds: Gendered challenges to breastfeeding*. Penang, Malaysia: WABA.

Horta, B. L., Bahl, R., Martines, J. C., & Victora, C. G. (2007). *Evidence on the long-term effects of breastfeeding: Systematic reviews and meta-analysis*. Geneva: World Health Organization.

Horta, B. L., Kramer, M. S., & Platt, R. W. (2001). Maternal smoking and the risk of early weaning: A meta-analysis. *American Journal of Public Health, 91*(2), 304–307.

Ip, S., Chung, M., Raman, G., Chew, P., Magula, N., DeVine, D.,…Lau, J. (2007). *Breastfeeding and maternal and infant health outcomes in developed countries. Evidence report/technology assessment No. 153 (Prepared by Tufts-New England Medical Centre Evidence-based Practice Centre, under Contract No. 290–02–0022)*. AHRQ Publication No. 07-E007. Rockville, MD: Agency for Healthcare Research and Quality.

Jacknowitz, A. (2008). The role of workplace characteristics in breastfeeding practices. *Women and Health, 47*(2), 87–111.

Kaewsarn, P., & Moyle, W. (2000). Cultural beliefs and breastfeeding duration of Thai working women. *Breastfeeding Review, 8*(1), 13–17.

Kramer, M. S., Chalmers, B., Hodnett, E. D., Sevkovskaya, Z., Dzikovich, I., & Shapiro, S. (2001). Promotion of Breastfeeding Intervention Trial (PROBIT): A randomized trial in the Republic of Belarus. *Journal of the American Medical Association, 285*(4), 413–420.

Leon-Cava, N., Lutter, C., Ross, J., & Martin, L. (2002). *Quantifying the benefits of breastfeeding: A summary of the evidence*. Washington, DC: Division of Health Promotion (HPP) of the Pan American Health Organization (PAHO).

Li, R., Fein, S. B., Chen, J., & Grummer-Strawn, L. M. (2008). Why mothers stop breast-feeding: Mothers' self-reported reasons for stopping during the first year. *Pediatrics, 122*, S69–S76.

Liamputtong, P. (2011). *Infant feeding practices: A cross cultural perspectives*. New York, NY: Springer.

Liamputtong Rice, P. (2000). *Hmong women and reproduction*. Westport, CT: Bergin & Garvey.

Meedya, S., Fahy, K., & Kable, A. (2010). Factors that positively influence breastfeeding duration to 6 months: A literature review. *Women and Birth, 23*(4), 135–145.

Newton, N. (1971). Trebly sensuous woman. *Psychology Today, 71*, 68–71.

Ortiz, J., McGilligan, K., & Kelly, P. (2004). Duration of breast milk expression among working mothers enrolled in an employer-sponsored lactation program. *Pediatric Nursing, 30*(2), 111–119.

Osman, H., Lama, E. Z., & Wick, L. (2009). Cultural beliefs that may discourage breast-feeding among Lebanese women: A qualitative analysis. *International Breastfeeding Journal, 4*, 12.

Pang, W. W., & Hartmann, P. E. (2007). Initiation of human lactation: Secretory differentiation and secretory activation. *Journal of Mammary Gland Biology and Neoplasia, 12*, 211–221.

Pisacane, A. (2000). Nestlé's violation of International Marketing Code. Similar practices take place in Europe. *British Medical Journal, 321*, 960.

Raven, J. H., Chen, Q., Tolhurst, R. J., & Garner, P. (2007). Traditional beliefs and practices in the postpartum period in Fujian Province, China: A qualitative study. *BMC Pregnancy Childbirth, 7*, 8.

Rojjanasrirat, W. (2004). Working women's breastfeeding experiences. *American Journal of Maternal and Child Nursing, 29*(4), 222–227.

Scott, J. A., & Binns, C. W. (1999). Factors associated with the initiation and duration of breastfeeding: A review of the literature. *Breastfeeding Review, 7*(1), 5–16.

Sheehan, A., & Schmied, V. (2010). The imperative to breastfeeding: An Australian perspective. In P. Liamputtong (Ed.), *Infant feeding practices: A cross-cultural perspectives* (pp. 55–76). Dordrecht, Netherlands: Springer.

Sikorski, J., Renfrew, M. J., Pindoria, S., & Wade, A. (2003). Support for breastfeeding mothers: A systematic review. *Paediatric and Perinatal Epidemiology, 17*(4), 407–417.

Small, M. F. (1998). Food for thought. In *Our babies, ourselves: How biology and culture shape the way we parent* (pp. 177–212). New York, NY: Anchor Books.

Social Policy Division. (2009). *OECD Family database*. Retrieved from http://www.oecd.org/dataoecd/30/56/43136964.pdf

Sokol, E., Thiagarajah, S., & Allain, A. (2001). *Breaking the rules. Stretching the rules. Evidence of violations of the code of marketing of breastmilk substitutes and subsequent resolutions*. Penang, Malaysia: International Baby Food Action Network.

Staehelin, K., Bertea, P. C., & Stutz, E. Z. (2007). Length of maternity leave and health of mother and child—a review. *International Journal of Public Health, 52*(4), 202–209.

Stuebe, A. (2009). The risks of not breastfeeding for mothers and infants. *Reviews in Obstetrics and Gynecology, 2*(4), 222–231.

Tappin, D. (2001). Breastfeeding rates are increasing in Scotland. *Health Bulletin, 58*(2), 102–107.

Taylor, A. (1998). Violations of the Code of Marketing of Breast Milk Substitutes: Prevalence in four countries. *British Medical Journal, 316*, 1117–1122.

UNICEF. (2009a). *Early initiation of breastfeeding.* Retrieved from http://www.childinfo. org/breastfeeding_initiation.php

UNICEF. (2009b). *Infant and young child feeding.* Retrieved from http://www.childinfo.org/ breastfeeding_iycf.php

U.S. Department of Labor. (2006). *Women in the labor force: A databook.* Washington, DC: U.S. Bureau of Labor Statistics

Van Rossum, C. T. M., Buchner, F. L., & Hoekstra, J. (2006). *Quantification of health effects of breastfeeding: Review of the literature and model simulation.* Bilthoven: Ministry of Public Health, Welfare and Sports.

Visness, C., & Kennedy, K. (1997). Maternal employment and breast-feeding: Findings from the 1988 National Maternal and Infant Health Survey. *American Journal of Public Health, 87*, 945–950.

WABA. (2003). *Maternity protection at work campaign kit: ILO convention no. 183 and recommendation no. 191.* Penang, Malaysia: Maternal Protection Coalition.

World Health Organization. (1981). *International code of marketing of breastmilk substitutes.* Geneva: World Health Organization.

World Health Organization. (2001). *The optimal duration of exclusive breastfeeding: Report of an expert consultation.* Geneva: World Health Organization.

World Health Organization/UNICEF (2009). *Baby-Friendly Hospital Initiative: Revised, updated and expanded for integrated care.* Retrieved from http://www.who.int/nutrition/ publications/infantfeeding/9789241594950/en/index.html

{ Commentary }

Short-Term and Long-Term Effects of Oxytocin Released by Suckling and of Skin-to-Skin Contact in Mothers and Infants

Kerstin Uvnäs-Moberg

Sulaiman, Amir, and Liamputtong describe breastfeeding rates in different parts of the world/in different countries and analyze some of the factors underlying the vast differences. A list of possible benefits induced by breastfeeding in mothers and infants is also given. The first aim of this commentary will be to give an extended and comprehensive description of the effect spectrum caused by oxytocin during breastfeeding beyond that of milk ejection. Based on the role of oxytocin as an integrator of behavioral and physiological adaptations during breastfeeding, the second aim will be to propose a possible connection between the frequent exposure of oxytocin and some of the long-term health-promoting effects seen following breastfeeding.

Oxytocin

Oxytocin is produced in the supraoptic nucleus (SON) and the paraventricular nucleus (PVN) of the hypothalamus. In the SON and PVN, oxytocin is produced in magnocellular neurons, which project to the posterior pituitary, which releases oxytocin into the circulation. Oxytocin is also produced in smaller parvocellular neurons, and oxytocinergic nerves project to many important regulatory areas in the brain (Buijs, De Vries, & Van Leeuwen, 1985).

Administration of oxytocin to animals has been shown to stimulate various social interactive behaviors (including maternal behavior), to induce an anxiolytic and calming effect, to decrease the pain threshold and inflammation, to increase well-being and mood, to lower blood pressure and cortisol levels, and to stimulate metabolic functions allowing nutrient assimilation and growth (Uvnäs-Moberg, 1998a, 1998b; Uvnäs-Moberg & Petersson, 2005). Most of these effects have been replicated in human males in response to administration of oxytocin as a nasal spray (Heinrichs & Domes, 2008).

OXYTOCIN-RELATED EFFECTS IN BREASTFEEDING MOTHERS

The suckling stimulus causes a pulsatile release of oxytocin into the circulation. Oxytocin pulses are linked to milk ejection and occur at approximately 90-second intervals (Jonas et al., 2009). Oxytocin, however, also influences maternal physiology and behavior via a release from nervous pathways that project from the PVN to relevant regulatory areas in the brain. Some of these oxytocin-related effects are as follows:

1. Oxytocin plays an important role in regulation of milk production, since prolactin secretion is stimulated via oxytocin-containing nerves in the anterior pituitary. In support of this effect, there is a strong correlation between prolactin and oxytocin levels in breastfeeding mothers (Jonas et al., 2009).

2. Breastfeeding mothers are less anxious and more socially interactive than nonbreastfeeding mothers. In part, these effects are mediated by oxytocin released in the amygdala. These changes correlate with oxytocin released during breastfeeding (Heinrichs et al., 2001; Jonas, Nissen, Ransjo-Arvidson, Matthiesen, & Uvnäs-Moberg, 2008; Nissen, Gustavsson, Widstrom, & Uvnäs-Moberg, 1998). In addition, maternal oxytocin levels have been demonstrated to correlate with the amount of interaction between the mother and the infant (Feldman, Weller, Zagoory-Sharon, & Levine 2007).

3. Breastfeeding is also associated with potent antistress effects, which are exerted by oxytocin released in areas involved in the control of the hypothalamic–pituitary–adrenal (HPA) axis and autonomic nervous tone. Each breastfeeding session is linked to lowered blood pressure and cortisol levels. A negative correlation between the mother's oxytocin and ACTH levels supports the inhibitory role of oxytocin on HPA axis function (Handlin et al., 2009; Jonas, Nissen, Ransjo-Arvidson, Wiklund, et al., 2008; Nissen et al., 1996).

4. Breastfeeding is also linked to important changes in digestive and metabolic functions in the mother. The levels of gastrointestinal and pancreatic hormones, such as gastrin, cholecystokinin, somatostatin, insulin, and glucagon, are influenced during breastfeeding, in a way that is consistent with optimized digestion, storing of nutrients, and recruitment of and transfer of energy to the mammary glands for milk production. These effects are exerted in areas involved in the control of vagal nerve tone, and oxytocin plays an important regulatory role. Somatostatin exerts inhibitory effects on the release of gastrointestinal and pancreatic hormones and also on gastrointestinal function. A negative correlation between oxytocin and somatostatin levels supports the positive influence of oxytocin on the function of the gastrointestinal tract (Uvnäs-Moberg, 1989, 1990).

As mentioned previously, all these effects are exerted in the brain via oxytocin released from oxytocinergic nerves. The reason why circulating oxytocin levels correlate with psychological and behavioral functions in breastfeeding mothers is that oxytocin is released in parallel into the circulation and into the brain during suckling (Kendrick, Keverne, Chapman, & Baldwin, 1988).

LONG-TERM EFFECTS OF OXYTOCIN

Some of the breastfeeding-linked effects become more strongly expressed after some time of breastfeeding. Maternal psychological changes toward increased social interaction and calm develop gradually over the first week postpartum and remain as long as breastfeeding lasts. Basal blood pressure decreases over time, and the release of cortisol in response to physical exercise is blunted (Altemus, Galliven, Carter, & Gold, 1995; Jonas, Nissen, Ransjo-Arvidson, Matthiesen, et al., 2008; Jonas, Nissen, Ransjo-Arvidson, Wiklund, et al., 2008).

The mechanisms underpinning the sustained effects during breastfeeding may be related to the effect of oxytocin to influence the function of other transmitter systems in a more long-term way. Repeated administration of oxytocin has, for example, been demonstrated to give rise to long-term effects in animal experiments (e.g., a sustained decrease of blood pressure and cortisol levels and an increased pain threshold and increased levels of gut hormones). The long-term antistress effects induced by oxytocin have been associated with an increased function of α-2 adreno-receptors, which exert an inhibitory action on central noradrenergic transmission, an important regulator of stress (Petersson, Alster, Lundeberg, & Uvnäs-Moberg, 1996; Petersson, Hulting, Andersson, & Uvnäs-Moberg, 1999; Petersson, Hulting, & Uvnäs-Moberg, 1999; Petersson, Uvnäs-Moberg, Erhardt, & Engberg, 1998).

LINK BETWEEN THE REPEATED EXPOSURE OF OXYTOCIN AND LONG-TERM HEALTH-PROMOTING EFFECTS OF BREASTFEEDING

As summarized earlier, oxytocin coordinates a pattern of physiological and behavioral/psychological adaptations in breastfeeding mothers. Some of these effects seem to become more pronounced the longer the duration of breastfeeding and may even persist after weaning.

It is possible that an increased sensitivity of the α-2 adrenoreceptors persists after the end of breastfeeding, in particular in women who have breastfed several children and for a long time. This would in part explain why breastfeeding seems to protect against cardiovascular diseases such as heart infarction, stroke, hypertension, and type 2 diabetes (Stuebe et al., 2009). The positive influence on weight loss may be related to increased recruitment of energy linked to breastfeeding, and the preventive effect against osteoporosis may be related to the anabolic effects on bone tissue caused by oxytocin released during breastfeeding (Nicks, Fowler, & Gaddy, 2010).

Breastfeeding has also, as mentioned in the chapter by Sulaiman, Amir, and Liamputtong, been associated with decreased occurrence of some types of cancers, such as breast, ovarian, and endometrial cancer. Interestingly, oxytocin has been demonstrated to decrease growth of these types of cancers (Cassoni, Sapino, Marrocco, Chini, & Bussolati, 2004). Whether oxytocin released during breastfeeding exerts a preventive effect on these types of cancers should be investigated. Given the many beneficial effects of oxytocin and the vast amounts of oxytocin the breastfeeding mother is exposed to, it is reasonable to assume that some of the long-term health-promoting effects of breastfeeding are a consequence of exposure to oxytocin.

Touch

Tiffany Field and Maria Hernandez-Reif describe some consequences of touch and pain in infants and their mothers and how massage can induce beneficial effects in mothers and infants presumably by activation of touch fibers. The third aim of this commentary is to give some complementary information on the structure and function of the sensory nerves that innervate the skin. The fourth aim is to describe the effects of skin-to-skin contact between mother and infant, a natural way of stimulating sensory nerves emanating from the skin, in a short- and long-term perspective.

As mentioned by Field and Hernandez-Reif, the skin is provided with receptors, which are activated in response to different physical and chemical modalities. The sensory nerves differ as to thickness and speed of transmission of nerve impulses. Evolutionarily older, thin unmyelinated C fibers transmit nerve impulses more slowly than the thicker myelinated fibers. The C fibers have been associated with pain, in particular chronic pain, and the myelinated fibers are supposed to mediate the sensation of touch. Recently a subpopulation of C-fiber afferents, the CT fibers, which are activated by stroking of the skin and which induce well-being, have been identified in humans (Olausson et al., 2008).

The nerve fibers mediating pain (noxious) and those mediating pleasant or non-noxious stimuli do not only give rise to the experience of anxiety and pain or calm and well-being, respectively. The activity of the HPA axis and the autonomic nervous system, for example, is also influenced.

Animal experiments show that noxious stimulation of the skin is linked to increased sympathetic nervous tone (e.g., increased blood pressure and increased levels of adrenalin) and to increased activity in the HPA axis as evidenced by an elevation of cortisol levels. By contrast, stimulation of nonnoxious fibers is accompanied by a decreased activity in the sympathetic nervous system and the HPA axis. In addition, some aspects of the vagal/parasympathetic nervous system are activated as evidenced by changed levels of gastrointestinal hormones.

These effects are in part exerted by reflex connections in the brainstem, but they also involve hypothalamic pathways. For example, noxious stimuli release corticotrophin-releasing factor (CRF) and vasopressin from the PVN in the hypothalamus. Corticotrophin-releasing factor and vasopressin not only activate the HPA axis but also increase the activity in some aspects of the sympathetic nervous system via nerves that reach areas involved in the control of the autonomic nervous system.

Nonnoxious stimuli, on the other hand, release oxytocin from neurons originating in the PVN, which will decrease the activity in the HPA axis and in the sympathetic nervous system. Aspects of the parasympathetic/vagal system are also activated. Pain threshold is increased and a calming effect is induced. Several of these effects are abolished after prior administration of oxytocin antagonists (Uvnäs-Moberg, 1998a, 1998b; Uvnäs-Moberg & Petersson, 2005, 2011).

SKIN-TO-SKIN CONTACT BETWEEN MOTHER AND INFANT

During skin-to-skin contact, both mothers and infants receive various types of nonnoxious stimuli. Touch, stroking, warm temperature, light, and moderate pressure constitute parts of this interaction.

Infants put on their mother's chest immediately after birth (or later) display an inborn breast-seeking behavior, they cry less, and their sensation of pain is reduced. Their skin temperature is increased as an expression of increased blood flow in the skin blood vessels, a sign of decreased sympathetic tone. Cortisol levels fall, as do the levels of the gastrointestinal hormone cholecystokinin (Bystrova et al., 2003; Tornhage, Serenius, Uvnäs-Moberg, & Lindberg, 1998; Widstrom et al., 1987).

All these effects are consistent with effects induced by nonnoxious sensory stimuli, which involve a release of oxytocin from neurons emanating in the hypothalamus. From a clinical point of view, skin-to-skin contact immediately after birth may reduce the negative consequences of the stress of being born (Bystrova et al., 2003).

Afferent sensory nerves in the skin are activated in the mother also, and a similar effect spectrum is induced. The mother's interaction with the child increases and she becomes calmer. Her cortisol levels and her blood pressure fall (Handlin et al., 2009; Heinrichs, Neumann, & Ehlert, 2002; Velandia, Matthisen, Uvnäs-Moberg, & Nissen, 2010). Maternal circulating oxytocin levels are raised in a dose-dependent way when the infant massages the mother's breast, but they do not display the pulsatility characterized by 90-second intervals that is caused by suckling and that leads to milk ejection (Matthiesen, Ransjo-Arvidson, Nissen, & Uvnäs-Moberg, 2001).

The effects of skin-to-skin contact can be used clinically. Repeated exposure to skin-to-skin contact, as during kangaroo care of premature infants, for example, gives rise to better bonding between the mother and infant, more milk production, and the infants growing and developing more quickly (Conde-Agudelo, Diaz-Rossello, & Belizan, 2003).

THE EARLY SENSITIVE PERIOD

Skin-to-skin contact in the immediate postpartum period gives rise to acute behavioral and physiological changes such as increased interaction between the mother and infant and decreased stress levels in both. Close contact during the early sensitive period has also been associated with better maternal bonding and interaction with the child several weeks later (Kennell, Trause, & Klaus, 1975; Klaus et al., 1972). In a study performed in Russia, mothers and infants exposed to 90 minutes of skin-to-skin contact after birth interacted in a more sensitive way 1 year later, and the children were better at coping with stress than those that were separated from their mother or even held by the mother but dressed in clothes (Bystrova et al., 2009).

In conclusion, close contact, in particular skin-to-skin contact between mothers (fathers) and infants, is associated with a bilateral increase in social interaction and bonding and with reduction of stress levels via stimulation of sensory nerves in the skin. Infant massage as described by Field may be a way of increasing the amount of the nonnoxious type of stimulation between mother and infant in order to induce better interaction and bonding between the mother and infant, to increase growth and development, and to reduce stress levels in the infant.

References

Altemus, M. D., Galliven, E., Carter, C. S., & Gold, P. W. (1995). Suppression of hypothalamic-pituitary-adrenal axis responses to stress in lactating women. *Journal of Clinical Endocrinology and Metabolism, 80*(10), 2954–2959.

Buijs, R. M., De Vries, G. J., & Van Leeuwen, F. W. (1985). *The distribution and synaptic release of oxytocin in the central nervous system.* Amsterdam: Elsevier Science Publishers BV.

Bystrova, K., Ivanova, V., Edhborg, M., Matthiesen, A. S., Ransjo-Arvidson, A. B., Mukhamedrakhimov, R., et al. (2009). Early contact versus separation: Effects on mother-infant interaction one year later. *Birth, 36*(2), 97–109.

Bystrova, K., Widstrom, A. M., Matthiesen, A. S., Ransjo-Arvidson, A. B., Welles-Nystrom, B., Wassberg, C., ... Uvnäs-Moberg, K. (2003). Skin-to-skin contact may reduce negative consequences of "the stress of being born": A study on temperature in newborn infants, subjected to different ward routines in St. Petersburg. *Acta Paediatrica, 92*(3), 320–326.

Cassoni, P., Sapino, A., Marrocco, T., Chini, B., & Bussolati, G. (2004). Oxytocin and oxytocin receptors in cancer cells and proliferation. *Journal of Neuroendocrinology, 16*(4), 362–364.

Conde-Agudelo, A., Diaz-Rossello, J. L., & Belizan, J. M. (2003). Kangaroo mother care to reduce morbidity and mortality in low birthweight infants. *Cochrane Database of Systematic Reviews,* (2), CD002771.

Feldman, R., Waeller, A., Zagoory-Sharon, O., & Levine, A. (2007). Evidence for a neuroendocrinological foundation of human affiliation: Plasma oxytocin levels across pregnancy and the postpartum period predict mother-infant bonding. *Psychological Science, 18*(11), 965–970.

Handlin, L., Jonas, W., Petersson, M., Ejdeback, M., Ransjo-Arvidson, A. B., Nissen, E., & Uvnäs-Moberg, K. (2009). Effects of sucking and skin-to-skin contact on maternal ACTH and cortisol levels during the second day postpartum-influence of epidural analgesia and oxytocin in the perinatal period. *Breastfeeding Medicine, 4*(4), 207–220.

Heinrichs, M., & Domes, G. (2008). Neuropeptides and social behaviour: Effects of oxytocin and vasopressin in humans. *Progress in Brain Research, 170*, 337–350.

Heinrichs, M., Meinlschmidt, G., Neumann, I., Wagner, S., Kirschbaum, C., Ehlert, U., et al. (2001). Effects of suckling on hypothalamic-pituitary-adrenal axis responses to psychosocial stress in postpartum lactating women. *Journal of Clinical Endocrinology and Metabolism, 86*(10), 4798–4804.

Heinrichs, M., Neumann, I., & Ehlert, U. (2002). Lactation and stress: Protective effects of breast-feeding in humans. *Stress, 5*(3), 195–203.

Jonas, K., Johansson, L. M., Nissen, E., Ejdeback, M., Ransjo-Arvidson, A. B., & Uvnäs-Moberg, K. (2009). Effects of intrapartum oxytocin administration and epidural analgesia on the concentration of plasma oxytocin and prolactin, in response to suckling during the second day postpartum. *Breastfeed Medicine, 4*(2), 71–82.

Jonas, W., Nissen, E., Ransjo-Arvidson, A. B., Matthiesen, A. S., & Uvnäs-Moberg, K. (2008). Influence of oxytocin or epidural analgesia on personality profile in breastfeeding women: A comparative study. *Archives of Women's Mental Health, 11*(5–6), 335–345.

Jonas, W., Nissen, E., Ransjo-Arvidson, A. B., Wiklund, I., Henriksson, P., & Uvnäs-Moberg, K. (2008). Short- and long-term decrease of blood pressure in women during breastfeeding. *Breastfeeding Medicine, 3*(2), 103–109.

Kendrick, K. M., Keverne, E. B., Chapman, C., & Baldwin, B. A. (1988). Microdialysis measurement of oxytocin, aspartate, gamma-aminobutyric acid and glutamate release from the olfactory bulb of the sheep during vaginocervical stimulation. *Brain Research, 442*(1), 171–174.

Kennell, J. H., Trause, M. A., & Klaus, M. H. (1975). Evidence for a sensitive period in the human mother. *Ciba Foundation Symposium, (33)*, 87–101.

Klaus, M. H., Jerauld, R., Kreger, N. C., McAlpine, W., Steffa, M., & Kennel, J. H. (1972). Maternal attachment. Importance of the first post-partum days. *New England Journal of Medicine, 286*(9), 460–463.

Matthiesen, A. S., Ransjo-Arvidson, A. B., Nissen, E., & Uvnäs-Moberg, K. (2001). Postpartum maternal oxytocin release by newborns: Effects of infant hand massage and sucking. *Birth, 28*(1), 13–19.

Nicks, K. M., Fowler, T. W., & Gaddy, D. (2010). Reproductive hormones and bone. *Current Osteoporosis Reports, 8*(2), 60–67.

Nissen, E., Gustavsson, P., Widstrom, A. M., & Uvnäs-Moberg, K. (1998). Oxytocin, prolactin, milk production and their relationship with personality traits in women after vaginal delivery or Cesarean section. *Journal of Psychosomatic Obstetrics and Gynaecology, 19*(1), 49–58.

Nissen, E., Uvnäs-Moberg, K., Svensson, K., Stock, S., Widstrom, A. M., & Winberg, J. (1996). Different patterns of oxytocin, prolactin but not cortisol release during breastfeeding in women delivered by caesarean section or by the vaginal route. *Early Human Development, 45*(1–2), 103–118.

Olausson, H., Cole, J., Rylander, K., McGlone, F., Lamarre, Y., Wallin, B. G., et al. (2008). Functional role of unmyelinated tactile afferents in human hairy skin: Sympathetic response and perceptual localization. *Experimental Brain Research, 184*(1), 135–140.

Petersson, M., Alster, P., Lundeberg, T., & Uvnäs-Moberg, K. (1996). Oxytocin causes a long-term decrease of blood pressure in female and male rats. *Physiology and Behavior, 60*(5), 1311–1315.

Petersson, M., Hulting, A., Andersson, R., & Uvnäs-Moberg, K. (1999). Long-term changes in gastrin, cholecystokinin and insulin in response to oxytocin treatment. *Neuroendocrinology, 69*(3), 202–208.

Petersson, M., Hulting, A. L., & Uvnäs-Moberg, K. (1999). Oxytocin causes a sustained decrease in plasma levels of corticosterone in rats. *Neuroscience Letters, 264*(1–3), 41–44.

Petersson, M., Uvnäs-Moberg, K., Erhardt, S., & Engberg, G. (1998). Oxytocin increases locus coeruleus alpha 2-adrenoreceptor responsiveness in rats. *Neuroscience Letters, 255*(2), 115–118.

Stuebe, A. M., Michels, K. B., Willett, W. C., Manson, J. E., Rexrode, K., & Rich-Edwards, J. W. (2009). Duration of lactation and incidence of myocardial infarction in middle to late adulthood. *American Journal of Obstetrics and Gynecology, 200*(2), 138.e131–138.

Tornhage, C. J., Serenius, F., Uvnäs-Moberg, K., & Lindberg, T. (1998). Plasma somat-ostatin and cholecystokinin levels in preterm infants during kangaroo care with and without nasogastric tube-feeding. *Journal of Pediatric Endocrinology and Metabolism, 11*(5), 645–651.

Uvnäs-Moberg, K. (1989). The gastrointestinal tract in growth and reproduction. *Scientific American, 261*(1), 78–83.

Uvnäs-Moberg, K. (1990). Endocrinologic control of food intake. *Nutrition Reviews, 48*(2), 57–63; discussion 114–131.

Uvnäs-Moberg, K. (1998a). Antistress pattern induced by oxytocin. *News in Physiological Sciences, 13*, 22–25.

Uvnäs-Moberg, K. (1998b). Oxytocin may mediate the benefits of positive social interac-tion and emotions. *Psychoneuroendocrinology, 23*(8), 819–835.

Uvnäs-Moberg, K., & Petersson, M. (2005). [Oxytocin, a mediator of anti-stress, well-being, social interaction, growth and healing]. *Zeitschrift fur Psychosomatische Medizin und Psychotherapie, 51*(1), 57–80.

Uvnäs-Moberg, K., & Petersson, M. (2011). Role of oxytocin related effects in manual therapies. In J. H. King, W., Pattersson M. M. (Eds.), *The science and application of manual therapy*. Amsterdam: Elsevier.

Velandia, M., Matthisen, A. S., Uvnäs-Moberg, K., & Nissen, E. (2010). Onset of vocal interaction between parents and newborns in skin-to-skin contact immediately after elective cesarean section. *Birth, 37*(3), 192–201.

Widstrom, A. M., Ransjo-Arvidson, A. B., Christensson, K., Matthiesen, A. S., Winberg, J., & Uvnäs-Moberg, K. (1987). Gastric suction in healthy newborn infants. Effects on circulation and developing feeding behaviour. *Acta Paediatrica Scandinavica, 76*(4), 566–572.

12

Developmental Optimization
Darcia Narvaez and Tracy R. Gleason

Anthropologists and other scientists involved in similar research consistently remark on how much the people from hunter-gatherer societies are "more intelligent, more alert, more expressive, and more interested in things and people around them than the average European or American" (Diamond, 1997, p. 20; see also Dentan, 1968; Everett, 2009). Why? What about the hunter-gatherer way of life might elicit engagement in the physical and social world more so than life in industrialized societies? Certainly the fitness requirements in physiologically harsh living conditions might make for a more severe culling of less intelligent genetic stock (Diamond, 1997). But could genes explain everything? We think not. As the study of epigenetics and developmental plasticity expands, the fact that early life factors, particularly psychological ones, influence developmental outcomes as much as genes, if not more, becomes ever more clear (Jablonka & Lamb, 2006).

In recent years, the field of developmental traumatology has emerged, which seeks to unravel the complex interactions among a child's genetic makeup, environmental stressors, and sensitive periods for child outcomes (De Bellis, 2010). Recent years have also put key elements of our distant past in higher relief (e.g., the health effects of high levels of vitamin D among our ancestors due to high skin exposure to sunlight; Cannell, Hollis, Zasloff, & Heaney, 2008). In this chapter, using ancestral practices as a baseline, we propose research into "developmental optimization," in which the complex interactions among genes, environment, critical periods, and the timing, intensity, and duration of experiences and their contexts are examined for their interrelationships and effects on the functioning of brain and body systems and implicated in child and adult outcomes. Our particular interest is sociomoral development, which includes personality characteristics such as empathy, conscience, and self-regulation. But we do not mean to imply that a developmental optimization framework is unrelated to other outcomes. It can also frame the study of intelligence, health, and other factors related to human well-being.

Human Nature and Moral Functioning

Darwin (1871) believed that morality was integral to human nature, emphasizing humanity's "moral sense" as a unique contributor to human evolution. In
Descent, Darwin (1871) identified several evolved components of the moral sense:
(1) pleasure in the company of others and sympathy or concern for their well-
being; (2) cognitive awareness allowing for comparison of past and future behavior, and dissatisfaction with mismatched expectations; (3) concern for social
rules constructed by the community, which, in concert with cognitive awareness,
fosters shame when group expectations are not met; and (4) habit or practice,
allowing for cultural transmission. Darwin assumed that these were commonly
held characteristics of humans, forming the backbone of any society.

But perhaps Darwin was too quick to assign these characteristics to innateness.
Evidence suggests that some of the characteristics may be on the decline in the
US population. Here are some examples. Concerning (1), contra the enjoyment of
sociality, single-person households are more prevalent than other types of households and single adults represent 50% of all adults (Johnson, 2009, along with the
fact that 50% of adults are single). Further, according to Cacioppo and Patrick
(2008), isolation and loneliness are increasing (recall *Bowling Alone* from 1995),
suggesting that the ability to get pleasure from social engagement is decreasing or
that modern forms of interaction are not fulfilling social needs (at the same time,
note the increase in the use of interactive social media). As for empathy, longitudinal analyses document a decrease in empathy among college students over the
last decades (Konrath, O'Brien, & Hsing, 2011; but note that other work suggests
that younger cohorts generally may show more empathy than older ones: Grühn,
Rebucal, Diehl, Lumley, & Labouvie-Vief, 2008). Regarding (3), the number of
families exhibiting antisocial behavior seems to be on the rise (Mooney & Young,
2006; Walker, 1993), antiheroes are celebrated in television and the media (Bloch,
2006), and cheating to get ahead is widespread (Callahan, 2004). More and more
communication is mediated by technology, but the quality of those interpersonal
exchanges are decidedly less socially and emotionally fulfilling than face-to-face
interaction (Turkle, 2011). Regarding (4), in the earliest years a child's ability to
conform to the requirements of formal schooling gives a measure of success or
failure in building habits appropriate for one's social context. The number of
children who arrive in kindergarten with behavior dysregulation appears to be
increasing, suggesting that many children have not mastered the requisite level
of self-regulation for early schooling (Gilliam, 2005; Powell, Fixen, & Dunlop,
2003) and/or that current practices in early childhood education and care are
developmentally inappropriate to prepare them for success in kindergarten. In
summary, the empirical work that addresses the characteristics of Darwin's moral
sense components suggests that they may be more epigenetic than genetic and
that modern society may not, or may no longer, be providing the necessary environment for their optimal manifestation.

Indeed, in chapter 1 (Narvaez, Panksepp, Schore, & Gleason, this volume), the authors described some of the evidence for the decline in well-being among US children and youth. Similar declines in moral and prosocial functioning are also apparent. For example, moral reasoning sophistication has been declining in college students, from postconventionality not to the next level down, conventionality, but to the lowest level, personal interests (Thoma & Bebeau, 2008). Moreover, in the past 50 years, "rates of maladaptive aggression and antisocial behaviors" have risen "in frequency and severity among children and adolescents" (Connor, 2002, p. 28). The picture is not good. At the same time, violent crime rates overall are down (Federal Bureau of Investigation, 2010), suggesting to some that morality has improved. But this view is only true if one takes morality to be "do no harm" rather than something more prosocial. Consequently, our concern is for the development and promotion of sophisticated social engagement and prosocial behavior, and for the facilitation of the developmental processes that bring them into being.

Setting the Stage for Moral Development Early in Life

Developmental psychology has made great strides in recent decades in identifying behaviors in early life that are foundational for moral functioning in adulthood. Underlying these behaviors are two important characteristics: self-regulation and concern for others. These attributes provide the foundation for social interaction, in that successful prosocial engagement with others requires both management of one's internal world, so as to move beyond personal concerns, and attention to the needs of others. Moreover, these qualities are characteristic of moral exemplars.

As a group, moral exemplars are more agreeable, conscientious, and open to new experience than the average person (Colby & Damon, 1991; Walker, 1999), and they show high regulation of emotion and successful management of stressful experiences. At the same time, they exhibit a higher than average affiliation with others (communion and compassion) and a higher than average sense of self-efficacy or agency (Frimer, Walker, Dunlop, Lee, & Riches, in press; Walker & Frimer, 2008, 2009), behavioral orientations associated with social engagement, and concern for the welfare of others. These components of personality develop over many years. Self-regulation, for example, is a complicated and long-term developmental task that includes physiological, emotional, and social components. Successful automatic self-regulation frees the individual to be able to focus on external concerns, such as the needs of others. In this sense, self-regulation is a necessary but not sufficient condition for the development of virtue. The second component, development of concern for others, depends on the construction of a brain that is relationally oriented and experienced in intersubjectivity, the emotional attunement that characterizes good early experience. The ability to act on concern for others emerges from experiences of mutuality, leading to the internalization of parental mores and the emergence of conscience (Kochanska, 2002). We examine the research on these two characteristics, which provides clues as to the kinds of early experiences that promote optimal moral functioning and can help in finding a proper moral baseline for human behavior. Because concern for others and the ability to act prosocially are necessarily dependent on good self-regulation (Kochanska, DeVet, Goldman, & Murray, 1994), we begin with the latter.

SELF-REGULATION

Self-regulation is a fundamental goal of successful development (Als, 1982) but is not the task of the child alone. It is by definition a social, and primarily dyadic, process that begins at (or even before) birth. The human infant is characterized by significant neurological immaturity, and thus even such basic physiological processes as regulating temperature and the sleep/wake cycle require support from a responsive, caring adult. Specifically, maternal sensitivity has been identified as an important component of an infant's physiological regulation (Moore et al., 2009; Spangler, Schieche, Ilg, & Maier, 1994). Failure to receive responsive care results in a maladaptive stress response in the infant. Indeed, even with custodial care that manages physiological regulation but is emotionally unresponsive, infants experience a heightened level of stress response (Gunnar, Larson, Hertsgaard, Harris, & Brodersen, 1992). A young child who is cared for with little warmth and responsivity, even if his or her physical needs are met, shows more depressed affect and fewer social bids than a child with a nurturing caregiver (Karrass & Walden, 2005).

Early life is a sensitive period for self-regulation development. Repeated experience of stress in early development can become an entrenched pattern that establishes a poor foundation for future development. Neglected and abused children show permanent changes to their neurological functioning as a result of poor vagal tone (Porges & Carter, 2010) and frequent hormonal imbalances (for reviews, see Lanius, Vermetten, & Pain, 2010; Schulkin, 1999). Poor physiological self-regulation is also linked to insecure or disorganized attachment to caregivers (Spangler & Grossman, 1993). On the other hand, attentive early caregiving results in what Fogel and colleagues (Fogel, 2000; Fogel & Branco, 1997) call a kind of "relational communication system," in which parent and child successfully modulate their behavior to achieve an optimal level of physiological arousal and coordinated action (Evans & Porter, 2009). Starting early in life, parental face-to-face interaction with infants often shows efforts to match infant affect, a process that leads to positive arousal and ultimately to mutual synchrony between parent and child later in the first year. Successful navigation of these processes is associated with measures of self-control (Feldman, Greenbaum, & Yirmiya, 1999). As Schore (this volume) points out, the mother–child relationship is critical to the foundation of emotion systems and the cultivation of right brain emotional signaling. Attachment behaviors are reflective of this deep neurobiological entrainment.

As the infant grows, the regulation of emotion becomes integral to the development of an attachment relationship (Schore, 2001; Sroufe, 1996). Security of attachment is highly correlated with measures of emotion regulation, such as impulse control and aggression (Egeland, 1983), through such physiological mechanisms as vagal tone shaping by caregiver touch (Carter & Porges, this volume). Beyond the attachment relationship and the neurobiological construction of the emotion systems through caregiver support in infancy, Morris, Silk, Steinberg, Myers, and Robinson (2007) identified three means by which parents shape emotion regulation beyond infancy: through the demonstration of particular emotions (i.e., modeling), as social references for situations in which children are unsure how to react, through the general emotional atmosphere parents provide in the family (e.g., marital relationship), and through direct tuition around emotions—at first helping children explicitly identify and manage their emotions and the emotions of others and subsequently suggesting ways in which children can cope with their negative emotions (in particular) on their own. All these co-constructions are facilitated by a good neurobiological base.

Social regulation builds on the physiological and emotional components of self-regulation. The development of a secure attachment relationship and well-shaped emotion systems in infancy sets the stage for creating and managing social relationships later in life. Theoretically, a secure attachment relationship provides a model of the self as worthy of love from others, creating the expectation that social relationships will be a beneficial and rewarding experience (Bowlby, 1979; Sroufe & Fleeson, 1986). Moreover, these relationships are thought to provide the infant and young child with the self-regulatory tools needed to manage stressful situations, whether social or not. Indeed, recent work in neurobiology has illuminated some of the mechanisms by which secure attachments facilitate healthy and adaptive strategies for coping with stress and novelty (Schore, 2001, this volume), and certainly associations have been found between early secure attachments and later relationships, both with adults (Erickson & Crichton, 1981) and with peers and friends (Hartup, 1983). As with emotion regulation, the development of social regulation continues to be a dyadic process throughout childhood as parents advise their children regarding social interactions, facilitate their participation in social groups, and model appropriate social behavior (Hartup, 1991). Even into adolescence, parents provide important resources to guide their children's emerging autonomy into the social world (Collins, Gleason, & Sesma, 1997).

CONCERN FOR OTHERS

In addition to the ability to regulate physiological, emotional, and social responses, the development of optimal moral functioning requires an external focus, in which the needs and desires of others are not only noticed but also given attention and concern. To behave in moral ways, a person must not only refrain from transgressions but also feel empathy for the plight of others and take some responsibility for their welfare. The ability to engage in these processes regularly and consistently requires resources beyond those needed to attend to the needs of the self.

The roots of empathy are apparent in newborns, who cry in response to the cries of other newborns (empathic distress), and it continues to develop throughout childhood under conditions of good care (Hoffman, 2000). Empathy is shaped particularly in the mother–child dyad of mutual coregulation. When the mother is sensitively responsive, she fosters the child's emotional attunement with others (Siegel, 1999). Concern for others emerges as the basic components of self-regulation are developing (Eisenberg, 2000). The intersubjectivity of the mother–child relationship fosters both empathy and self-regulation through a mutually responsive orientation (partners regulate themselves in response to the other; Kochanska, 2002).

Although the ability to refrain from wrongdoing—virtue as noncommission at its most basic level—requires a significant element of self-control (Grusec & Goodnow, 1994), evidence has emerged for the internalization of parental mores, the emergence of conscience, and the development of empathy as early as toddlerhood. Internalization of parental rules has been studied in young children as the ability to abstain from wrongdoing and the development of conscience. Grazyna Kochanska and colleagues have published extensively on this topic, demonstrating consistently and repeatedly that a child's ability to internalize parents' rules and successfully demonstrate conscience is directly related to the parent–child relationship and to maternal responsivity (e.g., Kochanska, 1994; Kochanska & Aksan, 2004, 2006; Kochanska, Barry, Aksan, & Boldt, 2008). The emphasis in this work and others like it (e.g., Laible, 2004a, 2004b) has been on the relation between a warm, nurturing social environment and not only compliant and caring behavior in children but also the desire to comply with parental requests (Grusec & Goodnow, 1994). Indeed, caregiver responsivity is related to cooperation and compliance in young children (Holden & West, 1989; Kuczynski, Kochanska, Radke-Yarrow, & Girniss-Brown, 1987; Parpal & Maccoby, 1985), and the relation between responsivity and outcomes such as early conscience is moderated by the security of attachment in the parent–child relationship (Kochanska, Aksan, & Koenig, 1995).

Virtue is not only about self-control but also about sympathetic action for others based on empathy. Although direct linkages between parent and child empathy do not always emerge in research (Strayer & Roberts, 1989), parent empathy may be associated with particular parenting practices such as low coercive control and encouragement of emotional expressiveness, even of negative emotions. These practices, in turn, relate to higher empathy in children (Strayer & Roberts, 2004). Socialization that includes parental warmth, but also the demonstration of prosocial behavior and explicit references to the reasoning for prosocial actions, appears to be most successful in eliciting prosocial behavior in children (Yarrow, Scott, & Waxler, 1973). Moreover, parents consciously and unconsciously inform their children to whom prosocial behavior should be shown and for whom empathy should be felt. For some families, such moral attitudes are applied to a specified in-group, such as family, a religious community, or a nationality. For others, ethical obligations are understood to apply to everyone (Oliner & Oliner, 1988).

The fact that caregiving is heavily implicated in the development of moral functioning comes as no surprise. Indeed, research in child development provides many clues for the practices that make up the kind of caregiving that results in prosocial, moral functioning. Even so, the standards we currently hold for exemplary moral behavior may, in fact, be only a fraction of our capacity. Our abilities to imagine the future, and to envision long-range effects of current decisions, suggest that we could be empathizing with our great-grandchildren and regulating our current behavior so as to benefit future generations. If so, satisfaction with current levels of sociomoral functioning, if indeed we are satisfied, may be unwarranted.

Getting the Baseline Right

To aim for developmental optimization, we suggest using our *ancestral human mammalian milieu* (AHMM) as a baseline. We gather the information for the AHMM from our catarrhine mammalian heritage, which is more than 30 million years old and was modified in the context of our small band gatherer-hunter (SBGH) ancestors. The human genus is presumed to have existed in the SBGH context for over 99% of its existence (Fry, 2006). Using the AHMM as a baseline, to the extent that we can draw information from it, is a logical and systematic way of developing a theory of the conditions for optimal human development. The AHMM baseline is especially useful when considering social and moral functioning because we have anthropological and explorer reports on the social and moral functioning of SBGH groups.

In addition to its basis in our evolutionary heritage, using the behaviors of SBGHs as a baseline for optimal human development has good face validity for the development of moral functioning. Members of nomadic foraging societies are reported to have pleasant and deeply prosocial relations and communities. Interpersonal violence is rare (for a review, see Fry, 2006). Small band gatherer-hunter societies tend to be amiable and egalitarian (more closely resembling our bonobo rather than our chimpanzee cousins; de Waal & Lanting, 1998). In these contexts, acting virtuously was most effective for survival and thriving (Everett, 2009; Fry, 2006; Thomas, 2006; Turnbull, 1983). Community members who did not act virtuously were expelled. The prosocial orientations shown by individuals in these groups have parallels with those of moral exemplars, and the parenting practices they use may as well (see Oliner & Oliner, 1988). Attending to these practices offers possible avenues for facilitating the development of a society that supports optimal moral functioning.[1]

---

[1] Note, however, that once human groups became larger and more complex, they often adopted raiding behavior, much like an overgrown chimpanzee group (Wrangham & Peterson, 1996). As humans, however, we have a powerful tool unavailable to chimpanzees and other apes: our

As noted in chapter 1 in this volume, early life experience for hominids involved (1) touch, being held or kept near others constantly; (2) caregiver prompt and appropriate responses to fusses, cries, and needs; (3) breastfeeding on demand frequently (2 to 3 times/hour initially) and on average 2 to 5 years; (4) cosleeping close to caregivers; (5) multiple alloparents, that is, frequent care by individuals other than mothers (fathers and grandmothers, in particular); (6) multiage free-play groups in nature; (7) high social embeddedness; and (8) natural childbirth (see Table 12.1). Because the merit of each of these was explained in chapter 1, we will not reiterate it here, but we can name these characteristics as mammalian-consistent.

Testing the Effects of Mammalian-Consistent Care

We have hypothesized that care consistent with that of the AHMM would be important to and facilitative of optimal sociomoral development (Narvaez, 2008). To that end, in several studies with our colleagues, we have been testing the effects of mammalian-consistent care on child moral development (Narvaez, Gleason, Cheng, Wang, & Brooks, 2012; Narvaez, Gleason, Brooks, et al., 2012; Narvaez, Wang, Gleason, Cheng, & Lefever, 2012; Narvaez, Wang, Gleason, Cheng, Lefever, & Deng, 2012). For two studies, we created a measure called the Family Life Attitude and Behavior Measure (FLAM), which we gave online to a few hundred American mothers and in a paper-and-pencil version to a similar group of Chinese mothers, all of whom had 3-year-old children. The FLAM is a survey that measures maternal behaviors and attitudes toward AHMM-consistent care (frequent touch, cosleeping, frequent and lengthy breastfeeding, multiple caregivers, prompt response to fusses and cries). The questionnaire also addresses child outcomes, such as manifestations of concern, empathy, and self-regulation (from the My Child measure; Kochanska et al., 1994) and inhibitory control as measured by the Child Behavior Questionnaire (Putnam & Rothbart, 2006).

In the American sample, several AHMM components emerged as particularly important for child sociomoral outcomes. In terms of empathy, mothers' reports of the choice to breastfeed and how long they breastfed were correlated with their reports of their children's empathy. Prompt responses to fusses and cries and reports of positive touch in infancy and currently also predicted child empathy. Interestingly, attitudes about touch also predicted empathy but were mediated by touch behaviors. In other words, a mother's attitude about how and how much she

---

larger, more complex brains. Even in contexts that may push us toward aggression and war (i.e., dwindling resources), we have the option of using our extensive creativity and problem-solving skills to choose prosocial and virtuous solutions to the issues that perplex us. The motivation to use our brains in such productive ways, however, depends on the kind of caregiving and support those brains receive early in life. We contend that such nurturance is to be found in caregiving practices that acknowledge and support our evolution as mammals: those of the ancestral human mammalian milieu.

should touch her child seemed to relate directly to whether she did so, and these behaviors in turn predicted her child's empathy. Empathy was also related to mothers' reports of how close their children seemed to feel to important caregivers. This result emphasizes the role of closeness in relationships for fostering empathy in young children.

Children's inhibitory control and self-regulation were also predicted by AHMM components. Again, breastfeeding predicted higher inhibitory control, and responsivity—prompt responses to fusses and cries—and current levels of positive touch both influenced inhibitory control and self-regulation. In general, a parenting orientation that emphasizes comforting touch, breastfeeding, and responsiveness to the child's needs was associated with positive sociomoral development in this sample.

Results from the Chinese sample were quite similar but not identical to those of the American sample. For example, the choice to breastfeed was again related to empathy, but breastfeeding length was related to the child demonstrating concern after wrongdoing. Responsivity predicted empathy, just as in the US sample, but was also related to concern, as were both positive touch in infancy and current positive touch. Touch also predicted self-regulation in the Chinese children, according to maternal report.

The similarities between the results for the American and Chinese samples suggest that caregiving experiences may be related to moral outcomes, such as empathy, in ways that are minimally affected by culture. Alternatively, US and Chinese culture may overlap sufficiently such that similar parenting practices result in similar outcomes. The ways in which culture influences the dynamic interplay between AHMM components and sociomoral outcomes remains to be explored. Contextual effects may mean that differences in the goals of socialization result in different AHMM-outcome connections.

We were also interested in whether AHMM consistency in parenting practices would relate to children's observable behavior, rather than just to mothers' reports of such behavior. The behaviors we chose to examine include those that tap sociomoral development, such as self-regulation, emotion recognition, physiological regulation, and empathy. To that end, we asked a new group of 50 mothers of 3-year-old children to fill out the FLAM, and in the lab, we measured a range of child outcomes, including but not limited to, children's physiological response to stress using cortisol, and tasks measuring emotion recognition (Ribordy, Camras, Stefani, & Spaccarelli, 1988) and inhibitory control (adapted version of the Stroop task; Gerstadt, Hong, & Diamond, 1994). Mothers and children were also observed in a free-play session together, which was coded using Landry's observation measure (Landry, Smith, Miller-Loncar, & Swank, 1997). Some of the child outcomes measured using this coding scheme include social engagement and self-regulation. We are still in the process of examining these data, but a few trends are emerging. For example, mothers' warmth (as measured by Landry) was related to children's ability to recognize the emotion of sadness and to inhibitory control. Children's social engagement was predicted by the mother's ability to show responsivity to her child, and her positive affect was related to physiological functioning.

Although these analyses are far from complete, the pattern that is emerging seems to suggest a connection between AHMM-consistent parenting behaviors and components of moral development, such as self-regulation and emotion recognition. Of course, in any of our studies, not every AHMM-consistent behavior is related to every outcome. Rather, the picture emerging seems to resemble a pattern seen for physiological health in terms of micronutrients like vitamins. Each vitamin targets particular systems or processes, yet for good health one needs a complement of vitamins. Similarly, each AHMM practice may facilitate particular outcomes, yet all practices are needed for good social, emotional, physical, and moral health. Clearly, we need to do more work to tease apart the mechanisms, mediators, and moderators of these relations to understand how early experience provides the building blocks for moral behavior in early childhood, and subsequently for exemplary moral behavior in adulthood.

Effects of Early Experience on Moral Functioning in Emerging Adults

Demonstrating a connection between parenting behaviors in infancy and early life and child outcomes at age 3 is useful, but it is insufficiently persuasive evidence that early experience plays a significant role in sociomoral functioning in adulthood. Triune ethics theory (Narvaez, 2008, 2009) makes the theoretical links between the neurobiological effects of early care and moral functioning later in life. Specifically, poor early care or trauma can lead to a disposition or propensity to use a self-concerned morality (a *safety* ethic) based in primitive survival systems, which represents either an externalizing or internalizing approach to moral interactions with others. Responsive early care, as that of the AHMM, and lack of trauma lead to a fully functioning *engagement* ethic—moral attunement with others in the present moment—based in full mammalian sociality. Care consistent with the AHMM also facilitates the *imagination* ethic, the ability to abstract from the present moment, consider alternative possibilities for more moral outcomes (*communal* imagination), and guide moral action. The imagination ethic, rooted in the prefrontal cortex and related structures, can also be driven by self-protection for a *vicious* imagination focused on long-term self-aggrandizement or be completely dissociated from emotion (*detached* imagination).

One set of evidence for triune ethics theory comes from attachment research in adolescents and adults. Those whose poor early care leaves them with overreactive stress response systems are more likely to experience personal distress instead of compassionate concern when under stressful interpersonal situations (Mikulincer & Shaver, 2008). Laboratory priming studies show that those who are primed for insecurity are less compassionate toward those in need (Mikulincer & Shaver, 2005). Further studies have examined the theoretical predictions of triune ethics theory.

For example, Narvaez, Brooks, and Hardy (2012) found that insecure attachment was related to favoring a safety ethical mindset, poor perspective taking, and low empathy. Secure attachment was related to agreeable personality, empathy, preference for an engagement ethical mindset, and a humanistic worldview. Engagement identity also strongly predicted integrity and moral action for the less fortunate. These findings are a first step toward demonstrating a more direct link between early experience and adult moral functioning.

Low Standards and Suboptimality

Right now, US culture has accepted low standards for childrearing as normative. This adoption of poor-quality care as normative appears to be grounded in three perspectives. First, it is undergirded by widespread cultural beliefs in children's resilience. After all, children survive and continue to develop in war zones and orphanages with minimal care, so that by comparison, low-quality daycare seems hardly problematic. These stressful conditions, however, compromise development in ways we are only beginning to understand (see, e.g., the NICHD Study of Early Child Care findings related to poor-quality care). Moreover, success in studies of resilience is not typically identified as empathy or social responsibility so much as graduation from high school and avoidance of incarceration. Second, the low standards currently held for childrearing are accepted because of the belief that children successfully adapt to their poor conditions (see Belsky, this volume). These adaptive behaviors, described and measured using partial evolutionary criteria—in which "success" is defined solely as reproducing a child[2]—hardly reflect well-being or a thriving life. Third, as understanding of the genetic roots of behavior has gradually increased, the belief that genes actually, and uniquely, control behavior has gained strength in the popular press. For example, when babies who died of sudden infant death syndrome were discovered to be more likely to have a deficit in serotonin receptors, researchers and reporters discussed this problem as genetic (Talan, 2010), rather than considering the epigenetics of serotonin receptor construction from breast milk and from touch (Lien, 2003). In short, these positions are exaggerated, if not completely wrong.

All development happens in a context, influencing gene expression, and during sensitive periods shaping personality, cognition, and social functioning. The phenotypes that are associated with particular genotypes are influenced by the confluence of events that surround their emergence. The same genotype can result in a range of phenotypes depending on the timing, intensity, and duration of environmental

---

[2] Although reproduction is often seen as a proxy for genetic success, determining actual genetic success is more complicated and requires a comparison with the success of the competition in terms of relative fertility and the success of offspring over several generations (see Lewontin, 2010).

effects (Oyama, 2000). However, it is our position that children with extreme insecure attachment (e.g., disorganized)—who demonstrate anger, alienation, aggression, and low empathy—are suffering much like Harry Harlow's (Harlow, Dodsworth, & Harlow, 1965) isolated monkeys. Their antisocial characteristics represent mammals who are neurobiologically damaged and emotionally undernourished. Even within the "normal" ranges of personality differences, we wonder if the phenotypic ranges have grown too large or become skewed from the effects of poor early care on neurobiology. The increase in psychopathology in US society may be owing to suboptimal support in early life, when the brain and body systems are built, given that early stressors are not easily remedied but have lasting effects on brain and behavior (Lupien et al., 2009).

What is the current context for families? Several societal indicators, such as the consistent rise in rates of psychopathology and actual data on stress experience from families (American Psychological Association, 2010), suggest that stress has become characteristic of far too many family environments. Caregivers need time and support to be responsive (Hrdy, 2009). The US society puts children in stressful environments that foster self-protective responses—detachment from others and vigilance for threats. Evidence clearly shows that stress-reactive brains, fostered by early stress experiences or lack of support, are less able to use their more relational and abstracting functions (e.g., Henry & Wang, 1998; Mirescu & Gould, 2006). In other words, stress can make you stupid over the short or long term (Sapolsky, 2004).

For all the reasons we have mentioned thus far, we surmise that Western brains are not developing optimally. In other words, from an evolutionary perspective, Westerners (or at least typically those from the United States) are neither optimal nor normal specimens (but this does not mean they have not been successful in reproducing with all the societal supports for child*bearing*, in contrast to child*rearing*, such as care for premature infants).

Epigenetics and Culture

Among our ancestors, survival would have been virtually impossible without the early life AHMM characteristics that foster secure attachment and the neurobiology that underpins it. For example, not breastfeeding would have led to early death, as would a lack of sociality (learned partly through play) or a lack of deep connection with the natural environment (see Gray, this volume). Very unlikely would have been a lack of touch, as social mammals die or become defective, nonreproductive adults if given only custodial, but no emotionally responsive, care (Bowlby, 1979). Being nonresponsive to a child would have been risky to the whole troop. Raising children with insecure attachment and the faulty neurobiology that accompanies it would have been dangerous for all concerned. Parenting consistent with the AHMM is vital for human well-being, and its absence represents a thwarting of fixed evolved practices that led to greater fitness long ago (see Narvaez, in press, for further discussion).

What catapulted humans into evolutionary success may, in fact, have been their *prosocial* and *cooperative* skills—particularly their ability to cooperate successfully in caring for their children (Hrdy, 2009; Roughgarden, 2009). Even today, one can distinguish between peaceful, prosocial cultures and more violent cultures by their childrearing practices; peaceful cultures practice AHMM-consistent parenting (Kemp & Fry, 2004; Montagu, 1978; Prescott, 1996). Cultures consistent with the AHMM also emphasize cultural narratives that lead to more peaceful behavior. Consideration of the AHMM context as a whole may be useful in our understanding of the development of morality and of moral exemplars.

A developmental optimization view takes the parenting of the long-standing AHMM as the evolutionary framework for developing optimal sociomoral functioning and offers a way to structure research. Within the AHMM framework, researchers can examine the specific effects of developmental timing for particular caregiving practices and their effects on later outcomes. Outcomes, shaped by epigenetic and developmental effects, include not only emotion and regulation systems and the human moral personality that results but also mental, physical, and social health.

Conclusion

Current Western human nature and culture are abnormal in terms of world history and world cultures (Sahlins, 2008), and yet conclusions about human nature and normal functioning are drawn regularly from studies of its members (Heinrich, Heine, & Norenzayan, 2010). If we accept Western culture as normal, then humans are on a fast train to self-demise. After all, Western culture is notably destroying humanity's habitat (Merchant, 2003). However, if we step back and examine the range of human characteristics, including social and individual characteristics, we can find evidence for societies that lived sustainably and peaceably for thousands of years (Fry, 2006; Lawlor, 1991). If we attend to their social and family practices, we may be able to restore some sensibility to our own childrearing practices, social structures, and supports for families, even within the aberrant constraints of modern Western culture, and thereby foster greater holistic intelligence.

Acknowledgments

The first author acknowledges the support of the Spencer Foundation and the University of Notre Dame Institute for Scholarship in the Liberal Arts. The second author acknowledges the Brachman-Hoffman Small Grants from Wellesley College.

We thank Douglas Fry and Margery Lucas for their comments on earlier drafts.

References

Als, H. (1982). Toward a syntactive theory of development: Promise for the assessment and support of infant individuality. *Infant Mental Health Journal, 3*, 229–243.

American Psychological Association. (2010). *Stress in America.* Washington, DC: American Psychological Association.

Bloch, A. (2006). *Deconstructing the American mythology: Revisionist Westerns and U.S. history.* Williamstown, MA: Williams College.

Bowlby, J. (1979). On knowing what you are not supposed to know and feeling what you are not supposed to feel. *The Canadian Journal of Psychiatry/La Revue canadienne de psychiatrie, 24*(5), 403–408.

Cacioppo, J. T., & Patrick, W. (2008). *Loneliness: Human nature and the need for social connection.* New York, NY: W. W. Norton.

Callahan, D. (2004). *The cheating culture: Why more Americans are doing wrong to get ahead.* New York, NY: Harcourt Harvest.

Cannell, J. J., Hollis, B. W., Zasloff, M., & Heaney, R. P. (2008). Diagnosis and treatment of vitamin D deficiency. *Expert Opinion Pharmacology, 9*(1), 1–12.

Colby, A., & Damon, W. (1991). *Some do care.* New York, NY: Free Press.

Collins, W., Gleason, T., & Sesma, A. R. (1997). Internalization, autonomy, and relationships: Development during adolescence. In J. E. Grusec, & L. Kuczynski (Eds.), *Parenting and children's internalization of values: A handbook of contemporary theory* (pp. 78–99). Hoboken, NJ: John Wiley & Sons.

Connor, D. F. (2002). *Aggression and antisocial behavior in children and adolescents.* New York, NY: Guilford Press.

Darwin, C. (1871/1981). *The descent of man.* Princeton, NJ: Princeton University Press.

De Bellis, M. D. (2010). The neurobiology of child neglect. In R. A. Lanius, E. Vermetten, & C. Pain (Eds.), *The impact of early life trauma on health an disease* (pp. 123–141). Cambridge: Cambridge University Press.

De Waal, F., & Lanting, F. (1998). *Bonobo: The forgotten ape.* Berkeley, CA: University of California Press.

Dentan, R. K. (1968). *The Semai: A nonviolent people of Malaya.* New York, NY: Harcourt Brace College Publishers.

Diamond, J. (1997). *Guns, germs and steel: The fates of human societies.* New York, NY: Norton.

Egeland, J. A. (1983). Bipolarity: The iceberg of affective disorders? *Comprehensive Psychiatry, 24*(4), 337–344. doi:10.1016/0010–440X(83)90062–90067

Eisenberg, N. (2000). Emotion, regulation, and moral development. *Annual Review of Psychology, 51*, 665–697.

Erickson, M., & Crichton, L. (1981). Antecedents of compliance in 2-year-olds from a high-risk sample. Paper presented at the biennial meeting of the Society for Research in Child Development, Boston, MA.

Evans, C. A., & Porter, C. L. (2009). The emergence of mother-infant co-regulation during the first year: Links to infants' developmental status and attachment. *Infant Behavior and Development, 32*(2), 147–158. doi:10.1016/j.infbeh.2008.12.005

Everett, D. L. (2009). *Don't sleep, there are snakes: Life and language in the Amazonian jungle.* New York, NY: Pantheon.

Federal Bureau of Investigation. (2010). *Crime in the United States* [Data File]. Retrieved from http://www.fbi.gov/stats-services/publications/reports__and__publications

Feldman, R., Greenbaum, C. W., & Yirmiya, N. (1999). Mother–infant affect synchrony as an antecedent of the emergence of self-control. *Developmental Psychology, 35*(1), 223–231. doi:10.1037/0012–1649.35.1.223

Fogel, A. (2000). Developmental pathways in close relationships. *Child Development, 71*(5), 1150–1151. doi:10.1111/1467–8624.00217

Fogel, A., & Branco, A. (1997). Metacommunication as a source of indeterminism in relationship development. In A. Fogel, M. P. Lyra, J. Valsiner, A. Fogel, M. P. Lyra, & J. Valsiner (Eds.), *Dynamics and indeterminism in developmental and social processes* (pp. 65–92). Hillsdale, England: Lawrence Erlbaum Associates.

Frimer, J. A., Walker, L. J., Dunlop, W. L., Lee, B. H., & Riches, A. (2011). The integration of agency and communion in moral personality: Evidence of enlightened self-interest. *Journal of Personality and Social Psychology, 101*(1), 149–163.

Fry, D. P. (2006). *The human potential for peace: An anthropological challenge to assumptions about war and violence.* New York, NY: Oxford University Press.

Gerstadt, C. L., Hong, Y., & Diamond, A. (1994). The relationship between cognition and action: Performance of children 3 1/2–7 years old on a Stroop-like day-night test. *Cognition, 53*(2), 129–153. doi:10.1016/0010–0277(94)90068-X

Gilliam, W. S. (2005). *Prekindergarteners left behind: Expulsion rates in state prekindergarten systems.* New Haven, CT: Yale University Child Study Center.

Grühn, D., Rebucal, K., Diehl, M., Lumley, M., & Labouvie-Vief, G. (2008). Empathy across the adult lifespan: Longitudinal and experience-sampling findings. *Emotion, 8*(6), 753–765. doi:10.1037/a0014123

Grusec, J. E., & Goodnow, J. J. (1994). Summing up and looking to the future. *Developmental Psychology, 30*(1), 29–31. doi:10.1037/0012–1649.30.1.29

Gunnar, M. R., Larson, M. C., Hertsgaard, L., Harris, M. L., & Brodersen, L. (1992). The stressfulness of separation among nine-month-old infants: Effects of social context variables and infant temperament. *Child Development, 63*(2), 290–303. doi:10.2307/1131479

Harlow, H. F., Dodsworth, R. O., & Harlow, M. K. (1965). Total social isolation in monkeys. *Proceedings of the National Academy of Sciences, 54*(1), 90–97.

Hartup, W. W. (1983). Peer groups. In P. H. Mussen (Gen Ed.), *Handbook of child psychology* (Vol. 4, pp. 103–196). New York, NY: Wiley.

Hartup, W. W. (1991). Social development and social psychology: Perspectives on interpersonal relationships. In J. H. Cantor, C. C. Spiker, L. Lipsitt, J. H. Cantor, C. C. Spiker, & L. Lipsitt (Eds.), *Child behavior and development: Training for diversity* (pp. 1–33). Westport, CT: Ablex Publishing.

Heinrich, J., Heine, S. J., & Norenzayan, A., (2010). *The weirdest people in the world?* RatSWD Working Paper No. 139. Retrieved from SSRN, http://ssrn.com/abstract==1601785

Henry, J. P., & Wang, S. (1998). Effects of early stress on adult affiliative behavior. *Psychoneuroendocrinology, 23*(8), 863–875. doi:10.1016/S0306–4530(98)00058-4

Hoffman, M. (2000). *Empathy and moral development: Implications for caring and justice.* New York, NY: Cambridge University Press.

Holden, G. W., & West, M. J. (1989). Proximate regulation by mothers: A demonstration of how differing styles affect young children's behavior. *Child Development, 60*, 64–69.

Hrdy, S. B. (2009). *Mothers and others: The evolutionary origins of mutual understanding.* Cambridge, MA: Harvard University Press.

Jablonka, E., & Lamb, M. J. (2006). The evolution of information in the major transitions. *Journal of Theoretical Biology, 239*(2), 236–246.

Johnson, B. (2009). New U.S. Census to reveal major shift: No more Joe Consumer. Ad Age White Paper 2010: America uncovers the marketing implications. *Advertising Age,* October 12. Retrieved November 28, 2010, from http://adage.com/article/news/ad-age-white-paper-joe-consumer-america/139592/

Karrass, J., & Walden, T. A. (2005). Effects of nurturing and non-nurturing caregiving on child social initiatives: An experimental investigation of emotion as a mediator of social behavior. *Social Development, 14*(4), 685–700. doi:10.1111/j.1467–9507.2005.00324.x

Kemp, G., & Fry, D. (Eds.). (2004). *Keeping the peace: Conflict resolution and peaceful societies around the world.* New York, NY: Routledge.

Kochanska, G. (1994). Beyond cognition: Expanding the search for the early roots of internalization and conscience. *Developmental Psychology, 30*(1), 20–22. doi:10.1037/0012–1649.30.1.20

Kochanska, G. (2002). Mutually responsive orientation between mothers and their young children: A context for the early development of conscience. *Current Directions in Psychological Science, 11*(6), 191–195. doi:10.1111/1467–8721.00198

Kochanska, G., & Aksan, N. (2004). Conscience in childhood: Past, present, and future. *Merrill-Palmer Quarterly: Journal of Developmental Psychology, 50*(3), 299–310. doi:10.1353/mpq.2004.0020

Kochanska, G., & Aksan, N. (2006). Children's conscience and self-regulation. *Journal of Personality, 74*(6), 1587–1617. doi:10.1111/j.1467–6494.2006.00421.x

Kochanska, G., Aksan, N., & Koenig, A. L. (1995). A longitudinal study of the roots of preschoolers' conscience: Committed compliance and emerging internalization. *Child Development, 66,* 1752–1769.

Kochanska, G., Barry, R. A., Aksan, N., & Boldt, L. J. (2008). A developmental model of maternal and child contributions to disruptive conduct: The first six years. *Journal of Child Psychology and Psychiatry, 49*(11), 1220–1227.

Kochanska, G., DeVet, K., Goldman, M., & Murray, K. (1994). Maternal reports of conscience development and temperament in young children. *Child Development, 65*(3), 852–868. doi:10.2307/1131423

Konrath, S., O'Brien, E. H., & Hsing, C. (2011). Changes in dispositional empathy over time in college students: A meta-analysis. *Personality and Social Psychology Review, 15,* 180–198.

Kuczynski, L., Kochanska, G., Radke-Yarrow, M., & Girniss-Brown, D. (1987). A developmental interpretation of young children's noncompliance. *Developmental Psychology, 23,* 1–8.

Laible, D. (2004a). Mother-child discourse in two contexts: Links with child temperament, attachment security, and socioemotional competence. *Developmental Psychology, 40*(6), 979–992. doi:10.1037/0012–1649.40.6.979

Laible, D. J. (2004b). Mother-child discourse surrounding a child's past behavior at 30 months: Links to emotional understanding and early conscience development at 36 months. *Merrill-Palmer Quarterly: Journal of Developmental Psychology, 50*(2), 159–180. doi:10.1353/mpq.2004.0013

Landry, S. H., Smith, K. E., Miller-Loncar, C. L., & Swank, P. R. (1997). Predicting cognitive-language and social growth curves from early maternal behaviors in children at varying degrees of biological risk. *Developmental Psychology, 33*, 1040–1053.

Lanius, R. A., Vermetten, E., & Pain, C. (Eds.) (2010). *The impact of early life trauma on health and disease: The hidden epidemic.* New York, NY: Cambridge University Press.

Lawlor, R. (1991). *Voices of the first day.* Rochester, VT: Inner Traditions International.

Lewontin, R. (2010). Response to comment on Not So Natural Selection from the May 27, 2010 issue. *New York Review of Books,* May 27.

Lien, E. L. (2003). Infant formulas with increased concentrations of α-lactalbumin. *American Journal of Clinical Nutrition, 77(6)*, 1555S–1558S.

Lupien, S. J., McEwen, B. S., Gunnar, M. R., & Heim, C. (2009). Effects of stress throughout the lifespan on the brain, behaviour and cognition. *Nature Reviews Neuroscience, 10*(6), 434–445. doi:10.1038/nrn2639

Merchant, C. (2003). *Reinventing Eden: The fate of nature in Western culture.* New York, NY: Routledge.

Mikulincer, M., & Shaver, P. R. (2005). Attachment security, compassion, and altruism. *Current Directions in Psychological Science, 14*(1), 34–38. doi:10.1111/j.0963-7214.2005.00330.x

Mikulincer, M., & Shaver, P. R. (2008). Adult attachment and affect regulation. In J. Cassidy, P. R. Shaver, J. Cassidy, & P. R. Shaver (Eds.), *Handbook of attachment: Theory, research, and clinical applications* (2nd ed., pp. 503–531). New York, NY: Guilford Press.

Mirescu, C., & Gould, E. (2006). Stress and adult neurogenesis. *Hippocampus, 16*, 233–238.

Montagu, A. (1978). *Learning nonaggression: The experience of non-literate societies.* New York, NY: Oxford University Press.

Mooney, J., & Young, J. (2006). The decline in crime and the rise of anti-social behaviour. *Probation Journal, 53*(4), 397–407. doi:10.1177/0264550506069364

Moore, G. A., Hill-Soderlund, A. L., Propper, C. B., Calkins, S. D., Mills-Koonce, W. R., & Cox, M. J. (2009). Mother-infant vagal regulation in the face-to-face still-face paradigm is moderated by maternal sensitivity. *Child Development, 80*, 209–223.

Morris, A., Silk, J. S., Steinberg, L., Myers, S. S., & Robinson, L. (2007). The role of the family context in the development of emotion regulation. *Social Development, 16*(2), 361–388. doi:10.1111/j.1467–9507.2007.00389.x

Narvaez, D. (2008). Triune ethics: The neurobiological roots of our multiple moralities. *New Ideas in Psychology, 26*, 95–119.

Narvaez, D. (2009). Triune ethics theory and moral personality. In D. Narvaez & D. K. Lapsley (Eds.), *Personality, identity and character: Explorations in moral psychology* (pp. 136–158). New York, NY: Cambridge University Press.

Narvaez, D. (in press). *The neurobiology and development of human morality.* New York: W.W. Norton.

Narvaez, D., Brooks, J., & Hardy, S. (2012). *A multidimensional approach to moral identity: Early life experience, prosocial personality, and moral outcomes.* Manuscript submitted for publication.

Narvaez, D., Gleason, T., Brooks, J., Wang, L., Lefever, J., Cheng, A., & Centers for the Prevention of Child Neglect. (2012). *Longitudinal effects of ancestral parenting practices on early childhood outcomes.* Manuscript submitted for publication.

Narvaez, D., Gleason, T., Cheng, A., Wang, L., & Brooks, J. (2012). *Nurturing parenting attitudes influence moral character and flourishing in three-year-olds.* Manuscript submitted for publication.

Narvaez, D., Wang, L., Gleason, T., Cheng, Y., & Lefever, J. (2012). *The ancestral early caregiving environment and child social, cognitive, and moral outcomes at age three.* Manuscript submitted for publication.

Narvaez, D., Wang, L., Gleason, T., Cheng, A., Lefever, J., & Deng, L. (2012). *Ancestral parenting practices and child outcomes in Chinese three-year-olds.* Manuscript submitted for publication.

Oliner, S. P., & Oliner, P. M. (1988). *The altruistic personality: Rescuers of Jews in Nazi Europe.* New York, NY: Free Press.

Oyama, S. (2000). *The ontogeny of information: Developmental systems and evolution (2nd ed.).* Raleigh, NC: Duke University Press.

Parpal, M., & Maccoby, E. E. (1985). Maternal responsiveness and subsequent child compliance. *Child Development, 56,* 1326–1334.

Prescott, J. W. (1996). The origins of human love and violence. *Journal of Prenatal & Perinatal Psychology & Health, 10*(3), 143–188.

Porges, S. W., & Carter, C. (2010). Neurobiological bases of social behavior across the life span. In M. E. Lamb, A. M. Freund, & R. M. Lerner (Eds.), *The handbook of life-span development. Vol 2: Social and emotional development* (pp. 9–50). Hoboken, NJ: John Wiley & Sons.

Powell, D., Fixen, D., & Dunlop, G. (2003). *Pathways to service utilization: A synthesis of evidence relevant to young children with challenging behavior.* Tampa, FL: University of South Florida, Center for Evidence-based Practice: Young Children with Challenging Behavior.

Putnam, S. P., & Rothbart, M. K. (2006). Development of short and very short forms of the Children's Behavior Questionnaire. *Journal of Personality Assessment, 87,* 103–113.

Ribordy, S. C., Camras, L. A., Stefani, R., & Spaccarelli, S. (1988). Vignettes for emotion recognition research and affective therapy with children. *Journal of Clinical Child Psychology, 17*(4), 322–325. doi:10.1207/s15374424jccp1704__4

Roughgarden, J. (2009). *The genial gene: Deconstructing Darwinian selfishness.* Berkeley, CA: University of California Press.

Sahlins, M. (2008). *The Western illusion of human nature.* Chicago, IL: Prickly Paradigm Press.

Sapolsky, R. (2004). *Why zebras don't get ulcers* (3rd ed.). New York, NY: Holt.

Schore, A. N. (2001). Effects of a secure attachment relationship on right brain development, affect regulation, and infant mental health. *Infant Mental Health Journal, 22*(1–2), 7–66. doi:10.1002/1097–0355(200101/04)22:1<7:AID-IMHJ2>3.0.CO;2-N

Schulkin, J. (1999). *The neuroendocrine regulation of behavior.* New York, NY: Cambridge University Press.

Siegel, D. (1999). *The developing mind: How relationships and the brain interact to shape who we are.* New York, NY: Guilford Press.

Spangler, G., & Grossmann K. E. (1993). Biobehavioral organization in securely and insecurely attached infants. *Child Development, 64,* 1439–1450.

Spangler, G., Schieche, M., Ilg, U., & Maier, U. (1994). Maternal sensitivity as an external organizer for biobehavioral regulation in infancy. *Developmental Psychobiology, 27*(7), 425–437. doi:10.1002/dev.420270702

Sroufe, L. (1996). *Emotional development: The organization of emotional life in the early years*. New York, NY: Cambridge University Press.

Sroufe, A., & Fleeson, J. (1986). Attachment and the construction of relationships. In W. Hartup & Z. Rubin (Eds.), *Relationships and development*. Hillsdale, NJ: L. Erlbaum.

Strayer, J., & Roberts, W. (1989). Children's empathy and role taking: Child and parental factors, and relations to prosocial behavior. *Journal of Applied Developmental Psychology, 10*(2), 227–239. doi:10.1016/0193-3973(89)90006–90003

Strayer, J., & Roberts, W. (2004). Children's anger, emotional expressiveness, and empathy: Relations with parents' empathy, emotional expressiveness, and parenting practices. *Social Development, 13*(2), 229–254. doi:10.1111/j.1467–9507.2004.000265.x

Talan, J. (2010). Serotonin abnormalities confirmed in sudden infant death. *Neurology Today, 10*(5), 14–15. doi:10.1097/01.NT.0000369546.51954.32. Retrieved February 10, 2011, from http://journals.lww.com/neurotodayonline/Fulltext/2010/03040/Serotonin__Abnormalities__Confirmed__in__Sudden__Infant.5.aspx

Thoma, S. J., & Bebeau, M. (2008). *Moral judgment competency is declining over time: Evidence from 20 years of defining issues test data*. Paper presented to the American Educational Research Association, New York, NY.

Thomas, E. M. (2006). *The old way: A story of the first people*. New York, NY: Sarah Crichton Books.

Turkle, S. (2011). *Alone together: Why we expect more from technology and less from each other*. New York, NY: Basic Books.

Turnbull, C. M. (1983). *The human cycle*. New York, NY: Simon and Schuster.

Walker, H. (1993). Antisocial behavior in school. *Journal of Emotional and Behavioral Problems, 2*(1), 20–24.

Walker, L. J. (1999). The family context for moral development. *Journal of Moral Education, 28*(3), 261–264. doi:10.1080/030572499103061

Walker, L. J., & Frimer, J. A. (2008). Being good for goodness' sake: Transcendence in the lives of moral heroes. In F. K. Oser & W. M. M. H. Veugelers (Eds.), *Getting involved: Global citizenship development and sources of moral values* (pp. 309–326). Rotterdam, The Netherlands: Sense Publishers.

Walker, L. J., & Frimer, J. A. (2009). Moral personality exemplified. In D. Narvaez & D. K. Lapsley (Eds.), *Personality, identity, and character: Explorations in moral psychology* (pp. 232–255). New York, NY: Cambridge University Press.

Wrangham, R. W., & Peterson, D. (1996). *Demonic males: Apes and the origins of human violence*. Boston, MA: Houghton, Mifflin and Company.

Yarrow, M. R., Scott, P. M., & Waxler, C. Z. (1973). Learning concern for others. *Developmental Psychology, 8*(2), 240–260. doi:10.1037/h0034159

{ Commentary }

Darwin et al. on Developmental Optimization
David Loye

Darwin would have been delighted with this splendid update for the work of so many of his aspirational offspring. Through intensive work over a decade I've found that if we look carefully into what Darwin (2004) actually wrote in many long ignored pages in *The Descent of Man*, we can see the original spark of observation or insight later to gain expansion and definition in the work of Bowlby, Erickson, Damon, Rest, de Waal, Harlow, Hoffman, Lewontin, Narvaez, Oliner, Schore, Yarrow, and many others whose work is so effectively identified in this vital integrative chapter.

The cross-multigenerational link between Darwin and us is perhaps most striking in the case of Darwin's long ignored emphasis on the correlates of love and moral sensitivity as the prime "higher agencies," which on page 403, *Descent*, first edition, and page 531, second edition, he specifically states take over as the "struggle for existence" (i.e., natural selection) drops in significance with the emergence of our species. This contention I found strikingly borne out with a computerized word count. Wholly contrary to the prevailing impression, where he wrote only twice of "survival of the fittest"—once to apologize for ever using the term—he writes 95 times of love and 92 times of moral sensitivity (Loye, 2004, 2010).

In pursuit of this first glimpse into the reality of the "other Darwin," I found that at most of the places in the original text where he writes of love or moral sensitivity he is further foreshadowing the work of his 20th- and 21st-century aspirational offspring. In most of the 95 places where he writes of love, for example, the focus is on nestling, caring, and nurturing of the child in a vast range of animals (including humans in the case of his own children, William and Annie). Likewise, in the 92 places for moral sensitivity, the focus is on instances of how this treatment of the child leads to adult caring for and acting on the behalf of others (Loye, 2010).

Where both Darwin and the authors of this chapter are headed with this neglected path is deeply meaningful and thought provoking. There are profound directions and undertones here.

For example, for both Darwin and Narvaez and Gleason, in the end the basic question is not just what optimizes moral development of the individual, on which the bulk of work in this area is focused, but how this level of concern relates to national and global moral development, and indeed, eventually the question of survival of the species.

In the case of individual moral development, the vital question raised is whether we can identify an "innate" set of early child-raising practices for optimizing human development—that is, a quasi-instinctual regimen for parents in a sense both prior to culture and cross-culturally held in common. In *Descent* and in *Expression of Emotion in Humans and Animals* (Darwin, 1998), and in by now scores of modern studies, can be found the supportive data. Implications here move on up in scale to the focus of, for example, Maslow's (1993) classic study of self-actualizers as moral exemplars and the trend thereafter for humanistic and positive psychology, or in the global ethic "movement" highlighted by the work of theologian Hans Kung (1996) and the development of the Global Sounding measure of human well-being and companion moral code I explore in *Measuring Evolution* (Loye, 2007).

In the case of national moral development, Narvaez and Gleason focus concern on the really rather horrifying hard body of current data showing that, contrary to what scores of blithe optimists believe, to an alarming degree, we are headed backward and downward in America.

This concern further underlines the question they raise about global development—and thereby the evolutionary course for our species—of the abnormality of the nature, priorities, and current track for Western culture (and this the best of choice, I feel compelled to add).

They get into this by noting the blindsided nature of research based just on studies of members of the prevailing culture—or us as we are today. I've been struck, for example, by finding the following pattern running through much research (e.g., Loye 2004; Piaget, 1997) and educational practice (e.g., Montessori, 1995; Seldin & Epstein, 2003). One finds a rough consensus for step-by-step advance during early childhood, which falls apart with the move on to the adult level—as tragically demonstrated by what happened to Kohlberg with the original Kohlberg Scale. In other words, we often seem to be on the right track with children hypothetically least yet shaped by the prevailing culture. But the hope falls apart as through the teens into adulthood the once hopeful child comes steadily under the barrage of steadily degrading cultural influence. "If we accept Western culture as normal, then humans are on a fast train to self-demise," Narvaez and Gleason write—a conclusion with which out of practically everything I have observed and written of over the past decade I heartily agree.

What's to be done? Narvaez and Gleason cut to the wisdom core of Darwin's original insight with their subhead "Getting the Baseline Right." Researchers gasping with overload, reluctant to consider one more seemingly alien database, may balk, but a widening body of study indicates Narvaez and Gleason are dead right in their conclusion that the baseline for saving us lies in the deep past and correlated subcultures today. They point to the emergent body of anthropological research showing the relation of the child-raising practices of our hunter-gatherer ancestors to the kind of adult outcomes we hope for and despair of gaining globally in modern life: an overwhelmingly amiable, egalitarian people, with a low degree of interpersonal violence and a high degree of moral sensitivity. They develop a measure for assessing moderns for favorable outcomes for this ancient ancestral child-raising regimen and find agreement with American and Chinese samples. By further probing the link in terms of Narvaez's exceptionally well-grounded triune ethics theory, they bring the correlative power of modern brain research into the picture with compelling results.

This bold opening of new territory for advancing the cause of developmental optimization, I suggest, can be greatly strengthened with attention to a still larger emergent body of research into the best baseline for us in the deep past. Integrating an extensive body of archeological, anthropological, and other studies bearing on the nature of the first step up from the hunter-gatherer stage into the peaceful, egalitarian, and highly creative first mass experiments in civilization—this is the work of cultural evolution theorist Riane Eisler (1987, 2000) and others identifying the developmental impact of partnership versus domination systems. Here again is a case of a replication in China (Min Jiayin, 1995, thereby hypothetically for Asia generally) of a model based on Western cultural work.

References

Darwin, C. (1998). *Expression of emotion in man and animals* (3rd ed.). New York: Oxford University Press.

Darwin, C. (2004). *The descent of man* (2nd ed.). London: Penguin.

Eisler, R. (1987). *The chalice and the blade: Our history, our future.* San Francisco, CA: Harper & Row.

Eisler, R. (2000). *Tomorrow's children: A blueprint for partnership education in the 21st century.* Boulder, CO: Westview Press.

Jiayin, M. (Ed.). (1995). *The chalice and the blade in chinese culture.* Beijing: China Social Sciences Publishing House.

Kung, H. (Ed.). (1996). *Yes to a global ethic.* New York, NY: Continuum.

Loye, D. Darwin, Maslow, and the fully human theory of evolution. In Loye, D. (Ed.). (2004). *The great adventure: Toward a fully human theory of evolution.* Albany: State University of New York Press.

Loye, D. (2007b). *Measuring evolution.* Carmel, CA: Benjamin Franklin Press.

Loye, D. (2010). *Darwin's lost theory: A bridge to the better world.* Carmel, CA: Benjamin Franklin Press.

Maslow, A. (1993). *The farther reaches of human nature.* New York, NY: Penguin.

Montessori, M. (1995). *The absorbent mind.* New York, NY: Holt.

Piaget, J. (1997). *The moral judgement of the child.* New York, NY: Free Press.

Seldin, T., & Epstein, P. (2003). *The Montessori way: An education for life.* Rockville, MD: Montessori Foundation Press.

Adaptations and Adaptations
Ross A. Thompson

The characteristics of early care that our hominid ancestors experienced have been a topic of continuing interest to those concerned with the emergence of human capacities. According to Narvaez and Gleason (this volume), early experience during our long species history typically included the following:

- Being touched, held, and kept near other people constantly, beginning from birth
- Caregiver prompt and appropriate responsiveness, particularly to fussing or crying that may signal danger or threat
- Breastfeeding on demand, resulting in frequent daily breastfeeding lasting on average for 2 to 5 years
- Cosleeping with caregivers
- Multiple alloparents, which may include older female kin (such as grandmothers and sisters) and fathers
- Play in peer groups with children of various ages
- Living in social groups (i.e., high social embeddedness)
- Natural childbirth

These are the characteristics most commonly associated with scientists' portrayals of the evolutionary heritage of humans. Although there is lively scholarly debate about how best to define the functional characteristics of the environment in which humans evolved and whether not one but several environments of human adaptation need to be analyzed (see Ball and Russell, this volume), it is nevertheless possible to proceed on the assumption that most, if not all, of these characteristics were likely to have been true of the early experience of our hominid ancestors.

Why is it important to understand early experience in the context of the physical ecology of human adaptation? One obvious answer is anthropological interest: Understanding the conditions affecting human evolutionary adaptation is important for its own sake. Its study advances Darwinian theory for the insights it offers into the selective pressures influencing the evolutionary development of the human species.

Often, however, scholars are interested in the physical ecology of human adaptation because of beliefs concerning its relevance to contemporary human behavior. It is not only that we exhibit the legacy of the adaptive processes shaping human evolution for millions of years, they argue, but also that the attributes of early human experience during these millennia are what humans are currently prepared for. To the extent that contemporary cultural patterns of early human care depart markedly from the adaptive practices that characterized our species during the large majority of our existence, they risk creating conditions that are inappropriate and potentially maladaptive for optimal human development to occur.

Such a view requires an incisive analysis of what is meant by the term *adaptation* and delineating its multiple meanings. It also renews provocative and important questions concerning the enduring impact of early experiences in human ontogenesis and their relevance to developmental evolutionary ecology. These are the issues profiled in this commentary.

Multiple Meanings of "Adaptation"

Viewed within the context of evolutionary theory, there are at least three kinds of "adaptation" in early childhood development that must be distinguished (see Bjorklund, 1997, 2007; Lamb, Thompson, Gardner, & Charnov, 1985).

The first, sometimes called *deferred adaptation*, is the most common way of thinking of evolutionary adaption in relation to childhood. It consists of the multiple ways that childhood experience is preparation for adulthood, and the evolved processes by which this occurs. Examples of deferred adaptations include childhood play as the preparatory rehearsal of adult skills and roles; the development of behavioral sex differences that anticipate adult differences in reproduction and parenting; the acquisition of language, cognitive, and behavioral skills that contribute to mature functioning; and many others. Deferred adaptations are thus relevant to the development of constructive adult capacities, and significant disruption of these processes in childhood risks rendering the adult less capable or competent.

The second kind of adaptation is called *ontogenetic adaptation,* and it has a significantly different function. Ontogenetic adaptations are those that facilitate the child's growth to maturity but do not necessarily have significant longer term implications for adult functioning. There are many ontogenetic adaptations in the early years, some associated with nursing, others with self-protection (such as fears of strangers and of separation in infancy), and others with social bonding. In each case, they function to ensure that the young of the species survive to reproductive maturity, but may have no enduring life span significance. Under species-typical circumstances, for example, newborn reflexes, stranger anxiety, or neonatal social imitation do not foreshadow adult competencies, even those that are phenotypically similar (such as imitative behavior later in life).

It is important to distinguish these two kinds of evolutionary adaptations, and also to distinguish them from *psychological adaptation,* which concerns the ontogenetic development of behavioral competence and psychological health. Most developmental research is concerned with adaptations of this kind that lead to constructive developmental accomplishments, and whether these are achieved depends on a variety of influences from the social environment, biological processes, and the child.

The challenge of developmental evolutionary ecology is specifying what kinds of adaptational processes are relevant to the characteristics of care in the environment(s) in which humans evolved. This requires a thoughtful analysis of the adaptational functions served by different practices. The importance of being held or kept near others almost continuously may have served, for example, as a means of protecting helpless offspring against predation or inadvertent abandonment. If they are ontogenetic adaptations of this kind, these practices may have no enduring significance once offspring have reached maturity. The social embeddedness of young children may have served a similar function of providing protection and nurturance, but may also have provided a means of ensuring that children had opportunities for social learning and peer play that constitute a deferred adaptation relevant to acquiring mature capacities. The importance of natural methods of childbirth, cosleeping with caregivers, and alloparenting can likewise be viewed as either ontogenetic or deferred adaptations depending on how the adaptive functions of these practices are interpreted. Clearly, to assume that practices characteristic of early experience in the context of human adaptation necessarily constitute evolutionary adaptations with lifelong consequences requires a more searching analysis of why these practices evolved in hominids and the adaptive functions they served.

The importance of these practices today depends on why they evolved, therefore, not simply that they were characteristic of human behavior during our species' evolution. Understanding their adaptive functions is important to determining what kind of adaptation they are, and also to identifying alternative practices of early care that may also have developed over the course of our biological heritage that could achieve the same functions. This is consistent with the principle of phenotypic plasticity: the view that there can be multiple phenotypes deriving from a single genotype depending on environmental conditions and other influences. The importance of phenotypic plasticity and the behavioral variability that results underscores the significance of focusing on the adaptive challenges of species evolution, not just a single set of evolved solutions to those challenges.

Whether these practices also promote psychological adaptation also involves complex considerations. Whether interpreted as ontogenetic or deferred adaptations, for example, practices such as alloparenting and caregiver responsivity may also contribute to a young child's sense of security and confidence in the environment of care. Indeed, many of the characteristics of early experience in the contexts of human adaptation can be regarded as psychologically adaptive practices for infants and young children, and there is supportive research evidence that this is true for several of these practices (see, e.g., Field & Hernandez-Reif, this volume). But it is not always true that evolutionary and psychological adaptation go together. As noted by Trevathan (this volume), high rates of morbidity and mortality related to childbirth in the contexts of human evolution compel caution about recommendations for a return to ancestral ways of giving birth. Likewise, Sulaiman, Amir, and Liamputtong (this volume) note that whereas breastfeeding confers biological and social benefits to young offspring, maternal work status may mediate whether such practices are psychologically adaptive for the mother (and thus perhaps also for her child).

It is important to recognize, therefore, that practices associated with early experience in the context of species evolution are not *necessarily* psychologically adaptive, even when they are determined to have been evolutionarily adaptive. Just as consideration of whether practices are deferred or ontogenetic adaptations requires an analysis of their biological functions, so too does consideration of whether practices are psychologically adaptive require an analysis of their functions in the current environment of early childhood care. It is possible, indeed, likely, that many aspects of human behavior in the context of species evolution would be deemed inappropriate, unnecessary, or maladaptive in contemporary cultural contexts.

Taken together, understanding the adaptive functions of practices of care in the environment(s) of species adaptation for hominid evolution can be fascinating and complex. Consider, for example, the importance of prompt and appropriate caregiver responsiveness. As a psychologically adaptive aspect of contemporary parenting, caregiver sensitivity has been found to be predictive of a secure attachment and a variety of other positive social and cognitive outcomes for young children (see reviews by De Wolff & van IJzendoorn, 1997; Laible & Thompson, 2007). It would seem sensible that, in the EEA, it would have also contributed to infant survival as an ontogenetic adaptation. But the picture may be more complicated. Caregiver responsiveness is likely to have contributed to nurturance and protection of human young that would be consistent with the inclusive fitness considerations of mother and child. But maternal inclusive fitness considerations are complex because they incorporate investment not just in the child's survival but also in the needs of several offspring at different levels of maturity as well as the mother herself, including her survival and future reproductive potential (Blurton-Jones, 1993; Clutton-Brock, 1991; Hrdy, 1999). At times, this requires adaptive trade-offs between the interests of the mother and the child. For example, the classic weaning conflict is, in biological terms, created by the discordance between the mother's diminished investment of energy resources in the child (with these resources redirected toward future reproduction) and the toddler's insistence on continued high maternal investment (see Trivers, 1985). Other kinds of adaptive trade-offs between maternal and child interests create the incentives necessary to move offspring toward greater independence. Viewed in this light, maternal solicitude is not an adaptive constant but is rather a biologically contingent phenomenon, and maternal prompt and appropriate responsiveness is adaptively time limited.

What does this mean for the importance of caregiver responsivity as a biologically adaptive feature of early experience in the context of species evolution? Is it an ontogenetic adaptation only during the preweaning period? Or does its adaptive significance change with the child's progressive maturity? What does this mean for its psychologically adaptive value in contemporary culture? Is it possible that an attribute of parenting that is biologically adaptive within a time-limited period in infancy inaugurates psychological processes today that are developmentally important in the long term, but which become independent of its biological foundations? These are the kinds of questions that are generated by an analysis of the multiple forms of "adaptation" associated with early experience in human adaptation and their current implications for healthy psychological development.

Parent–Child Attachment

Parent–child attachment is another illustration of this complex analysis and of the importance of different interpretations of adaptation. Bowlby (1969) viewed infant–parent attachment as an ontogenetic adaptation enabling the survival of young children to maturity but having no more enduring evolutionary function. Other scholars, working from the perspective of life history theory, have argued that attachment security is also a deferred adaptation (Belsky, Steinberg, & Draper, 1991; Chisholm, 1996, 1999). In this view, the security of attachment incorporates information concerning environmental support or challenge that inaugurates the development of alternative adaptive behavioral patterns of lifelong importance.

To Belsky, Steinberg, and Draper (1991), for example, the extent of the warmth and sensitivity of early care is an indicator of environmental support or risk that provokes a series of subsequent behavioral strategies—including the security of attachment, timing of pubertal maturation, onset of sexual activity, preferences in pair bonding, and eventual parental investment in offspring—that are each related to reproductive success in conditions of environmental security or challenge. In essence, children whose family experiences are characterized by high risk and challenge (and consequent parental insensitivity and child insecure attachment) are likely to develop reproductive strategies that are low investment and opportunistic, with children in warm, supportive families developing in the opposite manner.

Viewed in this light, the early quality of care provokes *facultative* (i.e., environmentally sensitive, rather than fixed) *adaptations* to prepare the organism for life in conditions of environmental support or challenge. There are thus multiple alternative behavioral adaptations arising from different conditions of early experience such that each behavioral pattern (e.g., secure attachment, insecure-avoidant attachment, etc.) is a facultative adaptation to different environmental conditions, consistent with the principle of phenotypic plasticity. Where facultative adaptations are concerned, therefore, there is no single behavioral pattern that is biologically adaptive in every environmental context. An important theoretical question in this life history analysis is whether the environmental conditions affecting parental care in one's infancy are probabilistically predictive of the environmental conditions of one's parental investment at maturity. There are many reasons to expect that this would not necessarily be so, rendering uncertain the long-term value of behavioral adaptations constituted on early conditions of care. Despite this, theorists with this life history orientation expect early security of attachment to be associated with the quality of other close relationships, especially romantic relationships, marital stability, and the quality of parenting (see, e.g., Belsky, 1997).

Many of these expectations are consistent with those of attachment theory. But the reasons for these predictions are very different for attachment theory and life history theory. To Bowlby and many of his followers, the behavioral consequences of early attachment security or insecurity are psychological adaptations deriving from the representations of self and others (i.e., internal working models) that attachment inaugurates. This is consistent with the mental health orientation of attachment theory. By contrast, life history theorists are interested in the behavioral manifestations of biological adaptations that evolved to promote reproductive success. The socioemotional competencies and psychological well-being associated with early attachment patterns are by-products of the more important inclusive fitness adaptations deriving from early patterns of care. The life history approach to understanding the adaptive significance of attachment security also leads to some novel expectations, such as the association of early attachment security with later pubertal maturation and the quality of adult romantic relationships, for which the relevant empirical evidence is mixed (Thompson, 2008, 2010).

In short, parent–child attachment can be narrowly viewed as an evolved process enabling helpless infants to survive to maturity, or instead as a catalyst for lifelong developmental pathways. These alternative interpretations of the adaptive significance of parent–child attachment have different implications for other aspects of behavioral development. Does the large research literature on attachment provide support for either perspective? Although contemporary attachment research does not provide anything close to a definitive judgment about these alternative views, it offers some suggestive perspectives (see Thompson, 2006, 2008). In general, the strongest associations between early security and later social and emotional functioning are in short-term follow-up studies in childhood. When early attachment is studied longitudinally in relation to adolescent or adult behavior, two conclusions are warranted by the research. First, although the security of attachment alone is not a robust predictor of later relationships and psychological functioning, it is more predictive when considered in concert with other indicators of the quality of early care. Because subsequent experience can transform as well as sustain the influence of early experiences, the best predictive models are those that combine early attachment with later measures of parental care (see, e.g., Sroufe, Egeland, Carlson, & Collins, 2005). Second, long-term associations between early attachment security and later behavior are also contingent on the stability of the relational environment. There are much weaker associations between early attachment and later functioning when there has been relational disruption and loss within the family, such as when parents divorce.

In short, early parent–child attachment security is most strongly associated with immediate behavioral competence, and its longer term effects are partially mediated by consistency and change in the relational environment. Such conclusions are consistent with Bowlby's original view of attachment as an ontogenetic adaptation and with alternative views that take into consideration that environmental conditions can change in ways that modify the effects of earlier adaptations. But this conclusion is tentative and provisional, offered primarily to illustrate the complex and provocative considerations required in understanding the "adaptive" functions of parent–child attachment.

Conclusion

Studying the adaptive processes influencing human development—whether ontogenetic, deferred, psychological, facultative, or any combination of these—involves understanding whether and how early experience is associated with later functioning (see Belsky, this volume). When biological adaptations are concerned, their effects may be limited to childhood or they may have lifelong consequences. Biological adaptations can be environmentally sensitive, such that different phenotypical outcomes derive from different ecological constraints or opportunities. Biologically adaptive processes may or may not contribute to psychologically adaptive outcomes. At times, understanding processes of biological adaptation requires estimating the trade-offs between conspecifics with overlapping, but not necessarily identical, fitness considerations.

What does this mean for understanding the significance of early experience in the environment of species evolution? In the end, it is not the *practices* of early care in this setting that are necessarily important, but rather the *adaptive functions* they served. In the human context of phenotypic plasticity, understanding how these functions were achieved in the environments of hominid evolution and how they are achieved in the current contexts of human development will contribute to our better understanding of their contemporary significance.

References

Belsky, J. (1997). Attachment, mating, and parenting: An evolutionary interpretation. *Human Nature, 8,* 361–381.

Belsky, J., Steinberg, L., & Draper, P. (1991). Childhood experience, interpersonal development, and reproductive strategy: An evolutionary theory of socialization. *Child Development, 62*, 647–670.

Bjorklund, D. F. (1997). The role of immaturity in human development. *Psychological Bulletin, 122*, 153–169.

Bjorklund, D. F. (2007). *Why youth is not wasted on the young: Immaturity in human development.* Oxford: Blackwell.

Blurton-Jones, N. (1993). The lives of hunter-gatherer children: Effects of parental behavior and parental reproductive strategy. In M. Pereira & L. Fairbanks (Eds.), *Juvenile primates* (pp. 309–326). New York, NY: Oxford University Press.

Bowlby, J. (1969/1982). *Attachment and loss. Vol. 1: Attachment.* New York, NY: Basic (Second edition published 1982).

Chisholm, J. S. (1996). The evolutionary ecology of attachment organization. *Human Nature, 1*, 1–37.

Chisholm, J. (1999). *Death, hope and sex: Steps to an evolutionary ecology of mind and morality.* New York, NY: Cambridge University Press.

Clutton-Brock, T. (1991). *The evolution of parental care.* Princeton, NJ: Princeton University Press.

De Wolff, M., & van Ijzendoorn, M. (1997). Sensitivity and attachment: A meta-analysis on parental antecedents of infant attachment. *Child Development, 68*, 571–591.

Hrdy, S. (1999). *Mother nature.* New York, NY: Ballantine Books.

Laible, D. J., & Thompson, R. A. (2007). Early socialization: A relational perspective. In J. Grusec & P. Hastings (Eds.), *Handbook of socialization* (Rev. ed., pp. 181–207). New York, NY: Guilford.

Lamb, M. E., Thompson, R. A., Gardner, W. P., & Charnov, E. L. (1985). *Infant-mother attachment: The origins and developmental significance of individual differences in Strange Situation behavior.* Hillsdale, NJ: Erlbaum.

Sroufe, L. A., Egeland, B., Carlson, E., & Collins, W. (2005). *The development of the person: The Minnesota Study of Risk and Adaptation from birth to maturity.* New York, NY: Guilford.

Thompson, R. A. (2006). The development of the person: Social understanding, relationships, self, conscience. In W. Damon & R. M. Lerner (Eds.), *Handbook of child psychology* (6th ed.). *Vol. 3: Social, emotional, and personality development* (N. Eisenberg, Vol. Ed., pp. 24–98). New York, NY: Wiley.

Thompson, R. A. (2008). Early attachment and later development: Familiar questions, new answers. In J. Cassidy & P. R. Shaver (Eds.), *Handbook of attachment* (2nd ed., pp. 348–365). New York, NY: Guilford.

Thompson, R. A. (2010). Attachment and life history theory: A rejoinder. *Child Development Perspectives, 4*(2), 106–108.

Trivers, R. (1985). *Social evolution.* Menlo Park, CA: Benjamin/Cummings.

Themes in Human Evolution

13

Play, Plasticity, and Ontogeny in Childhood
Anthony D. Pellegrini and Adam F. A. Pellegrini

The influence of "evolutionary heritage," phylogenetic history, and related terms, such as the environment of evolutionary adaptedness (EEA; Bowlby, 1969), on individuals' behavior and cognition has attracted interest by evolutionary-oriented psychologists, generally, and by evolutionary psychologists, especially those following the orientation of Cosmides and Tooby (1992) and the "Santa Barbara school" (Laland & Brown, 2002). As has been noted throughout this volume, evolutionary heritage, phylogenetic history, and the EEA are thought to reflect the evolutionary ecology of ancestral human hunter-gatherers. From this position, the selective pressures acting on these ancestral humans are hypothesized to have shaped the human genome in such a way that contemporary humans express these ancestrally shaped gene templates. This family of theories proposes that these templates play a large role in regulating the behavior and cognition of modern humans.

The other theme of this volume, the importance of early experience, stresses, implicitly at least, that certain factors during early ontogeny influence phenotypic plasticity. From this general view, individuals' ontogenetic development may be viewed as crucial for individual plasticity as early experiences provide opportunity for the immature organism to acclimate to (Bateson & Martin, 1999; Tinbergen, 1963; West-Eberhard, 2003) and construct their niches (Lewontin, 1982). That is, ontogeny affords opportunities for the phenotype to acclimate to and modify the environment it inhabits in order to maximize its overall fitness. The stress here is on the phenotype interacting with a variety of environments and genotypes during development, not following a generally defined program to an idealized environment or corresponding genotype. From these two points, we see a disconnect between the notion of the idealized environments and corresponding stress on unmediated genetic programs and a stress on the importance of early experience. That is, while these models recognize the importance of phylogenetic history, they do not make provision for the epigenetic transaction between individuals' genetic makeup and a variety of environments during ontogeny. In the latter case, the environment and genes affect each other during ontogeny and thus enable individuals to balance their ability to respond to and shape their given environments through phenotypic plasticity with maintaining some specialization. Our position, following Tinbergen (1963), is that in order to understand any set of behaviors or cognitions, we need to consider not only phylogenetic history but also ontogeny, as well as proximal and functional factors, simultaneously.

In this chapter, we contrast our position with an idealized evolutionary history and phylogeny position, as represented in evolutionary psychology, and its intellectual forbearer, sociobiology. In contrast to this, we stress the importance of developmental plasticity during early ontogeny and how play might affect the course of development, behavior, and possibly evolution. As we read it, some evolutionary psychological theory is a gene-centered approach that stresses the importance of the EEA, phylogenetic history, and genes as guides for human behavior and cognition and, correspondingly, minimizes the role of plasticity in human ontogeny. We show how epigenetic theories highlight the impact of the environment and behavior in the ontogenetic process as part of the organism's dynamic adaptation to ever-changing ecological niches (Bjorklund & Pellegrini, 2002). Play, as we will argue, is a paradigm example of a behavioral strategy used by juveniles to explore and subsequently acclimate to or alter their current niche. The variation in ability to use play as an acclimation strategy is hypothesized to impact evolution, assuming it contains some genetic basis (Bateson, 2005, 2011; Pellegrini, 2009; Pellegrini, Dupuis, & Smith, 2005; Spinka, Newbury, & Bekoff, 2001). To this end, in the final section, we outline ways in which play affects both ontogeny and phylogeny.

Sociobiology and Evolutionary Psychology

Theory and related hypotheses associated with the general field of sociobiology were pioneered by two evolutionary biologists, Robert Trivers (1971, 1972) and W. D. Hamilton (1964), and more widely popularized by two eminent biologists, E. O. Wilson (1975) at Harvard and Richard Dawkins (1976) at Oxford. Sociobiology arose, in part, as a counterpoint to group selection theory (Wynne-Edwards, 1962), a largely unexamined assumption that an individual's actions were naturally selected for in terms of their outcomes for the *group's* welfare. Group selection had been seen as the way to explain altruistic behavior (i.e., a behavior where the benefits to others are greater than those accrued by the actor). But group selection, as advanced by Wynne-Edwards, could not explain the complex patterns of selfish behavior that are actually observed in all animal species.

Traditionally, sociobiology takes the gene, and the individual as a carrier of genes, as central in understanding the genetic evolution of behavior, including social behaviors (Dawkins, 1976). That is, the individual, or more exactly the gene, is considered the unit of natural selection, with selection at the group level seen as largely unimportant (though see Boyd & Richerson, 1985; Wade & McCauley, 1984; Wilson & Wilson, 2007, for interesting discussions of "multilevel selection"). From this perspective, individuals act to maximize their own reproduction, or fitness, and the subsequent survival and reproduction of their offspring. Any benefits to the group, such as low levels of intragroup conflict, are seen as by-products of individual benefits; for example, low levels of conflict benefit individuals primarily (e.g., of both high and low social dominance rankings) and, as a by-product, the group, as an aggregate of individuals (e.g., by reducing group-level aggression). Consequently, if an organism's survival depends on some function that is influenced by the group, then there is selection on the individual to maintain the group's fidelity (Kerr et al., 2006).

Hamilton's (1964) kin selection theory was basic to defining sociobiology. His notion of "inclusive fitness" is defined as the sum of an individual's fitness plus the fitness of his or her kin weighted by their relatedness. Thus, it is more likely to "pay" (in terms of fitness) to increase the fitness of close kin (who are more likely to reproduce shared genes) than more distant kin, and especially nonkin. In other words, behavior that has costs for the individual performing it can still be selected for if it generates a net gain in fitness.

The primacy of the gene is also reflected in sociobiologists' views that genes guide ontogenetic development with little exogenous influence. As E. O. Wilson (1975, p. 145) put it:

The important point to keep in mind is that such phenomena as...the ontogenetic development of behavior, although sometimes treated in virtual isolation as the proper objects of entire disciplines...are really only sets of adaptations keyed to environmental changes of different durations. They are not fundamental properties of organisms around which a species must shape its biology.

This argument suggests that an organism's development is the result of an evolved *range of responses* to a variety of possible environments. That is, although genes do not "determine" behavioral expression per se, they prescribe the capacity for behavioral expression across a range of possible environments, shaped by natural selection. As such, Wilson's position implies that systematic changes in individual phenotypes are led by genes. Correspondingly, sociobiologists have examined behaviors as being functional or adaptive in the species' natural environment. Consequently, they have not paid much attention to ontogeny or the proximal mechanisms and constraints (e.g., such as environmental and phenotypic factors) that certain mechanisms might impact function and adaptation (Tinbergen, 1963).

The role of the environment and the phenotype in sociobiology and evolutionary psychology has, generally, been described in terms of a *range of reaction* (Gottlieb, 2003; Stamps, 2003; West-Eberhard, 2003), whereby genes prescribe a capacity to develop behaviors in environments that "trigger" (Wilson, 1975, p. 152) dimensions of that capacity. Different environments will facilitate or inhibit a phenotypic characteristic, but to similar extents for a genotype. Importantly, there is a unidirectional effect of genes on behavior, though these theorists acknowledge that the environment moderates that effect. Such an approach is compatible with traditional additive assumptions of behavior genetics analyses that apportioned variance to genetics and environment (Gottlieb, 2003).

However, this approach does not account, even at the gene level, for the molecular factors that interact with gene replication, transcription, and translation. Further, the environment inhabited by an organism, which could be a result of that organism's behavior (Lewontin, 1982), has been shown to affect genetic factors. For example, histone modifications of DNA, which influence chromatin structure and transcription rates, have been shown to be influenced by the environment of the particular cell or organism (Grunstein, 1998). This effect of the environment on gene expression is not independent of the organism's past experiences. Further modification of the histones, such as acetylation and methylation, has been shown to be a cumulative result of the cell's past experiences in different environments (Turner, 2002). Though these examples are only at the cell level, they are representative of a growing area of developmental biology where cell and organ growth are products of gene and environment interactions and consistent with a "norm of reaction," not a "range of reaction," position. In short, the latter position is a gene-centric approach, while the former stresses the transaction between phenotypes and genotypes.

Like sociobiology, evolutionary psychology shares a gene-centered view of human functioning, and it is seen by some as an offspring of sociobiology (e.g., Laland & Brown, 2002; Stamps, 2003); the centrality of the theories of Hamilton and Trivers were especially important in Cosmides's and Tooby's original work (Cosmides, 1989; Cosmides & Tooby, 1987, 1992). Cosmides and Tooby (1987) describe evolutionary psychology as the "missing link" between evolution and behavior. Also like sociobiology, evolutionary psychology is primarily concerned with function: The stated goal of evolutionary psychology is an adaptationist program aimed at recognizing specific functions (e.g., reproduction) associated with specific organs (e.g., the brain). From this position, the brain houses a variety of specific mechanisms (modules), and these mechanisms are adaptations that evolved to solve specific problems posed in the EEA and encoded in the contemporary genome (Tooby & Cosmides, 1992).

Evolutionary psychologists posit that modules and other forms of brain-based mechanisms reflect the selection problems faced by ancestral humans in the Pleistocene era. Specifically, modules reflect the specific cognitive mechanisms used to solve problems faced in the Stone Age. Thus, modern humans are walking around with Stone Age psychological mechanisms and applying them to contemporary problems associated with fitness. Modules are presented by evolutionary psychologists as "encapsulated units," each of which is independent of other modules. For example, a social exchange module should be independent of a language module (Cosmides, 1987; Tooby & Cosmides, 1992). A paradigm of a module cited by evolutionary psychologists is the language acquisition device proposed by Chomsky (1965, 1975) to explain the acquisition of syntax (although Chomsky himself does not support the view of independent modules—Chomsky, 1994, cited in Maratsos, 1998, p. 424). In short, evolutionary psychologists posit that these modules guide current cognition and behavior.

Evolutionary psychologists also assume, following their gene-centered orientation, that these mechanisms are "innate" (Cosmides & Tooby, 1987) and designed to solve very specific tasks; this compartmentalized modular view has been called a "Swiss army knife" view of the brain. Most important for our purpose is that these modules unfold within individuals with little guidance from the environment to solve specific problems through childhood and adulthood (Karmiloff-Smith, 1998; Laland & Brown, 2002). Specific to the role of the environment in motivating and shaping development, Tooby and Cosmides do discuss the coevolution of genes and the environment. They note that different aspects of the environment are "developmentally relevant" (Tooby & Cosmides, 1992, p. 84) at different periods in ontogeny. As a gene or set of genes is naturally selected over time, so too is the relevance of different aspects of the environment. While genes and environment interact, genes attend to only those aspects of the environment that are developmentally relevant, as determined by adaptations in the EEA. This environmental "trigger" view, as with sociobiology, is consistent with a reaction range, not reaction norm, of genes position (Gottlieb, 2003, p. 339). From this position, the role of experience during ontogeny is not central to evolutionary psychology and, by implication, minimizes the importance of proximal and ontogenetic factors (Tinbergen, 1963). As we will discuss later, evolutionary developmental biologists also stress the importance of modules, but for them, modules mean something very different: They take shape during ontogeny and facilitate flexible responses to the environment (West-Eberhard, 2003), a view that allows for greater flexibility in the interaction between behavior and evolution. We suggest that this flexibility is reflected and maximized in early ontogeny in children's play.

Epigenetic Theories

As noted earlier, the evolutionary psychology/sociobiology position is gene centered, with the assumption that population-level innovations in behaviors are due primarily to the effect of genetic mutation. In contrast to stressing the notion of the range of reaction, epigenetic theory stresses the *norm of reaction* view. Also as noted above, this occurs through histone modifications of DNA, which influence chromatin structure and transcription rates and have been shown to be influenced by the environment of the particular cell or organism (Grunstein, 1998). This allows for individuals' phenotypes to be significantly influenced by the environment in which the individual is embedded throughout ontogeny (Gottlieb, 2003; West-Eberhard, 2003). Indeed, the developmental trajectories of individuals with the *same* genotype are *not* predictable because of the role that the environment plays in influencing gene expression. Consequently, there is a true, nonadditive, interaction between genotype and phenotype, so that the relative phenotypic position of different genotypes may vary substantially and nonlinearly according to that organism's environment. In short, epigenetic theories turn the evolutionary psychology argument on its head by positing that behavior influences how natural selection might act at different periods of ontogeny and eventually evolution (Baldwin, 1896; Bateson, 1988, 2005; Bjorklund & Pellegrini, 2002; West-Eberhard, 2003). The take-home message here is that individuals are plastic, and this flexibility is exercised during early ontogeny to maximize phenotypes' acclimation to and, over multiple generations, adaptation to their environmental setting.

Epigenetically oriented theories, generally, posit that phenotypic (behavioral and cognitive) innovation is a response to environmental demands and is shaped by natural selection. We argue that play is a driver of developmental plasticity and behavioral innovation during early ontogeny. This type of innovation is possible during the juvenile period because children are well provisioned by adults (Burghardt, 2005, 2011). Indeed, one of the possible reasons for play being almost entirely limited to the juvenile period of development (though see Fagen, 2011) is that this period, especially for mammals, is characterized by parental protection and adequate provisioning (Burghardt, 2005).

Play may be especially important in the development of behavioral innovations in novel environments (Bateson, 2006; Fagen, 1981; Pellegrini & Hou, 2011). Behavioral (e.g., more or less vigorous locomotor play) and morphological (e.g., more or less developed skeletal and muscle systems) responses to environmental change are especially evident during early ontogeny. It is often the case that these changes comprise relatively independent behavioral subroutines and muscle systems, labeled as "modules" by some evolutionary biologists (West-Eberhard, 2003) and psychologists (e.g., Bruner, 1973). These modules, in contrast to those proposed by evolutionary psychologists (i.e., innate and remnants of the EEA), are the result of behavioral and cognitive recombination developed during ontogeny through exploration and play (e.g., Bateson, 1998, 2011; Bruner, 1973; West-Eberhard, 2003) and not due primarily to fixed genetic structure. Consequently, behavior can interact with the genotype in such a way that novel phenotypes are formed through behavior-induced environmental change that then result in a change in phenotype.

Pat Bateson, a behavioral biologist at the University of Cambridge, and his students have added considerably to our understanding of the role of early experiences, ontogeny, and play (e.g., Bateson, 1998, 2011; Caro, 1995; Caro & Bateson, 1986; Martin, 1982; Martin & Caro, 1985). Consistent with epigenetic theory, Bateson recognizes the role of behavior, especially play, during the juvenile period in shaping future development and impacting evolution. For Bateson, play can be the leading edge of adaptive change, a process he labels the "adaptability driver" (Bateson, 2006). Specifically, when organisms are faced with changes in their environment, changes in behavioral responses can be subject to natural selection and be adaptive if they foster survival and reproduction and contain some genetic basis. Responses to environmental change, especially if those changes are radical, require creativity in order to generate an array of responses that may work. Bateson suggests that play is an ideal candidate to be at the vanguard of this change.

As will be discussed in more detail below, in play, individuals take extant behavioral routines and recombine, eliminate, and add elements to form new behavioral modules. That such activity is intrinsically motivating means that the play will be sustained, thus increasing the likelihood of generating a solution during play. Once a play-generated solution to a problem is exhibited, it is likely to be used again by the originator and incorporated into the phenotype as a new "module," assuming that it confers some immediate benefit to the user. Additionally, it may then spread throughout the population, through social transmission (Boyd & Richerson, 1985; Pellegrini & Hou, 2011), when conspecifics have observed the effectiveness of the behavioral strategy. Furthermore, those individuals using the response should enjoy selective advantage over those not using it. Bateson, in keeping with his developmental orientation, stresses the fact that natural selection works on the phenotypes at all periods of the life span because of their influence on the fitness of the mature adult, assuming that the phenotypes are associated with additive genetic variation. From this position, play can have immediate benefits during childhood and also possibly deferred benefits at maturity. Clearly, children must survive childhood to reproduce later in development. Thus, the physically vigorous dimensions of rough-and-tumble play may be beneficial to immediate cardiovascular, muscular, and skeletal health (Pellegrini, 2011). Play may also have benefits deferred until maturity, as in the case of children practicing social roles that they will hold as adults, such as girls playing at grinding corn and boys hunting with bows (Bock, 2005).

The Specific Importance of Play

In this section we first define play. We then show how play relates to behavioral plasticity, primarily, through the formation of new behavioral and cognitive routines, or modules as defined by Bruner (1973) and West-Eberhard (2003), within individuals' reaction norms. Lastly, we speculate how these new modules can be adaptive and possibly naturally selected for.

We begin with a definition of play because the way in which a construct is defined is, to state the obvious, crucial for clarity in the scientific enterprise (e.g., Bem, 1995). The term *play* is used very loosely, often colloquially, even in the scientific literature, to label most forms of children's behavior, especially in the context of peer interaction. For example, in her seminal work on social participation, Mildred Parten (1932) labeled solitary *play* and parallel *play* (all our emphases) for forms of peer interaction that might not be play, according to many definitions. The labeling of children's general social behavior as "play" continues to the present, even in the seminal publications in our field (e.g., Fabes, Martin, & Hanish, 2003; Rubin, Bukowski, & Parker, 1998, p. 635).

A principled approach to defining play has been advanced by Gordon Burghardt (2005, 2011), whose categorical approach suggests that core criteria must be present for behaviors to be categorized as play; if not met, the behaviors are not play. The criteria include the following: The behaviors must be voluntary, observed in a "relaxed field," not functional in the observed context, and the behavioral elements must be exaggerated, segmented, and nonsequential in relation to the functional

behavior. A relaxed field is one where the individual, typically a juvenile, is well provisioned, safe, and healthy. Further, the child should voluntarily choose to engage
in some social, locomotor, fantasy, or object-directed activity that is not directly
functional. The nature and sequence of these behaviors should not resemble those
in a functional context. For example, a child could approach a peer with a "play
face," take an exaggerated swipe at the peer, fall to the ground, and then switch
roles, so the child's peers can hit at him or her.

The most important dimensions of this definition, from the point of behavioral plasticity and flexibility, are means over ends and nonfunctional criteria,
because they are antecedent conditions for children generating novel behaviors and
sequences of behaviors. That is, by not being concerned with the instrumentality of
a behavior, individuals are free to experiment with its form and place in novel behavioral and cognitive sequences, or "modules, as Bruner (1973) labeled them almost
40 years ago. Importantly, these criteria can be realized in each of the four domains
of play: locomotor (e.g., chasing a peer), object (e.g., piling blocks in different configurations), social (e.g., play fighting), and pretend (e.g., enacting domestic roles).
Further, each of these domains, with the obvious exception of social play, can be
either social or solitary. From this definition, play is a multidimensional construct
(Bateson, 2011) that reconfigures behavioral and cognitive processes, or modules.

To reiterate, we use the term *modules*, as used by some evolutionary biologists
(West-Eberhard, 2003) and Bruner, to label a process used during ontogeny as
a response to local ecological demands. From this position, modules develop as
a result of individuals interacting in different niches during ontogeny and differ
from modules described by evolutionary psychologists. For us, modules are relatively novel actions and cognitions constructed, within the bounds of their reaction norms, by individuals in response to new environments. With experience, these
rather diverse behavioral routines become more focused and relevant to the environments in which individuals are embedded. For evolutionary psychologists, on
the other hand, modules represent adaptations reflecting the EEA or some such
remnant of phylogenetic history.

Modules are formed in play, primarily due to the means over ends and nonfunctional definitional criteria of play that result in behavioral and cognitive flexibility.
This idea is not particularly new: Scholars from psychology (e.g., Bruner, 1972;
Sutton-Smith, 1967) and biology (e.g., Bateson, 2005; Burghardt, 2005; Fagen,
1981; Špinka et al., 2001) have posited links between play and creative responses
to the environment for over 40 years. The gist of these associated hypotheses is
that in the safe and well-provisioned context of play, characteristic of species with
an extended juvenile period, individuals place themselves into unconventional and
often disorienting positions or orientations. These novel situations afford opportunity to experiment with a variety of behavioral and cognitive routines and generate
novel, and possibly adaptive, responses, or modules. With repeated play experiences, the behavioral and cognitive routines can be used to solve problems at hand.
Stamps's (1995) example of locomotor play is illustrative. When placed in a new

environment, an individual (birds in Stamps's case) will first explore that environment and then play in it. Through locomotor play, the individual discovers new routes around the environment and eventually distills the optimal routes for possible foraging and escape routes from predators.

From this argument, individuals' play in new environments affords opportunities to read supportive and nonsupportive environments and then develop novel behavioral and cognitive routines that optimize life history decisions related to growth, survival, and reproduction. The comparative and human literatures are rich with examples of neonates "reading" the supportiveness of their environments, often through the responsiveness of their mothers (e.g., Chisholm, Burbank, Coall, & Gemmiti, 2005; Zahavi, 1977), and developing advantageous responses. Novel behavioral responses to these environments lead individuals to develop new phenotypes. We suggest that the ability to develop novel phenotypes depends on an individual's flexibility in play and can incur benefits, especially in novel and unpredictable habitats. Play is relevant to such life history changes because it is a relatively low cost way in which to develop alternative responses to new and challenging environments (Bateson, 2011). During infancy, mothers can afford opportunities to learn and develop new phenotypes (Bjorklund, 2006; Harper, 2005). An experimental example of this process comes from Steve Suomi's lab (2005), where, by controlling for the rhesus macaque's genotype, they were able to link changes in behavior to changes in dominance relationships and subsequent mating opportunity. The social behaviors monkeys learned through interaction with fostered mothers and play with peers resulted in these monkeys changing their behavioral trajectories from ones typically associated with their highly aggressive genotypes into behavioral trajectories of socially competent individuals. Further, the realized social status (i.e., social dominance) of the monkeys fostered by "normal" mothers was closely associated with the dominance of nurturant adults with whom they had a relationship. This elevated dominance status should, in turn, translate into the rehabilitated monkey mating with "competent" females (i.e., with a nonaggressive genotype).

Further, play with younger peers also enables maternally deprived monkeys to develop socially competent behaviors (Herman, Paukner, & Suomi, 2011; Suomi & Harlow, 1972). Play affords individuals opportunities to develop a successful phenotype, even for those individuals with maladaptive genotypic or socialization histories. In turn, behavioral modules developed during play can be evolutionarily relevant due to their potential effects on an organism's fitness, possibly by "widening" reaction norms beyond the juvenile period while not unduly sacrificing specialization. The ease (or low cost) with which play and play-related behaviors spread through the population allows for individual variation in levels and forms of play. Organic selection, also known as the "Baldwin effect," may be one of the mechanisms responsible for individuals' change in their own lifetimes when exposed to environmental change (Bateson, 2005). Organic selection is a way that traits or behavioral responses, especially to stressful environments, are transmitted across generations through non-Lamarkian means (Bjorklund & Pellegrini, 2000). The relation between fitness and play, in turn, creates an environment where certain play behaviors can be naturally selected for, assuming that an individual's play behavior is in some way related to additive genetic variation. Consequently, when juveniles mature, assuming these play behaviors translate into individual variation in fitness, there is a fitness landscape that selection can operate on.

Conclusion

There has been a marked increase in the invocation of evolutionary theories in the studies of human development. In this chapter, we use the case of play during the juvenile period as an example of how experience during early ontogeny can affect later development and possibly affect evolutionary processes. Rather than having human behavior and cognition being guided by modules reflecting the EEA and related forms of genotypic expression, we suggest a more transactional process between genes and ecology—one in which play during the juvenile period can enable individuals to adjust to and construct (Lewontin, 1982) niches—and that these strategies may be especially important in novel environments. Play enables individuals, after they have sampled their environments, to generate, in a rather low-cost manner, a repertoire of innovative behaviors that may be adaptive to their specific niche. This point was illustrated with experimental studies cited above of cross-fostered rhesus monkeys of differing genotypes. The initial phenotypic changes associated with play, such as increased exploration and cooperation, decreased aggression and stereotypic behavior, and dominance status was sustained across development. Selection should favor individuals exhibiting these new phenotypes relative to those who do not.

References

Baldwin, J. M. (1896). A new factor in evolution. *American Naturalist, 30*, 441–451, 536–553.

Bateson, P. P. G. (1988). The active role of behaviour in evolution. In M.-W. Ho & S. W. Fox (Eds.), *Evolutionary processes and metaphors* (pp. 191–207). London: Wiley.

Bateson, P. P. G. (2005). Play and its role in the development of great apes and humans. In A. D. Pellegrini & P. K. Smith (Eds.), *The nature of play: Great apes and humans* (pp. 13–26). New York, NY: Guilford.

Bateson, P. P. G. (2006). The adaptability driver: Links between behaviour and evolution. *Biological Theory: Integrating Development, Evolution, and Cognition, 1*, 342–345.

Bateson, P. P. G. (2011). Theories of play. In A. D. Pellegrini (Ed.), *Oxford handbook of the development of play* (pp. 41–47). New York, NY: Oxford University Press.

Bateson, P. P. G., & Martin, P. (1999). *Design for a life: How behaviour develops*. London: Jonathan Cape.

Bem, D. J. (1995). Writing a review article for *Psychological Bulletin. Psychological Bulletin, 118,* 172–177.

Bjorklund, D. F. (2006). Mother knows best: Epigenetic inheritance. Maternal effects, and the evolution of human intelligence. *Developmental Review, 26,* 213–242.

Bjorklund, D. F., & Pellegrini, A. D. (2002). *Evolutionary developmental psychology.* Washington, DC: American Psychological Association.

Bock, J. (2005). Farming, foraging, and children's play in the Okavango Delta, Botswana. In A. D. Pellegrini & P. K. Smith (Eds.), *The nature of play: Great apes and humans* (pp. 254–284). New York, NY: Guilford.

Bowlby, J. (1969). *Attachment and loss. Vol. I: Attachment.* New York, NY: Basic Books.

Boyd, R., & Richerson, P. J. (1985). *Culture and the evolutionary process.* Chicago, IL: The University of Chicago Press.

Bruner, J. S. (1972). The nature and uses of immaturity. *American Psychologist, 27,* 687–708.

Bruner, J. S. (1973). Organization of early skilled action. *Child Development, 44,* 1–11.

Burghardt, G. M. (2005). *The genesis of animal play: Testing the limits.* Cambridge, MA: MIT Press.

Burghardt, G. M. (2011). Defining and recognizing play. In A. D. Pellegrini (Ed.), *Oxford handbook of the development of play* (pp. 9–18). New York, NY: Oxford University Press.

Caro, T. M. (1995). Short-term costs and correlates of play in cheetahs. *Animal Behaviour, 49,* 333–345.

Caro, T. M., & Bateson, P. (1986). Ontogeny and organization of alternative tactics. *Animal Behaviour, 34,* 1483–1499.

Chisholm, J. S., Burbank, V. K., Coall, D. A., & Gemmiti, F. (2005). Early stress: Perspectives from developmental evolutionary ecology. In B. J. Ellis & D. F. Bjorklund (Eds.), *Origins of the social mind: Evolutionary psychology and child development* (pp. 76–107). New York, NY: Guilford.

Chomsky, N. (1965). *Aspects of a theory of syntax.* Cambridge, MA: MIT Press.

Chomsky, N. (1975). *Reflections on language.* New York, NY: Random House.

Cosmides, L. (1989). The logic of social exchange: Has natural selection shaped how humans reason? *Cognition, 31,* 187–276.

Cosmides, L., & Tooby, J. (1987). From evolution to behavior: Evolutionary psychology as the missing link. In J. Dupre (Ed.), *The latest on the best essays on evolution and optimality* (pp. 277–306). Cambridge, MA: MIT Press.

Cosmides, L., & Tooby, J. (1992). Cognitive adaptations for social exchange. In J. H. Barkow, L. Cosmides, & J. Tooby (Eds.), *The adapted mind: Evolutionary psychology and the generation of culture* (pp. 163–228). New York, NY: Oxford University Press.

Dawkins, R. (1976). *The selfish gene.* New York, NY: Oxford University Press.

Fabes, R. A., Martin, C. L., & Hanish, L. D. (2003). Young children's play qualities in same-, other-, and mixed-sex peer groups. *Child Development, 74,* 921–932.

Fagen, R. (1981). *Animal play behavior.* New York, NY: Oxford University Press.

Fagen, R. (2011). Play and development. In A. D. Pellegrini (Ed.), *Oxford handbook of the development of play* (pp. 83–100). New York, NY: Oxford University Press.

Gottlieb, G. (2003). On making behavioral genetics truly developmental. *Human Development, 46,* 337–355.

Grunstein, M. (1998). Yeast heterochromatin: Minireview regulation of its assembly and inheritance by histones. *Cell, 93*, 325–328.

Hamilton, W. D. (1964). The genetical theory of social behavior. *Journal of Theoretical Biology, 7*, 1–52.

Harper, L. V. (2005). Epigenetic inheritance and the intergeneration transfer of experience. *Psychological Bulletin, 131*, 340–360.

Herman, K. H., Paukner, A., & Suomi, S. J. (2011). G X E interactions in social play. In A. D. Pellegrini (Ed.), *The Oxford handbook of the development of play* (pp. 58–69). New York, NY: Oxford University Press.

Karmiloff-Smith, A. (1998). Development itself is the key to understanding developmental disorders. *Trends in Cognitive Science, 2*, 389–398.

Kerr, B., Delrue, M. A., Sigaudy, S., Perveen, R., Marche, M., Burgelin, I., et al. (2006). Genotype-phenotype correlation in Costello syndrome: HRAS mutation analysis in 43 cases. *Journal of Medical Genetics, 43*, 401.

Laland, K. N., & Brown, G. R. (2002). *Sense and nonsense: Evolutionary perspectives on human behaviour.* Oxford: Oxford University Press.

Lewontin, R. C. (1982). Gene, organism, and environment. In D. S. Bendell (Ed.), *Evolution: From molecules to men* (pp. 273–285). London: Cambridge University Press.

Maratsos, M. (1998). The acquisition of grammar. In D. Kuhn & R. S. Siegler (Eds.), *Handbook of child psychology. Vol. 2: Cognition, perception, and language* (pp. 421–466). New York, NY: Wiley.

Martin, P. (1982). The energy cost of play: Definition and estimation. *Animal Behaviour, 30*, 294–295.

Martin, P., & Caro, T. (1985). On the function of play and its role in behavioral development. In J. Rosenblatt, C. Beer, M-C. Bushnel, & P. Slater (Eds.), *Advances in the study of behavior* (Vol. 15, pp. 59–103). New York, NY: Academic Press.

Parten, M. (1932). Social participation among preschool children. *Journal of Abnormal and Social Psychology, 27*, 243–269.

Pellegrini, A. D. (2009). *The role of play in human development.* New York, NY: Oxford University Press.

Pellegrini, A. D. (2011). Locomotor play. In A. D. Pellegrini (Ed.), *The Oxford handbook of play* (pp. 172–184). New York, NY: Oxford University Press.

Pellegrini, A. D., Dupuis, D., & Smith, P. K. (2007). Play in evolution and development. *Developmental Review, 27*, 261–276.

Pellegrini, A. D., & Hou, Y. (2011). The development of preschool children's (*Homo sapiens*) uses of objects and their role in peer group centrality. *Journal of Comparative Psychology, 125*, 239–245.

Rubin, K. H., Bukowski, W., & Parker, J. G. (1998). Peer interactions, relationships, and groups. In N. Eisenberg (Ed.), *Manual of child psychology. Vol. 3: Social, emotional, and personality development* (pp. 619–700). New York, NY: Wiley.

Špinka, M., Newbury, R. C., & Bekoff, M. (2001). Mammalian play: Can training for the unexpected be fun? *Quarterly Review of Biology, 76*, 141–168.

Stamps, J. (1995). Motor learning and the value of familiar space. *American Naturalist, 146*, 41–58.

Stamps, J. (2003). Behavioural processes affecting development: Tinbergen's fourth question comes to age. *Animal Behaviour, 66*, 1–13.

Suomi, S. J. (2005). Genetic and environmental factors influencing the expression of impulsive aggression and serotonergic functioning in rhesus monkeys. In R. E. Tremblay, W. W. Hartup, & J. Archer (Eds.), *Developmental origins of aggression* (pp. 63–82). New York, NY: Guilford.

Suomi, S., & Harlow, H. (1972). Social rehabilitation of isolate-reared monkeys. *Developmental Psychology, 6,* 487–496.

Sutton-Smith, B. (1967). The role of play in cognitive development. *Young Children, 22,* 364–369.

Tinbergen, N. (1963). On aims and methods of ethology. *Zeitschirift für Tierpsychologie, 20,* 410–413.

Tooby, J., & Cosmides, L. (1992). The psychological foundations of culture. In J. Barkow, L. Cosmides, & J. Tooby (Eds.), *The adapted mind: Evolutionary psychology and the generation of culture* (pp. 19–136). Oxford: Oxford University Press.

Trivers, R. (1971). The evolution of reciprocal altruism. *Quarterly Review of Biology, 46,* 35–57.

Trivers, R. (1972). Parental investment and sexual selection. In B. Campbell (Ed.), *Sexual selection and the descent of man* (pp. 136–179). Chicago, IL: Aldine.

Turner, B. M. (2002). Cellular memory and the histone code. *Cell, 111,* 285–291.

Wade, M. J., & McCauley, D. E. (1984). Group selection: The interaction of local deme size and migration in the differentiation of small populations. *Evolution, 38,* 1047–1058.

West-Eberhard, M. J. (2003). *Developmental plasticity and evolution.* New York, NY: Oxford University Press.

Wilson, E. O. (1975). *Sociobiology: The new synthesis.* Cambridge, MA: Harvard University Press.

Wilson, D. S., & Wilson, E. O. (2007). Rethinking the theoretical foundation of sociobiology. *Quarterly Review of Biology, 82,* 327–348.

Wynne-Edwards, V. C. (1962). *Animal dispersion in relation to social behaviour.* Edinburgh: Oliver & Boyd.

Zahavi, A. (1977). The testing of a bond. *Animal Behaviour, 25,* 246–247.

14

The Value of a Play-Filled Childhood in Development of the Hunter-Gatherer Individual
Peter Gray

Children come into the world with drives and behavioral dispositions that are designed, by natural selection, to promote their development toward adulthood. Prominent among these is the drive to play. My aim here is to shed light on children's powerful drive to play by examining its manifestation in hunter-gatherer children. The human play drive, like all of our biological traits, was shaped from its earlier primate form during the hundreds of thousands of years when we were all hunter-gatherers. Therefore, an examination of the play of hunter-gatherer children may help us understand better play's natural forms and functions and lead to a better understanding of its continuing role in children's development today.

The pure hunting-and-gathering way of life is now nearly extinct, but as recently as 30 years ago, and to some extent even more recently, researchers could find and study hunter-gatherers, in various remote parts of the world, who had been almost untouched by modern ways. On the basis of such studies, anthropologists generally distinguish between two categories of hunter-gatherer societies (Kelly, 1995). One category, referred to as *delayed-return* or *nonegalitarian* hunter-gatherers, or as *collector societies*, are those who lived in fixed locations and exploited a rich local supply of food, commonly fish. They are characterized by food storage, relatively high population densities, resource ownership, hierarchical social structures, inherited status, and relatively high rates of violence and acceptance of violence as legitimate. Examples are the Kwakiutl of the American northwest coast and the Ainu of Japan. The other category, which is the one relevant to this paper, is that referred to as *immediate-return* or *egalitarian* hunter-gatherers, or as *band societies*.

Hunter-gatherers in this category live in small groups (bands) of roughly 30 to 50 persons each, including children, that move from place to place within a large but circumscribed area to follow the available game and vegetation. Wherever they are found, they have a highly egalitarian social structure, make decisions by consensus, own little property, share food and material goods within and even across bands, do not have means of long-term food preservation, have little occupational specialization except that based on gender, and generally reject violence as a legitimate way of solving problems. Archeological evidence suggests that band societies are more ancient than are collector societies and more likely to represent the living conditions of our preagricultural ancestors (Kelly, 1995). My focus in this chapter is exclusively on band societies, and when I use the term *hunter-gatherers*, unmodified, I am referring to band hunter-gatherers. Among the many band societies that were extensively studied in the last half of the 20th century are the *Jul'hoansi* (also called the *!Kung*, of Africa's Kalahari Desert), *Hazda* (of Tanzanian rainforests), *Mbuti* (of Congo's Ituri Forest), *Aka* (of rainforests in the Central African Republic and Congo), *Efé* (of Congo's Ituri Forest), *Batek* (of peninsular Malaysia), *Agta* (of Luzon, Philippines), *Nayaka* (of South India), *Aché* (of Eastern Paraguay), *Parakana* (of Brazil's Amazon Basin), and *Yiwara* (of the Australian Desert).

Findings from research into such societies have provided a challenge to scientists who are interested in human social nature. Whether we compare them to our great ape relatives or to humans living in agricultural or industrial societies, hunter-gatherers come across as far more egalitarian and altruistic than do members of other societies. The three African great apes to which we are most closely related—chimpanzees, bonobos, and gorillas—all live in groups in which high-ranking individuals regularly dominate and bully lower ranking ones and where battles for status are common (Boehm, 1999). All or at least most post–hunter-gatherer human societies seem, in various ways, to reflect the hierarchical structure of our ape heritage; those who are higher up exert power over those who are lower down, and large individual differences in wealth and privilege are tolerated and expected. And yet, perhaps for hundreds of thousands of years, human beings in hunter-gatherer societies lived in groups without dominant leaders, with what has been described as a "fiercely egalitarian" ethos (Lee, 1988), by means that ensured the equal distribution of food and material wealth among all band members.

How did hunter-gatherers maintain their egalitarian style of life? Christopher Boehm (1999) has proposed a quite convincing answer to that question. He contends that hunter-gatherer egalitarianism did not fall passively out of human nature, but was vigilantly maintained and enforced through social practices that he calls "reverse dominance." These practices included the condemnation and punishment of any individuals who displayed even incipient signs of domination, selfishness, or arrogance. In a standard dominance hierarchy, powerful individuals at the top control the rank and file; but in the hunter-gatherers' reverse hierarchy, according to Boehm, the rank and file collectively controlled anyone who might try to dominate others. The control was aimed specifically at deflating the potentially dominating person's ego, and it commonly involved ridicule or, in more extreme cases, shunning, which would stop only when the offending person expressed appropriate humility and ended the offensive behavior. The human hunting-and-gathering way of life apparently required an extraordinary degree of cooperation and sharing, far more than that exhibited by any of the great apes and more than that required for agricultural and postagricultural modes of human existence. According to Boehm, hunter-gatherer groups everywhere, perhaps independently in different parts of the world, invented the procedures of reverse dominance to achieve and maintain the egalitarian ethos that underlay their cooperation and sharing.

A Play Theory of Hunter-Gatherer Equality

Elsewhere I have proposed and elaborated upon a different theory—a *play* theory—to explain how hunter-gatherers maintained their egalitarian style of life (Gray, 2009). I see this theory as a supplement, not necessarily an alternative, to Boehm's reverse-dominance theory. I think both are true. My theory, simply put, is that hunter-gatherers maintained their egalitarian ethos by cultivating the playful side of their human nature.

Social play—play involving two or more playmates—is necessarily egalitarian. It always requires a suspension of aggression and dominance and heightened sensitivity to the needs and desires of the other individuals involved. Players may recognize that one playmate is better at the played activity than are others, but that recognition must not lead the one who is better to dominate the others. This is true for play among animals as well as for that among humans (Bekoff & Byers, 1998). For example, when two young monkeys of different size and strength engage in a play fight, the stronger one deliberately self-handicaps, avoids actions that would frighten or hurt the playmate, and sends repeated play signals that are understood as signs of nonaggression (Biben, 1998). That is what makes the activity a *play* fight instead of a real fight. If the stronger animal failed to behave in these ways, the weaker one would feel threatened and flee, and the play would end. The drive to play, therefore, requires suppression of the drive to dominate. My theory, then, is that hunter-gatherers suppressed the tendency to dominate and promoted egalitarian sharing and cooperation by deliberately fostering a playful attitude in essentially all of their social activities. The capacity for play, which we inherited from our mammalian ancestors, is the capacity that best counters the tendency to dominate, which we also inherited from our mammalian ancestors.

My play theory of hunter-gather equality is based largely on evidence, gleaned from analysis of the anthropological literature, that play permeated the social lives of adults in hunter-gatherer cultures—more so than is the case for any known, long-lasting post–hunter-gatherer cultures. Their hunting and gathering were playful; their religious beliefs and practices were playful; their practices of dividing meat and of sharing goods outside of the band as well as inside of the band were playful; and even their most common methods of punishing offenders within their group (through humor and ridicule) had a playful element (Gray, 2009).

In the remainder of this chapter, however, my focus is on the play of hunter-gatherer children, not adults. I will describe the conditions in which hunter-gatherer children played, the ways in which they played, and the means by which their play enabled them to acquire the skills, attitudes, and character traits essential to successful hunter-gatherer adulthood. I am concerned here with the development of the complete hunter-gatherer adult, but especially with the development of those traits that underlay hunter-gatherer egalitarianism. The data come primarily from the anthropological literature on children's lives in hunter-gatherer cultures and secondarily from a small survey that Jonathan Ogas and I conducted of anthropologists who had lived in and observed hunter-gatherer groups (described in Gray, 2009). For the survey, we asked researchers to fill out a written questionnaire pertaining to children's lives, especially their play, in the culture they observed. Ten different anthropologists completed and returned the questionnaire. Among them, they had studied seven different hunter-gatherer band societies (four in Africa, two in Asia, and one in New Guinea).

Before turning to the play of hunter-gatherer children, it would be worthwhile to consider the defining characteristics of human play. As form and function are related, the characteristics of play provide strong clues to play's developmental functions.

Defining Characteristics of Play

Like most categories of behavioral or psychological phenomena, *play* is a category with blurred edges. At least in our species, play can exist in matters of degree. We might speak of some activities as *full play* and of others as to varying degrees *playful*, depending on the degree to which they contain all of play's characteristics.

Play involves a convergence of characteristics, all of which have to do with the motives or mental framework underlying the observed behavior. Play scholars have used a wide variety of terms to describe or define their subject, but I think all of them can be boiled down quite well to the following five (Gray, 2009): Play is activity that (1) is self-chosen and self-directed; (2) is intrinsically motivated; (3) is guided by mental rules; (4) is imaginative; and (5) involves an active, alert, but nonstressed frame of mind. The more fully an activity entails all of these characteristics, the more inclined most people are to refer to it as play.

PLAY IS SELF-CHOSEN AND SELF-DIRECTED

Play, first and foremost, is what a person *wants* to do, not what a person feels compelled to do. Players choose what to play and how. Any activity motivated by coercion rather than choice is not play. In social play, players must decide together what and how to play, and they must do so in such a way that nobody feels coerced. Thus, social play provides continuous practice in the art of consensual decision making and getting along with others as equals.

The most basic freedom in play is the freedom to quit. Players know that playmates who feel coerced or in other ways dissatisfied will quit, and if too many quit the game ends. To keep the game going, players must satisfy not just their own desires but also those of the other players. The strong desire that children have to play with other children, therefore, is a powerful force for them to learn how to attend to others' wishes and negotiate differences. Even preschool children exhibit such abilities in the context of play (Furth, 1996; Garvey, 1974).

PLAY IS INTRINSICALLY MOTIVATED

Play is activity that, from the conscious perspective of the player, is done for its own sake more than for any reward outside of itself. Stated differently, it is activity in which means are more valued than ends (Vygotsky, 1978b). When we are not playing, what we value most are the results of our actions, but when we are playing, it is the activity itself that pleases us. Play may be goal directed, but the goal is perceived as part and parcel of the activity, not as the primary reason for the activity. For example, in constructive play, the goal is to build some object that the players have in mind. But the pleasure derives primarily from *building* the object, not from *having* the object once it is built.

In our culture, many of the activities that we call "play" are competitive. Competition can turn "play" into nonplay if rewards for winning extend beyond the game itself. "Players" who are motivated primarily by trophies, praise, or increased status outside of the game are not fully playing. Among animals there is a clear distinction between *contests* (including ritualized battles of bluff as well as actual fights), which are aimed at achieving dominance, and *play*, in which strivings for dominance must be set aside (Bekoff & Byers, 1998). Our competitive games are best understood as blends of contest and play. The blend can veer more in one direction or the other, depending on the degree to which heightened out-of-game status or other extrinsic rewards are present for winning. In this regard, it is noteworthy that hunter-gatherers are the only known human cultural groups that, as a rule, did not play competitive games (Sutton-Smith & Roberts, 1970).

A number of researchers have observed that, even in our culture, children playing naturally, without adult direction or adult audiences, rarely care much about winning (Fine, 1986; Gray & Feldman, 2004). In pickup games of baseball or soccer, for example, they may cheer wildly when their team scores a point, but they pay little attention to the final score and often don't even bother to keep score. This is especially true if they are playing in age-mixed groups; and hunter-gatherer children and adolescents always played in widely age-mixed groups (Gray, 2009; Konner, 1975).

PLAY IS GUIDED BY MENTAL RULES

As Lev Vygotsky (1978b) emphasized in his now-classic essay on the role of play in children's development, all play has rules. Children freely choose to play, but in so choosing they put themselves into a situation in which they must follow rules, not behave impulsively. The rules are concepts held in the players' minds, which give form to the playful activity. In a play fight, for example, the rules prescribe that you must mimic at least some of the motions of real fighting, but you must take pains not to really hurt the other person—no kicking, biting, scratching, or hitting hard, especially if you are the stronger of the two. In constructive play, a basic rule is that you must work with some chosen medium to produce or depict some specific object or design that you have in mind. In sociodramatic play, a basic rule is that each player must stay in character. If you are superman, you must not cry if you fall and hurt yourself; if you are the pet dog, you must walk around on all fours, no matter how uncomfortable it is to do so. Vygotsky contended that a major developmental function of play is to teach children how to inhibit their impulses and abide by socially agreed upon concepts of appropriate ways to act in particular situations, an ability that is important for all of adult life. Through play, children learn that inhibiting their impulses is not only necessary but is, ultimately, a source of pleasure.

PLAY IS IMAGINATIVE

Play, at least full play, always involves some degree of psychological removal of oneself from the immediate real world (Huizinga, 1955). Imagination, or fantasy, is most obvious in sociodramatic play, where the players create characters and a story line, but it is also present in other forms of play. In rough-and-tumble play, the fight is a pretend one, not a real one. In constructive play, the players know that they are building a pretend castle, not a real one. In formal games, such as chess, the players must accept the fictional world specified by the game. In the real world, bishops can move any way they choose, but in the fictional world of chess they can move only on the diagonals. The imaginative nature of play is, really, the flip side of play's rule-based nature (Vygotsky, 1978b). To the degree that play takes place in an imagined world, the players' actions must be governed by rules that are in the minds of the players rather than by laws of nature or impulsive instincts.

PLAY INVOLVES AN ACTIVE, ALERT, BUT RELATIVELY UNSTRESSED FRAME OF MIND

This final characteristic of play follows naturally from the others. Because play involves attention to means and to conscious mental rules, it requires an active, alert mind. However, because play is freely chosen rather than coerced, and because it is understood to take place in a fictitious world and to have ends that are inconsequential to real life, players are relatively free of psychological distress. Play is not always accompanied by smiles and laughter, and mental tension may arise as players strive to perform well; but, as play is always self-chosen, so is any mental tension that accompanies it. If the tension becomes too great, reaching the level of distress, the player is free to quit or to change the nature of the play at any time.

Much of the power of play for learning and creativity lies, paradoxically, in its apparent triviality. Because there is no out-of-game reward for success or punishment for failure, players are free to make mistakes, and therefore free to try out new ways of doing things and new ways of thinking. A great deal of psychological research shows that people are much better at learning new skills and solving problems that require creativity if they are led to believe that their activities are not being evaluated, and will not affect them in any lasting way, than if they are led to believe the opposite (Amabile, 1996; Geen, 1991). The tension and narrow goal-directedness created by concern for evaluation or for other real-world consequences tend to channel thought and action down well-worn paths and prevent people from exploring new ones. People who are already highly skilled at an activity perform better when the performance counts than when it doesn't, but the opposite is true for novices. The playful state of mind, therefore, appears to be the ideal state for learning new skills and conceiving of new ideas.

The Cultural Context of Children's Play in Hunter-Gatherer Bands

The cultural context in which hunter-gatherer children played was one of extraordinary indulgence of children's wishes, unlimited freedom to play and explore with little or no adult interference, exposure to all aspects of the adult culture, and continuous age mixing. This context contributed to the developmental value of their play.

INDULGENCE OF CHILDREN'S WISHES

A term often used by researchers to describe adults' general treatment of children in hunter-gatherer cultures is "indulgence," but a better term might be "trusting." The spirit of egalitarianism and autonomy that pervaded hunter-gatherer social relationships applied to adults' interactions with children just as it applied to adults' interactions with one another. The central tenet of their parenting and educational philosophy seemed to be that children's instincts could be trusted, that children allowed to follow their own wills would learn what they needed to learn and would begin naturally to contribute to the band's economy when they had the skills and maturity to do so. To illustrate this attitude, here are three comments concerning adult hunter-gatherers' treatment of children, each from a different observer of a different culture:

- "Hunter-gatherers do not give orders to their children; for example, no adult announces bedtime. At night, children remain around adults until they feel tired and fall asleep.... Parakana adults do not interfere with their children's lives. They never beat, scold, or behave aggressively with them, physically or verbally, nor do they offer praise or keep track of their development." (Gosso, Otta, de Lima, Ribeiro, & Bussab, 2005, p. 218)
- "Ju/'hoan children very rarely cried, probably because they had little to cry about. No child was ever yelled at or slapped or physically punished, and few were even scolded." (Thomas, 2006, p. 198)

- "Infants and young children [among Inuit hunter-gatherers of the Hudson Bay area] are allowed to explore their environments to the limits of their physical capabilities and with minimal interference from adults. Thus if a child picks up a hazardous object, parents generally leave it to explore the dangers on its own. The child is presumed to know what it is doing." (Guemple, 1988, p. 137)

From the perspective of a typical modern parent or educator, such indulgence might be expected to produce spoiled, unruly children, but apparently it does not, at least not within the context of hunter-gatherers' ways of life. Many researchers have commented on the cheerfulness and cooperativeness of hunter-gatherer children, and I have found no comments to the contrary. Here, for example, is what Elizabeth Marshall Thomas (2006, pp. 198–199) has to say about the Ju/'hoansi children she observed: "We are sometimes told that children who are treated so kindly become spoiled, but this is because those who hold that opinion have no idea how successful such measures can be. Free from frustration or anxiety, sunny and cooperative, ...the children were every parent's dream. No culture can ever have raised better, more intelligent, more likable, more confident children."

UNLIMITED TIME AND FREEDOM TO PLAY

Given this indulgent attitude, it is not surprising that children in hunter-gatherer societies spent most of their time freely playing and exploring, on their own, without adult direction and little if any adult interference. The general belief among most hunter-gatherer adults, borne out by centuries of experience, was that children educated themselves through their self-directed play and exploration (Bakeman, Adamson, Konner, & Barr, 1990). To our question, "How much free time did children in the group you studied have for play?" all of the respondents in our survey said that the children were free to play all day or almost all day, every day, from the age of about 4 (when they were weaned and began to move away from their mothers) on into their teenage years, when they began taking on some adult responsibilities (Gray, 2009). An exception to the general rule of complete freedom for hunter-gatherer children has been reported for the Hazda, where children are expected to forage for much of their own food. However, even for this group, researchers found that the children spent only about 2 hours per day foraging, in the rich vegetation near camp, and continued to play even while foraging (Blurton Jones, Hawkes, & Draper, 1994).

In no post–hunter-gatherer cultures have children been found to have as much time and freedom to play as did those in hunter-gathers cultures. In fact, research on groups of people transitioning from hunting and gathering to farming has shown that the more a family is engaged in farming, and the less they are engaged in hunting and gathering, the less free time the children have for play (Bock & Johnson, 2004; Draper, 1988). In farming families, girls are required to help with childcare and other domestic chores, and boys are required to work in the fields, beginning at a young age.

EXPOSURE TO ALL ASPECTS OF THE ADULT CULTURE

Although hunter-gatherer children usually played independently of adults, they were not segregated from adults. All of the adults in the band, most of whom were literally their aunts and uncles, cared for them and were ready to provide comfort and help when needed. All of the adults—with their different personalities, knowledge, skills, and foibles—were potential models to children of the kind of adult they might wish to become or avoid becoming. The children studied the adults and, in the privacy of their play, mimicked specific adults' actions and personalities, sometimes admiringly and sometimes mockingly (Turnbull, 1982). In our culture children may playfully mimic the heroes, villains, and fools that they see on television, but in hunter-gatherer cultures the models available to mimic were the real adults of their band, who represented the real ways of life toward which the children were moving.

Hunter-gatherer children could see first hand most adult activities, and those they didn't see they heard about as they listened to adult gossip, conversations, and stories. They were free to take part in all of the band's dances and ceremonies. They observed all activities that occurred in camp. They often accompanied their mothers on gathering trips. By the time they were young teenagers, boys were allowed to join men on some of their hunting expeditions. Thus, through observation and eager participation, they learned about the values, lore, and skills of their culture, and then they incorporated it all into their play.

Children not only observed adults using the culture's tools but also were allowed to play with those tools. In response to our question about toys that children played with in the bands that they observed, the respondents to our survey most often listed items that were either real or miniature versions of the tools used regularly by adults, such as bows and arrows, nets, knives, digging sticks, baskets, and mortars and pestles. Even very young children played with objects, such as sharp knives and burning sticks, that adults in our culture would deem too dangerous for children. Hunter-gatherer adults believed that children had sense enough not to hurt themselves with such objects and needed to play with them in order to become skilled at using them. There were some limits, however. The poison-tipped darts or arrows that adults used for hunting big game were kept well out of reach of young children (Thomas, 2006).

A number of hunter-gatherer researchers have commented that the children grew up in a play culture, of their own creation, which paralleled the larger culture within which it was embedded (Gosso et al., 2005; Shostak, 1981; Turnbull, 1961). In some cases the children would quite literally build a play village, of crude huts, a hundred or more yards away from the band's real encampment, which they would use as a base for acting out the full range of adult activities.

CONTINUOUS AGE MIXING AMONG CHILDREN AND ADOLESCENTS

Children and adolescents in hunter-gatherer bands played always in age-mixed groups. Even if the children had wanted to play only with age-mates, they would have been unable to. Because the bands were small and because births for any given mother were widely spaced (generally at least 4 years apart), few children would have found more than one or two other children within a year or 2 of their own age, and many would have found none (Konner, 1975). The typical hunter-gatherer playgroup might consist of half a dozen children ranging in age from 4 to 11 or from 8 to 15.

Age-mixed play offers unique learning opportunities beyond those present in same-age play (Gray, 2011b; Gray & Feldman, 2004). The most obvious advantage for the younger children is that it allows them to engage in and learn from activities that would be too dangerous or difficult for them to engage in alone or just with age-mates. To use Vygotsky's term, it allows them to play within their *zone of proximal development,* that is, at the realm of activities that are beyond their capacities to perform as individuals but within their capacities to perform in collaboration with more skilled others (Vygotsky, 1978a). In age-mixed play, older children provide natural supports, or "scaffolds," that literally or metaphorically raise the younger ones to higher levels. The scaffolds include physical boosts, hints, reminders, directions, and all sorts of help and instruction designed to keep the game going by moving the younger ones along. Such scaffolding occurs naturally and is seen whenever children of widely differing abilities play together at an activity that stretches the skills or knowledge of those who are less experienced.

But it is not just the younger children who benefit from age-mixed play. Older children consolidate their knowledge and expand on it through explaining concepts to younger ones. Even more important, older children exercise their nurturing instincts and gain a sense of themselves as mature and responsible through interactions with younger ones. The special educative power of age-mixed play lies in the asymmetry in knowledge and abilities coupled with play's general requirement that everyone's needs must be met (Gray, 2011b). To keep the game going, both the older and the younger ones must accommodate themselves to the needs of the others while still satisfying their own needs, and everyone learns in that process. That sort of ability to accommodate was particularly important to the hunter-gatherer way of life.

How Play Helped to Build the Hunter-Gatherer Person

Like children everywhere, hunter-gatherer children presumably played for the sake of play, with little conscious thought about its role in preparing them for adulthood. But inevitably they played at the kinds of activities, and in accordance with the kinds of attitudes and values, that prevailed in the adult culture that enveloped them. And so, through play, they educated themselves. Through play, they practiced the subsistence and artistic skills, the social skills and values, and the personal character traits required for hunter-gatherer adulthood.

PLAY AND THE DEVELOPMENT OF HUNTER-GATHERER SUBSISTENCE AND ARTISTIC SKILLS

It would be a mistake to assume that, because hunter-gatherer cultures were "simpler" than ours, children in those cultures had less to learn than do children today. The hunting-and-gathering way of life was highly knowledge intensive and skill intensive; and, because of the relative absence of occupational specialization, each child had to acquire essentially the whole culture or at least that part of it appropriate to his or her gender.

To become hunters, boys had to learn how to identify and track the 200 to 300 different species of mammals and birds that the group might hunt, how to craft to perfection the tools of hunting, and how to use those tools with great skill. Louis Liebenberg (1990) has argued convincingly that the origins of scientific reasoning lay in hunter-gatherers' animal tracking. Hunters combined the faint clues that they saw in sand, mud, or foliage with a vast store of knowledge, accumulated from their own experiences and from cultural transmission, to generate and test hypotheses about the size, sex, physical condition, speed of movement, and time of passage of the animal they were tracking (Wannenburgh, 1979). For example, they might infer that a certain antelope had passed by before a certain time of day by noticing that one of its footprints was overlain by the track of a kind of beetle that moves about only when the sun has reached a certain height in the sky (Thomas, 2006). Once a game animal was in sight, enormous skill was required to get close enough to it to shoot and hit it with a small poison-tipped arrow or dart. Researchers working in various hunter-gatherer societies found that hunting skills generally didn't peak until a man was 35 to 45 years old, evidence of continued learning in adulthood (Bock, 2002; Kaplan, Hill, Lancaster, & Hurtado, 2000).

It is no surprise that boys growing up in a culture where hunting was so greatly valued, so much talked about, and known to be so difficult would play and explore in ways that helped them to become skilled hunters. Hunter-gatherer children as young as 3 years old were observed to track and stalk small animals and one another in their play (Liebenberg, 1990). All of the respondents to our survey said that the boys in the culture they studied spent great amounts of time at playful tracking and hunting. The two respondents who studied the Agta—a culture where women as well as men hunt—noted that girls as well as boys in that culture engaged in much playful hunting. Young children might stalk and shoot at stationary targets, or at butterflies and toads, while pretending to hunt big game. By the age of 8 or 9 they might sometimes succeed in killing small mammals, which they would bring back to camp and cook, pretending they were adults bringing back big game. By their early teenage years they might sometimes join adults in real big-game-hunting expeditions, still in the spirit of adventure and play.

Successful gathering also required great skill and knowledge. Hunter-gatherer women—and men, too, to the degree that they gathered—had to know which of the countless varieties of roots, tubers, seeds, fruits, and greens in their area were edible and nutritious, when and where to find them, how to dig them (in the case of roots and tubers), how to extract the edible portions efficiently (in the case of grains, nuts, and certain plant fibers), and, in some cases, how to process them to make them edible or more nutritious than they otherwise would be. These abilities included physical skills, honed by years of practice, as well as the capacity to remember, use, add to, and modify an enormous store of culturally transmitted verbal knowledge. Researchers have found that the ability of hunter-gatherer women to gather and process foods efficiently increased up to the age of about 40, just as the ability of the men to hunt effectively did (Bock, 2005; Kaplan et al., 2000). It is not surprising, therefore, that young children, especially girls, spent much time playing with digging sticks and with mortars and pestles, and at games that involved finding and identifying varieties of plants.

As is true in other cultures, boys and girls in hunter-gatherer cultures segregated themselves by sex for some but not all of their play. Boys would play at hunting and other men's activities; girls would play at gathering and processing plant foods, birthing, infant care, and other women's activities; and both boys and girls would play at the many activities engaged in by both men and women. Our survey question about the specific kinds of activities observed in children's play elicited many examples of valued adult activities, beyond hunting and gathering per se, that children mimicked in their play. Caring for infants, climbing trees, building vine ladders, building huts, using knives and other tools, making various sorts of tools, carrying heavy loads, building rafts, making fires, defending against attacks from pretend predators, imitating animals (a means of identifying animals and learning their habits), making music, dancing, storytelling, and arguing were all mentioned by one or more respondents. Hunter-gatherer groups have rich traditions of music, dance, and stories, so it is not surprising that the children made and played musical instruments, sang, danced, and told stories in their play. Depending on the culture, they might also create beaded designs or other visual artwork.

The outdoor life of hunter-gatherers, including the need to flee from or fend off predators, requires that people of all ages and both sexes maintain fit and agile bodies. In agricultural and industrial societies, boys generally engage in much more vigorous physical play than do girls, but in hunter-gatherer societies both sexes engaged, nearly equally, in a great amount of such play (Draper, 1988; Gosso et al., 2005; Turnbull, 1961). They would joyfully chase one another around and, depending on topography, would climb and swing on trees, leap, swim, carry heavy objects, and perform all sorts of acrobatics in their play. They also practiced graceful, coordinated movements in their dances.

PLAY AND THE DEVELOPMENT OF HUNTER-GATHERER SOCIAL SKILLS AND VALUES

As I have already pointed out, social play, by its very nature, requires continuous cooperation, attention to and satisfaction of one another's needs, and consensual decision making. These are precisely the skills and values that are most central to hunter-gatherer social life. By allowing their children to spend essentially all of their time playing, hunter-gatherer adults allowed their children unlimited practice of the social skills and values that they held most dear. The age-mixed nature of the play, and the fact that it occurred in a cultural context where boasting or trying to prove oneself better than others was ridiculed, ensured that the play was even more cooperative and less competitive than is play in other cultures.

Using data from the Human Relations Area Files, John Roberts and his colleagues concluded that hunter-gatherer cultures were the only category of cultures that completely lacked competitive games (Sutton-Smith & Roberts, 1970). In a chapter describing Ju/'hoan children's play, Lorna Marshall (1976) noted that even games with formal rules, which could be played competitively, were played noncompetitively in the groups that she observed. All of the respondents to our survey stressed the noncompetitive nature of the play that they observed. For example, P. Bion Griffin commented that the only consistent rule of the play that he observed among Agta children was that "no one should win and beat another in a visible fashion."

Many of the games that hunter-gatherers played involved close coordination of the players' movements with those of the other players. This was true of all of their dancing and dancelike games, but it was also true of many of their other games. For example, in playful hunting with nets, the net-handlers and bush-beaters had to coordinate their actions just as adults had to in real net hunting. Another example is a tree-swinging game, in which children would coordinate their actions to bend a sapling to the ground and then release it all at once, so that the one who didn't let go would swing wildly in the treetop or be catapulted through the air (Turnbull, 1982). Such games, presumably, not only helped children learn to work together as a team but also helped bind them together emotionally as a community who cared about one another.

Several researchers have commented on the games of give-and-take played by hunter-gatherer infants with older children or adults (Bakeman et al., 1990; Eibl-Eibesfeldt, 1989; Gosso, 2005). Infants as young as 12 months old, or even younger, would delightfully give an object to the older playmate, then receive it, then give it again, and so on. The joy of such giving seems to lie in the instincts of all normal human infants. In a series of experiments conducted in the United States, nearly every one of more than 100 infants, aged 12 to 18 months, spontaneously gave toys to an adult during brief sessions in a laboratory room (Hay & Murray, 1982; Rheingold, Hay, & West, 1976). In our culture, such giving by infants is not much commented upon, but in at least some hunter-gatherer cultures it was celebrated, much like infants' early words are in our culture. Among the Ju/'hoansi, such giving by infants was deliberately cultivated. Grandmothers, in particular, initiated infants into the culture of sharing and giving by encouraging such games and by guiding infants' hands in the giving of beads to others (Bakeman et al., 1990; Wiessner, 1982). This is the one example of systematic, deliberate adult influence on children's play that I have found in the hunter-gatherer literature. No human trait was more important to the hunter-gatherer way of life than the willingness to give or share.

To be a successful adult hunter-gatherer, one must not only be willing and able to cooperate with others but also be able to assert one's own needs and wishes effectively, without antagonizing others. Practice at such self-assertion occurs in social play everywhere, as players negotiate the rules and decide who gets to play what part. In addition, hunter-gatherer children practiced such assertion more explicitly as they mimicked adult arguments in their play. For example, Turnbull (1982, p. 134) described, as follows, how Mbuti children, age 9 on up, playfully rehashed and tried to improve upon the arguments they had heard among adults:

> "It may start through imitation of a real dispute the children witnessed in the main camp, perhaps the night before. They all take roles and imitate the adults. It is almost a form of judgment for if the adults talked their way out of the dispute the children, having performed their imitation once, are likely to drop it. If the children detect any room for improvement, however, they will explore that, and if the adult argument was inept and everyone went to sleep that night in a bad temper, then the children try and show that they can do better, and if they cannot, then they revert to ridicule which they play out until they are all rolling on the ground in near hysterics. That happens to be the way many of the most potentially violent and dangerous disputes are settled in adult life."

PLAY AND THE DEVELOPMENT OF PERSONAL AUTONOMY AND SELF-CONTROL

The personality traits of the ideal hunter-gatherer are different from those of the ideal farmer (Barry, Child, & Bacon, 1959). Success in farming depends on adhering to tried-and-true methods. Creativity is risky, because if a crop fails a whole year's food supply may be lost. Moreover, farming societies are generally hierarchically structured, so obedience to those higher in rank is often essential to social and economic success. In contrast, success in hunting and gathering requires continuous, creative, intelligent adaptation to the ever-changing conditions of nature. For hunter-gatherers, the best assurance that food will arrive in camp on any given day derives from the accumulated efforts of diverse individuals and teams, each foraging in their own ways and using their own best judgments. The diversity of methods, coupled with the sharing of food among all members of the band, creates a hedge against the possibility that anyone will go for days without food. Thus, while the ideal farmer tends to be obedient, rule abiding, and conservative, the ideal hunter-gatherer tends to be assertive, willful, creative, and willing to take risks. A number of researchers have contended, quite reasonably, that relatively strict parenting promotes the rule-abiding obedience required of farmers and that permissive parenting promotes the self-initiative, creativity, and individual autonomy required of hunter-gatherers (Barry et al., 1959; DeVore, Murdock, & Whiting, 1968; Gould, 1969).

By definition, play entails continuous practice of self-initiative, creativity, and individual choice. Players must follow rules, but the rules always leave room for creative choices, and players are continuously free to modify rules to meet their wishes and prevailing environmental conditions. Moreover, players in a social game are free to quit if they don't like the rules and can't get others to change them. Likewise, hunter-gatherer adults and families who no longer wish to conform to the procedures of their band are free to start a new band or move to a more compatible neighboring band where they have relatives and friends (Ingold, 1999; Woodburn, 1982). Such mobility is unavailable to farmers, who are tied to the land that they cultivate. By allowing their children to play all day, hunter-gatherers allowed their children to develop fully the characteristics of personal autonomy that are essential to hunter-gatherer success.

Another trait of hunter-gatherers often commented upon by those who have observed them is their extraordinary self-control, especially their ability to remain cheerful in the face of pain and adversity. For example, after quoting another researcher about the cheerfulness of people in another hunter-hunter gatherer culture, Richard Gould (1969, p. 120) wrote: "Often I have had cause to notice this same good cheer and readiness to laugh and joke among the people of the Gibson Desert [hunter-gatherers in Australia], even when they are plagued by boils and heat, pestered by flies, and short of food. This cheerfulness seems to be part of a disciplined acceptance of frequent hardships which complaints would only aggravate."

Elizabeth Marshall Thomas commented similarly about the Ju/'hoansi whom she observed. As illustration, she recounted a scene in which a young Ju/'hoan girl had accidently stepped into a trap that a visiting biologist had set for a hyena far from the campsite. The teeth of the steel trap, which she could not open, had gone through her foot, and because the trap was fixed securely into the ground, she could not move it to sit down but had to stand on her nontrapped foot. She apparently stood, quietly and calmly so as not to attract predatory hyenas, until her uncle found her many hours later. Here are Thomas's words (2006, pp. 216–217):

> "I will always remember her calmness as we brought her to the encampment and dressed the wound. She had been alone, helpless, and in pain for many hours in a place frequented by hyenas, yet she acted as if nothing had happened, nothing at all. Instead, she chatted with other people about this and that in an offhand manner. To me, such composure in these circumstances did not seem possible, and I remember wondering if their nervous systems were the same

as ours. But of course, their nervous systems were the same as ours. It was their self-control that was superior. You can say that things are wrong, but you cannot show it. Your body language must suggest that everything is fine."

Lev Vygotsky (1978b) probably did not have this degree of self-control in mind when he wrote about the role of play in the development of children's capacities to control their impulses. Moreover, no researcher that I know of has suggested that hunter-gatherers' extraordinary self-control is developed through play. Yet, I suggest, it may be no coincidence that the same cultures that allowed their children the greatest freedom to play also produced people who seemed to have the greatest capacity for self-control. Children's strong drive to play leads them to ignore bodily discomforts and psychological irritations in order to continue following the rules of the game. In their physical play, children continuously dose themselves with moderate yet manageable amounts of fear, as they swing in trees, dive from cliffs, and engage in other thrilling adventures. In their social play, children may also often experience anger, to varying degrees, as will occur whenever people interact in close proximity over time. But to continue playing—which they strongly wish to do—they must find ways to control those emotions.

Learning to control emotions may, in fact, be one of the primary functions of play. Several researchers have supported an emotion regulation theory of play's functions, largely on the basis of play deprivation experiments with animals (Pellis, Pellis, & Bell, 2010). The most obvious behavioral deficits in monkeys and rats that have been deprived of play during their juvenile development involve emotional dysregulation. The animals show excessive, maladaptive, incapacitating fear and/or aggression when placed in stressful situations. Perhaps the extraordinary amounts of play engaged in by hunter-gatherer children helped to promote their extraordinary capacities to regulate their emotions in ways that were adaptive to their conditions of life.

Conclusion

By describing the universal identifying characteristics of play, the social conditions for play in hunter-gatherer bands, and the specific ways in which hunter-gatherer children played, I have in this chapter shown how hunter-gatherer children apparently acquired through play the skills, knowledge, values, and character traits essential to hunter-gatherer success. As Karl Groos (1901) pointed out long ago in his Darwinian analysis of human play, children come into the world predisposed to incorporate the adult activities that they see around them into their play and in that way become skilled at those activities. Consistent with this view, hunter-gatherer children played at all of the activities central to their culture, especially the most difficult ones.

The extraordinary play drive of human children was presumably shaped, from its earlier primate origins, by natural selection in the context of the hunter-gatherer way of life. Therefore, it may be no coincidence that the values, social skills, and character traits that seem to be part and parcel of all social play are precisely the values, social skills, and character traits that are essential to hunter-gatherers' egalitarian ways of life. Social play inhibits the drive for dominance; requires sharing, cooperation, and consensual decision making; fosters individual autonomy and self-assertion within a context of cooperation; and fosters the ability to control one's impulses and emotions. All of these apparently contributed to hunter-gatherers' abilities to survive.

This article has focused on play in hunter-gatherer cultures, but it is worthwhile to speculate about implications for our culture, today. Over the past half century, in the United States and other modern societies, there has been a continuous decline in children's freedom to play, especially in their freedom to play socially, in age-mixed groups, outdoors, away from adults (Chudacoff, 2007; Clements, 2004; Gray, 2011a). During this same period there has been a continuous rise—based on standard, unchanged measures—in childhood and adolescent anxiety, depression, feelings of helplessness, impulsiveness, and narcissism (Gray, 2011a; Twenge et al., 2010; Twenge, Konrath, Foster, Campbell, & Bushman, 2008; Twenge, Zhang, & Im, 2004). It seems quite plausible to me, based on the analysis of play's value presented here, that the rise in all of these forms of psychopathology may be at least partly a result of the decline of play (Gray, 2011a).

References

Amabile, T. (1996). *Creativity in context: Update to the social psychology of creativity.* Boulder, CO: Westview Press.

Bakeman, R., Adamson, L. B., Konner, M., & Barr, R. (1990). !Kung infancy: The social context of object exploration. *Child Development, 61,* 794–809.

Barry, H., Child, I., & Bacon, M. K. (1959). The relation of child training to subsistence economy. *American Anthropologist, 61,* 51–63.

Bekoff, M., & Byers, J. A. (Eds.). (1998). *Animal play: Evolutionary, comparative, and ecological perspectives.* Cambridge, UK: Cambridge University Press.

Biben, M. (1998). Squirrel monkey playfighting: Making the case for the cognitive training function for play. In M. Bekoff & J. A. Byers (Eds.), *Animal play: Evolutionary, comparative, and ecological perspectives* (pp. 161–182). Cambridge, UK: Cambridge University Press.

Blurton Jones, N., Hawkes, K., & Draper, P. (1994). Differences between Hazda and !Kung children's work: Affluence or practical reason? In E. S. Burch Jr. & L. J. Ellana (Eds.), *Key issues in hunter-gatherer research* (pp. 189–215). Oxford: Berg.

Bock, J. (2002). Learning, life history, and productivity: Children's lives in the Okavango Delta, Botswana. *Human Nature, 13,* 161–197.

Bock, J. (2005). What makes a competent adult forager? In B. S. Hewlett & M. E. Lamb (Eds.), *Hunter-gatherer childhoods: Evolutionary, developmental, and cultural perspectives* (pp. 109–128). New Brunswick, NJ: Transaction.

Bock, J., & Johnson, S. E. (2004). Subsistence ecology and play among the Okavango Delta peoples of Botswana. *Human Nature, 15,* 63–81.

Boehm, C. (1999). *Hierarchy in the forest: The evolution of egalitarian behavior*. Cambridge, MA: Harvard University Press.

Chudacoff, H. P. (2007). *Children at play: An American history*. New York, NY: New York University Press.

Clements, R. (2004). An investigation of the status of outdoor play. *Contemporary Issues of Early Childhood, 5,* 68–80.

DeVore, I., Murdock, G. P., & Whiting, J. W. M. (1968). Discussions, part VII: Are the hunter-gatherers a cultural type? In R. Lee & I. DeVore (Eds.), *Man the hunter* (pp. 335–339). Chicago, IL: Aldine.

Draper, P. (1988). Technological change and child behavior among the !Kung. *Ethnology, 27,* 339–365.

Eibl-Eibesfeldt, I. (1989). *Human ethology*. New York, NY: Aldine de Gruyter.

Fine, G. A. (1986). Organized baseball and its folk equivalents: The transition from informal to formal control. In B. Mergen (Ed.), *Cultural dimensions of play, games, and sport* (pp. 175–190). Champaign, IL: Human Kinetics Publishers.

Furth, H. G. (1996). *Desire for society: Children's knowledge as social imagination*. New York, NY: Plenum.

Garvey, C. (1974). Some properties of social play. *Merrill-Palmer Quarterly, 20,* 163–180.

Geen, R. G. (1991). Social motivation. *Annual Review of Psychology, 42,* 377–399.

Gosso, Y., Otta, E., de Lima, M., Ribeiro, F. J. L., & Bussab, V. S. R. (2005). Play in hunter-gatherer societies. In A. D. Pellegrini and P. K. Smith (Eds.), *The nature of play: Great apes and humans* (pp. 213–253). New York, NY: Guilford.

Gould, R. A. (1969). *Yiwara: Foragers of the Australian desert*. New York, NY: Charles Scribner

Gray, P. (2009). Play as a foundation for hunter-gatherer social existence. *American Journal of Play, 1,* 476–522.

Gray, P. (2011a). The decline of play and the rise of psychopathology in children and adolescents. *American Journal of Play, 3,* 443–463.

Gray, P. (2011b). The special value of children's age-mixed play. *American Journal of Play, 3,* 500–522.

Gray, P., & Feldman, J. (2004). Playing in the zone of proximal development: Qualities of self-directed age mixing between adolescents and young children at a democratic school. *American Journal of Education, 110,* 108–145.

Groos, K. (1901). *The play of man*. New York, NY: Appleton.

Guemple, L. (1988). Teaching social relations to Inuit children. In T. Ingold, D. Riches, & J. Woodburn (Eds.), *Hunters and gatherers 2: Property, power, and ideology* (pp. 130–149). Oxford: Berg.

Hay, D. F., & Murray, P. (1982). Giving and requesting: Social facilitation of infants' offers to adults. *Infant Behavior and Development, 5,* 301–310.

Huizinga, J. (1955). *Homo Ludens: A study of the play-element in culture*. Boston, MA: Beacon Press.

Ingold, T. (1999). On the social relations of the hunter-gatherer band. In R. B. Lee & R. H. Daly (Eds.), *The Cambridge encyclopedia of hunters and gatherers* (pp. 399–410). Cambridge, UK: Cambridge University Press.

Kaplan, H., Hill, K., Lancaster, J., & Hurtado, A. M. (2000). A theory of human life history evolution: Diet, intelligence, and longevity. *Evolutionary Anthropology, 9,* 156–185.

Kelly, R. I. (1995). *The foraging spectrum: Diversity in hunter-gatherer lifeways.* Washington, DC: Smithsonian Institution Press.

Konner, M. L. (1975). Relations among infants and juveniles in comparative perspective. In M. Lewis & L. A. Rosenblum (Eds.), *Friendship and peer relations* (pp. 99–129). New York, NY: Wiley.

Lee, R. B. (1988). Reflections on primitive communism. In T. Ingold, D. Riches, & J. Woodburn (Eds.), *Hunters and gatherers 1* (pp. 252–268). Oxford: Berg.

Liebenberg, L. (1990). *The art of tracking: The origin of science.* Claremont, South Africa: David Philip Publishers.

Marshall, L. (1976). *The !Kung of Nyae Nyae.* Cambridge, MA: Harvard University Press.

Pellis, S. M., Pellis, V. C., & Bell, H. C. (2010). The functions of play in the development of the social brain. *American Journal of Play, 2,* 278–296.

Rheingold, H. L., Hay, D. F., & West, M. J. (1976). Sharing in the second year of life. *Child Development, 47,* 1148–1158.

Shostak, M. (1981). *Nisa: The life and words of a !Kung woman.* Cambridge, MA: Harvard University Press.

Sutton-Smith, B., & Roberts, J. M. (1970). The cross-cultural and psychological study of games. In G. Lüschen (Ed.), *The cross-cultural analysis of sport and games* (pp. 100–108). Champaign, IL: Stipes.

Thomas, E. M. (2006). *The old way.* New York, NY: Farrar, Straus & Giroux.

Turnbull, C. M. (1961). *The forest people.* New York, NY: Simon & Schuster.

Turnbull, C. M. (1982). The ritualization of potential conflict between the sexes among the Mbuti. In E. G. Leacock & R. B. Lee (Eds.), *Politics and history in band societies* (pp. 133–155). Cambridge: Cambridge University Press.

Twenge, J. M., Gentile, B., DeWall, C. N., Ma, D., Lacefield, K., & Schurtz, D. R. (2010). Birth cohort increases in psychopathology among young Americans, 1938–2007: A cross-temporal meta-analysis of the MMPI. *Clinical Psychology Review, 30,* 145–154.

Twenge, J. M., Konrath, S., Foster, J. D., Campbell, W. K., & Bushman, B. J. (2008). Egos inflating over time: A cross-temporal meta-analysis of the narcissistic personality inventory. *Journal of Personality, 76,* 875–901.

Twenge, J. M., Zhang, L., & Im, C. (2004). It's beyond my control: A cross-temporal meta-analysis of increasing externality in locus of control, 1960–2002. *Personality and Social Psychology Review, 8,* 308–319.

Vygotsky, L. (1978a). Interaction between learning and development. In M. Cole, V. John-Steiner, S. Scribner, & E. Souberman (Eds.), *Mind and society: The development of higher psychological processes* (pp. 79–91). Cambridge, MA: Harvard University Press.

Vygotsky, L. S. (1978b). The role of play in development. In M. Cole, V. John-Steiner, S. Scribner, & E. Souberman (Eds.), *Mind in society: The development of higher psychological processes* (pp. 92–104). Cambridge, MA: Harvard University Press.

Wannenburgh, A. (1979). *The bushmen.* New York, NY: Mayflower Books.

Wiessner, P. (1982). Risk, reciprocity and social influences on !Kung San economics. In E. Leacock & R. Lee (Eds.), *Politics and history in band societies* (pp. 61–82). Cambridge, UK: Cambridge University Press.

Woodburn, J. (1982). Egalitarian societies. *Man, 17,* 431–451.

15

Rough-and-Tumble Play and the Cooperation–Competition Dilemma: Evolutionary and Developmental Perspectives on the Development of Social Competence

Joseph L. Flanders, Khalisa N. Herman,
and Daniel Paquette

Introduction

Mammals are highly dependent on social relationships throughout the life span. Humans, for example, are thought to have spent more than 90% of history living in hunter-gatherer societies (Gosso, Otta, Morais, Ribeiro, & Bussab, 2005), in which individuals typically belong to multiple social groups (Gosso et al., 2005; Suomi, 2005). Some social skills are likely to have emerged within such early environments of evolutionary adaptedness (EEA) to adapt to these social demands. However, underlying human social competence are deep-rooted and ancient neural systems governing attachment (Panksepp, 1998a), trust (Heinrichs, von Dawans, & Domes, 2009), and empathy (Preston & De Waal, 2002).

At the same time, humans and other social mammals face a lifelong challenge of competing for resources and access to mates. High status in a dominance hierarchy is highly desirable, as it affords preferential access to resources, greater longevity, and a high level of reproductive success (Wilson & Daly, 1997). On an ongoing basis, individuals—be it toddlers in a playgroup or the presidents of countries—face the universal challenge of maximizing their position within a social hierarchy without upsetting the relationships on which they depend for survival (Suomi, 1982). Thus, the presence of these two competing motivational systems, cooperation and competition, poses a complex, ongoing existential conflict for social mammals.

How is it that humans and other mammals develop the social competence necessary to adapt to the complexities of group living? What happens when individuals lack this competence? How and when do we intervene to prevent the development of psychopathology? In an attempt to address these questions, we propose that rough-and-tumble (R&T) play promotes the development of social competence, social cognition, and self-regulation by providing young mammals with embodied practice in activities that involve both cooperation and competition (Scott & Panksepp, 2003). Sadly, R&T play has been on the decline in North America as children have fewer opportunities to play in school (Miller & Almon, 2009), and adults have become less comfortable with aggressive play (Panksepp, 1993). The consequences of these trends are not entirely evident at this point, but the following examination of the role of R&T play in evolution and development suggests that we may be depriving children of important formative experiences.

Play and Social Development

The term *play* refers to those behaviors that are punctuated with positive affect, focus on process over the creation of a product, and are performed in nonserious contexts (Rubin, Fein, & Vandenberg, 1983; Smith, 2004). Because of the nonserious nature of play, individuals are able to interact with others in a manner that is largely free from normal consequences (Suomi, 1979b). This aspect of social play may explain why it is commonly interspersed with a range of social behaviors including fighting, fleeing, mating, and parenting behavior patterns, which are often expressed in gender-specific ways (Fagen, 1981; Power, 2000).

Social play in particular is thought to promote the development of social competence by providing individuals with opportunities to develop skills for group living. The design of social play supports this position, for it is a universal feature of childhood (Edwards, 2000) and is synonymous with the juvenile period in a variety of social mammals including humans (Fagen, 1981). Additionally, both the quantity and quality of social play correlate with measures of social competence (Rubin, 1982; Symons, 1978), and as children mature, play becomes both more social and more cognitively complex across development (Parten, 1932; Rubin, 1982; Smilansky, 1968). Finally, researchers have found that mammals deprived of companionship during peak play periods exhibit deficits in social competence (for a review, see Herman, Paukner, & Suomi, 2011; Pellis & Pellis, 2006). For example, researchers have found that rhesus monkeys and rats reared with their mothers but without peers during infancy tend to respond to affiliative or "friendly" social bids with heightened levels of agonism including aggression and fear-withdrawal behaviors as juveniles (Kempes, Gulickx, van Daalen, Louwerse, & Sterck, 2008; Pellis & Pellis, 2006).

Whereas immature individuals engage in various types of social play including contingent interaction, pretense, and games with rules, R&T play appears to be the most evolutionarily ancient and widespread type across social mammals and humans (Panksepp, 1998a). It consists of a variety of vigorous behaviors such as wrestling, grappling, jumping, tumbling, and running that would appear to be aggressive if not for the play contexts (Pellegrini & Smith, 1998). Panksepp (1998a, 1998b) has argued that the mammalian brain is hard-wired for R&T play based on the evidence that play behavior is homeostatically regulated: Juvenile rats will exhibit R&T play behaviors, which usually begins around 17 days of age, even if they have been prevented from engaging in any other prior play experiences, and will play even more vigorously if intermittently deprived of the opportunity to play (Panksepp, 1998a). However, these early impulses will only manifest themselves under the right environmental conditions. Rough-and-tumble play, like voluntary exploratory behavior, appears to emerge only when an animal is secure and content. Fear and hunger, for example, and associated states of deprivation quickly eliminate play behaviors. Young rats must have a secure home environment, for example, with abundant parental involvement, in order to play (Panksepp, 1998a).

Among humans, mothers are often the first to play fight with their infants, through tickling bouts and mocked acts of aggression (e.g., "I'm going to eat you! Ha! Ha! Ha!"). As motor coordination develops, children become more mobile and more active, and fathers increasingly become a favorite R&T play partner (Roopnarine, Hooper, Ahmeduzzaman, & Pollack, 1993). Fathers engage in more frequent R&T play with children than mothers, and both parents engage in more frequent R&T play with boys than girls (Panksepp, Burgdorh, Turner, & Gordan, 2003). Parent–child R&T play peaks around the time the child reaches 4 years of age (Pellegini & Smith, 1998). Children (especially boys) prefer physical play with either parent over any other form of play (Ross & Taylor, 1989). Rough-and-tumble play among peers begins to emerge at preschool age, peaks between 8 and 10 years of age, and trails off at the beginning of adolescence. It is more common in boys than girls across cultures (Carson, Burks, & Parke, 1993).

The most commonly studied form of R&T play occurs between peers. Blurton-Jones (1972) discusses the cues that differentiate R&T play from aggression in preschool children, following up on Harlow and Harlow's (1965) descriptions of play fighting in young rhesus monkeys. In play fighting contexts, children spend most of their time in close proximity; by contrast, during serious aggressive encounters, they come together briefly for aggressive acts and then flee rapidly from each other. Despite the subtle differences, children are typically highly adept at distinguishing playful from aggressive fighting (Smith & Boulton, 1990), regardless of their culture (Costabile et al., 1991).

Despite the prevalence of R&T play, it remains the least studied form of human play, probably because many people consider it disruptive and dangerous (Panksepp, 1993). Nonetheless, a recent increase in publications on R&T play over the last decade reflects a growing consensus that it is a highly important aspect of development (Paquette, 2004a; Pellegrini & Smith, 1998; Peterson & Flanders, 2005).

Evolutionary Functions of Rough-and-Tumble Play

The conservation of R&T play across mammalian species raises the question of whether these behaviors provide reproductive benefits. The importance of play in general in human evolution has been well described in the literature (e.g., Bateson, 2005). For example, Bruner (1976) argues that the prolonged juvenile period of humans, relative to other species, provides more time for play, and thus more time to develop sophisticated cognitive abilities. This hypothesis is borne out in neurobiological research on the development of the frontal lobes in animal play (e.g., Pellis & Pellis, 2006). However, consensus on specific function(s) of R&T play has not been reached. The prevailing theories over the past century have been that R&T play provides practice in the development of fighting skills (Groos, 1898) and/or establishing and reinforcing existing dominance relationships (Pellegrinii et al., 1998). During R&T play, participants employ a variety of mock aggressive behaviors in order to gain positional advantage over a partner (Pellegrini, 1988, 2002). However, most researchers have reported that adult monkeys, cats, and rats with little or no play experience during infancy still exhibit adequate fighting skills (Baldwin, 1969, 1986; Baldwin & Baldwin, 1973, 1976, 1977; Martin & Caro, 1985). Thus, more recently, efforts have been directed toward investigating the dominance theory of R&T play.

The design of R&T play is in accord with dominance theory, as higher rates typically are found for males than females, particularly in species where higher levels of aggression are found in males compared to females (DiPietro, 1981; Fry, 2005; Pellegrini, 2002). For instance, Paquette (1994) showed that adolescent chimpanzees use play fighting to negotiate status in their dominance hierarchy. Play interactions are a particularly interesting vehicle for dominance negotiations for those dyads with ambiguous dominance relationships. Participants are thought to use play to identify a partner's weaknesses and exploit this knowledge to gain social status. Recently, Fry (2005) found that adolescents living in a violent rural community displayed increasing levels of R&T play with age that was punctuated by more aggressive elements, whereas neither element was present in a nearby peaceful community.

One feature of R&T play that may pose a challenge to dominance theory is self-handicapping, if high rates persist into adolescence. If individuals are commonly disguising their true skill levels in order to play with a less skilled partner, gaining social status with a social partner via R&T play would be difficult. Observations of humans and animals have noted that play participants frequently handicap themselves during R&T play in an effort to match their partner's skill level (Aldis, 1975). Most dominant rats, for example, will let a subordinate peer pin them from time to time presumably to keep the peer interested in continuing play (Panksepp, 1998a). Unfortunately, there has been little empirical research on self-handicapping, with the exception of Thompson, Bekoff, and Byers (1998). As one would suspect, even less is known about developmental changes in rates of self-handicapping. Taken together, while there is some convincing support for dominance theory, more research is needed before any conclusions can be made about the impact of self-handicapping on the formation of dominance relations.

Recently, Peterson and Flanders (2005) hypothesized that the primary function of R&T play is the promotion of self-regulation skills. In a similar vein, Spinka, Newberry, and Bekoff (2001) posited that the main function of social play in general is the development of emotion regulation and motor coordination, both skills important for handling unexpected social conflicts. The design of R&T play may be uniquely suited for enhancing self-regulation: For instance, the practice of self-handicapping during R&T play probably involves the use of impulse control, moderation of strength levels, and planning and monitoring of social goals, all skills that reflect self-regulation. Furthermore, R&T play appears to exercise the neural circuits involved in regulating emotions and motor behavior: Gordon, Burke, Akil, Watson, and Panksepp (2003) reported higher metabolic activity within the frontal lobes of rats given the opportunity to play with peers compared to individually housed rats. Finally, both monkeys and rats with a history of play deprivation during infancy display a marked absence of self-regulation during social conflicts, including disproportionately aggressive and fearful responses (Harlow, 1969; Herman et al., 2011; Pellis & Pellis, 2006; Suomi, 1979a). Taken together, these findings support the proposition that R&T play may be important for developing self-regulation for navigating social conflicts.

Peterson and Flanders (2005) also hypothesize that R&T play furthers cooperation between social group members. While many of the elements of R&T play on the surface appear to involve aggressive behavior patterns, a social play bout appears to be functionally maintained not by imposing strength or social status, but rather by demonstrating sensitivity to the play partner. This feature could be described as the principle of "mutual enjoyment": R&T play partners are free to hit, push, and chase each other, but only as long as both partners are enjoying themselves. As soon as it stops being fun, the play interactions break down. In playing aggressively with you, I am learning to modulate my behavior with respect to yours; I am allowing your motivational and emotional states to shape mine; and I am adopting a shared frame of reference. Over time, this embodied appreciation of other gives rise to more abstract, social-cognitive abilities, such that one day, we are collaborating together on a research project. Thus, while there is an elaborate body of research demonstrating the physical, cognitive, emotional, and social functions of play, less attention has been paid to the manner in which play cultivates self-regulation. Play might be regarded as early social cognition.

Along these lines, Smith (2004) suggested that R&T play contributes to the development of perspective taking or theory of mind skills. In support of this proposition, young children who more readily adopt a shared play mindset with their mothers are more likely to be compliant with their requests (Kochanska, 2002). Along these lines, participating in R&T play with other prosocial partners also probably promotes other forms of social cooperation. For example, researchers have found that monkeys are more likely to help previous play partners than other group members (Biben, Suomi, & MacDonald, 1993; O'Neill-Wagner, Bolig, & Price, 2001), and that R&T play facilitates an infant hyena's transition from a family unit to a larger social group (Drea, Hawk, & Glickman, 1997). In sum, many features of R&T play appear to be directed toward developing self-regulation and cooperation, both skills that are necessary for resolving unexpected social conflicts.

The Role of Fathers in Human Rough-and-Tumble Play Development

Rough-and-tumble play has long been considered the domain of fathers. In comparison to great apes, humans are unique in the extent to which fathers are involved in parenting. While human fathers may give little or no direct basic care to children (Hewlett, 2000), they do adopt parental roles that are distinct from those of the mother (Le Camus, 2000). Human fathers play at least the role of provider of resources and protection for their spouses and children and, depending on the culture, assume various parental responsibilities, generally with boys at the end of childhood (Paquette, 2004a).

According to Le Camus (2000), paternal roles can be grouped together under the function of opening children up to the outside world. Fathers act as catalysts for risk taking, inciting children to use initiative in unfamiliar situations, to explore, take chances, overcome obstacles, be braver in the presence of strangers, and stand up for themselves (Paquette, 2004a, 2004b; Paquette, Eugène, Dubeau, & Gagnon, 2009). This parental specialization may have occurred phylogenetically with the emergence of the sexual division of labor (hunting for men and gathering for women) fostered, on the one hand, by the extremely high demands of the human infant due to its immature status and, on the other, by the growing complexity of the human societies to which the offspring must adapt (Paquette & Bigras, 2010).

Thanks in part to the great plasticity of human behavior, we are currently witnessing increased paternal involvement in Western industrialized societies, especially in middle socioeconomic families: Fathers are more involved in caregiving than before, with younger and younger children, and progressively more with girls, even in R&T play (Dumont & Paquette, 2008; Paquette, 2005; Paquette, Carbonneau, Dubeau, Bigras, & Tremblay, 2003). While fathers involved in caregiving become increasingly important sources of comfort for their children, studies show that such fathers continue to engage in vigorous, physical play with their children (Dumont & Paquette, 2008).

Paquette (2004a, 2004b) has suggested that fathers are primarily engaged in an "activation relationship" with their children, challenging them to confront and master the unfamiliar and unpredictable in the outside world. In particular, according to this evolutionary model, as men generally take more risks than women (Byrnes, Miller, & Schaffer, 1999), fathers are in the best position to teach children, especially boys, to socialize (regulate) their aggression, that is, to develop their skills and self-confidence in competitive situations, through the stimulation of risk taking, discipline, and father–child R&T play. It should be noted that in individualist societies (where autonomy and competition are valued), rather than in collectivist societies, the highest levels of interpersonal aggression, child–child and father–child R&T play, and also physical punishment of children are observed (Allès-Jardel, Schneider, Goldstein, & Normand, 2009; Paquette, 2004a).

Physical aggression appears in young children at an early age, around 8 or 9 months, and for the vast majority peaks between 15 and 24 months (Tremblay et al., 1999). At this age, most conflicts occur without physical aggression and consist of taking or attempting to take objects away from others (Coie & Dodge, 1998). The age of 2 years also corresponds to a period during which children establish a dominance hierarchy among themselves. The early age at which conflicts over object possession and dominance rank among children begin reveals a strong competitive tendency in children for environmental resources, even though aggressive behaviors are replaced later on in the majority of children by behaviors considered more socially acceptable.

According to Charlesworth (1988), the competition for limited resources that occurs in a social and intelligent species such as our own can manifest itself via five categories of behavior: aggression, intimidation, manipulation, deception, and cooperation. One study (Charlesworth, 1996) of children ages 4 to 8 years from four different cultures demonstrated that cooperation is an effective strategy in competition for access to play materials. Furthermore, preschool-aged children skilled at both cooperation and coercion obtain more resources in problem-solving situations (LaFrenière & Charlesworth, 1987).

Human competitiveness is also reflected in R&T play and war games, which both appear at around 2 to 3 years of age, primarily in boys' play. While R&T play typically involves physical contact between two partners without play objects, war games[1] tend to be symbolic, include objects (such as toy guns), and involve role-playing (e.g., as warriors or super heroes; Costabile et al., 1992). War games appear to be unique to our species, though they have only arisen in some cultural contexts. "In cultures where they appear, games this type are quite frequent: 50% of preschool-age children play them at least once a week at home, whether parents try to discourage them from doing so or not (Costabile, Genta, Zucchini, Smith, & Harker, 1992). Paquette, Bigras, and Crepaldi (2010) have hypothesized that war games permit children to learn about the social world on a "political" or strategic level, permitting them to explore power dynamics between groups (us versus them, good versus evil, etc.). Competitiveness cannot be suppressed but may be focused or channelled by adults to facilitate children's adaptation to their environment.

Father-Child Rough-and-Tumble Play and the Development of Aggression

There now appears to be sufficient research on the development of human aggression to formulate suggestions to help fathers (among others) make meaningful strides in curbing pathological aggression in children. Physically aggressive

---

[1] War games do not include video games.

behavior appears to be developmentally appropriate in the first 2 years of life. The subsequent preschool years appear to be a key period in the socialization of aggression, as most children bring those behaviors under self-control. However, a small percentage of children do not display the expected decrease in aggression during early childhood (Shaw, 2006; Tremblay, 2000). These children can be characterized as having an impulsive-aggressive temperament, for they are more likely to display uncontrolled and violent responses toward social partners. They also appear to have deficits in frontal lobe functioning (Séguin, Nagin, Assaad, & Tremblay, 2004; Séguin & Zelazo, 2005). A similar impulsive-aggressive profile has been noted in 5% to 10% of rhesus monkey populations (Higley, Suomi, & Linnoila, 1996; Mehlman et al., 1995; Suomi, 2004). In both humans and monkeys, reduced serotonergic activity underlies impulsive-aggressive temperament. More specifically, impulsive-aggressive individuals have been reliably found to have lower levels of the serotonin metabolite 5-hydroxyindole acetic acid, or *5-HIAA* (Higley & Linnoila, 1997), and a lower activity *l* variant of the *MAOA* gene polymorphism (Newman et al., 2005). Thus, there is strong evidence of a behavioral and biological basis for impulsive-aggressive temperament.

Impulsive-aggressive individuals are expected to engage in less play with others, due to a diminished capacity for self-regulation. In support of this hypothesis, impulsive-aggressive individuals tend to engage in rougher play with their peers, as well as lack the self-restraint needed to keep play from escalating into violence (Suomi, 1997). This pattern may be due in part to a higher threshold for sensory stimulation in impulsive-aggressive individuals. Evidence also indicates that aggressive children attribute aggressive intent to ambiguous social signals (Crick & Dodge, 1994). In sum, impulsive-aggressive temperament appears to present a considerable risk factor for poor psychosocial adjustment.

Several environmental factors are known to shape the development of aggressive behavior, including maternal education (Côté et al., 2007; Juby & Farrington, 2001; Nagin & Tremblay, 2001), maternal antisocial behavior (Caspi et al., 2002; Rowe & Farrington, 1997; Verlaan & Schwartzman, 2002), mother's age at the birth of her first child (Nagin, Pogarsky, & Farrington, 1997; Nagin & Tremblay, 2001), negative parenting and parent–child interactions (Côté et al., 2007; Juby & Farrington, 2001; Smeekens, Riksen-Walraven, & van Bakel, 2007), absence of a father figure in the household (Nagin & Tremblay, 1999), and family income (Pagani, Tremblay, Vitaro, Kerr, & McDuff, 1998; Sampson & Laub, 1994). Many of these studies were conducted with school-aged children or adolescents, but it appears that these risks apply to preschool-age children as well (Tremblay et al., 2004).

These findings indicate that even in the presence of an impulsive-aggressive temperament, children's experiences at home, particularly in the preschool years, impact their risk of being chronically aggressive. As the research reviewed here suggests, fathers appear to be optimally positioned to help socialize their children's aggression through R&T play (Panksepp, Burgdorf, Turner, & Gordon, 2003; Paquette, 2004a; Tremblay, 2003, 2006).

A series of studies investigated the role of father–child R&T play in the development of the ability to regulate aggressive behavior. An initial study explored the basic correlates of R&T play (Flanders et al., 2007). Using a simple questionnaire, parents were asked to provide information about the frequency and quality of R&T play with their children. Contrary to popular conception, the frequencies of father–child and mother–child R&T play were not significantly associated with problem behaviors such as physical aggression, hyperactivity, and opposition in children. However, children's self-regulatory functioning during R&T play, including their ability to stay calm and respond to instructions, was related to these behaviors. The correlations were maintained even after controlling for socioeconomic factors. These findings suggest that the self-regulatory deficits underlying some externalizing behavior problems are manifest during parent–child R&T play. As a result, parents might have the opportunity during R&T play to intervene and help their children overcome these deficits in a constrained and supportive context.

These findings point to an important role for parents in the development of physical aggression in children. In addition, they raise the possibility that there may be qualitative aspects of R&T play that determine whether it is conducive or destructive to the development of self-regulation in the child. A second study used observational methods to focus on a particular qualitative aspect of R&T play: the dominance dynamics in the play interactions (Flanders, Leo, Paquette, Pihl, & Séguin, 2009). Dominance here refers to greater access to resources or control over circumstances within the context of a social interaction (Hawley, 1999). In R&T play interactions, the dominant play partner is more likely to win or control the playfully aggressive confrontations. Dominance negotiation is an important behavioral feature of R&T play among rats (Panksepp, 1998b; Pellis & Pellis, 2006), chimpanzees (Paquette, 1994), and human children (Pellegrini, 1995a; Pellegrini et al., 1998) and is hypothesized to be important in father–child R&T play as well (Paquette, 2004a).

In the observational study, father–child play dyads were observed and videotaped during a 7-minute free-play session. The Play Regulation Coding Scheme (Flanders et al., 2009) was developed and validated to code for dominance during these play sessions. Data on R&T play frequency and the child's overall behaviors were also collected. The results indicated that for dyads in which the fathers of preschool-aged children were more dominant during play, more frequent R&T play was associated with a lower incidence of physically aggressive behaviors in everyday life. However, for dyads where fathers were relatively less dominant, more frequent R&T play was associated with higher levels of physically aggressive behaviors in everyday life. The overall amount of time the father spent with his child was controlled for in the analyses. Thus, parent–child R&T play can be associated with higher or lower levels of physical aggression, but the impact of R&T play on the child depends on the quality of the interactions between parent and child during R&T play. The self-regulation deficits that underlie chronic physical aggression in children appear to be evident during parent–child R&T play. Thus, a father who is more dominant during R&T play with his children is able to contain R&T play interactions and help his child grow through these deficits. A more lenient and permissive father cannot enforce these limits or scaffold the child's experience so that he or she learns to regulate aggression in other contexts where it is not appropriate.

A follow-up to this study (Flanders et al., 2010) examined the same children's self-regulatory competence 5 years later. The study demonstrated that among father–child play dyads in which the father was relatively less dominant, the frequency of R&T play predicted more physically aggressive behavior and poorer emotion regulation abilities 5 years later than in dyads where the father was more dominant. Physical aggression was not associated with emotion regulation, probably because emotion dysregulation is merely one of several potential triggers of physically aggressive behavior. These associations were found while controlling for the age of the child, the frequency of father–child play in general, and the overall time spent with the father. These findings are not only consistent with an initial study of preschoolers that demonstrated similar findings when these constructs were measured concurrently (Flanders et al., 2009) but also suggest a developmental process that expands beyond the preschool period into the school-age period.

Conclusion

The development of social competence takes shape in the preschool years. In this period, R&T play appears to foster the parent–child (especially father–child) bond, stimulate social cognition, and promote practical skills for group living. In parallel, children must learn to regulate the impulse to defend and expand their interests through the use of aggression—a job that is facilitated by the development of self-regulatory circuitry in the frontal lobes. Rough-and-tumble play may be an ideal context for children to learn skills for navigating the cooperation–competition dilemma they will face for the rest of their social lives.

Rough-and-tumble play may have been selected for to prepare social mammals for the complexities of life in dominance hierarchies. Given fathers' increasing involvement in childrearing in recent evolutionary history, they appear to be optimally positioned to use R&T play to socialize their children's aggression. Unfortunately, many children do not get the support, resources, and experiences necessary to develop the requisite social competence needed for group living. Individuals who always employ aggressive strategies may wind up socially isolated, which can prevent them from enjoying the benefits of close social relationships. On the other hand, individuals who only develop cooperation skills may not know how to defend or assert themselves in the many competitive situations that may arise. Neither of these outcomes is particularly attractive for our children. With the right balance of influences, children can develop a varied repertoire of social behaviors to cope with diverse competitive situations and embody some of the virtues of optimal social engagement, including authenticity, assertiveness, and leadership.

Rough-and-tumble play among peers can be seen as a proximate mechanism shaping young mammals' abilities to manage competition for limited resources. As such, it emerged long before the era of the EEA. By contrast, pretend or symbolic play, like any other cultural practice, was likely selected for during the EEA period, shaping children's adaptation to local physical and social environments. As such, symbolic play can help socialize children for a multitude of novel environments (see Pellegrini & Pellegrini, this volume), including, for example, the life of hunter-gatherers in the EEA, in which there are no competitive games (Gray, 2009). In this context, children are in mixed-age groups and parents are little involved in play. A range in age means diversity of strength, skill level, and cognitive ability, so each child tries to do his or her best without comparisons to the performance of others (Gray, 2009). Moreover, these ancestral cultural practices in general tend to encourage cooperation and limit dominance striving.

In contrast to Narvaez, Panksepp, Schore, and Gleason's position (this volume) that humans under optimal conditions are typically nonviolent and prosocial, we have suggested that humans are predisposed to both competition and cooperation. The optimal balance of these strategies will depend on the specific demands of a particular environment, and this balance is likely learned and consolidated through play interactions in childhood. Father–child R&T play is an excellent example, as it arose quite recently, in the context of our individualistic and competitive Western industrialized societies. More research on the topic could illuminate the role of these interactions on the social, emotional, and physical development of our children.

References

Aldis, O. (1975). *Play-fighting*. New York, NY, and London: Academic Press.

Allès-Jardel, M., Schneider, B. H., Goldstein, E., & Normand, S. (2009). Les origines culturelles de l'agressivité pendant l'enfance. Dans B. H. Schneider, S. Normand, M. Allès-Jardel, M. A. Provost, & G. M. Tarabulsy (Eds.), *Conduites agressives chez l'enfant: Perspectives développementales et psychosociales* (pp. 101–222). Québec: Les Presses de l'Université du Québec.

Baldwin, J. D. (1969). The ontogeny of social behaviour of squirrel monkeys (Saimiri sciureus) in a seminatural environment. *Folia Primatologica (Basel), 11*(1), 35–79.

Baldwin, J. D. (1986). Behavior in infancy: Exploration and play. *Comparative Primate Biology, 2A*, 295–326.

Baldwin, J. D., & Baldwin, J. I. (1973). The role of play in social organization: Comparative observations on squirrel monkeys (Saimiri). *Primates, 14*(4), 369–381.

Baldwin, J. D., & Baldwin, J. I. (1976). Effects of food ecology on social play: A laboratory simulation. *Journal of Comparative Ethology (Zeitschrift fur Tierpsychologie), 40*, 1–14.

Baldwin, J. D., & Baldwin, J. I. (1977). The role of learning phenomenon in the ontogeny of exploration and play. In S. Chevalier-Skolnikoff & F. E. Poirier (Eds.), *Primate bio-social development: Biological, social, and ecological determinants*. New York, NY: Garland Publishing.

Bateson, P. P. G. (2005). Play and its role in the development of great apes and humans. In A. D. Pellegrini & P. K. Smith (Eds.), *The nature of play: Great apes and humans* (pp. 13–26). New York, NY: Guilford.

Biben, M., Suomi, S. J., & MacDonald, K. (1993). Lessons from primate play. In K. MacDonald (Ed.), *Parent-child play: Descriptions and implications* (pp. 185–196). Albany, NY: State University of New York Press.

Blurton Jones, N. (1972). Categories of child-child interaction. In N. B. Jones (Ed.), *Ethological studies of child behavior* (pp. 97–129). New York, NY: Cambridge University Press.

Bruner, J. S. (1976). *Play: Its role in development and evolution*. New York, NY: Basic Books.

Byrnes, J., Miller, D., & Schaffer, W. (1999). Gender differences in risk-taking: A meta-analysis. *Psychological Bulletin, 125*(3), 367–383.

Carson, J., Burks, V., & Parke, R. D. (1993). Parent-child physical play: Determinants and consequences. In K. MacDonald (Ed.), *Children's play in society* (pp. 197–220). Albany, NY: State University of New York Press.

Caspi, A., McClay, J., Moffitt, T. E., Mill, J., Martin, J., Craig, I. W.,...Poulton, R. (2002). Role of genotype in the cycle of violence in maltreated children. *Science, 297,* 851–854.

Charlesworth, W. R. (1988). Resources and resource acquisition during ontogeny. In K. B. MacDonald (Ed.), *Sociobiological perspective on human development* (pp. 24–77). New York, NY: Springer-Verlas.

Charlesworth, W. R. (1996). Co-operation and competition: Contributions to an evolutionary and developmental model. *International Journal of Behavioral Development, 19*(1), 25–39.

Coie, J. D., & Dodge, K. A. (1998). Aggression and antisocial behavior. In W. Damon & N. Eisenberg (Eds.), *Handbook of child psychology: Social, emotional and personality development* (Vol. 3, pp. 779–862). New York, NY: Wiley and Sons.

Costabile, A., Genta, M. L., Zucchini, E., Smith, P. K., & Harker, R. (1992). Attitudes of parents towards war play in young children. *Early Education and Development, 3*(4), 356–369.

Costabile, A., Smith, P. K., Matheson, L., Aston, J., Hunter, T., & Boulton, M. (1991). Cross-national comparison of how children distinguish serious and playful fighting. *Developmental Psychology, 27,* 881–887.

Côté, S., Boivin, M., Nagin, D. S., Japel, C., Xu, Q., Zoccolillo, M.,...Tremblay R. E. (2007). The role of maternal education and nonmaternal care services in the prevention of children's physical aggression problems. *Archives of General Psychiatry, 64,* 1305–1312.

Crick, N. R., & Dodge, K. A. (1994). A review and reformulation of social information-processing mechanisms in children's social adjustment. *Psychological Bulletin, 115*(1), 74–101.

DiPietro, J. A. (1981). Rough and tumble play: A function of gender. *Developmental Psychology, 17*(1), 50–58.

Drea, C. M., Hawk, J. E., & Glickman, S. E. (1997). The emergence of affiliative behavior in infant spotted hyenas (Crocuta crocuta). *Annals of the New York Academy of Sciences, 807,* 498–500.

Dumont, C., & Paquette, D. (2008). L'attachement père-enfant et l'engagement paternel: Deux concepts centraux pour mieux prédire le développement de l'enfant. *Revue de Psychoéducation, 37*(1), 27–46.

Edwards, C. P. (2000). Children's play in cross-cultural perspective: A new look at the *Six Cultures* study. *Cross-Cultural Research, 34*(4), 318–338.

Fagen, R. (1981). *Animal play behavior*. New York, NY: Oxford University Press.

Flanders, J., Leo, V., Paquette, D., Pihl, R. O., & Séguin, J. R. (2009). Rough-and-tumble play and the regulation of aggression: An observational study of father-child play dyads. *Aggressive Behavior, 35*(4), 285–295.

Flanders, J. L., Séguin, J. R., Parent, S., Pihl, R. O., Zelazo, P. D., & Tremblay, R. E. (2007). *Psychometric properties of the Rough-and-Tumble Play Questionnaire.* Presented at the Society for Research on Child Development Biennial Meeting, April 2007, Boston, MA.

Flanders, J. L., Simard, M., Paquette, D., Parent, S., Vitaro, F., Pihl, R. O., & Seguin, J. R. (2010). Rough-and-tumble play and the development of physical aggression and emotion regulation: A five-year follow-up study. *Journal of Family Violence, 25*(4), 357–367.

Fry, D. (2005). Rough-and-tumble social play in humans. In A. D. Pellegrini & P. K. Smith (Eds.), *The nature of play: Great apes and humans* (pp. 54–88). New York, NY: Guilford Press.

Gordon, N. S., Burke, S., Akil, H., Watson, S. J., & Panksepp, J. (2003). Socially-induced brain 'fertilization': play promotes brain derived neurotrophic factor transcription in the amygdala and dorsolateral frontal cortex in juvenile rats. *Neuroscience Letters, 341*(1), 17–20.

Gosso, Y., Otta, E., Morais, M. L. S., Ribeiro, F. J. L., & Bussab, V. S. R. (2005). Play in hunter-gatherer society. In A. D. Pellegrini & P. K. Smith (Eds.), *The nature of play: Great apes and humans* (pp. 213–253). New York, NY: Guilford Press.

Gray, P. (2009). Play as a foundation for hunter-gatherer social existence. *American Journal of Play, 1*(4), 466–522.

Groos, K. (1898). *The play of animals*. New York, NY: Appleton and Company.

Harlow, H., & Harlow, M. (1965). The affectional systems. *Behavior of Non-Human Primates, 2,* 287–334.

Harlow, H. F. (1969). *Age-mate or peer affectional system*. Chicago, IL: University of Chicago.

Hawley, P. H. (1999). The ontogenesis of social dominance: A strategy-based evolutionary perspective. *Developmental Review, 19,* 97–132.

Heinrichs, M., von Dawans, B., & Domes, G. (2009). Oxytocin, vasopressin, and human social behavior. *Frontiers in Neuroendocrinology, 30*(4), 548–557.

Herman, K. N., Paukner, A., & Suomi, S. J. (2011). Gene X environment interactions and social play: Contributions from rhesus macaques. In A. D. Pellegrini (Ed.), *The Oxford handbook of the development of play* (pp. 58–69). New York, NY: Oxford University Press.

Hewlett, B. S. (2000). Culture, history, and sex: Anthropological contributions to conceptualizing father involvement. In E. Peters & R. D. Day (Eds.), *Fatherhood: Research, interventions and policies* (pp. 59–73). Binghamton, NY: Haworth Press.

Higley, J. D., & Linnoila, M. (1997). Low central nervous system serotonergic activity is traitlike and correlates with impulsive behavior: A nonhuman primate model investigating genetic and environmental influences on neurotransmission. *Annals of the New York Academy of Sciences, 836*, 39–56.

Higley, J. D., Suomi, S. J., & Linnoila, M. (1996). A nonhuman primate model of type II alcoholism? Part 2. Diminished social competence and excessive aggression correlates with low cerebrospinal fluid 5-hydroxyindoleacetic acid concentrations. *Alcoholism, Clinical and Experimental Research, 20*(4), 643–650.

Juby, H., & Farrington, D. P. (2001). Disentangling the link between disrupted families and delinquency. *British Journal of Criminology, 41,* 22–40.

Kempes, M. M., Gulickx, M. M., van Daalen, H. J., Louwerse, A. L., & Sterck, E. H. (2008). Social competence is reduced in socially deprived rhesus monkeys (Macaca mulatta). *Journal of Comparative Psychology, 122*(1), 62–67.

Kochanska, G. (2002). Mutually responsive orientation between mothers and their young children: A context for the early development of conscience. *Current Directions in Psychological Science, 11*(6), 191.

LaFrenière, P. J., & Charlesworth, W. R. (1987). Effects of friendship and dominance status on preschooler's resource utilization in a cooperative competitive paradigm. *International Journal of Behavioral Development, 10*(3), 345–358.

Le Camus, J. (2000). *Le vrai rôle du père*. Paris: Éditions Odile Jacob.

Martin, P., & Caro, T. M. (1985). On the functions of play and its role in behavioral development. *Advances in the Study of Behavior, 15,* 59–103.

Mehlman, P. T., Higley, J. D., Faucher, I., Lilly, A. A., Taub, D. M., Vickers, J., . . . Linnoila, M. (1995). Correlation of CSF 5-HIAA concentration with sociality and the timing of emigration in free-ranging primates. *American Journal of Psychiatry, 152*(6), 907–913.

Miller, E., & Almon, J. (2009). *Crisis in the kindergarten-why children need to play in school.* College Park, MD: Alliance for Childhood.

Nagin, D. S., Pogarsky, G., & Farrington, D. P. (1997). Adolescent mothers and the criminal behavior of their children. *Law & Society Review, 31,* 137–162.

Nagin, D. S., & Tremblay, R. E. (1999). Trajectories of boy's physical aggression, opposition, and hyperactivity on the path to physically violent and non violent juvenile delinquency. *Child Development, 70,* 1181–1196.

Nagin, D. S., & Tremblay, R. E. (2001). Parental and early childhood predictors of persistent physical aggression in boys from kindergarten to high school. *Archives of General Psychiatry, 58,* 389–394.

Newman, T. K., Syagailo, Y. V., Barr, C. S., Wendland, J. R., Champoux, M., Graessle, M., . . . Lesch, K. P. (2005). Monoamine oxidase A gene promoter variation and rearing experience influences aggressive behavior in rhesus monkeys. *Biological Psychiatry, 57*(2), 167–172.

O'Neill-Wagner, P. L., Bolig, R., & Price, C. S. (2001). Developmental aspects of play-partner selection in young rhesus monkeys. In J. L. Roopnarine (Ed.), *Conceptual, social-cognitive, and contextual issues in the fields of play* (pp. 111–124). Westport, CT: Greenwood Publishing Group.

Pagani, L., Tremblay, R. E., Vitaro, F., Kerr, M., & McDuff, P. (1998). The impact of family transition on the development of adolescent boys: A 9-year longitudinal study. *Journal of Child Psychology and Psychiatry, 39,* 489–499.

Panksepp, J. (1993). Rough and tumble play: A fundamental brain process. In K. MacDonald (Ed.), *Parent-child play: Descriptions and implications* (pp. 147–184). Albany, NY: State University of New York Press.

Panksepp, J. (1998a). *Affective neuroscience: The foundations of human and animal emotions.* New York, NY: Oxford University Press.

Panksepp, J. (1998b). Attention deficit hyperactivity disorders, psychostimulants, and intolerance of childhood playfulness: A tragedy in the making? *Current Directions in Psychological Science, 7,* 91–98.

Panksepp, J., Burgdorf, J., Turner, C., & Gordon, N. (2003). Modeling ADHD-type arousal with unilateral frontal cortex damage in rats and beneficial effects of play therapy. *Brain and Cognition, 52*(1), 97–105.

Paquette, D. (1994). Fighting and playfighting in captive adolescent chimpanzees. *Aggressive Behavior, 20*(1), 49–65.

Paquette, D. (2004a). Theorizing the father-child relationship: Mechanisms and developmental outcomes. *Human Development, 47*(4), 193–219.

Paquette, D. (2004b). La relation père-enfant et l'ouverture au monde. *Enfance, 2,* 205–225.

Paquette, D. (2005). Plus l'environnement se complexifie, plus l'adaptation des enfants nécessite l'engagement direct du père. *Enfances, familles, générations. Vol. 3: Paternité: Bilan et perspective.* Retrieved November 10, 2009, from http://www.erudit.org/revue/efg/2005/v/n3/012533ar.html

Paquette, D., & Bigras, M. (2010). The risky situation: A procedure for assessing the father-child activation relationship. *Early Child Development and Care, 180*(1–2), 33–50.

Paquette, D., Bigras, M., & Crepaldi, M. A. (2010). La violence: Un jugement de valeur sur les rapports de pouvoir. *Revue de Psychoéducation, 39*(2), 247–276.

Paquette, D., Carbonneau, R., Dubeau, D., Bigras, M., & Tremblay, R. E. (2003). Prevalence of father-child rough-and-tumble play and physical aggression in preschool children, *European Journal of Psychology of Education, 18*(2), 171–189.

Paquette, D., Eugène, M. M., Dubeau, D., & Gagnon, M.-N. (2009). Les pères ont-ils une influence spécifique sur le développement des enfants? In D. Dubeau, A. Devault, & G. Forget (Eds.), *La paternité au 21ᵉ siècle* (pp. 99–122). Québec: PUL.

Parten, M. B. (1932). Social participation among pre-school children. *Journal of Abnormal and Social Psychology, 27,* 243–269.

Pellegrini, A. D. (1988). Elementary-school children's rough-and-tumble play and social competence. *Developmental Psychology, 24*(6), 802–806.

Pellegrini, A. D. (2002). Rough-and-tumble play from childhood through adolescence: Development and possible functions. In P. K. Smith & C. H. Hart (Eds.), *Blackwell handbook of childhood social development* (pp. 438–453). Malden, MA: Blackwell Publishing.

Pellegrini, A. D., & Smith, P. K. (1998). Physical activity play: The nature and function of a neglected aspect of play. *Child Development, 69*(3), 577–598.

Pellis, S. M., & Pellis, V. C. (2006). Play and the development of social engagement: A comparative perspective. In P. J. Marshall & N. A. Fox (Eds.), *The development of social engagement: Neurobiological perspectives* (pp. 247–274). New York, NY: Oxford University Press.

Peterson, J. B., & Flanders, J. L. (Eds.). (2005). *Play and the regulation of aggression.* New York, NY: Guilford Press.

Power, T. G. (2000). *Play and exploration in children and animals.* Mahwah, NJ: L. Erlbaum Associates.

Preston, S. D., & De Waal, F. B. M. (2002). Empathy. *Behavioural Brain Research, 25,* 1–72.

Roopnarine, J. L., Hooper, F. H., Ahmeduzzaman, M., & Pollack, B. (1993). Gentle play partners: Mother-child and father-child play in New Delhi, India. In K. MacDonald (Ed.), *Parent-child play: Descriptions and implications. SUNY series, children's play in society* (pp. 287–304). Albany, NY: State University of New York Press.

Ross, H., & Taylor, H. (1989). Do boys prefer daddy or his physical style of play? *Sex Roles, 20*(1–2), 23–33.

Rowe, D. C., & Farrington, D. P. (1997). The familial transmission of criminal convictions. *Criminology, 35,* 177–201.

Rubin, K., Fein, G., & Vandenberg, B. (1983). Play. In E. M. Hetherington & P. H. Mussen (Eds.), *Handbook of child psychology. Vol. 4: Socialization, personality, and social behavior* (pp. 693–774). New York, NY: Wiley.

Rubin, K. H. (1982). Nonsocial play in preschoolers: Necessarily evil? *Child Development, 53,* 651–657.

Sampson, R. J., & Laub, J. H. (1994). Urban poverty and the family context of delinquency—A new look at structure and process in a classic study. *Child Development, 65,* 523–540.

Scott, E., & Panksepp, J. (2003). Rough-and-tumble play in human children. *Aggressive Behavior, 29,* 539–551.

Séguin, J. R., Nagin, D. S., Assaad, J. M., & Tremblay, R. E. (2004). Cognitive-neuropsychological function in chronic physical aggression and hyperactivity. *Journal of Abnormal Psychology, 113,* 603–613.

Séguin, J. R., & Zelazo, P. D. (2005). Executive function in early physical aggression. In R. E. Tremblay, W. W. Hartup, & J. Archer (Eds.), *Developmental origins of aggression* (pp. 307–329). New York, NY: Guilford.

Shaw, D. S. (2006). The development of aggression in early childhood. In H. E. Fitzgerald, B. M. Lester, & B. Zuckerman (Eds.), *The crisis in youth mental health: Critical issues and effective programs. Vol. 1: Childhood disorders* (pp. 183–203). Westport, CT: Praeger Publishers/Greenwood Publishing Group.

Smeekens, S., Riksen-Walraven, J. M. A., & Van Bakel, H. J. A. (2007). Multiple determinants of externalizing behavior in 5-year-olds: A longitudinal study. *Journal of Abnormal Child Psychology, 35*(3), 347–261.

Smilansky, S. (1968). Sociodramatic play as a type of play phenomenon. In S. Smilanksy (Ed.), *The effects of sociodramatic play on disadvantaged preschool children* (pp. 5–10). New York, NY: John Wiley and Sons.

Smith, P. K. (2004). Play: Types and functions in human development. In B. Ellis & D. Bjorklund (Eds.), *Origins of the social mind: Evolutionary psychology and child development* (pp. 271–299). New York, NY: Guilford Press.

Smith, P. K., & Boulton, M. (1990). Rough-and-tumble play, aggression, and dominance: Perceptions and behavior in children's encounters. *Human Development, 33,* 271–282.

Spinka, M., Newberry, R. C., & Bekoff, M. (2001). Mammalian play: Training for the unexpected. *Quarterly Review of Biology, 76*(2), 141–168.

Suomi, S. J. (1979a). Differential development of various social relationships by rhesus monkey infants. In M. Lewis & L. A. Rosenblum (Eds.), *The child and its family* (Vol. 2, pp. 219–244). New York: Plenum Press.

Suomi, S. J. (1979b). Peers, play, and primary prevention in primates. In M. Kent & J. Rolf (Eds.), *Primary prevention of psychopathology: Social competence in children* (pp. 127–149). Hanover, NH: Press of New England.

Suomi, S. J. (1982). The development of social competence by rhesus monkeys. *Annali dell'Istituto Superiore di Sanita, 18*(2), 193–202.

Suomi, S. J. (1997). Early determinants of behaviour: Evidence from primate studies. *British Medical Bulletin, 53*(1), 170–184.

Suomi, S. J. (2004). How gene-environment interactions shape biobehavioral development: Lessons from studies with rhesus monkeys. *Research in Human Development, 1*(3), 205–222.

Suomi, S. J. (2005). Mother-infant attachment, peer relationships, and the development of social networks in rhesus monkeys. *Human Development, 48*, 67–79.

Symons, D. (1978). *Play and aggression: A study of rhesus monkeys*. New York, NY: Columbia University Press.

Thompson, K. V., Bekoff, M., & Byers, J. A. (1998). Self assessment in juvenile play. In M. Bekoff & J. A. Byers (Eds.), *Animal play: Evolutionary, comparative, and ecological perspectives* (pp. 183–204). New York, NY: Cambridge University Press.

Tremblay, R. E. (2000). The development of aggressive behaviour during childhood: What have we learned in the past century? *International Journal of Behavioral Development, 24*(2), 129–141.

Tremblay, R. E. (2003). Why socialization fails: The case of chronic physical aggression. In B. B. Lahey, T. E. Moffitt, & A. Caspi (Eds.), *Causes of conduct disorder and juvenile delinquency* (pp. 182–224). New York, NY: Guilford.

Tremblay, R. E. (2006). Prevention of youth violence: Why not start at the beginning? *Journal of Abnormal Child Psychology, 34*, 481–487.

Tremblay, R. E., Japel, C., Pérusse, D., Boivin, M., Zoccolillo, M., Montplaisir, J., & McDuff, P. (1999). The search of the age of 'onset' of physical aggression: Rousseau and Bandura revisited. *Criminal Behavior and Mental Health, 9*(1), 8–23.

Tremblay, R. E., Nagin, D. S., Seguin, J. R., Zoccolillo, M., Zelazo, P. D., Boivin, M.,…Japel, C. (2004). Physical aggression during early childhood: Trajectories and predictors. *Pediatrics, 114*, E43–E50.

Verlaan, P., & Schwartzman, A. E. (2002). Mother's and father's parental adjustment: Links to externalising behaviour problems in sons and daughters. *International Journal of Behavioral Development, 26*, 214–224.

Wilson, M., & Daly, M. (1997). Life expectancy, economic inequality, homicide, and reproductive timing in Chicago neighbourhoods. *British Medical Journal, 314*, 1271–1274.

Play in Hunter-Gatherers

Barry S. Hewlett and Adam H. Boyette

The three chapters on play provide provocative insights and diverse theoretical and methodological approaches to the study of human play. Gray reviews hunter-gatherer ethnographic literature on children and hypothesizes that play is an important mechanism by which pronounced egalitarianism in hunter-gatherers is maintained. The chapter by Pellegrini and Pellegrini is a theoretical contribution to the study of human play. The authors are critical of hard-wired brain modularity approaches associated with evolutionary psychology, and instead advocate for an epigenetic or evolutionary developmental biology approach to understanding human play. They hypothesize that juvenile play is a prime mover in the development of behavioral "modules" that enable humans to adapt to novel or diverse local ecologies. Play is viewed as a creative process (recombine, innovate, and eliminate behaviors) that enables humans to rapidly adapt to changing environments. The behavioral modules that emerge in play can lead to genetic changes (ontogeny influencing phylogeny).

The chapter by Flanders, Herman, and Paquette focuses on rough-and-tumble (R&T) play. They review the child and nonhuman development literature and hypothesize that R&T play is (1) particularly important for the development of self-regulation and cooperation between group members and (2) primarily the domain of fathers and that fathers play a key role in the development of these abilities.

Pellegrini and Pellegrini and Flanders et al. have been conducting systematic research on play for years, and their chapters provide excellent overviews and current theoretical positions of these leading researchers. Gray is relatively new to studies of play but presents a nice summary of common representations of hunter-gatherers.

Play Research in the Context of Hunter-Gatherer Studies

Each chapter provides insights, new data, and theoretical exploration into human play. In this section, we examine their positions, data, and interpretations in the context of hunter-gatherer research, our field experiences, and studies of play. Few studies of hunter-gatherer play exist (see Bock & Johnson, 2004; Boyette, in preparation; Gosso et al., 2005; and Kamei, 2005, for exceptions). The Pellegrini and Pellegrini and Flanders et al. chapters cite more play studies from rats and monkeys than they do from hunter-gatherers. This is not their fault; many more systematic studies and data exist on rat and monkey play than on hunter-gatherer play. Although few studies of forager play have been conducted, they and other child development research on foragers provide a context for evaluating the results and generalizations from studies conducted in highly stratified industrial cultures with relatively unique social ecologies.

FATHERS AND PLAY

Flanders et al. state that "R&T play has long been considered the domain of fathers," then go on to describe others' and their own research about child–father R&T play. One sentence indicates culture may impact the frequency of R&T play (i.e., play may be more common in "individualist" cultures that value autonomy and competition than in "collectivist" cultures). However, data on Aka forager fathers (Hewlett, 1991) indicate they are rarely involved in R&T play and that "others," especially older brothers and sisters who provide care during infancy and early childhood, are much more likely than parents to provide all types of play (R&T, object mediated, face to face). Hewlett (1991) hypothesized that Aka fathers did not engage in R&T play because they intimately knew their children and could listen and read their children's needs rather than showing their love by stimulating them with vigorous play.

The collectivist–individual dichotomy is also problematic. The Ngandu farmer neighbors of the Aka are a collectivist culture (i.e., needs of the group valued more than the needs of the individual), but they highly value competition, while the Aka hunter-gatherers would be considered an individualist culture because they highly value and respect an individual's autonomy. Father–child R&T play may be particularly important in competitive cultures, but our observational data indicate Ngandu farmer fathers rarely play with their children.

The issue is that Flanders et al. give the impression that father–child R&T play is common, if not universal, and that it is an important way by which children learn to deal with the outside world. They probably did not set out to give this impression, but nowhere do they state that their studies apply only to Western or Euro-American cultures. Fathers' R&T play may be a particularly important process for Euro-American children to learn self-regulation because allomaternal care is limited and the nuclear family is relatively isolated by comparison to children in hunter-gatherer and other small-scale cultures.

Flanders et al. discuss aggression in children and cite several studies which indicate that most conflicts in infants and young children have to do with competition over objects. This is common in Euro-American and other cultures, but a recent study by Fouts and Lamb (2009) demonstrated that child conflicts among farmers were over objects but toddler conflicts among hunter-gatherers were over physical and emotional proximity to particular individuals.

Innovation and Play

The innovation and creativity functions of play hypothesized by Pellegrini and Pellegrini may be particularly important for Euro-American and other children in rapidly changing environments, but it is not likely to be as important in foragers in relatively stable environments (e.g., minimal impact by the outside world). Likewise, vertical (from parents) transmission of skills is important in relatively stable environments, whereas horizontal transmission (from peers, neighbors) is more adaptive in rapidly changing environments where regular updating is necessary. Humans are capable of both vertical and horizontal transmission to learn future skills or develop innovations for current survival, but their expression depends on their environmental context and either may include play.

Forager juveniles are the energizers of culture, but their role in innovation is not clear. Even in the domains of Aka dance, music, and body modification, the innovations adopted by others come from adults. Juveniles often adopt new dances and songs very quickly through play, but the innovations come from adults. The few modifications in subsistence techniques, such as net hunting, that we have observed have also come from adults. Spontaneous innovations in language or material culture have been observed in forager children's play, but these are often short-lived or remain within the context of children's culture and are not adopted by adults.

Pellegrini and Pellegrini do not provide human examples or studies to support the hypothesis that novel behaviors acquired in juvenile play are incorporated into a human culture, though they have examined this issue in another place (Pellegrini & Hou, 2011). Only laboratory studies of monkeys and chimpanzees are described. It would be beneficial to have an example of a human behavioral or cultural variant that emerged in play and became part of an adaptive module.

DEFINITIONS OF PLAY

Authors tend to select definitions conducive to their hypothesis. Gray lists five criteria of play, and four of the five criteria are characteristic features of social learning in hunter-gatherer childhood (see Hewlett, Fouts, Boyette, & Hewlett, 2011) or hunter-gatherer life in general. The pervasive nature of play in several domains of hunter-gatherer life may be a by-product of or at least amplified by cultural values, attitudes, and practices common to foragers rather than a specific mechanism that promotes egalitarianism as hypothesized by Gray. Pellegini and Pellegrini list four criteria of play from Burghardt (2005), and two of them (nonfunctional and exaggerated, segmented and nonsequential in relation to functional behavior) emphasize the creative or novel component of play behavior.

EVOLUTIONARY APPROACHES

Gray is the only author to use hunter-gatherers as an approach to understanding human nature. The chapter is consistent with evolutionary psychology as it identifies a human universal (play) that functions to maintain egalitarianism, but the chapter is inconsistent with an evolutionary psychology approach because it does not describe the recurring problem faced by hunter-gatherers that led to the selection for play with these functions. The chapter also does not discuss play in mammals or primates where the social learning and social competence functions of play are emphasized. We are not aware of studies that indicate play functions to maintain egalitarianism. Play does contribute to the social learning of egalitarianism in hunter-gatherers, but it also facilitates learning how to dance, share, make nets, cook, and so forth. Among farmers and pastoralists we know, play contributes to the social learning of gender inequality and competition.

Pellegrini and Pellegrini minimize the importance of evolutionary psychology and hard-wired approaches to human nature. Their chapter is consistent with a human behavioral ecology approach because it emphasizes phenotypic plasticity and strategies that enable individuals to adapt to relatively local ecologies and minimizes the importance of genetically hard-wired behaviors. We do not have the space here to discuss the various evolutionary approaches but advocate elsewhere for an integrated (evolutionary psychology, behavioral ecology, and evolutionary cultural anthropology) evolutionary approach to development (Hewlett & Lamb, 2002).

Culture or evolutionary approaches to culture are seldom mentioned in the chapters as influencing the nature or evolution of play. Culture evolves, has specific properties of its own, and can construct environments that influence play. Play is part of human nature and has deep phylogenetic and biological roots, but at a minimum, culture influences the frequency, nature, and potential evolution of play. For instance, chapters define play as having the following characteristics: (1) is voluntary, has minimal adult intrusion, and is self-motivated; (2) emerges when an individual is secure and content; and (3) includes imagination, reversal, creativity, and innovation. Based on our work (Hewlett et al., 2011), we identify characteristics of the culturally constructed environment of forager social learning as the following: Egalitarianism, respect for autonomy, and extensive sharing are core values. Children are socialized in a physically and emotionally intimate context. Learning is self-motivated and directed (directions from parents are rare). Socialization of trust of many others is common. Creativity is also valued as it is part of respecting an individual's autonomy, and dances and songs, for instance, generally allocate time for each individual to modify and improvise standard patterns.

Given the characteristic features of play, the forager's culturally constructed environment could amplify the nature, scope, and frequency of play. These and other dimensions of the forager's culturally constructed environment (e.g., camp size, mobility, lack of storage) could also influence the nature and evolution of play in a way similar to that proposed by Pellegrini and Pellegrini; that is, particular cultural niche construction leads to its own adaptations and potential genetic change.

FUNCTIONS AND CHARACTERISTICS OF HUNTER-GATHERER PLAY

A paucity of data exists on hunter-gatherer play, but the few published studies that exist suggest several functions and generalizations. Pellegrini and Pellegrini identify three general functions: (1) learning future skills, (2) learning skills for current survival and adaptation, and (3) a source of innovation to adapt to novel environments. The limited hunter-gatherer literature provides strong support for the first, some support for the second, and no support for the third. Existing studies indicate most play occurs while imitating subsistence (hunting-gathering), maintenance (cooking, house building), and expressive (dancing, singing) skills. However, Kamei (2005) describes some elements of Baka forager children's play that are essential to living with other children and have no relevance to future adult life. Innovations and improvisations take place in hunter-gatherer children's play, but no systematic evidence exists to indicate innovations are utilized, incorporated, or diffused into forager culture.

The few systematic studies that exist suggest the following generalizations:

1. Hunter-gatherer juveniles are more likely to play than juveniles in other cultures because (a) they have relatively more free time (few task assignments) than children in many other cultures (Bock & Johnson, 2004; Konner, 2010) and (b) several of the frequently mentioned conditions of play are common in foraging cultures.
2. Most juvenile play occurs when children imitate readily observable adult and older children's behaviors, such as subsistence, maintenance, and expressive activities (Bock, 2005; Kamei, 2005). Learning egalitarianism and sharing may take more explicit instruction, such as scaffolding and teaching, and may involve less play.
3. Rough-and-tumble play and competitive and aggressive play are relatively infrequent, while exploratory play is relatively common in hunter-gatherers (Bock & Johnson, 2004; Boyette, in preparation; Kamei, 2005).

Conclusion

The three chapters provide interesting and provocative ideas about the nature, functions, and evolution of play in humans, but they rely heavily on studies of play in highly stratified cultures or studies of play in rats and monkeys. In order to understand the nature of human play, we desperately need more systematic field studies of play in hunter-gatherers as this way of life characterized most of human history and will not exist much longer.

References

Boyette, A. H. (in preparation). Children's play and scaffolding non-aggression in a hunter-gatherer society.

Bock, J. (2005). Farming, foraging, and children's play in the Okavango Delta, Botswana. In A. D. Pellegrini & P. K. Smith (Eds.), *The nature of play: Great apes and humans* (pp. 254–284). New York, NY: Guilford Press.

Bock, J., & Johnson, S. E. (2004). Subsistence ecology and play among the Okavango Delta peoples of Botswana. *Human Nature, 15*, 63–81.

Burghardt, G. M. (2005). *The genesis of animal play: Testing the limits*. Cambridge, MA: MIT Press.

Fouts, H. N., & Lamb, M. E. (2009). Cultural and developmental in toddlers' interactions with other children in two small-scale societies in Central Africa. *Journal of European Developmental Science, 3*, 259–277.

Gosso, Y., Otta, E., de Lima, M., Morais, S. E., Ribeiro, F. J. L., & Bussab, V. S. R. (2005). Play in hunter-gatherer society. In A. D. Pellegrini & P. K. Smiths (Eds.), *The nature of play: Great apes and humans* (pp. 213–253). New York, NY: Guilford Press.

Hewlett, B. S. (1991). *Intimate fathers: The nature and context of Aka Pygmy paternal infant care*. Ann Arbor, MI: University of Michigan Press.

Hewlett, B. S., Fouts, H. N., Boyette, A. H., & Hewlett, B. L. (2011). Social learning among Congo Basin hunter-gatherers. *Philosophical Transactions of the Royal Society B, 366*, 1168–1178.

Hewlett, B. S., & Lamb, M. E. (2002). Integrating evolution, culture and developmental psychology: Explaining caregiver-infant proximity and responsiveness in central Africa and the USA. In H. Keller, Y. Portinga, & A. Scholmerich (Eds.), *Between culture and biology: Perspectives on ontogenetic development*. Cambridge: Cambridge University Press.

Kamei, N. (2005). Play among Baka children of Cameroon. In B. S. Hewlett & M. E. Lamb (Eds.), *Hunter-gatherer childhoods* (pp. 343–362). New Brunswick, NJ: Aldine Transaction.

Konner, M. (2010). *The evolution of childhood: Relationships, emotions, mind*. Cambridge, MA: Harvard University Press.

Pellegrini, A. D., & Hou, Y. (2011). The development of preschool children's (*Homo sapiens*) uses of objects and their role in peer group centrality. *Journal of Comparative Psychology, 125*, 239–245.

Perspectives and Counterperspectives

16

Perspective 1: Why Would Natural Selection Craft an Organism Whose Future Functioning Is Influenced by Its Earlier Experiences?

Jay Belsky

As Carter and Porges (this volume) make clear in their fascinating, phylogenetically informed chapter on the neurobiology of social behavior, the mammalian capacity for social communication was not present in our reptilian predecessors. Indeed, especially fundamental to the focus of this commentary on the effects of early social experience on later development is Carter and Porges' (this volume) insightful observation that "the phylogenetic transition from reptiles to mammals appears to be a shift from an organism capable of 'self-regulation' to an organism that is dependent at certain points in development on 'other regulation.'" This other regulation in mammals, of course, typically refers to the behavior and functioning of the mother, at least insofar as progeny are concerned. It is for this reason, no doubt, that so much effort has been expended characterizing variation in mother–infant interaction in rats, voles, and humans, to name three species that figure importantly in the contributions under consideration by Carter and Porges (this volume) and by Mileva-Seitz, Afonso, and Fleming (this volume). However, a focus on the determinants of parenting in both chapters, but especially in the latter, derives not just from an interest in why mothers parent the way they do, but from the underlying assumption that early experience in the mother–infant relationship affects not just the short- but also the long-term development of offspring. One goal of this commentary is to challenge, at least to a degree, this presumption.

The work presented by Mileva-Seitz, Afonso, and Fleming (this volume) is indisputably elegant in illuminating multiple determinants of mothering, in both rats and humans, just as is the work summarized by Carter and Porges (this volume) on the neurobiology of social behavior in voles. Of course, rats and voles afford much greater precision of inquiry, especially when it comes to illuminating biological processes shaping mothering. It is most fascinating to see how both hormonal processes and experiences influence the degree to which rat mothers engage in putatively species-typical mothering behavior. Carter and Porges (this volume) make clear, though, that it is not just mothering behavior that is influenced by hormonal processes, but also social behavior more generally.

An important, even if obvious, take-home message from both chapters is that rats, voles, and humans do not just behave in species-typical ways, but manifest within-species variation in social behavior in general and maternal behavior in particular. The same, of course, is true, most obviously, of humans as well. Just as importantly, there is also within-species variation in the extent to which hormonal and experiential factors shape social behavior and thus mothering. Thus, the fact that hormones like dopamine and oxytocin, as well as variation in developmental experience, have proven influential in shaping maternal and offspring behavior, sometimes via well-documented physiological pathways, should not be read to imply that all individuals within any species are equally susceptible to such effects. Moreover, in the case of humans, as Mileva-Seitz et al. (this volume) make clear, mothering is also affected by cognitive processes, which, not surprisingly, are less likely to be investigated in other species. Recall in this regard the intriguing—and original—findings showing that less sensitive mothers relative to more sensitive mothers, like teen mothers relative to adult mothers, manifest deficits in attention set shifting, impulsivity, and/or working memory.

Much, even if not all, of the work described in the two chapters under consideration focuses on processes or mechanisms by which early experience may influence later functioning, be those mechanisms social, physiological, or epigenetic, and thus addresses a fundamentally important developmental question: "*How* does early experience affect later development?" What is important to appreciate, however, is that such a focus on *proximate* determinants of human development is quite different, even if not entirely distinct, from *ultimate* explanations. And the fact is that few students of early experience ever raise the question posed in the title of this chapter involving *why* later functioning should be shaped by experiences early in life. Even critics of early experience thinking have not posed the issue in terms of natural selection, as I will do in the remainder of this chapter (Kagan, 1978; Lewis, 1997). In fact, even though the Carter and Porges (this volume) contribution is indisputably based on an evolutionary view of development, their evolutionary analysis is mostly phylogenetic—and insightfully so—and thus about reptilian–mammalian differences rather than the evolutionary basis of variation *within* species.

The basic premise underlying the remainder of this chapter is that natural selection has probably not shaped all humans—or perhaps voles or rats for that matter—to be (equally) susceptible to early experience effects of the kind that are the focus of much of this volume. Intriguingly, this possibility is actually empirically chronicled in the work on gene × environment interaction presented by Mileva-Seitz et al. (this volume, see Figure 6.6A). Recall that in investigating the effect of early life adversity on mothers looking away from the infant, these investigators discovered that only those mothers who carried one version of the DRD1 rs686 genotype were susceptible to early experience effects.

As it turns out, two distinct, though by no means mutually exclusive, evolutionary-inspired theoretical arguments advance the claim that individuals should vary in their developmental plasticity and susceptibility to environmental influence (Ellis, Boyce, Belsky, Bakermans-Kranenburg, & van Ijzendoorn, 2011)—and thus that much more attention needs to be accorded to this possibility than has typically been the case. These are Belsky's (1997a, 1997b, 2005) differential-susceptibility hypothesis and Boyce and Ellis's (2005; Ellis, Essex, & Boyce, 2005; Ellis, Jackson, & Boyce, 2006) biological-sensitivity-to-context thesis. Whereas the former has emphasized the role of nature in shaping individual differences in developmental plasticity, without excluding a role for nurture, the latter has emphasized nurture, without excluding nature. Additionally, whereas the theoretical argument for differential susceptibility leads to no specific hypotheses about susceptibility factors or mediating mechanisms, regarding these as essentially empirical questions, such concerns are central to the biological-sensitivity-to-context thesis (Ellis et al., 2011). Both models nevertheless predict that some children and perhaps adults will be more susceptible than others to both the adverse *and* beneficial effects of, respectively, unsupportive and supportive contextual conditions; Boyce and Ellis (2005) use the terminology of "orchids" and "dandelions" to refer to individuals who are, respectively, more and less susceptible to environmental effects. Each perspective is summarized in turn.

Differential Susceptibility

The view that children should vary in their susceptibility to rearing is founded on evolutionary logic that regards the dispersion of genes in future generations as the ultimate biological imperative and thus goal of all living things. Indeed, from the perspective of modern evolutionary biology, natural selection shapes living things not just to survive, but to reproduce. Importantly, such reproduction can be direct, as when one produces immediate descendants (i.e., children, grandchildren), but also indirect, as when one's kin—such as brother, sister, niece, or nephew—reproduce and, in so doing, pass on genes that they share, in varying proportions, with the individual in question. *Reproductive fitness* refers to the dispersion of one's genes in future generations, and *inclusive fitness* calls attention to the fact that one's genetic material is distributed both directly and indirectly. This evolutionary-biological foundation forms the basis for the differential-susceptibility hypothesis.

Because the future is and always has been inherently uncertain, parents residing in environments of evolutionary adaptation, just like parents today, could not have known (consciously or unconsciously) what childrearing practices would prove most effective in promoting the reproductive fitness of offspring—and thus their own inclusive fitness. As a result, and as a fitness-optimizing strategy involving the hedging of bets, natural selection would have shaped parents to bear children varying in developmental plasticity (Belsky, 2005). This way, if an effect of parenting proved counterproductive in fitness terms, those children not affected by parenting would not have incurred the cost of developing in ways that ultimately proved "misguided" when it came to passing on genes to future generations. Importantly, in light of inclusive-fitness considerations, these less malleable children's reduced susceptibility to parental influence would have benefited not only themselves directly but also their more malleable sibs—but indirectly, given that sibs, like parents and children, share 50% of their specific alleles in common. By the same token, had parenting influenced children in ways that enhanced fitness, then not only would more plastic or malleable offspring have benefited directly by virtue of parental influence but also, too, would their parents and even their less malleable sibs who did not benefit from the parenting they received, again for inclusive-fitness reasons (i.e., shared genes).

Such evolutionary reasoning leads directly to the proposition that children should vary in their plasticity and thus susceptibility to parental rearing and perhaps to environmental influences more generally. To be clear, though, this is not in any way a group-selectionist argument, but one that regards the individual as the unit of selection. After all, on the basis of the preceding analysis, it is considered adaptive for an *individual* child to be more *or* less malleable and to have siblings with contrasting susceptibilities, thereby accruing potentially direct and/or indirect benefits, and for an *individual* parent to bear children of both kinds, thereby benefiting directly (i.e., immediate offspring) and indirectly (e.g., grandchildren).

As noted already, without denying the possibility of environmental influences on malleability (see Pluess & Belsky, 2011), Belsky (1997a, 1997b, 2005) presumed that individuals varied for genetic reasons in their developmental plasticity. Not inconsistent with this view is extensive cross-species evidence that plasticity is heritable (Bashey, 2006; Pigliucci, 2007) and may function as a selectable character in and of itself (Sinn, Gosling, & Moltschaniwskyj, 2007). Indeed, one wild bird population shows evidence that selection favoring individuals who are highly plastic with regard to the timing of reproduction has intensified over the past three decades, perhaps in response to climate change causing a mismatch between the breeding times of the birds and their caterpillar prey (Nussey, Postma, Gienapp, & Visser, 2005). Also noteworthy is Suomi's (2006) observation that a single genetic difference distinguishes the two species of primates that fill multiple niches around the world from all others that inhabit singular and rather narrow ones, the presence (in some individuals) of the *5-HTTLPR* short allele, leading him to regard humans and macaques as "weed species." Although space does not permit consideration, extensive data on humans now reveal them to be differentially susceptible to all sorts of environmental experiences—for temperamental, physiological, and genetic reasons (for review, see Belsky & Pluess, 2009a).

Biological Sensitivity to Context

Boyce and Ellis (2005) argue that for adaptive reasons, children in both especially supportive and especially unsupportive developmental contexts should develop or maintain high levels of physiological stress reactivity, which they regard as a susceptibility factor and thus plasticity mechanism, that is, the endophenotypic instantiation of susceptibility to environmental influence. Thus, they expect a curvilinear, U-shaped relation between levels of supportiveness versus stressfulness in early childhood environments and the development of stress-reactive profiles, with high reactivity disproportionately emerging in both highly stressful and highly protected social environments.

In the case of children fortunate enough to grow up in particularly supportive contexts, Boyce and Ellis (2005) contend that it would be adaptive to be maximally influenced by the developmental environment. Indeed, the physical, behavioral, and psychological embodiment of the rich resource base provided by the family and the broader ecology would enhance the social competitiveness of the individual through the development of a broad range of competencies, thereby increasing his or her mate value and eventual reproductive fitness. In contrast, those growing up under harsh and dangerous conditions would increase their chances of survival and eventual reproduction by developing heightened vigilance to threat and thus being especially prepared to actively combat risks that they might face. For them, too, heightened physiological reactivity is presumed to be the vehicle for getting this developmental job done. Thus, it is Boyce and Ellis's (2005, p. 292) thesis that the stress-response system operates as a conditional adaptation, selected to enable individuals to fit environments that, starting early in life, would enhance their fitness prospects: "natural selection has favored developmental mechanisms (conditional adaptations) that function to adjust levels of BSC [biological sensitivity to context] to match familial and ecological conditions encountered early in life."

Conclusion

Both arguments also define individual differences in developmental plasticity to mean that some children and even adults will be more susceptible than others to both the adverse *and* beneficial effects of, respectively, unsupportive and supportive contextual conditions. This view is consistent with evidence summarized by Carter and Porges (this volume) showing that there is variability across individuals in how even hormones influence behavior and even more notably with the aforementioned gene × environment interaction work with humans carried out by Mileva-Seitz and associates (this volume). Especially important to appreciate is that this "for better and for worse" view of susceptibility to environmental influences (Belsky, Bakermans-Kranenburg, & van Ijzendoorn., 2007) contrasts markedly with traditional dual-risk/diathesis-stress frameworks that regard certain putatively "vulnerable" individuals as more likely than others to be adversely affected by unsupportive contextual conditions, while stipulating nothing about differential responsiveness to supportive conditions. Just as importantly, diathesis-stress thinking does not propose, as differential-susceptibility and biological-sensitivity-to-context theorizing does, that the very individual attributes that makes some individuals disproportionately susceptible to adversity simultaneously make them disproportionately likely to benefit from supportive ones (Belsky et al., 2007; Belsky & Pluess, 2009a, 2009b; Ellis et al., 2011).

Irrespective of whether plasticity is considered to be principally a function of nature or nurture—or their interaction—central to both evolutionary arguments under consideration is the claim that individual differences in plasticity have evolved. What this means, of course, is that it is probably misguided to regard many of the kinds of experiences highlighted in this volume to be equally influential to the development of all children. Unless such a possibility is entertained at the outset, it seems likely that research will both over- and underestimate the importance of early experience for human development—underestimating it for those who are highly susceptible while overestimating it for those who are far less malleable. As a result, whether one is looking at how early experiences shape hormonal and other physiological processes or how the latter themselves influence behavior, be it of mothers or offspring, investigators would be well advised to move beyond the study of "main effects." That is, they should consider the prospect that whatever hypotheses are guiding their inquiry, they will prove more accurate in the case of some rather than others.

References

Bashey, F. (2006). Cross-generational environmental effects and the evolution of offspring size in the Trinidadian guppy Poecilia reticulata. *Evolution: International Journal of Organic Evolution, 60*(2), 348–361.

Belsky, J. (1997a). Theory testing, effect-size evaluation, and differential susceptibility to rearing influence: The case of mothering and attachment. *Child Development, 68*(4), 598–600.

Belsky, J. (1997b). Variation in susceptibility to rearing influences: An evolutionary argument. *Psychological Inquiry, 8*, 182–186.

Belsky, J. (2005). Differential susceptibility to rearing influences: An evolutionary hypothesis and some evidence. In B. Ellis & D. Bjorklund (Eds.), *Origins of the social mind: Evolutionary psychology and child development* (pp. 139–163). New York, NY: Guildford.

Belsky, J., Bakermans-Kranenburg, M. J., & van Ijzendoorn, M. H. (2007). For better and for worse: Differential susceptibility to environmental influences. *Current Directions in Psychological Science, 16*(6), 300–304.

Belsky, J., & Pluess, M. (2009a). Beyond diathesis-stress: Differential susceptibility to environmental influence. *Psychological Bulletin, 135*, 885–908.

Belsky, J., & Pluess, M. (2009b). The nature (and nurture?) of plasticity in early human development. *Perspectives on Psychological Science, 4*(4), 345–351.

Boyce, W. T., & Ellis, B. J. (2005). Biological sensitivity to context: I. An evolutionary-developmental theory of the origins and functions of stress reactivity. *Development and Psychopathology, 17*(2), 271–301.

Ellis, B. J., Boyce, W. T., Belsky, J., Bakermans-Kranenburg, M., & van Ijzendoorn, M. H. (2011). Differential susceptibility to the environment: An evolutionary-neurodevelopmental theory. *Development and Psychopathology, 23*, 1–5.

Ellis, B. J., Essex, M. J., & Boyce, W. T. (2005). Biological sensitivity to context: II. Empirical explorations of an evolutionary-developmental theory. *Development and Psychopathology, 17*, 303–328.

Ellis, B. J., Jackson, J. J., & Boyce, W. T. (2006). The stress response systems: Universality and adaptive individual differences. *Developmental Review, 26*, 175–212.

Kagan, J. (1978). *Infancy: Its place in human development.* Cambridge, MA: Harvard University Press.

Lewis, M. (1997). *Altering fate: Why the past does not predict the future.* New York, NY: Guilford.

Nussey, D. H., Postma, E., Gienapp, P., & Visser, M. E. (2005). Selection on heritable phenotypic plasticity in a wild bird population. *Science, 310*(5746), 304–306.

Pigliucci, M. (2007). Do we need an extended evolutionary synthesis? *Evolution: International Journal of Organic Evolution, 61*(12), 2743–2749.

Pluess, M., & Belsky, J. (2011). Prenatal programming of postnatal plasticity? *Development and Psychopathology, 23,* 29–38.

Sinn, D. L., Gosling, S. D., & Moltschaniwskyj, N. A. (2007). Development of shy/bold behaviour in squid: Context-specific phenotypes associated with developmental plasticity. *Animal Behaviour, 75*, 433–442.

Suomi, S. J. (2006). Risk, resilience, and gene x environment interactions in rhesus monkeys. *Annals of the New York Academy of Sciences, 1094*, 52–62.

17

Perspective 2: Play, Plasticity, and the Perils of Conflict: "Problematizing" Sociobiology

Melvin Konner

For someone who has been thinking about the evolution of childhood since around 1965 and who finally published his "big book" on the subject (Konner, 2010), it is gratifying to see how the field has developed, expanded, and become increasingly "normal science," as exemplified in the chapters on play. While they are mainly theoretical, they represent a spectrum of approaches, and they help point the way forward.

Joseph L. Flanders, Khalisa N. Herman, and Daniel Paquette give cooperation a central role in human evolution, but they do so with a strong emphasis on the role of play, especially rough-and-tumble play. They argue that the self-handicapping that is universal in such play, and which has a long phylogenetic history, makes R&T play important in the developmental emergence of self-regulation in social situations, and that this in turn promotes the development of social cooperation and conflict resolution. They also give fathers a central role in the process, arguing that fathers are more likely than mothers to help children learn to interact with a wider world and also to manage social conflict. They also take the conflict itself seriously and provide support for the view that competition and dominance as well as cooperation are important in human development and have been important in human evolution. They recognize that one of the most effective domains of human cooperation occurs when we cooperate for the purposes of dominance and conflict. I might go further and argue that for most of human history, especially since the origins of agriculture, human cooperation has been directed frequently toward conflict and dominance, and that the absence of intergroup confrontations has usually been a temporary, albeit sometimes long-duration, lull in the series of conflicts (Konner, 2006).

Peter Gray's chapter describes five characteristics of play that, he argues, make it ideal for both transmitting hunter-gatherer skills, values, and culture and fostering an egalitarian lifestyle in adulthood: Play is self-chosen and self-directed, intrinsically motivated, guided by mental rules, and imaginative and involves an active, alert, but relatively unstressed frame of mind. Among hunter-gatherers, play occupies a great deal of children's time, although to say that it is all they do would be to miss the fact that in many hunter-gatherer cultures children provided much of their own subsistence, albeit often in a playful spirit (Konner, 2010). It would also deny them the substantial time they may need to observe adult activities—for example, going with their mothers on gathering trips and helping all along the way (Shostak, 1981). However, as Gray well understands, hunter-gatherer play groups are rarely peer groups but are instead mixed-age, mixed-sex groups that roam the area not too far from village camps engaging in foraging, games, exploration (looking for tracks they can tell their fathers about, etc.), and talking. Younger children learn from older children, and much of hunter-gatherer cultural transmission over time is done in this step-down, child-to-child fashion rather than from adult to child (Konner 1972, 1975, 2010). It makes little sense for competition and dominance to become an issue in a group of children who are different ages and sizes, and unlike in Western culture, boys and girls do not segregate to an extreme degree in middle childhood, so the sexes do not grow up in different cultures, at least before adolescence. All this seems geared to produce adults compatible with the egalitarian lifestyles characteristic of hunter-gatherers.

Anthony D. Pellegrini and Adam F. A. Pellegrini develop an argument giving play and the plasticity involved in play a central role in evolution. Following Patrick Bateson, they view play as an "adaptability driver" or cutting edge of plasticity, and, find this highly compatible with West-Eberhard's (2003) ideas about the complex role of plasticity in evolution as well as with recent discoveries about epigenetics. In contrast to Gray, this author, and many others, Pellegrini and Pellegrini reject the idea that there may be a mismatch between our environments of evolutionary adaptation (EEAs) and our current environment that our genetic endowments have not yet caught up with. These authors argue that there is no need for such a hypothesis, because, as the cutting edge of plasticity, play has adapted all along to the novel environments humans have encountered. However, they do not consider what Gray focuses on, which is not merely a change in the environments in which play occurs but an elimination of play from the lives of many children, either because of work or a combination of school and rigorously organized team sports. It is not obvious that this transition has been bad for children, but it is reasonable to hypothesize that reducing self-initiated, imaginative, intrinsically motivated play from children's lives completely could have some consequences consistent with the mismatch model.

The chapters in this section have in common a dissatisfaction with the self-assured genetic competition models of sociobiology and its heir, evolutionary psychology. They correctly emphasize the role of plasticity—whether in the form or service of cultural evolution, gene–culture coevolution, or adaptive play—in the larger evolutionary process; the fact that most conflict is ritualized or playful; and the role of cooperation in muting competition and the possibility that natural selection can operate at the level of the family or the group. These emphases are all to the good and certainly provide a counterweight to the emphasis on relentless competition and selection at the level of the individual or the gene. But these are not mutually exclusive possibilities.

Trivers (1974) and others highlighted parent–offspring conflict but focused on moments like weaning when the difference in adaptive goals is most clear; no one ever denied that parent and offspring share large domains of consonant interests. Rough-and-tumble play and ritual contests have always been of interest, but some violence is all too real. Group selection was ruled out by some sociobiologists but accepted as part of the picture by others, including by E. O. Wilson, the author of *Sociobiology: The New Synthesis,* who has been for the past few years one of its most prominent champions. Plasticity was never denied by anyone; it is obvious to all who study animal or human behavior. Cultural evolution and gene–culture coevolution are concepts that never receded from general discourse about evolutionary process.

But plasticity has limits, and models considering selection at the level of the gene or the individual have proven their value in *helping* to explain what we see in the living world and what we discern more dimly in the history of life. To the extent that their value has been exaggerated, their proponents should be criticized. But it will be a good day for evolutionary studies when we clear from our minds the dated notion that certain ideas are doomed to be pitted against each other in endless conflict. Those of us who de-emphasize the role of conflict in the natural world might also try to achieve compromise in these often ideological scientific conflicts as well.

References

Konner, M. (2006). Human nature, ethnic violence, and war. In M. Fitzduff & C. E. Stout (Eds.), *The psychology of resolving global conflicts: From war to peace* (Vol. 1). Westport, CT: Praeger Security International.

Konner, M. (2010). *The evolution of childhood: Relationships, emotion, mind.* Cambridge, MA: Harvard University Press.

Konner, M. J. (1972). Aspects of the developmental ethology of a foraging people. In N. G. B. Jones (Ed.), *Ethological studies of child behavior* (pp. 285–304). Cambridge, England: Cambridge University Press.

Konner, M. J. (1975). Relations among infants and juveniles in comparative perspective. In M. Lewis & L. Rosenblum (Eds.), *Friendship and peer relations.* New York, NY: John Wiley and Sons.

Shostak, M. (1981). *Nisa: The life and words of a !!Kung woman.* Cambridge, MA: Harvard University Press.

Trivers, R. L. (1974). Parent-offspring conflict. *American Zoologist, 14,* 249–264.

West-Eberhard, M. J. (2003). *Developmental plasticity and evolution.* New York, NY: Oxford University Press.

18

Perspective 3: The Emergent Organism:
A New Paradigm
William A. Mason

A Changing Perspective

A few decades ago, this particular book would not have been possible. During the last 50 years, fundamental changes have occurred in the concepts, methods, and basic assumptions of scientific psychology and related disciplines. A comparative psychologist starting a career in the mid-1950s of the last century could not escape the impression of intellectual ferment and upheaval. The ancient distinction between heredity and environment was being questioned (Anastasi & Foley, 1948; Beach, 1955; Hebb, 1953). The richness of the natural behavior of animals was being described in studies carried out in captivity and in the field (Carpenter, 1954; Hediger, 1955). Exciting new findings were appearing on exploration and curiosity, and discoveries were announced of cognitive achievements that challenged the stark stimulus-response paradigms of Pavlov, Watson, Skinner, and Hull (Butler, 1954; Harlow, 1951).

These changes amounted to a new perspective in psychology. In 1960, in the title to his presidential address to the American Psychological Association, Hebb referred to what was happening in psychology as "the American Revolution" (Hebb, 1960; see also Hebb, 1974). The principal ideas he touched on are now a part of the canons of the mainstream. He characterized psychology as a biological science whose principal business was the study of *mind*. By mind, he meant all forms of mental activity of the whole organism, human and nonhuman. "Mind and consciousness, sensations and perceptions, feelings and emotions" are appropriate objects of study (Hebb, 1960, p. 740). He emphasized, however, that these phenomena were inherently hypothetical and could only be approached indirectly and inferentially. Behavior is a basic tool in carrying out this process objectively. In addition, it is an interesting and important phenomenon in its own right.

Early Experience and the Ontogeny of Behavior

One of the most dynamic elements in the new perspective was the study of ontogeny. The role of experience in psychological development was traditionally associated with the nature–nurture issue. In contrast, in their 1954 review of early experience, Beach and Jaynes focused more on empirical results than their theoretical implications for a questionable causal dichotomy (Beach & Jaynes, 1954). Among the important influences on the increase in developmental research, they credited Hebb's *Organization of Behavior* (1949) and the work of Lorenz and other ethologists on imprinting (e.g., Hess, 1958; Lorenz, 1957). Whatever the source, within the space of a few years "early experience" became a hot issue. A conference on the topic was convened at Bar Harbor, followed by the founding of a new journal and an international society (Scott, 1973).

In 1954, while this research was gaining momentum, I began working with infant monkeys at the University of Wisconsin and had the opportunity to learn first hand about development and the importance of early experience. Our initial descriptions of the behavioral effects of moderate and severe environmental restrictions on rhesus monkeys appeared in the early 1960s (Harlow & Harlow, 1962; Mason, 1960; Mason & Sponholz, 1963). These initial reports were followed by more primate research documenting a broad range of effects of experience on the development of normal and abnormal behavior (e.g., Mason, 1967, 1971, 1973; Mason & Berkson, 1975; Mason, Davenport, & Menzel, 1968; Menzel, Davenport, & Rogers, 1970; Sackett, 1972; Suomi & Harlow, 1971).

Meanwhile, a second stream of research, originally carried out with laboratory rats, was making strides toward unraveling the complex neurological consequences of early experience, as well as adding new species and psychosocial variables to its agenda (e.g., Denenberg, 1970; Hennessy, 1986; Levine, 2005).

Developmental Models

These few examples do not do justice to the range and variety of developmental topics that were being investigated, nor to the outpouring of new information. Clearly, some sort of conceptual framework was called for to help integrate and organize this material. I was one of many to try. My aim was to present a general description of the normal process of social development of monkeys and apes and to indicate how it was influenced by experience (Mason, 1964, 1965). I drew on my personal experience and on the substantial literature on the early behavior of human and nonhuman primates. I also benefited greatly from the dynamic approach to development presented in general systems theory (e.g., Anderson, 1957; Ashby, 1960; Bertalanffy, 1968; Piaget, 1971; Reese & Overton, 1970; Schneirla, 1957). The influence of the systems approach is also evident in Bowlby's theory of attachment (Bowlby, 1969). The essential model is rooted in organismic biology (Bertalanffy, 1968). Within this framework, the individual is viewed as a self-organizing entity comprising different interacting, functionally defined organizational levels. The system is open, dynamic, and inherently changeable. All forms of development are the probabilistic outcome of influences originating from an active organism interacting selectively with a complex, variable, and uncertain environment (Brunswik, 1955). The general systems approach is particularly well suited to deal with the biological aspects of development, particularly the many forms and levels of early experience effects.

Beyond the relatively specific and varied theoretical and empirical contributions, I believe the research on early experience also contributed to a change in the basic foundational concepts of *experience*, the *individual*, and the *environment*.

Experience. This concept was usually construed as a relatively discrete event impinging on sensory receptors. The traditional generic concept of "stimulus" remains a useful shorthand for an independent variable in many sorts of scientific applications. It is obviously too narrow, however, to accommodate lots of important new findings. Existing data clearly indicate that many of the effects of early experience either escape detection by the sensory systems altogether or result in broad, often subtle changes that can have critical consequences for many aspects of psychological development. A host of well-documented examples include pre- and postnatal effects of nutrition, drugs, disease, stress, and environmental "enrichment." A more useful metaphor for causal effects encompassing all forms of experience is *information* (Oyama, 2000).

Individual. The *individual* as a psychological entity has been a foundational concept since the beginning of scientific psychology. In recent years, the concept has been greatly expanded and enriched, not only in science, but in Western culture as a whole. The sources are probably many. Spontaneity is recognized as an important quality of individual behavior. Within comparative developmental psychology, the model of the quiescent newborn mammal or bird that only acts in response to impinging stimuli is no longer tenable. Nor is the idea that the determinants of behavioral development can be categorically divided into innate and acquired (e.g., West-Eberhard, 2003).

The framework of dynamic systems theory has been a great help in thinking about individual development (Bowlby, 1969; Fogel & Thelen, 1987; Mascolo & Harkins, 1998; Mason, 2002). For example, an obvious place to begin to look for antecedents of primate behavioral development from a systems perspective is infancy. It has been known for many years that the neonatal primate is equipped (as are other mammals) with a sizable repertoire of behaviors that facilitate its adjustment to its mother and its early environment. In Piagetian terms, these are early *schemas*. Although these patterns are "species typical," contrary to the once popular view that their form and organization are fixed, they are capable of considerable flexibility and can adapt to existing circumstances in various ways, including simple, well-known forms of learning (e.g., Lipsitt, 1963; Mason & Harlow, 1959; Rovee-Collier & Gekoski, 1979). Of greater developmental significance, these early schemas are affectively charged and motivated and can join together. In a process called the *principle of component schemas*, primitive schemas with functional affinities and valence are combined into higher order schemas or emerging units (Mason, 2002). This is a dialectic and probabilistic process in which the developing individual is actively engaged with its environment, selecting opportunistically from what the environment affords. The emergent result of this process is the creation of major biologically significant concepts such as "mother," "food," "immature conspecific," and so on. The formation of component schemas into larger units is perhaps among the first examples of the emergence of basic concepts in some mammalian species.

Environment. After many years of debate, the dichotomous rendering of developmental determinants into "heredity" and "environment" is finished. The accepted view is that environmental and genetic influences are inextricably interwoven and both are essential to all development (Gilbert & Epel, 2009; Hamer, 2002; Oyama, 2000; West-Eberhard, 2003). Among the consequences of the demise of the nature–nurture dichotomy is an increased interest in the relationships between genetic and environmental influences on the developing phenotype. It is already clear that environmental influences can facilitate, sustain, guide, and constrain developmental processes rather than determine them directly. A well-known example of such an enabling condition is the research by Held and associates. Their findings show that giving an animal an opportunity to experience its own movements is key to its developing basic sensory-motor "reflexes" (Held, 1965). It is becoming increasingly clear that the social environment provides multiple opportunities to facilitate and shape species-typical development (e.g., Mason, 1978). As Bowlby understood, environments for the developing individual are always plural. One application of his concept of *environments of evolutionary adaptedness* might be to help account for a puzzling phenomenon, namely, a behavior that develops in one environment as a fixed and seemingly immutable species-typical pattern whereas in another, slightly different environment it develops in radically altered form or not at all. The obvious question is, What is the critical difference between similar environments that produces such disparate results?

Conclusion

Who can say how historians of science will regard the events of the past few decades of research on development? They will certainly recognize that important empirical advances have been made on all fronts, including anthropology, evolutionary biology, genetics, neurophysiology, and psychology, as evident in this volume. One might guess, however, that for the scientists participating in these events, the most exciting changes have been in new ideas about the natural world that their work has helped to create.

References

Anastasi, A., & Foley, Jr., J. P. (1948). A proposed reorientation in the Heredity—Environment controversy. *Psychological Review, 55*(5), 239–249.

Anderson, J. E. (1957). Dynamics of development: Systems in process. In D. B. Harris (Ed.), *The concept of development: An issue in the study of human behavior* (pp. 25–46). Minneapolis, MN: University of Minnesota Press.

Ashby, W. R. (1960). *Design for a brain. The origin of adaptive behaviour*. London: Chapman & Hall and Science Paperbacks.

Beach, F. A. (1955). The decent of instinct. *Psychological Review, 62*, 401–410.

Beach, F. A., & Jaynes, J. (1954). Effects of early experience upon the behavior of animals. *Psychological Bulletin, 51*, 239–263.

Bertalanffy, L. V. (1968). *General system theory. Foundations, development, applications.* New York, NY: George Braziller.

Bowlby, J. (1969). *Attachment and Loss. Vol. 1: Attachment.* New York, NY: Basic Books.

Brunswik, E. (1955). Representative design and probabilistic theory in a functional psychology. *Psychological Review, 62*, 193–217.

Butler, R. A. (1954). Curiosity in monkeys. *Scientific American, 190*, 70–75.

Carpenter, C. R. (1954). Tentative generalizations on the grouping behavior of non-human primates. *Human Biology, 26*(3), 269–276.

Denenberg, V. H. (1970). Experimental programming of life histories and the creation of individual differences: A review. In M. R. Jones (Ed.), *Miami symposium on the prediction of behavior, 1968: Effects of early experience* (pp. 61–91). Coral Gables, FL: University of Miami Press.

Fogel, A., & Thelen, E. (1987). Development of early expressive and communicative action: Reinterpreting the evidence from a dynamic systems perspective. *Developmental Psychology, 23,* 747–761.

Gilbert, S. F., & Epel, D. (2009). *Ecological developmental biology. Integrating epigenetics, medicine, and evolution.* Sunderland, MA: Sinauer Associates.

Hamer, D. (2002). Rethinking behavior genetics. *Science, 298*, 71–72.

Harlow, H. F. (1951). Primate learning. In C. P. Stone (Ed.), *Comparative psychology* (3rd ed., pp. 183–238). New York, NY: Prentice Hall.

Harlow, H. F., & Harlow, M. K. (1962). Social deprivation in monkeys. *Scientific American, 207*, 137–146.

Hebb, D. O. (1949). *The organization of behavior. A neuropsychological theory.* New York, NY: John Wiley & Sons.

Hebb, D. O. (1953). Heredity and environment in mammalian behaviour. *British Journal of Animal Behavior, 1*(2), 43–47.

Hebb, D. O. (1960). The American revolution. *American Psychologist, 15*, 735–745.

Hebb, D. O. (1974). What psychology is about. *American Psychologist, 29*, 71–79.

Hediger, H. (1955). *Studies of the psychology and behaviour of captive animals in zoos and circuses.* London: Butterworths Scientific Publications.

Held, R. (1965). Plasticity in sensory-motor systems. *Scientific American, 213*, 84–94.

Hennessy, M. B. (1986). Multiple, brief maternal separations in the squirrel monkey: Changes in hormonal and behavioral responsiveness. *Physiology and Behavior, 36*, 245–250.

Hess, E. H. (1958). "Imprinting" in animals. *Scientific American, 198*, 81–90.

Levine, S. (2005). Stress: An historical perspective. In T. Steckler, N. H. Kalin, & J. M. H. M. Reul (Eds.), *Handbook of stress and the brain* (Vol. 15, pp. 3–23). Netherlands: Elsevier Science and Technology.

Lipsitt, L. P. (1963). Learning in the first year of life. In L. P. Lipsitt & C. C. Spiker (Eds.), *Advances in child development and behavior* (Vol. 1, pp. 147–195). New York, NY: Academic Press.

Lorenz, K. (1957). Companionship in bird life. Fellow members of the species as releasers of social behavior. In C. H. Schiller (Ed.), *Instinctive behavior* (pp. 83–116). New York, NY: International Universities Press.

Mascolo, M. F., & Harkins, D. (1998). Toward a component systems approach to emotional development. In M. F. Mascolo & S. Griffin (Eds.), *What develops in emotional development?* (pp. 189–217). New York, NY: Plenum Press.

Mason, W. A. (1960). The effects of social restriction of the behavior of rhesus monkeys: I. Free social behavior. *Journal of Comparative and Physiological Psychology, 53*(8), 582–589.

Mason, W. A. (1964). Sociability and social organization in monkeys and apes. In L. Berkowitz (Ed.), *Recent advances in experimental social psychology* (Vol. 1, pp. 277–305). New York, NY: Academic Press.

Mason, W. A. (1965). The social development of monkeys and apes. In I. DeVore (Ed.), *Primate behavior: Field studies of monkeys and apes* (pp. 514–543). New York, NY: Holt, Rinehart and Winston.

Mason, W. A. (1967). Motivational aspects of social responsiveness in young chimpanzees. In H. W. Stevenson, J. E. H. Hess, & H. L. Rheingold (Eds.), *Early behavior: Comparative and development approaches* (pp. 103–126). New York, NY: John Wiley & Sons.

Mason, W. A. (1971). Motivational factors in psychosocial development. In W. J. Arnold & M. M. Page (Eds.), *Nebraska symposium on motivation* (pp. 35–67). Lincoln, NE: University of Nebraska Press.

Mason, W. A. (1973). Regulatory functions of arousal in primate psychosocial development. In C. R. Carpenter (Ed.), *Behavioral regulators of behavior in primates* (pp. 19–33). Lewisburg, PA: Bucknell University Press.

Mason, W. A. (1978). Social experience and primate cognitive development. In G. M. Burghardt & M. Bekoff (Eds.), *The development of behavior: Comparative and evolutionary aspects* (pp. 233–251). New York, NY: Garland STPM Press.

Mason, W. A. (2002). The natural history of primate behavioral development: An organismic perspective. In D. J. Lewkowicz & R. Lickliter (Eds.), *Conceptions of development: Lessons from the laboratory* (pp. 105–134). New York, NY: Psychology Press.

Mason, W. A., & Berkson, G. (1975). Effects of maternal mobility on the development of rocking and other behaviors in rhesus monkeys: A study with artificial mothers. *Developmental Psychobiology, 8*(3), 197–211.

Mason, W. A., Davenport, Jr., R. K., & Menzel, Jr., E. W. (1968). Early experience and the social development of rhesus monkeys and chimpanzees. In G. Newton & S. Levine (Eds.), *Early experience and behavior* (pp. 440–480). Springfield, IL: Charles C. Thomas Publisher.

Mason, W. A., & Harlow, H. F. (1959). Initial responses of infant rhesus monkeys to solid foods. *Psychological Reports, 5*, 193–199.

Mason, W. A., & Sponholz, R. R. (1963). Behavior of rhesus monkeys raised in isolation. *Journal of Psychiatric Research, 1*, 299–306.

Menzel, Jr., E. W., Davenport, R. K., & Rogers, C. M. (1970). The development of tool using in wild-born and restriction-reared chimpanzees. *Folia Primatologica, 12*, 273–283.

Oyama, S. (2000). *The ontogeny of information. Developmental systems and evolution* (2nd ed., Revised and Expanded). Durham, NC: Duke University Press.

Piaget, J. (1971). *Biology and knowledge: An essay on the relations between organic regulations and cognitive processes.* Chicago, IL: University of Chicago Press.

Reese, H. W., & Overton, W. F. (1970). Models of development and theories of development. In L. R. Goulet & F. B. Baltes (Eds.), *Life span developmental psychology: Research and theory* (pp. 115–145). New York, NY: Academic Press.

Rovee-Collier, C. K., & Gekoski, M. J. (1979). The economics of infancy: A review of conjugate reinforcement. *Advances in Child Development and Behavior, 19*, 195–255.

Sackett, G. P. (1972). Exploratory behavior of rhesus monkeys as a function of rearing experience and sex. *Developmental Psychobiology, 6*, 260–270.

Schneirla, T. C. (1957). The concept of development in comparative psychology. In D. B. Harris (Ed.), *The concept of development: An issue in the study of human behavior* (pp. 78–108). Minneapolis, MN: University of Minnesota Press.

Scott, J. P. (1973). The organization of comparative psychology. *Annals of the New York Academy of Sciences, 223*, 7–40.

Suomi, S. J., & Harlow, H. F. (1971). Monkeys at play. *Natural History, 80*, 72–15.

West-Eberhard, M. J. (2003). *Developmental plasticity and evolution.* New York, NY: Oxford University Press.

19

Perspective 4: Can Science Progress to a Revitalized Past?

G. A. Bradshaw

To achieve a psychology of liberation demands first that psychology be liberated.

—Ignatio Martín-Baró

The organizers of the conference "Human Nature and Early Experience: Addressing the 'Environment of Evolutionary Adaptedness'" and editors of this companion volume state: "In order for science to play an effective role in helping to reverse current negative trends in well-being, we need to foster a widespread understanding of the types of psychobiological needs that humans possess as a result of their evolutionary nature" (Narvaez, Panksepp, Schore, & Gleason, this volume). To this end, a number of papers review diverse models related to theories of human evolution with a focus on developmental contexts.

Roughgarden and Song (in press) propose replacing the standard evolutionary stable strategy (ESS) and related models with an alternative view of human interactions. Instead of envisioning evolutionary success as the outcome of processes of conflict along genetic time scales, they argue for a theory from management science where developmental economics are grounded in more intimate time scales and in a much more cooperative atmosphere: Parent–child interactions are not so much hostile as they are "honest." In another chapter, Fuentes (in press) brings an anthropologist's perspective to review various models including niche construction. Both papers focus on the importance of relational aspects of development and a kinder, gentler interpretation of humanity than what neo-Darwinians describe. Human behavior, psychology, biology, and evolution are no longer considered a linear progression of interacting yet individually intact entities. Instead, they are seen as the unfolding of linked relational processes of cooperation.

The book chapters provide a range of theories and explanations for why people turn out the way they do. The question is: Which one is "right?" Certainly, choice is somewhat constrained by tractability. As Fuentes points out, there are intrinsic limits to substantiating one theory or the other: It's hard to ascertain the quality of interpersonal relationships from bones. But even so, the veritable library of well-crafted theories leaves the reader somewhat perplexed, faced with choosing one or the other model, much like the customer standing at the counter of a French pastry shop.

When confronted with such ambivalence, it is often an indication that we have encountered a framing error: Conclusions fail to provide solutions. Humanity, and nature, may have been redeemed with the embrace of these more benign interpretations of evolution, but it is questionable whether an extended tour of formalized biopsychologies has brought us any closer to fixing the problem motivating the research in the first place, namely, modernity's diminished childrearing competency that has been identified as a key factor responsible for moral decline so widespread and pernicious as to prompt predictions of the human species' self-demise (Narvaez & Gleason, this volume; Roughgarden & Song, in press). The juxtaposition of Narvaez and Gleason, this volume. with Roughgarden, Song, and Fuentes prompts one to ask: Do we really need a mathematical model to advise us how to best care for our children?

This is not a facetious remark. In the closing remarks of their chapter, Narvaez and Gleason (this volume) hint at something of the same thing when they write, "Current Western human nature and culture are abnormal in terms of world history and world cultures, and *yet conclusions about human nature and normal functioning are drawn regularly from studies of its members*" (emphasis mine). In other words, science has convolved solution space with problem space by its exclusion of significant populations from the process of defining the conceptual baseline that shapes scientific inquiry. To conjure another metaphor, scientists are caught looking for solutions under a paradigm lamppost because it's the only place where science's light seems to shine. By failing to distinguish Western cultural values from its methodology, scientists limit science's capability to address the problems they ostensibly seek (Lavigne, 2003), thereby leaving science and society in a never-ending tautological bind.

Narvaez and Gleason identify something that is obvious to anyone who is not of Western culture: Millions upon millions of "data" (tribal peoples and nonhuman animals who have been dismissed, colonized, killed, and forced to become "Western") are omitted when it comes to defining statistical and value-based norms and practices. What is notable, and refreshing, about the work of Narvaez and Gleason, this volume. is that they speak as *scientists*. What they say is very much what social scientists have argued for decades yet has been largely absent in the biological sciences. Neuroscience is now consonant with the call for democratization of epistemic and cultural authority, to orient enquiry "from the point of view of the dominated instead of the dominator" (Martín-Baró, 1994, p. 14), that has followed successive social and political liberation movements (Bracken, 2002; Kirmayer, 2006). By recognizing that amicability, empathy, egalitarian politics, conscientiousness, and rarity of interpersonal violence characterizes whom they dub as hunter-gatherer small band (HGSB) peoples, Narvaez, Gleason, and others have jumped from neurons to not only neighborhoods but also nations. Other neuropsychologists such as Allan Schore have also expanded the scale of dialogue by linking what goes on inside to society at large, the conscious and unconscious collective, with the result that "a large number of disciplines in both the sciences and the arts are now experiencing a paradigm shift from explicit conscious cognition to implicit unconscious affect" (Schore, 2011, p. 77).

The suggestion that an *ancestral human mammalian milieu* (AHMM) replace Western culture as an alternative baseline for "developmental optimization" quietly recontextualizes the entire Western culture and episteme from a position of monopoly to a minority. The conceptual tether that has kept science hostage to the political agenda of Western hegemony has been dissolved by an honest scientific appraisal of the neuropsychological playing field. This instantly reconfigures the relationship between the Western academic community's theories and methods and those of other cultures. Instead of merely being "museum artifacts" and "ethnographic data" (Martin, 2009) in service to science, HGSB peoples join as epistemic players and, as they appear to excel as developmental optimizers, leaders of social innovation.

Until very recently, the rationale for studying non-Western traditions and nonhuman species was that they teach us why we Westerners became the way we are. Even with postcolonial sensibilities, non-Western epistemes have tended to be regarded as politically correct add-ons or interesting counterpoints to Western models. The same holds for animal research. "Animal models" used in experiments and studies are justified mainly by their ability to yield insights into humans (Shapiro, 1998). Now, in parallel with the new moral neuropsychological analysis of cross-cultural human development, a trans-species neuropsychology has emerged. A comparable, cross-species leveling has taken place with the explicit acknowledgment that the brains, behavior, and minds of all vertebrates, humans included, run on the same unitary model (Bradshaw & Finlay, 2005; Bradshaw & Sapolsky, 2006).

Germaine to the topic at hand, discovery of ways to promote prosocial psychological and socioecological well-being of children and families, science's trans-species leveling does something else. The AHMM expands to a simple AHIM (animal, human-inclusive, milieu). Not only does trans-species science expand the all-too-narrow definitions of normative, but it also compels modern human society to regard other species as moral and cultural exemplars and eschew ethics and behavior that destroy animals and their societies. As our neuropsychological peers, other species qualify for what we Westerners have coveted for ourselves: life, liberty, and the pursuit of all sorts of things including the right to be happy. Yes, rats have the right to laugh, too, and to do so without the specter of being condemned to laboratory life.

This is big news. First, the banners under which Western society marches, progress and capitalism, start looking less like holy grails than they do instruments of trauma. To be fair, the West is not the only human culture culpable of destruction. However, the past half millennium qualifies the West and its adherents for a unique place in human history as the engineer of the Sixth Great Extinction: an unprecedented sequence of genocides that have afflicted human and nonhuman species throughout the planet. The political and economic agendas that caused these geno-cides and undermined positive sociomoral parenting in tribal human (e.g., father-lessness in African American and South African families; Flood, 2003; Hunter, 2006) and animal (e.g., great ape captivity, Capaldo & Bradshaw, 2011; elephant psychological and cultural breakdown, Bradshaw, 2009; Bradshaw & Schore, 2007; Bradshaw, Schore, Brown, Poole, & Moss, 2005) societies are also responsible for today's sociomoral crisis in modern communities. Dramatic moral decline and its neuropsychological correlates directly map to Western cultural and political con-structs. Subsequently, while various models of evolution may explain the mechan-ics of sociomoral decline, the real, meaningful "discovery" is that the symptoms scientists now seek to cure are generated by a politicoeconomic agenda embraced by Western culture. The fact that violence and asociality are no longer confined to any particular social-ecological setting means "the modern West can no longer be quite distinguished from its victims" (Pfaff, 2005, p. 48). Given that tribal people such as the Columbian Nukak have lost half their population to disease and sui-cide since 1988 after first contact with Westerners and continue to figuratively and literally lose ground (Survival International, 2010), coupled with dire predictions of mass extinctions within decades, there may not be anything left on the planet *but* "abnormal" behaviors.

Subsequently, because cause and cure derive from the same system, solu-tions must entail something other than minor tweaking of one model or another. Preventing systemic trauma requires disabling social institutions that cultivate unhealthy behavior (Herman, 1997). This also means that science has to see to its own intellectual and ethical spring cleaning: The political constructs that promote diminished childrearing competency make up the endoskeleton that gives form and substance to science's mandates, concepts, and methods. To help restore moral health, scientists need to make science congruent with the entirety of its knowledge, that is, articulate a transcultural and trans-species episteme, and embrace a par-adigmatic shift that redefines progress as a revitalization of the past.

Second, the proposed AHMM/AHIM paradigm expands epistemic authority, how and who gets to say what is right or not, to include others outside the "abnor-mal" minority. If, as Narvaez and Gleason demonstrate, definitions of a normative population and attendant sociomoral models are compelled to reflect an AAHM (or, as suggested here, an AHIM), then so must epistemic membership. As progeni-tors of the dominating episteme, the scientific community is also a cultural outlier and "abnormal." Subsequently, if, as Western science shows by its own criteria, that other—tribal humans and species—is not inferior, then scientists are not entitled to claim the moral or epistemic high ground. Scientists are ethically and logically obliged to learn and accommodate tribal epistemes. Does this mean engaging in a Doolittle kind of science and culture where we talk to the animals?

Yes, it does. If there is any doubt that a democratic episteme can be created with other species, one needs only to look to science itself for illustration. In an ongoing study of the evolution of trans-species consciousness at the Great Ape Trust, Iowa, bonobos and humans show that very little keeps the species apart when a common, meaningful episteme and communication medium is made available (Savage-Rumbaugh, Wamba, Wamba, & Wamba, 2008). Through a participatory action research (PAR) project, bonobos and humans created a bill of rights whose content is nearly identical to that of human bills of rights; human and nonhuman showed comparable competencies as researchers when they shared authorship of the scientific publication describing these findings (Bradshaw, 2010, 2011).

So, then, what role can Western scientists play in helping steer modern society to increased prosocial behavior? The answer is straightforward: Begin to promote and live like those cultures that embody all the things we say we want for children and families in the present society: empathy, prosocial behavior, compassion, peace, and real, species-democratic sustainability. We can take our pick of prosocial empaths: elephants, parrots, tortoises, and practically every tribal culture who lived before European colonization. This is not to say that some tribal precontact cultures have no room for improvement: Certain rituals and practices raise ethical flags. Further, the radical contrast between conditions when HGSBs reigned and now means that some traditional practices are no longer congruent with the current environment and need to be suspended or re-evaluated (e.g., whale hunting; Thompson, 2007). However, in the main, nearly all offer viable and *vital* ethical and psychological alternatives consistent with scientific findings (and plain common sense) to remedy current social ills.

In the realm of scholarship, the answer is easy. We need more scientists like Narvaez to speak openly and with academic rigor on the topic. However, there are reasons that the topic is not discussed in broader mainstream academic circles. To dismantle science's epistemic monopoly and Western society's privileged dominance that have been obtained through violent suppression of other societies directly threatens the status quo. As C. G. Jung noted, fear of the other runs deep: "The primitive was a danger to me" (Jung, 1961, p. 112). Intellectual honesty also forces refashioning of a human identity and relinquishment of outmoded myths about nature's nature as "red in tooth and claw" (Bradshaw & Tick, 2009 Narvaez, 2011). The global socioecological unraveling we witness daily demonstrates beyond any doubt that animals simply don't do what we Western cultural adherents have done and do. It's time that scientists rectify an inaccurate myth.

All in all, this leaves modern humanity with a profound sense of embarrassment, if not humiliation, that our hunter-gather ancestors, tribal peoples, and animals may have it tough in the rough-and-tumble world of subsistence (Gray, this volume), but they *live*, not merely survive. Perhaps the biggest lesson that scientists and society learn from Narvaez, Schore, and others is that the point of evolution is not survival, but life. Now that science's own light has expanded the solution space, the question is this: Are we, who claim to be dedicated to reversing moral and ecological decline, sufficiently honest morally and ethically not only to each other but also to our constituency—the public, politicians, and funders? Will Western civilization and science desist from making knowledge and power equivalent in favor of linking "knowledge and morality" as hunter-gather and animal societies do (Deloria, 1996, p. 223)? Will we turn the incredible mental power and passion that drives research into an instrument of moral liberation? These are the critical questions and tasks that the science community now faces.

References

Bracken, P. (2002). *Trauma: Culture, meaning and philosophy*. New York, NY: Wiley.

Bradshaw, G. A. (2009). *Elephants on the edge: What animals teach us about humanity*. New Haven, CT: Yale University.

Bradshaw, G. A. (2010). We, Matata: Bicultural living amongst apes. *Spring Journal, 83*, 161–183.

Bradshaw, G. A. (2011). An ape among many: Animal co-authorship and trans-species epistemic authority. *Configurations, 18*(1–2), 15–30.

Bradshaw, G. A., & Finlay, B. L. (2005). Natural symmetry. *Nature, 435*, 149.

Bradshaw, G. A., & Sapolsky, R. M. (2006). Mirror, mirror. *American Scientist, 94*(6), 487–489.

Bradshaw, G. A., & Schore, A. N. (2007). How elephants are opening doors: Developmental neuroethology, attachment, and social context. *Ethology, 113*, 426–436.

Bradshaw, G. A., Schore, A. N., Brown, J., Poole, J., & Moss, C. J. (2005). Elephant breakdown. *Nature, 433*, 807.

Bradshaw, G. A., & Tick, E. (November 6, 2009). Of pachyderms and paratroopers. *Huffington Post*. Retrieved from http://www.huffingtonpost.com/ga-bradshaw/of-pachyderms-and-paratro__b__349107.html

Capaldo, T., & Bradshaw, G. A. (2011). The bioethics of Great Apes: Psychiatric injury and duty of care. *Animals and Society Policy Series*.

Deloria, Jr., V. (1996). *God is red*. Golden, CO: Fulcrum Press.

Flood, M. (2003). *Fatherhood and fatherlessness, discussion paper no. 59*. Manuka, Australia: Australia Institute.

Fuentes, A. (in press). Preliminary steps towards addressing the role of non-adult individuals in human evolution. In D. Narvaez, K.Valentino, A. Fuentes, J. McKenna, & P. Gray, *Ancestral Landscapes in Human Evolution: Culture, Childrearing and Social Wellbeing*. New York: Oxford University Press.

Herman, J. (1997). *Trauma and recovery: The aftermath of violence, from domestic abuse to political terror*. New York, NY: Basic.

Hunter, M. (2006). Fathers without *Amandla*: Zulu-speaking men and fatherhood. In L. Richter & R. Morrell (Eds.), *Baba: Men and fatherhood in South Africa* (pp. 99–107). Pretoria, South Africa: Human Sciences Research Council.

Jung, C. G. (1961). In A. Jaffe (Ed.), *Memories, dreams, reflections* (pp. 272–273). New York, NY: Pantheon.

Kirmayer, L. J. (2006). Beyond the 'new cross-cultural psychiatry': Cultural biology, discursive psychology and the ironies of globalization. *Transcultural Psychiatry, 43*(10), 126–143.

Lavigne, D. M. (2003). Marine mammals and fisheries: The role of science in the culling debate. In N. Gales, M. Hindell, & R. Kirkwood (Eds.), *Marine mammals: Fisheries tourism and management issues* (pp. 31–47). CSIRO.

Martin, C. L. (2009). Forward. In G. A. Bradshaw (Ed.), *Elephants on the edge: What animals teach us about humanity* (p. ix). New Haven, CT: Yale University.

Martín-Baró, I. (1994). In A. Aron & S. Corne (Eds.), *Writings for a liberation psychology.* Cambridge, MA: Harvard University Press.

Narvaez, D. (2011). Blog comments to: Narvaez, D. (April 17, 2011). What you think about human nature and evolution may be wrong. *Psychology Today* blog: Moral Landscapes. Retrieved April 23, 2011, from http://www.psychologytoday.com/blog/moral-landscapes/201104/what-you-think-about-evolution-and-human-nature-may-be-wrong

Pfaff, W. (2005). *The bullet's song: Romantic violence and Utopia.* New York, NY: Simon & Schuster.

Roughgarden, J., & Song, Z. (in press). Incentives in the family I: The family firm, an evolutionary/economic theory for parent-offspring relations. In D. Narvaez, K.Valentino, A. Fuentes, J. McKenna, & P. Gray, *Ancestral Landscapes in Human Evolution: Culture, Childrearing and Social Wellbeing.* New York: Oxford University Press.

Savage-Rumbaugh, S., Wamba, K., Wamba, P., & Wamba, N. (2007). Welfare of apes in captive environments: Comments on, and by, a specific group of apes. *Journal of Applied Animal Welfare Science, 10*(1), 7–19.

Schore, A. N. (2011). The right brain implicit self lies at the core of psychoanalysis. *Psychoanalytic Dialogues, 21*, 75–100.

Shapiro, K. J. (1998). *Animal models of human psychology: Critique of science, ethics and policy.* Seattle, WA: Hogrefe and Huber.

Survival International. (2010). *Progress can kill.* Retrieved December 2, 2010, from http://www.survivalinternational.org/

Thompson, A. (2007). Makah elder speaks: Interview with Alberta Thompson. *Earth First!! Journal.* Retrieved from http://www.earthfirstjournal.org/article.php?id==39

Wright, J. (2010). Lessons from the wolves. *Izilwane.* Retrieved April 17, 2011, from http://www.izilwane.org/lessons-from-wolves.html

20

Perspective 5: Earliest Experiences and Attachment Processes

Howard Steele

This comment focuses exclusively on attachment and how Bowlby's theory (1956/1979, 1969, 1973/1980, 1982) has been successfully deployed in developmental research, pioneered by Mary Ainsworth, documenting individual differences in infants' and toddlers' attachment patterns evident in observable behavior upon reunion following two brief separations from the parent (Ainsworth, Blehar, Waters, & Wall, 1978). As well, this comment highlights adult patterns of attachment evident in the language adults use to make sense of their attachment histories and derive meaning to inform their behavior as parents (Main, Hesse, & Goldwyn, 2008). In focusing on language and meaning, this comment highlights the relevance of higher order cognitive and moral processes in adults that enable the kind of recognition urged by many of the chapters in this book of how our contemporary Western environment, and the parenting choices typically followed, deviate markedly from the environment of evolutionary adaptedness (EEA) or context in which we evolved, representing significant social, moral, and mental health risks. A focus on the Adult Attachment Interview (AAI) is called for because the AAI is the most powerful predictor of infant patterns of attachment to have emerged from 35 years of research on the predictors and consequences of infant–parent attachment. And these infant patterns of attachment, as multiple chapters in this book have alluded to, merit close attention because it is infant attachment security that has been longitudinally linked to optimal social, emotional, and moral outcomes across the childhood years into adulthood (e.g., Sroufe, 2005). Curiously, maternal responses to the AAI account for 25% of the variance in infant–mother attachment security, whereas reliable observations of maternal sensitivity over the first year account for only 10% (van Ijzendoorn, 1995).

Thus, while advocating sensitive and responsive caregiving behavior by parents, we should also aim to encourage an overall valuing of attachment, coherence, and reflective functioning (Steele & Steele, 2008a) vis-à-vis the project of parenting and the wider social and political context in which we live. As Narvaez, Panksepp, Schore, and Gleason (Chapter 1, this volume) make clear, we cannot skirt the challenge to embrace an assumption about human nature, as Bowlby (1956/1979) did, that infants are born into this world oriented toward "goodness" and "concern for others," not "sin" or "violence." Narvaez and Gleason (Chapter 12, this volume) underscore how Bowlby was aligned with Darwin in making this assumption, which put him in direct opposition to not only Christian doctrine but also its equivalent in Bowlby's psychoanalytic world, that is, both Freudian and Kleinian worldviews. Yet, even if one assumes an innate aggressive drive operating in human life, one can embrace the parenting and societal goals articulated in this book as consonant with teaching the value of concern for others and instilling a moral sensibility in children (and damaged older folk in need of rehabilitation), who may not otherwise develop in this direction. All this is possible provided we do not think of early neurobiological pruning and myelination, powerful though these processes may be, as destiny.

There is much recent and accumulating evidence that the fundamental influence on the infant's earliest (and ongoing) attachment experiences is the parent's state of mind concerning attachment, reliably measured with the AAI (George, Kaplan, & Main, 1996) and an associated systematized approach to rating probable past experiences regarding and current state of mind concerning attachment (Main et al., 2008). As of 2008, there were reported in print more than 10,000 individual responses to the AAI, the majority of these from clinical samples (Bakermans-Kranenburg & van IJzendoorn, 2009). This means there is an expansive archive of information about how parents *think and feel* about their earliest (and later) attachment experiences and the powerful impact this has on their infants' earliest experiences and evolving thoughts and feelings concerning how to respond when distressed, and specifically the extent to which mother, father, or other familiar caregivers are likely to be available and responsive. Notably, a mother's response to the AAI predicts the extent and type of security/insecurity there will be in the infant–mother relationship, while a father's response predicts security/insecurity in the infant–father relationship (Steele, Steele, & Fonagy, 1996). This body of evidence speaks for embedding any event-based specific suggestions (e.g., to breastfeed or cosleep at nighttime) made to expectant or new parents in a nuanced appreciation of psychological processes and mental states that ultimately are responsible for the development of a secure infant–mother and infant–father attachment, observable between 12 and 18 months (Ainsworth et al., 1978). This phenomenon, the *process* of attachment, is what maternal and child health initiatives should be advocating together with encouragement of specific practices (e.g., breastfeeding or cosleeping) with support of mothers and allomothers (Hrdy, 2000), to provide sensitive and responsive care following infant cues over the first year of life and beyond.

Attention to the mental state and emotional needs of the mother (or father) is called for even with respect to recommending obviously beneficial parenting practices. For example, breastfeeding has multiple advantages including economic, social, psychological, physiological, and immunological benefits for mother and baby. Thus, it is now robustly recommended by pediatric science. Historically, medical and social pressures were otherwise. As Trevathan (this volume) points out, between 1950 and 1970, only 20% of newborn human infants in America were breastfed. And while we may decry this phenomenon, there is no suggestion that feeding type (breast or bottle or both) is predictive of whether an infant is securely or insecurely attached. It is the *state of mind of the mother* (Steele & Steele, 2008b) as she thinks about and delivers care, including the feeding of her baby, not whether the feeding is via breast or bottle, that fundamentally determines whether the baby will be a securely attached toddler (Britton, Britton, & Gronwaldt, 2006; van IJzendoorn, 1995).

A generation of longitudinal attachment research has shown this outcome, security of attachment to mother and/or father in the second year of life, to be the most reliable predictor (from diverse measures obtained in the first 2 years of life) of long-term mental, emotional, and social health outcomes extending from early childhood to young adulthood (Grossman, Grossman, & Waters, 2005; Sroufe, 2005). And it is mothers of securely attached infants who have been shown to display heightened levels of sensitive responsiveness (picking up and soothing) to their 6-month-old infants when the babies fussed or cried in the middle of the night (Higley & Dozier, 2009).

In other words, just as we know that infants (and probably adults) are differentially responsive to the environment (see Belsky's comment, this volume), parents should be supported to make informed empirical choices about labor, childbirth, and early postnatal care that *work for them*. It is our job as early childhood educators and parenting researchers to assure new parents that attachment is a process, not dependent on any single event or specific parenting practice. Attachment relationships are built up via thousands of interactions, and attachment security (or insecurity) reflects the pattern of interactions *over the first year of life* and beyond. Specific experiences in the first month of life, or in the first hour, or in the context of being born *may or may not be* indicative of the pattern of attachment that the child will develop.

We can be sure that the choices mothers and allomothers make will continue to be fraught at times, but this is not new. As Hrdy (2000) wrote, the contemporary dilemmas facing a mother who juggles concerns over career, child(ren), spouse, extended family, and friends are consistent with our long evolutionary history. The trade-offs and bargaining a mother engages in with herself and others, in order to ward off danger and maintain security for herself and her family, are not unique to the modern or postmodern world. Rather, these processes are a continuation of the profound struggles for survival faced by women ever since the hominid form we recognize as our own evolved in the Pleistocene era, some 10,000 to 1.6 million years ago. At times, deeply felt ambivalence toward pregnancy and motherhood, stemming from a range of life-threatening conflicts, is the rule and not the exception across species and across evolutionary epochs. In every era women have sought to improve their inclusive fitness (i.e., the chances that they will successfully reproduce and raise offspring who might, in turn, survive to reproduce themselves). Yet, whether or not this latter success is realized depends greatly on the care provided by the mother and the caregiving input she elicits from others, for example, father, grandmother, older child(ren), *over time*. This being said, recent evidence points to how close attention to mother–infant interactions at 4 months (when a characteristic pattern of relating is consolidating) are predictive of infant–mother attachment at 1 year of age (Beebe et al., 2010). In any case, imposing a prescription for mothers about how labor, delivery, the first hour after birth, feeding, and nighttime sleeping should proceed may be liberating, but at the same time it may be anxiety or guilt inducing, *especially for the parent with a vulnerable state of mind regarding an adverse attachment history*. Care may be needed to help some mothers free themselves of restrictive fears, born of past trauma, and enjoy the attachment process, including the range of practices that ordinarily facilitate the normative process.

The take-home message (Beebe et al., 2010) concerning the earliest attachment experiences, and the promotion of survival typified by security, is a goldilocks story. Parents succeed when they maintain their calm and monitor their own emotional states and those of their children—guessing as best they can, and seeking clarification. At the same time, it is prudent advice to seek to maintain a middle path, navigating between under- and overresponsiveness. With underresponsiveness, the infant is likely to feel rejected; with overresponsiveness, the infant is likely to feel overrun or interfered with—thus the virtue of the middle way.

A profound interference with a parent's capacity to navigate this middle path is seen in those parents who respond to the AAI whose 20 questions about childhood attachment experiences, upset, separation, loss, and trauma show that past experiences of loss or trauma are *not* resolved (Main et al., 2008). Some respondents to the interview show lapses in the monitoring of speech and reason in respect to the loss/trauma, such that past trauma overwhelms attentional and emotional resources *in the present moment*. The terms *absorption* and *guilt* are often apt descriptors of AAI narrative material showing evidence of unresolved mourning. Parents who provide such interview responses are likely to be highly fragile in the parenting role vis-à-vis a new infant. The likelihood in this context is not so much one of underresponsiveness or overresponsiveness as one of being frightened (by the past and by the new infant) or frightening toward the infant. Save for in the most extreme cases of purposeful abuse, these are unintended fearful actions that erupt and profoundly unsettle the infant. As a consequence, during the 20-minute Strange Situation observation, involving two brief (moderately stressful) separations, it is the infants of these frightened parents who show anomalous frightening behaviors upon reunion. They cover their faces, hide, cry uncontrollably, or freeze. From an evolutionary perspective, these are all adaptive responses in the face of an overwhelming threat, but for these infants, the great threat is the return of the parent.

Fortunately, there are reliable tools (with the Strange Situation Procedure) to track the evidence of these disorganized–disoriented infant attachments and (with the AAI) the unresolved mourning regarding past loss or trauma associated with them. Deploying these tools in clinical prevention and intervention work holds the promise of altering the caregiving environment for the parent and the child so that young children may thrive socially and emotionally and develop secure attachments, *because* parents are helped to better realize the dream of being the kind of parent they hope to be, underpinned by an age-appropriate understanding of their children's needs and potentials and a state of mind that locates past loss or trauma *in the past* (Steele, Steele, & Murphy, 2009; Steele, Murphy, & Steele 2010).

A parent for whom loss or trauma experiences are *not* unresolved is likely to possess a high level of reflective functioning (Steele & Steele, 2008a), namely, the capacity to guess well at the complex motivations underlying behavior in the self and others and to distinguish appearances (wishes) from reality. Such reflective parents (and readers) of this important book on human nature and parenting will be well positioned to see the reality described, that is, how far we have drifted from the good lessons we learned in the EEA in which we evolved. It is not too late, we must hope, to regain the solid ground from which concern for others and goodness flourishes.

References

Ainsworth, M. D., Blehar, M. C., Waters, E., & Wall, S. (1978). *Patterns of attachment: Assessed in the strange situation and at home.* Hillsdale, NJ: Lawrence Erlbaum.

Bakermans-Kranenburg, M. J., & van IJzendoorn, M. H. (2009). The first 10000 Adult Attachment Interviews: Distribution of adult attachment representations in clinical and non-clinical groups. *Attachment and Human Development, 11*(3), 223–263.

Beebe, B., Jaffe, J., Markese, S., Buck, K., Chen, H., Cohen. P., Barick, L., Andrews, H., & Feldman, S. (2010). The origins of 12-month attachment: A microanalysis of 4-month mother-infant interaction. *Attachment and Human Development, 12,* 3–141.

Bowlby, J. (1956/1979). Psychoanalysis and child care. In J. Bowlby (Ed.), *The making and breaking of affectional bonds* (pp. 1–12). London: Tavistock Publications.

Bowlby, J. (1969). *Attachment and loss. Vol. I: Attachment.* London: Hogarth Press and the Institute of Psycho-Analysis.

Bowlby, J. (1973/1980). *Attachment and loss. Vol. II: Separation.* London: Hogarth Press.

Bowlby, J. (1982). *Attachment and loss. Vol. III: Loss.* London: Hogarth Press.

Britton, J. R., Britton, H. L., & Gronwaldt, V. (2006). Breastfeeding, sensitivity and attachment. *Pediatrics, 118,* 1436–1443.

George, C., Kaplan, N., & Main, M. (1996). *Adult Attachment Interview* (3rd ed.). Unpublished manuscript, University of California at Berkeley.

Grossmann, K. E., Grossmann, K., & Waters, E. (2005). *Attachment from infancy to adulthood: The major longitudinal studies.* New York, NY: Guilford Press.

Higley, E., & Dozier, M. (2009). Nighttime maternal responsiveness and infant attachment at one year. *Attachment and Human Development, 11,* 347–363.

Hrdy, S. B. (2000). *Mother Nature.* London: Vintage (Random House).

Main, M., Hesse, E., & Goldwyn, R. (2008). Studying differences in language use in recounting attachment history. In H. Steele & M. Steele (Eds.), *Clinical applications of the Adult Attachment Interview* (pp. 31–68). New York, NY: Guilford Press.

Sroufe, L. A. (2005). Attachment and development: A prospective, longitudinal study from birth to adulthood. *Attachment and Human Development, 7,* 349–380.

Steele, H., & Steele, M. (2008a). *Clinical applications of the Adult Attachment Interview*. New York, NY: Guilford Press.

Steele, H., & Steele, M. (2008b). On the origins of reflective functioning. In F. Busch (Ed.), *Mentalization: Theoretical considerations, research findings, and clinical implications. Psychoanalytic Inquiry Book Series, 29* (pp. 133–158). New York, NY: Analytic Books.

Steele, H., Steele, M., & Fonagy, P. (1996). Associations among attachment classification of mothers, fathers and their. *Child Development, 67,* 541–555.

Steele, H., Steele, M., & Murphy, A. (2009). The Adult Attachment Interview: A clinical tool for facilitating and measuring process and change in psychotherapy. *Psychotherapy Research, 19,* 633–643.

Steele, M., Murphy, A., & Steele, H. (2010). Identifying therapeutic action in an attachment-based intervention with high-risk families. *Clinical Social Work Journal, 38,* 61–72.

van IJzendoorn, M. J. (1995). Adult attachment representations, parental responsiveness and infant attachment: A metaanalysis on the predictive validity of the Adult Attachment Interview. *Psychological Bulletin, 117,* 387–403.

21

Perspective 6: Nurturant Versus Nonnurturant Environments and the Failure of the Environment of Evolutionary Adaptedness

James W. Prescott

Scientific evidence has been accumulating since Bowlby's (1951, 1953) original contributions regarding how attachment of every newborn/infant child to his or her mother lies at the core of our humanity (Bowlby, 1951, 1953, 1969/1973; Cook, 1996; Dalai Lama, 1999; Montagu, 1952; and others). Bowlby's view has been reiterated by Hrdy (1999, p. 98), who states: "It was the mother who continuously carried the infant in skin-to-skin contact-stomach to stomach, chest to breast. Soothed by her heartbeat, nestled in the heat of her body, rocked by her movements, the infant's entire world was its mother"—its **Environment.**

Hrdy (1999) notes that "...no wild monkey or ape mother has ever been observed to deliberately harm her own baby" (p. 179). From whence does the source of maternal violence against the offspring of *Homo sapiens* and violence against mother by her offspring come? There are multiple causes. Bottle-feeding may be perhaps the single worst invention of the 20th century, as it deprives the infant/child of not only essential physical nutrients that are absent in formula milk but also the essential sensory-emotional nutrients that can only be obtained at the breast of the mother—touch, movement, smell, and taste of the mother's body—that forms the foundation for intimacy, pleasure, and love of mother and of women throughout adulthood (Prescott, 1968, 1971, 1975, 1997, 1996, 2002, 2005).

Despite the fact that John Bowlby (1953) warned that "one must be beware of a vested interest in the institutional care of children!" (p. 182), children spend an increasing amount of time in daycare rather than with their mothers. Instead, as the Western African proverb says: "It takes an entire village to raise a child" (a village of caring, usually related, adults). The environment of environmental adaptedness (EEA) included many allomothers (Hrdy, 1999). With the rise of the nuclear family and single motherhood in the last 100 years, the extended family and alloparents have all but disappeared.

Cook (1996), following in the footsteps of Bowlby (1951, 1953), has documented the failure of maternal–infant/child bonding as placing nations at risk for depressive and violent destructive behaviors.

Cross-cultural studies have long identified the failure of affectional bonding in the mother–infant/child relationship and adolescent sexual behavior as predicting depressive, destructive, violent, and drug-addictive behaviors (Bacon, Child, & Barry, 1963; Barry, 1982; Barry, Bacon, & Child, 1967; Barry & Paxon, 1971; DeMause, 1982; DeMeo, 1998; Ember & Ember, 1997; Ford & Beach, 1951; Prescott, 1975, 1977, 1979, 1980, 1989b, 1990; Rohner, 1975; Russell, 1972; Textor, 1967).

Distinctions must be made between ethnologies of single-culture studies (Chagnon, 1968; Crocker, 1990; Freeman, 1983; Harner, 1972; Liedloff, 1975; Mead, 1928; Nance, 1975) and multicultural studies, as provided by Textor (1967), Prescott, (1975, 1979, 1990), Rohner (1975), Russell (1972) and DeMeo (1998).

The errors made by Mead (1928) in *Coming of Age in Samoa*, corrected by Freeman (1983), could have been prevented by using a multicultural approach. It is well known that science is not based on a sample size of ONE. Wade (2010) has questioned whether anthropology is a science.

A different scientific model is called for where neurobiological studies of impaired brain–behavioral development in maternal–infant-deprived primates and other mammals have been documented (Berman, Berman, & Prescott, 1974; Bryan & Riesen, 1989; Coleman, 1971; Floeter & Greenough, 1979; Heath, 1975; Laudenslager, Reit, & Harbeck, 1982; Prescott, 2001a, 2001b, 2005; Riesen, Dickerson, & Struble, 1977; Saltzberg, Lustick, & Heath, 1971; Struble & Riesen, 1978; Teicher, 2000), which, along with the cross-cultural studies of tribal cultures by Prescott (1975, 1977, 1979, 1980), have confirmed Bowlby's (1951, 1953) conclusion that "mother-love in infancy and childhood is as important for mental health as are vitamins and proteins for physical health" (p. 182); Dokecki (1973).

Research by Cannon (1939), Cannon and Rosenbleuth (1949), and Sharpless (1969, 1975) on denervation supersensitivity (sensory deprivation) on nervous system functioning have defined the types of neurophysiological mechanisms that mediate the behavioral pathologies of maternal–infant separation (somatosensory deprivation—functional deafferentation; Prescott, 1971). There are bound to be other interpretations including the long-term epigenetic (environmental) influences of maternal–infant interactions (see Meaney's contribution to this volume).

Figure 21.1 is a photo collage that documents the emotional/social/sexual disorders of failed maternal–infant/child bonding that has lifelong effects (Prescott, 1977). Raine, Brennan, and Mednick (1994) found that birth complications combined with early maternal rejection at age 1 year predispose one to violent crime at age 18 years. Herman-Giddens et al. (1999) found that the World Health Organization (WHO) International Classification of Diseases (ICD-9) cause-of-death coding underascertained child abuse homicides by 61.6%. Numerous additional studies could be cited here.

Figure 21.2 depicts a Centers for Disease Control and Prevention map of breast-feeding duration distribution of the 50 states for the year 2004 with this writer's overlay of 2004 infant mortality rates for these states; the figure shows that breast-feeding bonding prevents infant mortality and suicide. Here are specific findings:

- Ninety percent (9/10) of states with less than 15% of children breastfeeding at 12 months have the highest infant mortality rates.

ASPECTS OF HUMAN AFFECTIONAL DEVELOPMENT 435

Fig. 1. "Swinging" surrogate reared monkey freely interacts with human attendant.

Fig. 2. "Stationary" surrogate reared monkey avoids interacting with human attendant.

Fig. 3. Two 8 month old isolate reared monkeys who avoid touching and social interaction.

Fig. 4. Two normally reared monkeys touch and cuddle one another.

FIGURE 21.1 *Photo collages of infant separation and bonding adult violence, sexual dysfunction, and child abuse consequent to mother–infant/child somatosensory affectional deprivation. From Prescott, J. W. (1977). Phylogenetic and ontogenetic aspects of human affectional development. In R. Gemme & C. C. Wheeler, (Eds.), Progress in sexology. Proceedings of the 1976 International Congress of Sexology. New York, NY: Plenum Press. http://www.violence. de/prescott/pis/1977paper.pdf; http://www.violence.de/prescott/letters/SSAD_PICS.pdf*

ASPECTS OF HUMAN AFFECTIONAL DEVELOPMENT 437

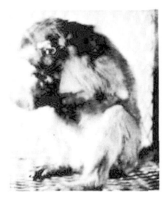

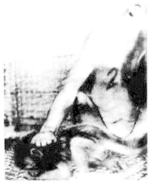

Fig. 5. Self-biting and self-mutilation of an adult isolation reared rhesus.

Fig. 6. Motherless mother crushing 20 day old infant to the floor.

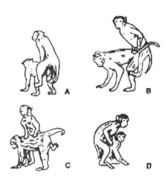

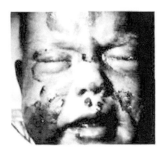

Fig. 7. Normal sexual posturing in the normal male & female rhesus (A, B). Abnormal sexual posturing in the isolation reared male & female rhesus (C, D).

Fig. 8. Physical pain in child abuse: 3 month old child with scaled milk thrown on its face.

FIGURE 21.1 *(continued)*

- Eighty-three percent (10/12) of states with greater than 25% of children breastfeeding at 12 months have the lowest infant mortality rates.

Prescott's (2001c, 2005, 2007) breastfeeding studies on tribal cultures found the following:

- Seventy-seven percent (20/26) of tribal cultures where weaning age is 2.5 years or greater have absent or low suicides.
- Eighty-two percent (14/17) of tribal cultures where weaning age is 2.5 years and greater and that support youth sex have absent or low suicides.

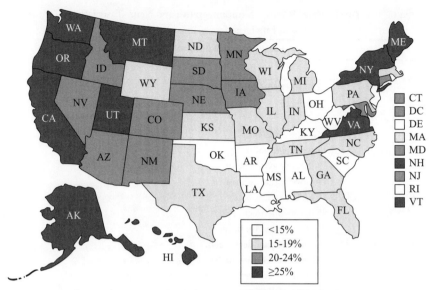

FIGURE 21.2 *Centers for Disease Control and Prevention map of breastfeeding duration by states with overlay of infant mortality for the year 2004 by this author, which shows that breastfeeding bonding prevents infant mortality. From Centers for Disease Control and Prevention. (2008). Breastfeeding practices—Results from the National Immunization Survey. Atlanta, GA: Author. http://www.cdc.gov/breastfeeding/data/NIS_data/index.htm; http://ttfuture.org/fi les/2/pdf/jp_bonding_prevents_infant_mortality.pdf*

Also see http://ttfuture.org/files/2/pdf/jp_bonding_prevents_infant_mortality.pdf and http://ttfuture.org/blog/1181, listed in References.

Regrettably, breastfeeding studies rarely report on breastfeeding beyond 1 year, even though the social/behavioral benefits of breastfeeding may be best realized by breastfeeding for 2.5 years or beyond (Christian & Sege, 2010; Prescott, 2010c).

Overpeck, Brenner, Trumble, Trifiletti, and Berendes (1998) have identified risk factors for infant homicide, and Vennemann et al. (2009) have documented that breastfeeding prevents infant mortality, yet these continuing statistics are ignored by the health science communities.

PAIN and **PLEASURE** are encoded in our two cultural/biological brains and determine who and what we become and whether we are placed on the life path of peace, harmony, happiness, and egalitarian relationships or on the life path of violence, alienation, depression, and authoritarian/destructive relationships (see Table 21.1; http://www.violence.de/prescott/letters/Our_Two_Cultural_Brains.pdf).

Moses Maimonides, in *The Guide of the Perplexed* (1190), stated, "The bodily pain caused to that member is the real purpose of circumcision" (III: 49); and female genital mutilation is noted as a federal crime (Palfrey, 2010), but not by the American Medical Association (2011), which opposed all legal efforts to ban male circumcision. http://www.violence.de/prescott/letters/PETITION_The_Hague.pdf

TABLE 21.1 Two Cultural Brains—Neurointegrative and Neurodissociative—That Are Formed by Pain and Pleasure Life Experiences Encoded in the Developing Brain

		Limbic-subcortical emotional brain	
		Pain	**Pleasure**
N	**P**	**Theistic Religions**	
E	**A**	**Patrilineal**	
O	**I**		
C	**N**	Gender Inequality	
O		**Sexual puritanism**	
R		Addictive synthetic drugs	
T		Authoritarian control	
I		Pain is a moral good	
C		Depression-violence-war	
A		**Neurodissociative Brain**	
L		**Science of pain-depression**	
		Biomedical Health Model	
		Legislative gender inequality	
		Politics of Betrayal	
	P		**Earth Religions**
	L		**Matrilineal**
	E		
B	**A**		Gender Equality
R	**S**		**Sexual liberty**
A	**U**		Natural botanical drugs
I	**R**		Egalitarian freedom
N	**E**		Pleasure is a moral good
			Joy-happiness-peace
			Neurointegrative Brain
			Science of pleasure-happiness
			Biobehavioral health model
			Legislative gender equality
			Politics of Trust

James W. Prescott, Ph.D. Presented at: Society for the Scientific Study of Sex: "Sex and the Brain" Midcontinent & Eastern Regions June 13–16, 2002 Big Rapids, MI, and Society for Cross Cultural Research 32nd Annual Meeting Feb. 19–23, 2003. Charleston, SC. From: Prescott, 2005. http://www.violence.de/archive. shtml

DVD: *THE ORIGINS OF LOVE & VIOLENCE: SENSORY DEPRIVATION AND THE DEVELOPING BRAIN.* 2008 http://ttfuture.org/violence

http://www.violence.de/prescott/letters/Our_Two_Cultural_Brains.pdf

The equal protection clause of the 14th Amendment has yet to be recognized for the protection of male children (Prescott, 1989a; http://www.violence.de/prescott/ truthseeker/genpl.html; http://www.violence.de/prescott/letters/GMC_is_Torture. html; http://pediatrics.aappublications.org/cgi/eletters/peds.2010–0187v1#50189; http://mgmbill.org/usfgmlaw.htm).

PAIN and **PLEASURE** form the neurobiological bridge from the neurobehavioral sciences to the philosophies and theologies of moral behavior, where the neurobehavioral sciences can rightfully question the moral assumptions and assertions of various moral theologies concerning **PAIN** and **Pleasure** (Prescott, 1972, 1975, 1989a, 1995; World Health Organization/UNICEF, 1990). Narvaez (2008) rightfully notes the neurobiology of our multiple moral behaviors.

Beauvoir (1949/2010) identified gender inequality as the principal plague upon humanity by quoting Pythagoras (c. 550 BC): "There is a good principle that created order, light and man; and a bad principle that created chaos, darkness and woman." Prescott (1975, 1995) has further identified the philosophical and religious foundations for violence against women, which place a high moral value on pain and suffering and view pleasure as a threat to moral salvation.

Single-culture studies are informative. For example, the ethnology of the Canela by Crocker (1980) chronicles the extinction of an ancient culture that is nonviolent, matrilocal, and highly nurturant, with *pleasure not pain as* a central principle of cultural life. Matrilineal/matrilocal cultures are near extinction. However, a science of moral behavior cannot be built upon any single cultural study—science does not exist with a sample of *one*. Thus, I conducted a study of the quantitative 400-culture sample of Textor (1967) showing the link between early care or its absence (specifically, touch—baby carrying and breastfeeding) and the formation of peaceful or violent societies (Prescott, 1975; Russell, 1972).

Conclusion

The rise of the medical/pharmaceutical corporate complex has rendered Bowlby (1951, 1953), Montagu (1951, 1971), Bronfenbrenner (1970), and many others irrelevant, as we have lost the capacity to learn from history the importance of mother love and to form a different brain for different moral behaviors (Dalai Lama, 1999; Prescott, 1995, 2002). "What mothers are to their children, so will man be to man" (Montagu, 1952, pp. 247–248). An environment of sensory-emotional deprivation has destroyed the environment of evolutionary adaptedness. The failure of evolutionary adaptedness is species extinction—there is no evolutionary adaptedness to a violent environment, as our violent death statistics on homicide and suicide over the past millennia attest.

The Conference on Violence held by the National Institutes of Health (1994) holds little promise for future adjustments to the status quo: "To date, investment across all Institutes and ICDs (Institutes, Centers, Divisions) in violence-related research has been minuscule relative to the total NIH budget (i.e. 0.5%)," which indicates the low research priority given to child abuse and neglect and violence. This pattern seems not to have changed. http://www.violence.de/prescott/dvd/NIHR_1994.html (Chambly, D. A., 1974).

Unless we change course, the future is bleak for *Homo sapiens.*

References

American Medical Association. (2011). American Medical Association House of Delegates adopts new policies during final days of semi-annual meeting. Press Release, November 15, New Orleans.

Bacon, M. K., Child, I. L., & Barry, III, H. (1963). A cross-cultural study of correlates of crime. *Journal of Abnormal and Social Psychology, 66*(4), 291–300.

Barry, III, H. (1982). Cultural variations in alcohol abuse. In I. Al-Issa (Ed.), *Culture and psychopathology* (pp. 309–338). Baltimore, MD: University Park Press.

Barry, III, H., Bacon, M. K., & Child, I. L. (1967). Child, definitions, ratings, and bibliographic sources of child-training practices of 110 cultures. In C. S. Ford (Ed.), *Cross-cultural approaches.* New Haven, CT: HRAF Press.

Barry, H., & Paxon, I. M. (1971). Infancy and early childhood cross-cultural codes 2. *Ethnology X*(40), 466–508.

Berman, A. J., Berman, D., & Prescott, J. W. (1974). The effect of cerebellar lesions on emotional behavior in the rhesus monkey. In I. S. Cooper, M. V. Riklon, & R. S. Snider (Eds.), *The cerebellum, epilepsy and behavior.* New York, NY: Plenum. http://www.violence.de/berman/article.html

Bowlby, J. (1951). *Maternal care and mental health.* Geneva: World Health Organization.

Bowlby, J. (1953). *Child care and the growth of love.* Baltimore, MD, and London: Pelican/Penguin. http://www.violence.de/prescott/letters/BOOK_OF_THE_CENTURY BOWLBY.pdf

Bowlby, J. (1969/1973). *Attachment and Loss* (Vol. I & II). New York, NY: Basic Books.

Bronfenbrenner, U. (1970). *Chairman, minority report of forum 15: Children and parents. 1970 White House Conference on Children.* Washington, DC: Superintendant of Documents. http://www.violence.de/prescott/dvd/Nixon-1970-WHC.pdf

Bryan, G. K., & Riesen, A. H. (1989). Deprived somatosensory-motor experience in stumptailed monkey neocortex: Dendritic spine density and dendritic branching of layer IIIB pyramidal cells. *Journal of Comparative Neurology, 286*, 208–217.

Cannon, W. B. (1939). A law of denervation. *American Journal of Medical Science, 193*, 737–749.

Cannon, W. B., & Rosenbleuth, A. (1949). *The supersensitivity of denervated structures.* New York, NY: MacMillan.

Chagnon, N. A. (1968). *Yanomamo: The fierce people.* New York, NY: Holt, Rinehart and Weston.

Chambly, D. A. (1974). *NIH research on antisocial, aggressive, and violence-related behaviors and their consequences* (p. 138). Bethesda, MD: National Institutes of Health, April.

Christian, C. W., & Sege, R. D. (2010). Policy statement. Child fatality review. *Pediatrics, 126*(3), 592–596. http://pediatrics.aappublications.org/content/126/3/592.abstract

Coleman, M. (1971). Platelet serotonin in disturbed monkeys and children. *Clinical Proceedings of the Children's Hospital, 27*(7), 187–194. http://www.violence.de/coleman/article.html

Cook, P. S. (1996). *Early child care: Infants & nations at risk.* Melbourne: News Weekly Books.

Crocker, W. (1980). The Canela (Eastern Timbira). *An ethnographic introduction. Smithsonian Contributions to Anthropology. Number 33.* Washington, DC: Smithsonian Institutional Press. http://www.violence.de/prescott/dvd/Canela.pdf

Dalai Lama. (1999). *Ethics for a new millennium*. New York, NY: Riverhead Books/Penguin Putnam.http://www.violence.de/prescott/letters/BOOK_OF_THE_CENTURY-DALAI_LAMA.pdf

De Beauvoir, S. (1953/2010). *The second sex* (a new translation of the landmark classic by Constance Borde and Sheil Malovany Chevallier/Introduction by Judith Thurman). New York, NY: Alfred A. Knopf.

DeMause, L. (1982). *Foundations of psychohistory*. New York, NY: Creative Roots.

DeMeo, J. (1998). *Saharasi*. Greensprings, OR: Orgone Biophysical Research Lab.

Dokecki, P. R. (1973). When the bough breaks ... what will happen to baby. Review of: Rock-a-bye Baby. Time Life Films (Lothar Woff, Ex. Prod.) *Contemporary Psychology.* 18:64.

Ember, C. R., & Ember, M. (1997). Violence in the ethnographic record: Results of cross-cultural research on war and aggression. In D. L. Martin & D. W. Frayer (Eds.), *Troubled times. Violence and warfare in the past.* Amsterdam, The Netherlands: Gordon and Breach Publishers.

Flaherty, J. (1978). In the Court of Common Pleas of Allegheny County, Pennsylvania. Civil Division. *McFall v Shimp* No. GD 78–17711. http://www.violence.de/prescott/letters/McFall_v_Shimp.pdf

Floeter, M. K., & Greenough, W. T. (1979). Cerebellar plasticity: Modification of Purkinje cell structure by differential rearing in monkeys. *Science, 206,* 227–229. http://www.violence.de/prescott/Floeter_Abs.html

Ford, C. S., & Beach, F. A. (1951). *Patterns of sexual behavior*. New York, NY: Harper and Brothers.

Freeman, D. (1983). *Margaret Mead and Samoa. The making and unmaking of an anthropological myth.* Cambridge, MA: Harvard University Press. http://www.violence.de/prescott/dvd/Samoa.pdf

Harlow, H. F. (1958). The nature of love. *American Psychologist, 13,* 673–685.

Harner, M. J. (1972). *The Jivaro: People of the sacred waterfalls*. New York, NY: Natural History Press.

Heath, R. G. (1972). Physiologic basis of emotional expression: Evoked potential and mirror focus studies in rhesus monkeys. *Biological Psychiatry, 5,* 15.

Heath, R. G. (1975). Maternal-social deprivation and abnormal brain development: Disorders of emotional and social behavior. In J. W. Prescott, M. S. Read, & D. B. Coursin (Eds.), *Brain function and malnutrition: Neuropsychological methods of assessment.* New York, NY: John Wiley.

Herman-Giddens, M. D., Brown, G., Vberbiest, S., Carlson, P. J., Hooten, E. G., Howell, E., & Butts, J. D. (1999). Underascertainment of child abuse mortality in the United States. *Journal of the American Medical Association, 282*(5), 463–467.

Hrdy, S. B. (1999). *Mother Nature. A history of mothers, infants, and natural selection*. New York, NY: Pantheon Books. http://www.violence.de/prescott/letters/BOOK_OF_THE_CENTURY-HRDY.pdf

Laudenslager, M. L., Reit M., & Harbeck, R. (1982). Suppressed immune response in infant monkeys associated with maternal separation. *Behavior and Neural Biology, 36,* 40–48.

Liedloff, J. (1975). *The continuum concept: In search of happiness lost*. New York, NY: Addison Wesley Publishing.

Maimonides, M. (1190). *The guide of the perplexed* (translated by Shlomo Pines, 1963: Part III, Chapter 49). Chicago, IL: University of Chicago Press.

Mead, M. (1928). *Coming of age in Samoa*. New York, NY: William Morrow & Co.

Montagu, A. (1952). *The natural superiority of women.* New York, NY: Collier Books. http://www.violence.de/prescott/dvd/Natsup.pdf

Montagu, A. (1971). *Touching: The human significance of the skin.* New York, NY: Harper and Row Publishers.

Nance, J. (1975). *The Gentile Tasaday. A Stone Age people in the Philippine rain forest.* New York, NY: Harcourt Brace Jovanovich.

Narvaez, D. (2008). Triune ethics: The neurobiological roots of our multiple moralities. *New Ideas in Psychology, 26,* 95–119.

Overpeck, M. D., Brenner, R. A., Trumble, A. C., Trifiletti, L. B., & Berendes, H. W. (1998). Risk factors for infant homicide in the United States. *New England Journal of Medicine, 339*(17).

National Institute of Child Health and Human Development/National Institutes of Health. (1968). *Perspectives on human deprivation: Biological, psychological, and sociological.* Washington, DC: National Institute of Child Health and Human Development, National Institutes of Health, Department of Health, Education, and Welfare.

Palfrey, J. (2010). *Letter of clarification of American Academy of Pediatrics on female genital cutting (FGC).* Retrieved from http://pediatrics.aappublications.org/cgi/eletters/peds.2010–0187v1#50189

Prescott, J. W. (1971). Early somatosensory deprivation as an ontogenetic process in the abnormal development of the brain and behavior. In I. E. Goldsmith & J. Moor-Jankowski (Eds.), *Medical primatology 1970.* Basel: S. Karger. http://www.violence.de/prescott/mp/article.html

Prescott, J. W. (1972). Before ethics and morality. *The Humanist, November/December,* 19–21. http://www.violence.de/prescott/humanist/ethics.html

Prescott, J. W. (1975). Body pleasure and the origins of violence. *The Futurist, April.* [Reprinted in *The Bulletin of the Atomic Scientists,* 1975, November.] http://www.violence.de/prescott/bulletin/article.html

Prescott, J. W. (1977). Phylogenetic and ontogenetic aspects of human affectional development. In R. Gemme & C. C. Wheeler (Eds.), *Progress in sexology. Proceedings of the 1976 International Congress of Sexology.* New York, NY: Plenum Press. http://www.violence.de/prescott/pis/1977paper.pdf

Prescott, J. W. (1979). Deprivation of physical affection as a primary process in the development of physical violence. In D. Gil (Ed.), *Child abuse and violence* (pp. 66–137). New York, NY: AMS Press. http://www.violence.de/prescott/letters/IM_BF_H.pdf

Prescott, J. W. (1980). Somatosensory affectional deprivation (SAD) theory of drug and alcohol use. In D. J. Lettieri, M. Sayers, & H. W. Pearson (Eds.), *Theories on drug abuse: Selected contemporary perspectives.* NIDA Research Monograph 30, March 1980. Rockville, MD: National Institute on Drug Abuse, Department of Health and Human Services.

Prescott, J. W. (1989a). Genital pain v genital pleasure. Why the one and not the other. *The Truth Seeker, July/August.*

Prescott, J. W. (1989b). Profiles of affectionate (peaceful) v non-affectionate (violent) tribal cultures. *The Truth Seeker, July/August.* http://www.violence.de/prescott/letters/Social-Behavioral_Characteristics.pdf

Prescott, J. W. (1990). Affectional bonding for the prevention of violent behaviors: Neurobiological, psychological and religious/spiritual determinants. In L. J. Hertzberg et al. (Eds.), *Violent behavior. Vol. I: Assessment and intervention* (pp. 110–142). New York, NY: PMA Publishing. http://www.violence.de/prescott/Violent_Behavior_1990.pdf

Prescott, J. W. (1995). Violence against women: Philosophical and religious foundations of gender morality. *New Perspectives, March/April.* http://www.violence.de/prescott/women/article.html

Prescott, J. W. (1996). The origins of human love and violence. *Pre- and Perinatal Psychology Journal, 10*(3), 143–188.

Prescott, J. W. (2001a). Along the evolutionary biological trail. Book review: Mother Nature: A history of mothers, infants, and natural selection (S.H. Hrdy). *Journal of Prenatal and Perinatal Psychology and Health, 15*(3), 225–232. http://www.violence.de/prescott/reviews/hrdy.html

Prescott, J. W. (2001b). Only more mother-infant bonding can prevent cycles of violence. *Cerebrum, 3*(1). [Lt. Ed re, Teicher, M. R.: Wounds that time won't heal: The neurobiology of child abuse. *Cerebrum*, 2001, 3(1).] http://www.violence.de/prescott/reviews/cerebrum.doc

Prescott, J. W. (2001c). *America's lost dream. Life, liberty and the pursuit of happiness.* The Association for Prenatal and Perinatal Psychology and Health, 10th International Congress, Birth—The Genesis of Health. The Cathedral Hill Hotel, December 6–9, 2001. http://www.violence.de/archive.shtml

Prescott, J. W. (2002). How culture shapes the developing brain and the future of humanity. *Touch the Future Newsletter, Spring.* http://www.violence.de/prescott/ttf/cultbrain.pdf

Prescott, J. W. (2003). *Our two cultural brains: Neurointegrative and neurodissociative formed by pain and pleasure from life experiences encoded in the developing brain.* http://www.violence.de/prescott/letters/Our_Two_Cultural_Brains.pdf

Prescott, J. W. (2005). Prevention or therapy and the politics of trust: Inspiring a new human agenda. *Psychotherapy and Politics International, 3*(3), 194–211. http://www.interscience.wiley.com; http://www.violence.de/prescott/politics-rust.pdf

Prescott, J. W. (2007). Why breastfeeding mothers are important. *The Mother, September/October.* http://www.themothermagazine.co.uk/, http://www.artofchange.co.uk/

Prescott, J. W. (2010a). *Genital mutilation of children is torture.* E-letter to the American Academy of Pediatrics protesting the position of the AAP Committee on Bioethics that supported female genital cutting (FGC), April 29. http://pediatrics.aappublications.org/cgi/eletters/peds.2010–0187v1#50189

Prescott, J. W. (2010b). Infant/child homicide, breastfeeding bonding and parental care. E-mail letter to *American Academy of Pediatrics* Policy Statement on Child Fatality Review: Investigation and review of unexpected infant and child deaths *Pediatrics, 104*, 1158–1160. Published online September 29, 2010, http://pediatrics.aappublications.org//cgi/content/abstract/126/3/592

Prescott, J. W. (2010c). *Breastfeeding bonding prevents infant mortality and suicide.* http://ttfuture.org/blog/1181

Raine, A., Brennan, P., & Mednick, S. A. (1994). Birth complications combined with early maternal rejection at age 1 year predispose to violent crime at age 18 years. *Archives of General Psychiatry, 51*, 984–988.

Riesen, A. H., Dickerson, G. P., & Struble, R. G. (1977). Somatosensory restriction and behavioral development in stumptail monkeys. *Annals New York Academy of Science, 290*, 285–294.

Rohner, R. P. (1975). *They love me, they love me not: A worldwide study of the effects of parental acceptance and rejection.* New Haven, CT: HRAF Press.

Russell, E. W. (1972). Factors in human aggression. Cross-cultural factor analysis of characteristics related to warfare and crime. *Behavioral Science Notes, 4*, 275–312.

Saltzberg, B., Lustick, L. S., & Heath, R. G. (1971). Detection of focal depth spiking in the scalp EEG of monkeys. *Electroencephalography and Clinical Neurophysiology, 31*, 327 333.

Sharpless, S. K. (1969). Isolated and deafferented neurons: Disuse supersensitivity. In Jasper, Ward, & Pope (Eds.), *Basic mechanisms of the epilepsies* (pp. 329–355). New York, NY: Little Brown & Co.

Sharpless, S. K. (1975). Disuse supersensitivity. In A. H. Riesen (Ed.), *The developmental neuropsychology of sensory deprivation.* New York, NY: Academic Press.

Struble, R. G., & Riesen, A. H. (1978). Changes in cortical dendritic branching subsequent to partial social isolation in stumptail monkeys. *Developmental Psychobiology, 11*(5), 479–486.

Teicher, M. H. (2000). Wounds that time won't heal: The neurobiology of child abuse. *Cerebrum, 2*(4), 50–67.

Textor, R. B. (1967). *A cross-cultural summary.* New Haven, CT: HRAF Press.

Vennemann, M. M., Bajanowski, T., Brinkmann, B., Jorch, G., Yucesan, K., Sauerland, C., … the GeSID Group. (2009). Does breastfeeding reduce the risk of sudden infant death syndrome? *Pediatrics, 123*(3). Published online 2 March. http://pediatrics.aappublications.org/cgi/content/abstract/123/3/e406

Wade, N. (2010). Anthropology a science? Statement deepens a rift. *New York Times,* December 9. http://www.nytimes.com/2010/12/14/science/14anthropology.html?_r=1&ref=science

Whiting, J. W. M., & Child, I. L. (1953). *Child training and personality.* New Haven, CT: Yale University Press.

World Health Organization/UNICEF. (1990). *Innocenti declaration.* Florence, Italy: Author. http://www.violence.de/prescott/letters/WHO_InnocentI_Declaration.pdf

22

Perspective 7: "It's Dangerous to Be an Infant": Ongoing Relevance of John Bowlby's Environment of Evolutionary Adaptedness in Promoting Healthier Births, Safer Maternal–Infant Sleep, and Breastfeeding in a Contemporary Western Industrial Context

James J. McKenna and Lee T. Gettler

Bowlby's Attachment and the Environment of Evolutionary Adaptedness in Retrospect: Who He Was, What He Did, How, and Why?

Grounded as it was in empirical evidence, John Bowlby's simple conclusion that "…the infant and young child should experience a warm, intimate, and continuous relationship with his mother (or permanent mother substitute) in which both find satisfaction and enjoyment" (Bowlby, 1951, p. 13) is certainly as appropriate now as it was some 62 years ago when it was first suggested; and yet, it seems that we have quite a distance to go toward implementing his recommendation, as work in this volume documents. The interplay of historically recent sociocultural and political forces and even legal factors leading to intransigent medical policies or positions is part of the reason. Ethnic and class-based health disparities contribute, too, coupled with tenacious Western social values and cultural ideologies aimed at transforming infants and mothers into who we want them to be, rather than who they actually are. That said, continuing creative research and disseminating it remain key. In that regard, given the persuasiveness of the findings presented in this volume, we owe much to these researchers as well as to the explanatory power of Bowlby's environment of evolutionary adaptedness (EEA). Given all that has been learned subsequent to Bowlby's death, he would be the first to acknowledge its inaccuracies while applauding Ball and Russell's attempts to eliminate them.

We know that this is true because in formulating the basic tenets of attachment theory, those closest to him were continually impressed by Bowlby's "strategy," wherever possible, to "meticulously test intuitive hunches against available empirical findings and concepts from related domains," according to Bretherton (1992) in her historically rich review and detailed account of his scholarship. No doubt Bowlby's familiarity with and admiration of Darwin's work and his sought-after intellectual associations with psychologist Jean Piaget; biologists J. M. Tanner and Julian Huxley; general systems theorist Ludwig von Bertalanffy; ethologists Robert Hinde, Harry Harlow, Niko Tinbergen, and Konrad Lorenz; and anthropologist Margaret Mead played a role in the etiology of his remarkable "polymathic" scholarship (see Bretherton, 1992; Kraemer, Steele, & Holmes, 2007; Metcalf, 2010).

Perhaps it was due to an active engagement with an unusually broad array of eclectic scholars that Bowlby anticipated—indeed, proposed—one of the major tenets of evolutionary psychology and evolutionary medicine, the significance of the possible conflict between rapidly changing cultural practices and the more conservative, evolved, or biological-based needs of contemporary actors, in this case, mothers and infants, about which Trevathan (this volume) and Ball and Russell's (this volume) research shed so much practical light (see especially Trevathan, Smith, & McKenna, 2007). Indeed, Bowlby's theoretical formulations, however imperfect, continue to provide the best explanations as to why it is that sometimes, despite cultural norms, mothers still exhibit behaviors that often just "feel right" (after Ball, 2002), whether recommended against or not (e.g., by medical or public health agencies), as they likely retain selective salience (i.e., they feel right because evolutionarily speaking, they *are* right, which is to say, adaptive).

Bowlby's delineation of the proximate mechanisms involved in the development of mother–infant, infant–mother attachment, all from a species-wide perspective, remains one of the most cogent, inclusive, and integrative ever argued. And his model was prescient in more ways than one. For example, he foresaw the immense significance of predation in shaping human evolution, a force recently emphasized and readdressed by Hart and Sussman (2008). He also recognized the connections between the infant's intense helplessness and the need for enriched maternal–infant contact and sensory-based communication that we now suspect have correlates to the rise of empathy and superior cognitive capacities that preceded (see Narvaez & Gleason, this volume) and, indeed, were prerequisites for language itself, according to Tomasello (2009).

It is clear that Bowlby also understood what years later Myron Hofer would call "hidden regulatory mechanisms" intrinsic in the regulation of developmental processes, especially of altricial mammals. Using embryology as a metaphor, Bowlby wrote that if growth is to proceed smoothly, the tissues must be exposed to the influence of the appropriate organizer at certain critical periods. In the same way, if mental development (of the infant) is to proceed smoothly, it would appear to be necessary for the undifferentiated psyche to be exposed during certain critical periods to the influences of the psychic organizer—the mother (Bowlby, 1951, discussed in Bretherton, 1992).

A Methodological Revolutionary?

But it was not just the innovative application of evolutionary concepts used to intro-duce the importance of maternal–infant contact and communication to attach-ment, so relevant to Ball and Russell's (this volume) and Trevathan's (this volume) arguments, nor the exquisite descriptions of the relevant proximate mechanisms that underlie it that catapulted Bowlby's contributions to historic dimensions. His methodological corrections were aimed at eliminating what he deemed serious defi-ciencies associated not only with his own field, psychoanalysis, but also with related subfields, including pediatrics and developmental psychology.

Recall that Bowlby's exegesis of attachment theory argued for both observing and analyzing the human mother–infant relationship outside of the biomedical or psy-choanalytical offices mothers and infants visited. At the time, such advocacy consti-tuted not only a heretical strategy but also an intellectual insult, at least as interpreted by his colleagues (Bretherton, 1992). Without apologies, he nullified the sufficiency—indeed, the legitimacy—of psychoanalytical armchair theorizing. He insisted that an understanding of the infants "tie" to its mother, its meaning, and the processes that create it, and the consequences of living without it could only be understood through detailed observational studies of what mothers and infants actually do (and why) rather than from inferences drawn *exclusively* from developmental histories aimed at describing what mothers and infants *supposedly* think or feel.

If that wasn't enough, even more daring was his reliance on data derived from studies (and people) outside the Western industrialized context. Situating his the-ories as he did within the context of living hunters and gatherers, naïve as it might have been, he aimed to elucidate the kinds and types of ancestral selective pressures he imagined savannah-living, Pleistocene mothers and their infants might encoun-ter. This approach was unprecedented, especially the notion that the kind of data derived could have any significance whatsoever to contemporary infants living in an industrialized nation.

He "Bested" Anthropologists, Too!!

In fact, we are slightly embarrassed to say that Bowlby co-opted his anthropology colleagues, too, beating them (as it were) at their own game, and, in the process, he also might have revealed some anthropological ethnocentrism and a surprising blindness as regards the utility of applying one of the most powerful theories of all, evolution, to explain infant–maternal behavior in relationship to clinical health and disorders. Nobody before Bowlby, including Darwin himself, had ever applied evo-lutionary concepts in the context of human infancy and maternal care quite so suc-cinctly and with such frankness and, yet, integrative detail. Bowlby was adamant that an understanding of contemporary mothers, infants, and the relationships they develop could never be accurately explained without first considering the original context and selective pressures within which they evolved that gave them adaptive meaning. Much of the recent emergent field of evolutionary medicine derives its validity and explanatory power from this one observation inspired by Bowlby and initially (in our opinion) used most effectively by biological anthropologist Melvin Konner in 1972 (see also 1976).

Defending this view took a lot of courage, as Bretherton (1992) describes. Bretherton (1992) reports how in his last work, a biography of Charles Darwin, Bowlby could have just as well been talking about himself, when he said of Darwin: "Since causes are never manifest, the only way of proceeding is to propose a plausible theory and then test its explanatory powers against further evidence, and in comparison with the power of rival theories. Since most theories prove to be untenable, advancing them is a hazardous business and requires a courage Darwin never lacked." (Bowlby, 1991, p. 412, cited in Bretherton, 1992).

To this we add, a "courage" that Bowlby never lacked, either!!

To What Did Bowlby Object as Regards Psychoanalytical Assumptions and Procedures?

Influenced by Donald Winnicott, his senior distinguished colleague, who once observed: "There is no such thing as a baby, there is baby and someone," Bowlby pushed further to identify the specific processes and mechanisms by which mothers and infants "attach" or fail to attach, and why the quality of that relationship significantly impacts adult psychological well-being and resilience, itself a concept that at the time could not be taken for granted in the same way that it can now. Conceptualizing attachment as a physically intimate process, and accumulative, one within which the extreme neurological immaturity of the human infant at birth renders the infant incapable of self-regulation, he suggested basically, in our own words, that there is nothing that the infant can or cannot do that makes sense except in light of the mother's body and/or her related care and commitment.

In fact, still using the vocabulary of psychoanalysis, he collapsed the child's "ego" and "superego," as Bretherton (1992) describes, to that of the mother when he argued:

> It is not surprising that during infancy and early childhood these functions are either not operating at all or are doing so most imperfectly. During this phase of life, the child is therefore dependent on his mother performing them for him. She orients him in space and time, provides his environment, permits the satisfaction of some impulses, restricts others. She is his ego and his superego. Gradually he learns these arts himself, and, as he does, the skilled parent transfers the roles to him. This is a slow, subtle and continuous process, beginning when he first learns to walk and feed himself, and not ending completely until maturity is reached.... Ego and super-ego development are thus inextricably bound up with the child's primary human relationships. (Bowlby, 1951, p. 53, cited in Bretherton, 1992).

Orphaned Monkeys and the Harlow Connection

Likewise, Bowlby rejected contemporary psychoanalytic explanations for the child's libidinal tie to the mother in which "need satisfaction was seen as primary and attachment as secondary or derived" (see Bretherton, 1992; Kraemer et al., 2007). For example, Freud argued that by eliminating the infant's hunger, the infant develops with the mother, the "object of attachment," a "discriminating" bond that eventually is extended beyond the mother to the infant's social nexus. The legitimacy of Bowlby's doubt about the primacy of satiation as a prerequisite for attachment was, of course, vindicated. Harlow's experiments on orphaned rhesus macaque infants showed that upon separation, if given the choice, these primate neonates consistently avoided clinging to the feeding (wire rim) surrogate mother, favoring instead clinging to a soft, cuddly, terrycloth mother who offered no food but nonetheless provided something more useful (i.e., "contact comfort") and apparently enough emotional security to facilitate attachment (Harlow & Zimmermann, 1959).

It is a historical curiosity, however, that it was this study showing that feeding was less important than Freud had argued teamed with prevailing Western cultural attitudes of the period, especially that bottle-feeding with formula or cow's milk obviated the need or desirability of breastfeeding, that likely prevented Bowlby from ever fully appreciating the overall critical role that breastfeeding has to his mother–infant attachment framework. Indeed, breast milk delivery plays a crucial part in promoting infant survival itself, as well as in myriad other aspects of the human infant's social and psychological development and physiological regulation by the mother including (but not limited to) attachment (see Konner, 2010; McKenna, Ball, & Gettler, 2007). Collectively, our current understanding of the importance of breastfeeding, across primate species, to mother–infant health and development (biological and social, respectively) complements (and partially underlie) Bowlby's evolutionary conceptualization of the mother–infant relationship.

Hanging on to Freud, in Part?

Even though Bowlby rejected Freud's interpretation of the origins of infantile sociality, he borrowed his explanatory strategy of identifying "component instincts" to describe what he conceptualized as discrete, innate, infant reflexes and behaviors he believed were relevant to the development of attachment just as they were, he imagined, in the Pleistocene as they evolved in the "environment of evolutionary adaptedness"—behaviors such as the infant's ability to visually track the mother's face to facilitate mutual gazing (i.e., communication). Smiling (and/or not smiling), another indentified proximity-maintaining mechanism, was needed perhaps to convince and motivate the mother to care and to invest, just as crying at separation could induce retrieval, and not crying (when held) could affirm the mother's special status. Sucking, grasping, clinging, the Moro reflex, scrambling both on and off the mother's body, and "following" her accordingly all constituted survival-related behaviors ("perceptuo-motor mechanisms" he called them) developing independently and functioning to obtain nutrition, promote maternal protection, keep the mother close, and become attached (Bowlby, 1969).

To What Did Anthropologists Object as Regards the Environment of Evolutionary Adaptedness?

Criticisms of the concept of the EEA focus on Bowlby's misconception that there was only one, and that a single marginalized Kalahari foraging society, the !Kung, could suffice to act as a proxy for explaining the diversity of evolving others that dotted the paleoanthropological landscape, as Ball and others describe (see also Foley, 1996; Hrdy, 1999; Irons, 1998). Present evidence clearly reveals that variable hominin forms coexisted and emerged in multiple and diverse ecological contexts ranging from heavily terrestrial to semiterrestrial to largely arboreal, making a simple, monolithic hominin spatial niche to assess human origins as regards any single attribute unlikely (Konner, 2010).

Also true is that, as originally conceptualized, the EEA failed to acknowledge earlier but just as relevant adaptations that evolved before the Pleistocene, such as the reduction of the number of young born among primates, delayed maturity, increased brain size, and a dependence on learning (but see Ball and Russell's reconceptualiztion of this issue, this volume). As mentioned, Bowlby also missed the connections between the evolution of breastfeeding and nighttime mother infant cosleeping, two subjects strangely absent in much of his synthetic writings despite the significant role they play in promoting emotionally based communication so important to (but not required for) attachment itself.

Additional recent criticism by Hrdy (1999) suggests that Bowlby either ignored or thought little about "maternal agency," the idea that mothers are not all the same but, more important, that they don't share the same reproductive opportunities and goals or have the same access to resources at any given time and, hence, will vary in the degree to which they will choose to invest in an infant or not, and when. Although we speculate here, Bowlby seemed not to appreciate how a woman's immediate ecological, social, or economic circumstances rather than her biology could be determinative. As Hrdy (1999) puts it: "Continuous contact and proximity and carrying may be what infants want but it might not be what mothers want or more importantly what they can provide." Similarly, throughout various stages of human evolution, a woman's contingencies, status, and roles changed tremendously, and depending on the ecology and culture in which she lived, as is true for men, she could have been more or less encumbered by her biology, affecting her reproductive choices. In other words, "a mother today, whether in New York, Tokyo or Dacca, is not just a gatherer caught in a shopping mall without her digging stick" (Hrdy 1999, p. 105). Fair enough.

Beyond Its Weaknesses

As is the way of good science, however, Bowlby's framework continues to stimulate critical insights that are used to correct and make more precise his own initial formulations—especially new ideas concerning the importance of shared care (alloparenting) rather than, as he argued, a singular concept of the mother as being able to meet all of her infant's needs, by caring for her infant alone. Konner (2010) summarizes the increased survivorship in infants whose relatives "assist" the mother, as does Hrdy (2009). These data and ideas are complemented by Gettler's (2010) hypothesis showing how direct male care in the form of infant-carrying behavior likely coevolved alongside a responsive underlying male physiology mediating reproductive hormones, especially testosterone, cortisol, and prolactin, that seem to reapportion themselves depending on what kind of reproductive effort is required: mating or parenting. As Gettler demonstrates using comparative data, male carrying behavior, like Hrdy's female allomothers, could have helped reduce daily energy demands among evolving hominin mothers, therein significantly shortening the human birth interval while helping to expand hominin population densities. The unique ability of early *Homo* forms to be able to support two (or more) dependent offspring simultaneously, without compromising child survival, let alone to do so in the context of giving birth to the least neurologically mature primate of all, the slowest developing and the most dependent on the mothers (or someone's) body for the longest period of time, was no easy feat.

Surely, then, Bowlby's contention that infants could only attach to one caregiver at a time, a concept referred to as monotropy, was a mistake. Indeed, the conclusion drawn from Hrdy's and Gettler's models is that humans are, indeed, best considered cooperative breeders. Hrdy (2009) suggests that shared care alongside the mother's more intense and still critical investment in her infant had the dual benefit of promoting the need for enhanced human empathy alongside a unique human capacity for understanding the "shared intentionalities" of others, and to develop a "theory of mind," which Tomasello (2009) argues constitutes an incomparable intellectual achievement unique to humankind.

Human Birth Ancient Midwives and Doulas: Improving the Experience of Birthing Women in the Western Hospital Setting Using Research Inspired by the Environment of Evolutionary Adaptedness

Framed by Bowlby's intellectual formulations of attachment theory described in terms of the EEA, we welcome the opportunity to comment further on the remarkable ongoing studies of mothers and infants by Trevathan (chapter 8) and Ball and Russell (chapter 9).

Broadly speaking, Wenda Trevathan's research focuses on the evolution (possibly) of humankind's oldest profession, midwifery, and the role of the "doula" or woman companion who assists and supports birthing/breastfeeding in mothers, shortening labors, and improving outcomes, all in relationship to the unique natural history of human childbirth. It is from a universal species-wide perspective, then, and a perspective fully documented by her own first-hand observations of mothers birthing and interacting with their babies in the first few hours following parturition that Trevathan explains why for mothers (and infants), the quality of the birth environment is not a trivial issue. Characteristics of the birthing environment as Trevathan discusses can negatively impact a mother's confidence and her success at breastfeeding and, as recent research suggests, have potentially deleterious effects on her child's epigenome. This idea is based on findings from a Swedish team that examined DNA methylation in leukocytes among infants born by elective cesarean section versus those born vaginally. Vaginal births were associated with significantly lower DNA methylation in infant white blood cells compared with cesarean births, the interpretation of which (see Schlinzig, Johnson, Gunnar, Ekstrom, & Noman, 2009) remains elusive.

Perhaps no researcher explains better than Trevathan how and why the breadth of the hominin pelvic architectures, specifically the birth outlet, was being reduced to accommodate bipedalism at the same time that fetal head size (and developmentally later, adult brain volume) was becoming larger to accommodate culture. The intersection of these conflicting adaptations known colloquially as the "obstetrical dilemma" forced the birth of an increasingly less neurologically mature, secondarily altricial dependent hominin infant. Trevathan argues that the emotions among women in labor motivating them to seek out and develop ties to other women who can assist them during this critical period are adaptive and reduce potential perils and complexities that a prolonged labor poses, and one in which the infant is born facing away and not toward the mother, as is true for almost all other primates.

Trevathan offers five specific suggestions consonant with the EEA as to how to improve a woman's birthing experience in a Western, urban hospital setting: (1) permit the presence of a supportive, female assistant; (2) have the mother give birth to the infant while in the upright or squatting position, taking advantage of gravity and the natural contours of the woman's body; (3) delay cutting the umbilical cord until it stops pulsating to maximize oxygen and iron retention; (4) keep the mother and infant in continuous contact, permitting maternal embracing, soothing, and massaging of the infant, stimulating respiration and breast milk production and reducing infant heat loss; and (5) support and encourage breastfeeding.

Where Should Babies Sleep? An Anthropological No-Brainer!!

"The tasks for those who use attachment theory to guide their research or their clinical work are to see where the ideas already formulated can aid understanding, to recognize where they need **supplementing** from elsewhere, and to accept that there are probably many fields on which they shed no light" (Bowlby, 1982, p. 313, emphasis mine).

Ball and Russell's work is remarkably complementary to Trevathan's, given that it concerns what we should do with infants after they are born, specifically where infants should sleep and the significance of breastfeeding. However, before delving into these issues, they first offer a new description of the EEA to "supplement" (to borrow Bowlby's own word used previously) critical elements of Bowlby's version. Along with McKenna (1986; McKenna, Mosko, Dungy, & McAninch, 1991), Ball's pioneering studies document the functional interconnections between breastfeeding and mother–infant cosleeping, highlighting the developmental context within which infant sleep evolved. Thus, she portrays an arrangement likely representing humankind's oldest sleeping and feeding arrangement. Both in terms of practical suggestions and the production of new knowledge, the depth and trajectory of both Trevathan's and Ball's ongoing studies reflect the best of what an integration of a resilient theory with imaginative empirical investigations can produce.

For example, Ball and Russell's more precise and expanded version of the ancestral environment (AE) was specifically designed to pinpoint in what context and sequential chronology human parent–infant sleep contact (and breastfeeding) emerged, disappeared (in relationship to "evolutionary recent cultural changes"), and then reappeared in the present, at least in Western industrialized settings. In their expanded version of the AE, Ball and Russell conceptualize a phylogenetically older and more comprehensive AE starting first with an initial generic period of mammalian reproduction and associated infant care practices that continued to evolve through at least three other periods. They begin their model (AE-1) denoting the rise of placental mammals, birth of live young (viviparity), and lactation, followed by a second period (AE-2) marked by the evolution of precocial mammals, specifically primates with low-fat and -protein and high-sugar-content milk, that evolved toward a third period (AE-3) in which neurologically immature infants (hominin) are born who cannot cling and who develop the largest primate brain relative to body weight of all.

At this point Ball and Russell describe an additional four subphases, what they aptly call "new cultural environments" (NCEs), designating NCE-1 as denoting the emergence of the "medicalization of childbirth" (anesthesia–hospital birth technology, infection control) and NCE-2 as the stage wherein scientific infant care associated with the invention of formula and the rise of parenting "experts" (i.e., "scientific" parenting) emerged. They then describe a third NCE-3 that involves opposition (or at least an alternative) to the NCE-2, with institutions such as UNICEF and the World Health Organization (WHO) introducing Baby-Friendly Hospital Initiatives that work to restore components reminiscent of the original AE-3 (i.e., uninterrupted breastfeeding, skin-to-skin and maternal–infant sleep contact, and/or rooming-in).

Ball and Russell's model incorporates recent culture changes (new considerations) as an attempt to correct Bowlby's EEA and to answer (in part) his critics. Their model ends somewhat where the system of infant care and maternal experiences began, with the NCE-4 (at least hypothetically). It denotes the acceptance and encouragement of "ancient infant care practices," finding utility in 21st-century

Western environments with "parent–infant sleep contact" alongside exclusive, infant-initiated nighttime breastfeeding being the norm.

Ball's creative attempt to make more historically useful Bowlby's underlying premise is remarkable given that it is offered in the context of so much more. Her own data, in addition to that collected by others (see McKenna et al., 2007, for review) in the home, hospital, and laboratory settings, lead not only to an appreciation of the importance of mother–infant cosleeping but also the real and potential deleterious consequences of not doing so: Solitary infant sleep is now known to be an independent risk factor for sudden infant death syndrome (SIDS; see McKenna et al., 2007, for review). Nighttime separation for sleep of the infant from the mother is of course a recent cultural innovation, as is the adoption of bottle-feeding (cow's milk, artificial formula) that made such sustained nighttime mother–infant separation possible. Cow's milk and formula are more calorically dense than is human breast milk, therein fostering artificially prolonged, consolidated infant sleep. While the positive effects on breastfeeding while bed-sharing are now accepted (i.e., bed-sharing increases the number of breastfeeds per night and lengthens the duration of months mothers are willing to continue to breastfeed), mother–infant cosleeping in the form of bed-sharing is not common in many Western societies due to fears of maternal overlay or suffocation. In fact, cosleeping in the form of bed-sharing is aggressively opposed by Western medical authorities to the extent that from vitriolic public campaigns against bed-sharing, it could be inferred that parents who choose to practice it are thought irresponsible, ignorant, or both (Gettler & McKenna, 2010). Ball's work and others has provided empirically based research that raises critical questions and research that effectively challenges the legitimacy and appropriateness of such claims and rhetoric (see McKenna & Ball, 2010).

It is worth noting that Ball was the first to comment on the universality of the sleeping positions adopted by breastfeeding, cosleeping mothers and infants, a mother–baby bodily orientation reported on by almost every investigator that has directly observed mothers and infants sleeping together on the same surface. This instinctive position makes maternal overlay highly unlikely, it should be noted. It is absent among nonbreastfeeding (i.e., formula- or cow's milk–feeding) bed-sharing mother–infant dyads, however, suggesting that at least in the Western setting perhaps bottle-feeding infants might not sleep as safely on the same surface with their mothers as do breastfeeding babies.

Consider, for example, that breastfeeding bed-sharing infants are always laid on their backs, giving them access to the breast (and not prone, a culturally constructed practice that caused an epidemic of tens of thousands of Western infant deaths from SIDS), with the mother sleeping laterally, facing and curled up around her infant, and the infant's head level with the mother's breast, in the space created between the mother's arm, which rests above the infant's head. The mother's knees are drawn up under her baby's feet. Moreover, as regards sleep architecture, bed-sharing promotes lighter sleep among breastfeeding bed-sharing infants and mothers (compared to when the dyad sleeps separate from one another) with social and sensory exchanges occurring continuously between them, making the ability to respond to each other increasingly more likely. Cosleeping in the form of bed-sharing significantly increases maternal-induced infant arousals, giving the infant practice in arousing quickly and effectively. Given the fact that "arousing to breathe" is one of the infant's most important defenses against hypoxia and specifically prolonged apneas suspected to be involved in SIDS, such "practice" could prove protective (see McKenna et al., 2007, for review).

In Sum: "It's Dangerous to Be an Infant"

As Konner (2010) reminds us, it *is* dangerous to be an infant, and especially one that is immobile and cannot cling to someone and, "proximity-maintaining behaviors" not withstanding, still cannot altogether control who will care for them and how, even when lucky enough to be born into a world in which predation is not at all likely. Bowlby seemed to understand this and tried to figure out first and foremost what human infants are up against and what in their limited repertoire they can do about it if given a chance. The process of creating attachments was Bowlby's answer to the human infant's vulnerability, and he was right, even though he might not have appreciated that, along with the mother, often the more motivated and attentive caregivers there were, the better (i.e., the greater likelihood of survival).

He never envisioned nor expected that an evolutionary-based perspective and the knowledge acquired by its use could ever serve as an easy endpoint, or that inferred general principles could be translated into specific practices applicable to all in any simple static way. How we can apply what we learn about humankind's evolutionary prehistory and from other cultures as regards what seems to constitute more universal human needs and attributes will be tricky no matter what. This is because as critics of the EEA rightly point out, ever-changing sociocultural and technological microenvironments change the functions of otherwise previously useful behaviors sometimes rather quickly. Identifying how observations and existing related, diverse lines of evidence can be integrated into theories that raise practical research questions is the first step, however, and perhaps a bit easier than later steps (e.g., assessing the results and then translating them into strategies and recommendations aimed at improving maternal–infant health). These challenges remain, but Bowlby surely gave us a powerful jumpstart.

Final Thoughts

It was the pain of separation that Bowlby himself experienced as a young boy, what he saw in the sad faces of his younger patients, and what he heard described in the tragic narratives of his older patients that prompted him to identify and explore what attachment is, what separation does, and how and why its effects often serve to diminish the vitality of the human psyche. The conference papers published in this volume surely document what Bowlby dedicated his life to. Perhaps unsurprisingly, it is the negative consequences of related types of separation and loss that tie together the works of the three researchers and others mentioned here. Bowlby's "conceptual framework," as he preferred to call it, which describes the evolved critical role that the mother–infant relationship and supplemental caregivers play in healthy human development, remains foundational, in spite of its flaws, and provides the relevant context to which all that is human must at some point make more than passing reference. Trevathan addresses the effects of separation and psychological isolation on a birthing woman, while Ball and Russell speak eloquently to our culture's unfortunate insistence on separating breastfeeding mothers and infants (or any parent–infant pair for that matter) for nighttime sleep, denying them all the sensory exchanges on which an exceedingly vulnerable and neurologically immature human infant depends.

So we end as we began by giving credit to Bowlby, who provided the intellectual justification and reasons, both moral and scientific, for building on his remarkable legacy. Kraemer et al. (2007, p. 306), whose eloquent and astute editorial served to inform this paper, say it best: "Bowlby looked forward to a time when children's rights would be respected universally without the need to 'champion' them, a task to which he was uniquely suited by his life experience, his endowment and his distinguished nature." We could not agree more.

Acknowledgments

The authors acknowledge that John Bowlby's history and especially his theoretical differences with Freud discussed here and other aspects of his work relied heavily on a remarkable paper on the origin, history, and development of Bowlby's scholarship, what amounts to a detailed, semibiographical review of his life, authored by Inge Bretherton, *Developmental Psychology* (1992), 28, 759–775.

Gary Metcalf's historical review of Bowlby's interdisciplinary contacts and the history of his institutional contacts throughout his life also was instrumental in shaping the contours of this paper and to him we also would like to extend our appreciation. See: John Bowlby: Recovering a systems scientist. Copyright 2010 International Society for the Systems Sciences.

We also would like to thank Darcia Narvaez especially for the time and effort invested in the conference and subsequent volume.

References

Ball, H. L. (2002). Reasons to bed-share: Why parents sleep with their infants. *Journal of Reproductive and Infant Psychology, 20*(4), 207–222.

Bowlby, J. (1951). *Maternal care and mental health.* World Health Organization Monograph Serial Number 2.

Bowlby, J. (1969). *Attachment.* New York, NY: Basic Books.

Bowlby, J. (1982). *Attachment and loss* (Vol. 1, 2nd ed.). New York, NY: Basic Books.

Bowlby, J. (1991). Ethological light on psychoanalytical problems. In P. Bateson (Ed.), *The development and integration of behavior* (pp. 301–313). Cambridge, MA: Cambridge University Press.

Bretherton, I. (1992). The origins of attachment theory: John Bowlby and Mary Ainsworth. *Developmental Psychology, 28*, 759–775.

Foley, R. (1996). The adaptive legacy of human evolution: A search for the environment of evolutionary adaptedness. *Evolutionary Anthropology, 4*(6), 194–203.

Gettler, L. T. (2010). Direct male care and hominine evolution: Why male-child interaction is more than a nice social idea. *American Anthropologist, 112*, 7–21.

Gettler, L. T., & McKenna, J. J. (2010). Never sleep with baby? Or keep me close but keep me safe: Eliminating inappropriate 'safe infant sleep' rhetoric in the United States. *Current Pediatric Reviews, 6*(1), 1–6.

Harlow, H. F., & Zimmermann, R. R. (1959). Affectional responses in the infant monkey. *Science, 130*(3373), 421–432.

Hart, D., & Sussman, R. (2008). *Man the hunted: Primates, predators and human evolution.* Boulder, CO: Westview Press.

Henderson, J. M. T., France, K. G., Owens, J. L., & Blampied, N. M. (2010). Sleeping through the night: The consolidation of self-regulated sleep across the first year of life. *Pediatrics, 126*(5), e1081–e1087.

Hrdy, S. (1999). *Mother Nature: A history of mothers, infants and natural selection.* New York, NY: Pantheon.

Hrdy, S. (2009). *Mothers and others: The evolutionary origins of empathy and mutual understanding.* Cambridge, MA: Harvard University Press.

Irons, W. G. (1998). Adaptively relevant environments vs. the environment of evolutionary adaptedness. *Evolutionary Anthropology, 6*(6), 194–204.

Konner, M. (1972). Aspects of the developmental ethology of a foraging people. In N. G. B. Jones (Ed.), *Ethological studies of child behavior* (pp. 285–304). Cambridge: Cambridge University Press.

Konner, M. (1976). Maternal care, infant behavior and development among the !!Kung. In R. B. Lee & I. DeVore (Eds.), *Kalahari hunters and gatherers* (pp. 218–245). Cambridge, MA: Harvard University Press.

Konner, M. (2010). *The evolution of childhood.* Cambridge, MA: Belknap/Harvard University Press.

Kraemer, S., Steele, H., & Holmes, J. (2007). A tribute to the legacy of John Bowlby at the centenary of his birth. *Attachment and Human Development, 9*(4), 303–306.

McKenna, J. J. (1986). An anthropological perspective on the sudden infant death syndrome (SIDS): The role of parental breathing cues and speech breathing adaptations. *Medical Anthropology: Cross-Cultural Studies of Disease and Illness, 10*(1), 9–92.

McKenna, J. J., & Ball, H. (2010). Early infant sleep consolidation is unnecessary barrier to breastfeeding. E-Letter in *Pediatrics,* http://pediatrics.aappublications.org/cgi/eletters/126/5/e1081; doi:10.1542/peds.2010–0976, November 2 in response to *Pediatrics, 126*, e1081–e1087, originally published online October 25, 2010.

McKenna, J. J., Ball, H., & Gettler, L. T. (2007). Mother-infant cosleeping, breastfeeding and sudden infant death syndrome: What biological anthropology has discovered about normal infant sleep and pediatric sleep medicine. *Yearbook of Physical Anthropology, 50*, 133–161.

McKenna, J. J., Mosko, S., Dungy, C., & McAninch, J. (1991). Sleep and arousal patterns of co-sleeping human mother-infant pairs: A preliminary physiological study with implications for the study of the sudden infant death syndrome (SIDS). *American Journal of Physical Anthropology, 82*(3), 331–347.

Metcalf, G. (2010). *John Bowlby: Recovering a systems scientist.* Copyright 2010 International Society for the Systems Sciences.

Schlinzig, T., Johnson, S., Gunnar, A., Ekstrom, T., & Noman, M. (2009). Epigenetic modulation at birth—altered DNA methylation in white blood cells after Caeserean section. *Acta Pediatrica, 98*, 1096–1099.

Tomasello, M. (2009). *Why we cooperate.* Cambridge, MA: Boston Review Book.

Trevathan, W., Smith, N. J., & McKenna, J. (Eds.). (2007). *Evolutionary medicine and health: New perspectives.* London: Oxford University Press.

Conclusion

23

The Future of Human Nature: Implications for Research, Policy, and Ethics

Darcia Narvaez, Jaak Panksepp, Allan N. Schore, and
Tracy R. Gleason

Human nature is often described as selfish (Dawkins, 1976) and violent (Pinker, 2002, 2011; Wrangham & Peterson, 1998). Such views of human nature are contrary to the views of most societies throughout most of history (Sahlins, 2008) and contrary to data about prehistory (Fry, 2006). Most alarming, the belief that human nature is evil, or at least fundamentally self-interested, may lead to treatment of children in ways that violate humanity's evolved, social, mammalian heritage and, ironically, result in the outcomes that are feared. In other words, neglect, trauma, and abuse result in poor physical and mental health, as well as in diminished capacities for prosocial behavior, "proving" the evilness of human nature. The "enthusiasts of evolutionary egoism" fail to recognize "their ethnocentrism by taking certain of our customary practices as proof of their universal theories of human behavior" (Sahlins, 2008, p. 2).

The research evidence showing that human beings are malleable and highly responsive to their earliest experiences is quite sound. As demonstrated in the contributions of this volume, early experience sets up the morphology and functioning of the brain and body systems. The social mammals emerged over 30 million years ago with a particular set of parenting behaviors, represented in their human variation in the environment of evolutionary adaptedness (EEA; Bowlby, 1980). Current culturally-derived childrearing practices diverge from these evolved, species-typical practices, potentially undermining the evolved human nature benefits that were common among foraging hunter-gatherers. Thus, at all points of human evolution, the nature of human nature depends on the ontogenetic niche. When the niche moves far from the expected environment for a social mammal, the ensuing trouble is not surprising. And we see trouble for health and social well-being throughout societies where certain traditional cultural practices, such as extended periods of attachment bonding, breastfeeding, cosleeping, and alloparental care, have diminished.

In light of the findings presented in this volume, we have two sets of recommendations. One set is for researchers in the human and health sciences regarding how they might think about applying the volume's content to their areas of study. The other set of recommendations is for citizens and policymakers on how they might attend better to human needs in ways that promote optimal development.

Recommendations for Future Research Across the Life and Social Sciences

ESTABLISH A BASELINE FOR EVOLVED HUMAN FUNCTIONING

Scientists have been starting with the assumption that the members of the US population typically studied are in the range of normality (i.e., in intelligence, emotional well-being, personality) and represent optimal development of the human genus. Such assumptions need to be made explicit and tested. In psychology, the population usually studied and generalized from is rarely representative of worldwide human nature, let alone our ancestral human personality and psychology (Henrich, Heine, & Norenzayan, 2010). According to our thesis, those raised with the fewest evolutionarily appropriate supports may be less flexibly intelligent and cooperative than those with the most supports. We recommend that scientists work to establish what is considered optimal by using as a baseline consistency with evolved, expected care informed by an understanding of cross-mammalian emotional needs. How much an individual's experience matches evolved, expected care and the supports required for optimal mammalian brain functions may be measurably linked to child and adult outcomes, as has been shown in recent animal studies (Weaver, Szyf, & Meaney, 2002). Those with early experiences that match the fulfillment of ancestral mammalian needs may give us the best estimate of evolutionary typicality. For example, just as we have learned recently of widespread human deficiencies in vitamin D because most Westerners are not spending their days exposed to the sun to the same degree as our ancestors (Cannell, Hollis, Zasloff, & Heaney, 2008), our bodies and brains may be becoming deficient in other ways compared to our ancestors. We need to know which deficiencies, especially interpersonal and emotional deficiencies, matter and how they matter before we can design interventions to prevent or alleviate long-term detrimental outcomes (see Narvaez, in press, for further discussion).

ATTEND TO BASIC NEEDS

We also recommend that researchers attend to the basic emotional and motivational needs of the mammalian brain, especially the early developing social-emotional right brain (Schore, 2012; Semrud-Clikeman, 2011), throughout the life span, in the context both of personality development and of medical vulnerabilities (Smith & MacKenzie, 2006). Comparable cross-species mammalian affective needs should be considered when doing research relevant to other mammals. Perhaps the greatest ill effect of living in cultures that do not follow the better side of our ancestral heritage is the stress it causes as the infant is developing its physiological and psychological competencies. Decades of studies have shown that diminished resilience to stress (e.g., sustained cortisol elevations following environmental challenges) commonly leads to diverse ill health effects both inside the womb and after birth (Chrousos &

Gold, 1992; Lupien, McEwen, Gunnar, & Heim, 2009). We suggest that a link needs to be made between our suggested evolved, expected care and later outcomes. We follow with a few examples of how research can be informed by these concerns.

EXAMINE CURRENT EPIDEMIC PROBLEMS IN LIGHT OF EVOLVED, EXPECTED CARE

Childrearing practices coevolved with the increasing helplessness of the human infant at full-term birth of 40 to 42 weeks (Trevathan, 2011). In recent decades, not only has the understanding of needy babies been minimized, but babies are increasingly born prematurely for a host of reasons (World Health Organization, 2012). This trend only increases the need to use evolved caregiving practices to ensure healthful outcomes. Current epidemic problems may benefit from accounting for the presence or absence of evolved, expected care.

Sleeping disorders, including sudden infant death syndrome (SIDS). Reports from foraging societies indicate that children and adults typically sleep in physical proximity with abundant touch. Typically, in Western culture, people sleep alone or with a single other person, and sleep labs test individuals in isolation. An orientation informed by evolutionary principles suggests that physical isolation might be tested as one possible cause of poor sleep. Caregiving in the United States typically isolates infants from close human contact for long periods of time, resulting in limited caregiver responsiveness and curtailed breastfeeding (Centers for Disease Control and Prevention, 2004). Additionally, we know from animal studies that a dearth of touch in the early years is related to underdevelopment of serotonin receptors (Kalin, 1993). Caregiving practices that include isolation likely influence serotonin and other brain system development during maturation, including various more specific prosocial neurochemistries such as endogenous opioids and oxytocin (Meinischmidt & Heim, 2007). For instance, infants with faulty serotonin receptors are more likely to die of SIDS (Audero et al., 2008; Paterson et al., 2006). These findings suggest that investigation of cosleeping versus sleeping in isolation might reveal important individual differences in sleep quality and have significant implications for neurodevelopment.

Depression. Faulty serotonin receptors are associated not only with sleep disturbances but also, at least among adults, the likelihood of depression (Caspi et al., 2003). Depression is an important avenue for research given that the United States has an epidemic of depression in real numbers (U.S. Department of Health and Human Services, Substance Abuse and Mental Health Services Administration, 1999) as does the rest of the world (World Health Organization/World Organization of Family Doctors, 2008). Because of the dearth of affectionate touch, pursuant to John Bowlby's theories of attachment, Prescott (1996) came to the conclusion that most children in the United States are susceptible to somatosensory affectional deprivation, a condition related to depression, violent behavior, and stimulus seeking. Prolonged social isolation of animals can promote all these symptoms, but the neurobiological links to behavior and outcomes need to be made.

Mental health and birth experience. In the ancestral EEA, birth took place in circumstances similar to those of other animals (except assistance may have become necessary over the course of evolution; Trevathan, 2011). In our ancestral past, infants and mothers were not subject to the interruptions in natural processes that accompany giving birth in the United States (Wagner, 2006), which is now commonly envisioned as a medical procedure. An orientation consistent with evolutionary principles would suggest that each intervention by medical personnel should be studied for its effects on infant brain development and on entrainment between mother and infant. Common cultural practices and their effects should also be studied. For example, birthing practices can be examined for their psychological as well as physiological effects. Insel (1997) pointed out that although it is used routinely in birthing practice, little research has been performed on the effects of synthetic oxytocin (Pitocin) on the infant or on the emerging mother–infant relationship. Liu and colleagues (2007) reviewed hospital practices and their detrimental effects on infants. More psychological research needs to be conducted in these areas. Moreover, the modern medical advances that have so significantly reduced infant and maternal mortality during the course of childbirth might be enhanced even further by efforts to study and ameliorate the stressful and potentially long-lasting effects of specific, and possibly unnecessary, medical procedures. Since World War II (when most births became hospital births, now approximately one-third being cesarean), depression and anxiety rates have climbed, reaching epidemic proportions in the United States and around the world (U.S. Department of Health and Human Services, Substance Abuse and Mental Health Services Administration, 1999; World Health Organization/World Organization of Family Doctors, 2008). Could the relation be causal?

Mental health and early caregiving. As noted in the introductory chapter, ancestral parenting practices (e.g., natural childbirth, no separation of mother and child, lengthy and frequent breastfeeding, constant touch, responsivity to needs, multiple adult caregivers, free play in nature) have declined in recent decades. Are these declines linked to compromises in mental and physical health? Some evidence suggests a connection. For example, the National Institute of Child Health and Human Development, Early Child Care Research Network (2004) has concluded that emotion dysregulation and poor attachment at 6 months depress performance in later assessments of social and cognitive capacities. Likewise, postnatal experiences may influence the manifestation of autism in genetically susceptible individuals (Morrow et al., 2008). The quality of early environments, especially opportunities for self-initiated, playful social engagements, may determine the incidence of attention deficit/hyperactivity disorder–type problems later in life (Panksepp, 2007). Moreover, these issues appear to be on the rise. About 21% of US children ages 9 to 17 have a diagnosable mental or addictive disorder associated with some demonstrable impairment, which reflects rate increases compared to the past (Haggerty, 1995). Further evidence is discussed in this volume: Breast milk has the amino acids that promote serotonin synthesis; touch increases prosocial hormones such as endogenous opioids and oxytocin, and these neurotransmitters and hormones are all implicated in mental health (Panksepp, 2003). More recently, type 2 diabetes and depression have been linked to one another (Golden et al., 2008), suggesting holistic organismic dysfunctions. Similarly, disorders in stress reactivity (e.g., the hypothalamic–pituitary–adrenal axis) are linked to physiological and psychological ailments (Chrousos & Gold, 1992). Clearly, careful and causal mapping of caregiving practices to physical and mental health outcomes needs to be done.

Medical toxins. The annals of medicine abound with possible iatrogenic diseases from the use of modern medicines in infants, from possible toxic factors that may cause autism, to the use of antiepileptic medications after the first febrile seizure leading to various developmental delays, to the excessive use of antibiotics in infancy, which may promote asthma (Kozyrskyj, Ernst, & Becker, 2007). Although the scientific database on such demographic findings is weak, for obvious reasons, causal studies on humans would be unethical, so animal studies might be conducted to illuminate any connections.

EXAMINE THE EFFECTS OF THE MISSING EVOLVED AND EXPECTED CARE ON HEALTH AND IMMUNITY, INCLUDING CANCER

The gravest outcome of practices inconsistent with evolutionary principles may be the stress caused as infants' physiological systems are maturing. Decades of studies have shown that poor stress responses (e.g., elevated and poorly regulated cortisol) can lead to many ill health effects (Chrousos & Gold, 1992). Many other specific factors deserve to be investigated.

Early affection and vagal tone. As pointed out by Carter and Porges (this volume), the quality of vagal nerve functions may be dependent on the quality of early nurturing. As a cholinergic inflammatory pathway, the vagus nerve communicates with the spleen to control immune function (Kessler et al., 2006). Nurturing physical touching by the caregiver fosters proper vagal tone, which influences multiple biological, including emotional, regulations (Calkins, 1997; Donzella, Gunnar, Krueger, & Alwin, 2000; Porges, 1991; Porter, 2003). Further work needs to be done on the timing, type, and length of touch for developing good vagal tone. Perhaps "baby wearing" is required for optimal vagal tone development.

Infant feeding, stress, and eating disorders. The mother's diet during gestation influences preferences of the child after birth (Leathwood & Maier, 2005). As with psychobehavioral maternal care practices (Meaney, 2001), there may be nutritionally mediated snowballing transgenerational effects. Feeding decreases stress response under maternal absence (Rosenfeld, Ekstrand, Olson, Suchecki, & Levine, 1993), suggesting a relation between nonoptimal early care, high levels of stress during development, and eventual overeating. This hypothesis deserves investigation. In addition, bottle-feeding may encourage overfeeding (Li, Fein, & Grummer-Strawn, 2008).

Excessive separation distress, crying, and depression. The impact of early social loss on depression has been well documented (Bowlby, 1980; Heim & Nemeroff, 2001), but other factors may well influence rising rates of depression. For example, a popular childrearing standard encourages parents to allow little babies to cry themselves to sleep, with the presumption that this is the best course for family homeostasis as well as development of independent attitudes. The emphasis behind this practice is on learning to self-soothe at an early age, rather than gradual acquisition of these skills through mutual regulation with a caregiver. A host of reasons both psychological and neurochemical suggest that such practices may be directly or indirectly linked to the ongoing epidemic of depression (Watt & Panksepp, 2009), but causal connections have yet to be established (although see Middlemiss, Granger, Goldberg, & Nathans, 2012, for evidence of longterm elevated cortisol in babies after crying is extinguished).

The marginalization of natural play. Much is being written about our failure to provide children with opportunities for joyful engagements with each other and with nature. Such practices may have long-term consequences on a variety of mental health parameters, for natural social play may be an experience-expectant process that helps certain forms of neural maturation with benefits for the development of higher executive brain functions (Panksepp, 2001, 2007). Comparisons of children who do and do not engage in such play would be relatively easy to conduct, although longitudinal work in this area would clearly be most informative.

CONSIDER ECONOMIC OUTCOMES

Early life experiences lead to lifelong outcomes that affect mortality and morbidity (McEwen, 2003). Heckman (2008) has marshaled data showing that life outcomes for American youth are worsening, especially in comparison to 50 years ago. He presents substantial evidence that improving early care for children provides an estimated 10% return on investment (an underestimate since health costs are not included). Even small changes in early caregiving practices could reap enormous economic rewards in adulthood. For example, infant formula diets lead to greater health care costs (Ball & Wright, 1999—upwards of $13 billion (Bartick & Reinhold, 2010), whereas greater length of breastfeeding is linked to greater upward social mobility as an adult (Martin, Goodall, Gunnell, & Smith, 2007).

Recommendations for Policy, National Initiatives, and Ethical Orientation

If science is to be of service to society, scientists need to step up and advocate for sound policies and practices warranted by empirical evidence. Speaking up for the welfare of children is an ethical responsibility for all those in the profession, particularly when the profession is supported by taxpayer dollars. We suggest that the following actions be taken by the psychological, psychiatric, and medical associations and their members.

POLICY STATEMENTS

Formulate policy statements on parenting. As noted by mental health researchers and confirmed with experimental data, poor parenting increases across generations, with cascading and accruing deleterious effects of deficient early childhoods (Perry, Pollard, Blakely, Baker, & Vigilante, 1995; Weaver et al., 2002). We must figure out how to mitigate these generational snowballing effects. We advocate a precautionary principle regarding parenting practices. If we take to heart our evolved caregiving practices and the evidence we have thus far, then we must reframe some current childrearing practices as "risky," such as formula feeding (Walker, 1993), sleeping in isolation (McKenna & McDade, 2005), institutional daycare (Belsky, 2001), "crying it out" (Blunt Bugental, Martorell, & Barraza, 2003), lack of skin-to-skin contact (Morelius, Theodorsson, & Nelson, 2005), and parenting in isolation (Amato, 2007). Policy statements could explicitly support breastfeeding, safe cosleeping, caring touch, and responsive caregiving (much along the lines of those advocated by Attachment Parenting International). Policy statements on parenting could also advocate "best parental practices" education for all members of a society, including college students, among whom we authors find widespread misunderstanding of infants' and children's basic needs.

Formulate a policy statement on structuring society and institutions to support children and families. With an eye toward prevention of mental and physical health problems due to poor early experience, professional organizations can advocate greater societal support for children and families. Specific suggestions could be made for social-governmental policies where parents and families are central in social planning and taxpayer support (e.g., extensive nutritional education, optimal psychobehavioral care, increased availability of maternal and paternal leaves and play sanctuaries for children; see Calnen, 2007, for a review). Institutional supports for breastfeeding and childcare, such as sensitive workplace daycare as well as local breast milk banks, would ensure that the burden of childcare would not fall exclusively on mothers or prevent them from working. What is more, neighborhood community and family support systems are essential for all new parents, but particularly for those who are struggling financially. Poverty for 6 months or more in early life has long-term detrimental effects (Brooks-Gunn & Duncan, 1997), and children reared in poverty are more likely to be depressed throughout their life course than those with sufficient financial resources (Gilmana, Kawachia, Fitzmauricec, & Buka, 2002).

Support for children and families is particularly crucial for improving mental health outcomes. After all, the effects of having a depressed or overly stressed mother in early life are lifelong (e.g., Ashman, Dawson, Panagiotides, Yamada, & Wilkinson, 2002). Although maternal depression is viewed as a "relatively common deviation in early experience" (Dawson, Ashman, & Carver, 2000, p. 699), we propose that it is tragically "common" because our social environments are not meeting human mammalian needs. As already noted, too much stress in early life, especially early social deprivation, leads to hyperactive stress or hypoactive response systems (Kertes, Gunnar, Madsen, & Long, 2008; Schore, 2012). Policies that acknowledge and try to amend the plethora of stressors experienced by parents may have long-term benefits not just for individuals, but for society as a whole.

NATIONAL INITIATIVES

Establish a national database on the relation of early experience to mental health.
Ever since the work of Rene Spitz (1947), abundant evidence has emerged
regarding how powerfully social neglect affects mental health outcomes. As we
have noted, the literature on the consequences of child abuse and neglect on
future psychiatric problems is constantly growing (e.g., Teicher, 2002; Schore,
2003, 2012). Many of these effects can be modeled in animals so as to help work
out the details of the underlying brain mechanisms (Panksepp, 2001). A national
database on child neglect and abuse effects could be a significant contributor to
this effort (as suggested by Dawson et al., 2000). We suggest an extensive federal
initiative to establish a substantive database on how such vicissitudes affect the
developmental landscapes of both animals and humans. Only when we explicate
the toxicity of particular environments and practices can we work deliberately
to eradicate them.

*Establish a research initiative focused on how the missing evolved, expected care
may affect mental health at all ages.* How do early caregiving environments contribute to well-being throughout the life span? For example, throughout most of
human evolution, isolation at any time was most likely rare (Lee & Daly, 2005).
Today, loneliness from lack of satisfying social contact is on the increase and is
related to poor immune function, greater stress response, higher blood pressure,
and greater depression (Cacioppo & Patrick, 2008).

ETHICAL RESPONSIBILITY

*Psychologists as professionals should be advocates for the optimality of early
experience as part of their ethical responsibilities.* The American Psychological
Association has position papers on mental health, but they emphasize intervention. We propose that *prevention* and *developmental optimization* be major priorities. "Thrive by five" should be a national motto for childrearing practices.
The field and its cousin fields know enough now to make critical recommendations. The inferred nature of evolved, expected care from modern anthropological studies and the cross-species or naturalistic approach to mammalian social/
brain development can form the starting assumptions for optimizing human
development and well-being. Divergences from these standards represent risks
that must be assessed. To ignore the long arm of evolutionary adaptation is to
risk ill-adapted persons who cannot approach with equanimity and intelligence
the problems humanity faces, which are exacerbated by increasingly poor child
upbringing. These are ethical concerns and should be considered in professional
ethical standards.

Psychologists should advocate for humane treatment. Gawande (2009) has
reminded us that solitary confinement for a mammal constitutes the greatest torture. Extended confinement leads to psychopathy. As an extension of its position

on torture, which applies primarily to noncitizen combatants, psychological and psychiatric associations should prepare a position paper against solitary confinement, which would also apply to US citizens. Such a paper would advocate humane treatment of those who are confined whether in prisons, hospitals, or nursing homes.

Conclusion

The recommendations for research and policy outlined here make the assumption that evolved, expected care and mammalian needs are the default (perhaps "without fault") grounding for evidence-based examination of how different environments contribute to optimal functioning. The onus of "proof"—or scientifically, the "weight of evidence"—should be shifted to those who argue for maintaining the status quo of arbitrary or convenient cultural practices that go against basic human/mammalian needs.

When societies forget the past and the mammalian nature of their citizens, they seem prone to set up detrimental cultural practices based often on arbitrary belief systems. No matter how cognitively sophisticated such systems may seem (e.g., Huxley, 1932; Rogers & Skinner, 1956), engineering mammalian nature, without a full consideration of the benefits and harms of different childrearing practices, is unreasonable and often tragic. The current epidemic of autism, where an estimated 1 in 88 children is diagnosable, symbolizes the problems we may face, as most agree that environmental toxins and stressors in early life contribute to it (e.g., Good, 2009; Panksepp, 1979). Ill-advised practices and beliefs have become normalized without much fanfare, such as the common use of infant formula, the isolation of infants in their own rooms, the belief that responding too quickly to a fussing baby is spoiling it, the placing of infants in impersonal daycare, and so on. We recommend that scientists and citizens step back from and reexamine these common, culturally accepted practices and pay attention to their potentially lifelong effects.

At the same time, we recognize the great neural and psychological resilience that human children and other animals can exhibit in the face of adversity (Kagan, 1997). This resilience has been a key argument of those who do not see "thrive by five" early childhood policies to be wise investments in child development, physical, and mental health. For a counterpoint, see the Organization for Economic Cooperation and Development (2009), which uses international data to support early investment. Human resilience, as measured to date, does often indicate that the harm done in childhood can be partly reversed by later enrichments (Lester, Masten, & McEwen, 2007). However, none of these studies have yet focused clearly enough on the intrapsychic emotional qualities of lived lives, nor on flourishing.

Psychology and related fields are undergoing a paradigm shift, challenging the cognitive model of human development with a social-emotional model grounded in neurobiology. The shift comes none too soon. "Think of the investment that evolution has made in the child's brain.... For most of history, civilizations have crudely ignored that enormous potential. In fact the longest childhood has been that of civilization, learning to understand that" (Bronowski, 1973, p. 425). The available clinical evidence already strongly suggests that the harm wreaked by early deprivations will, more often than not, leave lifelong psychological scars. The long-term costs to humanity may be even greater. Societal investment in optimizing health and wellbeing cannot come too soon.

References

Amato, P. R. (2007). The impact of family formation change on the cognitive, social, and emotional well-being of the next generation. *The Future of Children, 15*(2), 75–96.

Ashman, S. B., Dawson, G., Panagiotides, H., Yamada, E., & Wilkinson, C. W. (2002). Stress hormone levels of children of depressed mothers. *Development and Psychopathology, 14*(10), 333–349.

Audero, E., Coppi, E., Mlinar, B., Rossetti, T., Caprioli, A., Banchaabouchi, M. A., ...Gross, C. (2008). Sporadic autonomic dysregulation and death associated with excessive serotonin autoinhibition. *Science, 321*(5885), 130–133.

Ball, T. M., & Wright, A. L. (1999). Health care costs of formula-feeding in the first year of life. *Pediatrics, 103*(4), 870–876.

Bartick, M., & Reinhold, A. (2010). The Burden of Suboptimal Breastfeeding in the United States: A Pediatric Cost Analysis. *Pediatrics, 125* (5):e1048-1056. doi:10.1542/peds.2009-1616

Belsky, J. (2001). Developmental risks (still) associated with early child care. *Journal of Child Psychology and Psychiatry and Allied Disciplines, 42*(7), 845–859.

Blunt Bugental, D., Martorell, G. A., & Barraza, V. (2003). The hormonal costs of subtle forms of infant maltreatment. *Hormones and Behaviour, 43*(1), 237–244.

Bowlby, J. (1980). *Attachment and loss. Vol. 3: Loss: Sadness and depression.* New York, NY: Basic Books.

Bronowski, J. (1973). *The ascent of man.* Boston, MA: Brown, Little and Co.

Brooks-Gunn, J., & Duncan, G. J. (1997). The effects of poverty on children. *The Future of Children, 7*(2), 66–71.

Cacioppo, J. T., & Patrick, W. (2008). *Loneliness: Human nature and the need for social connection.* New York, NY: W. W. Norton.

Calkins, S. D. (1997). Cardiac vagal tone indices of temperamental reactivity and behavioral regulation in young children. *Developmental Psychobiology, 31*, 125–135.

Calnen, G. (2007). Paid maternity leave and its impact on breastfeeding in the United States: An historic, economic, political, and social perspective. *Breastfeeding Medicine, 2*(1), 34–44.

Cannell, J. J., Hollis, B. W., Zasloff, M., & Heaney, R. P. (2008). Diagnosis and treatment of vitamin D deficiency. *Expert Opinion Pharmacology, 9*(1), 1–12.

Caspi, A., Sugden, K., Moffitt, T. E., Taylor, A., Craig, I. W., Harrington, H., ...Poulton, R. (2003). Influence of life stress on depression moderation by a polymorphism in the 5-HTT gene. *Science, 301*(5631), 386–389.

Centers for Disease Control and Prevention. (2004). *Breastfeeding: Data and statistics: Breastfeeding practices—results from the National Immunization Survey.* Atlanta, GA: Author. Retrieved from http://www.cdc.gov/breastfeeding/data/NIS__data/index.htm

Chrousos, G. P., & Gold, P. W. (1992). The concepts of stress and stress system disorders. Overview of physical and behavioral homeostasis. *Journal of the American Medical Association, 267*, 1244–1252.

Dawkins, R. (1976). *The selfish gene.* New York, NY: Oxford University Press.

Dawson, G., Ashman, S. B., & Carver, L. J. (2000). The role of early experience in shaping behavioral and brain development and its implications for social policy. *Development and Psychopathology, 12*, 695–712.

Donzella, B., Gunnar, M. R., Krueger, W. K., & Alwin, J. (2000). Cortisol and vagal tone responses to competitive challenge in preschoolers: Associations with temperament. *Development Psychobiology, 37*(4), 209–220.

Fry, D.P. (2006). *The human potential for peace: An anthropological challenge to assumptions about war and violence.* Oxford University Press, New York.

Gawande, A. (2009). Hellhole. *The New Yorker*, March 30.

Gilmana, S. E., Kawachia, I., Fitzmauricec, G. M., & Buka, S. L. (2002). Socioeconomic status in childhood and the lifetime risk of major depression. *International Journal of Epidemiology, 31*, 359–367.

Golden, S. H., Lazo, M., Carnethon, M., Bertoni, A. G., Schreiner, P. J., Diez Roux, A. V., ... Lyketsos, C. (2008). Examining a bidirectional association between depressive symptoms and diabetes. *Journal of the American Medical Association, 299*(23), 2751–2759.

Good, P. (2009). Did acetaminophen provoke the autism epidemic? *Alternative Medicine Review, 14*(4), 364–372.

Haggerty, R. J. (1995). Child health 2000: New pediatrics in the changing environment of children's needs in the 21st century. *Pediatrics, 96*, 807–808.

Heckman, J. (2008). *Schools, skills and synapses. IZA DP No. 3515.* Bonn, Germany: Institute for the Study of Labor.

Heim, C., & Nemeroff, C. B. (2001). The role of childhood trauma in the neurobiology of mood and anxiety disorders: Preclinical and clinical studies. *Biological Psychiatry, 49*(12), 1023–1039.

Henrich, J., Heine, S. J., & Norenzayan, A. (2010). The weirdest people in the world? *Brain and Behavioral Sciences, 33,* 61–135.

Huxley, A. (1932). *Brave new world.* London: Penguin.

Insel, T. J. (1997). A neurobiological basis of social attachment. *American Journal of Psychiatry, 154*(6), 726–735.

Kagan, J. (1997). Conceptualizing psychopathology: The importance of developmental profiles. *Developmental Psychopathology, 9*, 321–334.

Kalin, N. H. (1993). The neurobiology of fear. *Scientific American, 268*, 94–101.

Kertes, D. A., Gunnar, M. R., Madsen, N. J., & Long, J. D. (2008). Early deprivation and home basal cortisol levels: A study of internationally adopted children. *Development and Psychopathology, 20*, 473–491.

Kessler, W., Traeger, T., Westerholt, A., Neher, F., Mikulcak, M., Mrrüller, A., ... Heidecke C. D. (2006). The vagal nerve as a link between the nervous and immune system in the instance of polymicrobial sepsis. *Langenbecks Archives of Surgery, 391*, 83–87.

Kozyrskyj, A. L., Ernst, P., & Becker, A. B. (2007). Increased risk of childhood asthma from antibiotic use in early life. *Chest, 131*(6), 1753–1759.

Leathwood, P., & Maier, A. (2005). Early influences on taste preferences. *Nestlé Nutrition Workshop Ser Pediatric Program, 56*, 127–141.

Lee, R. B., & Daly, R. (Eds.). (2005). *The Cambridge encyclopedia of hunters and gatherers.* New York, NY: Cambridge University Press.

Lester, B. M., Masten, A., & McEwen, B. (Eds.). (2007). *Resilience in children. Annals of the New York Academy of Sciences* (Vol. 1094). New York, NY: Wiley-Blackwell.

Li, R., Fein, S. B., & Grummer-Strawn, M. (2008). Association of breastfeeding intensity and bottle-emptying behaviors at early infancy with infants' risk for excess weight at late infancy. *Pediatrics, 122*, S77–S84.

Liu, W. F., Laudert, S., Perkins, B., MacMillan-York, E., Martin, S., & Graven, S., for the NIC/Q 2005 Physical Environment Exploratory Group. (2007). The development of potentially better practices to support the neurodevelopment of infants in the NICU. *Journal of Perinatology, 27*, S48–S74.

Lupien, S. J., McEwen, B. S., Gunnar, M. R., & Heim, C. (2009). Effects of stress throughout the lifespan on the brain, behaviour and cognition. *Nature Reviews Neurosciences, 10*, 434–445.

Martin, R. M., Goodall, S. H., Gunnell, D., & Smith, G. D. (2007). Breast feeding in infancy and social mobility: 60-year follow-up of the Boyd Orr cohort. *Archives of Disease in Childhood, 92*, 317–321.

McEwen, B. S. (2003). Early life influences on life-long patterns of behavior and health. *Mental Retardation and Developmental Disabilities Research Reviews, 9*(3), 149–154.

McKenna, J., & McDade, T. (2005). Why babies should never sleep alone: A review of the co-sleeping controversy in relation to SIDS, bedsharing and breast feeding. *Paediatric Respiratory Reviews, 6*(2), 134–152.

Meaney, M. J. (2001). Maternal care, gene expression, and the transmission of individual differences in stress reactivity across generations. *Annual Review of Neuroscience, 24*, 1161–1192.

Meinischmidt, G., & Heim, C. (2007). Sensitivity to intranasal oxytocin in adult men with early prenatal separations. *Biological Psychiatry, 61*, 1109–1111.

Middlemiss, W., Granger, D.A. Goldberg, W.A., Nathans, L. (2012). Asynchrony of mother–infant hypothalamic–pituitary–adrenal axis activity following extinction of infant crying responses induced during the transition to sleep. *Early Human Development, 88*(4), 227-232.

Morelius, E., Theodorsson, E., & Nelson, N. (2005). Salivary cortisol and mood and pain profiles during skin-to-skin care for an unselected group of mothers and infants in neonatal intensive care. *Pediatrics, 116*, 1105–1113.

Morrow, E. M., Yoo, S.-Y., Flavell, S. W., Kim, T-K., Lin, Y., Hill, R. W., …Walsh, C. A. (2008). Identifying autism loci and genes by tracing recent shared ancestry. *Science, 321*(5886), 218–223.

Narvaez, D. (in press). *The neurobiology and development of human morality.* New York, NY: W. W. Norton.

National Institute of Child Health and Human Development, Early Child Care Research Network. (2004). Affect dysregulation in the mother-child relationship in the toddler years: Antecedents and consequences. *Developmental Psychopathology, 16*, 43–68.

Organization for Economic Cooperation and Development. (2009). *Doing better for children.* Paris: OECD Publishing.

Panksepp, J. (1979). A neurochemical theory of autism. *Trends in Neuroscience, 2,* 174–177.

Panksepp, J. (2001). The long-term psychobiological consequences of infant emotions: Prescriptions for the 21st century. *Infant Mental Health Journal, 22,* 132–173.

Panksepp, J. (2003). Feeling the pain of social loss. *Science, 302,* 237–239.

Panksepp, J. (2007). Can PLAY diminish ADHD and facilitate the construction of the social brain? *Journal of the Canadian Academy of Child and Adolescent Psychiatry, 10,* 57–66.

Paterson, D. S., Trachtenberg, F. L., Thompson, E. G., Belliveau, R. A., Beggs, A. H., Darnall, R., ...Kinney, H. C. (2006). Multiple serotonergic brainstem abnormalities in sudden infant death syndrome. *Journal of the American Medical Association, 296*(17), 2124–2132.

Perry, B. D., Pollard, R. A., Blakely, T. L., Baker, W. L., & Vigilante, D. (1995). Childhood trauma, the neurobiology of adaptation, and "use-dependent" development of the brain: How "states" become "traits." *Infant Mental Health Journal, 16,* 271–291.

Pinker, S. (2002). *The blank slate: The modern denial of human nature.* New York, NY: Viking.

Pinker, S. (2011). *The better angels of our nature.* Viking: New York.

Porges, S. W. (1991). Vagal tone: An autonomic mediatory of affect. In J. A. Garber & K. A. Dodge (Eds.), *The development of affect regulation and dysregulation* (pp. 11–128). New York, NY: Cambridge University Press.

Porter, C. L. (2003). Coregulation in mother-infant dyads: Links to infants' cardiac vagal tone. *Psychological Reports, 92,* 307–319.

Prescott, J. W. (1996). The origins of human love and violence. *Pre- and Perinatal Psychology Journal, 10*(3), 143–188.

Rogers, C. R., & Skinner, B. F. (1956). Some issues concerning the control of human behavior: A symposium. *Science, 124,* 1057–1066.

Rosenfeld, P., Ekstrand, J., Olson, E., Suchecki, D., & Levine, S. (1993). Maternal regulation of adrenocortical activity in the infant rat: Effects of feeding. *Developmental Psychobiology, 26*(5), 261–277.

Sahlins, M. (2008). *The Western illusion of human nature.* Chicago, IL: Prickly Pear Paradigm Press.

Schore, A.N. (2002). Dysregulation of the right brain: A fundamental mechanism of traumatic attachment and the psychopathogenesis of posttraumatic stress disorder. *Australian and New Zealand Journal of Psychotherapy, 36,* 9–30.

Schore, A.N. (2012). *The science of the art of psychotherapy.* New York: NY. Norton.

Semrud-Clikeman, M., Fine, J.G., & Zhu, D.C. (2011). The role of the right hemisphere for processing of social interactions in normal adults using functional magnetic resonance imaging. *Neuropsychobiology, 64,* 47–51.

Smith, T. W., & MacKenzie, J. (2006). Personality and risk of physical illness. *Annual Review of Clinical Psychology, 2,* 435–467.

Spitz, R. (1947). *Grief: A peril in infancy* [[film]]. University Park, PA: Penn State.

Teicher, M. (2002). Scars that won't heal: The neurobiology of child abuse. *Scientific American, 286*(3), 68–75.

Trevathan, W. R. (2011). *Human birth: An evolutionary perspective.* New York, NY: Aldine de Gruyter.

U.S. Department of Health and Human Services, Substance Abuse and Mental Health Services Administration. (1999). *Mental health: A report of the Surgeon General.* Rockville, MD: Center for Mental Health Services, National Institutes of Health, National Institute of Mental Health.

Wagner, M. (2006). *Born in the USA: How a broken maternity system must be fixed to put women and children first.* Berkeley, CA: University of California Press.

Walker, M. (1993). A fresh look at the risks of artificial infant feeding. *Journal of Human Lactation, 9*(2), 97–107.

Watt, D. F., & Panksepp, J. (2009). Depression: An evolutionarily conserved mechanism to terminate separation-distress? A review of aminergic, peptidergic, and neural network perspectives. *Neuropsychoanalysis, 11*, 5–48.

Weaver, I. C., Szyf, M., & Meaney, M. J. (2002). From maternal care to gene expression: DNA methylation and the maternal programming of stress responses. *Endocrine Research, 28*, 699.

World Health Organization. (2012). *Born too soon: Global action report on preterm birth.* Geneva: Author.

World Health Organization and World Organization of Family Doctors. (2008). *Integrating mental health into primary care: A global perspective.* Geneva and London: Author.

Wrangham, R., & Peterson, D. (1998). *Demonic males: Apes and the origins of human violence.* Boston, MA: Houghton Mifflin.

{ ABOUT THE EDITORS }

Darcia Narvaez, Department of Psychology, University of Notre Dame, 118 Haggar Hall, Notre Dame IN 46556; Phone: 574–631–7835; Fax: 574–631–8883; e-mail: dnarvaez@nd.edu

Jaak Panksepp, Baily Endowed Chair of Animal Well-Being Science for the Department of Veterinary and Comparative Anatomy, Pharmacology, and Physiology, College of Veterinary Medicine, Washington State University, Pullman, WA 99162; e-mail: jpanksepp@vetmed.wsu.edu

Allan Schore, Department of Psychiatry and Biobehavioral Sciences, University of California at Los Angeles David Geffen School of Medicine, 9817 Sylvia Ave, Northridge, CA 91324; e-mail: anschore@ucla.edu

Tracy Gleason, Department of Psychology, Wellesley College, 106 Central Street, Wellesley, MA 02481–8203, Phone: 781–283–2487; Fax: 781–283–3730; e-mail: tgleason@wellesley.edu

{ INDEX }

Note: Page numbers followed by *n, t* and *f* refer to notes, tables and figures.